Every Nook & Cranny: A World Travel Guide

Book 1

(Have Will Gunna Travel)

Faye Day

Library of Congress Control Number:		2016900772
ISBN:	Hardcover	978-1-5144-4463-4
	Softcover	978-1-5144-4462-7
	eBook	978-1-5144-4464-1

Print information available on the last page.

Rev. date: 02/10/2017

To order additional copies of this book, contact:
Xlibris
1-800-455-039
www.Xlibris.com.au
Orders@Xlibris.com.au
721776

DEDICATION

To my son Michael for the inspiration and my daughter Selina for the encouragement (and the title!), with all my love. I hope you enjoy the book.

Pictures on the cover are:

Chocolate Box Cottage Eastnor England

Temple Guardian China

West Meon Hampshire UK

Delicate Arch, Arches National Park Utah USA

Sigiriya Lady Sri Lanka

Japanese Garden Compton Acres, Dorset England

African Market

Small Welsh Harbour

Stonehenge Wiltshire England

CONTENTS

INTRODUCTION

I feel privileged to have seen most of the world in great depth. The reader could do worse than follow the routes outlined in my book. I realise that there is a considerable amount of description but would hope it assists readers to travel the world vicariously through my eyes, specifically those for whom it is not otherwise possible.

There was nothing particularly remarkable about my first trip except perhaps that it set the pattern for a lifetime and started me on a career that spanned almost 30 years. The year was 1969, and I went to Singapore, by sea, on the *Centaur.*

Those first years were all spent in Asia, and although it was a challenge, I feel privileged to have seen it comparatively unspoilt, before package tourism was ever invented. A good example of the changes becomes obvious when comparing my first two trips to Thailand, which I shall illustrate later. Tourism is a two-edged sword: on the one hand it benefits the economy but on the other contributes to the decline in genuine friendship and hospitality as hordes descend and come to mean solely a source of money.

The first chapters of my book are the least interesting because I had very little to work with. I regret not keeping the letters that I sent to my children because they would have become the basis for this autobiographical travel narrative. I would encourage the reader to persevere!

A question I am frequently asked is why I travel alone. The answer is selfish: because I prefer to be independent and can cover more territory. By moving on as soon as I have seen the sights, I can often cover two destinations in a single day rather than sitting in a hotel room on my own. Even with only two people, 50% of the time one must be prepared to consider excursions not of your choice, and most women love to follow an activity in which I never indulge unless to purchase food – shopping! The biggest disadvantage is the single supplement cost of accommodation.

But the question most often asked – 'What is your favourite destination?' – is impossible to answer because each has its own attractions, for example, Canada for scenery, Spain for architecture, Papua New Guinea for excitement.

One of my main concerns when I travel for extended periods (up to five months) is the disaster zone that is my garden when I return; as a friend quoted to me, plants die but weeds never perish!

Some readers may be interested to know how I became involved in travel. In 1974, with King's Holidays, one of the leading agencies in Perth, I planned and prepaid for a trip that was extremely adventurous at that time. It was only because I had done so much research that I was able to extricate myself from the many problems that occurred, such as accommodation having to be paid for twice because remittance had not been received, and other incidents alluded to in my story. On my return to Australia, the concerned manager of the company consulted with me in my home and ultimately offered me a free trip to Asia in compensation. In addition, because of my experience, he said that if I was prepared to act as tour escort I would also be provided with accommodation.

I did two trips for King's and an equal number for Vacations Unlimited before being offered a tour by American Express to Ladakh in India. As it transpired, this did not sell, but because it sounded so fascinating, not having been accessed by Westerners before, I decided to take the trip as an individual traveller. The itinerary had not been well planned, and I incurred a severe bout of altitude sickness due to flying to Leh, situated at 11,500ft, direct from Delhi at sea level. Nevertheless, I believed it worth pursuing, made contact with local agents, and enquired of American Express whether they intended to persevere with the programme, which had not sold for two years. They readily agreed to my taking it over, and changing it to a more workable trip, I ran it successfully for 11 years, with the support of John Young from the *Sunday Times* who always gave me an editorial. He has my undying gratitude.

This is the first book of a series, and DVDs illustrating every chapter in detail are available.

SINGAPORE & MALAYSIA 1969

1969 saw my inaugural overseas trip, with my then husband, on the *Centaur* to **Singapore**, but it was not my first sea voyage. Prior to that, at the age of 11, I had sailed with my parents from Perth to Melbourne on the 28,000-ton Orient Liner *Orcades*. From here, we took our car across Bass Strait to Launceston on the ferry SS *Taroona*, which subsequently suspended service and left us stranded. My parents then leased a hotel and our holiday turned into a stay of nearly five years!

On board the *Centaur*, we met the Singapore Amateur Boxing team, which had been in Western Australia for a competition. We spent considerable time with them in Singapore, and many became long-standing friends. Arrangements to make the journey had been a spur of the moment decision because my uncle, who had been seconded to the Malaysian Air Force for some years, was due to retire and was leaving the country. In fact, our visit was cut so fine that my relatives had already left their home in Kelantan on the east coast and were staying in the grand (at that time) Malaysia President Hotel in **Kuala Lumpur**, where we joined them for a few days. I have pictures of the impressive pool area, the dining room hung with fishing nets and floats, and our family group in the bar, where I was wearing a beautiful beaded and sequined pink satin dress tailored in Singapore, complemented by beaded Italian sandals also purchased in that city. Accompanied by my aunt, uncle and cousin, we visited the well-maintained **Zoo**, with the usual exhibits: tiger, leopard, cassowary, giraffe, rhinoceros, and even an Australian emu. I have a photograph of myself in front of the floating restaurant holding one of the twig brooms used by sweepers. The ever-entertaining monkeys snatched my husband's sunglasses and actually imitated wearing them!

But first I must return to our stay in Singapore, where we spent time enjoying the gracious hospitality of our friends in the boxing team. One of the most intriguing venues was the old **Bugis Street**, enlarged on in the next chapter. In those early years, we did all the touristy things, like riding in a trishaw for the first time, visits to **Kranji War Memorial** and the notorious **Changi Prison**, and watching snake charmers with cobras. I was persuaded to hold the flute and drape one of the less lethal, beautifully marked specimens around my neck. I photographed many of the picturesque Malay *kampongs* sited in coconut groves, which have since disappeared. The decorative sunburst was a popular addition on gables of these thatch- or tin-roofed wooden houses. Built on stilts for, I assumed, circulation of air, they also had long shutters allowing access to cooling breezes.

Back then, I only used a simple camera with black and white film. I have pictures of an old three-storey apartment building with an external spiral staircase and washing hanging on a balcony, street stalls with unhygienic cooking conditions (bucket and basin next to a large open drain in the street), and shophouses with open shutters overhead and plants growing out of decaying walls. In those days, by our standards, living conditions in **Chinatown** appeared appalling. We saw a lovely Chinese temple, its roof enhanced with curled corners and ornate dragons, and in contrast, ugly high-density multistorey housing with washing strung on bamboo poles, extending from most balconies like colourful flags.

Crossing into **Malaysia** with our Indian driver-cum-guide, we saw women tapping rubber trees and the remarkable **Batu Caves** in **Selangor**. Set in lush surroundings, these were located at the top of a steep staircase (276 steps) with a host of small figures above the entrance. After visiting the **Lake Gardens** and impressive **National Monument** in honour of the nation's fallen heroes, we joined my aunt and uncle at the horse races in Kuala Lumpur. This was an extraordinary experience because of the fact that we, as Europeans, were totally surrounded by heavily armed police in helmets. It was the time of their *Mederka* (freedom) or Independence Day celebrations, which had the previous year been cause for serious rioting.

I remember little about the capital, founded by tin miners in 1857, except for its remarkable Moorish-style railway station (1910) featuring numerous spires and cupolas and, opposite **Mederka Square**, the distinctive **Sultan Abdul Samad Building** with its clock tower and spiral stone staircase.

Moving on to **Penang** (Pearl of the Orient) by taxi, we endured such a hair-raising ride, swerving in and out of traffic and careering around bends, pedestrians and animals, that I decided to bypass the mountainous road to the Cameron Highlands and continue straight through **Ipoh**. At that stage, I was not accustomed to heights (Western Australia being so flat) and had yet to experience some of the nightmare journeys of later travels! En route, I photographed a heavily laden bullock cart and a small Chinese temple. In Penang, I took pictures of palm trees lining the water immediately outside our hotel room, a novelty at that time. We took the funicular, built in 1923, up 692m **Penang Hill**, where we saw monkeys scampering on well-tended lawns. In the **Temple of the Azure Cloud** (**Snake Temple**, 1850), I again draped myself with another of these surprisingly silken serpents; venomous pit-vipers, they were supposedly rendered harmless by the smoke of burning incense! Constructed in 1850, the temple was dedicated to a Buddhist priest believed to possess incredible healing powers. According to local folklore, on the night of completion, snakes slithered out of the jungle to inhabit the structure. The doorway of the Thai **Chayamangkaloram Temple** was flanked by impressive colourful guardians with beaming faces, which towered above ornate figures with clasped hands. I took pictures of more *kampongs*, a woman working at a well, and a busy market with ladies in different styles of traditional dress. Two stall holders selling meat and chickens, all hanging in the open, had cigarettes dangling from their mouths, and trishaw drivers were protected from the elements by paper umbrellas. I was fascinated by a village built on stilts over the water, with washing hanging in front of houses and boats moored at the boardwalk. At **Ayer Itam**, the elaborate seven-storey **Million Buddhas Precious Pagoda** reared beyond tiered roofs of **Kek Lok Si Temple**, the curled corners of their eaves carved to resemble leafy vines. Women in wide-brimmed straw hats were working to clean verges, and I photographed policemen wearing side arms, which were not issued to Australian forces in the '60s or '70s. People flocked to Penang for the beaches, and the capital, **Georgetown** (after King George III), was not a priority. In 1786, the island was ceded to the British, named Prince of Wales, and remained under colonial rule until 1957.

Back in Singapore, the next venue was **Tiger Balm Gardens** (1935, now **Haw Par Villa**) depicting scenes of Oriental mythology, the afterlife, and ancient beliefs and superstitions. I took pictures of an ornate figure in the Thai section (with 'King Kong' in the background) and other tableaux in the weird displays. Monkeys, which have since been removed, were a menace in the **Botanical Gardens** – a combination of primary jungle and formal beds – and a clock tower behind old go-downs (warehouses) on the wharf at **North Boat Quay** composed the vista from a bridge. Taken from a boat, ancient mould-encrusted shophouses with washing outside windows and *sampans* in front completed my pictures. Further along the **Singapore River**, the dilapidated wooden houses were in a sorry state of disrepair.

On other occasions, I accompanied a girlfriend to Singapore, made a trip on my own, and took another with a male companion, with whom I rode the monorail on **Sentosa Island**. Here, we visited the two **Surrender Chambers** containing 91 life-sized figures comprising tableaux of these historic events. Now linked to the city by a causeway, originally Sentosa could only be accessed by ferry or a cable car from **Mt Faber** where, with a jolt, one was flung suddenly and unceremoniously out of the station to find oneself immediately suspended high above the water – quite a frightening experience. On this occasion, we stayed at the New Otani on the banks of the Singapore River; I have experienced many of Singapore's hotels and even stayed at the HUDC Chalets on **East Coast Parkway**.

An incident that illustrated Singapore's British heritage and a confusion of cultures occurred when I invited the entire boxing team to tea on their reciprocal visit in 1971. Surprised and somewhat flustered when they all turned up at 3pm as I was endeavouring to prepare the evening meal, they similarly wondered why there was no 'cuppa' forthcoming. In a complete misunderstanding, they had arrived for afternoon tea when they had been invited to dinner!

Back in those far-off halcyon days, Malaysia Singapore Airlines (MSA) was a joint venture, and knowing many of the crew members it was not a problem to be upgraded to first class, a fantastic way to travel but not worth the extra money! After splitting into a separate entity, until Singapore Airlines gained popularity, the aircraft were never booked to capacity, and as a consequence, service excelled. After the break-up, I was presented with a set of stainless steel cutlery with the MSA logo.

SINGAPORE 1970

In 1970, we made a return visit to **Singapore** with the Western Australian Amateur Boxing Association and, as honorary officials, were fêted at the various receptions and cocktail parties. As the only woman on the team, it took a while to adjust, and then I was accepted as 'one of the boys' – until an extremely amusing and interesting encounter when we went as a group to **Bugis Street**. The 'girls' seemed reluctant to approach our table, and the boxers blamed my presence, so I left them to their own devices and joined the transvestites, where I enjoyed a most fascinating evening. Treating them as females (some were gorgeous and put me to shame!), they readily accepted me, and we spent considerable time discussing clothes and family whilst they bought me drinks, all much to the consternation of my companions who were still ignored so, much amazed, they apologetically came and asked me to return. I formed quite a friendship with one (I forget 'her' name) who, on successive visits, preferred to sit and talk rather than work, even though trying to save money for *the* operation. I have a photograph of the two of us together – what a revelation! Because they had to produce identity cards, many daily crossed the border from Malaysia as boys, but the transformation was astounding; these glamorous individuals would be difficult to recognise as male unless one was aware. All types of deviant behaviour went on in Bugis Street, but mostly committed by intoxicated tourists; it could be threatening at times and not a place for the faint-hearted.

My first pictures are of the **Pasar Malam** or **Night Market**, where neon lights flashed Chinese characters, followed by film of a friend handling a six foot snake. Scenes of the old wharves show huge crates, '60s cars, clusters of *sampans*, dilapidated weathered shophouses, and dingy warehouses that have since been converted to colourful upmarket eating establishments. Amongst figures in big straw hats working on the verge was a woman staggering under the load balanced on a pole across her shoulders, a typical Asian sight but one new to me on that trip. This contrasted with peaceful scenes in the **Botanical Gardens**, where a fountain sat in the centre of a lake reflecting tall trees, and an orchid enclosure displayed 20,000 plants. Pathways and steps wound amongst verdant vegetation that included ferns and trailing vines, and a red wooden bridge overlooked a small waterfall splashing down rocks. In a more classical part of the grounds, colourful flowerbeds made a show in lawns and around the base of large trees, and flowering red bougainvillea grew over a pergola in a swathe of green grass kept immaculate by sweepers with straw brooms. A clump of lipstick palms with the distinctive red stem stood out amongst other exotic foliage, and the inevitable monkeys, including mothers with babies clinging to their belly, scuttled at my approach. **MacRitchie Reservoir**, near Thomson Road, was also a popular spot for walking.

We took a cruise past moored *sampans*, a line of open-air restaurants on **Clarke Quay**, the old **Customs House**, depressing dwellings with washing in front and struggling pot plants making futile attempts at beautification (all gone under the development of a modern Singapore), and into the huge harbour, once rated the world's largest port and now ranked third. Sailing further, we came to a fascinating community built on stilts over the water, with ladders leading from the surface and walkways between wooden houses, all with tall shuttered windows. Disembarking, we wandered past food stalls and trees with trailing lianas to traverse the plank pathways within the village, where washing hung on bamboo poles, one lady rinsed articles in an enamel basin, and some houses were enhanced with colourful potted plants. In 1970, we stayed at the Hotel Malaysia, out of the city centre in the suburb of **Tanglin**, with a waterfront view that has long since disappeared due to land reclamation. A large traffic circle in front had flowerbeds and a central fountain with many jets.

Vistas from our hotel room revealed the rooftop gardens and pool, a couple of European-style buildings with a dome and turret respectively, red tiled roofs of old shophouses, and stunning flame trees in full bloom. In those days, one could find tradesmen working in the streets, and walking past the open-fronted shops, I encountered a figure squatting on the roadway near a barrow, drinking tea, and a lad repairing a bicycle, a popular form of conveyance back then. A magnificent doorman in elaborate Oriental costume stood outside the Ming Court Hotel, which featured a foyer with planters and long glass chandeliers hanging three floors from a skylight, and I took film of large sculpted panels on the façade of the Hilton Hotel in **Orchard Road**, which was the poshest area in the early '70s.

We were privileged to attend the wedding of a family member of our popular Malay guide, the well-known and favoured 'Happy' – so called because of his permanent big smile – and his wife Rokie. A sign outside announced *Selamat Datang* (Welcome), and a large awning had been set up in the yard to shade long trestle tables ornamented with orchids. People were preparing huge quantities of rice in large boilers for the many guests expected to come and go throughout the day, and a band and vocalist entertained with Malay songs. I had worn a new pantsuit tailored from *kain songket*, a traditional Malay fabric into which gold or silver threads are woven. Requesting to assist in the festivities, I was given the task of washing the right hand of seated guests with water poured from a silver ewer into a bowl. Platters were laden with food, and chickens still ran in the yard – around the huge vats of rice being stirred with a long paddle! In the palm-lined street, a man selling peanuts, which he placed in cone-shaped rolled paper, sat on a low stool at a portable table. We watched as the bridal couple, dressed in gold and walking slowly beneath colourful decorations held aloft, passed gathered locals and well wishers to enter the house. There they sat side by side, both with solemn expression and the bride with head downcast, as people gesticulated and bowed obeisance. The bride's mother attempted, unsuccessfully, to encourage her to raise her face for my camera, and I had a photograph taken with them on their dais. It was a very enjoyable day.

We visited **Haw Par Villa** (mentioned previously) in **Pasir Panjang**, one gaudily painted tableau featuring a man bound to a stake whilst his entrails were cut out! Meant to portray the punishments of hell and results of the evils of adultery, gambling and drinking, one depicted a distraught wife running towards a drunken man fatally struck by a car, with a circle of people playing cards below. A white concrete goat stood on artificial rock amongst cement flowers and trees, and gigantic red-and-white fish with bulging eyes and spines along the back swam in simulated sea. A man lay supine with a sword in his right hand – and a bloody knife through his temple! The scene of a shipwreck showed one survivor standing on the back of a turtle, people clinging to the sinking vessel, and others floundering in the water or in the jaws of sharks. Ferocious gods, beautiful goddesses, and life-sized animals, including a rhinoceros (popular with small children who sat on its back) and tiger, were also represented.

Like so many flying banners, washing hung from poles extending from almost every window of high-rise apartments. Due to lack of space, the city spread up instead of out, but each housing complex had shops and restaurants aplenty, and living in such proximity the tenants enjoyed these and other communal facilities, interacting far better than in Western society; there was not the isolation and loneliness associated with our cities. The climate was also conducive to getting together in the cool of the evening. Deep roadside gutters were indicative of the heavy tropical downpours that can flood in minutes, and ceramic-tiled streets were common. In **Chinatown**, some of the ancient shophouses coated with grime and mould featured red or green wooden shutters, and tarpaulins protected food stalls and markets lining the narrow streets, all of which have disappeared in favour of produce behind glass. Chinatown was a bustling area, where people ate at all hours of the day and night. Washing was suspended across the streets, and paper lanterns swayed above sidewalks congested with crates, utensils and wicker baskets. Fruit and vegetable stalls provided plenty of colour, meat hung in the open, and nurtured by the humid conditions, greenery (including ferns and even trees!) sprouted from cracks in walls. Trishaws plied up and down, and bicycles and cars wended slowly through the conglomeration, where chickens sat in wire cages, and a man was washing the plucked birds and depositing them on the pavement! Platters and basins of unrecognisable dried foods and spices were displayed amongst fresh greens, corn, cauliflower, cucumbers and carrots; in those days, it held all the fascination of the mysterious East. I watched a lady selecting a fish from the range in large metal tubs in which water circulated from hoses. Her choice was sold by weight gauged by a handheld balance – an old kerosene tin holding the purchase at one end and weights the other. The item was then transferred to a clear plastic bag containing water, which was tied at the top for easy transportation and a hole punched for air. In the midst of it all, a man lay flat on his back on the footpath – sound asleep! There were remnants of sculpted decoration on some architraves, pillars and arched windows, and in the interior of one house I could see paper lanterns hanging. Other cages contained live snakes and animals, and a man was stirring a huge steaming boiler with trussed chickens on the ground nearby. Vendors were seated on low stools, a man emptied a basin into a street well beside a food stall stacked with bowls and trays of eggs, and another was preparing *dim sums* at a table next to where I ate with friends; it was none too hygienic, and I recall eating at a popular venue late at night with rats scurrying along the drains! On another street, where fabrics were sold amongst the fruits and vegetables, colourful umbrellas sheltered barrows, and a covered market displayed yet more fresh produce including coconuts, eggs and oranges, whilst pyramids of dried sardines sat in the hot sun. Many sellers squatted behind produce laid out on mats on the roadway, and in those bygone days, ladies still wore the *cheongsam*. Less evident examples of Chinese cuisine were bear paw, bird's nest, frogs' legs, live monkey brains, chicken testicles, and the more mundane snakes, pigeon and fish head. Also in Chinatown were the **Death Houses** in **Sago Lane**, where old people went to die – a sobering reminder of man's immortality. This collection of rooms had a wreath and black and white banner out front, but I understand that they do not exist today, although shops in Sago Street still make paper houses and cars to be burnt at funerals. Here, on a street stage, I also saw a colourful *wayang* (Chinese opera) with glittering costumes and lurid makeup. These were frequently performed at the Festival of Hungry Ghosts to appease and honour departed spirits believed to wander the earth at that time. The spectacle of weeping maidens and fierce warlords stroking their long beards was accompanied by clashing cymbals, clanging gongs and the banging of drums. **Temple Street** led to the exquisite Indian place of worship described in the next section on Singapore. In a more upmarket area of town, a large floral clock kept time outside the John Little store, and nearby fabled **Change Alley** marketed all manner of merchandise beneath its tarpaulins.

Singapore is one of the most progressive and tidiest cities in the world but has lost a lot of its character, and even Chinatown has become very sterile. An indication of this was the removal of notorious Bugis Street, where I spent many a fascinating evening in the party atmosphere created by colourful transvestites, prostitutes and gays. The area was originally allocated for Bugis settlers, a seafaring and trading society from the Celebes who became master shipbuilders, but in the 1970s it degenerated into a den of iniquity and was 'cleaned up' in the 1980s. Also changed dramatically is the island of **Sentosa**, which used to be called **Pulau Blakang Mati** (Back of the Dead). Once a burial place for local pirates, with British hilltop forts, in 1970 it was an undeveloped piece of real estate belonging to the army, where we attended a party with friends in the service.

Singapore was a very different city then. Now it is a big, busy, and exceptionally clean modern metropolis with only a hint of its colourful past. But a landmark of Singapore that will never change is the white colonial **Raffles Hotel** (1887), named after Sir Stamford Raffles (who arrived in 1819) and with an ambience reminiscent of Somerset Maugham; in fact, he stayed here, as did Rudyard Kipling, Joseph Conrad, Charlie Chaplin and Noël Coward, whose names appear in the guest book. Maugham wrote *The Moon and Sixpence* from his suite in the hotel. Also unchanged is the central grassed area called the **Padang**, with the **Singapore Cricket Club** at one end and, diagonally opposite, the **Old Supreme Court**, **St Andrews Cathedral**, and **City Hall** with its Corinthian columns. It was on the steps of the latter, in 1945, that Admiral Lord Louis Mountbatten accepted the Japanese surrender.

Interestingly, the walls of the cathedral are coated with an extremely hard plaster concocted from shell lime, egg whites and sugar.

Unfortunately, the ultra-modern Singapore has priced itself out of the market, it has become prohibitively expensive and no longer an economical holiday.

THAIPUSAM

On my second visit to **Singapore**, I was introduced to the macabre, almost ghoulish festival of **Thaipusam**, a Hindu ritual in which scores of penitents, in order to atone for sins and give thanks to Lord Subramaniam, walk barefoot over hot streets. They cover a distance of three kilometres, from **Sri Srinivasa Perumal Temple** in **Serangoon Road** to **Sri Thandayuthapani Temple** in **Tank Road**, carrying *kavadis*: steel frames weighing up to 32kg (70lb) gaudily decorated with peacock feathers, flowers, chains and paper ornaments, and threaded with long spikes that spear the body. The more affluent amongst the population pay others to perform this feat and endure the agony on their behalf! Some were adorned with limes hung on hooks imbedded in the skin, and all were accompanied by friends and family members who were chanting, dancing, playing tambourines, and carrying burning incense in pottery jars, the heady fumes of which became quite intoxicating as I followed the procession in the heat of the day. Other devotees, their eyes rolling back in their head, appeared in a trance-like state as steel skewers were threaded through their tongue by priests – without a drop of blood being spilt. The religious believe that this is due to divine intervention, but a white powder (probably a coagulant) was placed in the mouth beforehand. Still others had chains attached to a skewer inserted through both cheeks, and a couple had their cheeks pierced by spears as thick as a finger. One of the latter also carried a *kavadi*, a picture in its centre surrounded by iridescent balls – like shining baubles on a Christmas tree! Each end of the majority of steel spikes through tongue or cheeks was ornamented with a spade, trident or star. I took film of a young lady, her eyes closed, having tongue *and* cheeks pierced, the priest using visible force to insert the skewers; I shudder to watch it now without the anaesthetising effect of the incense! With eyes half open, the pupils disappeared upwards to expose only the whites; she was definitely in a hypnotic trance.

At the first temple, festivities were preceded by ritual cleansing with water before commencing the long walk. One young woman passed out and was supported by her followers, whilst another flung her arms wildly about and had to be restrained and subdued. In contrast, a youth sat contemplatively, his legs crossed and head bowed. Adorned with all the trappings, one penitent held the hand of a toddler in a pink dress. Some of the penitents even attempted dance steps with the tall *kavadis* nodding time, and a girl in a yellow sari, her hands clasped, was gyrating and frenetically jumping up and down. She had to be supported and guided before taking up her burden across one shoulder and continuing her frantic movements.

Beautifully dressed in elegant saris, women had their long dark hair garlanded with fresh flowers. A man was chopping coconuts with a machete, and some followers carried food (probably offerings) on platters. One man in a dhoti, his face pierced and body garlanded with artificial flowers, performed a comparatively energetic jig whilst carrying the *kavadi* on one shoulder. A woman indulged in a wild frenzy whilst she anointed the forehead of a male participant. Smoking incense was held between the two, and from a tray holding burning flame she selected some herb that she slapped on the man's chest and placed in his mouth; the face of a female companion was filled with anguish. The fanned fumes caused at least one person to collapse and others to stagger, another wore heavy anklets with many silver bells attached, a girl swayed back and forth with a silver urn on her head, a man spun in circles with his ungainly crown, and I saw one wedge-shaped *kavadi* like a miniature shrine. Towards the conclusion, devotees became more agitated and, finally reaching their destination, were relieved of their burdens and the skewers removed – and indeed there was no blood! At the end of the route, I took pictures from above the temple.

Rather than just a bystander observing from a distance, I was caught up in the pandemonium and participated in one of the most fascinating experiences of my travel career. The ceremony bore all the hallmarks of mass hysteria or hypnotism and at the time, although utterly absorbing, was almost too gruesome to watch; in fact, when I showed the film to my daughter's class I lost half the pupils!

In total contrast, I also spent time around the pool at the Raffles Hotel and watched people practising their drives at a golf course, where a caddy was collecting balls beneath a multihued umbrella – presumably for protection!

BALI 1970

In 1970, I made my first trip to **Bali**, where most tourism centred on the beaches. On that occasion, I stayed at the Segara Village in **Sanur**, where a giant wooden fish and lobster inhabited the strand, also made gay by red and white striped triangular sails on outrigger canoes, called *prahu*, which lined the shore; a cloud-shrouded island lay in the distance. I took film of the lush tropical garden surrounding my accommodation and encountered graceful girls balancing elaborate towering offerings on their heads as they made their way to a celebration. Bali practices a form of the Hindu religion akin to animism in which plants, stones and animals, as well as people, are attributed with spirits, hence the many festivals with offerings of flowers and fruits for which the island is renowned.

In the uninspiring capital of **Denpasar**, I photographed the four-faced Brahma image in the centre of an intersection and a boy with a mongoose clinging to his arm. I visited one of several monkey forests and the royal temple complex of **Mengwi**, with its moated sanctuary, **Pura Taman Ayun** built in 1634, and weathered wooden shrines crowned by odd numbers of progressively smaller *merus* (tiers), ranging from three to eleven. A superb free-standing gateway constructed of red brick with an intricately carved stone surround and wooden doors looked stunning superimposed on a blue sky, unblemished except for a few fluffy white clouds. Baths at the **Goa Gajah** (**Elephant Cave**) had water flowing from urns held by mournful-looking statues. The cave, constructed in AD 917, acquired its name from an elephant figure and statues of the god Ganesh found at the entrance. In lush surrounds containing a small natural waterfall, other baths, enjoyed by ducks, had greenery cascading down one wall and water pouring from the mouths of animals. I came across one shrine with exquisite illustrations.

At **Lake Batur**, a thick plume of vapour issuing from the crater of **Mt Batur** (1,717m) mingled with bruised clouds overhead to produce a bleak and brooding mood of this occasionally rumbling volcano. Displaying a black lava flow down the side, it rose within the rim of an older caldera wherein lay the lake, which is seven miles in diameter and called 'the navel of the world' by the Balinese. Passing rivers and gently waving palms, the tour took me down country roads with glimpses of green terraced rice paddies or *sawahs*. Topped with dry grass, adobe walls fenced compounds where many palm trees flourished, and we came to a gateway accessed via a set of steps flanked by stone figures, with tall slender bamboo decorations, symbolic of Bali, swaying at the base.

Joining a group, I took a *prahu* to **Turtle Island**. We paddled past people poling canoes, and the shallow water was so clear that it was possible to distinguish coral, weed, and even starfish on the bottom. As we approached the island, a few houses were visible beneath palm trees on the shore, and the many multicoloured triangular sails on craft moored in the blue harbour made a striking picture. Wandering around this seemingly timeless peaceful community, even more years behind its primitive mainland counterpart, we came to another quiet anchorage where only a couple of luxury yachts were berthed. Following behind a man carrying a live creature in a large wire cage slung across his back, we walked across a narrow causeway with water both sides – in which other men were engaged is some activity – and came to an enclosure holding the huge turtles for which the island is named. I sauntered around the settlement with its thatched dwellings, rough stone fences, and bright blue crabs, appearing ungainly with only one red and white pincer as large as their body, skittering along the ground and burrowing into the earth. Quite aggressive, they attacked each other with this single claw. There were, of course, the ubiquitous tiered temples, and I filmed villagers walking down narrow streets created by the high stone walls.

Back in the turquoise waters of Bali, a row of crude shops (where I ordered some tailoring), stone gateways, and bamboo groins lined a white beach with palm trees and a jungle backdrop. It has since changed considerably with the erection of modern luxury hotels and sophisticated shopping centres. At that time, the Segara Village was amongst the best, its pool surrounded by flowering bougainvillea and palms, but it became run down, as did the hallmark for many years, Hotel Bali Beach, when alternative beachside locations were developed.

I have wonderful film of one of Bali's interminable religious ceremonies, conducted on **Sanur Beach**. Bright long-handled silk parasols, together with the colourful attire of the people and multihued sails in the background, formed a cheerful basis for this activity that involved the sea. Women carried offerings, which included the cleverly woven bamboo creations combined with flowers and fruits, in silver containers on their heads, and a priestess dressed in white, flowers in her hair, was anointing the gifts with holy water. People, their hands clasped in prayer, were also blessed. There were several small shrines and, quietly sitting near elaborate intricately woven bamboo decorations, a live white duck! A procession of ladies in colourful *sarong kabaya* anointed a tall decorated bamboo throne shaded by two colourful umbrellas, and the prayers, smoke wafting from small fires, and other rituals, including the sprinkling of holy water and strewing of petals, continued for some time. Eventually, the duck was also blessed, garlanded with flowers, and taken to the water's edge, where I do not know if it was released or killed in sacrifice. Executing graceful slow-motion movements, small groups chanted and circled around other participants and objects, and the whole fascinating ceremony, with prayers, anointing, and the occasional dog joining the festivities, went on for hours – I was grateful not to be Hindu!

Film of the Bali Beach Hotel, with its bar in the pool, lily ponds, and exotic gardens with bougainvillea, fragrant frangipani and birds, together with the finale of a brilliant red sunset, concluded my trip record.

On this occasion, I purchased a Barong mask for my daughter, who was only little at the time. I hung it on the wall of her bedroom, but it frightened her so much that I had to remove it!

SINGAPORE 1971

En route to the east coast, where I was lodging in a beach bungalow, I photographed houses cocooned in lush tropical foliage at the edge of a tranquil river – with tin toilets on stilts over the water! I took pictures of a man with his boat, a woman gathering washing, and smiling people outside wooden dwellings with corrugated iron or palm-thatched roofs. These constituted neat Malay *kampongs* (compounds), the majority of which have since disappeared because in small Singapore the land is so valuable. Huge fish traps made of bamboo stakes, with a small wooden hut (*kelong*) on stilts at the end, extended into the choppy sea of the Malacca Strait, and I stopped to watch an extremely colourful (and stridently noisy) Chinese opera (*wayang*) enacted on a gaily decorated stage in the street. The lavish costumes and headdresses were striking, and the usual magician also performed. To one side of the huge tent, next to food stalls where trays of eggs were stacked beside an open fire, a barber was cutting the hair of a client.

In another *kampong*, a man wearing a long checked sarong, his torso bare, was sweeping with a twig broom, and people waved and called greetings from a verandah. In the age-old tradition, a woman wearing a wide-brimmed straw hat carried a load suspended from each end of a pole across her shoulders, and I took film of a makeshift store in a quiet back street, but it was impossible anywhere to escape the children who clamoured to be in photographs. I have pictures of friends taken in a private home and of **Sri Mariamman Indian Temple**, the oldest in Singapore. First built around 1827 and dedicated to Mariammam, goddess of rain, and mother-goddess Devi, its wedge-shaped exterior displayed a wealth of colourful ceramic images, including many-armed gods. On **Queen Elizabeth Walk**, I have footage of myself holding the head of a long snake draped around my neck and the 'charmer' blowing a bulbous 'jewel'-encrusted flute – I was even smiling! Another played as a deadly cobra emerged from a basket; I thought it was probably harmless, but the owner and his accomplice seemed genuinely apprehensive as they endeavoured to make it rear up. I ate at a street stall with a valued Chinese friend, Lawrence, who has since passed away, and filmed the harbour from a beautiful garden setting.

Haw Par Villa was always a source of much (albeit bizarre) entertainment, with garish tableaux depicting macabre scenes of torture, regal figures, larger-than-life gods, a concrete crocodile with gaping jaws sequestered in cement trees, and even 'King Kong'. Gambolling on the lawns of the **Botanical Gardens**, I encountered playful monkeys, including mothers with offspring that they carried clinging to their belly. More occupied a bench onto which they sprang from a nearby tree, whilst others clambered amongst the massive system of twisted and tangled vines around the trunk. As well as cultivated flowers, lush ferns and foliage, there was a verdant wilderness area, a display of orchids, and a lovely Victorian-looking white gazebo: a lacy structure surrounded by colourful flowerbeds in manicured lawn with tall trees in the background. I saw plants trailing over a pergola near mixed succulents, multihued blooms, crotons and conifers, and a Renaissance-type garden where a red floral border defined the pathway circling a lily pond with tall reeds in the centre. Situated in the middle of a grassed expanse, this was in turn enclosed by bougainvillea and trees behind a low box-shaped hedge, and the whole was encapsulated by a high green wall of cascading creeper.

I came across two boys carrying goats almost as big as themselves, who posed with cheerful smiles. Accompanied by a friend named Wong, I climbed a lookout tower in nicely landscaped grounds with a white pagoda, small pavilion, and pergola. The panoramic views revealed a vast industrial area. I was also invited by Wong to be his guest at the exclusive **Singapore Country Club** for an enjoyable few hours. On one visit, I enjoyed the **Chinese Garden** (**Yu Hwa Yuan**), which featured an arched entrance, curved bridge, twin pagodas, lotus blooms, weeping willows, and a courtyard with playing fountains. In comparison, the **Japanese Garden** had shrubs, hillocks, stone lanterns, and a tea house.

ASIA 1972

THAILAND

Thailand, the ancient Kingdom of Siam, is the only country in Southeast Asia never to have been colonised. Its history can be traced back to 3600 BC when it is widely believed that the village of Ban Chiang was man's first Bronze Age civilisation.

Bangkok

Beginning in **Thailand**, I was greeted outside my hotel in **Bangkok** (established as the capital in 1782) by an elephant – which shook hands with its trunk! Inside, a lovely ornamental pool was encompassed by trailing vines. My first visit was to the **Thai Royal Palace**, surrounded by walls built in 1783 and with multi-tiered gables, each apex bearing a graceful curved spire, their gold gleaming even in the dull conditions. Called *chofa*, these spires are believed to represent the mythological Garuda (half bird, half man), and gold is considered effective in placating spirits. Stone lions and guardians stood at one entrance and fearsome multihued figures (*yakshas*) with tusks like warthogs at another. As described in a subsequent chapter, colourful carvings in exquisite detail appeared on lintels and gables, temple bells lined eaves of many-tiered red-and-green tiled roofs, and tall wooden pillars and exterior walls were heavily decorated. One structure had a frieze of gilded Thai figures around the base.

The beautifully maintained grounds featured topiary trees, and it was here that I found the **Temple of the Emerald Buddha** (**Wat Phra Kaeo**), seat of this guardian image of Thailand, a 2ft-tall statue created from green jasper atop a towering gold altar. Believed to have been created in Patna, India, in 43 BC, there is much conjecture as to its true origin. According to legend, after 300 years it was transported to Sri Lanka whence, en route to Burma, it landed in Cambodia as the consequence of a shipwreck. When the Thais captured Angkor Wat in 1432, it was taken to Laos and finally Chiang Rai, where it was hidden. It reappeared by chance in 1434, when lightning struck the temple wherein it was housed and a stucco image fell to expose the solid jade Buddha within. It was relocated several times before its final resting place in Wat Phra Kaeo.

On the opposite bank of the **Chao Phraya River** stood the **Temple of Dawn** (**Wat Arun**), its many pagodas patterned with floral mosaics made up of millions of tiny porcelain fragments. The **Temple of the Golden Buddha** contained a 3m-tall 5½-ton image that was revealed in 1955 when it was dropped from a crane and the outer plaster casing, used to conceal its true value, damaged.

On a rice barge tour of the *klongs* (waterways), happy children swam in the murky canals, men balanced on heavy floating logs, and steps led to the water from tin- or thatch-roofed wooden houses on stilts, some beautified with potted plants, all enmeshed in palms and tropical growth, and one with a distinct lean, appearing in imminent danger of collapse! We passed typical Thai structures with *chofa* on the gables of red-and-green tiled roofs and more topiary art, a monastery with orange-robed monks, people bathing and poling canoes and, suspended overhead, huge fish traps. Washing was strung on poles, bananas and bamboo grew at the water's edge, thick clumps of water hyacinth undulated gently up and down with the movement of the *klong*, and red hibiscus was reflected on the surface. The hyacinth, an introduced weed, was taking over Thailand's waterways until the development of a new industry: the harvesting and drying of the plants to be woven into fine furniture and accessories. We negotiated narrow canals where cascading creepers, red flowers and palms were also mirrored in the still waterway. Naked children waved, and we encountered a colourful shrine on a wooden deck. Stopping at a farmhouse, boys were riding a water buffalo with massive horns (I also sat on its broad back for a photograph), children and women in traditional attire were seated near a large decorated ceramic urn on an elevated porch, and skinny-looking cocks were housed beneath wicker cages, which were raised to allow them to attack each other with the lethal spurs on their legs.

Continuing by boat, food was being prepared on open verandahs above the water, whereas in the canal, a lady was washing clothes and a man performing ablutions. It seemed incongruous to see television antennas in such a primitive setting. Rustic local shops were interspersed amongst housing lining the bank, we passed a long wide line of floating logs on which men stood in order to direct its passage, and there were always the reflections. Like gondolas in Venice, boats were moored to posts in the water, and we passed one full of fresh produce being rowed fore and aft by ladies in large straw hats, whilst another sold her wares to householders on a landing outside their dwelling. We began to encounter a lot more activity, finally entering a local floating market with healthy-looking vegetables for sale. Passing under a small wooden bridge, I saw more people washing and bathing, open-fronted shops with goods in baskets, and a policeman blowing a whistle – whilst standing on the roof of a ferry to direct river traffic! We were approaching the congested main market, where steam issued from a cooking pot on a boat selling hot food.

Disembarking briefly, we walked along wooden decking past stalls and houses, the latter secluded behind trees and potted shrubs. Boarding once again, we came to a pretty garden behind a stone levee, tendrils of red and white bougainvillea making a lovely picture as they reached to the water. Squatting on a small jetty, a lady was industriously occupied with enormous ceramic jars, whilst another, shaded by a large paper umbrella, paddled her canoe containing utensils possibly holding hot food. Banana plants were much in evidence, and more people were washing clothes and bodies on steps. One canoe held a load of coconuts, and laundry hung on lines above plants, baskets, and large pottery urns on many of the wooden verandahs; water lapping just below caused me to wonder how often they flooded.

Back in the city, people knelt before a small golden Buddha image in a shrine festooned with garlands of colourful flowers. Thirty-two kilometres from Bangkok, I visited the famous **Rose Garden**, where the show commenced with a parade of beautiful girls in costume (described more fully in a later chapter) led by drummers and a couple wearing large masks. However, this time they were joined by dignitaries shaded by a large silk parasol, riding on the back of an elephant adorned with a red scarf. There was a full *gamelan* orchestra, and the programme consisted of dances (one executed with bamboo poles), kick boxing (the combatants praying before the bout), both pole and sword fighting, and a mock wedding ceremony. On this occasion, I watched two bulls locking horns as they tussled in an outside arena where tribal dancers were beating drums, their wonderfully hued costumes contrasting with the rich green of the surroundings.

My next visit was to the **Bridge on the River Kwai** and the moving **Kanchanaburi War Cemetery**, where lie the remains of 12,399 of the 60,000 allied POWs who were forced to work on the infamous Burma 'death' railway and died from beatings, starvation, disease, exhaustion, and other forms of brutality and maltreatment. Emotive inscriptions on headstones, repeated in the war cemeteries of several countries, I have quoted elsewhere.

Chiang Mai

Flying above a patchwork quilt of rice paddies, I arrived at the moated city of **Chiang Mai** (founded 1296) in the north of Thailand, where I watched a farmer using a buffalo to till a waterlogged field, its surface shining like silver and newly planted rice apparent behind. Others worked with what appeared to be foot-operated lathes. In this rural environment, a woman in the conical coolie hat toted baskets on a pole across her shoulder, and in lush surroundings, woven houses roofed with dried banana leaves were lodged behind sapling fences. A man shouldering lengths of bamboo walked the narrow embankment between paddies, whilst others stooped to plant the rice.

Handlers sat on the necks of working elephants as they hauled teak logs, others used their trunks and long tusks to roll and stack them. In the muddy jungle environs of an elephant training camp in the **Mae Sa Valley**, this was a more authentic demonstration than that in the Rose Garden in Bangkok. A man carrying a load of bananas adroitly negotiated the miry incline. I had come here to visit hill tribes such as the **White Karen** and **Meo**, also known as **H'Mong**. It was considerably cooler in this elevated region, where wispy cloud rested on hills, waterfalls bordered by verdant vegetation tumbled over stepped rocks to a swiftly flowing brown river, and bullock carts lumbered along bucolic byways. A beautiful small temple had gables inlaid with glittering slivers of blue glass, a feature that I was to find in these northern locations on my third trip to Thailand many years later. Partially covered by undergrowth, a superb structure had figures in relief on one side and spires on top, and a tall *stupa* (dome-shaped Buddhist monument) inundated with sprouting greenery appeared like a giant fir tree!

Travelling by jeep over some of the worst roads that I had experienced, with ruts up to two feet deep in mud, we reached a village where the self-contained populace eked out a meagre living, their thatched houses ensconced in jungle surrounds. The growing of poppies being a major source of revenue, many suffered the effects of long-term exposure to opium, which they smoked in *bongs*. Women wove the black fabric for their tribal dress, men fashioned the silver worn by both sexes, and both men and women smoked the distinctive pipes. One man gave a demonstration of firing a crossbow, and children, also in ethnic costume, spun tops. I purchased a tribal necklace, purportedly created by the chief of the village, with a pattern beaten into a square piece on the end of a heavy chain attached to a circular yoke; from memory it cost around $10 and is about 98% silver. Horses were used for transport in this primitive community, which had rudimentary farming implements and few facilities but gloried in stunning panoramas over surrounding valleys, even though under a leaden sky at the time of my visit. One young woman, a babe on her back, was obviously dressed for tourists – specifically, me! She wore the long pleated costume (traditionally trimmed in red and/or blue embroidery and tied with a red sash) over trousers, with a headdress and silver necklace, the latter similar to that which I had bought. She carried a red and blue woven bag, one of which I also obtained, and held a red parasol.

On the return journey to Chiang Mai, we came across many people walking along the muddy verge. I was taken to **Wat Phra That Doi Suthep**, its staircase – up and down which traipsed many folk dressed in auspicious red – flanked by giant undulating multi-headed *nagas* (serpents) with crocodile images underneath. At the top, I found a complex with orange-robed monks, gilded umbrellas, and carvings. People prayed, lit joss sticks, and plastered shrines with thin sheets of gold leaf. Chiang Mai had an interesting history of intermittent warfare with Burma, the devastated city at one stage remaining a ghost town for 20 years, inhabited only by wild tigers, roaming elephants, and monkeys clambering over decaying temples.

On one of my overseas trips, I spent a couple of days in **Pattaya** as a guest of the Royal Cliff Beach Resort, followed by two days at the Weekender Hotel (also complimentary) near where I attended an extravaganza called **Alcazar**. Billed as the best cabaret show in Asia, it featured troupes of beautiful transvestites. As a destination, Pattaya did not have much to recommend it, but it was pleasant to stay in the ambience of five-star surroundings.

JAPAN

Honshu

Continuing my journey, I flew above dense cumulus cloud to **Tokyo**, where I was welcomed by a guide who informed me that my hotel was in flames. Alarmed by this statement, I arrived to find it covered with scaffolding, hence,

Japanese having difficulty with the 'r' sound, *frames* became *flames*! A similar mispronunciation in Indonesia had me referred to as 'Pay' Day – luckily not May Day!

Tokyo was just a fishing hamlet before the founder of the Tokugana Shogunate (rulers of Japan until 1867) moved there in 1590 with tens of thousands of retainers and their families, as well as merchants, labourers and craftsmen, to establish a new settlement. It then became, as now, one of the world's major cities but is today burdened with the added problem of traffic and the associated noise, pollution and bustle. My memories are sketchy, but the amazing underground shopping centres stand out because of the enticing displays to lure customers; necessarily attractive due to the high cost of merchandise, they were difficult to resist. I also vividly recall eating at a restaurant in the popular **Ginza**, the nation's most famous shopping district where, being pushed for time, I turned up the gas jet under my self-cooked meal on the table. Seated adjacent, a chubby peroxide-blonde Japanese lady (can you imagine such a thing!) hopped up and, excitedly saying something unintelligible, lowered the heat. Apparently, eating is an art and meant, like the tea ceremony, to be consumed at leisure, but because of my haste, I turned the flame up again, whereby she promptly readjusted it – this pantomime continuing until I had finished my repast!

First sights of glorious **Nikko** included verdant green mountains and fields and the vermilion, typically bowed, 28m (92ft) wooden **Shinkyo Sacred Bridge** (or **Snake Bridge**) across the ravine of the **Daiya River**. According to a 1,200-year-old legend, a priest coming to the Daiya River found the current too strong to cross and prayed to Buddha and the gods for help. Jao Gongen, the deity of reptiles, instantly provided him with a bridge of red and blue snakes, hence the alternative name. Climbing the tortuous zigzag road of the **Irohazaka Slope** by car, we came to the spectacular 97m (318ft) **Kegon Waterfall**. Flowing from **Lake Chuzenji** along the **Ojiri River**, it plunged with a tremendous roar (at a rate of three tons every second!) into a yawning chasm also featuring 12 minor falls – **Juni-Taki**. Splashing to the bottom, it burst in clouds of spray before thundering onwards, in a foaming white wash, over stepped boulders enclosed by towering perpendicular rock walls and dense growth in contrasting shades of green. The flow continued down the **Kegon Valley** to meet the Daiya River. I believe that the cascade freezes in winter, which would make an amazing spectacle.

Falling from the **Yukawa River** into Lake Chuzenji, overlooked by 2,484m (8,149ft) **Mt Nantai**, was the beautiful **Ryuzu** (**Dragon Head**) **Waterfall** that divided around a pretty foliage-covered rock formation. Still in Nikko, I visited the **Toshogu Shrine** (1636, but rebuilt in 1815 following destruction by fire) lodged amongst tall timber, which included some 1,000-year-old cryptomerias – Japanese cedars. Its elaborate five-storey (35m/115ft) wooden **Goju-no-to Pagoda** and eye-catching bonsai collection were secluded behind a red boundary wall, the *torii* (gate) bearing *shimenawa* – paper origami shapes expressing the existence of gods – hanging from a rope below the lintel. Entering here, one finds the complex of exquisite elaborately carved buildings that compose the shrine and many lanterns: 102 of stone, 17 of copper, and 2 of iron. The **Sacred Stable** bore the celebrated **Three Wise Monkeys**: Hear no Evil, Speak no Evil, See no Evil, but I have no pictures.

Next on the agenda was the giant 11.4m (37.4ft) **Daibutsu** or **Great Buddha**, a seated bronze image at **Kamakuru**. This was followed by something totally different: a black volcanic sand beach with shallow surf and people lounging under gay umbrellas. A drive through lush countryside revealed a rare clear view of **Mt Fujiyama** (3,776m/12,388ft) in the distance, its symmetrical cone rearing against cloud and blue sky. Travelling by ferry, I passed a large red *torii* in the water and a replica of an old-time sailing vessel, its figurehead depicting an angel blowing a horn. Riding in a cable car over a crater, fumes issued from between yellow sulphur-encrusted rocks, and in total contrast, I later experienced a traditional Japanese **Tea Ceremony**, an elegant exercise performed with graceful and leisurely ritual movements but a long protracted way to make a cup of tea! After spending the night at a hotel with shrouded vistas of Mt Fuji, next morning it proved to be exceptionally clear, and in haste to take a picture before my tour departed I put my diamond watch on top of my suitcase, inadvertently forgetting it. Picking up the case to leave, it dropped, unnoticed, onto the floor. In a testament to the unassailable honesty of the Japanese, it was returned to me two days later at a venue some miles distant!

Again travelling by coach, we passed fish or eel farms and came to 17th-century **Nagoya Castle**. In the region of **Ise**, I observed women pearl divers in action; apparently trained to hold their breath for long periods, they submerged with neither snorkel nor oxygen tank. A vast area of water was covered with rafts to which workers were attaching seeded oysters in order to artificially create the precious gems.

In **Nara**, first capital in the year 710, the spotted deer were so tame that I became quite intimidated when surrounded, one large-antlered specimen actually eating the luggage tag from my bag! I visited the obligatory wooden temple, with a large stone lantern in front and deer peeping between rows of smaller lanterns on pedestals lining the walkway. A line of metal lamps hung from eaves above a moat. Glorious gardens in **Kyoto** featured a lily pond, bamboo grove, an artificial waterfall, trees in mossy surrounds, and an enclosure fenced by colonnaded corridors. This contained typical raked white pebbles around large boulders, a style of garden known as *karesansui*, representing mountains and rivers (or continents in the ocean) and also peace and tranquillity. Encompassed by soaring trees, including a few with bright red foliage, a lake bordered by tall grasses reflected the **Kinkakuji** or **Golden Pavilion** – which was anything but! Originally constructed in 1397, it was rebuilt in 1955 after being burnt. This beautiful site also boasted tiny cascades, topiary, and a rock-ringed pool with small creeper-covered stone bridges and stepping stones across the water. I found Japanese children to be impeccably well behaved and came across two small boys chasing butterflies with nets. Tiny private courtyards also featured lovely gardens.

On the road again, we drove past many opulent houses with green fields in the foreground and forest behind. Reaching **Hiroshima**, I saw another large red *torii* in the water, a multi-tiered red pagoda in dense greenery, and a *torii* flanked by stone lions. The latter led to a shrine with *torii* now high and dry at low tide, pavilions with the signature red posts and eaves, and stone lanterns. More deer frequented this venue, and there was a second multistorey red pagoda in green surrounds. Crossed by a small curved bridge, a pool in another tranquil garden held many koi. To one side, a thin stream of water fell to rocks mirrored on the still surface.

Kyushu

I visited both sites on which the atomic bomb was dropped by the **Enola Gay** in WWII, Hiroshima and Nagasaki on **Kyushu**, the only evidence at the former being the point of impact: a blackened shell with a skeleton-like dome silhouetted against the sky. In the modern bustling 20th-century city that had risen rapidly from the rubble, this had purposely been left standing as a memorial, and it loomed as a poignant reminder of the terrible destruction possible to be wrought by man. The emotive museum was full of disintegrated clothing and shocking photographs, including one that made the newspapers of the world, that of a naked girl, burnt by napalm, running screaming down a road. It was a disturbing and thought-provoking experience. From a high vantage point, I took photographs of this amazing thriving city constructed in just a few short years.

Continuing to the town of **Nagasaki**, we passed busy little tugboats and a shipyard where, in slipways, some of the biggest vessels in the world were being built. Hoisted on stakes, a massive undulating cloth serpent reared its ugly head in the street, and a huge contemporary statue sat amid fountains with jets spraying water at different heights, a symbol of the lack of this life-sustaining fluid following the bombing. Strolling along the streets, I observed people in doorways engaged in varying activities. These included a man mending his nets and a smiling lady washing clothes in a blue plastic basin. Another, in *gaeta* (wooden clogs) and *kimono* girdled by the *obi*, walked with a sunshade; most of the populace in Japan wore Western suits and dresses. In fact, I had one contact in the country, which had been given to me by a friend from tennis on whose behalf I had taken a parcel, and at our first meeting she brought along her traditionally attired sister because she thought that I may not see the costume elsewhere! Neither the sister nor Miss Niwa, a kindergarten owner in Osaka, spoke English, so an employee acted as interpreter. After my return home, we corresponded and exchanged gifts for some years; on one occasion, I sent a toy koala with which the children were delighted, naming it Bobby.

From Nagasaki, I travelled past rice terraces to the totally fascinating spa town of **Beppu**, where I stayed in the fantastic Suginoi Hotel. This enormous complex even contained a skating rink, ten-pin bowling alley, theatres, restaurants, bars, a banquet hall, conference room, and at least three mineral baths, one of which was festooned with vines trailing from the ceiling and flourishing in the humidity. I plucked up the courage to experience one of these public bathing venues (for ladies only), where I was allocated a tiny square of towelling that I could not decide where to place! I was instructed to sit on a wee three-legged wooden stool in order to wash before entering the pool, where no soap was allowed. Set on pathways amid luxuriant palms, each stool had an individual tap with a mirror above. Having bathed, I adjourned to the large pool in the centre of the room, in the middle of which was a huge aquarium, its colourful fish silently drifting to and fro, adding to the serenity. Different sections contained water in varying degrees of heat, and first immersing myself in the coolest of these, I worked my way upwards, but not to the most extreme, which would surely have proved almost intolerable unless one was accustomed. As it transpired, I enjoyed the spa tremendously and, feeling surprisingly refreshed, even went in search of others, some for mixed bathing, although I did not indulge.

Each guest in the hotel was issued with a white terry-towelling robe and many wandered around identically attired. A humorous incident occurred when, wearing this same article, I ate in one of the restaurants. An elderly Japanese gentleman, who had obviously been agonising over the dilemma for some time and was in a quandary as to whether he would cause offence, arose from his seat and approached to enquire if I was aware that my gown was crossed in the manner of a male – left over right! Although due to ignorance on my part, my apparent lack of courtesy must have irritated him considerably. Under an orange awning at the end of the hotel's Olympic-size swimming pool, a stage had massed red flowers on the sides and a painted backdrop of Waikiki Beach in Honolulu. The thermal area, which was crossed via a wooden bridge, had over 3,000 natural springs. Although not as awe-inspiring as some, it was still impressive. Steam erupted from fumaroles in an area of thick forest that extended to stands of conifers on the omnipresent mountains. Ladies were working with rocks to create new attractions. A short cruise revealed fishing boats with a small sail at the back, bobbing up and down on the waves.

Back on land, we passed haystacks, people reaping crops, and a man sitting on a seawall, his wares protected by a red and yellow umbrella. To celebrate the opening of a new venture, large floral bouquets were adorned with messages in Japanese, and a courtyard was irrigated by an intermittently 'nodding' bamboo pipe activated by water. Lovely gardens, where women were cutting grass with scythes, incorporated an artificial hill created to represent Mt Fuji, a lake teeming with koi, and a pergola resembling a row of red *torii*.

Mt Aso, belching dense clouds of odorous vapour, was the closest that I had ever come to an erupting volcano. We were not permitted to approach the rim of the crater, but even from the foot it was an awesome spectacle. Encountering a more extensive thermal area, I have film of boiling pools and steam rising from large expanses amongst eerie primeval surrounds shrouded in mist. Eggs were being cooked in a basket lowered into one exceedingly blue pool with a roaring fumarole emitting thick vapour at the side. Dense clouds of steam also poured forth from fissures beside a lily-covered pond with willows overhanging pink and white flowers amongst the large upturned pads. Red salvia lined the edges and another red pergola was secreted in the lush background, fumes issuing around it contributing to an illusion of the structure being engulfed by flames. In order to relocate a huge palm tree, women were dragging it by hand, and I looked down into a small concrete enclosure housing a massive crocodile. As I watched, it closed gaping jaws with a snap, and many coins had been thrown around it for luck. Nearby, a ferocious red figure looked like an image direct from hell, and cheeky monkeys scampered across the ground, groomed each other, or swung from trees, one vigorously bouncing up and down on a swaying branch. A woman swept the compound with a twig broom, and I filmed an interesting study of a Japanese mother with a child on her back and a monkey with offspring, both surveying each other intently. Many had young and their antics were very amusing. My pictures concluded with the bright red rear of one of these animals walking away – a shot I titled 'The End'!

I embarked on a tour of the **Inland Sea**, but it was disappointing because it was polluted by smog from industrial sites. We sailed past many small islets and mountains, the latter sometimes almost indiscernible in the thick smoky fog, so consequently I do not have much of a record. Whenever we moored at a dock, vendors traded with passengers. In spite of the hazy conditions, or perhaps because of them, the setting sun turned the surface of the water to gold.

Honshu

Back on the island of Honshu, heavy stone outer walls announced 16th-century **Osaka Castle** with its surprisingly delicate five-storey (42m) pagoda on mammoth stone foundations and animal figures under the eaves. It was surrounded by a wide water-filled moat crossed by a wooden bridge, and many women in straw hats kept the approach clean. Miss Niwa, together with her sister and the translator, took me to lunch at a traditional Japanese restaurant with a gigantic imitation crab moving its claws above the entrance! A fascinating aspect of Japanese eating establishments, which I had never seen before, was the realistic plates of plastic food, including ice cream and sweets in parfait glasses, on shelves in display cabinets as an indication of particular dishes. Paper lanterns and white banners with Japanese characters hung above the entrance to a small shrine containing gladioli, pink and white lilies, a shining brass urn, and lighted candles in front of a moss-cloaked image flanked by two bell-shaped objects. The white banners adorned many doorways, one new enterprise sported the congratulatory floral tributes, a red wall was decorated with a mythical beast created from tiles, and paper lanterns, all with the same illustration, hung under the eaves of another shop. These were my last images of Japan before flying over very green mountains and winding rivers to Seoul, capital of Korea, where I stayed for just 24 hours but stepped back many years in time.

I spent one night in a typical Japanese *ryokan*, where I slept on a *futon* placed on a *tatami* mat covering the raised floor of the sleeping area. The Japanese-style bathroom had a deep but very small square tub. I also rode in the fabled **Bullet Train**.

KOREA

Seoul

All manner of goods, from flowers to fish, were displayed on dirty narrow streets in the hot sun, women wore the striking and colourful traditional dress with a long voluminous skirt dropping from the bustline, and there was still a large American army presence. In fact, I met up with an officer who escorted me to a street where precious gemstones, from the size of a small fingernail to an egg, were sold by vendors squatting on the sidewalk. It was here that I purchased one of the best bargains of my life: two large topaz or smoky quartz. I acquired both for the princely sum of four Australian dollars each, thinking that even if fake they were attractive. On arriving home, I had them valued (tongue in cheek) at one of our larger jewellery stores. The first assumption was that they looked too perfect to be genuine, but on closer scrutiny through an eyeglass, the jeweller requested me to leave them with him. They both proved to be authentic and back then were valued at $50 each. The problem was that even using only nine-carat gold, it cost me in excess of $100 dollars to have one mounted into a ring because the setting had to be shaped to my finger to support the weight. However, to this day it is much admired and still one of my favourite pieces; the other remains in its little silk bag!

Street scenes included men bowed under extraordinary loads, which they carried on their backs in wooden frames braced by straps around the forehead and chest or shoulders, and one toted a large assortment on his head. From an overpass, I looked down on a motorcycle policeman in blue shirt and black trousers directing traffic, and from this vantage point I observed dressed chickens in boxes, a table displaying drumsticks (the feet still attached) on paper, produce in large square baskets, and even puppies destined for the kitchen! These were for sale beside blackened 100-year-old eggs at the foot of the staircase. Unbeknown to me, I was served dog in a restaurant and it was one of the few times that I have become violently ill whilst travelling. Greens were piled on the pavement, garlands of garlic hung from walls, and large hessian bags were filled with some type of vegetable – whilst men swept and shovelled muck from drains in front! Cooked foods and meat chopped with a tomahawk and weighed by handheld scales were also sold, but it was difficult to get pictures in the bustling crowded streets.

Bicycles seemed to be the principal form of transport, but cars, buses, and heavy carts trundled by hand also travelled the main eight-lane highway.

I photographed a youth with a guitar and many women with loads on their heads. A man carried two large cans suspended from a pole across his shoulders, whilst a smiling lady carried her child on her back, nestled in a type of quilt tied around the waist. Bicycles were laden with stacked boxes, and one man hefted an impossibly large basket into which he deposited paper picked up from the road with a long pair of tongs. I saw fruits or vegetables being wheeled in a large barrow, a man almost disappearing beneath a pile of greens, and some of the loads in the wooden frames towering above the head of the bearer. Eggs were plentiful amongst the fresh produce, and a lady dressed in pink and white carried a similarly attired girl on her back.

I visited a complex of temples with a lurid green pool and came across an ancient wooden city gate on solid stone foundations. I encountered grapes and other fruits in large basins and live seafood in plastic buckets aerated with running water. The entire city seemed to be one big market, and a venue under canvas was full of fascinating sights, smells and sounds. Dried foods were heaped in baskets, and a lady balanced several tiers of garlic on her head. Dressed in a beige waistcoat and trousers, white shirt, hat, and shoes, an elderly man with a long white beard sat on a bench beneath a tree. Ladies demurely hoisted their long skirts as they mounted steps and one, a child sound asleep on her back, was inspecting items on offer. The view from my hotel room was of high-rise buildings with washing on lines outside rooftop dwellings. After an absorbing few hours, a huge memorial bade me farewell, and I moved on to Taiwan.

TAIWAN

The Chinese name means Terraced Bay, the Portuguese Ilha Formosa translates as Beautiful Isle, and both are apt.

Taipei

Altogether different, it was clean, policemen wore neat brown uniforms, and large brilliant green dragonflies alighting on plants also provided an introduction.

One of the most impressive things in **Taiwan** was the magnificent **National Palace Museum**, exhibiting priceless ancient artefacts all smuggled out of China. Not normally a museum person, I could have devoted an entire day to this venue with its treasures of artwork, jade, porcelain, bronze, enamel, lacquer ware, tapestries, and scrolls spanning 30 centuries. The other outstanding feature was the Marble Gorge. Classical Chinese buildings amid lush greenery, tree ferns, willows and lily ponds characterised the island, together with water in rocky recesses and abundant rice terraces. Possibly contributing to the green environment, a thermal area was comprised of different-coloured pools and steaming fumaroles. A dejected-looking water buffalo stood in a muddy puddle, and I saw a large temple complex with typical curved corners on the roofs. Sweepers trundling carts moved along streets that were considerably cleaner than Seoul, and a customer wearing the conical straw hat perused food displayed in a glass case. I wandered through the inevitable market, where goods were arrayed in large baskets, and ate at a street stall. From a small harbour, I surveyed many fishing boats at sea and walked through a village with narrow dirt streets, stone houses, and washing on poles. My hotel, the Mandarin, its red entrance flanked by stone lions, had a feature garden with imitation birds on decorative rocks lodged amongst foliage. The view from my window looked out across brown roofs and workers in green fields to the city beyond.

Taroko Gorge

Flying south over a tall mountain range, I joined a private tour by car to the marble **Taroko Gorge**, with a typical Chinese gateway (*pailou*) at the entrance. A fantastic feat of engineering, the road was blasted through rock to create 38 tunnels. Between the tunnels, hewn passages with wide overhangs provided views across the narrow chasm, its steep tree-covered sides (up to 3,000ft) enclosing the **Liwu River**. An attractive scene was composed of a red oriental-style building situated above a beautiful lacy waterfall tumbling over boulders to the rocky watercourse below. In places, the lush slopes gave way to sheer walls of white marble, and it was a pristine environment full of elusive butterflies. Plummeting down a verdant mountainside, a high ribbon waterfall appeared in the distance, and where the canyon narrowed even further, water churned through the confining white marble walls. The clean air produced wonderful vistas of green mountains against a blue sky, clear except for a few puffs of white cloud. At one section, we came upon men harvesting the marble: levering large slabs that smashed as they tumbled down the face of the cliff to be broken further by hammer and collected by workers below. We encountered more cascades surging down the looming sides and over huge boulders at the bottom, and a steep stepped pathway led to a small red-roofed rotunda amongst trees on top of a ledge. At one stage, we crossed the **Bridge of Motherly Devotion** flanked by white marble lions and with railings of the same material. With the opposite side almost close enough to reach out and touch, I could see water swirling below small caves in the rock, and we passed a natural formation, its flat surface shaped like a map of the island. At the end of this awe-inspiring highway, I was taken to see how the marble was cut into thin slabs by machine and witnessed a cultural dance performance by girls in extremely colourful tribal costumes with elaborate headdresses.

HONG KONG

Then it was on to **Hong Kong**, and the first sights that greeted me were high-rise apartments and scenes of appalling poverty, with washing hanging around tumbledown shacks and people working on the litter-strewn ground. Travelling by car, we came to a mass of ducks surrounding a house on stilts in the water. The simple subject of stakes reflected on the still surface made a surprisingly interesting picture in the subdued lighting. Traversing rural countryside with green fields and mountains in the background, we came to the 18th-century walled **Hakka** village of **Sam Tung Uk**, its two-storey stone houses hemming in narrow alleyways, and the ladies wearing large straw hats with a black fringe around the brim. People still cultivated small plots that they watered by hand, walking between the rows with watering cans filled from a nearby well and suspended from a pole across the shoulders. On the strait between the **New Territories** and mainland **China**, I observed *junks* with their distinctive sails unfurled.

The signs of the city, which extended right across roadways, were an attraction in themselves, both during the day and by night when they provided a blaze of colour. In Chinese and English, they announced places such as Kowloon Silk Store, Fuji Topless high class nightclub with sophisticated hostesses, Honeycock Restaurant, Champagne Dance Hall, Sky Room Bar, Sheila's, and Crown Radio. Divided into two districts, **Kowloon** (Nine Dragons) on the mainland and **Hong Kong Island**, the Star Ferry ran frequently between the two, and at a few cents, the fare was very cheap. Way back then, I enjoyed shopping, and the **Stanley Market** and **Temple Street** night market were good sources of bargains. However, I found that the people could by extremely rude, one shopkeeper even telling me to leave his store because I was just looking! In those days, it was still a British colony, and it is my belief that the populace, being politically unable to enter China and unable to afford travel to Japan, were frustrated by their situation as virtual captives in a veritable high-rise cement jungle of just a few square kilometres.

MACAU

Catching the hydrofoil, I went on a 65km (40mi) day trip to Portuguese **Macau**, passing motorised fishing *junks* en route. The island was named for a Chinese girl called A-Ma who took passage with a fishing fleet and was credited with its miraculous salvation when threatened by a great storm. According to the story, after walking ashore and climbing a nearby hill, she was taken to heaven and a temple built on the spot where she landed: A-Ma-Gau.

From a prominent position, I obtained views of the city and the Chinese mainland across a narrow stretch of water, my film uncannily taking on a red hue at this point! More *junks* were at anchor in the harbour and loads of fresh fish for sale in baskets on the wharf. People lived amid the clutter of baskets and barrels on their craft, washing hung on decks, and one had a row of chickens or ducks strung by the neck under an awning. In the shopping precinct, I saw a curtain of this same product – pressed flat! Walking along a tree-lined promenade, I encountered trishaws elaborately decorated for some festival and visited a temple with intricately carved tableaux along the roof capping and around the entrance. The most outstanding sight in Macau, atop a steep staircase, was the ruined **St Paul's Cathedral** with only the façade left standing; built in 1602, it was destroyed by fire in 1835. With a cross on top and decorative pillars, statues and sculpting – which included the Virgin flanked by a peony and chrysanthemum (representing China and Japan respectively), a Chinese dragon, Portuguese ship, and a demon – it was highlighted by an indigo sky, also visible through its empty doors and windows. There were a couple of other impressive buildings from a bygone era, but mostly the narrow cobbled streets were a collection of old shophoucses and high-rise apartments. On stepped, appropriately named **Ladder Street**, I saw mothers with babes on their backs and many schoolboys in white shirts and black shorts. I came across a street of antiques, a woman carrying a live fowl by the legs, food carts, baskets of produce, and the inevitable washing hanging overhead. In one area, laundry was draped amongst green plants flourishing on balconies, and here the signs were nearly all in Chinese. I took film of a man taking parts from a live snake for medicinal purposes. In 1999, the administration of Macau also reverted to China.

Back in Hong Kong, double-decker trams were plentiful, and I visited the area of **Repulse Bay**.

PHILIPPINES

The archipelago, discovered by Ferdinand Magellan in 1521 (he was killed 20 days later by Cebu chieftain Lapu-Lapu) and claimed for Spain, is made up of more than 7,100 islands. Following the Spanish, it came into the hands of America and finally attained independence in 1935. In 1942, Japan invaded the country and General Douglas MacArthur, together with Filipino troops, resisted the advance until ordered by President Roosevelt to retreat. It was then that he made his famous *I shall return* promise, which he duly did, seizing control from the Japanese in 1944. The Philippines achieved full independence again in 1946.

Luzon

Flying over flooded fields, I landed on the island of **Luzon**. Entering **Manila**, a palm tree lying across the waterfront boulevard gave an indication of the ferocity of storms that had recently ravaged the country. Other battered palms stood amongst fishing boats, where nets hung to dry and makeshift stalls and food carts catered for the crowd. Travelling by car, I saw people washing clothes in the centre of a rapidly flowing river, horse-drawn traps, and tin-roofed houses surrounded by banana plants, the huge leaves of which were being utilised by villagers to shelter from the rain as they walked along jungle paths. Weathered and blackened with mildew in the damp environment, a wonderful old stone gateway was surmounted by animal figures.

I embarked on a trip by Filipino *banca*, a dugout canoe fashioned from the wood of the *lawaan* tree, to the fabulous **Pagsanjan Falls**. Paddled up the 90m/300ft-high gorge by two boatmen, we passed vegetation that included palm trees, banana plants, creepers, and dense undergrowth. I saw local people in canoes and washing by the water's edge, men loading coconuts onto a barge, waterfalls veiled in mist and, where the river narrowed between towering green walls, trees almost creating a roof overhead. The volume of the swiftly flowing river had been swelled by the heavy rains, and as we approached churning white rapids, the boatmen alighted on slippery boulders in order to haul the canoe up; I was terrified lest they lose their grip and I went hurtling downstream again! One cascade tumbled hundreds of feet in a white ribbon, but others were delicate sprays providing a misty canopy above. In the wet conditions following the flooding, it was one of the most inspirational ventures that I have undertaken and was climaxed at the end of the gorge by the thundering 23m (75ft) Pagsanjan Falls hitting the surface of the water and throwing up clouds of spray. At that time, the only construction at the falls was a small rustic hut, but no doubt progress has caught up and it is no longer an isolated unspoilt spot. Then came the return trip, which needless to say was considerably faster (with a stop to bail out the canoe!) and took some skilful manoeuvring on the part of my boatmen. Encountering the comparatively quiet stretches again, people were still washing on the banks and loading boats, which were reflected on the surface. Pagsanjan (or Magdapio) featured in Francis Ford Coppola's film *Apocalypse Now.*

Manila was full of first-time experiences, such as bars with large genuine notices telling patrons to deposit all guns and weapons with the cashier – shades of the Old Wild West! One evening, a male partner and I were accosted in the street by a tout who wanted to show us the city by night, a proposition to which I would never normally succumb. He was a real 'bruiser'; with seemingly no neck and a head resting on broad shoulders, his nickname was 'Buddha Baby'. Having decided between ourselves that we would be safe with such protection, we first returned to the hotel where we made sure that he knew we deposited all our cash and valuables; he had said that we could reimburse him later. Well, it turned out to be one of the best and most intriguing episodes that I have ever experienced; never could I have seen such diverse and interesting aspects of this dynamic city, from luxury to the ultimate in bawdy, on my own. Our guide was known and acknowledged everywhere, but whether from respect or fear (because he seemed to represent the local Mafia!), I know not. Transported by horse-drawn carriage, we started at the upmarket end of town where he knew all the tricks, like carrying a concealed hip flask to avoid paying exorbitant prices. Our guide was extremely solid for an Asian, and I felt immensely sorry for the poor undernourished skin-and-bone horses being urged to trot on roads severely rutted by the rains, at one stage insisting that we get out and walk.

The finale was the sleazy **Fishers Club**, a darkened venue where girls performed X-rated acts with ping pong balls on the table at which we and others were seated, the men flicking lighters to see better. I do not know who was the more embarrassed, the girl on the table or me! But worse was to come. Just prior to departing, my two escorts adjourned to the toilet and left me standing in front of the panoramic window of a viewing room where girls were assessed as prospects by customers. I was mortified to find that I was assumed to be one of the 'hostesses' and gave my companions a piece of my mind when they returned some time later, but they just considered it very funny. Nevertheless, on the whole it was a remarkable evening, finishing up in the wee small hours with individual massages in a brothel, following which we were escorted back to the hotel, where we paid our guide a very reasonable sum. On a later visit to Bangkok (as tour leader), my party attended a live sex show where couples had intercourse on stage and obligatory drinks cost the earth!

As a total contrast, in **Manila Bay** I visited the island of **Corregidor**, site of General MacArthur's last stand in WWII, from where he possibly uttered the famous words *I shall return*. An amusing incident involved a car with heavily tinted windows provided by my tour company. An ex-official vehicle that once enabled corrupt politicians to travel incommunicado, whenever we approached a checkpoint, all traffic was halted and we were waved through because nervous guards were apprehensive about who might be aboard!

Motorised trishaws were a common method of transport in towns, but bicycles and pony carts were more practical in the countryside, where chickens ran around tin- or thatch-roofed woven houses on stilts nestled beneath coconut palms. People worked under crude shelters to produce coir from stacks of coconut husks. Tropical blooms made a splash of colour, rustic stalls sold necessities, a cooking fire flared in the open, and the usual washing was strung between trees; it was all very photogenic. Vendors clambered over buses as they attempted to sell their wares, and I had my first sight of the extremely colourful, brightly painted and garishly decorated *jeepneys*, with streamers flying and ear-splitting music blaring forth, one even sporting cymbals and a beribboned model horse on the bonnet. Evolving from modified war surplus American jeeps, the grossly overloaded vehicles were very prolific. The silver horse mascots proclaimed the driver's physical prowess and were a symbol of endurance. Incidentally, the most popular theory is that the name jeep evolved from the acronym GP, which stood for Government Purposes or General Purpose.

Next stop was a cemetery with huge elaborate mausoleums, some providing rooms inside for family members to mourn the deceased person on anniversaries and partake of food 'shared' with spirits of their ancestors. I was on my way, again by car, to **Baguio** and **Banaue**, site of renowned 2,000- to 6,000-year-old rice terraces in the district of the **Ifugao** (from *Ipugo* meaning Eaters of Rice), one of the world's ancient wonders, which I believe have since partially disappeared. Carved from mountainsides without the aid of metal tools, the terraces were a tribute to the heavens in thanks for the sustaining food, and if placed end to end they would have spanned halfway around the world. Isolated by the rugged mountains, in the days of Spanish colonisation the Ifugao managed to maintain their culture and customs. As one of the first to traverse the mountain road following the disastrous floods, in places we were obliged to wait whilst mudslides were still being cleared, and one could look back and see how the existing surface had been undermined – it was scary stuff.

We crossed a river by means of an old rusted landing craft from World War II; it was no wonder that the country had so many tragic accidents involving overcrowded ferries! Passengers balanced objects in rolled bamboo mats on their head (I seem to recollect some were live animals), and driving again, we passed colourful roadside fruit stalls laden with prime bananas, melons, and other tropical varieties. We visited a moving war cemetery, which really brought home the futility of conflict and the waste of human life; hill upon hill, almost as far as the eye could see, was inundated with small white crosses. At dusk I took film of fishermen wading slowly in shallow water and casting nets. The luminous glow filtering through cloud cover was mirrored on the surface to create an ethereal effect. As I wandered through a village still bearing signs of the recent floods, a huge pig lay asleep on the tiny porch of a rustic dwelling constructed from scraps of corrugated iron and wood.

Next day, we passed people working to repair damage and water buffalo pulling carts or just enjoying the wet conditions. In an embarrassing interlude, I lost a lot of respect for the International Red Cross. Requesting to see the floodwaters that were still raging in some areas, I was taken by my guide to a village where I was surprised to find the entire community gathering around me. Apparently, in order to gain access, my escort had informed them that I was from the above organisation, and with doleful expressions they clamoured around wanting information. None spoke English, so I only became aware of the situation after leaving, when I was told that in spite of millions of dollars in aid being poured into the country, to which Australia contributed a sizable amount, these people had received nothing and were in dire straits, funds having finished up lining the pockets of officials.

The houses, again built on stilts, were accessed by bamboo ladders. Wood was stacked in front, people pounded grain to make flour, one had goats feeding from a basket underneath, and of course washing hung on lines. Some more-affluent homes had decorative fences and neat little gardens where plants grew profusely in the humidity. Boats were stored beneath others, and we encountered a line of gypsy caravans crossing a bridge. Just prior to entering a narrow chasm, where the highway hugged a perpendicular cliff face on one side and dropped to a tumultuous river on the other, we passed roadside stalls, an impressive waterfall appearing to emerge from a cave, and local people walking along the verge. As we climbed higher, I could see the twists and turns of the tortuous road, and we came across a shrine to Our Lady in a rocky recess. At the highest elevation, the valleys below were filled with cloud, and thatched huts sat in cleared compounds surrounded by dense growth, in one of which a lady was washing articles in an enamel basin.

Finally arriving at the fabled terraces, the dwellings were dwarfed by entire mountains cut into narrow steps. I have a fantastic picture overlooking a flat-topped stepped green mountain with yellow ears of waving grass in the foreground and workers below. Most of the terraces were bare and gave the impression of giant brown staircases with green risers. A woman toting a conical-shaped basket slung from her forehead almost disappeared as she merged into foggy conditions created by low-lying cloud. In the town of Banaue, I was greeted by the usual market scenes, a man riding a sturdy mountain pony, and a goat and pig in the main street. Still extremely lush, one could look down on the river, waterfalls, and houses with tin or steeply pitched thatched roofs ensconced amongst banana plants, from one of which emerged a scantily clad male occupant. The serpentine river and its feeding tributary, green cultivated plots beside the stony bank, clusters of houses and the mountain backdrop, again with attractive grasses in the foreground, were a source of excellent photographs. More near-naked men worked collecting wood and bamboo, whilst others of these shy people scattered into the bush. I filmed a family group, including the dog, outside their home and obtained an amusing shot of a delivery driver in long gum boots (Wellingtons) and a blue shirt, his bare buttocks exposed as he bent over to deposit an unloaded box! In the river, skimpily attired people were bathing or gathering stones, and a man wearing just a breach clout carried a load of vegetation on his back.

Walls constructed with stones from the riverbed made an appearance, and vegetable mounds with patterned (e.g., circular) furrows created artistic patches interspersed with rice. In a reversal of colour, these flourishing paddies resembled green steps with brown risers. Using an adze, a man squatted to work on a block of wood, and trimmed timber tied in bundles lay nearby. Others, similarly employed, lived in crude shacks by the roadside. I came to an area where steeply stepped paddies filled with water appeared like a glass stairway, the often-seething river winding at the bottom. With gently waving rust-hued pampas in the foreground and the occasional bright red flower on the rim of a plot, it was the subject of striking pictures.

I filmed workers sorting coconuts and walked through a village where thickly thatched wooden storehouses, accessed by ladders, had discs inserted in the stilts or inverted cone-shaped wicker baskets on top to prevent rats climbing up. Inside one dwelling, flames of an open fire burned brightly, and sapling fences enclosed the compound where chickens, puppies and piglets ran around, two of the latter (one peculiarly striped) rubbing their itchy sides on wooden beams. They had a feed trough formed from a hollowed log, and a large mortar was fashioned in the same manner; it was a very primitive community. I watched people planting rice and marvelled at the way they traversed the narrow embankments between the paddies with ease; I found it extremely difficult even to negotiate my way into the village. Mothers carried babies in slings, a man was planing wood, another chopped bamboo, and a woman pounded grain. There were stacks of saplings, and children played happily, some chasing bubbles blown from a bamboo pipe. Holding a spear, an obviously important individual wore a vivid red cloak. We encountered men logging with machetes, women with loads of greenery on their heads carrying shovels, a man weaving with a ball of twine, and other men dressed only in loin cloths bearing sticks or spears. I walked past naked bodies bathing in the river and gingerly progressed along the top of a narrow ridge dividing newly planted rice; the further I went my legs turned to 'jelly' from fear of falling into the mud! In this village, a group of laughing children gathered around a lady using a hand loom to weave the colourful striped fabric from which skirts were made, another hung bright red skeins of dyed cotton on bamboo poles to dry. Many women wore a type of circlet on the head. My guide demonstrated the art of playing a flute by blowing with the nose, a man jogged with an enormous bundle of wood across bowed shoulders, and others, baskets on their backs, fished with spears. Storage barns had the appearance of huge haystacks, and I was shown an area of old overgrown cave dwellings.

Leaving this region, the landscape became stark, the road winding along brown mountains bearing scant vegetation and falling to a gorge confining a wider turbulent river, where men were collecting rocks. What appeared to be a small decorated wooden coffin lay askew in undergrowth at the foot of a cliff, and a high waterfall tumbled beside the road. As we climbed to the highest point on the Philippine Highway System (7,400ft), the cloud closed in, and I could see no further than the trees and grasses on the verge, conditions that made the road hazardous – the driver steering with his head out the side window! Reaching a small settlement, we refuelled at an old-fashioned hand-pumped bowser and continued on past more banana plants, lush growth, waterfalls, and thatched houses. Back in 'civilisation', I saw a girl sweeping with a twig broom, horse-drawn carriages, and people clearing weed from flooded fields.

Cebu

As a complete change of pace, I flew to **Cebu City**, on the island of the same name, where I saw the yellow stone pavilion with a red tiled roof housing the cross planted by Magellan during his voyage of discovery in 1521. Nearby **San Augustin Church** was the oldest Christian relic in the country. The island was known for making musical instruments, and I bought a cheap guitar, but it did not survive the journey because a join in the body opened with the change of climate, so I purchased an expensive Italian Eko in Singapore.

SINGAPORE

On this visit, I spent some time in the well-presented **Jurong Bird Park**, where exhibits included everything from exotic tropical birds to magellanic penguins. Amongst the more than 8,000 on show, I saw white birds like curlews with black heads and long curved bills, a mottled species with a large beak, another hopping in a peculiar manner on the branch of a tree, ostrich and cassowary, many types of colourful parrot, red ibis looking startling on bare branches, a flock of white long-necked water birds flying in a huge aviary with lush foliage, a bird with vivid red plumage camouflaged by a red long-leaved plant, more red ibis in a pond surrounded by philodendrons, and owls looking every bit as wise as reputed – one even winked when I zoomed in with the camera! There were also black and white hornbills, a row of small green birds hanging upside down, a beautiful black and white bird with a brilliant red head, and crowned cranes with their dainty feathery yellow crest. I identified brightly coloured macaws, beautiful pheasants, and birds of prey that included different species of eagle and hideous vultures. Together with the usual shimmering emerald variety, white peacocks wandered in grounds that even contained a small red Japanese wooden bridge. I also saw white swans, very pink flamingos in a large pool, big storks, and the impressive walk-in aviary, the world's largest, with the highest man-made waterfall – 30 metres.

MALAYSIA

Crossing the border (a long protracted procedure) with friends, I went to **Kota Tinggi** waterfall in **Johore Bahru**, **Malaysia**. A popular swimming hole cosseted in lush jungle vegetation, one can swim right beneath the 34m cascade, which falls with considerable force, but not recommended on weekends when it is crowded with tourists and locals alike! Nevertheless, I witnessed a lovely sunset through the palms. Next day, by the roadside back in Singapore, I encountered a monkey in an abysmally small cage and two of the largest snakes that I had ever seen – fortunately also in cages! Bird's nest ferns flourished in trees, and both natural and landscaped gardens were a feature of this island country.

On one trip, a transit stop at the airport in Kuala Lumpur provided a brief brush with fame when I received a hug from Mohammed Ali. On the occasion of my first visit to the United States, I shared a train compartment with Gretchen Christopher, lead female singer of The Fleetwoods, who insisted that I also share her snack.

Postscript

Macau is now one of the cleanest cities in the world, where not even the garbage is wasted. Collection is operated on an incentive basis, and contractors are paid for what they deliver to an incinerator that generates electricity for China.

ASIA 1974

In 1974, I organised a long trip to destinations where few people ventured at that time, and which ultimately launched me on my travel career. As it transpired, everything that could go awry, such as bookings not being confirmed or payments received (necessitating paying again on arrival), seemed to eventuate, and it was only because I had done so much research that I was able to extricate myself from these situations. On my return, following a meeting at home with the manager of Kings Holidays, through whom I had chosen to undertake the journey, I was offered a free trip in compensation, which would also include accommodation if I was prepared to act as tour leader because of my experience.

INDONESIA

With 13,667 islands, Indonesia is the largest archipelagic country in the world, stretching 5,120km (3,200mi) along the equator. It also has the greatest concentration of volcanoes (more than 400), most of which are dormant or extinct. The world remembers Krakatoa that shocked all humanity when it erupted in 1883, producing a tsunami that reached the west coast of America and caused the mountain to disappear, although it spawned a new island called Anak Krakatoa (Child of Krakatoa), which has grown to be very active, belching foul-smelling sulphurous gas and occasional solid debris. Registered in the *Guinness Book of Records* as the biggest volcanic eruption in history, the explosion was heard in Australia and Madagascar, and rocks and ash were blasted as far as Singapore. The ocean rushed to fill the caldera left in lieu of the mountain, and all settlements on the coasts of Java and Sumatra were buried or washed away, with the loss of 40,000 lives. Global weather patterns were affected for years.

The capital, Jakarta, on the island of Java, fell to Muslim forces in 1527 but was razed and renamed Batavia when seized by the Dutch in 1619. In 1941, they were swept out by the Japanese Imperial Army, which restored the name Jakarta, and it became independent under Sukarno in 1945.

Java

According to archaeologists, Java may well be one of the earliest places on earth to be inhabited by man. In 1891, the fossilised remains of what was to become known as Java Man (*Pithecanthropus erectus*) were found in Central Java. Believed to be half ape, half man, the creature must have lived some 500,000 years ago, at the beginning of the Pleistocene period when Java was connected to the Asian mainland. A later find, in 1931, revealed the more advanced but still not quite human Solo Man, believed to have lived 40,000 years ago. Still later, the 10,000-year-old remains of the first true *Homo sapiens* were unearthed in East Java.

Amongst the first things to confront me in **Jakarta** was the sight of people living under cloth shelters attached to corrugated iron fences and sleeping on the pavement. I observed food carts in the street, men with heavily laden baskets suspended from a pole across the shoulder, one toting chairs in a similar fashion, bicycles, and a shop selling caged birds. People were working with material resembling coir, and as usual all the children strived to be in photographs. Directly beside the railway track, I came across the appalling sight of people living under the same makeshift shelters. *Pedicabs* waited for customers, and I saw a long row of dwellings constructed from a conglomeration of odds and ends, with utensils in front and washing blowing in the breeze. One person was cooking over a smoking fire in an open-sided shelter, its roof consisting of plastic sheeting weighted with wooden planks. Similar accommodation continued alongside a murky brown river, and at that stage it was still somewhat of a culture shock to arrive from a modern progressive city to scenes of such abject squalor. From the muddy banks of the river, a man carting water in tin cans climbed a steep slope to a thatch-roofed woven bamboo house precariously perched on stilts amid banana plants and greenery. People were washing clothes, bathing, and even openly defecating in water flowing through a wide drainage ditch in a main thoroughfare!

The view from my hotel room showed six lanes of traffic, old houses with red tiled roofs, and uninspiring multistorey concrete blocks like boxes. Back at the railroad track, a market was in progress, the produce extending over the rails and having to be shifted at the advent of a train! Some vendors actually sat on the rail lines, whilst women in *sarong kebayas* selected from fresh produce, and children flew makeshift kites. A barber, his 'shop' set up beneath the shade of a tree by the river (a wooden chair in front of a mirror attached to the trunk), was attending to a client, and a lady, her posture extremely erect, walked past balancing a load of feathery material on her head, making it appear that she was wearing a high plumed headdress. I filmed more footage of life beside the railroad tracks, and in stark contrast, next I have pictures showing the grounds of my hotel near the beach in Bali, with thatched sunshades, stone lanterns, a bird aviary, pool, flowerbeds, and philodendrons climbing the trunks of palm trees.

Actually scheduled, *with a confirmed ticket*, to fly to Jogjakarta, I arrived at the airport only to find that I was not on the flight. After a protracted argument that became very heated, I demanded to speak with someone in authority and was escorted to an office, where I came to the realisation that an official had been offered a bribe and I had been 'bumped'. In the meantime, my flight had departed, and exceedingly upset, I yelled at the person in charge until he finally produced the flight manifest for the next departure, crossed off the name of another unfortunate passenger, and added mine to the list, the only problem being that the plane was headed for Bali and not Jogjakarta! However, I just wanted to leave and was farewelled with the words 'Lady, please don't come back again'! When I consider my reaction to others acting in this manner, I cringe at my own behaviour, but had I allowed myself to be intimidated by the belligerent attitude of the officer, meekly accepted the situation and not retaliated, I could have been stranded indefinitely.

To introduce a note of levity: a sign in the toilet at the airport showed a figure squatting with feet on the pedestal, superimposed with a big red cross.

Bali

My first pictures show people working with fibrous material spread to dry on the ground in front of an elaborate entrance. Constructed with small red bricks laid in patterns and adorned with lovely carved images, these ornate free-standing gateways to shrines and compounds were unique to Bali, often referred to as an island of 10,000 temples.

I attended a performance of the always entertaining **Barong Dance**. Accompanied by a *gamelan* orchestra, the colourful lion-like mythological Barong and monkey cavorted on stage. In this complicated tale of human sacrifice, a frightening witch and the mythological monster Rangda made an appearance. The show included a mock battle between his opponents and the Monkey King, who was finally disembowelled, the assailant drawing forth a string of sausages! The vibrantly hued costumes were striking, especially that of Kalika, disciple of Rangda, who transformed herself into a bird and was garlanded in a feast of colourful feathers. The Barong reappeared in the final act, together with his followers the *kris* dancers who, dressed in traditional black and white checked sarongs, their torsos bare, leapt about and, supposedly in a trance, stabbed themselves with lethal-looking *krises* yet remained unharmed. The *pemangku* (temple priest) sat cross-legged, and a woman with a tray of flowers knelt beside him as he sprinkled holy water. This doused the flame in a chalice-like vessel, creating smoke that wafted over the dancers. It was all fascinating and very energetic. Delicate maidens in lavish costumes, headdresses of frangipani crowning their long black hair, executed the traditional **Legong Dance**. In contrast to the dainty steps and graceful hand movements, there were comedy routines that caused me to laugh even though I understood not one word. Male performers also wore floral headdresses, and the stage was beautifully decorated. I also experienced the **Ketcak (Monkey) Dance**, inspired by events in the *Ramayana*, a Hindu epic that traces the abduction of Rama's wife Sita and attempts to rescue her from the evil King Rawana by Hanuman with his monkey army.

A tour through the craft villages of **Celuk** (gold and silver), **Mas** (woodcarving), and **Ubud** (painting) revealed verdant countryside where harvested rice paddies were filled with water, and we visited the 11th-century (another source quoted AD 917) religious hermitage of **Goa Gajah (Elephant Cave)** near **Bedulu**, where water issued from urns held by six weathered stone images on ancient baths excavated in 1925. The entrance, through the gaping mouth of a fearsome face with staring eyes (demon), was surrounded by carving depicting monsters, humans and forest scenes, with an eroded figure wielding a club to one side. I saw a fine triangular-shaped gateway and a small pavilion with sculptures on the stepped sides of its base, the thick thatched roof supported by a pillar at each of the four corners. I encountered small waterfalls, a narrow river, and everywhere dense jungle growth of ferns, bamboo, palm trees, and other exotic plants. Thatched roofs peeped above high stone fences covered with moss, and village roads were practically deserted. A man carried a load across his shoulders, and in those days many women were bare-breasted but shyly dropped a cover when foreigners approached. I photographed more of the intriguing gateways inserted with small wooden doors (one flanked by statues and frangipani), and we came to a walled 1,000-year-old sacred freshwater reservoir with springs bubbling up from below the surface and lovely reflections. This was **Tampaksiring**, and an ancient lichen- or moss-covered shrine located nearby was endowed with simple carving.

Finally reaching **Lake Batur**, I obtained excellent views of the volcano to the left and mountains opposite, even though the sky was overcast, its brooding clouds reflected in the grey water. Looking down on the artistry created by beige stubble-filled rice terraces and bright green banks, I could see people working. The panorama resembled a giant set of irregularly shaped brown and (where the rice was as yet unharvested) green steps from which erupted tall straight palms with feathery fronds on top, the whole making a stunning sight. Atop a steep staircase flanked by mythical figures, a white triangular entrance was covered in carving, and many rural mud walls were topped with the same dried grass or leaves that formed the thatching. I was on a private tour and taken to the neat home of my guide, where I was introduced to his family and took pictures of the compound, with a large pig in an enclosure and piglets running free. On the street outside, fluttering and swaying in a gentle breeze, long bamboo poles were bending at the top with the weight of intricate decorations made from the leaves. This is an art form at which the Balinese are extremely adept. A woman carried a large basket atop her head, and a naked man bathed in an irrigation channel; it was a way of life unchanged for centuries.

We arrived at the town of **Kintamani**, where I found horse-drawn traps, the inevitable bustling market with people eating at food stalls, and trucks converted to passenger vehicles, as much loaded on top as inside! A woman carried tiered baskets on her head, and a man was cleaning his teeth with a frayed stick. Under way again, we passed tiny thatched huts and palm trees in fields of tall green rice, eventually coming to a blue lake overlooked by more stepped paddies with an occasional splash of bright red foliage. The cluster of 22 tall temples at **Besakih**, their *merus* (tiers) tapering to a point, made interesting pictures silhouetted on a hilltop under a lowering sky with volcanic 3,142m (9,888ft) **Gunung Agung** behind. Called the **Mother Temple of Bali**, and the oldest, largest, and most important of Bali's estimated 20,000 *puras* (temples), possibly dating back to the eighth or tenth century, the three main sanctuaries were dedicated to the Trinity of Shiva, Brahma and Vishnu. My next photograph was one of the classical scenes of Bali: a man with a long flexible pole herding ducks along the verge. Other people walking beside the road toted baskets on their heads, and several couples each had a pig, the legs trussed, suspended upside down from a pole that they supported on their shoulders. Farmers worked their fields, whilst men and women washed clothes and bathed in a river. One woman led a tethered pig that others followed, a chicken ran along the top of a high wall, and I saw a man seated cross-legged on the ground playing a bamboo flute. Monkeys groomed each other or clambered up nutmeg trees and over photogenic mould-encrusted shrines in the sacred **Sangeh Monkey Forest**, no longer a safe venue because these inhabitants have become increasingly aggressive and are notorious thieves, stealing anything not firmly clutched! A busy produce market was the final stop before flying to where I should have been originally – Jogjakarta.

Java

Arriving in **Jogjakarta**, I saw decorated covered wagons pulled by oxen, and the exceptional 47m-high **Prambanan Hindu Temple** (AD 732), with a large deity and typical architecture featuring a wealth of carving on angular spires. For one thousand years it was Java's highest structure, lavishly decorated with motifs and sculpted panels, and the complex included temples to Brahma and Vishnu. Dedicated to Shiva, the main temple also contained a statue of his consort, Durga, and bas-reliefs depicted scenes from the epic *Ramayana*. Adorned with jewellery and elaborate headdresses, scantily clad figures with serene faces graced stone panels with embossed surrounds. There was a scene depicting a hunter aiming his bow and arrow at a garlanded deer, reliefs of winged figures with human heads, and monkey images. Standing in a recess with ornate sculpting above the lintel, a stylised lion was flanked by figures lodged above and below trees. A club-wielding deity with fiercely staring eyes knelt in the grounds. Being barely 25km from **Merapi Volcano**, Prambanan had been ravaged by both volcanic eruption and time. On the occasion of my visit, the immense weathered site exuded a wonderful aura because it was deserted.

Early next day, I was taken to the inspirational site of **Borobudur**, the largest Buddhist temple in the world, presenting a vision that can never be recaptured because it has now been restored. At that time, with early morning mist rising from the jungle, I saw its crumbling walls and tumbled *stupas* overgrown by the encroaching surrounds. With the overpowering atmosphere of time suspended in a capsule, it was an awesome spectacle, and in the all-pervading silence of this deserted venue, whispers seemed to be appropriate rather than disturb the ghosts of another era. Begun in the eighth century AD, 300 years before Angkor Wat and 200 years before Notre-Dame in Paris, it took 10,000 men ten years to complete. In 1814, it was rediscovered by Sir Thomas Stamford Raffles, and restoration by UNESCO only commenced in 1973, not even one year before my visit. Since then it has taken ten years and a cost of $24,000,000 to replace a million blocks and 450 of the original 504 serene statues of Buddha in varying sizes. It was still possible to distinguish the layout of this six-storey rectangular step pyramid, which was surmounted by three circular terraces with a central *dagob* (inverted cone shape or *stupa*) representing Nirvana forming the summit. Underneath each of the monumental *stupas* was an image of Buddha in various poses, and stone statues stood in niches on the walls. Mid-level stone panels, 120 in number, were enhanced with intricate tableaux telling the life story of Buddha. These included seated gods and goddesses, gatherings preceding and following passengers in an oxcart, and a scene depicting people in a grove of trees with an elephant. Altogether there were 1,460 reliefs, and the voluptuous figures bore a remarkable resemblance to those at Kajuraho in India. At the head of a steep flight of stairs, a doorway simulating a gaping mouth duplicated that by a contemporary culture (refer Bali). I was always amazed at how prehistoric civilisations built such high steps when they were small people – maybe a defence mechanism? Ranking with Angkor Wat, the Taj Mahal and the Great Pyramid, even today scholars are not sure if Borobudur is a step pyramid, temple, *stupa*, or place of pilgrimage. On the outskirts of the city, I encountered people bathing in a river and a group, one member sheltered by a paper sunshade, heading for a crowded cattle market with their sheep. Carrying infants in slings on their hips, women shopped from vendors sitting on the pavement with their goods, and I took pictures of typical thatched bamboo houses in a Malaysian *kampong* (most of which had disappeared in a modernised Singapore) with washing on a line and a figure working behind a bamboo fence.

EAST MALAYSIA (BORNEO)

Sarawak

Ruled from 1841 to 1941 by three white rajahs, Sarawak has a colourful history: wars with pirates, Dyak head hunters, and Malay and Chinese miners filled its past with mystery and excitement.

Back in the air again, we flew low over Borobudur, green fields in perfect squares, and plots filled with water like giant sheets of glass, all interspersed with a few houses and patches of trees. Following the course of a twisting river meandering through dense jungle, I could just make out mountains hidden in thick fog to one side. My first film on landing in **Kuching, Sarawak**, was of a woman carrying lengths of wood on her back in a tall basket slung from a band across her forehead. Walking barefoot on the stony road, she was accompanied by a small boy. I had come here to observe the life of the **Dyak** and **Iban** peoples living in communal *longhouses,* where several families cohabitated in partitioned palm-thatched or tin-roofed woven bamboo structures on stilts. Accessed via steps cut into a large log, with bamboo handrails, they had a split-bamboo *ruai* (verandah) running the length of the building, hence the name *longhouse.* Washing was threaded on poles suspended across this floor space, and fences were also constructed from bamboo. Women quickly gathered garments from the ground before hurrying indoors at my approach. Surrounded by mountains, and nestled as it was in thick vegetation that included banana plants, palm trees, splashes of red hibiscus, and bougainvillea, the village was very photogenic. I saw more women carrying loads in baskets on their backs, and different varieties of fern flourished beside a swiftly flowing stream. This was crossed by a primitive bridge created from a narrow branch, again utilising bamboo canes as handrails.

Back in the city, I saw the minarets and gold onion domes of the **State Mosque**, a towering elaborately carved totem depicting faces and figures, and the **Sarawak Museum** with a fine collection of tribal artefacts highlighting the cultural heritage and natural history of Borneo. An ornately carved and colourful item featured a toucan, tiny figures, and human skulls suspended from a crosspiece! An interesting note of trivia that I learned: kuching means cat in the Malay language, and the city was so called because it had a **Cat Museum** with exhibits from the world over, including a mummified example from Egypt, although I did not visit.

Then began a most exciting (although anything but comfortable!) trip to a Dyak village, commencing with a short flight to **Sibu**, where I embarked on a private river safari. Travelling by motorised longboat, my guide and I journeyed for an hour deep into the jungle, passing isolated habitations and a few people paddling laden canoes. This was followed by a walk that penetrated the enveloping rain forest, where epiphytes and creepers grew profusely on trunks – and I was forced to make use of a foul-smelling pit toilet with a crude wooden door! Ultimately reaching our destination, I was welcomed by the wife of the absent chief, in whose house, the sole individual dwelling, I was to stay overnight. I had taken nothing with me and possibly offended my hostess when I declined the offer of a used toothbrush – she probably considered me unclean!

Supported on poles about two meters high, these communal *longhouses* were built of wood, with the typical *ruai* running the length of the structure.

From large fibre mats spread on the decking, a woman was scooping grain by hand into a basket of similar material, which she carried indoors. Washing on poles seemed to delineate the individual residences, inside one of which was a chicken, and the interior was divided by low wooden partitions. I found it difficult to negotiate the steep steps hacked from a single log, this time without handrails, but the populace ran up and down with alacrity. Dugout canoes provided transport on the rivers, which were used as highways for communication between villages. Their source of drinking water, these same watercourses were also used for laundry, performing ablutions, cleaning teeth, and toilet functions; it was running water, but I certainly would have hesitated to enter, let alone drink it! We had carried our own food, including tinned fish, which we shared with these subsistence-living villagers who existed on a meagre staple diet of rice and a little green vegetable gathered from the jungle and cooked over an open charcoal fire. If someone was lucky enough to kill a wild boar, it was cause for great celebration in which everyone participated. The principle of these simple societies was one of caring and sharing: if anyone was ill or elderly, they were supported by the whole community. An experience that taught me a valuable and sobering lesson occurred when I tried to distribute lollies that I had taken, on advice from my guide, for the children. When offered to a child who already had a sweet, he held it up and indicated that I should give one to his friend. I could not help but think of the mad scramble that would have ensued had Western children been involved! It also taught me that the less you have, the less you have to worry about; these people were very happy.

In the evening, we were entertained by traditional dancing, which proved to be much more eventful than intended, although I was not aware until we departed the next morning just how perilous our situation became! Surrounded by the entire community, which included bare-breasted women and men high on *tuak* (the locally brewed rice wine), we were seated on the floor and dancers – coins sewn onto their elaborate costumes and wearing ornate headdresses, silver anklets and bracelets – performed in front of us. Accompanied by a *gamelan* orchestra, a youth executed skilful movements with a shield. At one stage, a man with elongated earlobes, his torso bare, and attired in a long loin cloth and feathered headdress, turned in a slow graceful manoeuvre whilst wielding a sharp *parang ilang* (long sword), and in so doing nicked under the eye of a child seated atop a pile of rice sacks behind. Great consternation broke out because the nearest medical help was miles away by river and road, but after the confusion abated, the entertainment continued. As mentioned above, it was only after we left that my Chinese escort, who had been justifiably terrified, informed me that as recently as the previous generation these people had been head hunters and he had feared for his life. Apparently, he had given them a substantial cash settlement to appease their wrath. This story brings to mind the blackened human skulls, decorated with dried grass, which were suspended from porch ceilings. A fire was built below, for what purpose I do not remember, and they were regularly 'fed' and given cigarettes, which bizarrely hung between teeth in naked jawbones below staring empty eye sockets! Succinctly, the Dyak indulge in ancestor worship and believe that in rituals the skull is endowed with the spirit. According to later reading, the area had also been the haunt for a roaring pirate trade.

I vividly recall spending an agonising night (pigs rooting with snorts, snuffles and grunts beneath the split-bamboo floor) dreading the necessity of having to use the toilet – the surrounding jungle! As is often the case, concern about the situation aggravated my need, and finally, at first predawn light, I ventured outside and squatted on the bamboo ramp leading to the door to relieve myself – hopefully unobserved! Later in the day, further downstream, I negotiated one of the rickety bridges, also accessed via a notched log, to see coffee growing, the plentiful clusters of beans still green. I saw more women in large coolie hats bearing loads, fruit on a *rambutan* tree, a demonstration of cock fighting (not nice to watch), a cane cage with some occupant hanging on a wall, a fisherman returning with his catch, and exotic jungle flowers. Then it was back downriver, after which I boarded an international flight to leave. Ever since that time, I have ceased to be critical of passengers who look disreputable; I was attired in the frock that I had slept in, with teeth uncleaned and long hair (fortunately plaited) a mess, whilst my shoes, which I later had to discard, were a disaster caked in mud!

Sabah

Flying above a dense canopy of tree tops, I arrived in **Kota Kinabalu**, **Sabah**, where my first pictures show a gorgeous spray of white orchids and my guide, in traditional dress that incorporated old coins, standing on the steps of a wooden house on stilts. These sights were followed by masses of blue water hyacinth, pink water lilies, purple flowering vines, and birds – which was about all I saw of Sabah! I had come to climb 4,101m **Mt Kinabalu**, but the weather was so bad that even helicopters would not attempt a landing.

SINGAPORE

Next stage on my trip was a flight over fishing traps to **Singapore**, where I was greeted by the familiar 8m-tall mythical **Merlion** (half fish, half lion) spewing forth its large jet of water into the harbour. Here, I spent time at the home of the Tan family, one of whose sons, Beng, was a chief steward on Singapore Airlines at that time, the other, Ray, my husband and I sponsored to migrate, together with his family, to Australia. The latter was a black belt in *Tae Kwan Do* (Korean martial art) and demonstrated his skill by breaking a brick, followed by three tiles balanced between two stools, with his bare hand. He concluded by breaking a wooden board with a foot. His father, announcing he would replicate the feat, approached and broke a tile – with a hammer!

A visit with other friends to the **Singapore Zoo**, by **Seletar Reservoir**, showed some interesting animals, including various African antelope, a rhinoceros emerging from the water and scratching its rump on a stump, gnus (two having a friendly tussle), and indigenous species. Birds included vibrant red ibis in a rocky pool ringed by tree ferns, palms, lawn and shade trees, less-than-colourful flamingos inhabiting a larger area, other long-legged water birds, an ostrich performing a mating ritual, and crested cranes. Big cats such as a leopard paced in small concrete cages, a jet-black panther sharpened its claws on a trunk, a Galapagos tortoise was feeding in a grassy enclosure, and crocodiles lay in a pool. It was the first time that I had seen the Komodo dragon, which were basking on rocks and flicking their long tongues, and the ever-entertaining orangutans included one washing face, hands and head with incredibly human-like actions. Two were swinging from branches and interacting whilst another, leaning on a fence, hooked the dextrous toes of one foot on top and nonchalantly urinated! One lay flat on its back, legs and arms splayed as if sunbathing, another stood in the attitude of an old man and scratched, and yet another pounded some object with a stone; I could have watched their amusing antics all day. The restaurant overlooked a beautifully landscaped pond, and final exhibits were a cassowary, a handsome tiger in an open enclosure bounded by a low wall and moat, a zebra rolling in the dirt, and playful otters.

This trip coincided with the annual **Chingay** procession, with eye-catching floats and different groups marching in uniform, the latter including gorgeous girls in colourful traditional costumes with floral headgear. Flicking a whisk, a white-haired long-bearded figure travelled behind a gigantic tiger. Amongst the floats were a huge bright yellow pith helmet and oversized boot, a teapot, an orange, a duck, pumpkin, and a 'toy' train full of passengers, including a jack-in-the-box and Disney characters Mickey Mouse and Goofy. These were followed by a Chinese-type carriage, a pagoda, a giant fish and turtle, figures in a wheeled trap drawn by replica horses, and a Chinese pavilion. Figures waving streamers stood on an elevated platform above animated animals (people in costume), and a multihued conveyance held performers from Chinese opera.

Interspersed with the floats were Chinese dragons, clowns riding bicycles, people in masks waving colourful ribbons, and others brandishing banners or huge flags (of various colours but predominantly red) on 18ft poles, which were the theme of the Chingay festival. More dragons and more red flags, over which acrobats executed backward somersaults in the air, were followed by a man on a unicycle and jugglers, the latter all dressed in black trousers, white shirts and red cummerbunds. Lovely Chinese girls with large fans came next, followed by tall figures in a variety of gay garb striding on stilts: one, with a black beard and bare belly, wearing red trousers and shirt and wielding a lethal-looking sword, another with a bowl of flowers. Then came more flags, dragons, and banners – it was a very lengthy parade! Held aloft on sticks, two extremely long dragons, undulating up and down, intermingled with mammoth flags supported by men having to run to maintain balance, one in a blindfold. A drummer preceded yet more flags, a lion, and an acrobat, more people flourished the colourful squares, and more floats bore elegantly adorned Chinese maidens. A man juggling knives, more dragons or lions with snapping jaws, flags, a horned serpent gnashing teeth at bystanders, and larger flags, one almost collapsing on the huge crowd, brought up the rear.

BANGKOK, HONG KONG & SINGAPORE 1976

Bangkok

In 1976, I escorted my first tour for Kings Holidays, to Bangkok, Hong Kong and Singapore, and my first pictures record some of the typical Thai architecture with red-and-gold multi-spired roofs.

Our trip began with a tour, by converted rice barge, of the *klongs* (canals) in **Bangkok**, which provided a perfect illustration of the impact of mass tourism on a country. When I had taken this excursion four years previously, it had been a new venture with barely a dozen people on the boat, and we visited one farmhouse, where a demonstration of cock fighting took place. On this occasion, we were obliged to queue for some time whilst a number of vessels were boarded, and several farms were employed. Counterweighted fish traps sprouted amongst palm trees along the lush banks, and we negotiated narrow channels with, in places, tall grasses forming a dense wall each side or branches of trees creating a canopy overhead. Wooden houses, bamboo poles draped with laundry on their verandahs, were built right over the water, and women washed clothes at the river's edge. Seated on wooden decking, a woman doused herself with water scooped in a basin, whilst others bathed in the dirty-looking brown river on which floated thick clumps of pretty water hyacinth. Others poled canoes, and one couple was vigorously soaping their hair and torsos on steps. These were also the repository for a large pottery jar and utensils, with washing hanging above and potted plants on shelves behind.

Our passage was marked by cheery greetings, beaming naked children waved happily from a small jetty, and everyone seemed gainfully employed. We passed one of the huge fish traps lowered into the water, a long line of barges, and another typical Thai structure, its steeply pitched red and green tiled roof, gables and eaves decorated with gold carving, and a white tower rearing behind. Standing in front, monks were washing dishes in a bucket as water lapped over the step at their feet. It was amusing to see policemen standing on the roofs of passenger boats to direct congested river traffic. Briefly disembarking at a boardwalk, I have comical film of a white monkey sitting on the head of a baby elephant, the latter using its trunk in an endeavour to extract something from the pocket of a gentleman wearing a white suit and carrying a white pith helmet. Seated on a bench, he was eventually forced to leave! Obviously meant as a tourist attraction, a second monkey was held by their handler. We came to **Wat Arun** on the **Chao Phraya River**, its many elaborately sculpted multi-tiered spires, the tallest 79m, also endowed with a few statues, and I photographed the elegant golden prows, carved with mythical figures, of royal boats in their sheds.

At the **Rose Garden**, a procession of beautiful sombre-faced girls in blue-and-lemon silk garments, ribbons hanging from flowers in their hair, carried offerings wrapped in shiny orange cellophane. On stage, they performed a dance with the traditional graceful hand movements, their fingers capped with long golden nails. Together with male partners, all in bright costumes, others executed similar motions without the artificial nails, and this was followed by couples dancing (or rather hopping) between pairs of bamboo poles. Arranged in a cross, these were moved in and out by other participants seated on the ground. Demonstrating total contrast, a display of fighting with adroitly twirled poles was followed by a mock wedding ceremony in which the colourfully dressed 'bridal' couple had their hands anointed over brass urns full of red petals. This was the culmination of the show, and we adjourned to the beautiful grounds, where we watched a circle of men skilfully manipulating a ball, from one to the other and high into the air, using all body parts (shoulders, back, head, knees, and so on) except the hands. Also outdoors, I have film of a dance performed by exquisite hill tribe girls, red flowers in their long jet-black tresses and dressed in ethnic attire, the black fabric enhanced with coloured stripes. Coincidentally, I was dressed in a black frock, the skirt bordered by large red flowers, and with the biggest snake that I had ever seen draped around my neck, so heavy that I could hardly stand upright. Embarrassingly, it kept flicking its tail under my short skirt, an action that I kept trying to prevent with my free hand!

Steeply pitched, tiered red-and-green roofs, a forest of graduated spires – at least one encrusted with ceramic flower motifs – and topiary trees denoted the **Royal Palace**. Surely one of the most ornate in the world, its eaves were lined with temple bells, gables featured glittering glass mosaics, gilded figures, and wonderful carved floral work, and there was one gleaming gold *chedi* (spire) soaring into a blue sky.

Travelling overland, I have pictures of working windmills, rice paddies, and the furrows of irrigation channels between palm trees. Excellent views from a bridge showed speeding motorised craft creating tremendous washes in one of the *klongs* and the legendary floating market where vendors, mostly wearing blue and shaded with large straw hats, sold every conceivable item. These included fresh vegetables and meat, the latter butchered, arrayed on boards across the front of the vessel, and weighed on handheld scales. Items were both bought or sold from boats, some paddled by mothers with babies. Joining the motley throng, I photographed greens in baskets or tied in bundles, a red plastic basin full of live turtles clambering over each other, fresh fish, and people ladling hot food.

Next, we visited the **River Kwai**, and even this had changed considerably, it was now a crowded venue with tourist facilities – there had been nothing there before! We trooped onto a floating restaurant beside the notorious bridge for lunch, which seemed incongruous when one remembered the significance of the site and how the POWs were starved. A trip upriver to the emotive **Chungkai War Cemetery** revealed floating houses, stands of feathery bamboo amongst the verdant growth, and mountains beyond. Emblazoned in large letters on a marble plaque at the entrance were the words *Their Name Liveth For Ever More*, and here again it seemed more 'commercialised'; on my first visit it had been a truly isolated well-cared-for patch in dense jungle. As previously, I spent time perusing the moving inscriptions on gravestones of men who died far too young. They carried such quotations as: *And God shall wipe all tears from their eyes*; *Some corner of a foreign land that is forever England*; *All you had hoped for, all you had you gave*, and *Peacefully sleeping, free from pain*: *we would not wake him to suffer again*. Returning to walk on the bridge, another moving experience, we then visited the Australian graves at **Kanchanaburi War Cemetery**, the familiar words of the ANZACS on at least one gravestone: *At the going down of the sun and in the morning we will remember.*

We visited a temple with a towering gilded image standing between smaller figures, its right hand raised to signify the *mudra* (sign) of dispelling fear. The steps leading to the temple were flanked by beneficial multi-headed *nagas* (water serpents). Also altered dramatically, for the worse, was the traffic chaos in the capital, the ubiquitous *tuk-tuks* (motorised trishaws) dicing with death whilst weaving their perilous path in and out. As a group, we attended one of the famous shows in **Patpong**, where live sex acts were performed on stage whilst the audience consumed exorbitantly priced alcoholic beverages.

Hong Kong

In **Hong Kong**, the graceful lines of a seven-storey pagoda stood in stark contrast to an austere modern white tower, and we visited the fantasyland of **Aw Boon Haw Gardens** (1935), on the same principle as Haw Par Villa in Singapore. Its colourful concrete images from myths and fairy tales included beasts, birds and dragons, a rotund laughing Buddha, and macabre scenes of torture. These featured an emaciated figure with staring eyes and pointed teeth, wielding a spiked mace.

This was followed by a trip to crowded **Aberdeen Harbour**, where smoke from cooking fires issued from the higgledy-piggledy assortment of congested boathouses, and washing hung overhead as, being lunchtime, people were using chopsticks to eat from china bowls. I could not even imagine living in such proximity to neighbours! Taking the funicular up **Victoria Peak**, we took the usual photographs of city skyscrapers at our feet and **Victoria Harbour** beyond. The peak tram began operation in 1888, cutting a three-hour trip via sedan chair carried by coolies to eight minutes.

Further afield, we found houses on stilts over the water and more washing on poles. Wearing a black trouser suit tied with a red sash, and shielded by a large straw hat with a black 'skirt' around the brim, a **Hakka** lady was carrying two baskets suspended from a bamboo pole – bamboo had an infinite number of uses! This was **Lok Ma Chau** observation point at the border post that overlooked the **Shenzhen River**, rice paddies, duck ponds, and mainland China. A similarly attired elderly couple, the man with a coolie hat and long white beard, sat as they had every day for some years, posing for pictures. Wearing the traditional curtained hat, a child had a puppy in a sling on his back. We proceeded to the ancient walled village of **Sam Tung Uk** (described previously), where several of the tribal people mingled about or attempted to sell souvenirs.

From the water, we obtained a close encounter with more tightly packed boathouses, the inhabitants going about their daily life on board and moving to and fro in *sampans*, the city in the background. Negotiating our way through larger shipping in the harbour, our guide pointed out a vast bare slope on the mountain looming behind the city, the result of a massive landslide that had destroyed many buildings. Making a fantastic sight as it turned, a large *junk* under full sail passed us by, and I took film of Hong Kong's incredible **Kai Tak Airport**, one of the busiest in the world. With yachts in the foreground, every three minutes aircraft from every part of the planet were landing or taking off from the runway over the water, banking steeply to clear the mountains.

Extending across roadways, the host of city signs looked tremendous at night, their neon lighting advertising businesses, restaurants, topless bars, clubs and pubs, with names like Red Lion Inn, Kismet, Bloom Bar, Pleasure, Fat Lee Medicine Co., and Clover Clothing, all in English and Chinese. At a market, itinerant vendors sold produce from baskets on the pavement, including fresh vegetables and fish, which were being scaled as I watched, and a butcher, his meat hanging in the open, was doing a roaring trade. Goods were piled on the sidewalk outside open-fronted stores with ramshackle dwellings above (the inevitable washing outside), and a man walked by pushing a cart containing a colourful array of miscellaneous items. In one of the shops, a man wearing a mask was working with a pile of flock or kapok, obviously used to stuff pillows on display.

From my hotel window, I looked down on activity in the tiny yards of houses on rooftops, where a man tended a couple of struggling plants and a woman was washing. This she hung to dry on a precariously balanced pink plastic pole. Hong Kong's Happy Valley Racecourse is world renowned, and Wong Tai Sin Temple is popular with locals because it has a reputation for useful horseracing tips!

Back on the water, I have film of two more *junks*, one with a red sail, and women in headscarves fishing from a *sampan*. On a punt guided by rope, we were ferried across a narrow waterway to the tiny village of **Tai O**, former haven for smugglers and pirates on peaceful **Lantau Island**, twice the size but so different from nearby Hong Kong. I have almost obscene pictures of dried ducks, pressed flat and hanging for sale, and scenes showing boats and houses with a barren brown mountain backdrop. In contrast, a high vantage point overlooked a blue bay with many small islands, and the final sight was **Po Lin Tze Monastery** on 750m (2,460ft) **Ngong Ping Plateau**.

Acquired as a spoil of the first Opium War in 1842, Hong Kong was a British colony for 156 years; it was handed back to the Chinese in 1997. The

Opium Wars evolved when Britain traded the drug, produced in India and exported by the East India Company, in answer to the demand for silver in payment for the huge quantities of tea imported into Britain from China, the only place that it was grown. Alarmed at the damage wreaked on society and the country's loss of silver earnings, the emperor declared a ban on opium imports, but the British continued to smuggle the illicit cargo up the Pearl River. In 1839, with the drug now India's largest export, the Chinese confiscated and destroyed the British stockpile in Canton, thus precipitating hostilities, after which victory saw the island ceded to Britain in a 99-year lease. It was not always a prosperous place, when the English took over, it was purely a community of farmers and fishermen, but a huge influx of refugees from China, seeking their fortune, assured such appalling conditions that when the bubonic plague struck in 1894, it raged for 30 years and claimed more than 20,000 lives!

Useless information: as well as tea drinking itself, the Chinese invented the teapot.

Singapore

Singapore is tiny, a mere 41km × 22km, but a giant in commerce and progress; every time I went, I saw massive changes in this showcase of Asia. Her origins can be traced back to the seventh century, and like many another island, she existed initially as a trading port: *junks* came from China laden with tea and other precious goods, tall-masted ships of the Bugis arrived from Indonesia filled with ebony, camphor and ivory, and from Borneo, Java and Sumatra came cargos of pepper, nutmeg, cinnamon, cloves, coriander and batik fabrics. Today it is a candidate for the world's busiest port and literally a crossroads of the oceans.

But in spite of its modern façade, Singapore still retains traces of its history such as that Grand Old Lady of the East, the **Raffles Hotel**. Opened in 1887 by the Armenian Sarkie brothers, it was patronised by princes, maharajahs, lords, film stars like Douglas Fairbanks and Mary Pickford, and the great authors Noël Coward, Rudyard Kipling, Joseph Conrad and Somerset Maugham, who wrote *The Moon and Sixpence* in his suite overlooking the Palm Court. It closed its doors in 1942 when taken over by the Japanese for high-ranking officers but reopened in 1946. The celebrated Singapore Sling cocktail was first concocted here, and in its time, it has seen everything from a Dutchman who used to drink up to eight bottles of gin a day to a tiger in the billiard room. Other relics of the city's past include the **Supreme Court**

(1939) with its dome and Corinthian pillars, and **City Hall** (1929), facing the green of the **Padang** where cricket was an institution. The formal surrender of the Japanese forces to Lord Louis Mountbatten in September 1945 took place on the steps of City Hall.

Truly a harmonious multi-racial society, shopkeepers in **Arab Street** sell basket ware and exotic fabrics, in **Chinatown** you can purchase powder scraped from antelope horn to relieve high fever, and in **Little India** one can find silver and brassware, garlands of fresh flowers, silk saris, spices, and *dhobi* shops, still laundering clothes by boiling in a cauldron and beating them on stone slabs.

ITALY 1976

Rome

My first trip to **Italy** was at the instigation of neighbours who had not visited their homeland since migrating to Australia many years earlier and invited me to accompany them. We began our tour in **Rome**, traditionally founded by Romulus in 753 BC, where the view from my solitary small window constituted my first photographs: the well created by four multistorey walls enclosing a tiny courtyard and washing hanging outside sills holding a few potted plants!

The Eternal City was endowed with more than its fair share of churches, which were soon to become commonplace, but initially I was enthralled by the sight of a huge cathedral, its dome, clock tower, and statues around the parapet. It was also my first experience of al fresco dining, unknown in Australia at that time, and I filmed nuns crossing in front of a towering column with a figure of the Virgin cradling the Holy Child on top, horns possibly representing the devil at her feet. There were many other buildings with domes, statues, tableaux in relief, and arched porticos, but it is too long ago to remember each specifically. One trio of white alabaster figures looked stunning against the clear unblemished blue of the sky, and each end of a large symmetrical structure was surmounted by twin winged images in chariots, each drawn by four horses. The superb panorama from an elevated position overlooked this white edifice and revealed an equestrian statue in the forecourt, trees and well-tended lawn to one side, and ruins in a sunken compound at my feet. Descending, I passed a second looming pedestal with a statue on top and entered the archaeological site, consisting of barely more than pillars and blocks of stone, after which I found myself in front of the mammoth white building, which turned out to be the **Vittoriano Monument**. Featuring a wealth of sculpture, it was built between 1885 and 1911 to honour King Vittorio Emanuele II. Another striking white statue featured intertwined figures against a startling blue sky, and a beautiful painting on an ancient brick wall was protected by a wooden awning. Flowering bougainvillea formed the foreground to a statue of an impressive male figure, naked except for a cape, restraining a rearing horse; other images lined the parapet above.

My rambles brought me next to the **Roman Forum**, from the seventh century BC, with its triumphal arch, **Arco di Septimo Severo** (**Arch of Septimius Severus**) erected in AD 203 to celebrate the Roman victory over the Parthians, and other familiar remains that need no explanation. Then it was on to the **Colosseum**, the 50,000-capacity stadium begun in AD 72 by Emperor Vespasian. Nearby, the highly decorated monumental **Arco di Constantino** (Constantine) was built to commemorate his victory at a battle in AD 312. The Colosseum was the symbol of Rome even in the Middle Ages; Bede wrote: *When the Colosseum falls, Rome shall fall – and when Rome falls the world will end.* It has been damaged by earthquakes several times, used as a source of stone and marble for later generations of builders, more recently affected by pollution and vibrations caused by traffic and the Metro, but still it stands. Outside this monumental structure, making a splash of colour against the grey stone walls, horses harnessed to red-wheeled wagons stood waiting for tourists, but strangely very few people were in the arena. I have a picture of my neighbour, Frank, standing next to a centurion's suit of armour; the Romans were (and still are) small people. More soaring columns had figures at the apex, and statues were everywhere.

Sicily

En route to **Sicily**, we passed **Mt Vesuvius**, crenellated towers, a huge figure of Christ, arms outstretched, on a peak, wonderful hilltop villages, photogenic ruins, a little yellow church with a white bell tower in a green valley, a hill surmounted by a cross on a tall pedestal, and the remains of a castle on the summit of a mountain, dominating the small town at its foot. On arrival in **Messina** from **Reggio di Calabria**, I met the extended family, who could not speak a word of English, and my friends being fed up with translating, I was deposited in a pension whilst they became ensconced with relatives and took off for remote villages, not nominating a date of return. The room in which I was installed was so stifling that I spent the hours therein naked, and such was the bad smell issuing from the drain that I was obliged to keep a plug in the sink and fill it with water. There was no bath; a shower down the hall cost extra and it is amazing how adept one can become at performing ablutions in a sink! Sicily was the home of the Mafia, and the whole of Italy formed an unholy alliance whereby religion and the mob tolerated each other in a strange coexistence.

My initial pictures in Messina were of the 12th-century **Cathedral** and its elegant **Campanile**, which housed the world's largest **Astronomical Clock**. At noon, a rampant gilt lion, waving a flag and turning its head, stood above two maidens who struck the large green-tinged bells, between which stood a golden cockerel flapping its wings. Led by an angel, other images paraded below, and underneath them again were tableaux and a second group of gilded images, with the Holy Ghost in the form of a bird circling above. On one side, a huge dial featured the 12 signs of the zodiac. The main portal of the cathedral was enhanced with figures and slender spiral pillars, and I saw yet another towering column bearing a religious image. Located near the bell tower, the **Fontana di Orione** (1553) commemorated Orion, mythological founder of the city, and was constructed by a pupil of Michelangelo on the occasion of the completion of an aqueduct making the houses of Messina the first in Sicily to receive running water. A typical Italian masterpiece, it had life-sized figures on top, naked females supporting the upper of two basins, and images representing the rivers Tiber, Nile, Ebro and Camaro reclining around the lower edge.

I went with my friends to the wonderful town of **Taormina**, capital of Sicily in the ninth century, spectacularly sited in mountainous terrain and tumbling in terraces down to the sea below. In one narrow street, balconies with decorative wrought-iron railings lay overhead, and an archway covered in greenery spanned one end. A white cross crowned a mountain overlooking the narrow and sometimes stepped alleys, where potted plants occupied balconies and bougainvillea cascaded down walls with coloured awnings. Flowers also lined parapets, pines grew at a higher altitude, and palms were mixed with orange trees in streets where art was displayed and colourful tables and chairs arranged for outdoor dining. Stone balustrades, ornate façades, statues, vibrant flowering trees, and multihued blooms against stone and whitewashed walls completed the picture. Trees festooned with a mass of blossom stood outside an attractive old church and bell tower, and I looked down on a narrow roadway with a sheer drop to the sea on one side and a curtain of vivid purple bougainvillea draping a wall on the other. There were colourful umbrellas, fountains in pretty walled gardens, and in streets that were a blaze of colour and overflowing with greenery, a passive donkey, lethargically flicking its tail, stood patiently on steps whilst being loaded with tiles. Flags were flying, and high up on one of the surrounding peaks was a castle.

Wandering amongst ruins overlooking the town, I could pick out several towers and **Mt Etna** to the west. The remains constituted part of the ancient **Teatro Greco**, a third-century BC amphitheatre, second largest in Sicily, dramatically suspended between sky and sea. A view over the ocean showed a rocky island with a solitary house, many boats in the harbour, and red umbrellas on a spit of land. We ate lunch under a canopy sheltered by red bougainvillea in an open-air restaurant perched halfway up this eyrie on **Monte Tauro**. Roving costumed musicians played a tinny flute and tambourine, and we had vistas of the bay, the island in the centre, rock tors and caves at the waterline, and buildings atop perpendicular cliffs opposite.

This being my first trip to Europe, Taormina impressed me as the prettiest village that I was ever likely to see; in fact, so much so, that I arose at 4am to catch a train and revisit it a few days later, and despite the intervening years and much experience, I have not changed my opinion, still considering it to have been amongst the ultimate in Mediterranean destinations. Walking in the deserted city before dawn, I was accosted by a policeman on a bicycle who wanted to know why I walked alone at that hour. He had no English, so we communicated in elementary German, and he decided to accompany me for safety. Eventually, a patrol car pulled up and enquired what he was doing, so I finished up with a ride to the station. I became aware that there was good reason for this precaution and the constable's obvious concern when, at a later date, I was followed by a cruising car and, again, by a man who ducked behind vehicles whenever I turned around, until I finally approached a police officer. On another occasion, in the shoulder to shoulder river of humanity moving through a flea market, a stranger slipped an arm around my waist, from which I could not extricate myself until I diverted swiftly behind a stall; it seemed that Italians did not just pinch bottoms anymore!

To fill in time, I took a four-day tour of the island, which traced a route through **Catania**, **Syracuse**, settled 734 BC, **Agrigento**, founded 582 BC, with temple ruins dating from this period, and **Palermo**, but I do not remember where particular points of interest occurred so will just give a general description. First was a magnificent cathedral with statues below stunning murals on the exterior and, amongst other intriguing sights, two crafted horses (one black, one white) that with their riders reached three storeys high. Balloon sellers created a festive atmosphere, and I was lucky enough to witness a procession of clergy bearing a towering spire covered with automated religious figures, some of which revolved around a sunburst with a face in the centre. The ornate façade of another mammoth cathedral featured soaring columns, statues, an eagle clutching a coat of arms, and recumbent cherubs. There were other pillared buildings, statues on pedestals, flowering trees, and a huge fountain, its central figure rising above life-sized images frolicking on the backs of gigantic fish. One lovely sculpture (minus the hands) was attired in robes so finely wrought that the stone appeared soft and delicate.

I recall visiting an ancient medieval village where, under its eaves, an old slate-roofed building was enhanced with murals portraying elegant figures, and decorative designs appeared on columns and around recessed windows. A simple fountain stood in the courtyard opposite an open-fronted stone tower, apertures in its wooden floors accessed by a series of ladders. An attractive church featured a fresco in the arch above the portal and interesting slender spires on top of its tall free-standing gable. Small medieval bricks were used in the construction of a round tower and crenellated walls with corner bastions. Crossing over the drawbridge and under the portcullis, a beautiful courtyard was revealed, one wall covered with a black and white diamond pattern and colourful murals that included St George and the Dragon. Wooden balconies ran around three sides and there were arched portals and windows. A second court, with vines and coats of arms on the walls, contained a laden orange tree in a hexagonal planter. Another illustrated wall was the backdrop to well-maintained gardens.

On the move again, a figure on a rearing horse surmounted a pedestal bearing deep relief of remarkable battle scenes, which included armoured knights using shields to parry lances. The inevitable castle topped a hill beyond a body of water reflecting a picturesque bridge and trees, and I have film of a monumental sculpted arch, buildings above a high embankment with steps leading to the water, and a tower looming behind ramparts atop a steep rise, the lower slope featuring a lovely garden. Views taken overlooking the city show a massive steeple towering above all else. A statue on a tall pedestal stood in front of wide steps, flanked by images, leading to a classical pillared building with a dome and carved pediment. This was situated at one end of an arched stone bridge, together with which it was beautifully reflected in the river.

A large double arch across the roadway connected two four-storey buildings, and one grand edifice featured multiple columns and a pyramid-shaped roof with a tapering spire. There were the customary statues on buildings and parapets, an elegant colonnaded courtyard, and a second huge memorial with tableaux in deep relief around the base. A structure resembling an aqueduct spanned the thoroughfare between two round towers, and larger-than-life figures were dwarfed by the tall pillars of a monstrous white cathedral with several domes and an incongruous multi-tiered brick carillon. The inevitable images topped a column in front. Streets were paved with flagstones and trams ran down the middle. Caressed by gently flowing water, a moss-coated dark rock formation was crowned by a black winged figure, and naked stark white images mounted the sides. I saw buildings with corner turrets and several more impressive statues on pedestals, including one with a reclining white lion on the plinth. A huge cathedral sat atop a distant hill, a mighty arch was surmounted by a charioteer driving six horses, and I found an elaborate clock tower with murals above a niche containing a figure on horseback. From immaculate gardens with an artificial lake, I obtained another view of the chariot-topped arch, which had a reclining image below an equestrian figure at each end.

Entered beneath a portcullis, austere fortifications with an enormous corner tower enclosed a massive compound; however, its appearance was somewhat softened by ivy draping sections of the forbidding walls. A peaceful grassed courtyard had a long reflective pool and flowers in front of a loggia, and a third was surrounded by a colonnade. The antithesis of this moated castle was the **Palazzo dei Normanni** in Palermo, which contained the **Cappella Palatina**, a jewel-like chapel designed in 1130, every inch inlaid with precious marbles and exquisite mosaics recounting Old Testament stories, created with coloured glass onto which gold leaf had been applied. Sadly, my movie camera was not equipped to capture indoor photography, so I do not have a record of this.

After two weeks in Sicily, I felt that it was an incredible waste of time and decided to take off on my own. Realising that I could not communicate with the family, I sought out an interpreter from the 7th Fleet of the United States navy stationed in the Mediterranean, and at that time berthed in Messina. Feeling not a little desperate, I brazenly bowled up to one of their aircraft carriers and called out to find if they had anyone on board who spoke Italian. When I explained my plight, they were extremely obliging, providing me not only with someone to translate but also a car and driver to take me to the home of the mother to get an indication of when my friends were due to return. Coincidentally, they arrived as we were speaking, but in between times I had been invited to an evening on the ship, which I accepted with alacrity. That was an experience in itself, and I was entertained royally. I was taken by tender to the USS *Mitscher* guided missile destroyer moored in the harbour and was immensely impressed at how the United States looked after their servicemen; there were no women sailors on board in those days. I recollect having freshly popped, buttered and salted corn in the officer's mess whilst watching a special screening (for me) of the film *Jaws*, which I had not seen before. This proved quite hilarious, because having viewed it probably many times before, immediately prior to the scary episodes someone would grab me from behind, and naturally I would scream – much to everyone's amusement! But I must say the sailors were all very polite and respectful, I was called ma'am so many times that I felt like the queen. I was also photographed in front of one of their big guns emblazoned, in large letters on the side, with the words: DANGER MAN KILLER!

One thing that sticks in my mind about Sicily was the incredible ice cream; surely the best in the world, the cones came served with fresh whipped cream on top!

Milan

The first stop on my solo jaunt was **Milan**, Italy's second largest city, where the amazing **Cathedral** – one of the world's largest Gothic edifices and fifth largest cathedral, commissioned in 1386 and taking 500 years to complete – had fine images of saints, important people and a few animals (3,200 created between 1397 and 1812) on the roof and façade. Small tableaux included one showing a man holding the head of a decapitated foe on which he rested his right foot. The 108m spire was surmounted by a gilded copper statue of the Madonna; beautifully executed towering brass doors, one with cherubic faces beneath the stone lintel, a second flanked by the heads of lions, portrayed biblical scenes, and the whole was crowned with a lacy parapet and veritable forest of slender spires (135) reaching skyward. There was a highly decorated archway to one side and, facing the cathedral, a statue of King Vittorio Emanuele mounted on a horse (a popular roost in the large square full of pigeons – and people), a white lion on the plinth. The corner of a nearby edifice featured a huge figure with a winged horse, and another stunning structure had fluted Ionic columns, numerous life-sized figures around the parapet, and a sculpted frieze encompassing the third-floor balcony. From the rear, the backlit cathedral took on the appearance of an enormous set of organ pipes, and I almost expected to hear an orchestral symphony with a host of angelic voices. In the vicinity was a soaring hexagonal tower and ornate lamp standards, also a repository for birds. There were many other elaborately decorated archways, through some of which I observed beautiful courtyards with flowers and hanging plants.

For the first time, I encountered the mammoth half-naked male forms supporting lintels on their bowed backs, which were to become a familiar sight in Europe, but the renowned **La Scala Opera House** (**Teatro alla Scala**, 1778) was an uninspiring ordinary-looking edifice. Four lovely frescoes representing Europe, Africa, Asia and North America adorned lunettes beneath the 47m glass dome of the **Galleria Vittorio Emanuele II**, an arcade with iron-and-glass barrel-vaulted ceilings connecting the Duomo and La Scala; statues were visible through an arch at one end. Dwarfed between 'modern' bland grey buildings was an attractive old brownstone church with a central clock tower. The **Church of Santa Maria delle Grazie** housed da Vinci's *Last Supper.*

Venice

Magical **Venice**, with its 118 islands, some 160 canals, more than 400 footbridges, and a plethora of churches, domes and towers in surprising squares, where artists were painting and that one seemed suddenly to stumble across by accident, is described in detail in a more recent chapter; it had not changed in the 30 intervening years. I purchased a charcoal drawing that, although not the most appealing, I had filmed at various stages of development, and it still hangs in my lounge room. Remarkably good pavement art was also an attraction. Murals on exterior walls of buildings along the **Grand Canal**, statues, arched windows, sculpted façades, the 16th-century **Rialto Bridge**, colourful window boxes, **Ca' d'Oro**, and the incredible beauty and opulence of **St Mark's Square** were not spoiled by overexposure and to this day remain a treasured memory. An **Astronomical Clock**, the bells on top rung by Moors cast in metal, stood cater-corner to the stunning **Cathedral**, tables and chairs were set up for al fresco dining, and huge Italian flags fluttered proudly in the piazza. Venice was full of gondolas, many moored to posts in the water and bobbing in the wash from boats. Religious images were prevalent, as was the lion of St Mark. It would be impossible to take a bad picture of Venice, and I have wonderful film of narrow streets, many churches, little canals crossed by tiny bridges, and walls bedecked with plaques, small shrines, greenery, flowers – and washing! Other well-known landmarks included the **Bridge of Sighs**.

On this occasion, I visited the islands of **Murano** and **Burano**, the first renowned since the 13th century (one reference said seventh century) for its glass, the latter, with its own leaning tower, for lace. I watched as old ladies sat in the sun creating the beautiful intricate patterns by age-old methods. Just as fascinating were its waterways and colourful fishermen's houses with fancy dormer windows. At the entrance to the Grand Canal, a large golden globe supported by kneeling figures had another standing on top. As with the old saying *All roads lead to Rome*, every avenue in Venice seemed, eventually, to bring me back to St Mark's Square.

Florence

My next destination was **Florence** (**Firenze**), centre of European life 500 years ago and the Renaissance in the 14th, 15th and 16th centuries. It was the home of the **Galleria degli Uffizi** (1574), Dante, Machiavelli, Michelangelo, and the Medici family, Florence's ruling class, which came to power as bankers and financed a large part of Europe's Cultural Revolution. They organised festivals of musical drama that came to be known as opera. Here, I found the magnificent **Cattedrale di Santa Maria del Fiore** (**Duomo**), with the largest brick dome in the world, designed by Brunelleschi and admired by Michelangelo. Begun in 1296 and taking almost 150 years to finish, its amazing pink, white and green façade took on a glowing honey-coloured tone in the sun. This incredible edifice also featured a square bell tower, spiral pillars, rose windows, elaborate carving on walls and doors, murals in tympanums, and many figures in niches and atop pilasters. Balanced on the backs of tortoises at the corners of its plinth, an obelisk stood in front of a smaller church with an ornate gable and black-and-white Arabic-style arches. A long arcaded building to one side had colourful images on plaques in the spandrels, and a second obelisk stood in a circular grassed expanse encompassed by tiered gardens with statues in recesses on top. Bridges spanning the **Arno River** included the familiar **Ponte Vecchio**, built in 1435, with its gold and silversmith shops (originally the domain of tanners and butchers who tossed leftovers into the river!), and surprise, surprise, there was a castle on a distant hill. In the 16th century, Grand Duke Ferdinando II decreed that the tanneries close because of the diabolical odours wafting towards his palace.

From the **Giardino di Boboli** (**Boboli Gardens**), I overlooked a large pool with a central sculpture, well-ordered gardens with fountains, and the vast city with the graceful 82m-high marble **Campanile**, designed by Giotto in 1334, and red dome of the Duomo rising above all. Back at street level, an ancient crenellated tower stood isolated from other structures, and a reproduction of Michelangelo's *David* appeared in a garden setting. Another panorama from a high vantage point revealed the green of a copper dome and many more towers, including the 94m-high crenellated **Torre d'Arnolfo** of the **Palazzo Vecchio** (1298–1314). Up here, I found beautiful gardens with pathways meandering between lawns and flowering beds, and superb views of a defensive wall, the river, and many of the bridges, with the city as a backdrop. A striking black and white church with a colourful mural on a gold background above its central window stood at the top of a flight of steps, and I obtained a wonderful overview of the free-standing tower mentioned above.

Back in the centre, I have a picture of a bronze statue in a sunlit square, framed by the black arch of an elaborate doorway in deep shadow. The focal point of Florence had to be the celebrated **Piazza della Signoria**, surrounded by elegant buildings and full of sculptures creating an outdoor gallery. Here, one finds Michelangelo's *David* (another replica) and other larger-than-life images outside the entrance to the Palazzo Vecchio, with stone lions reposing above its portal. To one side, the 14th-century **Loggia della Signoria** was also a showcase for sculptures, and amongst them were battling opponents, a lion, graceful entwined figures, a bronze statue of Perseus brandishing the head of Medusa (by Cellini), and Giambologna's final work, *Rape of the Sabin Women.* It was also the site of a large market, where I purchased a grey suede skirt and fur-trimmed jacket for a ridiculously low price. To the left, when facing the palazzo, was Ammannati's massive **Fountain of Neptune**, and I came across a set of glorious gilded or copper doors embossed with intricate scenes in a surround composed of smaller figures and heads. Mounted police made a nice picture, and patrolmen with tall white helmets wore side arms, which were not carried by our force at that time. An archway revealed a pretty courtyard and plaques adorned some walls, but I did not appreciate Florence as much as I should have because I had become overwhelmed by art and majestic buildings.

Pisa

From Florence, I headed to **Pisa**, where the first attraction I saw was the tiny, but ever so ornate (spires, statues, embossed doors), 14th-century **Chiesa di Santa Maria della Spina**, constructed to house a thorn from Christ's crown and situated on a sidewalk by the Arno. Reaching the grassed **Piazza dei Miracoli** (Square of Miracles), I visited the no-less-ornate 12th-century Romanesque **Cathedral**, the **Baptistry**, and the fabled 180ft **Leaning Tower**, although I did not climb. The bell tower, with its 16ft lean, was subsequently closed, and in 1994 six hundred tons of lead ingots were used, unsuccessfully, to anchor the north foundation. Lesser-known works were a representation of Romulus and Remus with the wolf, and the tangle of arms and legs in a colossal piece atop a tall pedestal. The cathedral, with a striped effect created by green and cream marble, was the perfect foil to demonstrate the lean of the tower, then around 14ft, which has since been arrested. Begun in 1064, the cathedral featured four tiers of fine columns above the entrance, diminishing in number towards the top, whereas the round Baptistry, started in 1155 and finally finished in the 14th century, had slender pillars circling the first floor and fancy gables around upper levels. Other edifices not so well documented included one with a decorative parapet, plaques, and delicate arched windows, an interesting small church, a façade ornamented with grey-and-white frescoes, and a free-standing tiered gable with a multitude of fine columns. An indeterminate stone animal stood atop an ancient yellowing wall.

Naples

Travelling by train, I passed ancient remains and a very long aqueduct before arriving in **Naples**, where both pizza and Sophia Loren were born. On this first occasion, I enjoyed Napoli, although on my second visit it was a dangerous, depressed and dirty city that left a lot to be desired, but nevertheless much loved by its inhabitants. In 1976, there were still horse-drawn carts, as well as escutcheons above doorways, the usual domes, a magnificent fountain, and statues in recesses and on parapets, gables and façades. The massive square **Castel Nuovo** (from 1279) presented forbidding dark bulwarks and crenellated towers, but the white stone of its triumphal entrance arch, **Torre della Guardia**, was marked by statues in niches, dainty tableaux in relief, and a figure atop the pediment. An outstanding building had a group of statues on top, and nearby, also bedecked with a host of images, was the monumental **Fontana di Nettuno** (1601) by Bernini.

At the Garden Hotel, I had a pleasant surprise when I received a phone call from my bosun friend from Messina, Gene, which I took in the once opulent, but now neglected and unused, enclosed rooftop garden. Having somehow traced my movements (shades of the CIA!), I was contacted via ship to shore radio and we spent the day travelling by bus along the tortuous **Amalfi Coast**. Displaying extraordinary vistas and cliffs plunging to incredibly blue water, it was even described by Homer in his Odyssey as 'steep rocks hanging over waves'. We stopped for a brief look at **Sorrento** and visited the island of Capri.

We arrived on **Capri**, once home to Emperors Augustus and Tiberius (and Gracie Fields), at the **Marina Grande**, where white and a few pink stucco buildings cascaded to the sea. Rearing behind the town and harbour was a church tower and another columned façade, and houses were perched atop perpendicular cliffs. Making its way up to the **Piazza Umberto**, the bus hugged the mountain and offered views of bare crags in a turquoise ocean. I have stunning film overlooking a town, its mountain backdrop, and surf breaking on a small strip of black sand beach far below. Harnessed to a gay cart, a beribboned horse waited for tourist trade, and I have pictures of a second harbour with many small boats, pink and white buildings, a church tower, and a background of incredible mountains. Gene and I made the hour's walk to the palatial remains of **Villa Jovis**, one-time residence of Tiberius and best preserved of the Roman houses. Walking back, the **Arco Naturale**, a massive rock arch through which views of the ocean were visible below, made an impressive sight, as did vistas of the rugged limestone coastline and pinnacles in the water. The symmetrical façade of a church had a pleasing striped effect created by the use of different colours of stone, a man rode a donkey up one of the steep streets, and I obtained excellent views of the **Faraglioni**: three rocks erupting from the sea. Unfortunately, because of limited time, we could not visit the **Grotta Azzurra** (**Blue Grotto**), but from the ferry back to Naples, I took great pictures of a church and buildings on a precipitous outcrop and the clutter of coloured houses and domes along the mainland waterfront.

We took a tour to fascinating **Pompeii**, destroyed in AD 79 by the eruption of Vesuvius that killed 2,000 people when the city was buried beneath ash. On reflection, it would have been preferable to visit the site independently because too little time was allocated by the guide and I felt that I did not see enough. However, even at that time, very little of the artefacts and decoration remained in situ, most having been transferred to museums. There were remains of several temples, theatres, baths, and a few villas with murals, mosaics and statues. The latter included a sculpted head beside a well and a small black statuette in the centre of a tiled pool (now dry) in a courtyard. The frescoes included three figures above an undulating snake in a small niche with a carved pediment atop miniature pillars. Plenty of fluted columns remained in the well-laid-out streets, together with remnants of shops and a brothel. As I recall, unearthed bodies were remarkably preserved, frozen in the act of movement as if they perished instantaneously.

Rome

It proved difficult to cope with the hassle of traffic and crowds after a day with company but I soon adjusted. Back where I began, in **Rome**, Neptune stood in the central arched recess behind a fountain, the others containing clustered figures including Roman soldiers. I found a barbican gateway in defensive walls, and even though the blaze of flowers was missing, I enjoyed the **Spanish Steps** (1725). On my subsequent visit, the obelisk and twin towers of the **Trinità dei Monti Church** at the top were marred by construction and scaffolding. I took film of the amazing second-century **Colonna di Traiano** (**Trajan's Column**) built to celebrate the victories of Emperor Marcus Aurelius, its spiral of minutely detailed reliefs depicting battles against Dacian armies. Considered one of the foremost examples of ancient Roman sculpture, it was surmounted by an image of St Peter, replacing a golden statue of Trajan in the Middle Ages. I was overawed by the blinding white **Trevi Fountain**, created between 1732 and 1762, which in spite of increased crowds, did not disappoint on my second trip. Also outstanding were the three magnificent fountains in **Piazza Navona**, one with a naked Poseidon doing battle with a giant octopus. All are described in a later book.

My next pictures show an elaborate church, more detail of the Vittoriano Monument, and an obelisk flanked by naked men with prancing horses. I admired artwork on a russet-toned hexagonal building before once again finding myself drawn by the allure of Trevi Fountain. More fantastic sculpting preceded a visit to remnants of Roman architecture and another glimpse of the Colosseum and surrounds, which included a small Parthenon-type construction. Standing alone above the **Circus Maximus**, I was filled with such a sense of awe that I could almost hear the chariot wheels thundering as they raced around the arena. A stone tower stood beside a multistorey white arch with many recesses, which at one time probably held statues, and a round structure was encircled by monstrous pillars supporting the roof. I took photographs, from inside and out, of the Roman Forum and its impressive arches of Titus (**Arco di Tito**) and Septimius Severus. Another impressive building had symmetrical domes, and a white church with statues on the façade featured many spires.

Trevi Fountain

Driving a chariot drawn by four high-stepping bronze horses, the sculpture of a winged Victory appeared insignificant atop a massive white edifice, and I took film of attractive bridges including **Pont Sant'Angelo**, which led to the mighty **Castel Sant'Angelo** meant as a tomb for Emperor Hadrian. First constructed by Hadrian in AD 136 as an approach to his mausoleum, the bridge collapsed and was rebuilt incorporating parts of the original. Added in the 17th century, the angels now adorning both sides were sculpted by Bernini and his pupils. The castle was converted to a fortress for popes in the sixth century AD and named by Pope Gregory the Great after he beheld a vision of an angel above the structure, heralding the end to a plague in Rome. In 1277, it was linked to the Vatican palaces by a passageway, often used by popes in times of threat. Visible to one side was **St Peter's Basilica**, the largest church in the world, its dome designed by Michelangelo. Amongst its treasures, the *Pietà* was the only work by Michelangelo to carry his signature – on the sash across the Madonna's breast. I made a visit to the **Vatican**, where St Peter's dominated the mammoth **Piazza San Pietro**. Also designed by Bernini, the basilica was flanked by two semi-elliptical colonnades with statues on top, each made up of four rows of Doric columns numbering 284 in total. Two highly decorative clocks graced the corners of the basilica's façade. The obelisk (AD 37) in the centre of the square was brought to Rome from Heliopolis by Caligula and erected in 1568; the city had the largest number of obelisks (13) brought by emperors from Egypt. Here again were comparatively few people, and I was astounded in 2006 to find it necessary to queue for almost two hours, without shelter, in unbearably hot sun (it was a year of record high temperatures), so I gave up the attempt. On this occasion, the colourful Swiss Guards made imposing figures.

Another obelisk, made in the 14th century for Pharaoh Seti, was brought from Heliopolis to Rome by Augustus, to celebrate the conquest of Egypt. It was placed in the Circus Maximus until 1589, after which it stood in the **Piazza del Popolo**. Laid out in 1538, this piazza was characterised by adjacent 17th-century Baroque churches: **Chiesa di Santa Maria dei Miracoli** and **Chiesa di Santa Maria in Montesanto**, one with a magnificent sculpted frieze. Statues and fountains adorned terraced gardens of the **Villa Borghese Park** diagonally opposite. Following a brief walk in these gardens, I photographed another clock tower, steeples, and ruins before moving on to the commencement of the **Appian Way**. Hardly changing in 30 years, it is described in detail in the 2006 chapter (book 4).

Returning to Rome, I took a train to **Ostia Antica**, founded by the Romans in the fourth century BC at the mouth of the river Tiber. It became a great port, and later a strategic centre for defence and trade, but declined in the 5th century AD when barbarian invasions and a malaria outbreak led to the abandonment of the city. Over time, it was buried to a depth of two floors in river silt, which contributed to its survival, and it was re-established in the ninth century by Pope Gregory IV. Now situated a considerable distance inland, it nevertheless provided a good insight into a working port. Points of interest in the vast arena included restaurants, laundries, shops, portals, public meeting places, a theatre and bath houses. I encountered faded murals and well-preserved floor mosaics, the latter including fish, animals, a head and torso with a long serpentine tail, a figure on a mythical beast, and three in a horse-drawn vehicle. A floor featuring a naked female surrounded by animals retained some colour, as did an almost complete surface with designs in octagonal shapes. Another featured pink-toned flower motifs in circles, and yet other images were highlighted by their floral border. The partially damaged dainty statue of a kissing couple (I do not know if it was original) stood on a small pedestal in the centre of a colourful geometrically patterned floor.

With grass sprouting amongst the ruins, creeper climbing walls, and wheel ruts still evident in overgrown roads, the deserted site was extremely atmospheric. Some buildings were reasonably substantial, one even displaying a sculpted figure, others merely foundations or tumbled blocks of stone. I found broken plaques on walls – one reading *tempio Roma a. . . sto* (I could not make out the last word) – many free-standing pillars, and in the **Terme di Foro** (thermal baths), even a row of *forica* – stone toilets! Near the entrance stood the impressive 15th-century **Castello di Guilio II**, and I have film of another barbican with a strange stark white pyramid in front, a photogenic bridge over a milky blue river beside a monastery, and murals in niches, but I am not sure where they were taken. In a recess beside an entrance, a beautiful relief depicted a lady, a long-necked bird at her side, reclining under a tree. Sculpted figures also graced the top of the doorway, which was flanked by Corinthian columns. My final picture, taken in the Villa Borghese Park, was of a large white sculpture depicting a naked man kneeling at the feet of an aloof-looking woman, his head cradled in her lap.

Train travel in Italy was economical and efficient, but when traversing mountainous terrain it had the disadvantage, due to many lengthy tunnels, of affording only sporadic glimpses of the fabulous coastal scenery and picturesque towns. Merely serving to whet my appetite, I vowed to explore the region at a later date.

INDIA, NEPAL & SRI LANKA 1977

INDIA

In 326 BC, Alexander the Great of Macedon crossed the Indus determined to add the fabulous country of India to his list of conquests. He successfully defeated the powerful kings of northern India but also exhausted his troops and subsequently withdrew. Chandragupta Maurya took advantage of this power vacuum and proclaimed himself king in 321 BC. The hotel chain is named in his honour. His son, Bindusara, was the father of Ashoka, the greatest and noblest ruler that India has known.

India, land of contrasts: bullock carts and jet planes, stark deserts and lush forests, blue jeans and silk saris, soaring skyscrapers, sumptuous palaces, and tiny thatched cottages.

Bombay

1977 saw the beginning of a love affair with **India**, which to this day remains one of my favourite destinations. The first of many trips, it was a comprehensive journey on which I made a complete circuit of the large subcontinent, never thinking that I would return; little did I know that it was to become the country that I have visited the most. In order to cover as much territory as possible, I flew between destinations, making in the region of 29 flights in 35 days!

Starting in **Bombay**, where I stayed at the YWCA, I filmed the 26m-high **Gateway of India** (1924–27), a massive yellow basalt arch built on the waterfront to commemorate the visit of King George V and Queen Mary in 1911, when India was considered Britain's 'Jewel in the Crown'. Bombay, also known as Bollywood, supports a thriving film industry, the largest in the world, with 67,000 produced since 1931, but I find Indian movies very naïve, even a kiss is just suggested as a couple disappear behind trees! One of the world's most populous countries, it was also vibrant and full of colour, as distinct from China, which on my first visit I found drab and monochromatic, with the majority of people dressed in the blue Mao suit and cap. Here, men wore white shirts and black trousers, and I photographed women clad in bright saris with gleaming copper or brass pots and trays on their heads, an art practiced from childhood, to which I attribute their perfect posture. These I filmed on a visit to the celebrated but unspectacular seventh-century **Elephanta Caves**, dedicated to Shiva the Destroyer, on **Gharapuri Island**. Like those at Ellora and Ajunta (described later), they were hand-carved using only a pick, hammer and chisel. Around the first century AD, this island was the capital of the Silahara dynasty. From across the water, I took film of the gateway with the famed Taj Mahal Hotel, listed as one of the 13 finest in the world, in the background.

The very English-looking **University** with its soaring **Rajabai** clock tower stood opposite an elegant classical building set in landscaped grounds, and yet people were living in poverty beside the road, along which water sellers peddled the precious liquid from large barrels on hand-pushed carts. I was surprised at the Western influence in many of the grand buildings, outside one of which I had my first encounter with a beggar (a woman carrying an infant), and there was even a red double-decker bus. There were structures with Eastern-type cupolas, and the **Prince of Wales Museum** was an outstanding domed edifice in immaculate surrounds. The foundation stone was laid by George V on his first visit to India, as Prince of Wales, in 1905. Buses, cars and motorcycles vied with oxcarts for position in busy streets, where there appeared to be no road rules. The **Hanging Gardens**, built in 1881 on top of the reservoir supplying water to Bombay, were the site of the gruesome **Towers of Silence** where, out of respect for the sacred soil that they believe should not be corrupted by rotting flesh, devout Parsis took their dead to be devoured by vultures. However, thankfully nothing was visible except these hideous birds hovering above the top. The sect originally came from Persia, having fled persecution in the seventh century AD, and in 2007 I visited similar burial towers in that country.

Bombay, now **Mumbai** again, began life as a cluster of islands inhabited by aboriginal fisher folk, the *Koli*, who built a shrine to the mother-goddess

Mumbadevi, from which evolved the name of the settlement. Ceded in 1549 to a Portuguese botanist and physician for Rs537, a number of beautiful churches were constructed. The city was then gifted as dowry to Catherine of Braganza on the occasion of her marriage to Charles II of England in 1661. In 1668, it was leased for £10 to the East India Company, which was responsible for much of the gracious architecture, and thus began the development of one of the world's largest cities and the finest port in the East. Later in my trip, on an overnight transit in Bombay, I was confronted with a general strike that brought the city to a standstill. I was advised not to leave the airport because there was no accommodation available and for fear that I would not be able to return in time for my flight. However, I negotiated with a taxi driver who declared that he could find me a room and vowed to pick me up the following morning. Taking the risk, I was deposited in a cheap hotel with a rowdy air-conditioning unit and bells going off all night – it was a brothel! Nevertheless, I was duly collected as promised and made my connection in spite of the traffic chaos.

Aurangabad

From Bombay, I went to the market town of **Aurangabad**, of itself not impressive but access point for the remarkable cave temples of Ellora and Ajunta, the latter hidden for centuries in dense undergrowth until relocated, by accident, in 1819 by a British army officer in pursuit of a tiger. Within a few years of discovery, vandals had left their mark on paintings that had survived intact for the better part of one thousand years. En route to the former, I took pictures of colourful people in the dry dusty countryside and the slender 60m-tall **Chand Minar** (**Tower of the Moon**, 1435) rising in front of a 200m-high mound originally known as Devagiri or Hill of the Gods, with the battlements of **Daulatabad Fort** (1187) on top.

The 34 Buddhist, Hindu and Jain cave temples at **Ellora**, constructed between the fourth and tenth centuries AD, were never 'lost' but abandoned and used by local villagers as dwelling places. Cooking and heating fires destroyed much of the painting but extensive carving remains. The almost incomprehensible feat of chiselling these caverns out of solid rock, working from the top down with primitive hand tools, remains a monumental achievement estimated to have taken several generations. Using an ingenious system of mirrors to provide light, their sculptures portrayed perfectly proportioned figures and life-sized elephants through to intricate patterns. The evil mythological king Ravana was shown crushed underfoot by Shiva the Destroyer, one of the Hindu Trinity, the others being Brahma the Creator and Vishnu the

Preserver. Hewn columns supported roofs and domes excavated from looming rock walls, a good example being **Kailash**, the largest monolith ever created. Cut from a single gargantuan block, it was composed of a gateway, pavilion, courtyard, assembly hall, vestibule, sanctum, and the free-standing **Pillar of Victory**. Over three stories high and excavated by 7,000 labourers over a 150-year period, it was approximately twice the size of the Parthenon and lavishly sculpted with epic themes.

The 30 subterranean Buddhist *chaityas* (chapels) and *viharas* (monasteries) of **Ajunta** dated from the second century BC and were abandoned by their builders more than 600 years before the discovery of America. Subsequently forgotten by civilisation for a thousand years, which ironically was responsible for their preservation, they rank amongst the greatest archaeological discoveries of modern times. Carved out of a horseshoe-shaped cliff encircling a deep valley, the caves were created over a period of eight or nine hundred years (from about 200 BC to AD 650) and contained artworks in various stages of decay. The frescoes were executed on white lime plaster applied over a surface of clay mixed with cow dung and rice husks, and colours were obtained from vegetable and mineral substances. Before reaching Ajunta, I obtained a magnificent panorama over the entire complex from a hillside above and, once in the valley, followed the path leading around the temples where, as they came towards me down a flight of steps, I filmed three barefoot pilgrims, all carrying staffs and dressed in white robes and turbans. In a rocky bed lined with trees, a quiet river traced the U-shape of the valley, and there was a small waterfall. Here, larger-than-life images of Buddha, each with a serene countenance, were interspersed with many smaller representations. I also photographed a group of monks, all with black beards, wearing the familiar orange and yellow robes.

Both Ellora and Ajunta had exquisite detailed paintings from the fifth century, but due to lack of light I was unable to record them. These illustrations depicted the life of Buddha, celestial musicians, palaces peopled by bejewelled princes and princesses, retinues of attendants, dancers performing to the sound of silent lutes, bazaars, warhorses in colourful trappings, richly caparisoned elephants, monkeys, peacocks, and a host of other images. Whilst the Buddhist caves presented calm reflection on the philosophy of Buddhism, their Hindu counterparts acquired an almost violent vitality, with gods and demons engaged in conflict, Lord Shiva flailing his eight arms (signifying omnipotence) in anger, rampaging elephants, swooping eagles, and entwined lovers. Squirrels scampered over steps, and from the interior one could survey surrounding hills and plains. By comparison, the Jain caves were very austere, like a series of boxes, and completely devoid of ornamentation on the exterior but still exhibiting colourful illustrations and engraved script within. Nearby, a white mosque stood in the shadow of stark hills.

On the return trip to town, I observed a group of women working on the roads – supervised by a man! Dressed in cotton saris displaying wonderful combinations of colours, they were breaking stones, carting them in baskets balanced on their heads, and depositing them to be spread with shovels; it was a shock to my pampered Western upbringing! The bus also passed a busy market where flames leapt in an open fireplace. I saw carts and bicycles on the dirt road, the ubiquitous cows, adobe dwellings, people working in fields, a goatherd wandering with his flock along the verge, and people just sitting outside thatched roadside shanties. Balancing bundles on their heads, family groups also walked along the edge of the road, and I noted mausoleums, haystacks, piles of wood in front of tin-roofed red or white houses, an archway in an ancient stone wall, grazing cattle, and laden bullock carts, but the thing that surprised me most was the comparative emptiness in a land that I had always believed to be wall-to-wall people.

Back in the rural ambience of Aurangabad, named for Aurangzeb, last of the great Moguls, a startling white building with several domes was located behind a reservoir featuring a fountain in the middle and an artificial waterfall. Another beautiful white structure, with a red sandstone colonnade, was reflected on the mirrored surface of a quiet pool. Although without sealed roads, Aurangabad contained an impressive Mogul-type gateway with cupolas and boasted the **Bibi-Ka-Maqbara**, a smaller version of the Taj Mahal, on which it was modelled between 1657 and 1661 in memory of the wife of Aurangzeb, son of Shah Jahan. Surrounded by four minarets, the base and dome were constructed of marble from Jaipur, but the remainder was stone covered with decorated stucco and not a patch on its illustrious counterpart. Street scenes included wandering pigs, a man pulling string attached to a long pole in order to operate a primitive device, people winnowing a pile of grain placed on matting, others squatting with goods in baskets (weighed by handheld scales), and the busy little black-and-yellow motorised trishaws.

Travelling by taxi, I visited a site of ancient mausoleums, pausing to watch bullocks being led back and forth to draw water from a well by means of a skin bag. I observed a lady with a pitcher on her head, a herd of goats ambling through the arched gateway in a stone wall, and a cow browsing near women unloading handmade bricks from the back of a donkey, which they stacked to dry in the sun. In this arid area, many men wore colourful turbans with white shirts and *dhotis*: a long loincloth with one end brought between the legs and tucked in at the waistline. The *dhoti* was sometimes favoured even in the capital, Delhi, where I saw the very funny sight of a well-to-do Indian, possibly a lawyer, hurrying down the courthouse steps, a briefcase in one hand and the other securely anchoring his private parts!

People congregated in a busy square where another elegant archway seemed out of place between ramshackle stalls. Freshly cooked foodstuffs were arrayed in heaps on a table next to an outdoor clay oven, which had utensils and a metal platter of ball-shaped concoctions on the edge. A pile of dry branches (for fuel) was placed to one side, and I saw a bread barrow and a colourful vegetable stand. A pair of oxen with extremely long curved horns pulled a wagon, a lady toted a bundle of saplings her own length on her head, a man carried a glistening metal container, children played in the street, and a figure sat on the pavement with produce for sale. We came across a large stone well where a youth was drawing water in buckets, animals and wagons stood in front of crude thatched dwellings, and huge baskets were stored next to a pile of dried grass on the roof of a porch, which was held down with rocks and supported by posts created from slim tree trunks. I enjoyed a close encounter with the carved pink sandstone minaret mentioned above, other heavily laden oxcarts plodded by, and a man wheeled a barrow full of fresh fruits. Solitary cows roamed everywhere, but I guess they all belonged to someone. We passed an isolated derelict-looking housing development for the poor, erected by donation from some benevolent philanthropist whose white bust stood on a pedestal near flags at the entrance – and was the best thing there! Some of the shelters were barely more than grass humpies, and many did not even appear to have a roof.

Udaipur

What a transformation greeted me on arrival in **Udaipur** (founded 1559 by Maharana Udai Singh) with its famous 18th-century Lake Palace Hotel on a tiny island in **Lake Pichola**. Formerly known as **Jag Niwas** and until comparatively recently the summer residence of the Maharana, it seemed to rise directly from the water. I took a boat to the hotel, which afforded grand views of the traditional architecture of the city. The immaculate grounds of the building included an internal courtyard with a rotunda at one end and the scalloped arches of an open corridor on one side. Pathways encompassing irregularly shaped patches of lawn formed patterns around a reflective lotus pond, tables and chairs were placed beneath umbrellas around the edge, and purple bougainvillea climbed pillars of the colonnade behind. Another grassed inner patio, this one containing a central fountain and twisted streamers suspended overhead, was being set up with tables and chairs for dinner.

Emerging from the surface of the lake, the stone figure of a woman, an urn upon her head and wearing a filmy gossamer-like shroud that clung to her wet body, served as a roost for pigeons. There were many fancy cupolas and a number of balconies with carved balustrades; bi-level gazebo-like turrets faced the lake, and inner walls were decorated with exquisite floral designs created with chips of coloured glass, which shone in the sunlight to foster an illusion of living plants. Other flowers and vines with bunches of grapes were formed with inlaid marble as in the Taj, but sadly many of the pieces were missing. Every inch of this ancient edifice, from the top of its cupolas to the bottom of its swimming pool, the slender carved columns, fountains and filigree screens, was marble. At night the court was lit by coloured lights. I stayed in these opulent surroundings, where I had a huge black marble bathroom but with antiquated plumbing and fittings. This brings to mind another occasion on which I had an old-fashioned bathtub on four feet, and when the plug was pulled out, the water escaped all over the floor – the outlet was not connected to a drain!

A second island held the companion **Jag Mandir** used in the 17th century, and the **Monsoon Palace** could be seen atop a distant hill. Visiting a site of ancient stone ruins, I saw a man in white (with a red turban) accompanying two ladies in elegant saris, one blue and one red, glittering with appliquéd mirrors that caught and reflected the sun as they moved.

At the lovely 18th-century **Saheliyon-ki-Bari Gardens**, a square tank in an inner courtyard, entered via a scalloped arch, had black marble pavilions at each corner; a similar white marble structure in the centre, water cascading from its domed roof, contained red flowers. Pale pink walls were accentuated with purple bougainvillea. Other fountains stood in smaller ponds, and gentle sprays erupted beside pathways to form soft curtains of water. A large circular pool with elephants around the circumference contained lotus blooms and a four-tiered central fountain, the latter featuring delicately crafted flowers and white birds spewing water from long beaks. Water also issued from the trunks of the elephants.

Outside this peaceful haven of flowers, fountains and trees, a sign at the entrance reading *Let thy voice be low*, I was again confronted by the noise, hustle and bustle of busy streets. Here, I encountered donkeys and a camel moving with its graceful steady gait, all laden with straw. Pony traps cantered by, and a line of women carrying tiers of goods on their heads were all dressed in red saris; this royal colour was much favoured by the ladies of Udaipur. A group with bundles of saplings was lounging against a wall, one with a ring through her nose well before the current craze of body piercing, and a woman was seated on the pavement with a basket of fresh flowers. Threaded and sold in lengths, these were often used to adorn the long dark tresses, on which they looked delightful. Bicycles and cows wove between vendors pushing food carts, other people balanced what could have been sugarcane or bamboo on their heads, and an oxcart, the horns of the beasts painted red, wended its way through the congestion in a narrow street. A woman with a straw broom was sweeping outside one of the whitewashed buildings, its doorway flanked by colourful illustrations of richly garbed figures mounted on an equally elaborate horse and elephant, customary in houses where a marriage had taken place.

From the **City Palace**, I obtained a splendid panorama over Udaipur and the compound below, where an elephant was chained in a stable! The **Peacock Courtyard** displayed arched windows, a wealth of intricately carved walls inset with peacocks composed of thousands of tiny coloured glass slivers, and a marble floor with a black and white zigzag pattern. Cupolas on numerous turret-like balconies were a prevalent characteristic, as were scalloped arches. Here again, I saw beautiful murals portraying elegant images – and a somewhat ill-proportioned horse with a massive body on fine stubby legs. My next pictures show the richly carved **Jagdish Temple**: the god Vishnu painted on one side of a doorway and every surface bearing small three-dimensional tableaux depicting images with beatific features in erotic positions. The main entrance of the temple was guarded by a life-sized stone elephant – and an armed sentinel because of the treasures therein – and opposite, a finely wrought arch led to a narrow alleyway. Here also were many pilgrims, and I observed a man with items slung from a pole across one shoulder, more pony traps and straw-laden camels, flower sellers, and several homes with frescoes, including one with an illustration of a man herding a spotted cow, its neck adorned with garlands. Finally, I photographed a couple of exotic birds, including a kingfisher perched on the topmost point of a pine tree.

Jodhpur

Heading to **Jodhpur**, the main city of **Rajasthan** on the edge of the **Thar Desert**, I encountered remnants of ancient fortifications. Jodhpur was founded in 1211, but the city was built by Rao Jodha in 1459, and his descendents ruled until Indian independence in 1947. The Rajputs, illustrious warriors high on the Indian cast system, were the former rulers of north-western India. **Rajput** princes had an average of nine wives; Raja Man Singh of Jaipur had 1,500! The term for the riding breeches evolved from the attire of local men.

I started in **Mandore**, the early capital five miles north, which despite being on the fringe of the desert was green, with abundant trees, fountains and artificial lakes, but I remember it most for the compelling **Shrine of 300 Million Gods**. To the right of this were stunning intricately carved sandstone *chhatris* (cenotaphs, literally 'umbrellas') of former rulers, incorporating arches, domes, cupolas, and windows like lacework executed from a single slab of stone. Peacocks, the native bird of India, were plentiful here, and for the first time I realised that these heavily plumaged birds could fly. They perched atop the pinnacle of a tapering tower located near a wonderful cenotaph, its fluted pillars supporting arched eaves sheltering delicate sculpting underneath. A large stone cat, prey in its mouth, embellished the roof of a porch with another tall tower looming above. Amongst the many lavishly carved and ornamented structures in the grounds, a dainty rotunda sat in a pool. I took close-up pictures of the fine tracery in windows and discovered the beautiful artwork of the impressive **Hall of Heroes** in recesses behind flowering bougainvillea. Carved from a single rock, this consisted of polychrome statues depicting women warriors, each with eight hands holding weapons of war and such mundane domestic items as jugs. Similarly, a colonnaded corridor held tableaux, also carved from a single mammoth slab, which included a life-sized multi-headed horse and various gods. All executed in white, these featured black accents such as moustaches. Cheeky monkeys and small birds inhabited the grounds, which were beautified with topiary, some shaped into perfect spirals. A reservoir provided an elevated viewpoint looking out across other traditional architecture and the stark surrounds of the vast boulder- and scrub-strewn desert terrain, also called home by gregarious monkeys. In the state once known as **Marwar**, meaning Land of Death, this barren outlook was weird, almost chilling in its contrast to Mogul-style gardens with their bridge across a man-made canal and maze of immaculate green stepped lawns, fountains, trees and flowers. Together with the complex just described, it all appeared like a mirage or some elaborate optical illusion.

In the dusty streets of Jodhpur, men sat astride haughty camels, and the fabulous **Mehrangarh Fort** (1459) crowned an adjacent hill. A visit to the fort began at the **Victory Gate**, erected by Ajit Singh to mark a military defeat of the Moguls in the 18th century. A cloak of shadow lent an even gloomier ambience to its grim exterior, which belied the exquisite carving found within. A steep ascent to the summit was marked by the handprints of 15 maharajah's widows who committed *suttee*, death by immolation when husbands were killed in battle, rather than suffer at the hands of the enemy. It was still possible to see evidence of these conflicts in marks left by cannon balls on outer walls. From ramparts lined with heavy artillery, the panorama embraced as far as the eye could see: over the sprawling city, towers, temples, and a nearby white mosque dazzling against its dull brown rocky backdrop. Inside the fortifications, the looming 500ft lotus-patterned and lace-worked sandstone façade concealed palaces with mirrored rooms, murals, sumptuous brocades, marble-topped furnishings, gold decoration, and tinted panes – so that royal ladies could literally see the world through rose-coloured glasses! Apparently, the 200-year-old **Thakat Vilas Palace** within the fort was resplendent with floor to ceiling murals depicting marches, feasting, wars, games, weddings, religious rites, beautiful women, proud men and palace pets in minute detail but was not open to the public. On the way back, I saw a camel kneeling to drink at a waterhole, another pulling a cart, and a large cenotaph in the desert. In the town, I was aware of camels being ridden, many hauling loaded wagons, the usual cows, donkeys bearing loads of dried grass, trishaws, a great number of people walking (the men sporting white *dhotis*, shirts, shawls, turbans, and even white beards), bicycles, motorbikes – and the occasional car! Rajasthan remains my favourite state after Kashmir.

Jaipur

There was no mistaking the pink city of **Jaipur**, founded by Maharajah Sawai Jai Singh in 1727, also in Rajasthan and another of my favourite places. Only 13 when he became ruler, Jai Singh was dubbed 'Sawai' (prodigy) by Mogul emperor Aurangzeb who ruled in Delhi at that time, a title still retained by the princely house of Jaipur. Elaborate multilevel buildings were either constructed of pink sandstone or painted in that colour (with white trim), often with open pavilions on top. A classical example was the superb rose-pink and white five-storey curvilinear-topped **Hawa Mahal** (**Palace of the Winds**), built in 1799 by Sawai Pratap Singh. Protruding from its façade, honeycombed bay windows allowed ladies of the court to look down undetected on activity in the streets below. Jaipur was also the site for the **Jantar Mantar**, largest of five observatories built throughout the country in the early 1700s by Jai Singh. Well before its time, it featured massive yet precise stone and marble instruments, including a sun dial and zodiac signs for charting horoscopes.

Jaipur also boasted a lakeside palace and the imposing early 17th-century **Amber Palace**, traditionally approached mounted on a gaily painted elephant decked in colourful trappings; the towers and bastions of another fort topped a ridge behind. The **Ganesh Pol** (gate) was adorned with vivid 300-year-old murals like those of Jodhpur, and within the massive outer walls I observed marble columns surmounted by elephant heads (each with a lotus in its trunk), gardens, and exquisite detail on the **Jai Mandir**. The glistening **Sheesh Mahal** was literally a glass palace, its walls and ceilings covered with mirrors, which reflected flames from lighted candles to simulate shimmering stars in a night sky. The concave ceiling in one room was shaped to fit snugly over the back of an elephant! Filigree marble windows overlooked public places, enabling them to be discretely observed by ladies in the Maharani's quarters unseen by those below. An inner courtyard demonstrated an interesting rudimentary system of air-conditioning in which water pouring down a ribbed marble channel was cooled by breeze blowing through perforated marble screens each side. From the gardens could be seen other towers on surrounding hills. There was an area that had the semblance of an open pillared audience hall, and I came across many decorative cupolas. Other fine paintings included one of the elephant-headed god Ganesh being fanned by ladies-in-waiting. The tale of how Ganesh received his head is a fascinating one that the reader should investigate. Briefly, the eldest son of Shiva and Parvati was mistakenly beheaded by his father. Persuaded by Parvati to restore him to life, Shiva ordered his servants to bring him the head of the first creature they encountered, which happened to be the wisest of animals, an elephant. I found façades with delicate designs, scalloped niches with intricate inlay, and rich stained glass. Looking from above, I could see gardens laid out like a patterned Persian carpet extending into **Maota Lake** and a town nestled in a valley of the encompassing hills.

On the return journey to the city, I observed the third lake palace and camel carts. Back in Jaipur, I came across a breathtakingly beautiful building with ornamentation like delicate white lacework, street stalls, decorative arches sheltering murals, and again very few motorised vehicles in the wide streets. Originally constructed to accommodate elephant processions, they were lined with exceptional pink buildings, many exhibiting sculpted bay windows, domes, cupolas, and false façades. A particularly impressive pink and white archway, through which a series of arches was visible, had a scalloped top surmounted by twin cupolas. Although wide, the streets were crowded with camel carts, hand-pushed barrows, bicycles, pony carriages, motorised rickshaws, and colourful pedestrians. A white pig skittered across the road, a man pushed a cart of green vegetables, and a lady in a black *burqa* (outer garment covering the head and body) carried a child. Balancing an enormous basket of the puffy bread called *puri* on his head, a man walked past a figure in a red turban playing a traditional stringed instrument, whilst another was seated on his *charpoy* (hemp-strung bed) smoking a *hookah*. The original city was guarded by a fortified wall with seven gates, but it had expanded outside that perimeter.

Amritsar

Bypassing Delhi at this time, I went straight to **Amritsar** and the **Golden Temple** in the **Punjab**. Amritsar, the name is derived from *amrit sar* meaning pool of nectar, was founded in 1574 when the fourth Sikh guru made his home by the pool, believed to have miraculous healing powers. The temple is of great religious significance to the mainly Sikh population; like Mecca for the Muslims, it is every Sikh's desire to visit it at least once. Located in the centre of a vast tank in an immense walled compound, it was accessed via a causeway leading from the marble-tiled walkway surrounding the cistern. So named because the dome and upper portion were covered with around 400kg of the precious metal, I did not find the temple particularly outstanding, considering some of the surrounding buildings just as impressive. Inside the edifice, flower sellers offered garlands of orange and yellow marigolds. The white marble walls were inlaid with animals, birds and floral work created with semi-precious stones as in the Taj. Polychrome figures appeared in scalloped niches above doorways. Amongst the devotees praying around the perimeter of the sacred water were many in the signature bright blue robes with pointy-toed shoes, a sheathed sword at their waist, steel-tipped pike in hand, uncut hair covered by a turban, and sporting a beard – the five symbols of the Sikh faith. It was near this hallowed site that the celebrated epic *Ramayana* was written.

Amritsar's other claim to fame (or infamy) was the **Jallianwala Bagh**, a quiet garden with the red sandstone **Flame of Liberty**, erected to commemorate the day in 1919 when British General Dyre ordered soldiers to fire on a gathering of men, women and children who were meeting at this spot to demonstrate for independence. On this tragic day, around 2,000 defenceless people were slaughtered, and walls still bear the marks of bullets. Independence was finally achieved 29 years later. More congested street scenes revealed red-turbaned police, an elegant white building with a cupola, narrow alleys into which enclosed carved wooden balconies projected overhead, a row of parked bicycles, participants in a protest march holding aloft red banners, heavily laden figures, and everywhere the imposing statuesque Sikhs.

Srinagar

Crossing the addictive scenery of the snow-clad **Himalayas**, I made my first trip to **Srinagar** (1,768m), in **Kashmir**, where I found bare poplars, sullen clouds, and cold hazy conditions. I had prearranged to stay in one of the legendary houseboats (described in detail in a following chapter) but on arrival found that I was not expected and the accommodation not prepared. In compensation, the extremely apologetic owner insisted that I stay free of charge, and thereafter developed a friendship that endured for some years when he became my agent in Kashmir. Accessed by canopied *shikara*, my houseboat was made cosy by a *bakhare* (stove) on which a kettle stood all day to provide hot water for tea or *kahwa*: green tea with cardamom and cinnamon. The dull overcast sky, mountains, naked poplars and boats were perfectly mirrored in the still waters of **Lake Dal**, making the entire world appear grey, but back from the shore the land was blanketed in snow like a white tablecloth. Roofs were also covered with the white precipitation and blended into surroundings where the colour of evergreen conifers was bleached by the icy environment to produce a black and white universe. On closer inspection, it was like being transported into a Christmas card; branches heavily laden with snow drooped overhead and threads of icicles hung from drifts. Mountains in the distance displayed smooth unblemished surfaces of pristine white, and people walked with *kangri* (cane baskets holding clay pots full of hot coals) held beneath their heavy woollen *pahrans* (cloaks), making them appear pregnant. Icicles also hung from eaves; stacked logs and stone fences were made picturesque with snow, which served to beautify even ugly surroundings, and narrow rivulets wound paths like ink across the white ground. Other people were covered from head to ankles in blankets, and a figure with a pail stooped between tin-roofed dwellings constructed with small bricks to collect water from a stream running too swiftly to freeze. Amongst the clutter of houses by the shore of the **Jhelum River**, I saw people washing utensils in the bitterly cold water on which ducks, seemingly oblivious, still swam. A figure ladled liquid into a woman's container, and a man swathed in woollen garments smoked a *hookah* whilst squatting in his open-fronted store. Occupying the lower level of two- and three-storey wooden buildings, shops sold clothing and utensils amongst an astounding mish-mash of items.

The 400-year-old **Hari Parbat Fort** commanded a prominent place atop a hill, and from my position I could see a cemetery and large building like a palace in the foreground. The **Hazratbal Mosque** contained a hair of the prophet Mohammed brought from Medina over one thousand years ago. Ruins attested to a civilisation in this 5,200ft valley as early as 3 BC, when a settlement was founded by Mogul Emperor Ashok, but it was Akbar in the 16th century who made it great.

Encircled by mountain peaks, this vale filled with fluffy white clouds has been described as a bowl of whipped cream, and indeed, at that time, with no radar or radio communication, it sometimes took days to be able to fly in. I recall being stranded in Amritsar for three days, attending the airport each morning only to be told that there was no flight. Aircraft had to fly into Srinagar before noon because conditions deteriorated later in the day and so, much depending on the weather further to the north, departure from Amritsar could never be predicted until the plane actually landed! A flag was raised when it was first spotted, but oft-times it by-passed Amritsar to make its deadline. When I eventually boarded a flight, the beaming ground crew came up to me in the aircraft before take off and said, 'You are lucky today'! In the intervening period, Indian Airlines had put me up in a leading hotel but one that was under renovation, and the room, with his and her bathrooms, tiffany lamps on bedside tables, and a red velvet swing suspended from the ceiling, was also full of builders' tools and sawdust!

In these cold winter days, there was not the frenetic activity that I was to find on subsequent visits, or the bewildering variety of goods spilling onto the streets. On the outskirts, fields were divided into small snow-bound plots, but nothing was being cultivated. From below, I took pictures of deserted pavilions in the **Mogul Gardens** on their hillside perch, and even the houseboats looked sad without the flower sellers' *shikaras* and other customary lake traffic. But on close encounter, even though moored amongst brown lotus, they were just as appealing as always. The serenity of the lake, apparent at any time, was even more so in tranquil water that, without a ripple to mar the surface, mirrored other boats as I relaxed and drank tea beneath the fretwork canopy on my sundeck. Opposite, occupants of an onshore house were buying fruits and vegetables from a vendor in a *shikara* containing a smoking coal fire.

Delhi

After a brief visit, not wanting to be marooned again in bad weather, I flew back to **Delhi**, the capital and most Westernised of Indian cities, with impressive buildings and monuments but where they still used lawnmowers pulled by cattle! In other places grass was trimmed with scythes. Accommodation was cheap at that time, and I stayed at the government run Ashok Yatri Niwas for around $11 per night. **New Delhi** revolved around a grassy ring called **Connaught Place**, from where roads radiated like the spokes of a wheel through a series of concentric circles. Around the centre ran **Connaught Circus**, and it was near here that my room was located. The radial road of **Janpath** led eventually to **Rajpath**, site of the annual Republic Day parade, where I found a grass-filled arena with a lofty stone rotunda, the **India Gate**, and the imposing red-and-white sandstone **Parliament Buildings**. Further along, I came to the 16th-century sandstone and marble **Mausoleum** erected for emperor Humayun, said to have been the inspiration for the Taj Mahal. Set in attractive gardens, the tomb was an impressive monument, and when viewed through the arched gateway indeed resembled the Taj. Other noteworthy ancient structures stood nearby. In contrast, I visited the **Raj Ghat** (Gandhi Shrine), a plain black marble slab at the place where he was cremated in 1948, enclosed by low white walls in a vast expanse of green lawn. It was inscribed with Gandhi's last words, *Oh God*, in Hindi, bright orange marigolds were placed on top, and people came to venerate the beloved leader all through the day. From here were visible the domes and 130ft-high minarets of the huge **Jama Masjid** (mosque), the last building constructed by Shah Jahan (of Taj fame), between 1644 and 1658, and I experienced a lugubrious encounter: the cruel and distressing sight of a muzzled black bear made to dance on its hind legs.

In the distance, the famous Red Fort (1638–47) also stood out, and I entered the area of **Old Delhi**, the walled city built by Shah Jahan in the 17th century. In front of the mosque I came to the fascinating, congested and busy bazaar of **Chandni Chowk** (**Silver Street**, established 1650), in Mogul times the biggest commercial centre of the East and richest in the world. Here, a man with a bicycle was selecting a live hen from a crate, and pedal rickshaws were abundant. It contained all the ingredients of a teeming Indian city: colour and drabness, hope and despair, affluence and poverty, cleanliness and filth, lassitude and frenetic movement, hospitality and antagonism; however, I found the push and shove in the ancient narrow lanes quite intimidating.

The mosque itself, largest in India, was capable of holding 25,000 worshippers. Surrounded by a towering crenated wall with corner bastions, it was accessed via a mammoth gate, surmounted by cupolas, at the head of a massive staircase on which people sat or reclined. I did not enter but went instead to the **Red Fort**, commissioned by Shah Jahan in 1638 when he moved the capital from Agra back to Delhi, which also featured looming walls with gates topped by cupolas and, as the name suggests, was constructed from red sandstone. Inside, arched pavilions were full of local people and visitors, and I saw beautiful embossed white marble walls and a room with exquisite inlay work. Scattered around the grassed compound were many buildings with scalloped arches and cupolas, including the **Diwan-i-Am** (**Hall of Public Audiences**), pillared **Diwan-i-Khas** (**Hall of Private Audiences**), and the white **Pearl Mosque** built by Aurangzeb, son of Shah Jahan, in 1659. It was within this magnificent setting, in a room with a solid gold ceiling and walls studded with valuable gems, that the renowned **Peacock Throne** was originally lodged until looted by the Persians in the 18th century.

Agra and Fatehpur Sikri

My next destination was **Agra**, which surprised me in its simplicity. Home of the arresting **Taj Mahal**, it was virtually just a village with donkeys, chickens and pigs wandering the streets. Outside whitewashed adobe cottages, surrounded by their belongings and utensils, people appeared to have set up house on the pavement, one lady squatting to wash brass platters in a basin. The Taj Mahal is synonymous with India, how could one visit the country without seeing it? Built by Shan Jahan in memory of his adored wife Mumtez Mahal, who died giving birth to her 14th child in 1629, it took 20,000 stonecutters, masons and jewellers labouring more than two decades to construct.

It was from Agra that I visited the fantastic abandoned city of **Fatehpur Sikri**, built as a capital but due to lack of water only inhabited for 11 years, from 1574 to 1585. The court relocated to Lahore before returning to Agra 15 years later, and the streets became the haunt of wild beasts. En route, I encountered a large flock of vultures. It must have been a wondrous city because it still conveyed an aura of elegance and grace in the well-preserved buildings, ornamental pool, and even a huge chequerboard, where scantily clad dancing girls were used as live pieces! The city was protected by an artificial lake on one side and 10km of 10m-high walls with 11 battlemented gateways on the other three; built in 1576, the mighty **Buland Darwaza** (**Victory Gate**) was, at 54m, India's tallest arch. Although constructed from stone, the various structures with their dainty cupolas enhancing rooflines still appeared delicate. Rows of cupolas also topped the mighty walls and monumental gateways. The **Audience Chamber** of Akbar the Great contained the **Pillar of Truth**, a central octagonal column with a massive ornate capital, blossoming like a flower, upon which he sat and from which radiated walkways used by his advisors, who imparted wisdom; lesser subjects stood below to listen to discussions and record events. On a lighter side, the emperor had a splendid pavilion built for the Royal Astrologer, and another, known as the **Ankh Michauli** or **Blind Man's Buff House**, where he is said to have enjoyed games such as hide and seek with the ladies of his harem, although further research indicated that it could have been the **Treasury**. Surrounding a courtyard, rooms with blue enamelled roofs made up the living quarters for one of his wives; fine carpets covered the floors, and rich silken cushions were spread for her ladies to rest upon in perfumed air.

Akbar was the third of the great Moguls and grandson of Babur who swept with his hordes through the Kyber Pass, but in spite of having many Muslim, Christian and Hindu wives and concubines, at the age of 26 he was childless. The city was created in 1569 when Akbar, seeking to beget a son, made his way on foot to consult a holy man said to perform miracles in the tiny village of Sikri, 40km from Agra. However, content with his life in the desert, the simple seer in dusty white robes, sheltering beneath a stone canopy, refused to accompany him back to Agra. When his wife became pregnant the elated emperor decided to build a walled place of splendour, with fountains, drainage and air-conditioning systems (already described), palaces, mosques, mansions and monuments to rival the city that he had left behind; this was Fatehpur, meaning Victory. A white marble mausoleum to the saint, where women still petition for the gift of children, sat in a courtyard. There was even a tusk-studded tower erected in memory of Akbar's favourite elephant, which performed the role of judge and executioner; accused prisoners were thrown before the fierce animal and if ignored it proclaimed their innocence, but the guilty were trampled. A quote from the annals of an English traveller of the 1500s who visited Akbar, one Ralph Finch, states that *The king hath 100 elephants, 30,000 horses, 1,400 tame deer, 800 concubines and such other store of leopard, tiger, buffalos, cocks and hawks that is very strange to see . . . Fatehpur is a great city, much greater than London.* Here also were rooms with exquisite detail in decoration, inlay work, lacy sculpted stone, marble window screens, and a mutilated painting of battling elephants. The **Panch Mahal** was a five-storey structure with innumerable pillars surrounding open galleries, each successively smaller than that below, surmounted by a small pavilion. Surveyed from behind carved balustrades, the view from on high encompassed numerous cupolas, the pool, crenated walls, gardens, and the surrounding countryside.

Not only a great builder, Akbar was a patron of artists and left a legacy of exemplary works, including some of the finest miniatures ever produced. In this period, colours were obtained using ochre, kaolin, terra verde, carbon black, malachite, azurite, lead white, madder

Panch Mahal

lake, indigo, gold, silver, lapis lazuli and *peoni* – a yellow substance extracted from the urine of cows fed on mango leaves! We drove back past a lake nurturing waterbirds and through photogenic villages with people gathered in front of thatched and whitewashed adobe cottages. We passed goats, carts, a figure on a crude litter (people often slept in the cool of the open air), and cattle in a field.

Agra's **Red Fort**, built from 1565 to 1572, predated that in Delhi by three quarters of a century, but was every bit as imposing as its counterpart. Adjoining the broad **Jumna River**, the 70ft-high crenellated outer wall was almost two miles long, and within its boundary reposed the richly decorated **Musamman Burj**, where the imprisoned Shah Jahan lived out his life gazing across at his beloved Taj Mahal. With its domed roof and four slender minarets at the corners, the Taj needs no introduction or explanation, although my initial reaction was one of disappointment because it was smaller than I had envisaged and dirty with the passage of countless hands touching the yellowed marble for good fortune. Interestingly, the minarets lean slightly outwards to avoid damage to the monument should they fall. Far more imposing for me was the towering 90ft-high red and white gateway – intricately patterned, inlaid with verses of the *Qur'an* (Koran), and crowned by cupolas – and the symmetrical red sandstone mosques at each side of the actual tomb. Located at the end of a long reflecting pool with fountains in the centre and lined by lawns and trimmed trees, the Taj was still a site of constant pilgrimage, and on subsequent visits I found the often deserted alternative places of worship to be venues where I could escape the crowds and contemplate the edifice and its surroundings in peace and tranquillity, adding a different dimension to my appreciation. One could not help but be in awe of the sheer emotion that emanated from this masterpiece dedicated to love, with its white marble panels embossed with flowers and walls inlaid with semi-precious stones, an art that survives in Agra to this day. In a single blossom measuring just 2.5cm square could be found 64 different inlays of jasper, agate, lapis lazuli, carnelian and bloodstone. Foundations on the opposite side of the river marked the site where it is believed that Shah Jahan contemplated erecting himself a counter-balancing black mausoleum to be joined to the tomb of his wife by a black and white bridge, but he was interred before it could come to pass. He was finally laid to rest beside Mumtez in 1666.

In 1977, the Taj was closed for the first time in 300 years because of the war with Pakistan. During this time it was camouflaged with straw matting, wildflowers, vines and grass because the pilots of Pakistani bombers were using its reflection under moonlight to guide them to important targets.

Peasant people, the men in cloaks and turbans, the barefoot women in gay saris and heavy silver anklets, wandered in groups across the marble patio around the outside of the shrine, which was ornamented just as lavishly on the exterior as within. But I deviate from my description of the Red Fort, which also featured dainty cupolas, carved balustrades, delicate arches and, similar to that in Delhi, an open gallery with a forest of columns. Here also was the **Palace of Mirrors**, its walls set with tiny concave circles of reflective glass, which in the dim light twinkled overhead like myriad stars. In the evening, the sun sets the red sandstone walls of the fort afire.

I watched as a pair of cattle was used in an age-old method to rotate a rudimentary wheeled mechanism, the purpose of which was not immediately apparent. I saw more people mounted on camels and women collecting water from a communal well, which they carried in brass urns on their heads. My next pictures show the dramatic contrast between classical sculptures in a museum and a modern tiled floor in which every square carried a different design.

Khajuraho

I moved on by air to the little visited (at that time), isolated and fairly inaccessible village of **Khajuraho** with its fabled erotic temples. These fascinating enigmatic structures were built by the Chandelas of the warrior Rajputs, but for what reason and why so many has remained unanswered because nothing else was left amongst the mute hills and silent lakes, although the carvings speak with eloquence of a bygone era when chariots rolled in battle, men traded, and beautiful women adorned themselves with exquisite finery. According to mythology, the father of their race, Chandra the moon god, descended from heaven to embrace the peerless Hemavati, daughter of a Benares priest, as she bathed in the moonlight waters of Rati Lake. On departing, he told her that she would give birth to the founder of a valorous race, and it was his dynasty that raised the temples.

The external tableaux portrayed explicit sexual acts, including bestiality and masturbation, but these images comprised barely 10% of the whole. Only 22 of the original 85 temples built between AD 900 and 1100 remained, but these were extraordinary in detail and depicted voluptuous and nubile bodies, their supple limbs in graceful poses and lascivious embraces. Worshipped as the main force of creation, women were a favourite subject, with facial expressions and elaborate hair styles faithfully reproduced. Like the pyramids of Egypt, it took thousands of craftsmen working every daylight hour, centuries to create these works of art, which showed the entire range of human activity and emotions. In keeping with the preference for female form, maidens were featured at daily chores such as washing hair, writing letters, gazing in mirrors, playing with balls, singing, applying henna, and strumming instruments. There were sensitive interpretations of kissing couples, mothers with babies, and musicians, as well as more sombre subjects of horsemen in military processions, camels, elephants, crocodiles, wild boar, and hunting scenes showing a deer, its neck pierced by an arrow. They were erected by scantily clad followers of a sect of Hinduism that saturated sexual pleasures with divine qualities, and each temple was formed with a series of peaks culminating in a tall spire, symbolising the Himalayas where the gods were supposed to reside. Although depicted with elaborate headdresses and heavily bejewelled, the images were either naked or dressed in flimsy transparent garments, and I also saw demons, beasts, and gods or mythical figures with the heads of animals, carrying axes.

Busily foraging, pretty grey squirrels with black and white horizontal stripes created havoc amongst red flowers at the site. An oblong structure was surmounted by an elephant, and a white temple with red bougainvillea in the foreground was startling against the rich blue of the sky. Reflected in a swampy patch surrounded by long grass, a wading bird made an attractive picture, a stepped steeple was enhanced with fine floral decoration, and I came across an image of Ganesh. A massive stone elephant was housed in an open pillared gallery, and a second stood in a garden. Pilgrims anointed an image on the staircase at the entrance to one towering temple, and I found representations of group sex. Ducks glided in a large tank, the steps of which were crowded with people performing ablutions and washing clothes. A sculpted figure crouched in front of a life-sized lion-like *leogryph* (the Chandela emblem) rearing beneath a carved awning, and more large stone elephants appeared small amongst sculpting on the façade of a mammoth temple with bulbous towers. Again, I saw barefoot pilgrims wearing chunky silver anklets, but monkeys were the only permanent occupants.

In the dusty dirt streets of the small village, I saw a lady doing her laundry, many desert tribesmen, and a white product spread on the road. This also appeared on large trays at a crowded market place, along with vegetables in baskets on the ground. One house was coloured a deep pink, others white, but there was absolutely no modern intrusion in this rural community as I battled my way through rickshaws, carts, bicycles, vendors selling lengths of fabric, people toting produce on their heads, dogs and spices. Dried grass and even a dead tree sprouted on parapets of dilapidated stone buildings from a grand era long gone.

Away from the market, a narrow dirt street was occupied only by a solitary pedestrian and a cow. The men were once again attired in white, and ladies wore bright saris of a single colour, as distinct from the multihued garments of the poorer people seen to date. Dressed in deep red, one woman sat with a basket whilst her companion winnowed grain on a woven platter, another fanned a cooking fire, and others squatted in doorways. The market spilled into a large dusty arena, where I observed a boy chewing on a length of sugarcane, a man selecting a cauliflower from a lady seated on the ground, many with baskets on their heads, a man with a live chicken under one arm, and numerous other fascinating cameos of life in this rustic setting with a way of existence unchanged for a thousand years. I saw dung that had been formed into cakes, spread to dry, and piled into beehive-shaped heaps for later use as fuel. The compound in front of a house was a jumble composed of a cart, goats and a bullock, a litter, stacks of wood, and baskets of produce. I photographed dahlias twice the size of a man's hand, and visited a nicely landscaped well-maintained site of ancient temple ruins, where vibrant red-flowering bushes highlighted the rust colour of the old stone. The one remaining complete structure, a squat tower consisting of two strangely rounded tiers, was carved with fine floral work. Outside a gateway guarded by two unusual polychrome beasts, I filmed monks in the maroon robes of Tibetan lamas, more at an elaborate well, one walking with a bucket, and others seated on stools. My last pictures in this area show monuments like ornate mausoleums and a complicated piece of artwork with many figures of people and animals. It was all an amazing experience.

NEPAL

Kathmandu

In the air once again, I flew over winding rivers in remote areas of northern India and alongside the snow-covered Himalayas to reach another cloud-filled valley into which we descended to **Kathmandu** (4,423ft), capital of **Nepal**. This was very different, with towering red pagodas and no vehicular traffic in the central **Hanuman Dhoka** (**Durbar Square**). A living museum, it featured incredible buildings, a wealth of statues, and the **Big Bell** and

200-year-old **Drum**, said to be the largest in Nepal. Two white porcelain beasts flanked a decorative blue and gold doorway, to the left of which, from his place under an umbrella, a huge red-robed image of Hanuman, monkey god from the *Ramayana*, protected the 17th-century **Royal Palace**. Red pagodas reared behind the white walls of the compound, its entrance guarded by similar fabled creatures with the all-seeing eyes of Buddha above. It boasted wooden doors in a highly ornate multihued archway filled with small figures. Standing to attention in red uniforms with white baldrics and belts and red turbans, the human palace guard looked striking.

Nargarkot

Before spending time in Kathmandu, I made a side trip to **Nargarkot** (7,200ft), from where it was possible to see beautiful bucolic panoramas of hillsides with terraced fields harbouring quaint red-and-white houses and, in the distance, 8,850m (29,035ft) **Mt Everest**, Mother Goddess of the Winds. After rising in the extremely chilly wee hours before dawn, I was taken to a place where this perfect environment bore witness to a brilliant sunrise, the glowing red orb emerging below a bank of black cloud which was backlit at the edges. It created the illusion of looking at the world upside down, and in a strange phenomenon the sun was triplicated to appear like a series of spheres. I saw the tops of surrounding peaks bathed in a pink glow, which as the 'three' suns rose higher was transformed to pristine white. Everest, in the far distance, actually appeared lower than its neighbours; it was an awesome sight. The meaning of the Tibetan name for Everest, Chomolungma, was Mother Goddess of the Universe, and the Nepalese name, Sagarmatha, meant Churning Stick in the Sea of Existence.

Patan

Then it was on to **Patan** or **Lalitpur** (City of Beauty), founded between AD 289 and AD 299 on the southern bank of the sacred **Bagmati River**, and once a separate little country. Here, chickens ran in the street, a woman was lifting a huge pottery urn to take indoors, and a man was stitching with string to seal a sack. A white *stupa*, on the steps of which women rested heaped baskets of wood carried on their backs, stood out amongst red buildings with bundles of tied saplings leaning against the walls. Constructed of small bricks with wooden framework and posts, the buildings were attractive, and spires rose from a cluster of *chortens* (dome-shaped Buddhist monuments) near where women washed and collected water from a communal well. Some structures were enhanced with exquisite woodcarving of animals, figures, decorative designs and latticed screens, others with ornate sculpting on wooden doorways and balconies. Narrow streets and squares were brick paved, and many of the multi-tiered pagodas featured the distinctive Nepalese metal 'tongue' suspended from the roof. Amongst heavily cloaked people in the misty light of early morning, I saw a man squatting in a doorway smoking an unusual bulbous pipe. A small pavilion atop one roof was crowned by a row of gleaming metal spires with cone- and flag-shaped ornamentation on the points, and the 'tongue' was adorned with a face. A tall column with a figure at the apex stood at each end of **Durbar Square**.

The streets were a bewildering array of architectural delights – a feast of fantasy. There was a spire with a decorative metal umbrella on top (a common sight in Asia), more towering pedestals surmounted by images, fretwork screens, a white-capped brick *stupa*, intricately carved columns, colourful tiles, temple bells, elaborately sculpted brackets beneath eaves, carved canopies, lion guardians, and the statue of a god in a wall recess. In an around it all was a mass of interesting people: men working on the pavement or carrying goods suspended from a pole across the shoulders, women in homespun skirts and shawls with baskets slung from their foreheads, a woman shampooing her hair, others collecting water in brass or pottery vessels, a barber using a cutthroat razor to shave a customer seated next to vendors selling vegetables and unknown substances on the sidewalk, a woman washing clothes in a basin near cows and a dog, two walking backwards and forwards to wind thread – and always the cattle. The steps of an open-sided five-storey pagoda were flanked by sculpted animals; beginning with man and elephants and ending with lions, they became successively smaller as they ascended.

Without the distraction of traffic noise, temple bells resounded everywhere, and one ancient brick wall was endowed with a painting. Bearing many utensils, a group congregated at yet another well, and I found faded artwork featuring Parvati, the ten-armed goddess of battle, above a doorway and an arch with greenery sprouting from the top. I followed behind a woman wearing many rings in her ears, again before the modern trend, and came across a brick edifice overpowered by its richly carved woodwork. I encountered a white tower, many more pagodas, an immense stone lion, and more ornate brass roof decoration. A huge winged figure, hands clasped as if in prayer, knelt in front of a building, people were mounted on an elephant (live), and even a couple of cars wended slowly through the cluttered maze. This was Kathmandu but the above description applies to both cities; I do not recall where the demarcation came (on my film) because Patan was a smaller version of the capital. There were markets, monuments and shrines everywhere, flags flying, and mythical monsters silhouetted against the sky. Looming over larger-than-life monkey-like figures at each side, an imposing image with glaring eyes was Bhairav, the God of Terror.

However, the most bizarre attraction was that of the **Living Goddess**, a 200-year-old tradition of virgin worship begun when the king seduced a young girl who died. To atone, he conducted a search for the perfect child, believed to be a reincarnation of the goddess Taleju, who was established as an object of veneration until puberty. To this day, a five year old with no physical blemishes, fears or bad traits is selected and installed in the **Kumari Ghar**, where she can be viewed (for a fee!) at a window. Once a year, until she leaves at adolescence, she is taken out in procession. With heavily kohl-rimmed eyes and a spangled forehead she made an extraordinary apparition, but when I attempted to take a photograph she instantly disappeared, not to return. It is believed that any man marrying her will immediately die.

Flower sellers made a spectacular display near another ornately carved temple, but the most inspiring sight was the 2,000-year-old **Swayambhunath Chaitya** (*stupa*). One of the most ancient in the world, it consisted of an austere white sphere dominated by a gilded copper umbrella above a helical spire, the sphere in turn atop a square structure with the all-seeing eyes of Buddha on all four sides, surveying a host of subsidiary *stupas*, shrines and sacred pillars. I have an amusing photograph of a rickshaw driver in his vehicle, head lolling to one side, bent legs spreadeagled – and sound asleep! A slightly different pagoda had five progressively smaller round tiers, their circumferences skirted with fluttering cloth. Viewed through temple bells, the unique rooftops, surrounding hills, and a temple on a distant rise provided the basis for superb pictures. I also found a big ceremonial drum and, hidden under eaves, colourful highly erotic carvings similar to Khajuraho, supposedly to shock the virgin goddess of lightning so that she would not strike!

Towards evening, the skyline was a tapestry of spires, and another monumental building had a tapering tower and pillared porticos above a colonnade circling its hexagonal foundations. I encountered a cow near a massive metal lion, a giant bell suspended beneath an arch, a courtyard with small animal figures around a golden spire, a pair of life-sized stone elephants ridden by *mahouts* (also stone), a man coming from a well with a gleaming brass water pitcher balanced on one shoulder, and barefoot women bowed beneath loads of wood on their backs. Temple bells and the images atop pillars were silhouetted against the dusk, and an extremely long 'tongue' hanging from ornamentation on the roof of an elaborate pagoda extended down three levels. Just when I thought I had seen it all and was saturated with the splendours of this ancient city, I came to an even more ornate structure with a heavily carved pediment above a doorway and colourful artwork on the brick façade.

INDIA

Varanasi

As a change of pace, but still with religious connotations, I went from Kathmandu to the holy city of **Varanasi** on the muddy banks of the sacred **Ganges River**. Here, most hours of the day but especially at dawn, thousands of people including many holy men, lined the banks, bathed, washed garments, filled ornate brass jugs, exercised on the *ghats* (steps), or simply sat in the lotus position (cross-legged) with hands clasped in contemplation – along with goats, cows, pigs and pigeons. Varanasi, formerly **Benares**, is the oldest continually inhabited city in the world, having attained glory as a centre of Hinduism long before Rome had become known or Athens established its might. A contemporary of Babylon, Nineveh, and Thebes, it was already ancient when Lord Buddha came to Benares in 500 BC and has for 3,000 years been the spiritual centre of India, the Hindu equivalent of Amritsar (for Sikhs) and Mecca (for Muslims). Many came here to die and were cremated on one of the waterfront burning *ghats*, where fires and smoke could be seen all day. In fact, one of the first things that I saw was four men shouldering a bamboo litter bearing a flower-swathed corpse. Families who could not afford cremation simply floated their shrouded dead on the water, a disquieting sight with which I was confronted when paddled along the river. I saw others heading to the crematoria with bodies carried on litters, but in spite of its grisly connotations, it was a colourful and vitally interesting venue. Reminiscent of Udaipur, I saw a white doorway illustrated with colourful figures, flowers and birds; a white cow lay in front. Large flowers graced the pillars of an arched entry, which led to a porch with an elephant and richly attired images depicted on the wall, but the focus and fascination of Varanasi lay in the *ghats*. I took a boat moored at the foot of the steps; people bathed nearby and others carried containers to collect the sacred water.

White cows also wandered in this congested area, where umbrellas were erected for shelter from the sun, and the spires of temples rose above the conglomeration of higgledy-piggledy buildings seeming to fall over each other in their descent to the river. The tower of the **Durga Temple**, comprised of many pinnacles clustered around a central spire, was considered by worshippers to be the universal soul surrounded by individual souls. The domain of monkeys, one was perched on the head of a garlanded stone lion in the black and white tiled entrance hall, around which bells hung between intricately carved pillars. Paintings in the **Tulsi Manas Temple** depicted lovely maidens and charioteers in the epic story of the *Ramayana*, and behind pink walls in the grounds of the university, I was surprised to find a life-sized stone rhinoceros in a pool at the soaring white marble **Shiva Temple**. There were other illustrated buildings, but Varanasi and the activity of the *ghats* were best appreciated from the water, my short excursion revealing more corpses awaiting cremation on the steps, many brown bodies bathing, boats hoisting patched sails, the body in the water mentioned earlier, thick smoke from funeral pyres, and many, many towers.

Calcutta

To quote the words of the musical: *Oh Calcutta!* Portuguese ships traded here in the 16th century, and in 1690 the East India Company raised the British flag. Ten years later **Fort William** was built on the banks of the **Hooghly River**, near where the bridge soars today. Capital of the British administration until 1912, this one-time showcase of Victorian grandeur, India's largest city, was now a place of constant day to day struggle for survival for the vast majority living on its overcrowded streets.

Smog-riddled **Calcutta**, the world's fourth largest city, was unmistakable because it was the only place still retaining hand-pulled rickshaws that, along with large hand-operated flat carts, buses, bicycles, horse-drawn surreys, bullock wagons, cars and motorcycles, clogged the city's streets. I have described my affinity for this bustling, overpopulated and depressing, but at the same time exciting metropolis, in a later chapter. A demonstration of the extremes was illustrated by the squalor and abject poverty as opposed to the sparkling white marble monument of the **Victoria Memorial** with its reflective lake on one side of the **Maidan**, a green sward where Hastings, the first governor-general of India (1773 to 1785), once hunted tiger. This white marble palace, a tribute to the days of pomp and ceremony associated with the Raj, cost around one million dollars to build back in the 1920s. Some say it was modelled on St Paul's in London, others a poor attempt at rivalling the Taj.

Calcutta was home to teeming millions of illiterate people, many of whom were literally born, lived and died on its streets and, again in contrast, was the birthplace of Tagore, winner of the Nobel Prize for Literature, who passed away in 1941. Congested roadways resounded with the continual blare of horns, bells in the hands of rickshaw drivers, and the constant cries of hawkers, and yet there was the serenity of temples and the **Botanical Gardens**. The Hooghly, a tributary of the Ganga, flowed through the city, and at one end of its 1,530ft steel cantilevered **Howrah Bridge**, at that time the largest of its kind and third largest in the world, lay the railway station, where wall-to-wall people virtually set up residence: sleeping on mats and cooking – a direct opposite to the calm oases of five-star hotels. It was bad luck if one needed a ticket in a hurry because a few hours were required to weave between 'lodgers' and departing and arriving passengers to effect the transaction, which often necessitated being shunted from one counter to another several times!

Adjacent to another grand edifice, an elaborate temple had silver figures on the back of a shining metallic elephant standing beneath a canopy decorated with peacocks. A wall inlaid with flowers of coloured glass or semi-precious gemstones was also enhanced with blue peacocks, and an equestrian statue stood atop a white arch on the grassed Maidan. The **Zoological Gardens** were a rare treat on two accounts: the attractive lakeside setting with birdlife in the trees and an exhibit of the magnificent rare white tiger, albeit pacing back and forth in a small cage. In a nearby enclosure, Bengal tigers demonstrated the marked difference between the two. Pure white deer and a rhinoceros also featured.

Back amongst the hustle and bustle, people washed clothes and bodies under street faucets, carted water in buckets, and lit cooking fires outside lean-to shelters beneath which they lived in the filthy streets – and past which walked prosperous businessmen attired in suits! A line of protesting workers carried placards and a barber squatted on the curb to shave a customer, yet Royal Calcutta Golf Club was the oldest outside Scotland, the birthplace of the sport.

Hyderabad

En route to **Hyderabad** (founded 1589), I passed mausoleums and fish ponds, and I have pictures of an embossed archway and a circular tablet depicting copulating animals. Sited in rocky terrain, sprawling **Golconda Fort**, built by the Kakatiya dynasty in 945 to 970, had the appearance of a ruined city, with the exception of graceful minarets towering above a crenellated wall on the hilltop. From this higher elevation, several domes were evident outside the perimeter, and I located sculpted figures ornamenting a doorway cut into an immense looming boulder. Mammoth rock tors had been incorporated into the walls as a natural defence, and there was evidence of a system for water, but the only inhabitants now were goats. Within arched recesses were dozens of small niches that would at one time have been receptacles for objects and very beautiful. Surrounded by archways, a bare courtyard had a well in the centre.

The impregnable fort fell only once, when Aurangzeb, after an eight-month siege and believing rumours of hidden gold, bribed a traitor to open what was later called the **Victory Gate**, which was studded with huge iron spikes to prevent elephants from battering it down. Capital of the Golconda Sultanate (the name comes from *golla konda* or shepherd's hill) between the years of 1518 and 1687, it remained much as it was when one of the world's wealthiest courts. A source of fabulous legends (and the Koh-i-Noor and Hope diamonds!), it was very photogenic. Thirteen miles from Hyderabad was the lovely turquoise **Osman Sagar** (lake), which was a total antithesis to the deserted fort. The minarets, spires and domes of mosques made striking pictures silhouetted against the skyline, and I saw many buffalo being doused with water and washed by their attendants in the **Musi River**.

In the city itself, I found the **Nehru Zoological Park**, which featured more magnificent Bengal tigers, happily in an open wooded enclosure, monkeys, and storks foraging in a green algae-covered pool, but the highlight, in the heart of ancient **Hyderabad**, was the renowned **Char Minar**. Referred to as the 'Arc de Triomphe of the East', this 200ft-high arch with four elaborate minarets was built to celebrate the end of a plague in 1591. It was surrounded by the **Lad Bazaar**, which included the famous **Street of Bangles**, where a myriad of these colourful delicately spun-glass circles were sold.

Madras

Next, I found myself in southern India, a region of unique temples like truncated pyramids. The façades of these extraordinary edifices were embellished with thousands of ornate figures. My first stop was **Madras**, called by its citizens Vanakkam or Bright Jewel and capital of India's southernmost state, **Tamil Nadu**. Here, I visited **Kapaliswarar Temple** dedicated to Lord Shiva, its wedge-shaped *gopuram* (tower) composed of many tiers bearing exceptional images and behind which, bordered by colonnades, I found a large tank with a shrine in the middle.

Madras developed from the anonymous fishing village of Madraspatnam and was the first firm foothold for a burgeoning alien empire when the British landed on its shores in 1640. They built **Fort St George** and the oldest Anglican Church in India, **St Mary's**, consecrated in 1680; Robert Clive, one of the founding fathers of British India, was married here in 1753. The church also bears reminders of Elihu Yale, early Governor of Madras and founder of Yale University in America. Colonel Wellesley had an association with Madras, as did the Duke of Wellington who defeated Napoleon at the Battle of Waterloo. Tradition and faith record the arrival, a few years after the Crucifixion, and martyrdom in AD 78 of the apostle Thomas to whom a basilica was erected.

Mahabalipuram

Intending to return at a later date, I did not stay long in Madras but moved on to **Mahabalipuram**, the seventh-century seaport on the **Bay of Bengal** where, apart from the singular temples, street scenes offered the same trishaws, laden carts, bicycles and pedestrians (but few cars), and a woman stacked kindling near a thatched dwelling. The town was known as **Mamallapuram** by the third- to ninth-century Palavas and succeeding generations of Tamils and has, since my visit, reverted to this name. En route, I saw a cluster of white temples, a palm-fringed tank with a pavilion in the centre, and a 1,000-year-old mammoth stone block carved to resemble a chariot with four massive stone wheels, the pavement in front lined with flower sellers and beggars. Ruled by the dynasty of Palavas more than 1,000 years ago, Mahabalipuram was best known for its monumental bas-reliefs on granite boulders and the wonderful 17th-century **Shore Temple**, with figures on its stepped spires and guarded by a row of stone bulls, together with at least one mythical lion, atop walls. At high tide, seawater lapped against these same surrounds.

Cave temples and elaborate carvings epitomised this relaxed and quiet old fishing village, but the major attraction was a set of five temples, called *rathas*, hewn from roof to steps out of 6m-tall stone blocks. A life-sized elephant stood in their midst, and lying between two temples was an indolent bull (Nandi) cut from the same stone. Referred to as **Krishna's Butterball**, a balancing rock looked precarious but had remained stationary for hundreds of years. Amongst the largest bas-reliefs in the world was **Arjuna's Penance**, a 27m/90ft-long 8m/30ft-high boulder constituting part of a cliff face and sculpted with an array of over 400 figures. Representative of creation in its entirety, these included an old hermit, his arms outstretched in penance, and a cat mimicking the action: standing on hind legs with front paws extended.

Other images portrayed lions, gods, beasts, birds, life-sized elephants, men, monkeys searching coats for nits, dancing figures, deer (one scratching with a hind leg) and snakes. A natural vertical cleft in the middle, down which it was believed water once ran, was supposed to represent the **Ganges**. The entire work seemed full of movement and life.

Tiruchirapalli

In **Tiruchirapalli**, temples still retained vestiges of colour, and figures appeared to support the weight of upper levels across their shoulders. Another mighty stone carriage had elephants on corners at the top. Many *swamis*, their foreheads decorated with ash, mingled with the crowd; women with baskets of limes and bananas squatted near a chalk drawing on the sidewalk, and I passed a lotus-filled tank, at the edge of which a man was vigorously soaping and washing his white goat! Amongst the plethora of wedge-shaped *gopurams*, one heavily accented in turquoise and pink featured floral decoration and images full of animation. Colourful figures on horseback and elephant respectively, stood one each side of the entrance to a large enclosure. The **Rock Fort**, crowned with a shrine to the god Ganesh, loomed 300ft above the **Teppakulam Sacred Tank**, in the centre of which was a pavilion.

SRI LANKA

Colombo and Kandy

Ceylon reverted to its original name in 1972. Our word serendipity comes from the Arab name for the country: Serendib. Flying to **Sri Lanka**, meaning Resplendent Land, I stayed only briefly in **Colombo**, at that time dirty and depressing, before moving on to the idyllic lush and green highlands of **Kandy**, with views of the lake from my accommodation. Here, I found a typical island paradise, with working elephants amongst palm trees, and roads winding between verdant greenery that included banana plants. Coconuts were heaped beside the verge, ponies pulled thatch-roofed carts, narrow streams bounded by grassy banks gurgled over stones, people washed in a wider stretch of water, bats flew overhead or hung upside down in trees (like large black seed pods!), and emerald mountains reared at higher elevations. At the **Royal Botanical Gardens**, dating from the 14th century, I saw topiary, a gorgeous display of many and varied orchids and other exotic blooms, a dripping fountain draped with a cloth of creeper, and glorious red- and pink-flowering trees. The lake, mist-shrouded peaks, and wide waterways made for beautiful pictures, whilst flourishing fields of grain and a temple with bamboo decoration put me in mind of Bali.

Sigiriya

A highlight of any visit to Sri Lanka must be the 640ft-high **Rock Fortress** of **Sigiriya** with its fabled fifth-century frescoes of seductive females. This fortified retreat was established when Prince Kasyapa, coveting the throne, led a palace revolt in about AD 473, overcame his father King Dhatusena, and walled him up alive! Kasyapa being the son of a concubine and legally a bastard, his half brother Moggalana, the rightful heir, fled to India to plot revenge. Fearing the wrath of his brother if he returned to exact retribution, Kasyapa built himself a luxurious palace on a rock summit accessed via a perilous stone stairway. Originally approached through the gaping mouth of a stone lion, only the paws, each claw as tall as a man, now remained. The retreat even had a water tank hewn out of the hilltop.

About halfway up this lofty eyrie, the still captivating 22 semi-nude bejewelled Singhalese beauties lay in a natural protected pocket. Kasyapa reigned for 18 years before his brother eventually returned with troops to challenge him, whereupon, in the heat of battle, he fell upon his own dagger and committed suicide. Another story goes that instead of waiting in his impenetrable sanctuary and pouring hot oil down on his rival, he rode out at the head of his army on an elephant, which became bogged in a swamp and, deserted by his soldiers, he killed himself. Succumbing to my fear of heights, I did not make it above the paintings; nevertheless, the panorama from the entrance, over fields, a reservoir, and other remains peeping above dense jungle inhabited by monkeys and lizards, was awesome. Commonly referred to as the eighth wonder of the world, Sigiriya was declared a World Heritage Site in 1982.

Anuradhapura

The next destination, **Anuradhapura**, was established five centuries before Christ, deserted in the ninth century, and rediscovered by the British in the nineteenth. Called moonstones, elaborately carved semicircular slabs depicting elephants, horses and what appeared to be ducks, marked the entrance to some buildings, and 1,600 remaining pillars testified to the magnificence of the **Brazen Palace**, so named because its copper roof (long since gone) could be seen for miles around. Originally constructed in 135 BC and standing nine storeys high, the palace burned to the ground and was rebuilt in the 12th century. **Royal Baths** filled with green algae-coated water were now the realm of turtles. Here one finds the 12m/40ft-high **Aukana Buddha**, perhaps the best preserved rock sculpture in Asia. A statue of Buddha in the lotus position sat atop a short flight of steps flanked by two lions. At that time, this little visited site with remains of many monastic buildings and a few statues was the preserve of a solitary cow contentedly grazing on well-tended grass. Here also was the **Bo Tree**, which grew from a sapling of the very tree under which Buddha attained Enlightenment. Supposedly brought to Sri Lanka by a daughter of Emperor Ashoka, it was planted over 2,220 years ago and was the oldest tree in the world.

Polonnaruna

At **Polonnaruna**, the 11th-century Singhalese capital, was located the spectacular **Gal Vihara**, which featured in the film *Baby Elephant Walk* starring Elizabeth Taylor. Here were three Buddhas sculpted from a single rock face. The standing image was 23ft high, the seated figure, with typical elongated earlobes, slightly smaller, and the recumbent Buddha 44ft long. A huge *stupa* or bell-shaped *dagoba* was practically hidden by dense growth. These structures were built over a relic of Buddha or one of his followers and varied in size from two feet in circumference to those larger than all but the greatest pyramids of Egypt. An edifice that I recall as a library was probably the **Trivanka Image House**, with vibrant murals of court life in its interior. Here again was another impressive figure in high relief, many pillars, browsing cows, and a lily-covered pond. Wild blue hibiscus made a pretty sight, and far-reaching views from a height were tremendous. Along the road, we passed an elephant ambling down the centre with his keeper, thatch-roofed adobe houses with primitive murals and sapling fences, a traditional cremation site, an area of plain square pillars sprouting like a forest of stone, and startling white *dagobas* in green surrounds, one ringed by a wall bearing sculpted elephant heads.

Kandy

Back in Kandy, the immense **Dalada Maligawa** (**Temple of Tooth**), founded in the 17th century, was said to house a tooth of Buddha smuggled into the country secreted in the hair of a princess more than 1,600 years ago. It was surrounded by a moat said to be filled with turtles but blanketed with minute green plant life. Also bright green was the water in a tank, its tiered sides with steps leading down to the reflective surface. Other photogenic ruins reared above a canopy of green foliage, and I saw a delicate waterfall and an elephant with exceptionally long tusks, flapping its ears and swaying its head to and fro.

A rare experience was provided by a visit to the newly established elephant orphanage, where babies were being fed from beer bottles full of milk. I did not realise that they were born with a rough coat of bristles (eventually shed); this I discovered on patting one hardly bigger than a large dog, whereby, considering its size, it trumpeted an almighty bellow. It frightened the wits out of me and on questioning the keeper as to whether it objected to being stroked he replied that, quite to the contrary, the roar indicated that he loved it! Elephants use their trunks for many purposes: to touch and caress each other, breathe, drink, trumpet, obtain food from low on the ground or up to five metres, lift objects from a tiny twig to a mighty log, use as a snorkel whilst swimming, scoop up dust to shower themselves for coolness, lift newborns or discipline calves, rub or scratch using a stick, swat flies with a small branch, spar, hold a mates tail, blow warm air, and flick rocks, wood or other objects at intruders.

If I were to sum up Kandy in one word, that word would be serendipity.

INDIA

Madurai

I flew back to Madras and moved on to **Madurai**, one of India's most ancient cities, its history going back six centuries before Christ. The emperors of Greece and Rome conducted trade with the ancient city. Here were more temples and tanks, the principal one being the fantastic **Meenakshi Sundareswarar** dedicated to the consort of Lord Shiva. This featured five terraced *gopurams* over 150ft high, each inundated with carving and colourful graphic statues, again in turquoise and pink, including multi-armed gods with fearsome faces, regal figures seated on an elaborately adorned bull, and images in all manner of poses. The ceiling of the colonnade encircling the central sacred **Tank of the Golden Lotus** was decorated with psychedelic *mandalas* (symbol representing the universe), but even more interesting was the buzz of ceaseless chatter amongst the multitude of worshippers armed with bowls of coconut and flowers. According to legend, the tank was once used to judge literary works; manuscripts of worth floated on its discerning waters whilst those lacking merit sank like stones. In its **Court of a Thousand Pillars**, each one was alive with carvings. *Gopurams* on other temples were even more brightly hued, and one was crowned with the fierce countenance of a mythical beast reminiscent of Bali.

The city of Madurai, the most ancient home of **Tamil** culture, was founded more than 2,500 years ago and, as with most cities in southern India, had the ambience of a small town. But also as in many cities of the subcontinent, I saw people living amid rubbish and under makeshift shelters erected against walls. I was struck by the strange sight of a mother and baby, both with startling yellow peroxide hair! Near a hall of many pillars, a man was milking a cow in the street, another sat cross-legged on the pavement turning the wheel on a hand-operated sewing machine, and girls were dexterously threading flowers for sale, the massed blooms creating a feast for the eye amid the squalor. Jasmine, sulphur-yellow dwarf chrysanthemums, roses and marigolds were strung on lengths of wet banana stem fibre, measured from finger tip to elbow, and sold for 50 *paise* a strip. Also in sharp contrast to the sordid conditions, bright Hindu paintings adorned walls, and stone columns were carved to represent rampant green dragon-headed lions.

Trivandrum

Trivandrum was the antithesis of Madurai, featuring **Kovalam Beach**, with thatched huts amongst palm trees and attractive European-style buildings with gables and turrets, one being the pink and white **Napier Museum**. The name derives from Thiruananthapuram, the abode of the scared serpent, Anantha, on which Lord Vishnu reclines.

Cochin

Flying over **Cochin**, where Christianity first came to India, one could simultaneously observe the virgin jungle, **Kerala** backwater, and palm-studded coast, its swaying fronds mistaken by Vasco da Gama for people waving in welcome. At one time called Queen of the Arabian Sea and Venice of the Orient, Cochin was the port for the fabled land of incense and myrrh, which attracted traders from the court of Kublai Khan and 'to which King Solomon's ships sailed a thousand years before Christ' to be loaded with timber for construction of a temple in Jerusalem, gold, ivory, peacocks, coir, pepper, herbs, and aromatic spices such as cardamom, cloves and star anise. It was already known to the Romans, Grecians and Chinese before being colonised by Portugal in the 16th century. Arabs, the Dutch and English all left their imprint on the town.

Pyramids of vibrantly hued powders made an indelible splash of colour on street stalls, policemen wore tall cocked hats, shorts and long socks, people used enamel utensils to wash themselves on the road verge, and fishermen threw their nets from dugout canoes, whilst larger vessels hoisted square sails like white sheets. Lining the shore, fish traps appeared like enormous fragile butterflies as they hovered overhead, and a white church stood out amongst the green foliage. A picturesque pink church was also sequestered amongst palms, and I watched as men in white *mundus* (a type of short sarong), their bare black backs glistening with sweat, hauled on the rock-weighted ropes attached to the pole that raised and lowered one of the huge cantilevered nets into the water – to produce only a small catch. A white goat strolled along the seafront, and the flapping fish were put into baskets from which they were then taken, weighed, and sold straight away.

I entered the **Church of St Francis**, the oldest European church in India, built by the Portuguese in 1503 and containing the tombstone of Vasco da Gama who died here in 1534, his remains later moved to Lisbon. I visited the fascinating 400-year-old synagogue at **Mattancherry**, where I was amazed to find Indian Jews, descendants of a colony of refugees from Roman dominated Jerusalem following the destruction of the second temple in AD 70, and in 1969 only numbering one hundred. Built in 1568, the synagogue, featuring Chinese hand-painted tiles, was destroyed by the Portuguese in 1662 and rebuilt two years later. I observed people working with coconut husks to produce coir and surveyed the many different craft moving backwards and forwards in the water. At the beach, I recollect clusters of beautiful pink frangipani, a pavilion on the strand, long boats being poled, larger shipping and, seen from the sea, good views of modern and conventional buildings, the latter with towers and cupolas.

Further north, lay Kozhikode, its original name of Calicut giving rise to the cotton cloth calico, which is still made here.

My final pictures show the appalling poverty where hundreds of families, the detritus of humanity, were living in crude cloth and cardboard shelters beside the airport runway in Bombay; naked children ran around and one person was making an attempt at sweeping. This was followed by virgin mountains and pristine white cloud before descending and landing in the bustling port of Hong Kong en route back to Australia.

India was full of poor people with a rich past.

Two events for which I do not have specific dates stand out: a dust storm like an impenetrable beige wall that approached with frightening rapidity up the **Jumna River** in **Agra**, and from which we sheltered in the Taj, and an occasion on which I had purchased, at the request of a male friend, a blue whip with a brass-studded handle and plaited thong. On this same trip, in order to demonstrate the art to my group, I had both hands extensively tattooed with henna, and thus, dressed in a short skirt and with the whip lashed around the outside of my suitcase (that was too small to contain it), I arrived back at Perth airport. If ever I was to be detained by customs, I thought it would be now!

More customs stories

After one trip to **Leh**, my final stop en route to the airport was to purchase a kilo of red chilli powder, which I deposited on top of the clothing in my suitcase. I arrived at the terminal to find a notice listing prohibited items: knives, guns, *krises*, aerosol sprays, flammable liquids and the usual assortment, but added to the bottom it specifically mentioned 'chillies powder'. I wondered if they feared that a terrorist would approach the cockpit with a handful of this 'lethal' condiment and demand to be flown to an alternative destination. I considered it ludicrous, but in retrospect, I guess if thrown into the eyes it could cause considerable damage. I did not get caught with my illicit substance!

Security at Indian airports was always strict, even before the threat of terrorism. Women were frisked, some even having their long hair examined for concealed items, many were forced to waste a photograph to prove that a camera was what it claimed, and on certain strategic sectors, even at transit stops, all baggage was removed from the aircraft and placed on the tarmac. Passengers were obliged to alight and identify each piece (strictly by the claimant), which was duly marked by a police officer or official before one was allowed to reboard. At times, I felt female customs officers were a little too diligent in their duty, poking and prodding every item, particularly cosmetics, which in my opinion was prompted purely by curiosity in the days when tourists were a novelty. Oft-times, things like hairspray had to be surrendered but were consigned, appropriately labelled, to the care of the captain, to be returned at the end of the flight. This is no longer possible.

In a similar incident to the above, I *did* break the law when, on a trip to **Singapore**, my husband rang me to say he had 'fixed' customs and to spend all my remaining money on radios. These I laid on top in my case, but the closer we came to **Perth** the more anxious and nervous I became because of the knowledge that I was contravening regulations. My agitation must have been obvious, because on arrival, I was not met and conducted through as expected, the official afraid to approach me and alarmed at what I might be carrying! Again, I was not searched.

In 1977, I also went to **Bali** as tour leader for Kings Holidays.

NEW ZEALAND 1978

I have described both Canada and Norway as God's own country but have one of the greatest practically on my doorstep. New Zealand encapsulates the best of all destinations and has the advantage of being small and compact; it is a world in miniature, with beauty and changing vistas revealed around every corner.

In 1978, together with my husband, we hired a car and travelled for five weeks in **New Zealand** – **Aotearoa** (Long White Cloud) to the indigenous **Maori**.

North Island

Beginning in **Auckland**, my first pictures show a wooden bridge secreted amongst massive tree-ferns and tall foliage, which was typical of the lush environs encountered all over the islands but particularly in the south. I also noticed exotic flowers and tree trunks nurturing colourful orange fungi, mosses and minute ferns. A black and white bird with a red bill and legs resembled a Jabiru stork, and a grey bird with a striped chest and red beak had modified wings remarkably like a penguin. Accommodation in New Zealand was very good; our first night on the road was spent at a motel with a unit overlooking lovely flowerbeds and lawn. Also excellent (and cheap) were the dairy products and fruits, which included huge strawberries and some, like boysenberries, not previously tasted. Having our own vehicle, we could load up with large bags of fresh produce and prepare our own meals because many places provided kitchen facilities.

I recorded an impressive memorial, a beautiful river, a lovely green lake, and a huge tree covered in red blossoms. Magnificent gardens featured a vine-covered pergola, water lilies, and a conservatory displaying giant tree ferns, trailing plants, coloured and variegated leaves, orchids, bromeliads, the carnivorous pitcher plant, a pure white bell-like flower that looked like a petticoat with an overskirt, hanging baskets, massed flowers including anemones in multiple colours with blue hydrangeas, striking orange tiger lilies, palms and succulents. Next on the agenda was the **Auckland Museum**, its **Polynesian Court** exhibiting carved Maori meeting houses, food storage buildings, totems, and images such as a *tiki* with a protruding tongue. In Maori mythology, tiki was the first man and found the first woman in a pond, but there are several deviations to this story. Pride of place was a war canoe, the only one preserved intact, made in the 1800s from a single *totura* log hollowed with an adze. After a long history, which included being presented to a Maori chief in exchange for a piebald stallion in 1853, it finished up in this museum in 1965. Given the name **Te Toki Tapiri** (Tapiri's Battleaxe), it was 82ft long 6ft wide and could carry one hundred men!

The delicate 'wedding cake' clock tower of the university reared behind garden beds and a floral clock in extensive green lawns, and we wandered wooden boardwalks through the quaint (a word I use often in conjunction with New Zealand) shopping precinct of **Parnell Village**. This revelled in timber buildings with wooden balustrades on verandahs and balconies, slender turned posts, bay windows, fine fretwork or wrought-iron filigree, striped awnings, brick paving, and even an external spiral metal staircase painted white. Most establishments were white, but there was the occasional bright red, pink or green wall; it was all extremely photogenic.

Our next attraction was the superb **Whangarei Falls**, cascading in a sheer drop to a green pool in dense forest, but there were many such in a land blessed with so much water. We were heading towards the small seaside town of **Russell** in the beautiful **Bay of Islands**. Here, I have pictures of an old-time three-masted wooden schooner, a Maori meeting house with an image crowning the roof, and an elaborate longboat. Although lower, a second set of falls generated a greater volume of water, and in contrast, we came to a glorious and peaceful turquoise bay with a tiny tree-covered island in the centre. As the name suggests, the area was dotted with small islands and was a Mecca for yachts, often moored in secluded coves. Russell's little white **Christ Church** was surrounded by weathered gravestones and a white picket fence. We took a boat trip around dozens of islets, traversing water that changed in colour from cobalt blue to aqua, hues so intense that they appeared unreal.

Although cloudy, it was a fine day, with sun glinting off the water. Sailing past the aforementioned schooner, heavily wooded shores, rocky outcrops, grottoes, and a penguin floating on the surface, we eventually reached **Piercy Island**, literally just a rock with a hole in the middle. The same as that off the east coast of Canada, and with almost the same name, we navigated right through. This grey monolith was virtually denuded of plant life, but hundreds of seabirds were wheeling around, and on its leeward side the ocean was a stunning shade of emerald. We encountered a vessel ploughing forward under a billowing red and yellow spinnaker, other formations with apertures, rock tors, and waves crashing into caverns.

Pompellier House, site of the signing of the Waitangi Treaty, was also located in the Bay of Islands. At **Kerikeri** we took in the **Maori Stockade** with its two underground bunkers, **Rua Kumara** and **Rua Kiore**, the purpose of which I am not sure. Dwellings inside the palisade also featured the figure with the protruding tongue. The first stone building in New Zealand, erected here in 1833 as a storehouse and refuge for a Maori leader, stood on the waterfront, with a little white church on a grassy knoll behind. I have memories of houses with colourful cottage gardens in this tiny settlement. Continuing on, we passed an area of gentle green inclines dropping to white sand dunes and an extraordinarily blue ocean before retracing our steps south, back to tall timber, verdant undergrowth, and a river bubbling over white rocks in a ferny glade. New Zealand's kauri forests in the north date back 60,000 years, they survived the Ice Age but fell victim to man and have become depleted. More lush scenery, including hillsides with massed tree-ferns, was followed by willows bending graceful boughs above a reflective surface.

Arriving in **Rotorua**, we stayed in the Puhi Nui Motel where we had the luxury of a private thermally heated pool. Here, from outside the high hedged perimeter, we saw the **Maori Royal Palace**, its ornately carved red gates set in an archway formed by totems, their eyes composed of gleaming puha shell. Similar images appeared on roof capping and eaves; gables were adorned with designs. Flowers in a conservatory featured the Dutchman's pipe, and relieving an expanse of green lawn, a show of colour was provided by blue and pink hydrangeas and a tree with gorgeous feathery pink blossoms. A three-storey mansion in bucolic surrounds overlooked a quiet waterway spanned by several bridges, and we drove along a highway enveloped by tall trees.

Many places in Rotorua were endowed with carved red figures, and the smell and steam from thermal springs was evident everywhere, even emanating from grates in the road! There were numerous active areas, probably the most visited being **Whakarewarewa**, right in town and enclosed by a log fence topped with small *tiki* guardians. Here, in close proximity, one finds clear deep-blue pools of hot water through to boiling viscous mud ponds that plip and plop in an alarming manner, spewing the liquid earth some distance. Here also was the impressive **Pohutu Geyser**, which erupted frequently, spraying a towering fountain of hot water skywards. Other sections consisted solely of fissures in the ground spouting thick clouds of the pungent sulphur-smelling steam into the atmosphere. Also containing small red totems, even a nearby graveyard was ringed by the eerie vents.

Much of the land was barren and grey, but the hot springs probably served to provide beneficial nutrients because the immediate surrounds were quite lush, and from a distance it appeared as if smoke billowed from a hundred fires. It was a phenomenon equalled only by America's Yellowstone National Park. A busy stream rushed alongside steaming fumaroles, and there were strangely still areas reflecting white clouds and the brilliant blue of the sky. One calm pool, encompassed by ferns and mirrored trees, possibly contained fresh water. Also located behind a palisade, another replica Maori village featured an arch depicting a couple embracing below a series of faces, the whole created in auspicious red. A red *tiki* stood in long grass beside a blue pool, and a cairn belched smoke near a green sward. Standing on the shore of **Lake Rotorua**, the red and white **Chinemutu Church** was built in a half-timbered style unique to Rotorua, and much evidence of Maori culture and tradition appeared around town.

We visited the idyllic **Taniwha Trout Springs**, teeming with fish, flowers and ferns. A white wooden bridge crossed the crystal clear stream, ducks swam in the water, and drooping willows lined the banks. Colourful beds enhanced a grassy dell, shy deer hid amongst the foliage, and water (this time cold) bubbled up from the mouths of springs in the river bed. Long strands of waving green weed made patterns beneath the surface, and in one densely wooded area there was a small but powerful cascade. I have film of another lovely little white church and the attractive half-timbered buildings and grounds of **Government Gardens**, where people were playing croquet on the lawn. Even here, steam issued forth from rock vents at the edge of a landscaped pond in the foreground. There was a gracious old bandstand, and carved red Maori figures ringed steps at the base of a tall monument with classical sculpted images.

Each of the spectacular thermal areas around Rotorua was unique, and we headed next for the awesome **Waimangu Valley**, where the activity could be seen from a long way off, literally appearing like a volcano erupting from a verdant green crater ringed by burning crags. To one side was an almost iridescent vivid emerald pool (and so named) partially covered by a peculiar green-tinged crust. Here, it was possible to take a boat across **Lake Rotomahana**, a body of cold water with scorching steam belching from fissures on the edge; the entire region fostered an illusion of fire. Even a walk through this dramatic primeval area was quite daunting because one had the impression of the earth just biding its time before a cataclysmic explosion. In fact, the narrow pathway, with steam virtually underfoot, had to be continually rerouted because of the changing direction of the boiling water. I was glad to leave! A few birds including black swans frequented the lake, which depending on the light and reflections of thick foliage, varied in hue from vibrant blue to a deep emerald.

Minerals produced interesting red hues in the rock wall encompassing a pool where, within its startling white rim, wisps of vapour wafted gently from water that was a wonderful shade of turquoise. There were rapidly rushing streams and a small waterfall, also appearing hot, in proximity to hissing and spitting thermal areas. Waving white pampas grasses added yet another dimension in colour, and brilliant blue patches were in places almost obliterated by a cloak of white steam. A region of silica terraces, with vertical stripes in hues of burnt-orange, red, yellow and brown, also contained coloured pools. Large green craters on hillsides appeared like extinct volcanoes. This extreme environment had developed unique life forms of multihued lichens, mosses, and specially adapted heat-tolerant plants. The algae that thrived beside the boiling waters had changed little since the beginning of life on earth. This accumulation of geysers, hot springs, mud pools, fumaroles, silica terraces and salt deposits were the ingredients of an outstanding attraction.

Back near Rotorua, I photographed more deer (a mother and fawn), discovered more beautiful falls in the vicinity, and visited a part of the park exhibiting such diverse features as bubbling ponds of black mud and delicate ribbons of water over stepped rocks. In a ferny grotto, I filmed a black and white pheasant and a peacock proudly displaying his magnificent plumage and quivering tail feathers to entice two white peahens that, totally unimpressed, turned their backs to peck at tidbits on the ground. In this area, I found one pool with a fascinating cloth of floating bubbles, the adjacent waters varying from blue to a seething black.

Leaving this desolate region of fumes and fumaroles behind, we passed a blue bay, yet another small white church, and superb river scenery with rapids flowing over rocks between green banks. The church was that of **Opotiki**, which has a fascinating but macabre history. The man who established it in 1860, Reverend K. S. Volkner, was hanged and decapitated in 1865 by a fanatical preacher. Dressed in the dead missionary's clothes, the assailant then delivered a sermon in the church with his victim's head beside him on the pulpit. He drank the reverend's blood from the Communion chalice, which he passed amongst the congregation, and finally tore out the eyes and swallowed them. Fighting broke out against a punitive expedition and a redoubt was built around the church, forming the centre of a frontier post from which the town sprang. The renegade preacher, Kereopa, was taken prisoner and hanged in Napier in 1872. Reverend Volkner's body was recovered and interred beneath the pulpit. There was also a giant sacred **Puriri Burial Tree**. According to ancient Maori custom, bones of important people were exhumed after interment, scraped and coated with preservative paint, then placed, in elaborate ritual, in caves or hollow trees to protect them from desecration by enemy tribes. This tree, with a 67ft girth, was estimated to be 1,000 years old and contained many bones and skulls, since removed. We came to a tall colourful totem surmounted by an eagle with spread wings and discovered white daisies in an area of unusually bare contoured hills. We followed the river as it traversed a narrow gorge then widened into an expanse of blue.

Travelling through **Gisborne** and back at the coast, a fine line of leisurely white surf made a marked distinction between the deep blue of the ocean and a black beach strewn with driftwood. Continuing southwest, a long curved pergola beautified with flowerbeds was an attractive addition to gorgeous landscaped gardens near the water's edge. This was **Napier** on **Hawke's Bay**, which I remember specifically for its splendid floral displays around street trees and in expansive lawns, the latter also featuring a floral clock. In the outstanding **Centennial Gardens**, a small waterwheel turned in a garden setting and a waterfall flowed down a cliff face. Here, bounded by attractive plants, I also found a murmuring rill running through a grassed section. **City of Flowers**, a title bestowed on many another, was deservedly applied to Napier. A dedication to fishermen, portrayed wearing sou'-westers and mackintoshes as they hauled in a laden net, was situated in the centre of a large pool.

It was here that I had my first encounter with a gannet colony when, at low tide, we rode on a bumpy tractor-trailer across the seashore at the base of rugged taupe and beige striated cliffs. On the opposite side of the glorious blue bay I could see the birds wheeling and landing amongst the seething white mass in a crater atop a stark grey ridge, which on reaching an observation point we ultimately looked down upon. The congested colony of these strikingly marked white birds – with a wingspan of two metres (6.6ft), a yellow head, perfectly etched black lines around the beak and eyes (that were a startling blue), and black tips on wings and tail – was also inhabited by many fluffy white chicks, and whilst some adults collected twigs for nests still occupied, others fed their similarly sized offspring with regurgitated food. There was much flapping of wings, and one bird was tossing and catching a stick with its beak, much like a child at play, whilst another settled carefully on an egg. Perched atop a rock ledge, an adult and pure white downy chick made an arresting picture against a rich blue sky. The birds dive for fish at speeds of 145km/h (90mph) from a height of 30m (98ft). I have described the squabbling and squawking of these vociferous birds at a later date so will not do so here. Others congregated on innumerable rocky outcrops that became islands at high tide. Usually an island breeder, this was the world's largest mainland colony (5,200 nesting pairs) and was located at the southern end of Hawke's Bay on **Cape Kidnappers**, so called because it was from here that Captain Cook's Tahitian interpreter was taken by local Maoris.

Passing another quaint church in the **Esk Valley** and a series of waterfalls in green surrounds, we headed north again, across to **Lake Taupo** and the lunar landscape of the thermal areas of **Wairakei** and **Waiotapu**. Here, we found steam emerging from boiling water at the bottom of deep cracks in the earth's crust, an indigo waterway beyond a series of opaque apple-green ponds, and a turquoise pool next to a large blue pond, its rim of stark white and vibrant red just discernable through the mist. A small warm waterfall caressed yellow sulphur-encrusted and red-tinged rock, the colours accentuated against the natural grey surface. I was at Waiotapu to record the daily display, at 10.15am, of **Lady Knox Geyser**, which erupts up to 21 metres.

Departing, we made for **Orakei Korako** (Place of Adorning, an apt title), where I was confronted with the best of nature's art in the most stunning and extensive silica terraces. Assuming the appearance of petrified cascades, they were coated with bright green algae at the waterline of a deep-blue lake, against which the rich earthy tones of the quartz deposits were striking. Apart from the tinted terraces, over a few of which hot water flowed, this site also contained an expansive area of clear pools with an amazing variety of colours like a veritable artist's palette. There was also a cavern, from the dark recesses of which one could look up to see palm trees throwing a lacy silhouette against the sky. In sharp variance to the orange silica steps, we came upon a river of vivid emerald green flowing between lush banks and dropping in fierce foaming falls to boulders in its bed. More mud pools spurted blobs larger than dinner plates, and in places where the clay had solidified, much of it had adopted a rust-red colour that contrasted dramatically with the white. Mosses enhanced some sections, and always there was the steam. As I negotiated a wooden walkway across sparse scrub in this extremely active area, a small geyser intermittently spouted water. The exceptionally green freshwater river led eventually to powerful **Huka Falls**, which churned in a white wash through a narrow chasm.

About this time we went to **Waitomo Caves**, featuring the usual formations but with the added attraction of fascinating glow worms, which I had never seen before. Entered by boat on a subterranean river with an underground waterfall, the **Glow Worm Grotto** was illuminated only by a myriad of these minute insects suspended on threads from the ceiling of the soaring chamber. Appearing as a million stars on an inky black sky, it was a magical sight. We visited a replica historic town, had our first glimpse of the snow-covered **Southern Alps** in the distance, and saw two more stunning falls. The first surged through black rock with feathery pampas grass in the foreground; the second was a wider gentler cascade in lush surroundings.

A conservatory contained palms and beautiful decorative plants such as coleus, their deep red leaves edged with green and so perfect that they almost appeared artificial. Flowers included red-and-purple fuchsias and brilliant purple cyclamen, their petals rimmed with white. In the grounds, beds of profusely blooming roses were interspersed with ponds containing fountains. We were in **Wellington**, and from this renowned **Rose Garden** I obtained a wonderful panorama over the city and harbour. Climbing roses enhanced an arbour with a waterfall in the background, and a second glasshouse was full of multihued blooms, including a red pelargonium with a frilled white edge, more fuchsias, bromeliads, and colourful hanging baskets.

South Island

From **Picton** we took the ferry to the picturesque port of **Lyttleton** on the **South Island** where, for the first time, we were really surrounded by mountains, with snow on distant peaks. Driving through **Westport** to **Greymouth**, we encountered glorious green rivers and virgin forest. I am sure New Zealand rivals Ireland for greenness, and lodged amid palms I found a white wildflower like a hollyhock. Reaching the west coast, we were confronted by rock formations in the sea, with waves pounding cliffs and surging into a cavern, but the lush growth and palm trees still flourished on top. We came to an impressive blowhole and a narrow passage along which foaming water churned and was forced up a tall slender chute to spurt fine spray. Wild water also burst through a hole in walls enclosing a confined space, and this area was known as **Punakaiki** (pancake) **Rocks** because of their remarkable resemblance to stacks of pancakes.

Clouds hung low in the valley as the elements played hide and seek with the environs, and we drove beside a boulder-strewn waterway where red fern fronds and tall flower heads with bell-shaped clusters made an appearance amongst the rich green foliage. Nurturing this wonderland that was nature's garden, narrow but high falls plummeted in stages through ferns, mosses and lush undergrowth. We moved south, through misty mountains with snow in the distance and rivers far below, over **Lewis Pass** (911m) and down to ground level, where I found picture perfect postcard scenes consisting of purple bells by the roadside, a blue river, green slopes, and snowy peaks rearing above low-lying cloud. Traversing **Burke's Pass**, we were once again on top of the mountains, and I photographed a charming white wooden church amongst conifers. Our destination was the fabulous milky blue **Lake Tekapo**, with its photogenic **Church of the Good Shepherd** constructed of stone from the shore and situated on a spit of land extending into the glacial water. The chancel window afforded a wonderful vista of the mountains and lake, its unreal colour augmented by barren grey hills behind and even eclipsing the blue of the sky. I passed an entire day seated at the picture window in our unit just appreciating this outlook. In the vicinity, I filmed a deep-blue lake; it was a strange phenomenon that bodies of water in close proximity could display such disparate hues. From this community of A-frame dwellings amid fields of purple, pink and white lupins, I watched a figure parasailing and admired a pale blue sunset sky with puffs of grey in a bank of rose-pink cloud. It looked amazingly like a glorious painting. With the advent of day, the same scene was transformed into a mass of white cloud across azure heavens. In the **Mackenzie High Country** around Tekapo, a tribute to the sheepdog stood ever vigilant atop a boulder.

From here, we headed for the alpine area of **Mt Cook**, known to the Maori as **Aoraki** (Cloud-Piercer), and even the onset of rain could not dim the breathtaking surrounds: green meadows full of colourful lupins at the foot of snow-capped peaks, a scene perfected by the appearance of a rainbow. Here again, as sullen clouds blew and swirled in strong wind gusts across the summit of mighty Mt Cook, on which I could discern distant glaciers, I spent the day engrossed in observation from the window of our protective self-contained hut secluded amid majestic pines. Mt Cook (3,754m/12,350ft) is part of New Zealand's Southern Alps, which extend from Milford Sound to Blenheim in the north. Next day dawned clear and sparkling, the wind again whipping cloud across the mountain. Investigation produced waterfalls, a milky green lake, and an expanse of blue water backed by green slopes, behind which a glaring white ridge stood out against the blue of the sky. Sunset striking the crest of Mt Cook transformed it to the palest pink, now decorated with a halo of pink cloud.

Next day, I was seated next to the pilot as we took off for a flight over the Alps in a ski plane, which landed on a snowfield hemmed in by awesome peaks and a blue glacier; it was one of my most memorable experiences. I have film of a second plane taking off and banking sharply to clear the mountains. Back on the ground, I photographed yellow alpine buttercups, waterfalls created by the melting ice, and more turquoise water, with willows and purple flowers on the bank.

We crossed a choppy **Lake Wanaka** to see primitive rock art depicting figures and animals created with red ochre, and prior to arriving in the east coast city of **Dunedin**, as far south as we ventured, I recorded a stone church, gardens with a shady creeper-covered pergola and willows overhanging a red wooden bridge, and round boulders like immense marbles on a stormy coastline, which could have been erratics distributed by glacial action (see Newfoundland, book 4). This city had many gracious buildings, none more so than 35-roomed **Olveston House** built in the Jacobean style between 1904 and 1906 and the well-known **Larnach Castle** with stone lions flanking steps to the entrance. Amongst the fine churches was the **First Church of Otago** featuring many spires and a most impressive steeple, and there was a fine turreted clock tower and imposing monuments. I have film of whales or dolphins offshore, and pictures of golden-yellow blossoms, waxy red fuchsias with their purple underskirts, a tree with vibrant red foliage, and a stately home that featured in brochures. It is probably not widely known that the city was called Dunedin because it is the Gaelic word for Edinburgh.

Heading west again, I have photographs taken from inside our unit at **Lake Te Anau**, followed by film of the lake and rugged mountains. Tracing the partially dry course of a wide river, which fluctuated from rushing water to calmer stretches below forested slopes, their crests bare and barren, we arrived at a place of perfect mirror reflections in the **Eglington Valley**, the like of which I have rarely seen. Traversing **Hollyford Valley** to the **Homer Tunnel** (only completed in 1953) and through it to the **Cleddau Valley**, looming green mountains with snowy summits crowded in on all sides. This led to renowned **Milford Sound**; just as breathtaking as all the pictures portray, it must surely rank as one of the best sights in the world – in fact, Rudyard Kipling called it the eighth wonder – with 265m (869ft) **Mitre Peak** perfectly reflected in quiet water. A boat ride along this incredible fiord took us past equally impressive pyramid-shaped and jagged mountains rising straight from its surface (dwarfing a small sightseeing plane), soaring cliffs, snowy vistas, virgin rainforest, stunning 500ft **Bowen Falls**, and numerous ribbon falls, including a slender stream from a hanging lake. On the return voyage, we sailed under the drifting spray and close to the foot of a second tumultuous fall, and in places pale delicate mosses and ferns at the waterline provided a contrast in colour. Adding to the enjoyment, we revelled in rare fine weather and sunny skies, with light sparkling on water in an area that receives 200 inches of rain in as many days. A solitary seal basked on a rock. At the conclusion, we drove past turbulent mountain streams, the water from melting snows swelling the volume to form fietrce falls that thundered through fine rocky chasms and poured across big boulders, creating whitecaps on the blue surface. At one stage, with water tumbling from a natural snow-topped amphitheatre, I was overawed by the majesty of my surroundings. The incredible scenes of rushing rivers, snow-capped green mountains, emerald and blue lakes, waterfalls such as beautiful **Falls Creek** by the **Milford Highway**, rocky ridges and beech forest were innumerable.

In stark contrast, which I appreciated because of the chance to experience the fiords in all their moods, we took a cruise on **Doubtful Sound** in conditions of steady rain and mist, which served to produce a multitude of additional falls. First crossing **Lake Manapouri**, where low-lying cloud and misty veils engendered an ethereal ambience, we made a brief stop to observe several olive-green *keas*, the New Zealand native parrot, which exhibited flashes of red underwing in flight. Boarding a bus to cross **Wilmot Pass**, I saw blackened trees with the beginning of new growth, and deep red, orange and yellow mosses and lichens on rock beside lovely roadside falls. I seem to remember that the sound had not long been open, and in 1960 it had been necessary to fly bulldozers and heavy equipment in by helicopter to construct this road connecting it to the West Arm of Lake Manapouri, New Zealand's deepest (400m/1,312ft), and well below sea level. At two dollars per centimetre, it was the most expensive road built in New Zealand.

It was still raining, and the swollen creeks and rivers put on a spectacular show, as did the myriad cascades. Commencing our boat trip on the actual sound, we passed a few yachts in a sheltered cove and many more scenes of grandeur, including shrouded peaks and green-clad surfaces alive with water plunging straight to the fiord. Other waterfalls could be seen behind densely wooded spits of land projecting into the sound, and again a rainbow added to the appeal. The ultimate splendour of these vistas evoked sensations of wonder for which I find mere words inadequate. Unfortunately, much of my filming had to be carried out inside the boat and was consequently marred by reflections on the glass. The sound was so named by Captain Cook in 1770 because once entered he was doubtful that he would get back out due to a lack of easterly winds in **Fiordland**.

Travelling north, we arrived in the quaint city of **Queenstown**, with its single-storey wood-and-shingle buildings, picket fences, stone church, old waterwheel at the head of the Mall, and even horse-drawn wagons in the street. But the highlight of Queenstown (for me) was the delightful **Botanic Gardens**, with water lilies and ducks adding interest to a pond crossed by a stone moon bridge, beautiful trees, and flowerbeds in spacious lawns. Idyllically situated at the foot of the **Remarkables Range**, the city faces **Lake Wakatipu**, on which it was pleasant to cruise aboard the TSS *Earnshaw,* and a view of which we obtained from our window. **Shotover Canyon**, offering thrilling jet boat rides, and rugged **Skippers Canyon** were both accessible from Queenstown. In keeping with its gold rush atmosphere, there was even a store called The Golden Nugget.

Not far from Queenstown we found picturesque **Arrowtown**, where white stone buildings included the inevitable church, and tiny wooden cottages were sequestered behind white paling fences. Gone was the lush vegetation of the fiords in this typical mining country of multihued hills near **Lake Hayes**. One slate-roofed stone structure had a pretty English garden that included bright yellow flowers and dark red hollyhocks. After more footage of sublime scenery, unbelievably green waterways, and innumerable falls, which included **Roaring Meg** in **Kawarau Gorge** and the gauze-like spray of **Orman Falls**, we drove through **Haast Pass** and came across pretty **Fantail Falls** right beside the highway. I found myself back at the coast, gazing over a turquoise ocean from wooded slopes at **Knight's Point**, where the **Tasman Sea** pounded black rock formations with an uncanny resemblance to the Twelve Apostles of Victoria's coastline in Australia. This was followed by the incredible mirror of **Lake Matheson**, banks of ferns and tiny colourful varieties like miniature gardens flourishing on logs, rollicking rivers, and white-capped mountains.

At **Westland National Park** we encountered both **Fox** and **Franz Josef Glaciers**. Walking alongside the former, I could look down on its cracked surface where black silt marred the blue of the ice. Meltwater flowed from beneath the dirty moraine, adjacent to which was a beautiful teal-blue pool with a sheer fluted rock wall looming behind. We took a guided walk that proved to be one of my most challenging feats; even though provided with steel-capped spiked boots and aided by steps that our guide cut into the ice with a pickaxe, I still had to be assisted across the slippery route. We found small pools that showed up vivid blue against the glare of the white surface and were extremely lucky to encounter an ice tunnel, which would not have lasted more than a day but through which it was possible to walk. The brilliant blue inside was something that I shall never forget.

Franz Josef (11km/6.8mi) was advancing at a rate of two to three metres (6.5 to 10ft) per day, ten times the norm! I filmed this second and bluer glacier making a statement against its background of white snow, a small white church with a steeply pitched red roof, more of the incredible surrounds that exhibited such a raw beauty, the ethereal view through the chancel window of **St James Church**, a waterfall in a rock cleft, and smooth perfectly rounded holes at the edges of the glacier's path, which had been created by boulders as they were swept along by the moving wall of frozen water. The ice face of Franz Josef was higher and its surface more creviced, making it prohibitive for hiking, but we did cross a rickety swinging bridge spanning a chasm, with water raging between massive boulders below and stones tumbling down the sides. Looking up from the base, myriad pinnacles were outlined against (and brighter than) the dull sky. Trickling down the grey walls confining the glacier, silver threads of water augmented the steady flow issuing from under the moraine. Like all natural features, Franz Josef was steeped in legend. The Maori name, *Ka Roimata o Hinehukatere*, means Tears of the Avalanche Girl, and the story was told of Hinehukatere who loved to climb the mountains and persuaded her lover, Tawe, to accompany her. When he fell to his death, her many tears froze to form the glacier. Leaving these weird and wonderful shapes of nature, we came to a larger waterfall, another area of mirror lakes, a beautiful rainforest walk, a wide river with a stony bed, and another totem surmounted by a bird.

And thus we arrived at **Christchurch**, in the centre of the **Canterbury Plains** farmlands, where I discovered policemen in tall helmets like London Bobbies and its distinctive cathedral that featured in so many pictures but was severely damaged by earthquake in 2011. Like its namesake, Christchurch was very English, with towers and turrets on gracious and stately buildings set in immaculate lawns. However, the **Town Hall** with its globular fountains and a large pool in the forecourt was contemporary. Flowing through the city and its beautiful gardens, the **Avon River** was crossed by photogenic wrought-iron and stone bridges; willows and other decorative trees lined the banks. I saw the elegant **Canterbury Museum** and a grand arched clock tower surrounded by flowerbeds. My sightseeing concluded with a hothouse and gardens, attractive stone buildings surrounding the campus of the university, a small wooden cottage with a brick chimney, a half-timbered structure, and a quaint house with shutters behind a picket fence. An oast house was now the Chateau Commodore, and a tiny church with fretwork around the steep gable and a free-standing bell tower was secluded in green forest. The very French **Hôtel des Pêcheurs** had red-and-white shutters, and rolling contoured hills descended to blue water.

Amongst other sights were the elusive kiwi, the **Putiki Maori Church**, a statue dedicated to **Pania of the Reef**, a lofty carillon, and an ivy-draped cottage, but I do not recall exactly where these were.

'And so (in terms of the old documentaries) now we bid farewell to New Zealand'.

SINGAPORE, HONG KONG & PENANG 1979

In 1979, I made two trips as tour leader for Vacations Unlimited, visiting Singapore and Hong Kong, followed by Singapore and Penang.

Singapore

Even then, **Singapore** was a clean modern city, with many interesting vestiges of its past relegated to history books. Aside from its pristine, almost sterile environment, the thing that never ceased to impress me was the lush plant life. The humid conditions being very conducive to growth, Singapore was famous for its orchids. On this occasion, my first pictures record gardens with a striking red and yellow variety. Here also was a group of serious-faced children, all dressed in white with the black Malay cap (*songkok*); it always amazed me how they kept so clean.

On a tour to the moving **Kranji War Cemetery**, I took film of emotive inscriptions on headstones that marked 'This Little Piece of England'.

Hong Kong

In what was at that time British **Hong Kong**, photographs taken from **Victoria Peak** show the city and harbour. A multi-tiered pagoda and other buildings of Chinese origin stood in the bizarre **Aw Boon Haw Gardens**, which displayed large colourful images representing characters from folklore and superstitious belief set in an artificial environment of rock and greenery.

Other pictures show *sampans*, most bedecked with washing, clustered cheek by jowl in the locality of **Aberdeen**. Washing also hung like flags on bamboo poles protruding from high-rise balconies.

We visited one of the few remaining old areas, the walled town of **Sam Tung Uk**, where women dressed all in black wore large straw hats with a black frill around the brim but without a crown. Inside the fortifications, the alleyways were narrow, and produce was peddled by ladies seated on cane chairs – a couple smoking pipes.

On a tour to the **New Territories**, ducks congregated in crude shelters or perched on wooden planks criss-crossing ponds, and we stopped to watch workers in fields. Two black-clad **Hakka** figures carried a basket suspended from a pole braced between their shoulders, whilst another, toting a pole with a basket of greens at each end, also had a sleeping child slung on her back and a jet-black puppy or goat in her arms. Looking from the hilltop of **Lok Ma Chau**, we could see mainland China across the water.

We rode to **Ocean Park** on the cable car; at over three kilometres, it was supposedly the longest in the world. A pretty pool near the entrance contained ducks, and our 'bubbles' passed above a gigantic seahorse sculpted in green turf on a hillside. At the show we watched orcas (killer whales) and porpoises in action, the latter executing the classical enormous leaps, 'walking' on tails (flukes), swimming on their backs, spinning whilst 'standing' erect, flicking balls with their flukes, waving this same appendage, and concluding with several leaping in unison. Performing seals, their bodies glistening black as they emerged from the water, also entertained. The usual comical antics included the clapping and waving of flippers, balancing a ball poised on top of a stick on the nose, and walking on flippers. One assumed an upright position atop a ball that it propelled whilst balancing another on its olfactory organ!

We visited gardens featuring waterbirds and falls in a lovely tropical setting, pools containing fountains, sculpted hedges, a floral clock in an expanse of lawn, exotic blooms, variegated and decorative leaves, vines climbing a pergola and lampposts, frangipani, lipstick palms, and turtles swimming in a lily-covered pond.

Singapore

On the second tour, taking a cable car to **Sentosa Island** we saw twin pagodas in the water and, bounded by covered corridors, a beautiful pond containing flowering lilies, water plants and colourful koi. There was also a lake fringed with drooping bamboo, which provided a good foreground to a dragon boat on the opposite shore and a tall pagoda beyond. Other pavilions faced a wooden bridge, moon gate, and rock formations in lily-covered ponds.

Singapore was no longer the shopper's paradise that it once aspired to, but it was still rewarding to take tea or a Singapore Sling, first concocted in 1915, in the elegant colonial ambience of the legendary **Raffles Hotel**, known as the Grand Old Lady of the East. Once more highly valued than gold and considered to have magical powers, jade was amongst infinite commodities from luxury items to tawdry trinkets offered for sale, but nothing except food from hawker stalls was cheap, and bargaining was expected. Worth seeing were the fabulous collection at the **House of Jade** and **Jurong Bird Park** with its cages of exotic multihued parrots, a flamingo pond, and walk-through aviary complete with waterfall and birds of bright red plumage flying free. We also visited the crocodile farm, where a mass of these prehistoric creatures slithered over each other, their jaws agape and wicked-looking yellow eyes unblinking.

High-rise buildings with the latest computer technology sat side by side with old shops selling dried fish, fried noodles, funeral offerings, incense, wooden clogs, paper umbrellas, sharks' fins, live frogs and turtles, birds' nests, and medicinal remedies such as ground pearls, snakes, ginseng roots, and powder scratched from antelope horn to relieve high fever. Old red-roofed houses where ancestors were still worshipped and classical structures including a Muslim mosque stood shoulder to shoulder with contemporary skyscrapers. Due to lack of space, everything went up instead of out, as testified by the innumerable blocks of high-rise housing referred to as vertical suburbs. Harsh edges of concrete were softened by landscaping, an excellent example being the ivy and antignon (Mexican rose or coral vine) cascading from freeway overpasses.

Singapore's early history is shrouded in mystery; the earliest known mention was in the third century when a Chinese account named it Pu-luo-chung (Island at the end of a peninsula), and from that time it has been a crossroads of trade. Pepper, rice, ginger, cinnamon, tortoise shell and sandalwood were amongst the lucrative lure for pirates that abounded on the seas. The next recorded stage in its history was the 14th century when it became part of the mighty Sri Vijayan Empire and was known as Temasek (Sea Town). It acquired the name Singa Pura (Lion City) when a visiting Vijayan prince saw an animal he mistook for a lion. The island has also had its share of invasions.

'Surprising Singapore' as it has been dubbed, clean and green, with the second highest standard of living in Asia after Japan, was founded in 1819 when Sir Stamford Raffles purchased it from the Malay ruler. The end of British domination came with the invasion and occupation by the Japanese during WWII, after which the local populace never fully regained confidence in their erstwhile masters. Following independence in 1965, Singapore's driving force was Prime Minister Lee Kuan Yew, grandson of a Hakka coolie from China, holding a double first degree in law from Cambridge University. As with today, even in the early 1800s Singapore had a strict moral code, and owners of gaming houses were publicly flogged. In the middle of the 19th century as many as 300 of its multi-cultural citizens per year were eaten by tigers! By this time, goods traded included Chinese tea and silk, ebony, ivory, gold dust, coffee, antimony, sage, nutmeg and other spices, pearls, rattan, cloth, opium, beer, whiskey and haberdashery. Also in this period, criminal rackets run by Chinese flourished.

The 1920s and '30s saw racial segregation between Europeans and Asians, the introduction of *tiffin* (tea), and a rather indulgent lifestyle. Literary lions Michener, Conrad, Kipling, Coward and Maugham all frequented the island state at some stage. At the time of writing, the Westin Stamford was the world's tallest hotel, and the population was comprised of 77% Chinese, 14% Malay, 7% Indian and 2% European, with 87% living in government built housing. Reflecting its prosperity, Singapore was said to have more golf courses per capita than any other nation on earth.

In 1981, I made two more trips to Singapore that have not been documented.

Penang

Penang was a typical tropical island: rocky bays with white sand beaches, palm trees and blue water, but one that I always found less than perfect, and on this occasion under sullen skies. Discovered in 1786, it was referred to as Pulau Pinang (Island of the Betel Nut) and had its early beginnings as the first British trading post in the Far East.

At the Casuarina Hotel in **Batu Ferringhi,** we were given rooms facing landscaped grounds and the ocean. We saw a temple with the obligatory dragons wending their serpentine way across the roof, which also featured exquisite carving of birds, flowers and figures. Other attractions included a complex with twin pagodas, a tiered gateway, and curled rooflines with decorative carving. We observed chimpanzees in an enclosure and, in jungle environs outside, a baboon clutching a baby with the wizened face of an old man. We visited the well-known **Wat Chayamangkalaram**, protected by colourful guardians with pointed ears and big toothy grins. Mythical multi-headed serpents also made an appearance. The compound contained ornate white towers with golden spires, reclining figures flanking a doorway, and elaborate sculpted gateways, one with a life-sized white elephant each side; it was very reminiscent of Thailand. In a beautiful jungle setting, we admired a natural waterfall cascading over stepped ledges of rock, the area also inhabited by Indian minor birds with their bright yellow bills, orange-and-yellow butterflies on self-toned blossoms, and red dragonflies. I took pictures of street vendors, a crowd of people around a truck decorated with floral wreaths (possibly a funeral), people on bicycles and, nestled in palm groves and dense foliage, thatched cottages with chickens running free.

PAPUA NEW GUINEA 1980

In 1980, I experienced one of my most memorable journeys: four weeks in **Papua New Guinea**. Until recently, PNG was a land of mystery, where tribes had evolved isolated by mountains; they developed many different languages and each thought that they were the only people on earth. Well into the 20th century, there existed a 'cargo cult' amongst some tribesmen who believed that aeroplanes brought gifts from the gods, and they built miniature runways as welcoming shrines. Before independence was attained in 1975, some people had never seen a wheel, but today modern technology exists alongside the primitive as mighty machines scoop ore from one of the world's largest open pit copper mines at Ok Tedi and a woman uses a digging stick to tend her *kaukau* (sweet potato).

Port Moresby

It was a challenging venture because of primitive conditions, lack of transport, and the extremely high cost; as a matter of fact, for the first time ever, I resorted to accepting invitations from strangers (expatriates) to stay in their homes. I found that organisation generally bordered on chaotic, and even after 30 years of self-rule the country still relied on the expertise of Australians to head major corporations. One example of the hospitality extended to me occurred in the **Port Moresby** offices of Air Niugini when, bypassing the disorganised crowd milling around the service desk, I wandered down passages in search of a representative. Entering a partially open door, I found the Australian manager, who invited me to sit, attended to my request, and because of a sudden tropical deluge insisted on driving me back to my accommodation! Although strong, the *kina*, named from the traditional shell currency, was still boosted by the Australian dollar, and I was regaled with many horror stories relating to exorbitant prices. In fact, tourism, only averaging 3,000 per year at that time, was actively discouraged as a result of too many people getting into trouble financially and because of bandits holding up vehicles on certain roads. Even before leaving Moresby, I met up with backpackers who had been incarcerated because they ran out of funds, their alarming tales causing me to panic and almost reducing me to tears – I was about ready to return on the next plane home!

I had been provided with one contact, whom I met in Port Moresby, and his first reaction was 'Why did you want to come here?'! In his opinion the country had nothing to offer, but I found it totally fascinating. It included, to this day, both the most exciting and disappointing times of my life, the first being my involvement in tribal warfare and the second, which I still cry about, the irreplaceable loss of all my film taken at an authentic bride dressing ceremony that I came across deep in the Highlands. A genuine ritual that it was a privilege to observe, the procedure included a bride auction conducted by an elder, possibly the father, who banged a long staff on the ground beside a row of blackened pigs' heads, presumably part of the dowry. Obviously, I could not understand a word, but it was an animated and rowdy exchange. Villagers, their faces gaily painted with red and yellow pigment, surrounded me, and others were cooking in pits dug in the earth, the food covered with hot coals and banana leaves. The bride herself was ensconced in a natural bower of greenery, where she was attended by female relatives and friends. It was a truly absorbing and unexpected encounter. I also lost film of a village where houses on stilts were built almost entirely over the water, with large verandahs in front serving to hold pigs, chickens and dogs in times of flood. Everyone here poled a dugout canoe, and I saw wee tots from a very young age (one wearing nothing but a colourful woollen beanie!) piloting their own craft. Understandably, this village was infested with mosquitoes, and I think that most of the population suffered from malaria.

However, my first pictures show Sydney, the Harbour Bridge and Opera House as I flew overhead en route to Port Moresby. I took film of thick cumulus clouds below the aircraft, a sight that never fails to impress.

Madang

Exotic tropical blooms were my only pictures in Moresby, a sprawling uninteresting city, and continuing by air, I flew low over staggering mountains and winding rivers to the primitive airport at **Madang**, where a horde of colourful tribal folk, the ladies carrying babes and with *bilums* (string bags) slung from their heads, lined a wire fence in front of the single-storey tin-roofed terminal building. During the Second World War, these gentle people were christened 'Fuzzy Wuzzy Angels' for their assistance to allied troops, and even the air hostess, a floral pattern emblazoned on the front of her bright yellow uniform and wearing sandals, had an enormous mop of tight black curls. So thick is the hair that it was not uncommon to see a pen, comb or other items carried therein.

I have pictures of a large black hornbill with a reddish-brown head, white tail, and outlandish white beak, as it hopped in comical fashion across lawn under an exotic flowering tree. Palm trees bordered the edge of a lovely lagoon, where a few people were enjoying the water, and a native, poised on rocks, fished with a long spear. Small houses were sheltered beneath palms, colourful leaves made lovely displays, the vibrant red ginger bloomed profusely, epiphytes and elkhorns flourished on the branches and trunks of trees, and I saw scarlet cock's comb. Papua New Guinea was home to the unique tree kangaroo, which I only managed to see caged, as were colourful parrots. However, in the vicinity of the 30m-tall white **Coastwatchers Memorial Light** – assuming the form of a candle and dedicated to those men who, during the war, stayed behind the lines to report on Japanese troop and shipping movements – numerous bats hung upside down in trees. Long-legged birds waded across the pads of pink lilies covering the surface of a pool, and menfolk fished from canoes whilst smiling women sat on the grass making *bilums,* the handles hooked around their toes. Surrounded by goods including many large melons, people were also seated on the ground in the interesting open-air marketplace. Another colourful venue, here I observed a lady with a baby cradled in the *bilum* strung across her forehead and others laden with purchases of fruits and vegetables carried in the same manner.

Towards evening, with subdued light shining on reflections in still water, I watched bats flying and took film of one with the cutest face peering at me from its upside down position in a wire enclosure. I stayed at the comfortable Smugglers Inn, which presented a pretty picture with lights glowing from where it stood in forest at the water's edge.

Angoram

I went to **Angoram** by minibus, along a dirt track lined with lush growth, palm trees and flame flowers, and where I encountered thatch-roofed split-bamboo houses sitting on stilts, remains of an old rusted WWII army tank, and the wreck of an aircraft from the same theatre of war, lodged where it had come down and almost covered by the encroaching jungle. Coming to a village market, people sat on grass under and around a makeshift shelter, and a 'dunny' at the end of a plank walkway was perched on piles over the water. At another location people were fishing, and although hot it was all very scenic and serene.

Sepik

Reaching a calm section of the mighty 1,123km (698mi) **Sepik River**, I took a cruise in a small boat launched from the Melanesian Explorer, on which I had embarked for a few days. Appearing like ghosts amongst reeds at the edge of dense jungle, slender white tree trunks were beautifully mirrored on the still surface, along with palms, breadfruit trees, red flowers, a white heron, tall grasses, creeper-entangled trunks and branches, trailing vines, and other tropical vegetation. It was one of those breathtaking river rides that never pall, always giving me great pleasure. A couple of small thatched huts and a few figures stood in a clearing under palm trees on a sandy bank, and we encountered different species of birdlife. People paddled their fragile-looking but surprisingly sturdy craft along the river, and in isolated places men were industriously chopping large logs or engaged in various other activities. Moored canoes were the only indication of habitation where dwellings were secluded in forest. Stopping in a village, I saw my first **Haus Tambaran** (**Spirit** or **Ceremonial House**), constructed of elaborate thatch and with a wonderful mask on the gable. Large naked male and female figures adorned carved totem poles erected in front.

Further on, we came to the **Kambaramba** water community described earlier, and the entire village turned out to line the bank and farewell us on departure. In another settlement, houses were roofed but without walls, and crude benches bordered one hard-packed earthen floor, in the centre of which a blackened pot was suspended over an open fire; a dog lay in front and the near-naked inhabitants stood nearby. Chickens and pigs wandered a will (the pigs even foraging near the cooking fire!), and in an amusing incident I saw a sow rear up to steal something from a bench, much to the consternation of the housewife, who chased it. Another figure was occupied chopping melon onto the ground as fodder for the animals. It was in just such a primitive village that I received a shock when I observed an old lady playing cat's cradle with a piece of string! I was astounded to think that this could have evolved in a race that had little or no contact with the outside world and were literally a prehistoric people living in the 20th century. Children were the same all over the planet, and those here blew bubbles with bamboo pipes or rolled wheels (cut from tin cans) nailed to sticks.

Passing a few laden canoes and a ferry boat, we reached a more substantial village featuring elaborately patterned thatched walls and decoration above open doorways, some with thatched canopies. People congregated beneath raised flooring that was accessed by ladders made from stout branches, and compounds were enhanced with palm trees, banana plants, colourful crotons, and birds. A bare-chested man held an exotic feathered friend in his hands.

The Sepik area was renowned for its carving, which was much sought after overseas and commanded huge prices; faces even featured on posts supporting flooring. The incredible masks were often painted or decorated with cowrie shells, and feathers or fibre were utilised for hair. Extraordinary costumes incorporating complete head masks were woven from a stiff material like that used for baskets. I watched a man creating the spade-shaped paddles, and other objects were embossed with figures. I saw a decorative model of a pig and a crocodile (*puk puk*) head complete with teeth – which looked genuine. Pigs were a sign of wealth, the more he owned being an indication of a man's worth. I was appalled when informed that they were considered more valuable than wives, who were obliged to suckle them! Ornaments were inserted into holes in the ear lobes of small children, and adults even carried cigarettes this way. Once again, villagers lined up on the bank to say goodbye, the advent of a visitor, particularly a foreign stranger, being a big event.

The river was a busy lifeline, and we passed canoes filled with naked black bodies, one vessel almost submerged and another with a smouldering substance in the stern. I believe that fire was often carried because in some places wood was unavailable. People were working with *sak-sak* (sago) on the banks, and we came across a rickety bridge, ducks, people washing, and many more dwellings, some featuring geometric designs on the cane or palm-matting walls, and many with the age-old display of laundry on lines. Above the doorway of a second *haus tambaran* (in different tones of thatch), a distinctive canopy protected a mask with a bone through the nose. In an activity often encountered, a lady was assiduously engaged in the involved process of producing the starchy product from the sago palm: scooping the pulp into a

wall illustrations

chute beside the river, dowsing it with water from a large ladle, and pressing to drain off the resultant liquid. This was collected and the residue from the palm discarded into the river where, on this occasion, a black and white duck was swimming, her brood of ducklings trailing behind.

A particularly photogenic scene consisted of a house lodged in a jungle clearing accessed by a flimsy bamboo bridge across a grass-edged lagoon, its surface covered with deep pink water lilies. Another spirit house, with extremely long spires at each end of the roof, stood in a grassed expanse surrounded by palm trees, beautiful red foliage and hibiscus. At yet another such venue, a mother suckled her infant unabashed whilst villagers executed a dance. Their faces painted white and etched with patterns, they were clothed in swaying grass skirts, elaborate feathered headdresses, garlands of flowers, and cowrie shell necklaces. One man clapped sticks together for rhythm, and they waved leaves or long palm fronds. In a concession to the missionaries, a couple of the women wore brassieres! It was a totally engrossing performance. I watched a man working underneath his house, every post of which bore a different design.

Moving on, we paused at several communities. The roof of one house had a carved bird, its wings spread, perched on the spire, and I filmed a man with raised scars, purposely inflicted, on his torso and arms. A sign of prestige, some were made to represent the marks of crocodile teeth or the ridges on its skin, and young men attaining manhood still underwent this skin cutting ceremony. Standing atop the ladder to his doorway, I have pictures of a white-haired elder wearing a colourful lap-lap and a large pendant depicting the face of a creature made with cowries. Much of my film is too dark to distinguish detail, but I have excellent footage of an eagle flying overhead, the magnificent jungle growth, and superb reflections. A thatched structure without walls displayed a wealth of absolutely stunning painted designs on the ceiling, and a wooden effigy stood on a beam below. One house had a decorated door, and another a multihued gable. Long red pods and enormous strange fruits hung from branches, and I witnessed the playing of the highly elaborate *garamut*, a drum formed from a hollowed tree trunk, two of which were fashioned to represent crocodiles.

ceiling art

On the move again, I saw a grassed airstrip, and we were passed by the out-of-place speedboat from our vessel disturbing the environment with its noise. Heading down narrow rush-enclosed waterways, we came to a tiny village displaying human skulls with blackened eye sockets and few remaining teeth – a reminder of ancestors or not long past cannibalistic rituals? At the death of a close relative, the bereaved person will cut off a finger above the second joint, which is then strung and worn around the neck. Wild orchids hung in clusters, but glorious bright blue butterflies proved illusive to capture on film. The biggest butterflies that I had ever seen were plentiful, including a vibrant green variety as big as a small bird. Papua New Guinea was home to the world's largest butterfly, Queen Alexandra's Birdwing, now sadly endangered. I photographed an interesting couple, the wife wearing only a grass skirt, her husband sporting flowers in his hair and bones or tusks through his nose. On the final night aboard, we were entertained by native dancers, their faces painted and attired only in breach clouts, feathers, and shell ornamentation.

Amboin

From Angoram, I flew in a small plane to **Amboin**, over nothing but jungle and brown ribbons of winding waterways with white clouds like polka dots above. As we progressed, the terrain changed to snaking rivers reflecting the colour of densely forested emerald mountains. Because it was only the departure point for onward travel, I have few pictures here: a butterfly with black, red and blue wings alighting on a bright yellow daisy and, in a green setting with large trees and hibiscus on rolling lawns, a native wearing armbands, a necklace, red flowers in his hair, a loin cloth tucked into a wide bark belt, and a bundle of grass on his backside. This apparition demonstrated the deportment and demeanour of someone strolling in an English garden!

Karawari

Boarding another light plane, I flew to the **Karawari River**, a large tributary of the Sepik. I particularly remember this trip because I was the sole passenger in a single engine cargo-carrying Cessna, and the weight was so critical that it was even necessary to weigh me! I vividly recall the pilot, whose name was Lenny, because it was the only time that I had ever seen sunglasses with yellow lenses. Flying a single engine plane above the mountains of PNG is dangerous business and a lot of pilots were Australian. Sensing my nervousness (especially when the stall light kept illuminating!), Lenny insisted that I take the controls and fly the aircraft. From then on, I had an absolute ball, trying to maintain the little image of a plane on the control panel at an even keel and banking the aircraft left and right; it certainly took my mind off my paranoia! I even have film of myself (taken by Lenny) to prove it. He promised that when he returned to pick me up he would take a different route and show me an outstanding gorge.

We approached low over Karawari Lodge (I had relinquished control by then!), situated on a green grassed plateau and surrounded by dense tropical growth. Listed in the book of the best hotels in the world, it was only accessible by charter aircraft or riverboat and was the sole habitation in what was previously a lonely isolated patrol outpost. I had the privilege of being the solitary guest, and I must say that my entire experience in this extreme district was superb. The dining room was located in a reproduced *haus hambaran* (with appropriate artworks), and my private plaited-grass reed-thatched cabin – where a barefoot native in pristine white padded silently on the wooden floor to bring me pre-breakfast tea and hot croissants as I lay in bed under a mosquito net – was ensconced in jungle on a high ridge overlooking the river and valley, where smoke from cooking fires wafted lazily and mingled with floating early morning mist. Later in the day, like a curtain rising on a captivating scene, this shredded and dissolved. The hotel even had a kidney-shaped swimming pool with bamboo decking, where orange, black and white butterflies flitted around orange and yellow lantana, and big colourful dragonflies settled on plants in the exotic garden surrounds.

Here, I undertook several more boat rides, with gauze-like cloud initially hanging like fog low over the water. Clumps of gorgeous red blooms drooped amid insignificant leaves, and I gazed overboard into reflections so perfect that I was overcome by an eerie sensation of floating upside down amongst the clouds. A lone bird skittering across the surface was the only thing to break the illusion. We passed laden canoes ferrying people and goods, one with a small broadly beaming boy and a dog in the bow. At the riverside, a woman with two naked children was squatting near a cooking fire to prepare food; on our return she was washing in the water. Deviating down narrow reed-lined canals, we encountered prolific birdlife. White heron, disturbed by our approach, took off from long grass at the water's edge, a cormorant, wings spread, perched on the topmost branch of a tree, and large grey waterbirds stood on a sandbank. Its long neck craned, one heron remained motionless, presenting a perfect mirror image on the unruffled surface, and at this point mountains were introduced to the panoramas. An isolated dwelling with only a naked child appearing to be in attendance had a lovely decorated gable. An old lady in a floral skirt held strings of fish, another filleted a catch, and some washed utensils in the water. With just a few craft propelled by paddles and no powerboats, the aura was one of peace and tranquillity, and the milieu was exceptionally beautiful.

A helicopter landed at Karawari, the tremendous downdraft from the rotor flattening surrounding foliage, and I was taken on a brief ride above the lodge and environs. Returning, I photographed a cuscus, a cute cuddly looking animal with big round eyes sitting in the fork of a tree. Numbers of large blue dragonflies with transparent wings, and others displaying fantastic iridescent colours of red, purple, blue or bronze alighted on the grass. Brightly hued monarch butterflies landed on leaves or blended with lantana blossoms.

Embarking on another cruise, I observed the beautiful white spider orchid and large orange bracts probably related to the ginger flower. His face decorated with white ochre, a man was hewing at the trunk of a huge sago palm with a long-bladed adze. Wearing only a grass skirt, a lady transferred the results of his labours into a woven basket, which was then taken to a similarly attired woman using a long-handled ladle to work with the pulp as described earlier. The sago was placed into a large container, boiling water poured onto it from a big iron cauldron sitting over an open fire, and the liquid stirred by another worker. Prepared vegetable (jungle greens) lying on a woven mat nearby was later added to the bubbling boiler. Dogs and villagers with painted faces – one bare-breasted female, her chest and arms also adorned – congregated around, many with lips and teeth stained red from chewing betel nut, and it was here that I witnessed the old woman playing cat's cradle. Seated on a log at the river's edge, a man with an elaborately decorated face was resplendent in an apron of foliage, a bunch of *asgras* ('arse grass', the name by which it is generally known), a bushy feather headdress, armbands created from coloured leaves, and a large shell pendant. A woman with a polka-dotted face sat cross-legged in front of another fire and, using the base of a small wooden bowl, pressed sago into a pancake. This she did on a metal platter like a shallow wok balanced on branches over the flames. Meanwhile, the container of sago, now a gooey coagulated mass, was being continuously stirred over smoking coals with a wooden spoon. Sprays of fabulous wild pink orchids were an incongruous sight, and wispy veils of vapour hung in the valley.

Back on the river, the different greens of the jungle were broken here and there by trailing red blooms, and many birds accompanied us downstream. We passed small communities sequestered in their luxuriant surroundings, and I even saw one house ensconced high up in treetops. Ashore, locals adroitly crossed logs spanning creeks, but they presented an intimidating challenge to me. Reaching another village, a man with a tusk through his nose, his daubed face giving a semblance of white glasses and wearing bead necklaces and long dangling earrings, was patting a white pig. Others, with heavily painted chests and features, necklaces, swinging grass skirts, tall feathered headdresses and leafy adornment, performed a circular dance to the beat of a *garamut*. A couple had naked children on their shoulders, and even the pig seemed keen to join in! The man playing the *garamut* chanted and stamped his feet, the jingle of tinkling bells around his calves beating time. A common piece of male apparel was the *koteka* (penis gourd), worn on the appropriate member and making it appear permanently erect – and large! The whole PNG experience was like living a page of history.

The silent brooding river was now churned a muddy brown, and long lianas hung over the water. I visited a village with roofs shaped like prows and boys shinning like monkeys up tall narrow palms for coconuts. We passed a short green airfield with a motionless drooping windsock and a light plane parked at one end. In a country that because of the harsh conditions had very little road infrastructure, many people owned a small plane as we would a car. Treacherous landing strips were an adventure in themselves: some on perilous mountain slopes and one that, due to an overnight deluge, became so waterlogged and boggy that we had to walk the entire length to assess its condition before taking off. Even taking this precaution, we were afterwards informed that bystanders held their breath as we barely cleared the treetops. On another occasion, a commercial flight took off with passengers seated on luggage in the aisle, and once, with a complement of crew as passengers on board, we flew with wingtips almost touching mountain sides, so perilously close that concern was expressed by the veterans of PNG aviation who declared 'What do these cowboys think they are doing?'. They appeared to be showing-off for the benefit of their colleagues.

At yet another settlement in its verdant emerald cocoon, natives in huge elaborate masks, one with a long proboscis-like projection, executed dances for me. A youth wore a red double hibiscus flower in his dark hair, and a toddler rolled a tin lid attached to the end of a pole. Altogether, I spent some days and covered the Sepik area quite extensively. On my final night at Karawari, Bob Bates, an Australian from Queensland and owner of Trans Niugini Tours, arrived to transfer me back to civilisation. When I expressed regret that Lenny did not turn up, he also offered to show me interesting highlights but first arranged, via pedal radio, the only medium of communication in this remote area, a lift (on a coffee truck!) to Wewak, which I had thought that I would have to miss due to lack of public transport.

Leaving Karawari, we flew low over a wrecked WWII aircraft in the jungle and Bob asked me if I had ever experienced weightlessness. Replying in the negative and hastening to be assured (emphatically!) that it was safe, he then proceeded to demonstrate by climbing, almost vertically, to a considerable height and then dropping rapidly; it was an exhilarating mind-blowing sensation. At the time, he was carrying one other passenger in the form of a native whom he was ferrying to work on a bulldozer at another isolated airstrip and whom he had not warned of his intention. When I gleefully requested to do it again, he just said 'Look in the back', and I immediately repented; the black-skinned fellow had turned positively green, and his eyes, showing enormous whites, were literally bulging out of his head!

I was deposited at a place that I do not recall but where vegetables were distributed over a grassy tract in a large local market crowded with men and colourful women with babies and *bilums*. Banana leaf was used for wrapping purchases. Buildings in this area had steeply pitched thatched roofs that extended right to the ground like alpine A-frame cottages, one elaborately decorated with intricate painted patterns. It was here that I joined my coffee truck for the ride in the cab to Wewak, at one stage finishing up partially overturned in a ditch! With no such luxury and the RAC (Royal Automobile Club), we just had to wait for a similar vehicle to pull us out, following which we forded a river, but there was no further mishap.

Wewak

In **Wewak** I was once again at the other end of the spectrum, the ocean, where a tall wooden figure like a totem stood on the beach. At **Cape Wom Memorial Park**, where the unconditional surrender of the Japanese Imperial Forces was signed, stood a curious monument covered with numerous relics from the war, such as helmets, rusted rifles and bayonets. According to my informant, this marked the beginning of the notorious **Kakoda Track**. I have my doubts but ventured a short distance along the trail, and even that was enough to convey a little of the horror that must have been the lot experienced by those unfortunates who lived and fought in the gruelling conditions of inexorable cloying heat, humidity, mud and mosquitoes along its appalling route. In contrast, there were some beautiful gardens and reflective ponds, near one of which a person washed whilst, in another, a man fished with a net. Bob picked me up with the plane, and after one brief stop, we travelled once more above lofty emerald mountains and big rivers.

Mount Hagan

And so we come to the most exciting episode and the crowning star in my travel documentary. I had been dropped off at the remote and desolate airfield of **Wapanemanda** (the only other facility being a couple of petrol bowsers) to catch a local minibus to Mount Hagan, situated at 1,690m in the **Central Highlands**, where most of the valleys were settled 10,000 years ago. Bob put me in the care of a native, admonishing him that *missi* was nervous and to *draivim isi*. Pidgin is a fascinating dialect and the common denominator (it is even used in their House of Assembly) in a land where there are in excess of 700 individual languages in the Sepik River area alone. They evolved because of tribes existing in complete isolation due to the sheer logistics of getting from one mountain settlement to another, and they make up 45% of the world's total. Pidgin was fairly simple to pick up, and expressions like *Yu wantok* (one talk, friend) *bilong mi* need no explanation. It can be quite comical; for instance, conversation is *toktok*.

From the outset, it was a captivating encounter because I boarded the bus as the only European amongst a crowd of indigenous people, mostly men wearing nothing but wet *asgras* and a tiny loin cloth in front. At one stage, the vehicle not being able to make it up a hill, everyone trooped out to push as it slipped and slid in muddy conditions to the crest. As we proceeded, I began to notice more and more men at the side of the road wearing *asgras*, their hair adorned with bird of paradise feathers and sunflowers. Some wore a pig-tooth necklace and/or a porcupine quill piercing their nose, and all carried spears (a few even steel tipped), bows and arrows, and one concession to the 20th century, a metal-bladed tomahawk. Arrows were fashioned from black palm and traditionally tipped with bone from the forearm of a male ancestor so that his spirit could guide the weapon to the enemy. Daggers were carved from the leg bone of a cassowary. I expressed interest rather than concern, until a man threw a stone at the bus, which was ultimately halted and we were all obliged to disembark. Tribal fighting was imminent and because passengers on the bus were members of both warring factions it was dangerous to continue. I was fortunate to strike up a conversation with the only person who spoke English, a young dark man working for the law courts in Goroka, and he explained the procedure to me as we sat together, on a rock, for the greater part of the day. At the commencement, three warriors bearing huge sheets of corrugated iron, used as shields and painted with geometric patterns, formed a row behind which the rest of the 'army' trotted up the road. Their adversaries were ensconced in hills to one side, and a battle ensued with arrows raining down on each party of protagonists. At one stage, a warrior with a spear through his leg was brought back to where I was seated, but being preoccupied they paid little heed to my presence. This particular conflict over land (others can involve women or pigs) had been waged for some years, and apparently it was all treated as a game, with defined rules of engagement; nevertheless, it could become quite serious, with loss of life and property. Eventually, around 5pm, the warfare was broken up by police dropping tear gas from helicopters, the crowd dispersed, and we continued on our way. To my sorrow, the film is not very clear, although I do have good footage of people running in panic at the arrival of many police armed with guns at the end. The wonder of it all was that this was no gimmick for tourists but absolutely authentic!

I was staying at Kimininga Hostel in **Mount Hagen**, run by a couple from Queensland, and next morning met up with correspondent Sean Dorney (who reported from the area for the ABC) and a cameraman who were in the Highlands to make a documentary on an alfalfa project. The previous day, having encountered the hostile losers from the conflict, they had faced aggression and, threatened with violence, had been forced to flee for their lives. Green with envy at my tale, they decided to hire a car and try to locate more activity. Requesting to join them, we set off with a local councillor to search for more antagonists, many of whom were public officials who discarded their Western dress to participate! We did not come across any fighting, but we did find a group heading for their *sing-sing* ground to prepare for the day's battle. This also turned out to be an amazing experience. We had to negotiate paths ankle deep in mud, and as for practically my whole time in PNG, I was afraid of slipping and falling with the camera. Then a remarkable event transpired. As I stepped gingerly through the mire, an unusually tall warrior attired in *asgras*, flowers and feathers, and armed with a handful of spears, came up behind me and, silently taking one of mine with his free hand, led me to the venue. This in itself was a privilege because women were generally banned from the *sing-sing* ground. I would have given anything to procure a photograph, and the cameraman was sorely tempted but did not want a European in his film.

Utterly enthralled, I watched the ensuing preparations during which the clan members were harangued by their chieftain, who was wearing an exceptional headdress of bird of paradise plumes – and silver tinsel! He told them (according to our interpreter) that having killed four men the day before they had achieved a victory, and he urged them on to even greater heights. Then a mock battle was enacted, which became progressively more enthusiastic, at one stage a warrior running towards us and lunging with his spear. I lowered the camera in alarm, but my companion kept filming and probably obtained some remarkable footage. Some carried decorated shields, and these fearsome-looking fellows regarded the camera with wariness and suspicion but eventually broke into beaming smiles that transformed their whole demeanour. Shortly after this, because they seemed to be getting a little too exuberant, we quietly departed, arriving back at the vehicle only to find that anything of value had been removed! Again, I saw police helicopters overhead, and on leaving we passed evidence of burnt out houses and destroyed trees. The two days had been the epitome of excitement and the ultimate adventure.

My biggest disappointment in Mount Hagan was not timing my visit to coincide with the big biannual *sing-sing* celebrations, although I did find colourful people and appreciated the cooler climate and magnificent scenery of the Highlands, where I discovered delicate but lovely waterfalls feeding an impressive river. The elegant bird of paradise, hornbills, beautifully coloured parrots, a majestic cassowary, and tree kangaroos were exhibited in a mini zoo, and fabulous butterflies in brilliant hues of blue, yellow, green and orange alighted on colourful leaves and flowers. If threatened, the tree kangaroo was capable of leaping 12 to 18m (40 to 60ft) from the forest canopy to the ground. I corresponded with the wife of the manager at Kimininga Hostel for some time after my return home, and on one occasion she related a most amusing story: it appears that they hosted a convention for government ministers, and when they departed so did half the blankets!

Continuing my journey, I photographed more wonderful scenery, clusters of red berries on coffee plants – and people, together with pigs, scavenging in a rubbish dump! At yet another village market, I saw vendors seated with coconuts, a few corn cobs and hands of bananas, one customer, naked except for a long striped loincloth, red necklace and knitted woollen beanie, mingling with more conventionally garbed men – a commonplace sight. I came across housing with very decorative rooflines, on one of which the ornamentation was sprouting leaves! A road sign supported by rocks read *Draivim isi isi ol wokman wok istap.* Another stated *Wok long rot ol kar mus stop sapos yu lukim red pela mak* (here a red stop sign was inserted). Literally translating as: Work along road all car must stop suppose you look red fellow make (stop sign), more precisely it meant: Work along the road all cars must stop when you see the red sign. Tall grasses provided an interesting foreground to mountains and rivers in ravines, and I filmed a native with a pale-toned spotted cuscus atop his head. With coiled tail, it clung to the dense mop of black curls as it turned in a circle. Many people plodded along the road, one shepherding a big black pig tethered by a rope, and others with bundles on their heads.

A fascinating fact revealed in the highlands was that of agricultural systems dating back 10,000 years, whilst people in Britain and northern Europe were still foraging and hunting. This predated cultivation of grain in the Middle East's 'fertile crescent', traditionally regarded as the birthplace of agriculture.

Asaro Valley

And so I came to the beautiful **Asaro Valley**, near Goroka, with a waterfall, lush vegetation that even included pink wildflowers, and a village with round thatched dwellings. This was home to the famed **Mud Men**, representing ancestral spirits who used to appear from the depths of the jungle to assist hard-pressed combatants in battle. A more feasible explanation states that in some distant past, tribesmen driven into the river by their enemies had emerged covered in mud, which frightened their attackers into retreat, and so the ritual was perpetuated. Pigs wandered around pits dug in the ground and lined with leaves in preparation for cooking. Called a *mumu*, food was eventually placed on top of a bed of hot coals or fire-heated rocks within, covered with leaves, and dirt shovelled on top. Finally, water was poured into the centre of the mound, causing steam to issue from around the edges.

Ghostly figures in grotesque masks, their bodies covered with white clay, wearing loin cloths of leaves and waving twigs, materialised like apparitions from behind houses. They performed a less than animated dance, after which they demonstrated the making of fire by rapidly pulling twine back and forth beneath two sticks held onto a piece of bark by the feet. When a spark was produced, the man picked up the bark and gently blew on it to create a lot of smoke, and presumably a small flame. They gave a display of archery ability – but most missed the target! Another created 'music' with a strange reed instrument.

Goroka

In **Goroka**, I was fascinated to see natives wearing grass skirts, necklaces and elaborate headdresses, carrying weapons, and sitting on the kerb with traffic moving to and fro!

Trobriand Islands

Yet another flight took me low over precipitous ridges, jungle, a maze of criss-crossing waterways and falls to the coral cays ringed by white sand and turquoise water that made up the tiny islands of the **Trobriand** group in **Milne Bay**. If possible, this little-visited part of PNG appeared even more primitive. **Kiriwina** had the only landing strip, with rudimentary facilities, and I was greeted by many semi-naked men and women carrying banana leaves or matting, which they used to shelter from the sun – a few actually had umbrellas. The voluptuous young girls wore short grass skirts, beads, and hibiscus in their hair, and some carried machetes. The only other native that I saw was a big black and yellow striped spider busily spinning its web.

At that time there was only one hotel, a rustic building with beach sand floors run by a European. It was not a little disconcerting to be served breakfast by amply endowed bare-breasted women, their busts at eyelevel when seated! Although flat, the atolls were still lush, with palm-fringed white sand enveloping blue lagoons, the water gently caressing the shore. People walked rutted tracks using the matting for protection from sun and rain. Simple huts, a shaded porch in front, stood on short stilts, but in contrast the tall narrow granaries were highly decorated. Men fished from boats or poled a type of outrigger canoe, and massive green butterflies made a stunning show amongst red hibiscus flowers. As everywhere, children were curious, and I was surrounded by naked and near-naked black bodies in a village where people waded through floodwater to reach their homes, which were set in a jungle clearing and circled this 'lagoon'. A most amazing fact of these islands was that crayfish crawled along the pathways and were there for the picking!

I spent an interesting afternoon taking tea with a lady anthropologist who was living in a sand floor hut on the beach in order to carry out research on the people. Canoes were drawn up onshore, and I was a magnet for the children. Carrying an infant on her hip, one attractive young girl was happy to pose for a picture, and a young boy without a stitch of clothing was hacking at a coconut with a long-bladed implement. Another figure sat on her stoop grating the flesh of this same fruit (actually a drupe) into a container. Laughing children blew bubbles with a bamboo pipe, and I filmed a mother and baby sitting in the doorway of their dwelling, on the porch of which was a big woven basket. Beautiful tropical flowers were abundant, and the inevitable washing was strung on lines – even though the people wore few clothes! Girls seemed to favour very full grass skirts, some incorporating different colours, and the men, shirts and/or colourful sarongs and the occasional T-shirt. I watched men fishing with spears and saw banana leaves spread flat on the ground, weighted with poles, and left to dry in preparation for thatching. A similar method was employed to dry shredded leaves for making the grass skirts. A particularly striking young woman with flowers in her hair and floral armbands, sat with a group atop a pile of material with which they had been working. I photographed a couple with elaborate floral headdresses and another with armbands of flowers, all three naked except for the grass skirt or breach clout. Surprisingly, there was no litter; I guess everything had a use. It rained a lot in this lush land and was still falling heavily under leaden skies as I made my way to the airport 'terminal' again.

For more than one hundred years anthropologists have studied the Trobriand Islands, being described by one early scholar as the Islands of Love.

Lae

I flew to **Lae**, where I photographed a tiny tot in a coloured grass skirt, the distressing sight of dead turtles (on their backs) and blackened wallabies (cooked and with entrails exposed!) on market stalls, the large and well-maintained war cemetery, and a magnificent waterfall plunging to a green pool at the bottom of a stony precipice covered with verdant growth. Axe heads found in the region have been dated at 40,000 years old. Interesting mountains in the area were crowned with perpendicular creviced bluffs. It was from Lae, in 1937, that aviator Amelia Earhart took off and flew into oblivion.

And so I said farewell to the most stimulating trip of a lifetime, one of my enormous regrets being that I was unable to undertake a journey deep into the Sepik area, where a white woman had never ventured or been seen by the local populace. It was proposed that I accompany an American travel writer on a private three or four day trek conducted by a man who had married a native woman and written books on the region, but the author contracted malaria and our guide refused to take me on my own, citing danger as the reason. In retrospect, it was a good decision because I do not think I would have handled the unremitting heat, tenacious jungle, and primitive conditions well. At one stage on the Sepik, I saw mosquitoes so thick that they literally resembled a dense black cloud.

I was disappointed not to have seen Rabaul because in 1994 this once beautiful city was destroyed by a violent volcanic eruption that left a wasteland buried in black ash, with broken structures and a tangled mass of ruins poking out of the mud like a scene of apocalyptic devastation.

Papua New Guinea was an ambitious venture, and looking back I marvel at achieving so much.

Sydney

A night in **Sydney** on the way home revealed an inner city waterfall, the **Cathedral**, the **War Memorial** in **Hyde Park**, the **Sky Tower**, beautiful formal flowerbeds in the **Botanical Gardens**, **Captain Cook's Cottage**, the historic **Rocks** area, the **Opera House** and **Harbour Bridge**, a clock tower with a contemporary sculpture in the foreground, old **Fort Denison** in the harbour, an arrangement of huge balls like silver bubbles in a forecourt, a fountain with figures (including Neptune) below the central image, and a second classical fountain, with combatants, a woman with a deer (Diana the Huntress?), and a pigeon (live) perched on the outstretched hand of a naked male on a pedestal in the middle.

A brief lesson in Pidgin:

Good Morning	Gud Moning
What is your name?	Kolim nem bilong yu?
Where are you from?	Yu bilong wanem ples?
I would like some coffee	Mi laikim sampela kofi
I would like to buy a newspaper	Mi laik baim niuspepa
How much does that cost?	Em i kostim hamas?

SOUTH AFRICA 1981

My first trip to the African continent was spent with my husband, at which time we hired a car for six weeks. Initial photographs record jacaranda trees in full bloom and the **Telecommunication Tower** in **Johannesburg**, situated on a plateau at 1,753m, followed by lovely landscaped gardens and the imposing granite **Voortrekker Memorial** in **Pretoria**, the latter surrounded by a wall holding full-sized reliefs of 64 wagons pulled into a *laager* (circle) as they were in the Battle of Blood River. Iron railings around the monument represented the *assegais* (spears) and shields of the **Zulu** warriors. Large embossed animals and delicate sculpted latticework enhanced the façade, and 216 steps led to the entrance, inside which the four walls were decorated with an Italian marble frieze depicting the history of the 1838 trek.

I took pictures of the large and beautiful protea flower and an equestrian statue at the edge of a reflective pool containing water lilies. Behind this, a fountain occupied the forecourt of a building with a central clock tower and columned portico. A fountain also stood in the courtyard of a mansion with bay windows, turrets and cupolas, decorative iron roof capping, fancy-shaped free-standing gables, and wide verandahs. Other statues stood in streets with impressive colonial and contemporary structures that included an orchestral shell. The wet bodies of a herd of metallic deer gleamed in the sunlight as they 'leapt' over arcs of water. I took film of the city from the glorious colourful terraced gardens of the semicircular **Union Buildings**, with towers crowning symmetrical blocks at each end. Wedding parties had assembled on the lawns for photographs, the rich colours of the attendants' outfits almost seeming to glow against their dark skin.

We attended an energetic performance of native dancing in an open-air auditorium at the **Gold Mine Museum**, where magnificent black bodies glistened in the sun, and fringed adornment swayed on kicking legs and stamping feet. Other dances were accomplished wielding decorated poles or flexible rods, and yet more by dancers who introduced a beaded headband to their costume. Forming a large circle, a few leapt and gyrated in the centre. The next group performed a frenetic dance with sun glinting off flashing swords, and a troupe of fearsome-looking Zulus, dressed in leopard skins and holding spears and animal hide shields, entered the arena preceded by drummers. A dancer with tall colourful feathers in his armbands (giving the impression of wings) gave a solo exhibition before being joined by a large company in another exuberant display, which included mock combats. The performers were all very black and looked marvellous in their various costumes. Executed to ferocious drumming, the show concluded with rapid gymnastics resembling the actions of a contortionist. Born as a mining camp in 1886, Johannesburg has produced one third of the gold mined worldwide since the Middle Ages.

We drove to an **Ndebele** *kraal*, where we found flat-roofed adobe houses and thatched *rondavels* ensconced behind high walls. Decorated with extremely colourful geometric designs, these were entered through a step-topped archway. The women were also very colourful, with beaded necklaces, rows of gold bangles almost covering the legs, and beaded anklets above bare feet. Travelling further, we came to a more traditional village with the addition of a different type of dwelling: a short tunnel forming the entrance gave it the appearance of a straw igloo! Women were working beneath a shelter created from saplings. Surrounded by exotic white flowers and cactus in savannah-like terrain, we saw a crude stone wall with a battlemented tower. Smoke issued from a flat-roofed adobe hut, also decorated but much less colourful, with washing in front and thatched *rondavels* nearby. We spent the night in one of these ethnic constructions, where we had to provide our own food but had a personal houseboy to cook it.

Next day, we came to the first of several stunning waterfalls that we were to encounter: emerging from a green pool, it plummeted down a perpendicular rock face and between moss-covered boulders to a river making its way through dense undergrowth. The surroundings were superb, with tall grasses forming the foreground to rugged cliffs rearing above forested slopes. We then proceeded to a couple of lower, but no less attractive falls cascading into water churned a muddy brown by their force.

Going through **Nelspruit**, we made a detour to the **Sudwala Caves and Dinosaur Park**, where life-sized replicas of these massive beasts, going back

300 million years, included tetradactyls, stegosaurus (with a brain no larger than a walnut but a nerve centre in the hip region that controlled movement of the powerful spiked tail), brontosaurus (the heaviest land animal ever known, weighing over 30 tons and 18m (60ft) in length but a herbivore with weak jaws and blunt teeth), tyrannosaurus rex (at 16ft high and 60ft long, the largest and fiercest predator, although its forelegs were ineffectual), triceratops (with horns like the rhinoceros), one resembling a prehistoric buffalo with a tremendous horn span, and a woolly mammoth or mastodon with gigantic tusks, precursor to today's elephant. Set in swamp and thick jungle with mountains in the background, they looked extremely authentic. Together with the usual formations, the actual caverns contained evidence of the first life on earth, *collenia*: limestone fossils of algae that existed more than 2,000 million years ago! The caves were the site of a bloody battle between two Swazi brothers claiming kingship, which resulted in the elder being beheaded and his followers slaughtered. H. Rider Haggard used this episode for his best-selling novel *King Solomon's Mines*.

Next on the agenda were the pretty **Bridal Veil Falls** and tall narrow **Lone Creek Waterfall**, both plunging down precipitous faces in the area of **Sabie** and the **Blyde River Canyon** where the rivers **Treur** and Blyde (River of Joy) meet. At 800m (2,630ft) deep and 24km (15mi) long, the canyon is the third largest in the world; the second, in Namibia, is described later. Marking the beginning of the ravine were the intriguing cylindrical cavities of **Bourke's Luck Potholes**, created by the swirling action of pebble laden floodwaters. Driving through the quaint 1870s gold mining town of **Pilgrim's Rest** and past scenic **God's Window**, we reached the breathtaking **Lisbon Falls**, which fostered growth of delicate mosses.

I have photographs of a striking white stone building with a turret, succeeded by magnificent landscaped grounds featuring flowerbeds, urns full of colourful blooms, a fountain, ponds, and shady pergolas, all set in vast lawns. This was **Graskop**, en route to **PheZulu** (meaning High Up) traditional *kraal* in Natal's **Valley of 1000 Hills**, a representation of a **KwaZulu** native village with elaborately thatched dwellings and indigenous people demonstrating culture, costumes and crafts. A couple wore the most amazing cowrie shell hair adornment, and bare-breasted women performed dances in a dusty compound overlooking a verdant green valley. This was followed by men in long loin cloths and feathered headdresses, chanting and executing high-stepping movements. It was very touristy, but entertaining because there were few people present.

By comparison, we entered a city where I noted several grand buildings, including one with domes and a double-storey pillared portico topped by a sculpted pediment. Another had cupolas on small turrets between ornate gables around the roofline, its attractive clock tower enhanced by similar features. A column in front had white figures around the base and atop the summit. We visited yet another set of beautiful twin falls (and one smaller drop) before arriving at a wide watercourse in the green foothills of flat-topped mountains, their creviced sides exhibiting unique rocky outcrops. Making a picturesque scene on undulating grassy slopes was a cluster of *rondavels*, outside one of which a man was industriously chopping wood.

In **Natal** we encountered the beautiful mountain and river scenery of the 300m/984ft-deep **Oribi Gorge**, one huge U-turn, appropriately called **Horseshoe Bend**, viewed from the plateau of a high bluff rearing above lush green slopes. This elevated position also provided panoramas of other chasms and farther valleys filled with dense growth. I have film of myself seated (apprehensively!) on **Overhanging Rock**, a large, aptly named jutting slab with the **Umzimkulwana River** far below and hazy mountains in the distance. Other formations were allocated names such as **The Pulpit** and **Needle**, and a rock tower was called **Baboon's Castle**. We came across a woman toting a bundle of long saplings on her head and a collection of thatched white *rondavels* near a fenced enclosure (probably for stock) with a horse grazing nearby.

Another town possessed a clock tower similar to that described earlier and a square surrounded by elegant colonial buildings with spired turrets, cupolas and domes. A steep street of neat terraced houses, mostly white but with a few pastel façades, had balconies overlooking tiny gardens or potted plants behind rendered brick fences. Hanging ferns, philodendrons, bright flowers, variegated leaves, multihued coleus, and trees hosting creepers, orchids, elkhorns and bromeliads were all highlights of an outstanding conservatory. It also featured palms, red and white anthuriums (actually a bract and also known as the flamingo lily), maidenhair fern, pelargoniums with rich purple, deep red (with frilly white edges) or pure white petals and, in the centre of a pond, a fountain with cherubs frolicking in the bowl. Figures on a pedestal appeared in a large outdoor pool. Passing a building resembling a mosque, we came to a peaceful river in a less dramatic setting than previously and, on a grassy plain, encountered a flock of ostrich with many young. I felt sympathy for two poor donkeys pulling a cart holding a large family of Africans. My next pictures were scenic: a stream threading through sparse greenery in a rocky valley, stone tors erupting here and there creating interest, and strange grey mountains in the distance.

Africa is the best place in the world for viewing wildlife. Having no concept of what to expect and imagining that it would be necessary to search diligently for animals, it was a revelation to realise that they were abundant – big tuskers almost within touching distance. With much excitement we entered **Kruger National Park**. Forty miles wide and stretching two hundred miles from the Crocodile River in the south to the Limpopo in the north, it is one of the world's largest wildlife sanctuaries (almost the size of Belgium), and in a short space of time, on a comparatively flat expanse, we found large black-and-white storks with long red bills and lanky legs. Our first game was bontebok, a large brown antelope with slightly curved ridged horns and a white blaze and rump. They were with young, which were beige in colour and without markings. At a pretty waterhole edged with trees and lush reeds, we managed to approach very close to a large blue heron. We observed many more deer, some too far away to identify, and white birds roosting in trees.

It was here that I suffered my first huge disappointment of the trip, the movie camera malfunctioned and I was forced to buy a simple still camera (for an exorbitant price!) within the park. Subsequent pictures of animals, except for one massive elephant with long curved tusks right beside our car, are quite minute because I did not have the facility of a zoom lens. I have a photograph of the wide, mostly dry riverbed that our camp overlooked and where animals came to drink in the evening. We discovered that it was possible, and indeed considerably cheaper, to stay at game reserves all over South Africa, and I became aware of specialised parks devoted solely to the elephant and mountain zebra respectively, the latter, where we spent one night, in the **Cape Province**. As a point of interest, South Africa's first hotel was established when guests of the country's founder liberally helped themselves to his cutlery, crockery and table linen, so he opened a hostelry outside the fort wherein he resided. The first boarding house, run by a mother and daughter, was a tent pitched next to their ox-wagon! The first bar was a corrugated iron shed that its owner dubbed 'Central Hotel'.

Kruger was very open, so in spite of being summer and the grass quite high, it was easy to distinguish giraffe, their long slender necks craning above trees. The ubiquitous springbok were plentiful, as were zebras. An interesting fact concerning the latter is that fat bellies are not an indication of good health; this is reflected by their manes, which should be standing upright. There were herds of wildebeest (gnus) and several sightings of the incredibly ugly warthog. Big stork-like birds perched on dead branches and we saw Grant's gazelle and waterbuck, a medium-sized antelope with a distinctive circular white patch on its rear. Monkeys with babies sat on the railing of a bridge. A huge solitary tree of enormous girth stood on the dry veldt, a herd of graceful impala sheltered in the meagre shade of another, and I was lucky to spot a female kudu in dense scrub. At one stage, in direct contravention of the rules and alongside a few people from other vehicles, we left our car to watch lions with a recent kill; however, they were so engrossed in feeding that they paid us no heed. The protected population of the park showed absolutely no concern for cars; in fact, we had to stop for a giraffe ambling directly across in front of us. We also came very close to a lone lioness, which wandered from the bush to sit languidly and panting beneath a shade tree at the side of the road.

On a guided walk with an armed guard (in slouch hat, khaki shirt, shorts, and long socks) we saw baboons, hippopotami enjoying a pool ringed by big boulders and tall growth, and weaver bird nests hanging like decorative baubles from the slender branches of a tree.

As we continued by car, the illusive cheetah made a rare appearance, and our visit concluded with more ostrich, brilliant red flame trees, mountain scenery, deer beneath the flat-topped acacia trees so synonymous with Africa, a monitor lizard sunning itself on a rock, and jungle-clad banks of a brown river.

Interestingly, an adult elephant deposits upward of 150kg (330lb) of dung per day! The Limpopo was immortalised by Rudyard Kipling in his book *The Elephant's Child.* He refers to it in the words: *to the banks of the great, green, greasy Limpopo River all set about with fever trees.* The fever tree is a species of acacia with bright yellow bark, which may account for its name because malaria sufferers often turn yellow. However, it is more likely that the name derives from the swampy areas where the trees are found, ideal breading grounds for malarial mosquitoes.

Swaziland

We spent a miserable Christmas Day attempting to enter **Swaziland**, a tiny monarchy that until the death of King Sobhusa II in 1982 had the world's longest reigning ruler. Approaching a remote border post, we were denied entry because we had not had cholera inoculations. Not wanting unnecessary 'jabs', our thinking had been that in the event of an outbreak it would be possible to obtain them at that time. In a confronting interview, no entreaty was going to satisfy or deter the implacable large black man in charge from carrying out his 'duty'. Adopting an arrogant attitude, he drew himself up to his full height, looked down on me, and declared 'I am the superior man here' – a backlash at white supremacy? After lengthy negotiation, one of his colleagues finally relented enough to indicate a rough road, not shown on the map, around the perimeter of the country, which took us the major part of the day to negotiate. Leaving the patrol post, we located a clinic where we were given the appropriate injections, but at the main border town, where we finally arrived late in the evening, we were not required to produce evidence or even asked about cholera shots!

The town was deserted, but we eventually managed to find a boarding house, closed but with a note and telephone number on the door, where the owner of the establishment was prepared to give us a room without meals. However, she later expressed sympathy by presenting us with a tray containing cold remnants of her own Christmas dinner! We went through places with names such as **Pig's Peak** and **Mbabane**, the capital.

South Africa

From Swaziland, we headed south to **Durban** with its strip of hotels facing the seafront along **Marine Parade**. Even considering the length of time that has elapsed, I remember a delicious meal of hot tongues and piccalilli in the dining room of one of these establishments, looking out at the promenade along which *rickshaws* plied, operated by Zulus almost completely enveloped in extremely colourful costumes and sporting the most extraordinary towering headdresses. We also witnessed a sidewalk performance by figures in masks. Interspersed with modern edifices, Durban featured some wonderful colonial buildings and the very beautiful black and white filigree-iron **Vasco de Gama Clock**, a monument to commemorate the first sighting of Durban by the Portuguese explorer on Christmas Day in 1497. A Japanese garden with the usual stone lanterns and red bridges was an incongruous sight, and Zulus popped up all over the place.

We continued to the two homelands of **Transkei** and **Ciskei**, the latter recently independent but already showing evidence of neglect, with few remaining street signs, broken windows, and three-foot-high weeds. Then it was along the **Garden Route**, which took us through **East London**, with an impressive **City Hall**, to **Fort Beaufort** with its **Martello Tower**. This was followed by **Addo Elephant National Park**, Port Elizabeth, **Plettenburg Bay**, with the Beacon Island Hotel on a rocky promontory in the water,

Knysna and **George** (named for George III) before arriving in Cape Town, where my pictures show magnificent gardens at the foot of mountains. Whilst in **Port Elizabeth**, we went to **Happy Valley Fantasy world**, a Disney-like attraction with colourful tableaux featuring figurines coated with ultra-violet reflecting paint and illuminated with stunning effect by ultra-violet lamps. Characters included Chillie Willie, Little Bo-Peep, Heidi, and Hiawatha. We also admired the graceful **Paul Sauer Bridge** spanning the **Storms River**. At **Oudtshoorn**, out of **Mossel Bay**, we visited the **Safari Ostrich Show Farm**, where they explained the development, from hatching to raising, of the world's largest bird and the production of merchandise, including plumes that once sold for R500 a kilo – no wonder feather dusters were so expensive! They even held novelty races, the jockeys, in colourful silks, riding bareback. A piece of trivia: ostrich eggs do not break if stood upon! North of Oudtshoorn, we visited the **Cango Caves** with their typical crystalline formations.

In between, I managed to get the camera attended to and commenced filming again at the **Drosdy Museum** in **Swellendam**. An eye-catching thatched white building, it had two gigantic pines flanking the pathway to the entrance, a long verandah shaded by grapevines, and a waterwheel and thatched white cottages in the grounds. Six miles south, we called into the **Bontebok National Park** on the banks of the **Breë River**. A coastal drive around the cape produced scenic vistas of gentle waves kissing a stony shore and mountains known as the **Twelve Apostles**, which put me in mind of the Remarkables in Queenstown, New Zealand. The unblemished blue of the sky was repeated in the turquoise water, the two separated by gradual green slopes. Here and there, bleached-looking rocks extended into the sea.

Established in 1652 as a victualing station for ships of the Dutch East India Company, **Cape Town** had its share of attractive buildings, including a tiny blue mosque on a corner. Towers, turrets and cupolas were mixed with the contemporary, and always there was the fantastic backdrop of **Table Mountain**. This distinctive massif, South Africa's most famous landmark, was 1,086m (3,560ft) high with pyramid-shaped monoliths, known respectively as **Devil's Peak** and **Lion's Head**, at each end. Palm trees, statues and a cannon featured in the gardens mentioned above, which from hazy recall, could have once been the location of a fort. Nearby, at the site of a weekend market on **Grand Parade**, stood an impressive edifice with a central clock tower, a stone balustrade forming the parapet, a carved pediment, and a columned porch at the head of stairs. Table Mountain also provided the backdrop to a horse atop the dome of a columned rotunda, a fountain in a large pond surrounded by flowers, and an extensive rose garden.

Taking the obligatory trip up mountains opposite the famed 'Table', we obtained an incredible overview of the sprawling city nestled in the lee of its protective mass with the ocean in front. It was a city of flowers and trees and the venue for another attractive conservatory. One unusual structure, with eight seated bronze lions flanking a set of steps leading to a colonnade, reminded me of Europe. Standing atop a pedestal at the base of the staircase was a figure with a rearing horse. This was the elaborate **Rhodes Memorial** (1912) on the slopes of Devil's Peak, the summit of which loomed behind. At the head of the stairs, a bronze bust of the founder of Rhodesia was inscribed with the words of his friend Rudyard Kipling: *Living he was the land, and dead his soul shall be her soul.* The nearby university was also composed of classical buildings featuring columns and pediments, and I observed other pillared porticos.

The **Botanical Gardens** displayed different types of protea – named after the Greek god Proteus who could change his shape at will – clusters of long red-and-white bell-shaped flowers (a variety of heath), and a tropical section with large cacti. Mountains formed the backdrop to a pond, its banks lined with lush growth that included tree ferns. I filmed examples of attractive Cape Dutch architecture with its distinctive rounded gables and, in beautiful grounds on the peninsula, the wine cellar of **Groot Constantia**, enhanced with a lovely white pediment featuring stucco cherubs with the fruits of the vine. **Marine Drive** revealed a bay with a bluff like Hawaii's Diamond Head on one side, and glorious sunny weather heightened my appreciation.

Approaching the **Cape of Good Hope Nature Reserve**, southernmost tip of the African continent, where the Indian and Atlantic oceans meet, we experienced an intimidating but nevertheless humorous incident when our stationary car was overrun by baboons. These included a mother with a baby clapping its hands, one of which another adult took hold in a surprisingly human-like action. Initially amusing, they became quite threatening, and we eventually endeavoured to dislodge them by slowly taking off, whereupon one of these aggressive animals, expressing its displeasure, jumped ferociously up and down on the hood. This resulted in a very large dent, which ultimately 'popped' with a mighty bang, frightening the wits out of us! In spite of this, I enjoyed the stark environment with its windblown scrub and dramatic coastal scenery, the waves pounding eroded rock formations far below. We continued around **Hout Bay**, the road winding above rocky beaches and pale-coloured sea-lashed cliffs with scant vegetation but affording superb panoramas of the fabulous mountains. Gulls perched on the guano-decorated representation of an animal surmounting a tall boulder at the water's edge, and I took pictures of luxury housing perched precariously above a bay, with at least one car parked on a flat rooftop accessed from the street!

Back it the city, I filmed elaborately shaped and decorated gables, a church with a fancy belfry above the entrance, the **Houses of Parliament**, a three-storey mansion with an elegant porch set in spacious grounds, and several other grand buildings, all of them white. In the vicinity of Cape Town we entered three of the gracious old homes, now museums: **La Gratitude**, Groot Constantia (mentioned above), and **Koopmans de Wet House** (1701) containing a priceless collection of Dutch colonial furniture, old silver, glass, Delftware and porcelain. Travelling through **Paarl**, we also visited the famous vineyards and wineries of **Stellenbosch**. It being off season, the world famous **Kirstenbosch Gardens** were denuded of flowers.

Two hundred and eighty-seven miles from Cape Town, but directly opposite as the crow flies, was the small coastal town of **Lamberts Bay**, where we stayed at the Marine Hotel. From the beach, we obtained excellent views of Table Mountain across the ocean before heading north for **Namibia**, at that time part of South Africa but since 1990 an independent country. Also from Lamberts Bay, we visited the second of four enormous gannet colonies that I was to encounter on my world travels, this one on a rocky promontory and also home to a great colony of cormorants. Described in more detail in the New Zealand chapter, I find these odorous locations packed full of noisy chattering birds absolutely fascinating. But prior to this we came across an old mill, a waterwheel, a photogenic church, and a lake with flamingos. These I managed to capture in full flight as they passed overhead, their long necks stretched out in front and legs behind. They made a great sight against a dull sky, which served to accentuate their pink colour.

At **Bird Island**, a multitude of cormorants with flapping wings and questing beaks, preened and interacted as they nested on boulders painted white with their droppings, one having an obvious altercation with a neighbour as it adjusted sticks in its nest. Waves created by a surging sea crashed beyond, and the horde of black bodies on the white rock presented an astonishing spectacle. Even more congested was the accumulation of gannets, which seemed to prefer being tightly packed and literally sat one on top of the other in every available space, with still more landing in their midst. At one spot the two species intermingled, and the contrast between the black birds and beautifully marked white gannets was striking; the whole was a seething mass of avian bodies and a scene of constant activity. I do not recall seeing any hatchlings, but many cormorants still sat on leafy nests, and one tended a charcoal grey chick as large as its parent. There was even a small group of jackass penguins waddling with their ungainly gait on a flat rock, one plunging into the breaking surf.

Namibia

Heading further north, making for **Fish River Canyon** on the fringe of the **Namib Desert**, we entered harsh terrain and saw our first baobab trees flourishing amid boulders. This was the complete antithesis of the previous few days, the desert best described by the name attributed to it by the **Nama** people: *Namib*, meaning Place Where There Is Nothing. It became progressively dryer and dryer, with low rises beyond stony windswept plains, scant scrub, a few cacti, African quiver trees, and initially no visible wildlife, although I did photograph a long-tailed black widowbird on a telegraph pole. Second only to America's Grand Canyon, and very similar in appearance except that it lacked the colour, the Fish River Canyon was situated in an extremely arid area with no animal life other than a few hyraxes: small mammals sometimes called rock rabbits. Known in South Africa as dassies, their closest living relative is the elephant! Barring some exotic red cacti and a solitary tall quiver tree, we saw no vegetation, and there was barely any water in the large bends of the river. Gazing down from the plateau at the rim of the gorge, fingers of rock pointed skywards from its creviced sides, and the whole world looked grey and dun coloured. It was exceptionally hot and we saw only one other visitor the entire day, which caused me to pause and reflect what could have eventuated in the extreme conditions had we incurred a breakdown, although as a precaution it had been necessary to sign in. Surrounded by flowering bougainvillea and palm trees, our accommodation was literally an oasis in the desert.

Back amongst evidence of civilisation, we drove down an avenue of lush palms, past a working waterwheel and huge aloe housing a massive weaver bird nest, to an area with more water and consequently a few trees and sparse greenery on rock walls. This led to the awesome **Augrabies Falls National Park**, where we stayed overnight. The local **Khoikhoi** name, The Place of Great Noise, aptly described this venue. Plunging in a tumultuous mass through a deep narrow ravine of the **Orange River**, the falls formed part of a gigantic whirlpool that illustrated the eroding power of water on granite as it completed its 18km surge down a gradient of 191m, the principal cascade being 56m and the force of the drop creating dense clouds of mist that trapped the sunlight to produce glorious rainbows. The passage of this roiling rampaging river had also sculpted interesting rock formations such as a giant toadstool, on which amazing multihued red, blue and yellow lizards scurried or just sat and absorbed the warmth. Secondary falls plummeted down sides of the gorge to join the main body of water. There were industrious bright yellow weaver birds flying in and out of their upside-down nests, and fairly tame Thomson's gazelle, easily recognisable by the black stripe on their sides, passed with their characteristic bounding action (called stotting or pronking) in front of our hut. That evening produced an incredible sunset with a mass of pink and grey cloud against a pale blue ceiling. I was disappointed that the heat finally defeated us; we did not venture further north to Windhoek or Etosha Game Reserve but turned south once again.

South Africa

In a changing environment, we came to a wide river, plentiful trees including spindly teak and the strange tree aloe or *kokerboom* (quiver tree), and flat-topped mesas with fissured sides, which in turn gave way to a blue lake with plentiful birdlife, mountain scenery, and a green boulder-strewn river with white sandy banks as we travelled back through the **Karoo** and historic **Matjiesfontein** (1884) in the hinterland. The latter, declared a National Monument in 1975, was literally another oasis in the desert, with a spired clock tower, a combination of colonial and Cape Dutch architecture, flame trees, beautiful gardens and lawns, a mansion with squat crenellated towers on the roof, and another featuring delicate iron lacework. There were statues, old-style street lamps, a large pool containing fountains and ducks, an attractive church, a birdbath and water lilies in a small pond, wrought-iron fences, an antiquated fuel pump between modern versions on the sidewalk, and even an English red double-decker bus! It was like something transposed from another time and place, appearing as a veritable mirage in the midst of austere surroundings.

Other places we went through included **Keetmanshoop** with an old Lutheran church, **Beaufort West** (founded in 1818) with its quaint **Town Hall** built in 1866 and now a National Monument, **Grünau** with unusual rock formations, and **Graaff Reinet** featuring the 1806 **Drostdy**, behind which was a picturesque complex of 19th-century cottages called **Stretch's Court**, once occupied by slaves. Here also was **Cape Dutch Reinet House** constructed between 1806 and 1812, with the world's largest grapevine at the back; planted in 1870, its stem had a girth of 2.38 metres.

We drove through the extraordinary **Valley of Desolation**, presenting a prehistoric landscape of tall rugged outcrops and dolerite pillars up to 120m (394ft) that gave the valley its name, and past the unique **Spandau Kop**, a stony mound atop a pyramid-shaped rise. In the **Mountain Zebra National Park** we saw acacia trees with huge thorns (and deceptively pretty pompoms of golden-yellow blossom!) and enormous red-and-green grasshoppers, as well as ostrich, deer, and of course zebra. A hillside of strange cacti, birdlife including a large grey heron amongst a flock of sheep, and Bushman art were other attractions. Underway again, we went through the spa town of **Aliwal North** to **Pietermarizburg**, with its wonderful red and white Victorian **Town Hall**, and crossed the 2,874m **Sani Pass** into **Lesotho**.

Lesotho

One of the world's poorest nations, here I suffered my second huge disappointment when I lost an exquisite marcasite bracelet hung with Australian charms, including a kangaroo, koala, the Sydney Harbour Bridge, a boomerang and an emu, to which I had added the Eiffel Tower and a gondola from Venice. I had worn it for 33 years since it was given to me at the age of 11 by my mother and am still greatly upset at its loss. Even the offer of a $100 reward in this very poor country produced no result.

I photographed the elaborate plaited hairstyles of indigenous girls, and we saw colourfully costumed tribal folk herding cattle, men on horseback at a village market, and decorated box-like houses. Friendly people typified the kingdom, and thatched stone *rondavels* were surrounded by tall flowering cactus, but there was little else of scenic value. We exited the country through the capital, **Maseru**.

South Africa

Entering the **Orange Free State**, we visited the **Willem Pretorius Game Reserve**, where the terrain was mostly flat open land with sparse vegetation. Wildlife included deer – I identified blesbok, red hartebeest, springbok, and one gemsbok or oryx – giraffe, tortoises with decorative shells, and birds such as the ostrich, guinea fowl, blue crane, long-tailed widowbird and various eagles. We witnessed the hilarious antics of a tortoise vocalising with loud grunting noises as it attempted to mount a female twice its size! Also in the park were a few colourful highly decorated houses of modern-day natives and intriguing dry-stone walls and remains of low corbelled huts belonging to the **Ghoya**, the first **Bantu** settlers. These were constructed with the round wall curving inwards until a hole of around 50cm remained, which was sealed with a single slab. At night the small entrance was closed by rolling a stone over the opening.

White birds covering a row of dead trees in a stretch of water produced the illusion of a profusion of blossoms. From here, we went through **Ficksburg**, with rock monoliths like castles dominating small *kopjes* (hills), to **Golden Gate Highlands National Park**, where gentle green slopes contrasted greatly with the huge (up to 140m) flat-topped yellow-and-white sandstone outcrops featuring open caves sculpted by wind and rain. We had one such outstanding vista from the window of our accommodation at the **Brandwag Holiday Resort**, others surrounded a picturesque lake. Here, we experienced another gorgeous sunset, the rose-pink and grey clouds appearing painted.

Leaving the park, I photographed a brilliant red bird on a barbed wire fence and *rondavels* of a different type, their dome-shaped thatch gleaming like bronze in the sun. Next, we came to the incomparable **Drakensberg** (Dragon's Mountain) with the colossal, instantly recognisable, natural 8km-long and 3,000m/9,850ft-high amphitheatre, which embraced everything in its foreground. It is known to the Zulu as *uKhahlamba*, the Barrier of Spears, a name said to imitate the sound of spears beaten against the great war shields. Here again, we stopped in a thatched hut, at the **Royal Natal National Park**, with a view of the amphitheatre from our small front patio and undulating green slopes leading to a massive rock formation looming behind. Guinea fowl with chicks inhabited the grounds, and it was an awe-inspiring location. Departing, we drove past gradually terraced fields, *kraals* with farm animals, and a small waterfall amid luxuriant growth with a mountain backdrop.

Now back in Natal, at **Larula Spa** I wasted considerable time in the frustrating pursuit of trying to film vibrant multihued birds flitting amongst rushes at the edge of a pond, where I also noted kingfishers and waterbirds. Displaying perfect reflections, this was located in a verdant meadow in front of our accommodation. Also on the property, in caves overlooking a bubbling river and green hills, I found excellent examples of the Bushman's art: stick figures but surprisingly sophisticated portrayals of large animals. Another striking sunset was preceded by a bank of mushrooming white cloud in a navy blue sky above a superb emerald landscape. Next day, I observed people fishing, and we followed the course of a river fluctuating between quiet pools and small cataracts splashing over rocks to an attractive waterfall.

It was in South Africa that we went to a **Carnivore Cuisine** restaurant, where all types of game, including zebra and kudu, were brought to the table and carved directly onto the plate from large skewers.

Zimbabwe

Flying into **Victoria Falls** in **Zimbabwe** – at that time it was too dangerous to drive – one could distinctly discern spray from the cataracts rising like steam from a fissure in the flat expanse of earth. Zimbabwe, on a 600m-high plateau between the **Limpopo** and **Zambesi** Rivers, only attained independence in 1980, under a black majority government headed by Robert Mugabe, after deposing the white Rhodesian Front government of Ian Smith following 14 years of turmoil, rebellion and bitter guerrilla warfare against two factions, one waged by Joshua Nkomo based in Zambia, the other led by Mugabe from Mozambique.

I took film as we flew low over the treetops on landing, and on that occasion we stayed at the A'Zambesi River Lodge, where I have delightful footage of a playful donkey chasing a large greyhound around and around a tree in front of the units. The frisky pair gambolled together for some time, the donkey ultimately getting down on its front knees to bray at the barking dog before retiring to the side of the pool, where it mischievously used its teeth to remove a mattress from one of the lounge chairs! Many vervet monkeys were foraging in bush by the river. A juvenile crocodile, its jaws gaping wide, was amongst others in a concrete pool, whilst larger representatives of these primeval beasts lay supine in a tangled mass, one monster displaying a set of terrible teeth and another slithering silently into the slimy green water. Weaver birds flew in and out of nests, gorgeous pink and white water lilies bloomed in a landscaped pond, a monstrous tree bore huge nuts, and a relaxed cheetah, lying in a shady patch behind a wire enclosure, turned to look directly into the camera.

At the falls, I was greeted by the statue of **Livingstone**, gazing forever across the awesome spectacle that he first introduced to the world in 1855. The grandeur of this site is something that has to be experienced to be believed. To quote Livingstone's words: *Scenes so lovely must have been gazed on by angels in their flight.* Falling 108m (354ft) from a point where the Zambesi is 1,700m wide, the force of the torrent (estimated at 545 million litres per minute in the rainy season!) sends up spray sometimes reaching a height of 500m, which maintains the surrounding rainforest. Plummeting with a tumultuous roar, at the period of this visit there was considerably more water than on my subsequent trip. As a consequence, it was lusher, with drops continually dripping from the trees and undergrowth that, added to the spray, caused one to become drenched in a short space of time. Waving grasses in the foreground of the mighty white wall made for superb photography as, from the opposite side, I zoomed in on Livingstone wrapped in his green cocoon on top. It was a sight almost impossible to comprehend, and I had to repeatedly convince myself that I was actually beholding in reality a vision hitherto only seen in books.

The environment was totally unspoilt by the intrusion of artificial structures, and one could peer unobstructed from right at the edge. Because of the spray, even huge boulders at the bottom were not always visible, and places where the gorge narrowed were viewed through a fine veil of mist. Numerous smaller cascades created delicate curtains that plunged to a beautiful white-capped blue-green river below, probably reflecting the colour of the sky and the dense green of its surrounds because at the top of the falls the Zambezi appeared brown. It was absolutely stunning from every vantage point: viewed through grasses and foliage, beyond the trunks and bare branches of trees, past rock formations, or with no foreground at all, but none more so than the **Flight of Angels**. This added an entirely new dimension because one could see along the entire length as the 'Smoke that Thunders' erupted from the crevice that opened dramatically from a perfectly flat plain. As the course turned back upon itself, the river revealed quieter sections running almost parallel. Around Victoria Falls I was able to obtain close-up photographs of deer.

Taking the **Sundowner Cruise**, we sailed past verdant banks with palm trees and clumps of long rushes at the water's edge. We saw several hippopotami, and I was fortunate to capture two hippo 'yawns' on film, albeit at a distance. After six hectic weeks, it was a most enjoyable and relaxing excursion, and although most of the passengers availed themselves of the unlimited alcoholic beverages on board (to their detriment!), I was content to indulge myself just watching the passing parade. At one stage, a beautiful rainbow touched the treetops, but the sunset that we had come to see was unremarkable. One evening, in the grounds of the Victoria Falls Hotel, we attended a cultural programme of dance and mime featuring elaborate costuming and a figure on stilts.

The splendour of the falls was a fitting farewell to Africa and remains one of my wonders of the world. I was disappointed not to get to Hwange Game Reserve, although the following week a group was taken hostage on the road and never heard from again. Their bodies were found some months later.

Mauritius

Flying back to Perth via **Mauritius**, home of the extinct dodo bird, we stayed at La Piroque Hotel in **Flic-en-Flac**. Cottages were set in a tranquil tropical garden featuring coconut palms, a pond, colourful birds, and flowering oleander, hibiscus and frangipani, with mountains in the background and the beach in front. A glass-bottomed boat ride showed us the reef and a different aspect of the wonderful mountains, their searching spires looming behind a white strip of sandy shore. Palms with bulbous trunks lined a pathway in **Pamplemousse Gardens** (established 1735), where a large pond contained huge up-turned pads of the Victoria regia lily. The more than 80 species of palm included the talipot, which is said to flower once after 60 years and then die. Black boulders littered the blue water in a sheltered bay, palm trees fringed its curve of white strand, and misty mountains formed the backdrop. A classical picture was created by a solitary palm leaning over a turquoise ocean with boats on the surface and puffy white clouds on the horizon. I took film of a luxury resort hotel on its own tiny island, a bed of massed anthuriums, jagged mountain crests, a green crater, the high but narrow **Cascade Chamarel**, and the eerie **Chamarel Coloured Sands**: low, smoothly rounded sand dunes composed of seven distinct colours (red, brown, violet, green, blue, purple and yellow) and completely encapsulated by thick vegetation (see Island Odyssey 2013, book 5).

In May and July 1981, I also made two trips to Singapore (not documented).

INDIA & SIKKIM 1982

INDIA

Delhi

My first sight on this occasion was of the 16th-century **Tomb of Humayun**, built by his queen. A monument similar to, and possible inspiration for the legendary Taj Mahal, but constructed of marble and sandstone, it had a sparkling white dome and a reflective pool in the centre of a palm-lined pathway leading to a colonnade encircling the mausoleum. It made an exceptional picture framed in the impressive arched gateway. This was the first important landmark in Mogul monuments. Incidentally, Humayun's son, the Great Akbar, and *his* son Jehangir, ruled from Agra and Lahore respectively; it was the latter's son, Shah Jahan, who brought the capital back to Delhi. Surrounded by trees and spacious lawns, a nearby structure had turrets at the corners and striped onion domes.

The 72.45m (243ft) fluted **Qutb Minar** (tower) was 14.5m (47ft) wide at the base, tapered to 2.5m at the top, and had four progressively smaller sculpted ledges around the perimeter. Of the five storeys, the lower three were red sandstone, the others marble and sandstone. Begun in 1193 by Delhi's first Muslim sultan, Qutb-ud-Din Aibak, it had withstood the test of time in near perfect condition and was inscribed with verses from the *Qur'an* and sayings of the prophet, the letters at the top larger so as to be read from the ground. Also in the compound, but not as well preserved, were the remains of India's first mosque, **Quwwat-ul-Islam**, with lovely carved pillars belonging to an earlier edifice and an archway with beautiful intricately embossed designs. Within the ruins stood a 24ft-tall iron column; raised in the fourth century and bearing lines of Sanskrit, it has stunned scientists because it has survived rust free. It is said to bring good luck if hands held behind the back can be joined around the wide shaft, and it has been rubbed shiny by many attempts at the feat. This complex was set in attractive grounds, but another extensive site was overgrown, with monkeys scampering on its partially tumbled stone walls. At a rural village where a horse was tethered near an outdoor clay oven, I came across an interesting group of people: the women in colourful cotton saris and silver jewellery, the men all in white.

Drummers preceded a lengthy procession that included large ceramic elephants on floats drawn by bullocks, a shrine borne on shoulders, and two floats ostensibly pulled by life-sized replicas of horses but pushed from behind by men. Participants with clapping sticks interacted whilst parading, and seven very young novice priests walked within a small enclosure cordoned off with bars held by a police escort. Dressed in yellow turbans and toning costumes with heavy silver jewellery at the yoke, each had a solemn angelic face. Others rode on an elaborate dais, one wearing a mask that the Jain often utilise to prevent harming even an insect. The sect has prospered in trade and commerce rather than agriculture because even tilling the soil involves taking the life of an insect. Here, an outstanding building was surmounted by cupolas supported on slender pillars, which were to become commonplace. There were also gold-spired domes and another tall fluted column. I saw donkey carts, trishaws, bicycles and motor bikes – but few cars.

Ladakh

In 1982, I made my first visit to **Ladakh**; *la* meaning pass and *dakh* many, thus: Land of Many Passes. Often referred to as the Roof of the World, it only opened to international tourism in 1980, and due to the remoteness and enormous difficulties associated with getting in and out, it was still comparatively unspoilt by Western influence. Situated at 3,505m (11,500ft), well above the tree line, the terrain was just sand, gravel and solid rock. Every blade of green had been cultivated, and the awe-inspiring mountains were overpowering, making me feel very insignificant. In my travels throughout Europe and the Andes in South America, I did not see anything to equal them in ruggedness and grandeur.

Due to extreme weather conditions, which caused the tarmac to crack and be constantly in need of maintenance, it was always a bumpy landing whenever I flew across the snow and ice of the **Himalayan Mountains** and **Karakoram Range** to the little known Tibetan community of **Leh** (aptly translating as Oasis) in Ladakh. Ethnically and linguistically part of **Tibet**, here I found heavily clad women sitting with small piles of vegetables spread on cloth on the roadway. Most wore a long bulky woollen garment called a *goncha* and the traditional headgear, like a winged top hat, known as a *gonda*. Carrying a laden basket slung on her back, one even sported ethnic footwear with turned-up toes. The dominating feature was the palace, built with huge stones carried from nearby without the aid of machinery. Their prayer flags fluttering, white *stupas* or *chortens*, dome-shaped monuments peculiar to Buddhism, sat on a stony rise behind stone and adobe dwellings with stone fences. Isolated buildings stood on desolate plains ringed by the snow-capped peaks.

On this first trip to Leh, founded in the 14th century, I stayed in a *yurt* hut at the Ladakh Serai in outlying **Stok** village, which had its own 19th-century palace still occupied by the royal family. As a guest in the village, I was privileged to attend a local celebration, which also played host to the queen. Unfortunately, having flown straight from sea level, I was suffering my first serious bout of debilitating altitude sickness, with nausea, vomiting, diarrhoea and excruciating headaches, which persisted for four days, so that I had to forgo the honour of being presented to her majesty, a well-loved figure every bit as regal as royalty should be, and with fine unblemished features even though she sometimes worked side by side with her people in the fields.

Feeling extremely sorry for myself, I witnessed competitive archery contests and just surveyed the fascinating faces around me as these descendants of the Mongols were intent on the games, and probably imbibing in *chhang*, a local alcoholic beverage brewed from *grim* (a type of barley), the staple diet of Ladakhis. The women, one of whom was spinning wool with a top-like spindle, all wore the tall hats and copious jewellery, and even the children were dressed in the long garb, one carrying a miniature bow and arrow. Many were adorned with the natural long-haired goatskin cloak that they never seemed to remove – summer or winter! A young lady in an elaborately bejewelled costume agreed to being filmed but kept her eyes downcast the whole time. With the background of snowy mountains and blue sky, it was a tremendous spectacle. At the conclusion, a very slow-moving dance was executed by men and women with sashes draped over their right shoulders; even those born to these high climes operated in slow motion, and I was continually admonished not to exert myself. It is my understanding that the Indian army, which mans this vast outpost, always confines new recruits to bed for some days until they acclimatise. I was also led to believe that, in reverse, locals descending from this altitude suffered the same symptoms.

Scattered around Stok were *chortens* bearing prayer flags and surrounded by *mani* walls. The latter consisted of flat votive stones chiselled with prayers in Tibetan script, or the mantra *Om Mani Padma Hom*: 'Hail to the Jewel in the Lotus'. After recovering, I was taken to several *gompas* (monasteries), which included 500-year-old **Spituk** overlooking the **Indus,** known in Hindu legend as the Lion River because it was fabled to pour from a lion's mouth. All very ancient, the monasteries had wooden balconies – those on one bowed with age – and contained frescoes, precious *thankas* (painted scrolls, some from the Potala Palace in Tibet) and 700- or 800-year-old statues. As well as the prized *thankas*, Spituk contained a collection of ancient masks and a 900-year-old temple dedicated to Kali, whose image had 35 arms on each side but except for a festival in January was kept covered. Comprised of ten temples, the 12-storey 800-year-old **Tikse** featured a *stupa* with coloured relief, ancient swords, statues, *thankas*, spectacular colourful *Tantric* illustrations on a wall, and a gigantic pillar, believed to be from Tibet, engraved with the teachings of Buddha. It was always easy to recognise the village of Tikse because it commanded an entire hill, with the monastery on top and a row of *stupas* at the base.

Entrance to another was via an arch surmounted by a *stupa* decorated with blue relief, and rubble littered the compound. I watched as a robed figure, a large load in a basket on her back and a child seated on her shoulders, walked past a series of *chortens* residing on a flat hilltop nearby. From the elevated position of this monastery, I looked down into the crater formed by its encircling rocky mountains, the irregularly shaped fields resembling vast crazy-paved flooring, and white summits visible in the far distance. Mounting ancient steps to the entrance, I found curtains on the façade billowing in the breeze, but the inside projected an aura of total peace and calm. The astonishing panorama from upper levels looked out over green fields, hilltop *stupas*, stands of poplars, bundles of brush on flat roofs (drying for winter fuel), and barren windswept stretches to the ever-present mountains. Only a few small white clouds relieved the almost unbroken blue of the sky, and I saw very little birdlife.

monastery in Leh

Others visited were **Shey** (1655), containing the largest Buddha – a two-storey (7.5m) seated copper and brass image gilded with gold, plated with silver, and studded with gems – and **Hemis** (1620), composed of several temples. This was the largest and wealthiest, with gold images, art pieces glittering with precious stones, and priceless ancient *thankas*, one believed to be the biggest in existence, exhibited only once every 11 years. The kitchen held a 12m-diameter copper vessel capable of cooking rice for 500 people! The *gompa* had an elaborate carved gateway that introduced colours of blue, yellow and maroon, and there was also stunning artwork on walls surrounding the compound. Inside were many wonderful ancient handwritten books wrapped in cloth, and monks were seated on the floor chanting and swaying as they turned the loose pages. I remember this particularly because of a very funny incident. At the time, I was wearing a pair of yellow slacks, on the right leg of which I had painted leaves and bright flowers. Standing beside one devotee, I was startled when he interrupted his religious observance to tug on my trousers and, smiling, make a comment that I could not understand!

Once again, the monochrome surroundings of sand, fields (this time brown), and mountains was astounding. I photographed a monk standing in an elegant carved doorway, but for the most part the buildings were plain and quite austere. Whilst every village had its own *gompa* (the word means 'a solitary place'), they were usually set apart, and one was isolated at the foot of bare mountains across a rock-strewn plain. Of those that I saw, one incorporated the immense boulders upon which it was built into the structure, but I do not recall which.

Back in the city, an old man with a white beard, old-style round glasses and a walking stick was spinning his brass prayer wheel, each revolution multiplying the number of praises within, and I took film of the narrow alleys and activity in the streets. This included people queued outside a butcher's shop with meat hanging between the open wooden shutters – surrounded by flying insects! There was *one* vehicle (a jeep) parked in the main street! The 16th-century nine-storey **Khar Palace**, resembling the Potala and housing the museum, featured some fine carved exterior woodwork, and here again I looked down on *stupas*, trees, people working in fields delineated by low stone walls, and the incredible mountains. Amongst the exhibits were antique artillery, large semi-precious stones (particularly turquoise), animal skins, 1,000-year-old *thankas* worked with pure gold and crushed gemstones, and royal crowns, costumes and jewellery that were hundreds of years old. Wearing the goatskin, an old lady sat cross-legged in the centre of a courtyard enclosed by covered walkways with grass piled on top to dry and fleeces hanging on rope strung between wooden posts supporting the roof. Towards evening, in the vicinity of my *yurt*, I filmed farmers bringing home horses and cattle (yaks), a figure toting a large mound of grass, and others loading the same material onto the backs of donkeys – of which only the legs, faces and ears were visible! Possibly due to the altitude, the sky seemed a lot clearer and the colour more intense, sometimes even royal blue, which outlined and accentuated the whiteness of buildings to perfection.

I took many more pictures of the arid terrain, isolated houses, stone fences, a green crop, buildings on rocky crags against the stark blue of the sky, a woman tending an open fire beneath a metal can, and a figure storing grass on the flat roof of a dwelling bearing swastikas (originally a Hindu symbol) on the wall. At one venue, a group was sewing the tops of jute sacks filled with grain, and I had my first close encounter with a yak (other than a stuffed one in the museum), albeit a scraggy moth-eaten beast.

A few interesting facts: The months in Ladakhi are based on the names of animals.

Their fascinating funeral rites dictate that the deceased person, wrapped in colourful garments, be lowered into a *purkhang* (an oven-like structure), below which a fire is lit and the corpse reduced to ashes. These are collected on the fourth day, mixed with clay, and fashioned into miniature *stupas* to be placed near a monastery. The ashes of prominent saints are kept in urns inside *stupas,* which along with *manis* are believed to ward off evil spirits. Usually, the youngest son of a house becomes a lama at a very early age.

Most sects are vegetarian, only consuming breakfast and lunch and abstaining from alcohol. The Ladakhi system of medicine is called *swaripa*, meaning 'the art of living'. Brahma was thought to be the first practitioner, indigestion the first disease, and hot water the first medicine! Called *amchis*, present day practitioners dispense herbal, mineral and animal drugs. Kernels of the apricot are crushed and utilised as lamp- and hair oil.

There being no timber, yak dung is primarily used as fuel. The hollowed-out horns provide containers for gunpowder, hooves are used for making glue, the hair for thick cloth and tents, and the tail acts as a *chanwar* – fly whisk.

Buddhism was brought to Ladakh by an emissary of King Ashoka as early as the third century BC.

Kashmir

With my nose glued to the window, I flew to **Srinagar** (1,768m), over the same captivating vistas of barren mountains giving way to snow-covered peaks, paths of glaciers appearing like roads in a forbidding terrain, and finally, green slopes as we approached **Kashmir**. Normally, I request an aisle seat because I suffer from restless leg syndrome and do not like having to clamber over bodies to move about, but for this flight a window seat is essential. The terror of the road was reserved for later trips, although the first time I was not so aware of it because I was enthralled with the passing panoramas.

At **Dal Lake**, I took film of vibrant blue kingfishers and large tracts of water covered with lotus leaves, which also surrounded my houseboat, New Royal Palace, belonging to my friend Gulam. Taken from the upper deck, I have pictures of a vendor selling vegetables from a *shikara* pulled alongside a boat opposite and others, including flower sellers with their bunches of brilliant blooms, plying back and forth. There is no more pleasant diversion than to float leisurely on these craft, surveying the wonderful fretwork-trimmed houseboats that reflect an era of gracious living, with trees in the background and lotus spread like a carpet in front.

As a complete change of scene, we took a trip into the pine-clad mountains, with an effervescent river winding through a deep valley at the foot. I was also taken to **Pahalgam**, stopping en route to visit remains of a ninth-century Mahadeva temple dedicated to Vishnu at **Avantipur** – founded by Avantivarman who reigned from AD 855 to 883 – before delving into the city streets of **Anantnag**. Here, I found three- and four-storey wooden buildings and at least one brick edifice featuring decorative wooden shutters and arched windows with delicately carved insets. Here also were several mineral springs, the largest believed to be the abode of Ananta, the serpent on which Lord Vishnu rests, and another a lovely blue with a domed pavilion in the centre. Along the way, peasants in rough clothing were bringing their horses, dogs, chattels, and stores of fodder down from the high country for the winter. The road to Pahalgam paralleled the path of the fast-flowing milky blue **Lidder River**, boulders in its bed creating rapids as it forged a path between stony shores bordered by flourishing fields at the foot of conifer-clad slopes. It was another of those sylvan settings that in many places took on the appearance of a painting. Other popular hill destinations were **Gulmarg** (described in the next chapter) and **Sonamarg** (Meadow of Gold, 2,740m), in a valley of silver birch and sycamore carved by the **Sindh River**.

Returning to Srinagar, I saw two men trundling a heavy wagon along roads lined with wooden buildings. Inhabited by bustling crowds, wandering cows and geese, the streets reverberated with the sounds of endless blaring horns and the jingle of harness on horse-drawn carts. Smoking *hookahs*, shopkeepers sat on the raised floors of their open-fronted stores selling goods such as tea, incense, plastic bags, piles of firewood, tin and copper cooking utensils, English candy, woodwork, pottery, cheap radios, shawls, and papier-mâché items. Sunset was particularly beautiful, and early next morning, with the lake still shrouded in mist, I took a boat ride to the floating market. I was paddled amongst the congestion of flower and vegetable *shikaras* – one piled high with green runner beans, others with squash and spring onions – and along picturesque narrow waterways where I encountered more kingfishers, lotus, rushes, and floating islands with abundant greenery, crops and ducks; it was a delightful experience in idyllic surrounds.

I was taken to the illustrious 400-year-old **Mogul Gardens**, the first with mountains soaring behind flowerbeds, lawns, trees, and a man-made canal with a waterfall and fountain. I am especially proud of a photograph utilising an arched doorway to frame a verdant mountain beyond a pavilion with a water chute and colourful garden in front. **Shalimar** featured attractive terraced gardens with flowering plants, trimmed bushes, and fountains in a stepped water channel. Bordered by red salvia and other vibrant blooms, this led to a glorious lake, also mentioned in the following chapter. With their watercourses, ponds, overhanging trees, and splashes of colour, the gardens radiated a perception of cool even in the humidity. Srinagar and its gardens were renowned for the celebrated chinar trees, originally brought from Persia and still existing only in that land and Kashmir.

I took pictures of the remains of 18th-century **Hari Parbat Fort**, constructed by Afghan governor Atta Mohammed Khan, and the wall around it built by Akbar between 1592 and 1598. Situated on a hill said to have grown from a pebble dropped by Parvati to crush a demon, it overlooked the smaller **Lake Nagin** (Jewel in the Ring), with fewer houseboats but also covered with massed lotus and circled by trees. Taking final film of a spired mosque on the **Jhelum River**, I headed south.

Goa

From a bus, I photographed the white dome and minaret of a mosque enveloping a tiny island in the ocean. I was approaching the palm-studded shores of **Goa**, at that time a debauched place full of long-haired, unkempt and degenerate hippies, dressed in sarongs, begging on the streets, and smoking marijuana, which made me embarrassed to be Caucasian. Only part of India since 1961, Goa was ruled for 451 years (from 1510) by the Portuguese, who called it Pearl of the Orient or Queen of the East. It had a decidedly Christian face, which seemed incongruous in predominantly Hindu India, and was at one time an important trading post for spices from Malaya, coral and pearls from Persia, and Chinese porcelain and silk. Saint Francis of Xavier founded a mission here before the Inquisition was set up in the late 16th century, portending a 250-year reign of terror during which hundreds of innocent victims were tortured and slain on charges of paganism. Following this, a disastrous plague in 1738 wiped out almost 250,000 people before, in 1750, the survivors abandoned the ravaged city and moved six miles down the **Mandovi River** to instigate a new community at the one-time fishing village of **Panaji**. Finding themselves in skirmishes not only with rival powers but the Goans themselves, who were becoming increasingly discontent with colonial rule, Portugal's days were numbered and came to a close when the economy faltered. Just prior to them being forced out, rich deposits of manganese and iron ore were discovered, and the mining and export of these products became the chief industry. Other small concerns of rice and flour mills, cashew and soap factories, and tile and brick plants were established.

In **Old Goa**, the red stone **Bom Jesus Basilica** (1594) stood out. It housed the remains of St Francis in a gem-studded silver casket entombed in a marble mausoleum. Across the square reposed the huge **Cathedral of St Catherine** (**Sé Cathedral**), its weathered white façade hardly preparing one for the 14 magnificent side chapels, each built in a different style, containing altars dedicated to the saint. Of its five bells, the **Golden Bell** is the largest in Asia. Seven kilometres from Panaji, the **Reis Magos Church** (1555) was dedicated to the three Magi: Gaspar, Melchoir and Balthazar. There were several other religious edifices of note (including mosques and temples), the **Viceregal Arch**, and white cottages standing beside a palm-fringed reservoir. Also beside the tank was another weathered white complex (this one with domes), an eight-tiered pagoda, and a soaring pole threaded with a series of discs – like a gigantic metal kebab! Yet another white church made a wonderful sight ensconced in thick jungle across a brown river. Further along the lush shoreline, people were washing clothes in the shallows around a sandbank.

Calcutta

Back in civilisation, naked children and people with utensils were using running water in a gutter to engage in the same pursuit mentioned above, and men seated on low stools on the sidewalk were being shaved. Pavements were inundated with rubbish, and washing hung on kerbside railing opposite lean-to shelters of the poor. This was my second visit to **Calcutta**, the world's fourth largest city, founded in 1690 on the banks of the **Hooghly River**. Named after the fishing village of Kalikata that once occupied the site, rickshaws were still pulled by barefoot boys with bell in hand, and women in elegant saris vied with cows for possession of the footpath. Calcutta is not a safe city, and I vividly remember being loudly berated by my landlady because I had worn diamond rings when walking the few blocks to her establishment. On subsequent journeys, I rarely wore jewellery of any description, except perhaps a plain wedding band as a precaution against being hassled as a single woman. In fact, on my return to Calcutta later in this trip, I just enjoyed the fascinating activity viewed from the security of my hotel room. In spite of its reputation, I enjoy the city because it is vital, vibrant and alive; people are literally born, live and die at all hours of the day and night on its crowded streets. Also on my return, I shared public transport with a well-to-do citizen who, because he felt vulnerable, refused to take a taxi at night, preferring to be surrounded by people.

But I am getting ahead of myself. Having sailed from **Bombay** to Goa on an overnight ferry, I considered it a pleasant relaxing interlude to include in one of my group tours. However, the return voyage was a complete disaster, which unfortunately caused me to change my opinion. Whereas the initial trip had been on a new vessel, the return was on a sister ship that was so bad it had been condemned, but for lack of a replacement was pressed into service. In direct contrast to the crew on the way down, the rude dining room waiters were dressed in extremely dirty white uniforms, and my cabin was infested with hordes of huge cockroaches, so many that one could not have avoided them if occupying the bunk! After several requests, the cabin was sprayed with a foul-smelling (and probably highly toxic) liquid, making it impossible to inhabit and forcing me to spend the night on deck! Arriving back in Bombay, I submitted a lengthy written report, but to no avail because not even an apology, let alone a refund, was forthcoming.

Bhubaneswar

From Calcutta I went to **Bhubaneswar**, capital of **Orissa**, a city with hundreds of ancient uniquely shaped and elaborately sculpted temples, all that remained of 7,000, going back to the seventh century, which once ranged around the sacred lake, **Bindusagar**. Decorated inside and out with figures, images of gods, animals and lotus, many related tales. The once white façade of an elegant building was enhanced with sculpted filigree-edged canopies above finely carved tableaux. Similar delicate work appeared around doors, windows and the parapet. I photographed the tenth-century **Mukteswar**

Mandir (temple) through a massive gateway, the arch of which seemed to have been hewn from a single immense boulder. Leaning against one of the gigantic pillars was an old bare-chested *sadhu* with a long white beard. Fishing with rudimentary traps consisting of a net attached to the base of sticks fashioned into a pyramid, young men were standing waist deep in a stretch of muddy, turgid and churning floodwater with greenery sprouting from ruins behind. One of the fluted curvilinear towers of the largest temple, 11th-century **Lingaraja Mandir**, featured a life-sized seductive maiden with little clothing but arms adorned with many bracelets, standing beneath a palm tree on an intricately carved background. Various other images graced a multitude of tapering towers, many appearing like stacks of stone *paratha*: a flat round Indian bread.

On contrast, the nearby rock-cut caves of **Udaigiri** were extremely plain. Located beneath heavy rock shelves, they were excavated in the second century BC. Underneath a monstrous slab of black stone, one such cave-like temple, **Chota Hathi Gumpha**, had embossed elephants flanking decorative carving around the arched doorway, another, **Ganesh Gumpha**, had life-sized sculpted elephants in front of a hewn colonnade, and a third, **Bagh Gumpha**, utilised the shape of an enormous boulder to simulate a tiger head, its gaping mouth forming the cave entrance. I had an interesting experience when I sat with two of the holy men in their place of meditation; one had taken a vow of silence and could not speak, but the elder was well educated and very entertaining. From an adjacent hilltop, I obtained an excellent overview of the complex secluded in its green bower. Back in the townsite, I saw a man cooking in an open-fronted stall, his gleaming tin utensils on the floor in front of brightly burning flames in a low adobe fireplace. I had intended visiting Konarak and Puri, but because of imminent flooding, and fearing to become stranded, I had to leave early.

Bombay

Adverse conditions in Orissa also meant that I arrived back in Bombay early, but being a Sunday, there was no assistance available at the airport, and none of the hotels that I attempted to contact would answer their telephone. Familiar with the Sea Green Hotel on **Marine Drive** alongside **Chowpatty Beach**, I requested the shuttle to drop me there. The driver acquiesced, but halfway into the one hour transfer he refused to honour the commitment, nominating an alternative location where I found a foyer crammed with people also wanting accommodation, always a difficulty in Bombay. Almost despairing, a young lad appeared from nowhere, grabbed my suitcase, which he deftly deposited on his head, and rushed out saying 'I have a room for you'. There was nothing for it but to follow him, around corners and up a steep flight of stairs leading from a doorway in a dark narrow alley. At the top, I was indeed given a room – for the extortionate (at that time) sum of $10. It turned out to be the filthiest that it has ever been my misfortune to inhabit, everything, including the fan, caked with dirt, and no bedding. I had to tip the boy to locate and provide me with an unbleached calico mattress cover. Wanting nothing more than a shower – this antiquated (also none-too-clean) facility was opposite – I backed out of the enormous double wooden doors of my lodging, threw home the massive bolt, and emerged from behind drapes that hung in front, only to be confronted with two huge dark truckie types in black singlets; I do not know whose jaw dropped the furthest, and I realised that I was in a brothel! Glaring, defying them to speak, I scuttled to the bathroom and locked the door. But that was not the end of it. Returning to the room, I investigated further and found a screen in one corner, behind it nothing but a metal grill for voyeurs to observe the antics when it was removed! Needless to say I left very early next morning.

Another brothel story, also in Bombay, concerns a forced stopover due to a massive strike that closed down the entire city. Advised not to leave the airport because of protest marches and lack of transport, I nevertheless managed to locate a taxi driver who vehemently vowed to return next morning and took me to a sleazy 'hotel' where, for obvious reasons, bells rang intermittently all night! At least it had an air-conditioner, albeit making an incredible racket, and I was able to rest. The driver did indeed pick me up in time for the flight.

Calcutta

Once again in Calcutta, from my window I filmed people around stalls crudely sheltered by plastic sheeting – one selling the betel nut concoction called *paan* that he wrapped in a leaf – rickshaws, a man collecting water from one of the government sponsored street faucets, a small boy trundling a huge flat-cart, and a vendor with a portable glass case containing fresh fruits, which he sliced and sugared (or salted) for buyers. Others carried a basket, a stack of metal containers, or a load of stools on their heads, and a man industriously sharpened knives and scissors on a foot-operated grindstone. A large procession appeared, its members bearing red banners featuring the hammer and sickle. To take my mind off a tortuous bus ride, I recollect once asking why they courted communism because it meant lack of freedom and independence; the enlightening reply was: 'Who wants to be free to starve'! After the protest march, a street sweeper armed with two short sapling brooms emerged, along with pony carts, a wagon with lengths of metal piping extending far out the back, people with buckets, and a man who was soaping himself from head to toe in a rich white lather, which he rinsed off under the faucet. Later, another parked his flat-cart, stretched out (legs askew) on top, and fell sound asleep for the night!

Apparently, the century-old **New Market**, originally Sir Stuart Hogg Market, with a Victorian wrought-iron roof, sold everything from cobra skin wallets and stuffed mongooses to snake charmer pipes and Christmas cakes, from electronics to cheeses, from champagne flutes to floral bouquets; in fact, all you may ever require in a lifetime. Under its clock, a meeting place for the entire city, one could run the gamut from flower sellers to smugglers.

There is a legend that Calcutta owes its origin to Job Charnock, an East India Company agent who married a Hindu woman that he rescued from her husband's funeral pyre.

SIKKIM

Darjeeling

I left Calcutta for my one and only visit to **Darjeeling** (of tea fame), this because it was difficult to access, having to fly to **Bagdogra** and then catch the famous 'toy train'. Plying its narrow gauge line, this crept up lush mountain slopes with verdant trees, creepers, ferns and entangled vines. It passed terraced tea plantations and pine-scented forests, crossed rivers in ravines capturing gossamer-like clouds, and wound through steep passes with waterfalls, all at hardly more than walking pace – 56 miles in seven hours! Situated 2,134m (7,000ft) above sea level, in the shadow of snow-clad Mt Kanchenjunga*, the world's third highest, Darjeeling was one of the popular hill stations established by the British and still very English in appearance, although much the worse for wear. Even now, in the neglect and broken windows, buildings bore signs of the backlash aimed at the British after they pulled out, but it was not difficult to visualise the opulence that once was. The land of **Sherpas**, the town itself was constructed in a series of steps, with only one small square, where colonials used to parade in the evening and which

* Known to the Sikkimese as Khangchendzonga, it is the guardian deity of the land, ensuring peace and prosperity, each of its five peaks crowned by an animal: tiger, lion, elephant, horse, and the mythological Garuda.

was, at that time, forbidden to Indians. I missed a wonderful opportunity in Darjeeling when – strolling along the **Maidan**, dressed in a suit, swinging a cane, and looking every inch the epitome of an English gentleman from the illustrious days of the Raj – I met a charming professor of music from a prestigious London academy, who offered for me to accompany him to an appointment with Tensing Norgay, sherpa to Hillary on his historic ascent of Everest, but sadly I could not spare the extra days before the meeting was scheduled to take place.

The railway track ran through the centre of town, between typically alpine buildings with steeply pitched roofs, decorative eaves around gables, and a few bay windows. I saw an authentic European clock tower and, amongst thick greenery at the Windamere Hotel (where I stayed), a traditional English garden, even to roses and tiger lilies, everything dripping moisture from the mist and rain. There was a little spired church hugging the side of a hill but views were obliterated by thick fog, although this had a beauty all its own as it nestled in the densely forested valleys. A crowd of spectators was watching a football game at an oval that appeared on the verge of oblivion. It was raining quite heavily as I approached a Hindu temple, where a white ox sat in an enclosure out front, colourful prayer flags hung limply, and a red-robed monk, surrounded by offerings and ringing a small bell, was seated beneath an umbrella. A poorer area had dilapidated stores, ramshackle wooden huts with washing hanging outside, chickens ranging in the wet street, and a youth herding cows.

Wearing the maroon robes of a Tibetan holy man, a monk was turning a row of large prayer cylinders (*chhosko*) at the colourful **Ghoom Buddhist Monastery** situated at 2,438m. The wheels send prayers to heaven according to the number within multiplied by the number of revolutions. Wearing a fan-shaped hat, a second monk produced a long alpine horn, its eerie sounds resonating in the still air. Metal lions reminiscent of China guarded the entrance, and the mist-shrouded temple was barely visible through the elaborately carved gateway, lending a ghostly aura to the scene.

Cauliflowers were arrayed on the footpath right beside the train line, people stood outside a small ornate shrine almost overtaken by its verdant surrounds, monks congregated on a balcony, and a lady seated on her doorstep beside the railway track was picking impurities from grain spread on a large platter balanced on her knees. Forming attractive pictures, isolated houses were perched at the tops of old overgrown terraces, with fronds of tall grass like sugarcane in the foreground. I caught the bus out on a foggy morning when it was impossible to see more than a few feet past the window. In what was to become a familiar sight, clamorous vendors crowded around the vehicle whenever we stopped.

INDIA

Simla

From back where I started, in Delhi, I went to the hill station of Simla, capital of **Himachal Pradesh**, and the lesser-known places of pilgrimage, Hardwar and Rishikesh. My route passed through the uninteresting city of **Chandigarh**, built purely as the capital of **Punjab** and **Haryana** states by a team coordinated by Le Corbusier.

The first sight encountered on the streets of **Simla** was a bent figure stirring the milky contents of a huge wok over an open fire. A glass cabinet contained the finished product of his labours, and a couple of gaily dressed smiling women seated on the ground in front of a stone wall were cooking corn on the cob over makeshift burners, which they fanned in unison with pieces of cardboard. Another was toting an enormous bundle on her head, and I saw many bicycles. A monkey scampering in front of a statue on a pedestal was the only pedestrian in a deserted side street. It was in one such street here that I had a brief skirmish with monkeys until rescued by a passer-by.

Featuring the same photogenic wooden shophouses, Simla also had a church with a square Norman bell tower, a half-timbered edifice, and some attractive colonial buildings, but it had its share of tumbledown structures as well. Again, a steeply stepped town, it overlooked similar mist-filled valleys to Darjeeling.

Kulu and Manali

Continuing my trip, I headed for Kulu and Manali in the Valley of the Gods, from where one can also access Leh. The long journey was made by bus, in which three people were crammed onto hard wooden seats designed for two, and almost as much was loaded on top as inside. The cabs were always decorated with an amazing assortment of plastic flowers, pictures, beads, ornaments, and/or religious objects and images, and it was disconcerting to observe drivers clasp their hands in prayer before commencing the journey! I remember being the object of much interest amongst the peasant people because I was a woman travelling alone, but their suspicion and reserve soon broke down, and I found it hard work when the elderly man I was seated next to tried to communicate. A short break in a mountain village revealed rakish and rickety structures, donkeys, and a man cooking *chapattis* in a clay oven. In stark contrast, seated on colourful cane chairs placed beneath a shady tree on the wide expanse of lawn in front of a mansion, a group was partaking of liquid refreshment.

Stopping for breakfast, I was invited by a fellow traveller, an Indian who spoke English, to accompany him to a street stall, its utensils blackened by flames, where I was introduced to fresh yoghurt and have enjoyed it ever since. At one stage, we halted at a red shrine with a lion painted on the façade, which everyone trooped off to visit, coming back with popcorn. Some of this was offered to me by my elderly travelling companion – from very dirty hands! Following the course of a wide, often boulder-strewn river fed by rushing streams and waterfalls, we drove through verdant mountains with lush undergrowth. We went through many small communities, stopping in one where I observed metal pans over an adobe fireplace with a pile of wood to one side, a lady winding wool from a spinning wheel, and cattle by the river. On the road again, we passed a huge herd of white goats and ladies in tribal dress, babes slung on their backs. Reaching our destination, fascinating **Kulu** (4,000ft), busy streets produced people selling food freshly prepared over cooking fires in drums, vegetables and fruits such as cabbages, onions and apples on rough stalls, chunks of coconut and other delicacies heaped for sale, roles of matting, and a host of interesting faces. Holding the hands of two small children, one lady was adorned with a gold nose stud and many earrings, well before the days of body piercing gaining popularity.

Underway again, we climbed still higher above the raging river, past crude wooden shacks, a solitary spotted goat (with three white legs and one brown!), and a flimsy suspension bridge. At 2,200m (6,000ft) in the lower reaches of the **Himalayas, Manali** was situated above the thundering **Beas River**, with a few houses built right into the hillside, prayer flags winding their way to the summit, and a white temple partially hidden in thick greenery. Not as easily accessible as other mountain retreats, I found I was the only tourist. Stooped figures swept the streets with brush brooms, and monks joined the shoppers around vegetables displayed in boxes on the ground. Women wore traditional dress, whilst the men were clothed in more conventional shirts and trousers but with the addition of an embroidered cap, and sometimes a shawl. Donkeys roamed the thoroughfares, horses were being herded across a wooden bridge, a woman cooked in the open, another squatted with utensils besides running water in the street, and a young lady stood combing her long black tresses whilst the rest of the family group enjoyed the sunshine; it had all the ingredients of a shabby mountain town overwhelmed by surroundings of incredible beauty.

A line of donkeys wended a zigzag path down a mountainside on the opposite bank of the turbulent river, and breathtaking scenes incorporating snowy ridges against a blue sky were framed between lower peaks with cloud on top. Looming behind massed boulders, dense stands of pine and cedar lined the banks of the blue river, the rocks in its bed creating whitecaps and small cascades. Overhanging rocky slopes, a long timber structure with carved ornamentation and latticework windows in a gallery, clung precariously to the mountainside. I observed stone fences and many large wooden or stone dwellings with slate roofs and covered wooden balconies running around the upper level, beneath which animals sheltered and abundant fodder was stored.

I came across sacred baths, an arch with script in Hindi and an image on top, a residence with elegant carved pillars and eaves, others with fine fretwork and carved window screens, and cows in the street. A *sadhu* with the mark of Vishnu on his forehead, a long white beard, and dressed in white, toted a metal container, a pile of kindling was stacked for fuel, and wonderful vistas of towering green slopes appeared through every gap in the buildings. A couple was spreading grass on a roof to dry and others distributed it around their courtyards. A young girl carried her sister on her back, smoke issued from a chimney, people washed clothes at the edge of a well, small children (one with a bare bottom!) used sticks to drive cows down steps and along flagged pathways, and women were washing utensils and collecting water from other communal wells; one bathed a baby. I saw a lady (wearing many bracelets, her ears completely covered in rings, and a large one through her nose – like a bull!) dousing the backside of a girl wearing only a shirt. People mounted the steps to a three-storey pagoda-like structure and rung a bell at the entry, a man smoked a *hookah* in the doorway of his shop, a cobbler worked next door, and three delightful children had the red caste mark* on their foreheads. I noticed a group of women donned in different-coloured headscarves squatting on the pavement (one smoking), a second temple with colourful prayer flags fluttering and, beside a food cart, a bearded and barefoot red-turbaned figure dressed in a short red sarong and carrying a gleaming brass pot. I photographed women washing their hair or doing laundry by the banks of the broiling river and placing the articles on boulders to dry. There was always a friendly smile

* Still prevalent in rural India, beneath the four main castes are the Dalits (formerly Untouchables), and it is from a Tamil Dalit group, the Paraiyars, that we get our word 'pariah'.

as people went about their various activities in the clear mountain air on a sunny (though chilly) day.

It was on a night portion of this excursion that, knowing the unseen horrendous conditions of the 'highway' we were travelling, I experienced the incident mentioned in the Calcutta section. On this particular bus, I was seated on the outside of the front seat, and tired from continually bracing my arms to prevent being flung to the floor as we negotiated the constant hairpin bends, I placed my foot on the engine cowling, whereby the driver immediately stopped the vehicle and refused to proceed any further until I removed it. In spite of the fact that the buses were exceedingly filthy – from refuse, people spitting or vomiting and, I am sure, even urinating – this object was sacrosanct!

Hardwar and Rishikesh

I returned to Delhi via the holy towns of **Hardwar** and **Rishikesh**, where temples with beehive-shaped towers, some highly carved, and one shining silver dome stood along the shores of the river. Here also were bathing *ghats* like those of the Ganges at Varanasi. A promenade extending into the water accommodated a clock tower, many sunshades, saris spread to dry, and people lining steps each side. Standing proudly with his formally attired son, I filmed a man dressed only in a long red loincloth and toting a white bag over one shoulder. There was a lot of activity in these busy places, with figures from saffron-robed *sadhus* to beggars wandering the streets. Crowds were bathing, and there were many bicycles, rickshaws, pony traps, and carts drawn by bullocks. Hardwar was a holy place full of temples, shrines, ashrams and dharamshalas; it was to Rishikesh that the Beatles came to practice transcendental meditation and also where *yoga* was born. Along the way, I saw a flock of vultures feasting on prey, and cattle resting in the compound of a group of houses. Two youths drew water from a deep well in the yard, and a *charpoy* sat under the overhang, supported by tree trunks, of a grass-thatched roof.

INDIA 1983

Between the years of 1977 and 1997 inclusive, I visited India a total of eleven times, nine as tour leader on my own successful programmes, but only a few are described (briefly) in this book. I returned in 2010 for the last time.

Delhi and Agra

In 1983, I led a tour to the subcontinent that began in **Delhi**. A scene that epitomises India: ladies in colourful saris, tiered brass pots on their heads, drawing water from a well was our first encounter, succeeded by men in white *dhotis* and turbans driving laden camel carts, and vultures in a field en route to Agra. We stopped at a village consisting of crude thatched shelters, under one of which an old man sat on a rickety *charpoy* (litter), and a beautiful young woman nursed a pensive wistful-looking child. Following our first glimpse of the gleaming **Taj Mahal** from across the **Jumna River**, we entered via the massive red and white gateway, the silhouetted arch of which provided a perfect black frame for the white monument. A beautiful image was also captured in its reflective pool lined with pine trees set in green lawns. Even after many visits, the embossed and inlaid marble never failed to impress me, but it was the red sandstone entrance to the tomb that took my eye, because not lauded as much, it was therefore surprising. Arabic script around the perimeter increased in size towards the top so as to be read from below.

Beneath eaves of Agra's **Red Fort**, heavy but intricately sculpted stone brackets were also outstanding, and these, together with its mighty bastions, delicate cupolas, and the scalloped arches in the multi-pillared **Audience Hall**, resulted in a triumph of Mogul architecture. At Kohinoor Jewellers in Agra, one could view a fabulous three-dimensional work embroidered with silk threads. Called *The Legend*, it depicted 24 wildlife scenes.

Precocious monkeys frequented 16th-century **Humayun's Tomb** in Delhi, which also displayed exquisite decoration on sandstone façades and was said to possibly be the inspiration for the later Taj. It was Humayun who originally presented the Koh-i-Noor diamond to the Persian Emperor, in order to raise an army against the Afghan, Sher Shah Suri, to whom he had lost his kingdom.

Kashmir

Then it was on to mystical **Kashmir** and the serene ambience of **Dal Lake**. Ringed by mountains and trees, amongst them many poplars, its renowned houseboats were reflected on a surface broken only by early morning flower sellers as they gently paddled *shikaras* filled with bright blooms, which included numerous long-stemmed gladioli in various hues. Here, one could almost commune with the gods, but onshore, the dusty streets of **Srinagar** city with their congestion and noise were an unwelcome antithesis. With a mostly Muslim population, women wore the black signifying *purdah*, but I think it was more to counteract the dirty conditions than any sense of piety! Handcarts trundled before open-fronted wooden shops vied with sedate cows, trishaws, bicycles, pedestrians, and the occasional car for space in the centre of thoroughfares. In front of a store selling melons, a vendor squatted at the roadside with a basket of produce, a man with bags of spices sat cross-legged beside him, and a barrow of fruits was shaded by an umbrella, but meat hung in the open.

On a tour through **Tangmarg** to **Gulmarg** (2,653m), I have pictures of a lovely fenced garden featuring roses, hollyhocks and an old-fashioned lamp in spacious lawns set with tables and chairs. Arriving at our destination, nestled in a valley encased by stunning mountain peaks of the **Pir Panjal** range, menacing **Nanga Parbat** (Naked Mountain, at 26,000ft the world's fifth highest) was to the north. Known as the Meadow of Flowers, in summer the grassy slopes of this hill town are transformed into expanses of colour by a profusion of wildflowers: bluebells, violets, daisies, forget-me-nots and golden buttercups. A ski resort in winter, it is also home to the highest green golf course in the world. In an attempt to counteract speed (as if such a thing was possible on India's congested roads!), the route to Gulmarg was lined with original slogans including: *If you are married to speed divorce her* and *Slow down there is no room in heaven.*

The following day, we embarked on a 96km trip past saffron fields (at that time bare) to **Pahalgam**. It is no wonder that genuine saffron is so expensive, it takes the filaments of 120 to 140 crocus blooms to obtain a single gram, or 75,000 flowers to make one pound! We stopped to photograph the beautiful blue **Lidder River**, burbling over its rocky bed in the **Lidder Valley**, and ate a picnic lunch in cool and inviting surroundings, where we observed groups of colourful gypsy people, accompanied by laden mountain ponies and dogs, bringing their sheep and goats to pasture at a lower level for the winter. Dense pine forests lined the banks, and high hills reared in every direction. Once a shepherd's village, at 2,134m (7,200ft) Pahalgam was lower than Gulmarg. As we continued to follow the rushing river, the fir-covered mountains seemed to become closer and higher. Patches of snow still adorned summits that, as we drew nearer, provided superb views of green valleys with the river running its twisting course along the bottom. Descending to the valley floor and crossing this waterway, lush pastures and forested slopes enclosed us on either side, the latter framing mountains with snow in crevices and topped by banks of white cloud in an otherwise blue firmament. Later, I saw men riding sturdy little mountain ponies along a stony riverbed between verdant green slopes with considerably more snow beyond.

Back in Srinagar, I have pictures of a gorgeous blue kingfisher on our houseboat, an eagle on a post in the water, a man with an enormous snake around his neck, and another selling peacock feather fans. My final film of the lake shows a cluster of flower sellers mirrored on the surface as they sat in their *shikaras*. A trip past the houseboats and along narrow waterways revealed ramshackle wooden shops on piles over the water, with goods from clothes to cans of soft drink displayed out front. A poignant sight was that of two dejected-looking sheep standing forlornly in a *shikara* moored in front of a butcher's shop, their fate dictated by carcasses hanging outside – a Mogul Arts 'Emporium' next door! We passed people paddling their small craft, ducks and hens in the grounds of old multistorey farmhouses onshore, floating gardens, massed pink water lilies, and flourishing greenery. We drifted beneath picturesque wooden bridges, saw more brilliant blue kingfishers, and passed sets of steps where people were washing, their laundry pegged on lines strung from building to building. Some colour had been introduced on façades, ducks congregated in front of a tumbledown wooden shack on stone foundations, and a man fossicked in the water whilst children waved from a bank where washing was strung between trees. I have photographs of the spire of a mosque rearing above houses along the banks of the **Jhelum River**, which according to legend was born when Shiva prevailed upon his consort

Parvati to appear in that form. He thrust his trident into the earth and the water sprang forth.

My next film, taken in the legendary 17th-century **Mogul Gardens**, features a girl in a jewellery-adorned ethnic costume seated cross-legged on green grass in front of a magnificent display of red blooms, all of which served to accentuate the colours of her dress. In grassed areas bordered by huge trees, abundant small fountains played in large pools surrounded by colourful beds, whilst cloud hung lazily below the crests of mountain tops beyond. In **Shalimar**, a water channel with central fountains flowed to a still lake. Crossing the lake and reflected on its surface, a tree-lined causeway was connected in the middle by a small stone bridge. Here again were the chinar (plane) and willow trees set in manicured lawns graced with predominantly red flowers. Created in 1619 by Emperor Jahangir for his queen, Nur Jahan (Light of the World), it was extended in 1727 by Shah Jahan, of Taj fame. In yet another, the pathways to moated pavilions were edged with brilliant red salvia. Altogether there were four gardens: **Shalimar Bagh** (meaning Garden of Love, around 400 years old), **Nasim Bagh** (Garden of Cool Breezes), **Chashma Shami** (Royal Spring), the smallest, laid out by Jahangir and completed by Shah Jahan in 1632, and **Nishat Bagh** (Garden of Pleasure or Bliss, 1633). Designed by Asaf Khan, brother of Nur Jahan, this had 12 terraces representing the 12 signs of the zodiac and was planted with cedar and cypress.

Ladakh

Ethereal conditions persisted as we made our way in four-wheel-drive vehicles to **Leh**, capital of **Ladakh**. Beginning in **Ganderbal**, on the banks of the **Sindh River**, it was 46 miles to **Kangan** and the start of dramatic scenery. At this first stop, cloud as fine as mist hung low on the mountains as we wandered past ramshackle sidewalk stalls with meat hanging in the open and hopeful hungry dogs underfoot. Near **Sonamarg**, tucked between mountains up to 4,877m, we passed goatherds with a large flock of white goats that they were herding beside the Sindh. Magical scenes, which except for the weather could have been in the Swiss Alps, were comprised of dense afforestation (mostly pines) on steep cloud-draped slopes and wildly rushing water churned into foaming white rapids as it tumbled over boulders. Hill people were leading a horse, craggy summits speared through cotton wool clouds, and waterfalls from small pockets of snow cascaded down sides of mountains to green alpine valleys. Viewed from a height, raging rivers assumed the guise of streams, and wooden villages appeared like miniature models. We went through an isolated rural town with makeshift dwellings and stores, sturdy horses, and a milling population dressed in *pahrans* (long woollen cloaks) and hats. Climbing again, we came to a dirty glacier melting right beside the road and found ourselves amongst patches of hard-packed snow and the remains of ice, which in winter connected the mountains enabling people to cross, but was now thawing and creating bridges with boisterous water flowing underneath. Transcending the tree line, the awesome scenery defied imagination, and we encountered more glaciers, icy rivers, rugged ridges, and snowy crests. I always felt insignificant when dwarfed by the grandeur and immensity of God's creation in this region.

Crossing 3,645m (11,578ft) **Zoji La** (*la* means pass) and now well above the tree line, we were confronted by foreboding sheer rock walls, snowy peaks framed between closer summits, and a lively river emerging from beneath a glacial bridge. We were now a lot closer to the sparse snow, and the rugged barren mountains took on a strange aspect as windswept gravel formed skirts around their bases. Encompassed by creviced tors, wide stony fields were criss-crossed with rivulets like a web of tangled lines, only present when the snow was melting. The vast expanse was compelling in its solitude. Houses nestled amongst trees near some sections of the watercourse, and it was incredible to witness how these staunch, stoic and steadfast people could make the stark, desolate and desert-like terrain bloom. We descended to the **Drass Valley**, second coldest inhabited place on earth with temperatures falling to a record –58°C (–50°F), and continued on to **Kharbu** before arriving at **Kargil** (2,740m) in the **Suru Valley**. Here, we made our overnight stop in very basic accommodation, all that was available on the journey. Captured in 1531 by Sultan Saiyed of Kashgar, Kargil was famous for its apricots and mulberry trees. I found crumbling, occasionally whitewashed adobe houses (one with an upper level accessed by a rickety ladder), roofs weighted down with rocks, the dome and minaret of a mosque, a bridge across the now raging river, and a typical illustration promoting the ideal family of four for illiterate peasants – but absolutely no traffic.

Underway again next morning, gravel and granite mountains and walls of brown rock towering behind lighter-coloured contoured hills made a dramatic contrast to thick bands of trees lining the wide river on the valley floor and flat-roofed adobe houses amid a patchwork of fields, the whole appearing like a stage in some vast amphitheatre. We encountered one hilltop community with box-like multistorey houses, and a building amazingly (and seemingly precariously) perched atop the point of a pyramid-shaped peak with white houses and a *stupa* at the bottom. We came to secluded **Mulbeck Monastery** decorated in the maroon colour of the monks, its prayer flags barely moving in the still air, and a mammoth 8m-high relief of a **Maitreya** (Buddha) believed to be around 2,000 years old on a rock face behind. Our vehicles were a magnet in this little visited part of the planet, and I photographed some fascinating faces with bemused expressions: full of wonder at the strange apparitions in their midst. In an isolated rustic local teashop where we paused for refreshment, a man was wearing the traditional tall hat with turned-up wings on the brim. These peasant people were incredibly dirty, and I doubt they washed regularly, if at all!

We came to an area with columns of rock and interesting colour contrasts in the sand and stone; a yellow patch was highlighted by a burst of sunshine. Far below, a herd of sheep or goats appeared near a ribbon-like strip of water in arid terrain, not even one blade of grass visible to relieve the starkness. The environment was the closest to a moonscape imaginable, and one particular site projected the striking beauty of starkly etched ridges, created by light and shade, below massed grey and white cloud, the whole like a painted canvas. Passing the beacon on the highest point, **Fatu La** at 13,479ft, we came to **Lamayuru Monastery**, Ladakh's oldest, dating back to the tenth century. Situated on and amongst rocky outcrops riddled with caves, it was cocooned by brooding mountains. This *gompa* was richly furnished with carpets, Tibetan tables, *thankas*, and tiny permanently lit lamps. A figure was ushering donkeys into a stone enclosure underneath a dwelling amongst a cluster with brush on the roofs, an old grey-haired lady in the ubiquitous shaggy goatskin shawl was eating the remainder of one of our boxed lunches, and long poles bearing prayer flags were erected next to a tall *stupa*. Buddhists believe wind carries the prayers to gods. From an elevated position, we looked down on items stored or drying on flat roofs. Incredible rock formations formed the basis of wonderful, almost unreal pictures, and a lady knelt beside an icy stream to wash her hair whilst her naked child splashed nearby. Another woman walked past with a load of greens in a huge basket on her back. In the distance, behind stark black ridges, startling snow-capped mountains made an appearance beneath fluffy white cloud in an intense blue sky.

Leh itself was a very ancient city, with crumbling buildings and a populace in ethnic dress. A man was skinning and butchering meat hanging in a grove of trees behind a white stone fence, and traditionally attired ladies sat on the pavement with surprisingly fresh vegetables for sale, which they weighed on handheld scales. An old man (I am sure the same one that I photographed the previous year!) sat on steps absorbed in the pursuit of spinning his prayer wheel, and the dominating palace loomed above narrow arched alleyways.

Monks in saffron robes conversed on the sidewalk, and donkeys were the main means of conveyance. Colourful garments hanging outside shops provided a stark contrast to the drab surroundings, and one lady, a sequined shawl covering her head, was industriously spinning wool by hand. At her side, glass bottles containing what I assumed was fuel were for sale, and a man with long grey hair, beard, and moustache was carrying a bundle of greens. I was lucky to observe the old-style headdress called a *perak*, its long 'tail' encrusted with large lumps of crude turquoise, the number of stones indicative of the wearer's wealth. Numerous prayer flags and white *stupas*, many with red spires, were scattered around. A wonderful stone-walled alley had a *stupa* on top of its ancient log-beamed mud vault. Rather than bartering, many years ago I learnt from one of my clients the art of trading. In a hilarious pantomime in Leh, she stood in a marketplace, her arms extended up the legs of a pair of tights whilst extolling their warmth and virtues to a male stallholder, who queried if men wore such things. With a perfectly straight face, she assured in the affirmative, and acquired a leather cap with fur earmuffs in exchange!

We visited the *gompas* described in the preceding chapter, and the village of **Tikse** was an awesome sight, its white buildings ascending the slopes of a dun-coloured mountain to the monastery on top, which was outlined against a deep blue cloudless heaven. Halfway up a bare cliff face, a huge painting decorated the rear wall of a recess housing a white structure. The terrors of the road journey I have described in the 1985 chapter on India.

We flew back to Delhi over the snowbound craters and crevices of the Himalayas, with black ridges peeping through and for once no cloud cover. As we approached the capital, a brilliant blue lake bordered by sheer mountains appeared, a sight only visible from the air. Our trip concluded with more of the marvellous Mogul architecture and a market in the city.

TAHITI, SOUTH AMERICA & EASTER ISLAND 1983

TAHITI

My nine-week journey began with a stopover in **Tahiti**, made famous by Paul Gauguin. From the plane I obtained my first look at **Moorea**, the absolute epitome of a tropical island, which I have not found before or since. Spectacular jagged green mountains, sheathed by cloud, erupted from a circle of aqua sea that was divided from the deeper-blue ocean by a ring of white surf crashing over the encompassing reef. In Tahiti, the main town of **Papeete** was a nondescript settlement, but yachts lining the bay, with Moorea in the background, provided pleasing pictures. My first priority was a 12-mile trip by ferry, over a choppy brown sea, to this neighbouring island. Looking back at Papeete from the boat, a couple of clock towers rose above the low buildings, a large vessel was moored in the harbour, a few houses mounted green hillsides, and a small plane was performing aerobatics.

Approaching the still shrouded mountaintops of Moorea, I could see rustic shacks amongst a thick fringe of palm trees along the shoreline, the mountains providing a verdant backdrop. We docked in a bay enclosed by these fantastic peaks, and finding that there was no transport, I was advised to go to the resort from where daily tours of the island were conducted. Attired in a bikini, matching top and long skirt with platform-soled shoes, I set out to walk. Climbing rapidly, I nevertheless appreciated the views, through stately palms, of a yacht anchored in a glorious blue lagoon ringed by a narrow strip of white beach and another at the end of a long jetty leading to thatched huts over the water. Sparsely populated, a few small houses materialised in bucolic settings of green valleys at the foot of rugged green ranges, now clear of cloud but still under an overcast sky. Banana plants and tall palm trees grew at the base of emerald green slopes descending almost vertically from knife-sharp creviced ridges.

Although hot and hard going, I was thoroughly enjoying the walk, but minutes were ticking by and I did not know how far away the resort was situated so I decided, for the first time in my life, to thumb a lift. There was very little traffic and I was disillusioned when the few cars passed me by – an indication of my age! However, eventually an almost toothless local man in a beat-up utility offered me a ride, which was just as well because I never would have made the distance to the hotel on foot. Arriving at the resort, I requested to be dropped off at the gate, but he insisted on proudly driving his foreign visitor right to the door. Embarrassed, hot and flustered, I entered the reception to enquire about a tour, which I was informed was not running that day but was available from another guesthouse. Sympathetic to my obvious distress, the thoughtful manager provided me with towels and told me to have a swim in the pool before transporting me to the alternate venue for a tour, which proved to be one of the most beautiful that I have ever undertaken. Nestled in the lee of mountains and opposite a white beach, the pool had a curtain of water at one end and thatched pavilions along one side; girls with large multihued wreaths of tropical flowers on their heads served drinks and snacks.

We travelled in an open charabanc-type vehicle, past graceful leaning palms, bright red bougainvillea, and secluded idyllic blue bays encompassed by mountains with many peaks. At the end of a dirt track bordered by tall palm trees, a lone tor stood like a solitary sentinel, its top piercing dark brooding cloud above. Several coves were enclosed by mountains falling sheer to the water, and in a stiff wind, palm fronds were blowing like banners. James Cook had an association with this island, which was also where scenes from the movie *South Pacific* were filmed. The thick vegetation was a showcase for the gorgeous red and yellow heliconia, frangipani and other exotic flowers, including one that was a mass of waxy-looking glossy red blossoms. Coming to another bay, peaks were visible through a forest of palms; I am at a loss for words to describe the exceptional beauty of this island and have yet to find its equal.

Moorea

With Paradis Tours, I did a Circle Island Tour of Tahiti, which included views of what was referred to as an upside-down hotel: reception was at the top of a hill, its rooms on floors that descended in steps towards the reef at the bottom. From here, I could see the heavy swell and waves pounding a green coastline, and we discovered a strange crab. We stopped at the homestead of James Norman Hall, author of *Mutiny on the Bounty* and other South Pacific novels, **One Tree Hill**, named by Cook, **Point Venus**, where he, Wallis and Bougainville landed in 1769, and the **Blowhole**, where the sea erupted through black lava rock with each surge of the waves. In complete contrast, we drove to the **Botanical Gardens** and **Gauguin's Museum**, passing emerald mountains with high but narrow waterfalls cascading down jungle-clad ravines, colourful crotons amongst palm trees, verdant growth in the foreground, and quiet inlets with low-lying cloud. The picturesque gardens featured ponds covered with pink water lilies, large-leaved philodendrons, exquisite pink and red ginger bracts, a cluster of dainty pink-tipped white flowers, several varieties of the magnificent heliconia, ferns climbing the trunks of trees, double pink hibiscus, delicate white iris with the appearance of orchids, other tropical flowers, including tiny blossoms creating a pyramid of pink, and of course palms. Completing the circuit, we passed rivers, more roadside crotons introducing colour into the green surroundings, and an extremely high but fine perpendicular waterfall. From the window of my room, I looked out at a tropical garden (featuring heliconias) to the sea beyond. Surrounded by white wooden lounge chairs and reflecting overhanging palms, the pool was right beside the ocean, with mountains in the background.

SOUTH AMERICA

In spite of extensive travelling completed since, South America remains a highlight because of its incredible bounty of diverse and outstanding attractions.

CHILE

There is a saying in Chile that when God created the world he had a handful of mountains, deserts, lakes, and glaciers left over, which he put in his pocket, but as he walked across heaven they all trickled out through a hole, and the long trail they made on earth was Chile.

Santiago

As distinct from the tropical paradise of Tahiti, on the flight to **Santiago**, capital of **Chile**, I observed the snow-capped **Andes** in the far distance. Taking an orientation walk from El Hotel de Don Tito, the first sight I encountered was a beautiful **Neptune Fountain** in front of the white sculpted dome, fluted Ionic columns, arches, and balustrades of an edifice set amid landscaped terraces and stone stairways on 230ft **Cerro** (hill) **Santa Lucia**, where the foundation of the city took place in 1541. From the top, I obtained wonderful views of the centre: square towers of modern high-rise blocks behind classical structures, and traffic like toy vehicles below. In other directions, the Andes formed the background to a church spire towering above buildings whilst, closer to hand, another church steeple loomed in front of a space needle amongst skyscrapers beyond. Also on the hill, a red brick fortress-like construction had a sculpted coat of arms above the arched entrance, crenellated walls and towers, and an old-style streetlamp in front. Everything was set in beautiful surrounds, with fountains, graceful drooping trees, palms, potted plants, and trailing creepers cascading down walls.

Walking around the perimeter, I found a statue encompassed by greenery atop a stone grotto with the white spire of a church rearing into a cloudless blue sky behind. An equestrian statue stood in a leafy plaza fronting a grey stone façade and adjacent stepped white tower, both with clocks – reading different times! Diagonally opposite, next to an all glass façade, were the twin towers of a church with a large image, one arm raised, above the entry and a statue on a pedestal in the forecourt. Further along, the plaza featured lawns with a small pond and a variety of trees. Passing an edifice with symmetrical square towers, round windows, and figures on the parapet, I came to an iron bridge along which stallholders, their produce shaded by umbrellas, were selling everything from fresh fruits and vegetables to large live crabs. My final picture was of yet another church, with twin spires and a rose window.

BOLIVIA

Despite its mineral wealth, Bolivia was the poorest country in South America.

La Paz

Flying alongside the Andes, the land became progressively more barren, the winding route of a ribbon of road appearing like a black snake twisting across a dry yellow plateau. The city of **La Paz**, at 3,632m (12,300ft) the world's highest capital, was nestled in a bowl-shaped crater.

Early next morning, I left on a tour to Tiahuanaco, passing through a quiet Indian town of virtually one street. An attractive church with a dome and symmetrical belfries, each with three bells, faced a large empty square containing only a monument and two Indian women in traditional dress sitting on a low wall. Many more of these ladies, in hard brown bowler hats, several layers of brightly coloured voluminous *polleras* (skirts), and knitted shawls were seated on the sand in an open market place, some with babies in striped multihued blankets on their backs. Amongst produce arrayed for sale on straw mats, I saw large red tomatoes, onions still retaining their green tops, bananas and eggs, with the usual handheld scales in evidence. I believe that there was also a market where remedies for various ailments could be bought from a witchdoctor. Donkeys stood outside a crude adobe hut roofed with corrugated iron, and I encountered a man ploughing with a team of oxen and a lady twirling a rope to herd sheep.

Tiahuanaco

Arriving at **Tiahuanaco**, I was made aware of one big advantage in travelling alone – I was the only one there! This added to the spellbinding aura of this mysterious venue. Centre of the pre-Inca **Aymara** civilisation, it dated back to 1580 BC, and flourished around AD 700 with a population of over 100,000, making it one of the biggest cities in the world at that time. Little remains today, but it is believed to be the oldest site in the Western Hemisphere, and some estimates put the ruins as far back as 10,000 BC. Discovered by the **Incas** about AD 1200, there were remnants of aqueducts and temples, but most awesome was the **Sun Door** bearing embossed Aztec-like figures and esoteric inscriptions, which have been interpreted to mean that the long-vanished people intended to return.

Sun Door

I saw a couple of large stone images and stellae in a court surrounded by low walls bearing sculpted heads; it projected quite an eerie ambience. Lying at 13,000ft on the **Bolivian Antiplano**, Tiahuanaco ranks amongst the world's great archaeological sites. On the return drive to La Paz, I observed men and women, the latter with bundles on their backs, trailing laden donkeys across the trackless waste of yellow sand, with only isolated telegraph poles and a group of thatched adobe cottages to break the monotony.

La Paz

From the window of my room, I had a view of the unique yellow stone lunar landscape on the outskirts of the city that was, in fact, called **Valley of the Moon**, and which I was later taken to see. Consisting of a vast collection of weird volcanic formations and needle-like pinnacles, it exhibited a dramatic contrast in colour to its immediate surroundings. Unfortunately, due to climbing directly from sea level to such a height, I contracted my second bout of acute altitude sickness, from which I did not recover until I descended three weeks later. It seriously curtailed my activities at Machu Picchu, and I suffered the most diabolical constant headache that I have ever endured, literally standing on my head in an endeavour to alleviate the excruciating pain. Photographs around the city included people in colourful clothing (some toting large loads of merchandise), old vehicles, wide paved squares, the twin steeples of 16th-century **San Francisco Church** on **Plaza Venezuela**, steep cobbled streets, stalls beneath crude shelters on pavements, **Casa el Turista** next to a none-too-hygienic-looking Clinica Dental – and guinea pigs rotating on a rotisserie, which I was too shocked to film! The majority of buildings were ugly, but one square was lined with ornate façades that included a bell tower. **Plaza Murillo**, with white statues on pedestals around the perimeter, housed the huge domed **Cathedral**. A monument occupied a grassy circle in front, and always the mountains loomed behind.

Lake Titicaca

Under cloudy skies, I commenced a two-day journey to **Cuzco** with a guide. We drove past a few cattle, cottages and crops to reed-rimmed **Lake Titicaca**, at 3,810 (12,664ft), the world's highest navigable lake, containing 36 islands. From the village of **Huatajata**, we crossed by launch to **Suriqui Island**, with a few scattered houses, scant trees, and a couple of llamas, and where, still making reed boats, I felt privileged to meet the man who had constructed Thor Heyerdahl's **Kon Tiki** raft.

Again travelling by road, we went to 17th-century **Copacabana**, a far cry from that in Brazil but nevertheless making a great picture situated on the edge of the lake at the foot of a pyramid-shaped mountain. Interesting light-hued buildings with towers, domes and cupolas surrounded checked paving, and there was a large Indian population because of a famous shrine containing a statue of the Virgin said to have miraculous powers. An ancient brownstone church with a dome and square bell tower had a simple small stone cross atop the modestly engraved rounded gable above the portal, and the roof and square tower of an asymmetrical church were topped with tiny spires. Plain buildings were fronted by a paved square with trimmed trees in small fenced gardens: oases of green in barren surrounds.

Setting out once more, we passed black and white alpacas grazing on sparse fodder and headed for the lake, where I saw a large flock of pink flamingos. A visit to the villages of **Pomata** and **Juli** revealed nondescript housing in streets with few cars and devoid of people. Twin bell towers graced an old church with carved images above the door, and a statue, the right arm outstretched, was just visible above and beyond tiled rooftops.

After spending the night in **Puno**, next day saw a visit by boat to the **Uros Indians**, thought to be direct descendants of the **Aztecs**, living on their fascinating floating islands literally built from the strong *totora* reeds that grew all around the lake. Houses and boats were also made from this medium, and the islands were spongy and soggy to walk on; continually sinking, it was necessary to constantly add more rushes to 'top them up'. The people also ate the tuberous roots. Such primitive damp living conditions were obviously unhealthy because I saw many snotty-nosed children, but the self-sufficiency of these people was amazing. The huts had sagging roofs, also constructed from reeds, and fresh sheaves were stacked everywhere. I saw people poling boats, many craft anchored to the shore, utensils outside doorways, a woman washing items in a tub, fish and blue crabs spread to dry (on reeds!), ladies creating embroidered articles for sale, and a reed church with a lopsided small wooden cross on the roof; in fact, many structures displayed a lean on this soft surface with rushes underfoot. Leaning from a boat, one person was cutting more reeds, and these craft were also used to ferry animals to small uninhabited islands to browse. The women always wore their long black hair braided, and amongst a group sitting in a wooden vessel used to transfer people and goods to and from the mainland, I saw one wearing an elaborate headdress. Forced from

Lake Titicaca

their traditional lands by the Incas, the Indians took to the lake to escape persecution and land taxes.

Sillustani

My next destination was the *chullpas* (tombs) at the archaeological site of **Sillustani**, located on a peninsula jutting into **Lake Umayo**. Situated on the lakeshore under dramatic dark skies with rolling cloud, and again deserted, the area was dotted with pre-Inca stone towers, a few foundations, and crumbling walls, but my biggest thrill was being able to pick up shards of ancient decorated pottery, which I doubt would be permitted, if indeed still in evidence, at any other historical location in the world. Created from rough stones, one interesting circular structure had a tiny low doorway and corbelled roof, and I noted a larger square building, cairns, and a couple of pitted towers, once rendered white. Obviously restored, a complete tower with a rounded top was constructed from large slabs of stone; it was all very atmospheric. We drove through dry rocky terrain in which it would seem impossible to produce anything; however, clusters of farm buildings with low stone walls appeared intermittently.

PERU

Columbus heard rumours about the fabulous wealth of a mysterious **Inca Empire**, the most powerful in the Americas, when he landed in the New World, but it took the Spaniard Francisco Pizarro to conquer it, subjugate its people, and create the brightest jewel in the crown of Spain.

Cuzco

Continuing on, next morning I caught the train for the long trip to Cuzco across the snow-swept **Antiplano**, bounded by glaciers and snowy mountains sometimes half hidden in scudding cloud. Many Indians sold handcrafts on stations and even boarded the train. Beautiful fur rugs featuring pictures created with pelts of different shades caught my eye, one depicting a grazing animal in front of a man seated on a block of wood to play a flute. For the princely sum of three dollars, I could not resist purchasing the fluffiest, softest pair of white slippers made from the coat of a baby llama. The people weave clothes from their wool, eat the meat, burn the dried dung for fuel, and use the animals for transport. The environment was one of stone and stubble with a few isolated houses amid scant trees, and we passed a huge colourful local market in open space beside the tracks. Villages consisted of once white houses behind high walls with tile coping, which lined narrow dirt streets with stone drains full of dirty water down the middle. One featured the attractive remains of an ancient arched stone bridge.

In **Cuzco** (at 3,310m), said to be the oldest permanently inhabited city in the Western Hemisphere, I had a convenient room in the lovely Hostal Corihuasi just off the main square, **Plaza de Armas**. An 18th-century house built on Inca terraces, it featured original colonial furniture and paintings, flowering plants in pots on a stepped stone wall, and stairs leading to a tiny courtyard. From an elevated position, I looked out across rooftops and watched a man leading a donkey with loaded panniers as they wended their way up the steep steps of a cobbled street. On arrival, I was given an infusion of coca leaves from which cocaine is made, but it served no purpose because it did not relieve my headache. It is estimated that income from coca equals that derived from legal export of tin, natural gas, petroleum, silver and zinc combined.

Pisac

Early next morning, I departed for a full day of sightseeing beginning with the huge weekly Indian market at **Pisac**. We passed a small river flowing below barren cloud-topped peaks, with a solitary swathe of green between the water and rocky terrain on the near side. Approaching Pisac, cocooned in a cradle of mountains, we halted for the view from a height showing the town spread out below, lines of cultivated conifers, and fields in a checked patchwork made up of different greens and browns. Blue and red awnings in a large central compound marked the location of the day's activities. The comparatively clean cobbled streets, lined with the now familiar white walls and red barrel-tiled roofs, were deserted because almost the entire populace attended the market, but I came across bakers removing the flat round bread, with the aid of long-handled paddles, from a huge clay oven under a roofed section of courtyard with a hand-pumped well in front. Facing a stone cross was a simple white adobe church with a bell tower.

the baker

Moving amongst the throng at the colourful crowded market, I discovered more of the fur rugs (this time worked with designs and llamas), utensils, food stalls, gay garments hanging on walls, bowler-hatted mothers with the numerous skirts and babes or purchases in stripped blankets on their backs, dogs, and vendors, many wearing white hats, sitting on the cobbles selling vegetables, which included the onions with tops, greens, carrots, and heaps of chillies spread on cloth. A few wore traditional ornate headdresses that resembled a fringed lampshade, and although most were reluctant to be photographed, one smiling lady with pink, maroon and white flowers atop a wide-brimmed hat was happy to oblige. A procession to Mass included mayors from surrounding villages, a few of whom I captured after the service. Carrying symbols of office, these were dressed in intricately woven *ponchos*, their heads covered with embroidered caps topped by hats like large upturned bowls strapped under the chin. A flowering tree overhung one wall, and mountains loomed directly behind some of the houses.

the market

Ollantaytambo

Leaving here, I was taken to an impressive site of Inca excavations above the canyon of the **Urubamba River**, near the town of **Ollantaytambo**. Here, gigantic irregularly shaped boulders of an ancient fortress were fitted so closely together that even a knife blade could not be inserted between them. With green fields below and cloud-draped creviced mountains opposite, it was particularly inspiring. Other remains included buildings and walls constructed with smaller stones, and the venue overlooked farmhouses and a couple of crude circular structures, also built of stone, for which I have no explanation. In the not-so-tidy town, I saw a house built onto the face of a mountain, vendor tables in a wide thoroughfare, a man staggering under the load of greenery on his back, and narrow cobbled streets in the shadow of the brooding range.

Cuzco

Back in Cuzco, the massive **Cathedral** facing Plaza de Armas featured twin towers, a dome, many small spires, and the **Capilla del Triunfo**, its symmetrical belfries each containing three bells. Begun in 1560 but not completed until 1654, the cathedral was constructed of stones culled from the destroyed palace of the Inca ruler, Viracocha, which originally occupied the site. In an effort to desecrate the Inca religion, the Spaniards also employed stone from the holy site of Sacsahuaman and even used the very sand spread on the plaza in mortar because it was considered sacred. The cathedral contained the **Great Monstrance**, a jewelled masterpiece of pearls and emeralds, and a painting of an Indian-looking Christ with his apostles – dining on guinea pig at the Last Supper! Judas had the face of the conquistador Pizarro, who began life as the illegitimate poorly educated son of a minor noble.

Over two miles in elevation, Cuzco was the fabled gold-laden capital of the Inca world more than 500 years ago but was razed in 1533 by Pizarro's Spanish conquistadors in search of its treasure. In temples filled with gold, which included monuments and ritual baths made of the precious yellow metal, they encountered more than even they foresaw and levelled the city in the looting. Rebuilt on solid stone foundations that were too difficult to destroy even by subsequent earthquakes, today it is a Spanish colonial city superimposed on an older civilisation of which the culture still endures.

The Incas worshipped the sun, source of all light and warmth, and originally the term Inca was only applied to the ruler, but the Spanish accredited it to nobles and priests, and it eventually encompassed the entire race. The Incas themselves were great builders of roads, bridges, tunnels, aqueducts, irrigation ditches, and stone stairways, all without benefit of the wheel, which apparently they never developed. Subjugated Indian peoples were consigned land work and tasks such as weaving, pottery making, and construction of fortresses, but not forced to revere the sun god. Their **Quechua** tongue is still the dominant language of five million Indians, but their history is sketchy because they developed no written or hieroglyphic word; meagre records were kept on knotted llama cords called *quipas*, and historians rely on accounts maintained by the conquistadors and missionaries.

Narrow cobbled streets were enclosed by tall buildings erected on top of the massive stone foundations, the upper levels whitewashed adobe and a few with small balconies. Because of low cloud cover, they appeared dark and gloomy, but two colonial houses with corner balconies stood out: one with a solid wooden balustrade, the other a turquoise building with lacy ironwork railing. Cuzco was full of impressive churches, and the symmetrical bell towers of **La Compañia de Jesús** also faced the central Plaza de Armas. I also visited the **Church of Santo Domingo** built over an Inca temple, **La Merced Convent** with its rich treasury, and the **Church of San Blas** featuring an intricately carved cedar pulpit.

Sacsahuaman

One mile from Cuzco, approached through a green valley, **Sacsahuaman** (a name I can never forget because my guide referred to it as 'sexy woman'!) was a mighty 15th-century fortress and parade ground for Inca warriors. One thousand feet long, it was again built from tremendous blocks of stone, some weighing 300 tons, perfectly pieced together without mortar so that even a razor blade could not fit between them. Cut from a quarry a mile distant, they were transported by levers, since both the wheel and pulley were unknown to the Incas. It was a feat that took 30,000 men labouring 80 years to complete! Attended by brightly dressed Indian women, llamas and sheep grazed on the grassy parade ground, a white statue of Christ, arms outstretched, stood to one side, and the site afforded magnificent views of the city, ringed by mountains. Clearly visible on its prominent square were the twin towers and domes of the two mighty churches and a fountain in the central grassed expanse. I also looked down on a formation of concentric stone circles explained as representing the eye of some deity, a fact only apparent from afar. From here, I was taken to the ruins of **Puca-Pucara Fortress**, **Kenko Amphitheatre**, and **Tambomachay**, a ritual bath with water gushing from a source yet to be located, and where, seated on a rock, a solemn-faced girl nursed a lamb in her lap.

Machu Picchu

I went to **Machu Picchu** (8,200ft) via a combination of train and bus, the latter negotiating a precarious road winding up a sheer slope with rapids in the brown Urubamba River below. This river dropped an incredible 1,000m (3,300ft) over 47km (29mi). Snow was visible on distant peaks as, surrounded by verdant cone-shaped mountains, we climbed a wall of the canyon, with lush vegetation filling the crevices and cascades tumbling to the narrow watercourse at the bottom. Some summits were shrouded in cloud, but most were a startling green, and from the top I could see the road snaking its way 1,350ft up the side of the ravine. Machu Picchu (Old Peak in the Quechua language) needs little explanation because it is exactly like the numerous pictures that predominate in brochures on South America. However, here I was not so lucky because the site was always crowded with sightseers clambering over and amongst the remains, although with patience I managed to obtain a few excellent photographs without people.

First seen by a European only in 1911, this remarkably preserved city, declared the Lost City of the Incas, survived because, ensconced in its ingenious isolated eyrie in the clouds, it was never found by the Spaniards. A maze of narrow streets, stone houses, and terraced emerald fields, it roosted on a concealing perch invisible from the ground, and it is uncertain whether it was constructed for ceremonial purposes or as a military stronghold. Around 1,000 people lived here until the last ruler died in 1571, after which the city was inexplicably abandoned. Apart from clearing the jungle growth, no restoration was deemed necessary; wooden struts or corbels still protruded from walls, and only the roofs, which were made of straw, had rotted and were missing. A self-sustaining community of more than 200 buildings, there were temples, baths, a sun dial, evidence of a drainage system, a large round tower, stone fences, and a sacrificial altar, all connected by endless stairways hewn out of solid rock. I took effective pictures framed by stone arches. Determined not to miss anything, I practically crawled around the site on hands and knees, and on arrival back at the hotel had to be carried from the bus whilst the management procured the services of a Spanish speaking doctor who administered an injection to enable me to catch the plane next morning – at last I was on my way down!

Machu Picchu

Arequipa

Again passing snowbound peaks, I flew south to **Arequipa**, dominated by the 6,000m (19,200ft) snow-capped extinct volcano **El Misti**. Palm trees grew in the large central **Plaza de Armas**, which was bordered by colonnaded buildings and the large twin-spired **Cathedral**, in front of which I later watched as crowds venerated a statue of Our Lady atop a flower-bedecked float with white doves flying overhead. I glimpsed a profusion of potted plants and flowering creeper in a private courtyard behind tall iron gates. Arequipa was called the White City because many of its buildings were constructed of ashlar, a smooth white stone carved from volcanic lava, which was enhanced with black wrought iron.

I visited the picturesque 16th-century **Santa Catalina Convent** (1579), a town in itself, with flower gardens, fountains and trees in several immaculate colonnaded courtyards paved with black and white checks, one of which held a large cross flanked by two smaller crosses. Incredible translucent rock was used for windows and skylights in the red and white buildings. I found carving on walls, a series of beautiful murals, floral bouquets in spandrels, an outdoor clay oven, a steep stone stairway, and vaulted alleys. Next to a deep empty well with steps leading to the bottom, a water channel ran down the middle of two rows of stone basins used for washing. Potted red geraniums cheered a white wall, and there were old-style lamps, white domes and, in a recess above the foundations, an outside fireplace where wood was burnt to furnish warmth for an indoor heating system. The whole imparted a serene atmosphere, but the reality was very different because cloistered in tiny dark cells with only a single window in the mud-brick walls, the nuns spent their life in contemplation and prayer. In a tomb-like recess beyond a small opening, her servant was condemned to endure a living death. At one time there were 180 of these depressing chambers.

Pisco

The next part of my journey took me by public bus across the **Atacama Desert**, the driest place on earth, with stretches where rain has never been recorded. We passed very little habitation: a few crude shacks selling things like Inca Kola, a rudimentary rest stop, a small settlement with some cultivation, and one dry dusty town. However, I found the landscape fascinating: taupe-coloured sands, black dunes, and smooth windswept silver hills containing a mineral that glinted in the sun. People selling snacks boarded the bus at various intervals, and at comfort breaks there was not even a rock for privacy. Screened by their full skirts and obviously wearing no undergarments, the women simply squatted beside the vehicle to relieve themselves, but I refrained from going! Towards the end of the trip, the road deviated to the coast, and the desert extended right to the edge; it was an incredible sight.

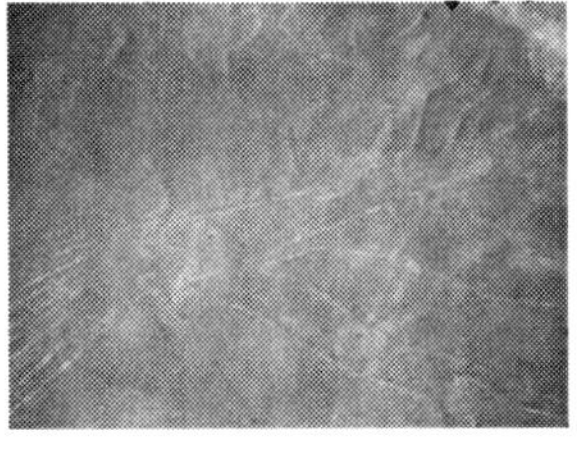

Nazca Lines from the air

Reaching my destination of **Pisco** (the grape brandy, basis of the 'pisco sour', comes from here), I stayed at the Hotel Paracas on the **Bahia de Paracas**. Literally an oasis in the desert, cool corridors surrounded a swimming pool, flowers, and lawn! My room had a private enclosed courtyard with a small garden and mosaic bench seat. My purpose here was a flight over the vast desolate plateau containing the mysterious **Nazca Lines**, with their perfect straight 'runways', triangles and illustrations. The latter included a monkey, hand, condor, hummingbird, parrot, spider, dog, pelican, heron, a lizard, and an enormous human figure, all only distinguishable from the air.

Interestingly, the 90m monkey and most other images were drawn with one continuous line. Climbing an observation tower situated overlooking the 'hand', one could appreciate, even more, the baffling puzzle confronting scholars because the engravings were shallowly etched into the hard surface and had withstood erosion by the elements since time immemorial, although one would imagine them to be easily obliterated by even just the simple accumulation of sand.

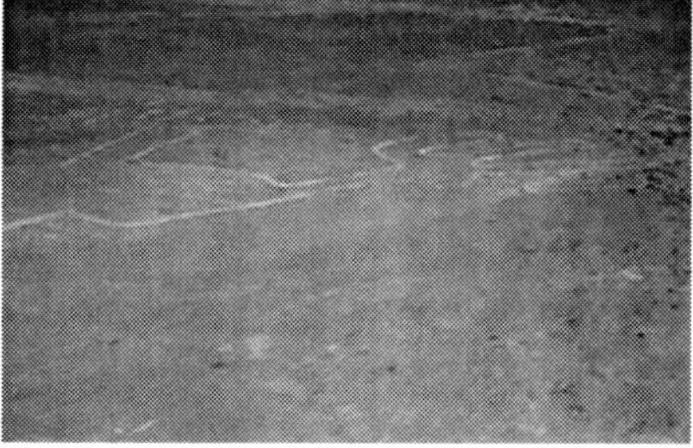
the hand from the observation tower

The dimensions were such that it was difficult to conceive of a primitive race having the ability, knowledge and instruments to create these accurate perspectives on the ground. Unfortunately, they blended into the monochrome surroundings and did not photograph well. The plateau was also marked by what appeared to be dry watercourses like a web of tangled lines. Whilst in Pisco I met an elderly author who had published a book proposing a logical explanation for the phenomenon, although I forget what it was, preferring to subscribe to the romantic theory of Erich von Däniken that they were created by extraterrestrial beings!

Lima

From Pisco, I travelled by bus to the capital, **Lima**, for an overnight stay at the Hotel Riviera. Known as the City of Kings, it was the most important metropolis in South America for more than three centuries, but I did not have time to absorb much more than the **Plaza de Armas**, bounded by imposing buildings with the usual towers and elegant façades. In a glass case on public view, the **Cathedral** housed the remains of Pizarro who, on a quest for gold, founded the city in 1535, after a massacre in which thousands of Indians – who were in awe of the white men and horses, both unknown in their world – were slaughtered; he was murdered in 1541. Adjacent sat the **Archbishop's Palace** with enclosed cedar balconies on the granite façade. Outside the gates of the nearby **Palacio de Gobierno** (**Presidential Palace**), guards in plumed helmets, white jackets with red epaulets and braid, red trousers and long black boots, stood at ease, rifles slung over the right shoulder and left hand behind their back. The thing that impressed me most was the prevalence of ornately carved wooden balconies, but I did not like Lima, it did not have a good 'feel'. Other things of note were a large equestrian statue and an outstanding white façade like a Gaudí creation, with fine pillars and a wealth of elaborate stuccowork. Superimposed on a white frontage, a dark stone portico had spiral pillars, delicate ornamental carving, and figures in niches, including a central image of the Virgin behind iron railing beneath a fluted shell.

ECUADOR

Quito

Again travelling by air, I flew directly above the snow-covered Andes to **Quito** in **Ecuador**, home of the so-called Panama hat and so named because it sits on the equator. Originally settled by Indians more than 1,000 years ago, Quito was conquered by the Incas in the 13th century, razed by Pizarro in 1533, and rebuilt by the conquistadors in 1534. This city had a European ambience, evidenced in many of its buildings (one even called Taberna Bavaria) and a fountain in front of a triumphal arch. Cloud was hanging almost at street level in the cooler climate of this higher elevation, 9,000ft above sea level, although still with palm trees, and the views from **Panecillo** (little bread loaf) **Hill** encompassed the city and surrounding green mountains. I looked out over a beautiful church with a dome, brown portico on the white façade (I saw this repeated often), and gardens in the forecourt. There was a white 'wedding cake' tower, statues on tall pedestals, two guardsmen (more casual than those in Lima), narrow paved alleys, old-fashioned three-branched lampposts, an ice-cream cart in a square, a market outside the white twin-towered **Cathedral** with its brownstone doorway, and even a white castle with arched windows, battlements, and a preponderance of red-topped turrets!

Ambato

I joined others to go to the weekly market at **Ambato**, one of the largest in South America. Fruits and vegetables in baskets and on carts beneath gay umbrellas, brightly dressed Indian ladies with garlands of beads, framed pictures next to tomatoes, citrus and bananas, ladies plaiting wool and one, seated on the pavement beside bundles of leeks, sewing an ethnic cap, breads and freshly cooked foods (including a row of corncob vendors), a woman carrying onions in her hand, and another (wearing rows of pink coral around her neck) asleep with her mouth open – all were cameos of this vibrant bustling place. Other subjects for my camera included piles of purple grapes and sliced pineapple on trays, the preparation of food, kebabs on a grill and whole fish frying in a pan, women with babes or bundles on their backs, rugs with traditional bird designs hanging on a wall, a heap of vibrantly coloured skeins of wool, an ice-cream cart, wooden bowls and spoons, woven bags full of spices, and clothing for sale; supervised by his mother, a young boy was trying on hats.

Back in Quito, I photographed more street scenes, including heavy relief of fruits, flowers and leaves on metal doors, decoration on parapets, more of the market activity in front of the cathedral, and a building with statues in recesses, intricate sculpted ornamentation, and solid spiral columns with ornate capitals.

Quito cathedral

The churches were rich in artworks, but I had no means of recording the images. Other side trips took me to the **Equator Monument** (**Mitad del Mundo**), where one can stand with a foot in each hemisphere, and to **Otavalo**.

Quayaquil and the Galapagos Islands

I flew to Quayaquil, where I changed planes for the charter flight to **Baltra** in the **Galapagos**, visited by naturalist Charles Darwin aboard HMS *Beagle* in 1835. Here, I transferred to the *Buccaneer* for a five-day cruise amongst these islands 1,000km (625mi) off the coast of Ecuador. Numbering 12, they are the peaks of gigantic underwater volcanos rising 7,000 to 10,000ft above the sea bed. Our first destination was **North Seymour**, where we saw prolific animal and birdlife, including the spectacular blue-footed boobies with their piercing yellow eyes and incredible bright blue plastic-looking feet. Frigate birds were characterised by their wide wingspan, splayed tail, and fascinating red bulbous sac at the throat, which they inflate to attract the female, and I observed grey-and-white dusky or lava gulls with red eyes, feet and legs. A booby nested near adorable pure white fluffy chicks as big as the parent bird, two pairs performed a courtship dance, one was nestled on an egg, and another sheltered its wobbly offspring, which looked hardly more than a day old. Small sea lions frolicked on a sandy beach whilst others lazed in the warmth, one opening a sleepy soft-brown eye at my intrusion.

The unattractive terrain was flat and rocky with low vegetation, but words cannot describe the wonder of being in this pristine primeval place. The wildlife was very trusting in the protected environment, showing absolutely no fear of man; in fact, boobies were nesting right on the pathway, from which it was forbidden to deviate, and did not move at our approach. Waves splashed onto a shore crowded with sea lions, which clambered over each other or emerged with sleek glistening bodies from the surf. One strained backwards in an awkward attempt to scratch its chest with a hind flipper, and I saw my first marine iguanas – unbelievably ugly but somehow appealing beasts! Other small birds included bright yellow warblers. A frigate flew overhead with the sac swinging from its throat like an inflated red balloon, and we saw huge albatross with their hooked beaks. In this venue, which had to be one of life's amazing experiences, I also came across a small red-headed lizard sunning itself on a rock and boobies sitting on eggs or feeding their young with regurgitated food.

We sailed on to **Point Cormorant** on **Floreana (Charles) Island**, also known by the Spanish name, **Isla Santa Maria**. Here, pale flamingos (apparently the depth of colour depends on their diet) were reflected as they waded and foraged in a shallow blue lagoon enclosed by a small section of white beach, a few trees, and hillier terrain including the volcanic cone of **David's Peak**. The water was so clear that I could see large fish and even discern the trail left along the bottom by a flamingo. I also saw a white bloom remarkably like the flower of a passion fruit. The seashore here was home to brilliant red Sally Lightfoot crabs (looking already cooked!), which scurried along the sand or looked startling against black lava rock lapped by gentle waves. Evidently made by giant turtles coming ashore to lay their eggs, tracks like those of large truck tyres led from the turquoise water, and separated from its flock, we encountered an ungainly white flamingo fledgling walking on stilt-like legs with knobbly knees. Disobeying the rules, we tried (without success) to shepherd it back to the lagoon. There were small wren-like birds, a few cacti, and I found a spiny anemone on the wet sand.

Moving on to **Punta Suarez** on **Española (Hood) Island**, I saw a small horizontally striped two-toned lava lizard, sea lions, and birds, which could have been petrels, Audubon's shearwater or noddy terns, plummeting like falling stones into the sea as they dived for fish. Taking to a small boat, we sailed around offshore rocks coated with guano; cacti like strange alien species sprouted from the top and sea lions basked amongst boulders at the base. Back onshore, mockingbirds or finches fluttered around many active sea lions, including young pups with big gentle eyes and soulful expressions. Two were engaged in a spat, and one just flapped a sandy flipper as it lay indolently between rocks. Most had disdainful expressions and, too lazy to turn around, one craned backwards to look at me. They varied in colour from light beige to dark brown. The rocks were inhabited by wonderful mottled red-and-green marine iguanas, with long claws and a spiny ridge along the backbone, feeding on exposed green algae. Both small and large birds were to be found here, including masked boobies and wave albatross, two of which I saw clashing bills. Coastal cliffs were pounded by a deep-blue sea, the surf erupting with dramatic effect in high white plumes through blowholes. Seals, their bodies gleaming, splashed in pools left by the spray.

Next morning, we disembarked at **Plaza Island**, where I saw a wading bird and a type of heron secreted in reeds, and pure black birds perched on rocks. This island contained the **Opuntia Cactus Forest**, a tree cactus like the prickly pear but with hairy trunks and standing maybe 20ft tall. The rocky shore provided a habitat for Sally Lightfoot crabs and lithe sea lions, many of the latter sporting and rolling in a turquoise ocean, and we were fortunate to witness the birth of a baby, an event that the ranger accompanying us (always a necessity) had never seen in three years. We watched as the attentive mother, with a beautiful golden coat, caringly cleaned and caressed her surprisingly active newborn cub. We also found frigate birds, the red-eyed lava gulls, and other small species. Here also, I had my first sight of the prehistoric-looking scaly yellow land iguana with its spines and loose folds of skin around the neck; in fact, one encounter was a little too close for comfort because one of the large reptiles charged at me! Admonished by the ranger to stand still (easier said than done!), it stopped, and he informed me that it was just attracted by the yellow slacks I was wearing!

land iguana

These remarkable creatures can move at an extremely fast pace, as they demonstrated when chasing each other through the flat red, yellow and green scrub dotted with white rocks and cactus. I noticed one large yellow monitor lizard and watched more birds plunging into the glorious cobalt blue water. The rocks were a haven for the snow-white red-billed tropic birds, with their long slender tails like fine quills.

In the afternoon, we visited the **Darwin Research Station** at **Academy Bay** on **Santa Cruz** (**Indefatigable**) **Island**, and it was here that I saw the enormous Galapagos tortoise, displaying disgusting table manners as they masticated greens into slimy mush (that dribbled down their open mouths) and snapped at each other as they fed! One laboriously emerged from a pool with a slow ungainly gait. Here also were more yellow warblers, wild lemon hibiscus, and brilliant red bougainvillea. The itinerary also included the islands of **Bartolome** and **Santiago** (**James**), and my last pictures were of red cliffs and birds nesting on a rocky outcrop in the water.

Back in **Quayaquil**, I filmed the imposing **Cathedral of San Francisco** with its large rose window and twin spiked spires. The park opposite contained an equestrian statue on a tall pedestal and several iguanas with long dewlaps (that help regulate their body temperature), their appendages and tails drooping as they lounged languidly along the branches of trees. An impressive building with Ionic columns, a plain pediment, and urns on the balustrade forming the parapet, also had relief around the arched entrance to a glass-roofed arcade. This featured sculpted long-robed figures, their arms crossed, standing on brackets immediately below the vault, and beautiful decorative glass panels under a dome. I saw vegetable barrows in the streets, and clothes hung above the sidewalk. My room overlooked a swimming pool in rainforest surrounds that included palm trees and large-leafed philodendrons, the latter even climbing around the arched stained-glass window of a church forming one wall of the courtyard.

Amazon

My next excursion commenced with a one-hour flight that took me from Quito, over the snowbound range of the Andes, and above the impenetrable canopy and crisscrossing rivers of the **Amazon** jungle, to **Lago Agrio**, whence I moved on to **Coca** by road. I had chosen to visit the **Rio Napo**, an isolated narrow tributary of this mighty river because the end near the city of Manaus was just a wide and bustling commercial waterway. This section epitomised my expectations of jungle: thick vegetation, different colours and varieties of fungi, exotic blooms (including one with tiny white florets emerging from a cone of green and purple bracts, which I had never seen before), huge buttressed trees, others with small red aerial roots – and large insects!

After checking into the Flotel Orellana, the first part of my journey was by dugout canoe down the muddy brown swift-flowing **Payamino River**, with overhanging trees and heliconias in the lush undergrowth but scant birdlife, to the tiny community of **La Floresta** (**San Carlos**). Here, we encountered a native house consisting simply of a thatched roof above open floor space. Built on stilts, it was accessed by steps cut into a tree trunk, at the top of which stood a dog. There was also a green parrot pecking in one corner, an open-weave basket like those used for poultry, a few utensils, pottery, and a variety of green vegetable for cooking – but no people.

kitchen

We passed several other crude dwellings tucked away amongst trees and one person paddling a canoe, but the native populace had been sorely decimated along the Amazon. As we returned to our 450-ton flat-bottomed floating hotel, we enjoyed a superb subtle sunset endowing the river with a golden hue.

Next morning introduced an exciting day, commencing with a jungle walk followed by a canoe trip around **Lake Taracoa**. Exotic tropical blooms included a tall variety with red flowers sprouting along the stem like gladioli, tubular yellow flowers emerging from a cone-shaped cluster of red bracts, a strelitzia, and the red and yellow heliconia; most were brightly coloured but I did see a pale pink wild hibiscus. Mammoth flanged trees hosted a multitude of epiphytes, and fungi included species in brown, white, apricot (with a scalloped edge), and a two-toned variety. We crossed marshy areas via narrow plank walkways with bamboo handrails and came across gorgeous giant butterflies in hues of green, turquoise, orange and black with white spots, and cobalt blue and black; there was no attempt at camouflage because they stood out starkly against the dense green foliage. Continuing by canoe, we passed dangling lianas, overhanging limbs, bromeliads in the clefts of trees, a bright yellow bird, brilliant blue kingfishers – and a snake slithering along a branch overhead. Clinging to a twig, a mass of furry black and white caterpillars with blue heads made an interesting picture. It was still and serene, with lovely reflections.

native house

This was also a five-day excursion, and after travelling up the **Jivino River** and being transferred by 'jungle bus', the third night was spent in **Limoncocha**, in a primitive lodge constructed from local materials and surrounded by dank steamy jungle. We were to sleep on bunks in a dormitory, and I was allocated an upper berth with a sheet; even in the evening it was very hot. My main concern was the necessity of having to make a 'visit' during the night; being conscious of having to descend from my lofty perch with just the sheet for cover (I sleep naked) and head for the rustic facilities, made me more aware of the call of nature. I lay awake for a long time listening to cicadas and watching fireflies through the screen but ultimately had to succumb (with difficulty) to the urge.

The thatched building was situated on a small rise facing a lagoon, and next day we were invited to participate in a boat ride to go swimming. The guide laughingly told us that the water was full of *pirañas*, which we took to be a joke until a boy was bitten. You have never seen people evacuate an area with such rapidity; I found it particularly difficult to scramble up the side of the canoe and feared losing the lower half of my bikini! There were indeed *pirañas* in the lagoon, which the local lads proceeded to catch, demonstrating their vicious razor-sharp pointed teeth. They were surprisingly small fish but with powerful jaws, and a school can shred small prey to bones in minutes. Back on the Jivino River, we went (once more by dugout) to **Monkey Island**, home to a colony of woolly monkeys where we also saw amazing ants carrying pieces of leaf many times their size, with which they 'marched' in formation. Again, we passed primitive native houses on stilts (many open sided), accessed from the river via steps cut into the muddy bank, where canoes were moored and people washed.

native houses

My fascination with this type of environment never wanes, and with over 400 species, the region around the lodge was apparently one of the richest in the world for bird colonies. Amongst many that I could not hope to name, I saw a type of marsh hen with a blue head.

Next morning, we visited the small catholic settlement of **Pompeya**, with an intriguing **Anthropological Museum** wherein I filmed a strange figurine. The quaint mission church was built in native style, its thatched roof and bamboo walls braced with struts in the form of a cross. Here also, we saw captive capybaras (or peccaries), the world's largest rodent, and once more aboard the Orellana we passed a local antiquated ferry called *Zulema*, like something straight out of the African Queen – I would not have been surprised to see Humphrey Bogart! Arriving back in Coca on the final day, I filmed interesting activity at crude food stalls lining the river. A hefty woman was kneading dough and rolling it into rounds into which she spooned a filling, and another fried balls of some concoction in a cast-iron cauldron over an open fire, transferring them with a slotted ladle to a tray beneath a cloth. Hands of green bananas lay on the ground, a man just sat reading the paper, and a mangy dog sniffed hopefully around the cooking area.

BRAZIL

The Portuguese arrived in the 1500s, followed by waves of immigrants and black African slaves. In 1808, the King of Portugal, fleeing from Napoleon, stayed in the colony of Brazil for 13 years. Returning to Portugal, he left his son as regent, who promptly declared himself king but was forced to abdicate. A period of dictatorships and military power was followed by democracy.

Rio de Janeiro

It was then on by air to **Rio de Janeiro** in **Brazil**, where I arrived in the early hours of Christmas Day, which also happened to be a Sunday. Thinking it an ideal opportunity to film the city without traffic (I was staying in **Copacabana**), I made my intention known to the management who, for safety reasons, because it would be deserted, strongly admonished me not to do so, even threatening to lock me in my room overlooking a busy landscaped traffic circle and a long tree-lined avenue bounded by high-rise, if I did not comply. I finished up spending this festive occasion watching Sampson and Delilah on my television – in Portuguese!

Next morning, I had a half day tour along the beaches, including **Impanema** of pop song fame. The famous green mountains formed a lovely backdrop to palm trees planted in a strip of white sand between a black and white paved promenade and the blue sea. Because I live on one of the world's best beaches, my attention was riveted on the buildings whilst most of the tourists were gawking at the ocean. Views across the bay showed the city at the foot of 1,299ft **Páo de Açúnas** (**Sugar Loaf Mountain**). The name derives from the mountain's resemblance to the conical containers, called 'sugarloaves', into which sugarcane was placed after boiling and refining during the 16th and 17th centuries. We drove up 710m (2,329ft) **Corcovado** (Hunchback), an ancient lava cone, to see the immense 700-ton 39m (130ft) statue of Christ the Redeemer with its outstretched arms. Finished in 1931, one of the hands alone was 3.2m (10ft) long! Unfortunately, it was shrouded in fog and the visage of the figure was not clear, but the wonderful panorama over the city and natural harbour of **Guanabara Bay**, even though misty, was magnificent. The tour also took in the **Tijuca Tropical Forest**, with a most attractive waterfall.

In the afternoon, I ventured into the centre, experiencing not a little trepidation because police would call me over and indicate, with sign language, that I should put the camera away, but because it had a wide strap around my wrist and I wanted to record my visit, I took the risk without incident. Even on my brief excursion, Rio exhibited a vibrant atmosphere, and one could not fail but be imbued with a sense of excitement; however, sadly it was also one of the most dangerous cities, as frequently pointed out to me. A quirk of the metropolis was the preponderance of Volkswagens in the streets. Amongst the classical buildings, an imposing edifice topped by a central dome had statues flanking the wide staircase leading to its columned portico and on the parapet above. Opposite, a crowded mosaic-paved boulevard had trees, vendor carts, statues on pedestals – and a plethora of pigeons! Following this walkway, I came to a grassed area with palms, a tall elaborate fountain, an obelisk, flowers, and a castle-like structure (or church) on a slight rise surrounded by greenery, which I had seen from the bus. My peregrinations eventually brought me to the impressive **Monument to World War II Heroes** at the bay. Housed in a vast open space, this consisted of two 150ft concrete pillars with a slab resting on top; an eternal flame burned underneath and sculpted figures represented the three armed forces. Sugar Loaf Mountain rose majestically in the background. Next, I came to the highly decorated **Municipal Theatre**, a small replica of the Paris Opera House, and walked through a market area where hammocks were hung for display. I came across interestingly adorned buildings and a large pool in the foreground of a futuristic structure with the appearance of a stepped Mayan temple. Finally, I took pictures of a strange construction like stacked boxes separated by pillared concourses and the **Cathedral** with its symmetrical bell towers, dome, and solid metal doors embossed with cherubs and floral decoration.

cathedral Rio de Janeiro

Whilst in Rio, I attended the most amazing, never to be forgotten, **Samba Spectacle**. Tall stately women with ebony skin, danced and paraded in voluminous, sequined, and vibrantly coloured costumes, their height doubled by towering feathered headdresses. In this world renowned **Plataforma I** show, there were also African themed costumes with zebra stripes. Others were dressed in white, black, silver or gold, and except for long ‘tails’, some wore very little at all! Rio even had a museum dedicated to the flamboyant Carmen Miranda, Brazil's famous actress and singer of the 1950s. Locals maintain that 'God made the world in six days and the seventh he devoted to Rio'.

Iguassu Falls

From Rio, I flew close above a wide tortuous brown river winding through an ocean of endless green to the entirely different spectacle of **Iguassu** (**Iguazú**) **Falls**, eighth wonder of the world and, at 85m (279ft), 93 ft higher than Niagara. Fifty-eight thousand tons of water per second pours over the southern edge of the **Paraná Plateau**, and I spent three days in this region without the overwhelming display ever palling. Over three kilometres (10,000ft) in length, 275 conjoined cataracts cascaded vertically or in steps down jungle-clad sides of the ravine, creating rainbows that hovered in the mist above; each individual fall an inspiration in itself. They form the boundaries of Argentina, Brazil and Paraguay (my only recollection of which is handmade dolls with nothing under their skirts except black pubic hair!) and I saw them from both sides.

Iguassu Falls

I stayed at the legendary four-star Cataratas Hotel on the Brazilian side, with a room overlooking the falls and a breakfast to die for! One could literally spend hours consuming delicacies on offer in the buffet, everything from a range of freshly squeezed exotic fruit juices, to a huge variety of hot and cold dishes, including meats, pancakes, hash-browns – you name it, it was there! Rhea, related to the emu, inhabited the grounds, one sitting throwing dirt over itself, the other foraging in the garden. Vibrantly coloured red-and-blue macaws roosted in trees – and one on the back of a chair at the poolside. A flock of small bright green birds wheeled and dived around the edge.

I have yet to make my mind up as to which of the two, Victoria or Iguassu, is my favourite, both having unobstructed views along natural pathways lined with thick jungle foliage of bamboo, which on this occasion consisted of palm trees, lianas, wild orchids, ferns, lichens and bromeliads, with puffs of white cloud in a blue sky. Big brilliant butterflies and birds, including a yellow-breasted toucan, were also an attraction at this outstanding venue. Some falls were mere narrow ribbons, whilst others were curtains of water many metres across, plunging down perpendicular faces to rocky shelves, where they erupted in a fountain of spray. As well as the glorious display flowing over the opposite bank, on the near side I took film from above the falls as I progressed to the dramatic culmination, **Union Falls** (the highest), spilling into **Garganta del Diablo** or **Devil's Throat** at the end. This was a circle of thunderous water tinged orange by mineral content, and fragile-looking dusky swifts flew in and out of nests hidden behind the force of the tumultuous cascade. One could not hear oneself speak against the constant roar of this wall of water, and mist formed a screen obliterating the opposite face of the abyss. Blowing in a steady stream, it rose in thick billowing clouds from the base of the massive volume falling from above. Making my way back, I obtained stunning photographs through the black branches of dead trees or with tall waving grasses in the foreground. Small active rainbow-hued birds also inhabited the lush wet foliage, as well as others, less colourful, with long tails. Butterflies included a black and white variety with red wingtips. Evening produced a wonderful sunset. Boats no longer being an option (for safety reasons), the climax of my visit was a helicopter flight over the dense jungle, hotel, river and falls, which included a terrifying descent into the Devil's Throat, the bottom hidden under an impenetrable column of spray.

Iguassu from the air

ARGENTINA

Buenos Aires

Next day, I crossed to the more prolific Argentinean side and viewed the spectacle from directly above the amazing falls, which gave the impression of being immersed in their grandeur. In the afternoon, I flew to the capital, **Buenos Aires** (City of Good Air), where I witnessed a spectacle of a different kind as, in an annual New Year tradition, cascading sheets of white paper and shredded accounts, receipts and records from the previous year rained down, in a veritable snowstorm, from office windows onto the city. In a land of *gauchos* (cowboys), cattle and *pampas* (fertile prairie), Buenos Aires was a sophisticated city. An orienteering walk brought me to **Casa Rosada**, the pink Palace of the Peron's facing the enormous **Plaza de Mayo,** which featured the white image of a female armed with a spear atop the 18m (61ft) **Piramide de Mayo** obelisk (1811) honouring Liberty and the May Revolution. Here also was **La Catedral**, with the tomb of General Jose de San Martin who helped liberate South America from Spain. By law, the president must be Catholic. A line of city maintenance trucks circled the plaza, waiting to clean up the paper overnight. **Avenue de Mayo** intersected with **Avenue 9 de Julio**, at 140m the widest in the world. Impressive structures in surrounding streets included that with a white-columned porch and deeply sculpted pediment. A nearby building was dominated by statues and a central tower, and a huge bronze memorial stood in front of a colonnade.

I went to the fascinating Italian district of **La Boca** (The Mouth), the original heart of the city inhabited in the 19th century by Genoese sailors and port workers. It was an assemblage of multicoloured stuccoed, timber, and corrugated iron houses with lacy iron balconies and brightly painted lattice and shutters. There were statues, murals on many walls, and moulded plaques, including one life-sized portrayal of a man on a raffia-seated stool playing an accordion. Stroking a bow across the strings of a box-like musical instrument held under the chin in the manner of a violin, a man performed in front of one of several statues in **Caminito Street**. In spite of the explosion of colour, it was evidently an impoverished section of the city, and washing hung on balconies above the main thoroughfare. One tiny store, a red and white awning above its window, had cherubs in deep relief below the sill and beneath the eaves; a heavily embossed plaque graced the wall to the right of the door. A large coloured bas-relief depicted a man with a guitar serenading a damsel on a balcony, and I walked past a picturesque tree-lined lake.

paper snow

Buenos Aires must have had a significant Italian heritage because even my hotel was called Italia Romanelli, and from my window I looked down on the mass of white paper caught in wires and inches deep around parked cars in the road. Sauntering again, I joined the people shuffling through the reams of paper in the white-coated streets, where I found a cathedral with Christ in a recess below the central tower, one of three crowned with green cupolas.

Other noteworthy buildings included the corner **Banco de Boston**, its bowed entrance ornately sculpted and statues on pedestals in front. I found myself back outside the palace, where guards stood at attention either side of the doorway. Whilst in Buenos Aires, I also attended a tango performance, its music once forbidden for its sensuality and passion, but which I did not find as stimulating as the samba show.

Ushuaia

The next part of my journey turned out to be a highlight of not only this trip but all my adventures before or since. Left to my own devices, I arranged an excursion to the world's southernmost city, Ushuaia, and on to El Califate near **Lago Argentino**, from where I joined a Spanish speaking group to see the Moreno Glacier. My flight was with the Argentinean Air Force (Aero Fuenza), which used their planes on domestic sectors, and being shortly after the **Falklands** (**Islas Malvinas**) War (numerous signs attested to the fact *Las Malvinas son Argentina's*), I was astounded to be offered passage in the cockpit. As with the Himalayas the previous year, we flew over one of those incredibly blue crater lakes only visible from the air.

On this my first visit, I found **Ushuaia** a fairly unattractive community of small but neat houses, a few flowers including multihued lupins, and buildings nestled in a valley ringed on three sides by snow-sprinkled mountains, the fourth facing the **Beagle Channel**. It had grown enormously on the occasion of my second visit, with touristy alpine-looking outlets selling souvenirs and cold weather apparel. Producing wonderful vistas of water, snow-dusted mountains and forest, the terrain made up for any shortcomings in the townsite. I took a channel boat trip between cloud-enveloped summits with wisps trapped in hollows, to investigate rocky offshore islets housing seal colonies and teeming with birdlife, but mainly cormorants. It also provided an excellent view of the township, where a clock tower rose above the low buildings. Raging over boulders and fed by a boisterous waterfall flowing through dense greenery, a wild blue river proved an additional attraction on a tour to an *estancia* (ranch), where I was introduced to the delights of the *parrillada* (Argentinean BBQ); whole carcasses were split and staked in front of open fires – it was delicious!

From here, once more in the cockpit, I flew to **El Califate** where I was separated from the group and lodged in a different hotel, with respect to which I felt rather chuffed at being able to negotiate compensations such as the inclusion of breakfast – in Spanish! Early next morning, we were transferred by bus to **Perito Moreno Glacier**, declared a Natural Heritage of Humanity by UNESCO, and the culmination of my South American odyssey. En route, we encountered blue bergy bits (an official designation for ice 3 to 15 feet above the surface) in the water, and on reaching our destination, snow-covered mountains reared behind the wall of ice. Totally unbeknown to me was the fact that this glacier, in **Lake Argentina**, is the only one in the world continually advancing over water, with the result that every four to five years it completely bisects the lake, causing the water level to increase on one side (up to 37m/120ft) until the pressure ultimately erodes the ice, forming a bridge to which, when aware of its imminent collapse, a privileged few descend en masse to witness the awe-inspiring spectacle that follows.

The news was received in the early hours of the morning, and by the time we arrived the immense volume of water, which had taken years to accumulate, was surging in a fierce torrent through the narrow chasm between the crevassed face of the blue glacier and the high bank on which we were seated. A remnant of the ice bridge, a solitary pillar, was all that stood on our side. This had to be the most exhilarating display of the incredible power of nature that one could hope to experience, the force of the water tearing away massive 300-year-old chunks of the glacier as big as multistorey towers, which fell with a resounding splash and huge plumes of spray, only to be tossed like a child's wooden building blocks down the rampaging waterway. Accompanied by a thunderous roar and the sharp sound of cracking ice, which could be heard at a distance of many miles, it took less than 24 hours after the demise of the bridge for the lake to reach equilibrium and the entire process to begin anew. Adding to the dramatic effect, low-lying cloud settled above the startling blue glacier. Reaching back with my mind, many things have become vague and without the aid of my films I would not recall them, but one memory that will never fade or diminish is the impact of that awesome spectacle.

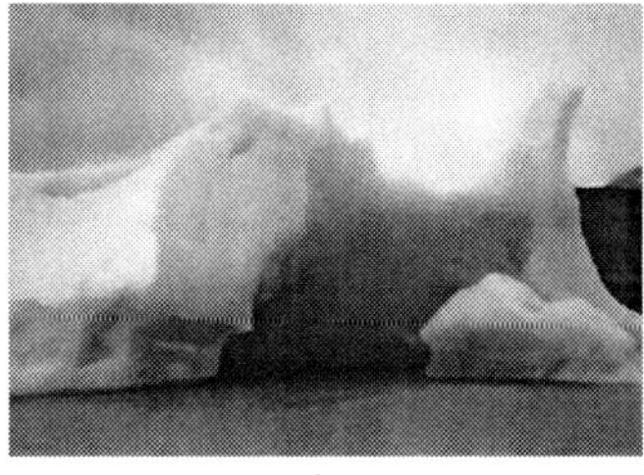
iceberg

Later, venturing by boat amongst the floating bergs (shades of the Titanic!), we encountered wonderfully sculpted shapes exhibiting different shades of brilliant blue, which stood out against the pristine white of the snowy mountain backdrop. Circumnavigating an exceptional semicircular formation, it caught the spasmodic light to give it a translucent effect, accentuating the rich blue of its interior and glinting off the edges with the sparkle of diamonds.

Even some of these were calving, and we saw the occasional bird, even an elusive condor, braving the icy conditions. This 'voyage' eventually led to another glacier, and our last sight, the aptly named **Grey Lake**, was full of bergy bits.

One eerie aspect of life in this Antarctic region was the length of daylight in summer, as a consequence of which the locals would participate in a night's entertainment such as the theatre before the evening meal, and I joined one such outing.

ARGENTINA to CHILE (Lakes Crossing)

After the outstanding episode of Moreno Glacier, I thought that nothing could compare, but the lakes crossing into Chile came a close second. Flying to **San Carlos de Bariloche** on the shores of **Nahuel Haupi** in the **Argentinean Lake District**, I found a delightful alpine town reflecting its first colonisation by Germans: stone-and-log buildings (and a tower) with steeply pitched roofs, and famed the world over for its chocolates – of which I sampled not a few! The two-day crossing was by a combination of ferry and road transport, each of the magnificent water courses, encompassed by verdant foliage that included pines and the occasional flowering tree, acquiring a different hue, and just a few patches of snow on crests beyond. It began with a cruise from **Puerto Pañuelo** (Pocket Handkerchief Port) to **Puerto Blest**, a picturesque settlement where lunch was taken. Surrounded by colourful gardens, dwellings behind log fences also featured pretty flower boxes below their shuttered windows, and I found a park with tall timber and glorious floral beds surrounded by green lawns. Bright blooms filled planters on the pavement, a spired church added interest, and shops (still selling chocolates!) included one with dormer windows and illustrations on the façade.

Initially it was cloudy, contributing to changes in the colour of the water, and many birds wheeled around our vessel. At one stage, we stopped at **Las Bosques Arraynes**, a fascinating cinnamon-bark forest, its leafy green canopy shading smooth contorted bronze trunks assuming fantastic shapes; in fact, it had been the inspiration for the environment in Walt Disney's Bambi! Continuing by bus to **Puerto Alegre**, we again took a boat, past thickly forested islets and a high waterfall, to **Puerto Frias**, and thence into **Chile**, where I left the remainder of the passengers to continue on and went by bus to **Puella**. Here, I spent the night in an idyllic location, the only guest in a small isolated establishment ensconced in woodland, with views from my window over the lake and distant snow-draped peaks. Behind the property, amongst abundant plant life that included bamboo, I discovered a beautiful multilevel waterfall, small birds, and flowers. I spent an enjoyable couple of hours walking and encountered water cascading through lush undergrowth, big bees buzzing around beautiful buttercup-yellow blossoms, rivers rushing over rocky beds, and superb mountain scenery. After breakfast, I cruised across **Lago Todos Los Santos** (All Saints Lake) to **Petrohué** for lunch, following which I continued by road along the shores of **Lake Llanquihue**.

The climax of this part of the journey, across waters alternating from turquoise and indigo to emerald green, with trees extending down steep slopes right to the edge, was stunning **Osorno Volcano**, its cone coated in perfectly smooth snow like icing on a cake and gleaming in the sun. Passing other pyramid peaks, one with a needle-sharp point, we sailed over surfaces displaying unbelievable blues, sometimes with whitecaps or a sunlit silvered sheen that made the verdant slopes almost pale into insignificance. At the conclusion of the cruise, we came to a gorgeous river where waving pampas formed the foreground to rapids racing between forested hills. We followed its course (by road) to a series of tumultuous waterfalls that crashed and boiled in a powerful surge of foaming white, through clefts, over and around boulders, to vivid emerald water. With mighty Osorno dominating the scene, the entire setting was one of ultimate splendour.

My night stop was the isolated but lovely stone-built Hotel Ralún set in landscaped grounds, its lawns and gardens surrounded by 1,000-year-old virgin larch forests that almost reached the shore of the crystal clear **Petrohué River**. At **Puerto Montt**, my accommodation, again near the water, was some miles out; a tiny shingled mill and working waterwheel were located nearby, and a white timber church with a tower and steeply pitched red roof lay in a field surrounded by trees. The only reason I have for remembering this town was the procurement of a fabulous hand-woven and -embroidered woollen coat with a hood, which cost me in the vicinity of $15! Sights included a sculpted pediment with colourful images, visible behind trees shaped like green lollypops, and a market with shellfish in wooden crates, fruits displayed beneath cane goods and woollen articles hanging from eaves (where I purchased my coat), and vegetables under cover – but fresh fish on the roadside in the open!

Santiago

After completing a large circuit and finding myself once more in **Santiago**, I took a tour with Gray Line to **Valparaiso** (Chile's main port) and the garden city of **Viña del Mar**, an area of luxury apartments overlooking a rocky coastline. Climbing like steps up hillsides, they were resplendent with hanging gardens and coloured umbrellas on patios. We passed a tiny bay with small fishing boats pulled up on a pebble beach and seagulls wheeling overhead, a working floral clock, many palm trees, and a castle-like structure atop rocks at the water's edge. Behind an iron grille, a large fountain graced the forecourt of the white **Palacio Rioja**, from where stairs led to a pillared portico.

Although some 2,630 miles long, Chile averages only 110 miles in width, and half the territory is occupied by the Andes, rising to an average of 10,000ft. The name Chile is derived from an Indian word meaning The End of the World.

EASTER ISLAND

The final destination of my trip was a four-day stopover in **Easter Island** (**Isla de Pascua** or **Rapa Nui**), 4,000km off the coast of Chile and the remotest inhabited island on earth, its nearest neighbour, 1,900km (1,180mi) away, is Pitcairn Island of Mutiny on the Bounty fame. At that time little visited, it is another of those places of which I prefer to preserve the mystery. The entire wave-pounded island was dotted with legendary *moai* (statues) left by a vanished civilisation. The story goes, that as guardians of the land they were originally erected facing out to sea, all their power issuing from the eyes. The small **Sebastian Englert Archaeological Museum** had a logical explanation for their construction and primitive method of transportation – anthropologists have concluded that this used up the last remaining trees – but I forget the details. One belief is that the all-powerful priests used their magical *mana* to make them walk.

On the occasion of my visit, there was no accommodation for tourists, and the occasional guest was lodged in a private home vacated by the occupant for the duration, the lady of the house coming in daily to cook and clean. The barren terrain had been totally denuded of trees, and even grazing for sheep was scarce, so the populace had turned to catching crayfish, of which there was an abundant supply and which became their staple diet. I presented a problem because I do not like these crustaceans and it was difficult to find a substitute! I imagine most people would dream of being able to indulge in this gourmet item every day, but I had to make do with rice and a little vegetable!

Under the impression that I was to have sole occupancy of the house, I was settling in (even humming to myself), when all of a sudden I was alarmed by an eccentric obese American who, materialising out of nowhere, entered through my doorway (covered only by a lace curtain), grabbed me by the hand, and whisked me into the bathroom. All the while jabbering excitedly, he explained the use of the shower and necessity for caution, indicating with rapid movements the dangers of exposed wiring! As it transpired, he was sharing the house and turned out to be exceedingly friendly, generous and obliging, a millionaire who in his time had owned a radio station and run for the United States Senate but spent a considerable part of every year on the island. In fact, he later married a local girl in a traditional ceremony and sent me photographs of the wedding. The family founded the extensive Cofrin Arboretum in Wisconsin. He called me Julie Andrews because I reminded him of the songstress, whose birthday incidentally is the day before mine and we are both vocalists. This is an appellation that has plagued me for many years because I do not particularly like her! Even a Chinese shopkeeper in the backstreets of Hong Kong remarked 'Do you know you look like Julie Andrews?'!

After I returned home, we corresponded for some months, until the occasion of his marriage; I even received a satellite phone call from Tahiti before the days when it became common technology. At that time, he was engaged in a project to raise one of the *moai*, a feat estimated to cost in excess of a million dollars and previously only achieved by Thor Heyerdahl, who had re-erected a small number. This great Norwegian explorer came here on the famous Kon Tiki expedition in 1947. The first Europeans to set foot on the island were members of a Dutch expedition under Admiral Jacob Roggeveen, which arrived on Easter Sunday in 1722 (hence the name), and James Cook landed in 1774. Most of the gigantic statues, up to 21m in height, weighing up to 300 tonnes and, except for one kneeling, all just heads or head and torso, were bareheaded, but a few sported a red topknot supposedly resembling a redheaded race. When first discovered, all the images, with the exception of unfinished works, were face down in the earth, and the eyes had been removed to destroy their power. At the archaeological zone of **Ahu Tahai**, restored *moai* made imposing pictures as they stood in a line on the shore, gazing inward for all eternity – with sightless eyes. I used one to effectively frame others in the series, and I have photographs of a tiny bird perched on a topknot, leaning statues, and many still lying on the ground.

Easter Island moai

Additional sites in this totally fascinating rocky and grass-covered dot in the South Pacific Ocean included the ceremonial village of **Orongo**. Here were prehistoric foundations of oval buildings and a row of corbelled dwellings created with crudely shaped flagstones laid horizontally, the doorways so low that it was necessary to crawl through. These remains were situated on the 1,300ft ridge of **Rano Kau** volcano, which loomed over the ocean, its awesome crater filled with pools of blue water, and rocks around the rim embellished with a phalanx of enigmatic embossed figures depicting the god Make-Make and the birdmen.

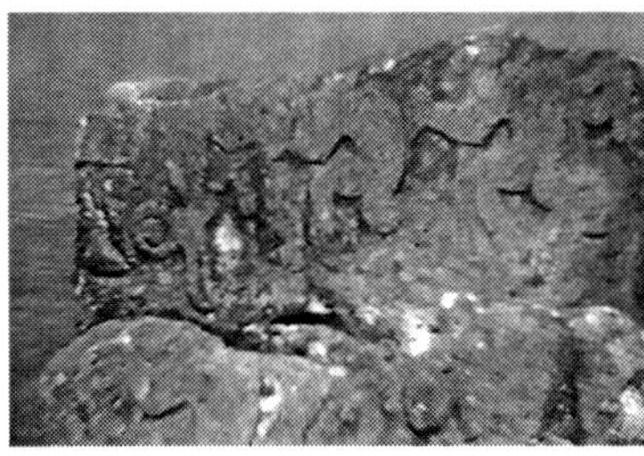

Make-Make and the birdmen

According to legend, men used to dive from the height and swim one mile in shark infested waters to an offshore rock in order to collect the first migratory sooty tern egg of the spring season, the clan chief of the servant achieving the feat and returning with the egg intact becoming birdman for a year. There was also a table where the virginity of maidens to be offered to the *Tangata Manu* (Birdman) was verified.

Douglass accompanied me to the quarry at **Rano Raraku** volcano from where the stone (volcanic tuff) was excavated and carved and which, along with seven perfect resurrected heads, contained approximately 180 apparently abandoned during various stages of construction, as well as a mammoth incomplete full-sized image lying on its back.

moai

For the most part the sky was blue, but a dramatic ceiling with black windswept clouds against an eerie white light enhanced the scene of a line of five. One particularly interesting figure had a sailing ship etched into the chest. I came across a petroglyph like a large fish, and my final pictures show *moai* silhouetted against the waning daylight.

I was also taken to a cave where cannibalism was once practiced. Lumber used for rollers depleted the forests, and resources to support the 4,000-strong population dwindled, so that the Rapa Nui degenerated into warfare and cannibalism. When Captain James Cook arrived, he found only 630 people scratching out a marginal existence. In 1875, just 155 islanders remained, but it once boasted an impressive culture: the Rapa Nui possessed the only written language in Oceania and espoused rock carving, tattooing, dance and music.

Scholars have yet to agree on the origin of the race that initially inhabited the island, but the weathered monuments have left a proud heritage for their humble descendants of today, and it was a tremendous conclusion to a great trip full of diverse attractions – truly the trip of a lifetime!

Postscript

German mathematician Maria Reiche believes that the Nazca lines are an astrological calendar of the ancient Peruvians.

The Galapagos were unknown until 1535 when the becalmed Bishop of Panama, Tomás de Berlanga, drifted 800 miles offcourse whilst sailing to Peru. He was unimpressed by the desolation of the islands but is credited with naming them after the huge tortoises. Decades later they fell foul of buccaneers hiding in sheltered coves after raiding Spanish ships, who introduced rats, cats, dogs and goats. The pirates were followed by whalers and sealers who decimated the wildlife to near extinction.

INDIA 1984

This trip began with the usual montage of market scenes: cooking stalls shielded by rough shelters, carts displaying fruits, including one piled with quarters of peeled pomelo, a man washing at a street well, people seated cross-legged on the pavement, bicycles, motorised trishaws, a horse and buggy, open-fronted food shops arrayed with cans and utensils, a man stirring the contents of a basin, and another fanning coals in a metal drum.

Sanchi

My first stop on this occasion was **Sanchi**, of great archaeological importance because of third century BC Buddhist *stupas* built by Emperor Ashoka, as a penance for horrors inflicted, to house relics of Lord Buddha and his disciples. Neglected and covered by time with sand and vines, they were thus saved from destruction by Mogul emperor Aurangzeb, who mercilessly desecrated every Buddhist shrine that he encountered. Rediscovered in 1811 by a British military officer, they were not properly restored until the early 1900s. The **Great Stupa** is the oldest stone structure in India; representing heaven embracing earth, it was a vast dome 36.5m (106ft) in diameter and 16.4m (42ft) high surmounted by a fenced square platform symbolising the heaven of the gods. It was guarded by a stone wall with four carved *toranas* (gateways) consisting of two uprights topped by a series of horizontal bars. These were covered with sculpted legends: the birth of Buddha was signified by the lotus, his enlightenment by the Bodhi tree, his teachings by the wheel, and his death (*nirvana* or salvation) by *stupas*. Buddha, at that period only depicted in disguise, was represented by symbols: footprints, umbrellas, ducks and geese (perhaps portraying his flock), and deer for the first sermon preached in a deer park near **Sarnath** 2,500 years ago. Carvings on the **South**

Gate depicted the birth of Buddha and showed Maya, the mother, standing on an open lotus whilst elephants shower her with water and dwarfs bestow garlands. It also features the story in which Bodhisattva (Buddha before attaining enlightenment) took the form of an elephant king with six tusks. The less favoured of his two wives, vowing to be reincarnated as the Queen of Benares in order to avenge her husband's favouritism, starved herself to death. Her wish fulfilled, as queen she ordered hunters to track down and kill the elephant king, but before this could be accomplished, the elephant handed over his tusks, an act so noble that the queen died of remorse. On the **East Gate** Buddha is represented as a riderless horse, renouncing wealth and leaving his father's house to begin his search for truth. The **North Gate** reveals Buddha walking on water whilst flames issue from his feet and angels bang drums. Another scene shows Buddha in the form of a bodhi tree, being offered a bowl of honey by a monkey. Elephants supported the architraves, whilst dainty *yakshis* (maidens) hung nonchalantly on each side.

Other carvings depicted trees, figures on horseback surrounded by designs and smaller images, female forms seated on antlered beasts and bulls, concentric circles, and figures astride kneeling elephants. Grotesque figures atop one gate looked amazing silhouetted against the sky. Near the South Gateway stood the remains of one of 30 pillars the emperor built throughout India. Ashoka's lion, four of which once adorned the column, is the symbol of the republic and can be found on every banknote.

Palms grew at the site, a herd of buffalo wallowed in a nearby pool, and from a rocky outcrop I obtained great views over a fertile green valley with abundant trees and a river. I walked down a stony and muddy village street bordered by adjoined thatch-roofed adobe houses (once whitewashed), outside one of which a woman was washing utensils and pottery jars. Chickens scurried underfoot, saplings were piled for kindling, a young girl, long black hair hanging down her back and a load on her head, was ambling with a white calf, people congregated at a well, and women walked past with gleaming brass urns stacked on their heads. Within this rural setting, I came upon the incongruous sight of a massive boulder bearing beautiful deep reliefs of a reclining figure and a large image wearing a loincloth, the latter surrounded by a host of smaller figures.

Bhopal

Quiet **Bhopal** was catapulted into world news in the 1980s following a nuclear accident. Once ruled mostly by Begums, enlightened women of the 19th and 20th centuries, it was clustered around two lakes built in the 11th century by Raja Bhoj, the **Great Lake** measuring four and a half miles by nearly two. The main points of interest were the beautiful mosques, which included **Taj-ul Masjid**, one of the largest in India. It featured a gold spire on each of three white domes looming behind the enormous stone entrance, itself with cupolas atop slender pillars on the corners. Flanked by multistorey octagonal towers surmounted by white domes, the colonnaded façade featured scalloped arches. The whole was enclosed behind a crenellated pink stone wall, and a small white-domed square tower stood outside. Viewed through its gateway, an attractive white temple was topped by two pink beehive-shaped towers flanking a taller similarly shaped white tower.

A cart pulled by a pair Brahman bulls carried two ladies in tribal dress, and I saw the remains of a large monument nearby. An elaborate ornamental arch indicated steps to the lake, where people were engaged in various activities. Birds and lions appeared amongst images on the stone gateway of an outstanding temple, its façade enhanced with heavy richly carved columns, figures, and stone screens with dainty fretwork. Supported by finely sculpted pillars, a balcony above the entrance also bore delicate designs. Nowhere but India have I seen this stunning intricate treatment of stone. Walls either side of the gateway were topped by a series of beehive towers, and there was a large crowd of worshippers.

Ahmedabad

Unlike the rest of India, in the state of **Gujarat** I found that few people spoke English, and the largest city, **Ahmedabad**, was the least progressive; working elephants competed on the roads with buses, trishaws, camel carts and cars – beneath large cigarette advertisements. It was a strange eclectic mix of modern and old: ugly square concrete blocks adjacent to structures with traditional arched balconies. The **Sidi Sayyid Mosque**, constructed in 1573 by a one-time slave of Ahmed Shah who founded the city in 1411, featured the **Tree of Life** in delicate stone tracery in a window. The ornately carved stone gateway of **Sidi Bashir Mosque** was flanked by the solid but finely carved **Shaking Minarets**, and I took film of a *mahout* riding an elephant, a group of excited children and, holding an infant, an obliging lady wearing a purple and red sari edged in blue, her arms adorned with many gold bangles. Hawkers, bicycles and motorised trishaws commandeered the road near a huge triple-arched city gate, and a cart drawn by a bullock with enormous horns plodded past. Here also, I found goats in the congested street outside a small temple with filigree stonework. The many signs were all in Hindi, a man wore a bright red turban, washing hung on balconies, and one strange building, either by design or accident, projected at odd angels.

Gujarat was Gandhi's home state, and his simple cottage, **Hridaya Kunj**, dating back to 1915, is now a National Monument. His ashram, on the west bank of the Sabarmati River, was the starting point for the celebrated 24-day 241-mile Salt March in 1930, when Bapu (the name by which Ghandi was affectionately known) and 81 supporters, which numbered 90,000 by the end, protested the unjust tax laws imposed by the British. Salt was a basic necessity that had been monopolised by the foreign government, and at the conclusion of his non-violent protest Gandhi went down to the sea at Dandi and picked up a pinch of salt, for which he was arrested one month later. As a result, thousands followed his example, and the fledgling Congress Party organised the illegal sale of salt all over the country; 60,000 were arrested, which ultimately led to the downfall of the British Empire in India. The emotive on-site museum displayed Gandhi's meagre possessions, including his glasses, sandals, spinning wheel, bowl, cutlery, *dhoti*, and bed sheet.

In nearby **Lake Kankaria**, constructed in 1451 by Sultan Qutb-ud-Din, lay a small island housing the **Nagina Wadi Summer Palace**. Stone buildings with domes and bay windows lined the shores of the lake, where a lady toted a tall load on her head and people sat on steps below the grassy bank. Washing draped the walls of a squalid shanty town, its tumbledown hovels erected from corrugated iron and timber, their makeshift roofs weighted down with sticks, stones and old car tyres. *Charpoys* lay in front of a few, and ladies created clouds of dust as they swept the dirty streets with handheld brooms made of twigs. In the townsite, camel carts again made an appearance, and long skeins of dyed yarn made a colourful display spread across the pavement or hung on lines to dry. Another famous landmark in Ahmedabad was the **Adalaj Vav** (1499), a well with series of steps leading to the water, and galleries at each of five levels, their richly carved pillars and walls decorated with leaves, flowers, birds, fish, and ornamental designs. Ramshackle food stalls nevertheless sold excellent produce, with much displayed in wicker baskets or burlap sacks.

Palitana

I travelled by small local train to the end of the line at **Palitana** (Abode of the Gods), where I found the most wonderful collection of 863 magnificent Jain temples atop 602m **Shetrunjaya Hill** – up 4,000 steps totalling four kilometres! But first it is worth repeating the journey, because as the solitary first class passenger and the only European face, I was virtually mobbed when it seemed that the entire village also bordered the carriage to surround and subject me to close scrutiny, avidly staring quite openly. The driver came to my rescue, using his authority to angrily disperse the crowd and taking me under his wing. The only one to speak some English, he invited me to look at his engine, proudly explaining that it had been made in Europe (I think Hungary), but when I came to dismount I found that my hands were covered in black grease! It had obviously given him kudos to be in charge of a *memsahib* and he made the most of it; although embarrassing, I found the whole episode very entertaining.

On attaining our destination, and after a most arduous climb (it took over two hours), with water sellers and optimistic porters hiring *dolis* (lift-chairs carried by two people) at regular intervals, I reached the gorgeous marble and stone shrines spanning a period of 900 years from the 11th century. Created by descendants of the craftsmen who fashioned the Dilwara shrines at Mt Abu (see below), this phalanx of temples glistened in the sunlight. Like the Muslims with Mecca and Sikhs with Amritsar, a devout Jain aspires to visit this sacred hill at least once in his lifetime. Pilgrims must be attired in clean clothes and climb barefoot or wearing non-leather footwear. The persistent porters followed prospective clients, the price becoming increasingly lower as we ascended. To my despair, I lost all my film and have no pictorial record of this wondrous place with its copious spires and fantasy of intricate carving, which I christened India's Disneyland!

Modhera

I moved on to **Modhera** to see the fabulous partially ruined **Sun Temple**, built by King Bhimdev I in AD 1026 and dedicated to the sun god Surya. Displaying a wealth of carving superbly crafted in exquisite detail, it sat above the *kunda* (reservoir); stone steps and terraces leading to the water were dotted with shrines containing images of several deities in various sizes. Amongst the profusion of minute designs and prolific figures on the main temple were images of four-armed gods and goddesses, the sun god riding seven horses, and curvaceous, voluptuous and nubile women, like those seen at Khajuraho (see India 1977), dancing and worshipping the *Shivalinga*. It was designed so that the rising sun at the equinoxes shone through the doors, the passing rays giving life and movement to the chiselled forms.

Mount Abu

After Modhera, I went to the delightful hill station of **Mount Abu**, which takes its name from Arbuda, the powerful serpent that rescued Shiva's sacred bull, Nandi, when it fell into a chasm. Perched in lush surrounds on the highest point of the **Aravalli Range**, 1,220m above sea level, this attractive town overlooked **Lake Nakki**, which legend states was excavated by fingernails of the gods. It featured at least two elegant buildings with a clock tower and arched colonnade respectively, flower gardens, and trees. A tremendous view from **Sunset Point** revealed the green lake, the town, and huge granite outcrops on verdant hillsides; it was a complete change from the dry dusty environs of Ahmadabad.

Again, I have very little to show for the superb, almost 1,000-year-old marble-hewn Jain temples of **Dilwara** because movie photography of the interior was not permitted, and the exterior gave little indication of the splendours to confront one within. The first temple (AD 1031) took 1,500 masons and 1,500 labourers 14 years to complete. Its domed hall contained 1,600 female figures playing musical instruments and 1,600 sculpted goddesses in fluid and graceful poses. Flawless marble imparted its own beauty in the second temple (AD 1231), where reliefs on panels above doorways, fine sculptures on ceilings and pillars, and carvings in every niche and corner (nook and cranny!) depicted ascetics, saints and worshippers.

A domed two-storey structure with ornate pillars occupied the roof of an open gallery also possessing carved columns and domes. The entrance to another venue was flanked by massive stone elephants with cropped trunks. Stark white temples stood out behind palm trees on a rocky slope, and whitewashed houses with tiled roofs were nestled in greenery. Also cocooned in dense growth and palms was an abundance of placid green and blue pools. A picturesque scene showed a pyramid-shaped mountain at the end of a valley enclosed by hillsides covered in lush growth. Palms lined a small watercourse at the bottom, flowers flourished in the foreground, and I came to a place where a tiered cascade tumbled over granite boulders surrounded by thick tangled jungle.

Jaisalmer

Leaving all this behind, I went to Jodhpur and on to 12th-century **Jaisalmer** in **Rajasthan**, where the cool blues and greens of Mt Abu gave way to the burnished yellow sand of the **Thar Desert**. From a distance, the solid yellow sandstone walls of the fortified city, its tall buildings towering above, loomed over the surrounding countryside making a most impressive sight. Founded by Ravel Jaisal in 1156, the entire town was carved out of golden sandstone.

A cow was the solitary occupant of a paved street cluttered with rubble but lined with multistorey stone buildings bearing dainty sculpting and balconies of stone lacework. These were the *havelis*, one-time homes of wealthy merchants. Men wore mainly white with coloured turbans, and two sat cross-legged on the pavement, together with a woman, engaged in the twisting of wool, one a classical figure all in white, even to his beard. Nearby, makeshift stalls stood beneath the city's encompassing stone walls and towers. An archway was adorned with motifs, and I came across colonnaded balconies with sculpted pillars, and a preponderance of exquisite filigree oriels worked in stone. The distinctive beehive-shaped towers of a Jain temple stood out above the flat roofs, and small images sat cross-legged on the front of lacy panels (*jalis*) forming the parapet of a building that also exhibited myriad delicate patterns incorporating flowers, fine tracery and latticework on its façade, pillars and scalloped arches. Other exquisitely ornamented structures displayed captivating designs on *jalis* and balustrades, under eaves, beneath stone balconies, on canopies above, and even on steps. Many featured fragile projections hanging like icicles from below eaves or bay windows.

sculpted window of a haveli

In every direction, visions of bygone splendour were revealed, examples of the absolute pinnacle of the artisan's achievement, and it was difficult to come to terms with such poverty surrounded by evidence of riches that could only be imagined in the one-time opulence of these vestiges of former glory. The multiple conical towers atop the Jain temple appeared at the end of a narrow street, and it was possible to access one of the flat roofs for a view across these and rounded domes, through openwork parapets, and down into narrow laneways. In the distance, outside the city and surrounded by scant trees, I could see another grand building with two towers.

There were ugly sides: in some places I found bare stone walls, debris in the streets, ancient unguarded staircases climbing façades, tumbled buildings, washing draped over parapets or hung on walls, and poles with a network of hideous electricity wires. Some opposing balconies were so close that they almost touched, and a calf stood drinking from a well in a courtyard where I observed a white wall with a mural depicting large images from religion or mythology. Shaded by a rare tree, a small open gallery, its white roof and dome supported by a forest of columns, stood out in contrast to the golden stone all around.

It was a blessing that there were no cars because I wandered aimlessly with my eyes always directed upwards, although one did have to avoid women bearing pottery jars on their heads and the occasional carts drawn by sedate camels as they negotiated the narrow passageways. In a few dark alleys light glinted off embroidered articles inserted with tiny mirrors, an art that is synonymous with Rajasthan. The **Salam Singh Ki Haveli** was a particularly breathtaking edifice surmounted by an overhanging rectangular section heavily carved underneath, its brackets in the form of peacocks. Curved stone canopies, their pointed ends appearing like dripping stalactites, covered the graceful arches of this highly embellished colonnaded balcony.

There was not a hint of cloud in the clear blue sky as I arrived, once again, at a part of the city directly beneath the rearing, round and crenellated towers of its fortress walls. Another incongruous splash of white was provided by an intricately carved and painted doorway below an elaborate stone balcony with an openwork parapet above. A white cow preceded me as it sauntered down a paved street, a goat foraged to one side, an isolated green door made a glaring statement, and a building with 'icicles' (a type of pendentive work) under the eaves featured a plethora of gorgeous stonework *jalis*, no two alike. Several *havelis* featured the pendentive formations under oriels and lace-like bay windows. I obtained wonderful street pictures through a decorative scalloped stone arch and tremendous views of the town from another rooftop. These included a tower composed of progressively smaller open galleries with stone canopies, surmounted by a cupola.

Back in the street, a man squatted near camels standing in the shade of old walls. A false façade featured lacy window screens flanked each side by an open corridor with bright sky visible through its arches. Pendentive work graced a balcony below, and lager stone 'stalactites' hung beneath a balcony adorned with ducks marching in line below wheel-like motifs and intricate sculpted patterns. Embraced on all sides by this overwhelming stonework, I found the detail of the delicate carving quite incredible. I encountered a house with a life-sized stone elephant on a ledge just above street level, the wooden shutters of its arched windows embossed with interwoven branches and their fine central columns made to resemble tree trunks. The coffered squares of huge wooden doors in an arched entrance were studded with embossed flowers. Finding myself once more back at the city walls, a cow stood near a vegetable cart and others gathered opposite food stalls, their makeshift awnings supported by slender trunks of felled trees. Vendors, some in the red robes of tribal ladies, were seated on the roadway surrounded by baskets containing surprisingly choice greens. It was a timeless city.

Outside the walls, I visited the site of ancient cenotaphs: round and rectangular monuments like gazebos, their cupolas, canopies and arches almost as decorative and alluring as the *havelis*. It was a dramatic venue established in stony terrain with cactus, cattle, a few stunted shrubs, and the walls of the fort city on its mound behind. The cenotaphs made a grand picture silhouetted against the unblemished blue of the sky, and there was a small tree-rimmed waterhole nearby. At the northern end of the city, the conical spires of Jain temples built by prosperous merchants and bankers in the 14th and 16th centuries clustered around the **Amar Sagar Tank**. Balancing brass jars on their heads, women entered via an arched gateway with enclosed stone balconies on the façade and cupolas on top. Beyond it I could see a domed structure in the water. Said to have been funded by a famous prostitute, the gate was built during the absence of the maharaja, who had refused permission for its construction because he felt that it was beneath his dignity to pass under it to enter the tank; however, a Krishna temple was added to the top so that he could not tear it down.

Khuri

Passing a solitary bird and two men wearing the *burnoose*, reflected in a narrow watercourse as they led camels across the endless tract of sand, I commenced my day trip to **Khuri**. A completely self-contained community of thatch-roofed adobe dwellings, the village expressed the epitome of desert life. Openwork created with mud bricks topped one compound wall, but the painted decoration seen on my subsequent visit was missing. Bowls sat on stoops, a woman was winding yarn into skeins, and another, wearing a red blouse, headscarf, and copious bracelets, an infant seated at her side, was churning milk into butter. This was achieved with the aid of an upright stick inserted through a hole in a crosspiece balanced on the rim of the container. Supported by tying it to a spindly branch leaning against a wall, the stick was agitated by means of a strap pulled rapidly back and forth – necessity being the mother of invention? A huge wicker basket was propped against the house and pottery jars, one with a brass drinking vessel on top, were scattered around. Other women, one in a colourful floral garment and bracelets, were stooping to sweep with brush brooms. Absorbed in some activity, a group of men sat in a circle on the ground.

Quite a few trees seemed to flourish in the inhospitable terrain, jars sat next to rickety *charpoys* outdoors, and sapling enclosures held chickens or served to protect meagre plants from marauding cattle. I came across goats near items drying outside a potter's, his wife in a red sari with gold bangles from her wrists to her shoulders, and a man sitting with one foot on the neck of a struggling, audibly protesting sheep, to clip the wool with locally forged hand shears.

Located a short distance from the village was a collection of cenotaphs, and a mixed flock of white sheep and black goats congregated at a large waterhole in barren surroundings. A donkey stood in the water, people filled containers, a camel sat for loading at the edge, and women walked with jars on their heads. Carrying a bucket that had been utilised to fill the leather bags, a child finally led the heavily burdened camel back to the settlement. Rustic ladders lent against walls, a woman was kneading something on the ground, and more women, one in a bright yellow sari, walked past toting jars. I made a short camel safari into the wind-sculpted sandhills to appreciate their classical knife-sharp ridges and wave-like ripples.

Back at the village, I discovered birds in a grassy patch where women, all dressed in red, were drawing water from a well. Standing on a stoop near an upended camel cart, stark black goats appeared like dark shadows against the dun-coloured adobe walls. Anchored by a stake in the ground, rope was stretched to strips of wood on which warp threads for a length of cloth had been attached, holding them taut in preparation for weaving with a handheld shuttle. At another house, a man and woman operated a rudimentary loom holding a wider piece of fabric. The eaves of thatched roofs were supported by bare, bent and twisted tree trunks, and neat compounds of compacted earth were regularly swept clean. I filmed the young lady in a colourful floral garment with a long pink chiffon-like head covering and a mark adorning her forehead, who was squatting to prepare my meal in a tiny unroofed annex. Surrounded by a gleaming brass bowl and other utensils, a knife, a pile of kindling, an assortment of sauces, and fresh cabbages and potatoes in a basket, she used a long-handled spoon to stir ingredients in a pot over the open clay fireplace.

Camels rested in the vicinity, a huge cast-iron cauldron with handles sat in the sand, a litter was upended outside a door, one dwelling was embellished with a geometric design in ochre and white, and round low-walled adobe enclosures included one with stepped triangles decorating the top. Dressed in colourful floral garb, a long orange *shayla* (scarf) and gold bangles, a young girl sat scrubbing and polishing a brass tray and bowls to a glowing golden sheen with the desert sand. A large stone mortar with a wooden pestle stood nearby. Two men in white robes and red and white turbans respectively, stood beside a horse resplendent in an embroidered saddle blanket and embossed silver and tooled leather saddle, but constantly flicking its tail due to irritating insects. It was getting late in the day, and people were making their way back to the village with herds of donkeys, the women in flowing robes and bearing bowls, the men walking with a staff or riding laden camels and donkeys. It completed a most fascinating and enjoyable experience.

Jodhpur

Travelling back through **Jodhpur**, the city and its entire surrounds dominated by the massive solid-walled fort on a bleak 120m escarpment, I found an interesting stone clock tower presenting a mixture of architectural styles and a domed open pavilion on a nearby rooftop. At the crowded railway station full of fascinating faces, tribesmen in white garments with red, yellow or white turbans made a colourful sight as they sat on the platform passing a *hookah* from one to the other. Someone walked amongst them with a begging bowl, and two *sadhus* with painted foreheads and long beards, their hair twisted into buns on top of their heads, and wearing short white *dhotis* but virtually bare-chested, held stout staffs and carried their meagre possessions in bundles across the shoulder.

Udaipur

In **Udaipur**, I visited the legendary **Lake Palace Hotel**, where flowers and colourful shrubs were the perfect foil for recessed white panels, their scalloped edges framing stylised trees, patterns and figures. Closer inspection of other panels revealed exquisite inlay work representing different flowers; created with slivers of coloured glass and mirrors, they sparkled like jewels in the sunlight. A domed gazebo stood at one end of a colonnaded courtyard enhanced by flowers in tubs, patches of lawn, trees, shrubs, and a fountain in the centre of a pond, with the occasional bird flitting to and fro. Through a scalloped archway, I photographed the imposing **Maharana's Palace** on the lakeshore, reflected, together with perfect puffs of white cloud, in the water. Further investigation of the hotel produced latticework stone window screens beneath decorative overhanging eaves, colourful mosaics, and an ornate multistorey turret.

Clouds and sky created the perfect backdrop for a series of free-standing arches with elaborate pillars and elegant decoration on top, and through which the white town and a stone rotunda were visible below. In the streets, I found a façade with a magnificent mural depicting regal personages, sheltered beneath an umbrella, riding in a *howdah* on the back of an enormous elephant decked in elaborate finery. On the opposite side of the doorway, along with people and patterns, a striking horse carried richly garbed figures. Another entrance was flanked by a couple of majestic tigers. This time I stayed onshore, at the small but friendly Saheli Palace.

Chittorgarh

From Udaipur, I moved on to **Chittorgarh** – and more Jain temples. A wealth of carving featured below the beehive-shaped domes of one topped by flags fluttering in a barely discernable breeze, but the main attraction, visible all over the city, was the square nine-storey **Jaya Stambha** or **Tower of Victory** (1458–1468), with small figures on the façades. Close to this tower, the ornate arched **Gateway to Mahasati** had images in recesses, and nearby Rajput remains were enveloped in green surrounds. Looking through the gateway, I gazed down upon the conical towers of a temple also set in lush greenery, with a long wall of the ruins (part of the fort) in the background. **Chittorgarh Fort**, considered the largest in India in terms of area, contained many attractions of which I saw only a few. The **Kalika Mata Temple**, dedicated to the goddess Kali in the 14th century, was originally an eighth-century sun temple damaged during the first sack of Chittorgarh. A solid high stone wall enclosing **Gaumukh Reservoir** had steps leading to the water, and **Padmini's Palace**, surrounded by a moat and reflected on its surface, was a small but interesting white structure. The 12th-century 22m-high **Kirti Stambha** (**Tower of Fame**) rose above a white dome and the conical spire of another Jain temple. It was in Chittorgarh that, in 1568, thousands of orange-robed Rajput warriors fought to the death with swords against besieging Mogul armies, whilst their women assembled in an underground chamber to die in honour by flame. This mass suicide by immolation, called *jauhar*, was traditionally performed by Rajput women in times of military defeat to avoid being dishonoured by their captors.

I was again travelling by train, and at the interminable stops, vendors with baskets of foodstuffs on their heads walked up and down the platform, whilst goats foraged on the tracks. In India, it seemed that as many people rode on the roof as in carriages, and at each halt waves of humanity would ascend and descend from this vantage point. In fact, at one stage we were delayed when the train halted to retrieve a body from the line, which I was led to believe was a frequent occurrence. I was still an object of much interest, and laughing men in pristine white with coloured turbans posed for my camera. At sunset, I obtained gorgeous film of palms and trees silhouetted against a brilliant red sky.

Sariska and Bharatpur

Sariska was my base for a visit to the world renowned **Bharatpur Bird Sanctuary**. In the township, I took fascinating film of men rolling dough, stretching it by flipping from hand to hand, and baking the flat round bread in a sunken clay oven, the finished product removed with the aid of a metal rod – and a degree of showmanship for my benefit! Low mountains lay beyond a grassy compound containing an open arched gallery, the surrounding plain wall nevertheless enhanced by a gateway with lovely lacy carving. A domed white building with many cupolas was mirrored in the placid green water of a tank, along with one of several stone rotundas that sat at intervals around its edges. Diagonally opposite, a second white complex had a backdrop of stony brown mountains with sparse green foliage. En route to the sanctuary, I came upon a remarkable cow draped in a floral blanket, its face bedecked with a mask of cowry shells and a garland of flowers circling green cloth covering its horns. Like the trains, people were boarding a bus with an equal number of passengers on top; I once spent a fortnight on these conveyances, their narrow hard wooden seats designed to accommodate two – and sold for three!

After the bustle of Indian cities, entering the oasis of **Keoladeo Ghana Sanctuary** in Bharatpur was like experiencing another world – tranquil and relaxed. Now known as the **Keoladeo National Park**, it was designated a World Heritage Site in 1984, and birds arrive from as far away as Siberia and China. They include ducks, geese, grey heron, storks, egrets, spoonbills, pelicans, cranes, kingfishers and ibis. My first encounter, a blue bird with a large orange bill, made a perfect picture posing on a dead branch, and the surroundings were beautiful: marsh, plenty of trees, a few flowers, palms, and copious birdlife. Common cormorants atop stakes in the water spread their wings in the classical manner to dry. Perched on bare black trees silhouetted against a pale sky, these same black birds became the basis of stunning photographs. Numerous wading birds were in evidence, but I had come to see the incredible migratory painted storks (actually a white bird with pink and grey markings), which alighted with their huge bulk atop flimsy twigs at the very tops of spreading trees, transforming them into something resembling, from afar, a canopy of swaying blossoms as they flapped their wings to maintain balance. With their long orange beaks and long spindly legs, they looked ungainly on their precarious perches, but it was a fantastic sight. A river afforded glorious reflections, some trees held a combination of the storks and cormorants, and I saw colourful parrots. The whole proved a fitting finale to an eventful tour.

INDIA GROUP TOURS 1984

June

En route to our initial destination, the **Taj Mahal** in **Agra**, we passed similar scenes as described in the 1983 chapter: a women in a sparkling sari crossing the road with brass pots on her head, animals around a *charpoy* in a compound, a woman operating a hand pump for her companion to rinse washing, and a thatched village where I photographed a wagon parked alongside white Brahman bulls resting under a tree. Twelve kilometres from the Taj, we visited **Akbar's Tomb** at **Sikandra**, an impressive monument in similar vein to that of Humayun, and passed huge hideous-looking vultures ripping, tearing and squabbling as they feasted on an unfortunate dead cow, their struggles creating clouds of dust in the parched earth. In complete contrast, we also encountered a herd of deer grazing sedately on green grass beneath trees.

After the Taj, I have film of trishaws, bicycles, and crowds of people in rural Agra, and then it was on to **Fatehpur Sikri**, begun in 1569 with the **Jama Masjid**. Here, framed by an archway, my film shows cupolas atop the **Panch Mahal**: a striking multilevel open pavilion. I also recorded the tiled courtyard incorporating a pachisi board, where Akbar is said to have sat on a low stool and used dozens of gaily dressed dancing girls as pawns, the white mausoleum of mystic Salim Chisti with its delicately carved lace-like marble screens, palaces and halls with solid and yet intricate sculpted stonework, and the mighty **Buland Darwaza** (**Victory Gate**) surmounted by a series of cupolas. This wonderful venue is described more fully in an earlier chapter. On this occasion, I have dramatic film of a diver leaping 80ft from the top of a massive pink sandstone wall to a murky green pool below.

My next pictures, taken on the road from **Srinagar** to **Pahalgam**, in **Kashmir**, show the gorgeous **Lidder Valley**, its winding blue river churned white by rapids. There were even pockets of snow in distant crevices. In this idyllic location, surrounded by conifers and stupendous mountains, we sat on the grassy bank to eat our picnic lunch. Rustic wooden farmhouses with chickens foraging in front, and tall narrow half-timbered buildings constructed with small handmade bricks provided subjects for following photographs. Mounting the pavement, a horse and rider stood under an awning outside the entrance of a shop to converse with someone therein! Seen from a height, additional vistas of the valley revealed the tree-lined river running through green fields. Enclosed by towering mountains, their ridges clearly defined by light and shade, the water reflected the colour of the brilliant blue sky above and was an awe-inspiring sight. Pictures of Pahalgam feature more ancient half-timbered buildings, fruits and vegetables displayed outside open-fronted shops, a narrow stepped street with wood stacked for winter, an individual exerting great effort to propel a heavily laden handcart, carcasses suspended from a beam in the open frontage of a butcher's shop, and rural people – all encompassed by the looming mountains.

August

The record of this trip begins at **Fatehpur Sikri**, with film of the same man plunging into the same green pool, causing a resounding splash that threw up a cloud of spray. Surprisingly, he emerged from his endeavour to reveal an amazingly fit elderly man, with white hair, a short beard, and attired only in a red breach clout.

This was my only film taken in Agra on this occasion and was followed, on the way to **Pahalgam** from Srinagar, by scenes of colourful statuesque women carrying water containers on their heads, others drawing the precious liquid from a village well, and a cooking stall under a crude thatched shelter with a wooden bench in front and flames leaping around pots on the clay fireplace. In one dusty street, dried dung was piled outside high adobe walls with wooden doorways leading to secluded compounds. We passed a line of camel carts and, in the town, wandered along a thoroughfare flanked by ancient tall wooden buildings with shutters overhead and vendors squatting in open shopfronts below. Two women were attired in bright purple from head to foot, the usual cows ambled amongst pedestrians, and again carcasses were hung in the polluted atmosphere. On the return journey, we came across a thatched village with bright red chillies spread on mats on the ground and strung on bamboo poles, making a vibrant splash of colour against the dull backdrop.

Back in **Srinagar**, founded in the third century BC by Ashoka, I have a photograph of a broadly beaming woman wearing a multicoloured floral garment, a knitted woollen hat, a nose ring, and a heavy silver necklace. By comparison, others in the plain black of *purdah* walked the congested streets where, amongst other things, brightly hued skeins of wool were hanging. Even though a city, Srinagar resembled a village inasmuch as pigs skittered, cows sauntered, and dogs scuttled. Reflected in the **Jhelum River**, the glaring silver roof of a mosque stood out amongst the drab wooden buildings along its banks. On a leisurely *shikara* ride, I filmed dense clusters of water lilies and tall poplars lining the shore, boats moored alongside huge but old and dilapidated multilevel brick and timber farmhouses with sheep and chickens in front, people propelling the canoe-like craft with spade-shaped paddles, and the tranquil waterways with **Hari Parbat Fort** on its hilltop in the background. Taken from my houseboat window, hung with curtains of traditional multihued hand-done crewelwork, I have pictures of trees and mountains beyond the peaceful serenity of **Dal Lake**.

We flew over the jagged dazzling white peaks of the **Himalayas** (for once scarcely hidden by cloud) and dry brown mountains of the **Karakoram Range**, between both of which **Ladakh** is cocooned, to the capital **Leh**, its nine-storey stone-built **Khar Palace** rearing above the town. Here, we visited a few of the ancient monasteries, their whitewashed buildings with wooden balconies standing out dramatically against the stark rock, which in turn stood out against a stunning, almost cobalt blue sky overhead. The inner courtyard of **Hemis**, ringed by four-storey wooden and whitewashed façades, had long fluttering prayer flags on towering poles in the centre. Walls displayed some exceptional artwork depicting Buddha-like images and an angry-looking red-faced demon or god, and the entire complex was nestled at the foot of lofty mountains. From the monastery, one could look down on a large spired *stupa* and the summits of lower, but still mighty mountains. Cloud descended quickly, covering the rocky terrain with a white blanket. I have pictures of group members standing beside one of our jeeps, and my film finishes with a scene of the incredible starkness relieved only by a few trees in a cultivated green valley ringed by the dominating mountains.

Ladakh, land of several passes (*la* means pass; *dakh*, several), lies on a plateau in the **Indus Valley**, between the world's two highest mountain ranges, Himalayas and Karakorams. At a height of between 2,900m and 5,900m it is, after the Tundra in Siberia, the coldest inhabited place on earth, with extremes of –40°C in winter to +38°C in summer. Although the **Indus River** flows through it, the land is hot, dry and arid. The annual rainfall is only about 5mm (2in.) and the population relies on the sun to melt winter snows for irrigation of their amazingly green fields.

The two-day road journey from Srinagar to Leh follows an ancient trade route through the **Zoji la**, along the **Drass River**, and into **Kargill** in the **Suru Valley** for an overnight stop. A few kilometres beyond Kargill stands a 2,000-year-old 8m-high relief of Buddha carved out of rock and, further still, the dramatic **Lamayuru Monastery** – see India 1983.

INDIA GROUPS & TREK 1985

My June tour in 1985 is not documented, but that in August was memorable for me because I undertook the trek described below.

AUGUST

Srinagar

Touching briefly on the group itinerary, I indulged my passion for markets by filming street scenes with colourful Kashmiri ladies wearing the *salwar kameez* (traditional suit of a long tunic worn over trousers) and gold bracelets, a *swami* carrying his staff and tin container, mounds of vibrantly hued powders, goods in baskets, wandering cows, and old cars. At one time, the vast majority of automobiles in India were locally made Ambassadors, all black and all identical. Trees and mountains provided a lovely background to a group of gypsies squatting by the roadside, amongst whom I observed several interesting faces. These included a shy girl with a winsome smile carrying a baby, and an old lady with long grey plaits, wearing an ethnic embroidered cap with a flap at the back, heavy earrings, bracelets, and a large decorative stud in her nose; I saw many such precursors to modern day body piercings. Items were being weighed on handheld scales, and a small child wore an elaborate embroidered and beaded headdress with earflaps. Holding a scruffy-looking infant, a second mother also wore the nose adornment, together with heavy necklaces; I was continually amazed at the obviously poor people who wore a wealth of jewellery. Several women were dressed in the elegant *salwar kameez* with its long matching scarf, and men wore turbans. I photographed some of the beautiful scenery of Kashmir that was all around us: dancing rivers, green fields, and a few houses in valleys at the bottom of tree-clad mountains with wispy cloud in blue sky above.

We were transferred by *shikara* to our houseboats on **Lake Dal**, its surface clothed in the pink flowers and large green leaves of the lotus, with willows and poplars amongst trees lining the banks. We were fortunate to be in an isolated location with tremendous views of the lake and mountains beyond.

Leh

Flying from **Srinagar** to the Tibetan community of **Leh** in **Ladakh**, over the majestic **Himalayas** that guard it, I was enraptured by vistas of glaciers and massive black pyramid peaks looming starkly above snow and ice cradled in craters. The age-old city of Leh, dominated by the remains of its 16th-century **Khar Palace**, resembling the Potala in Lhasa, was a warren of narrow streets enclosed by ancient mud-brick walls. Many alleys were covered by adobe archways reinforced with logs, one with a *stupa* on top. Situated at 3,500m, Leh is the world's second highest capital after La Paz in Bolivia and only accessible by road for three months of the year. Once a crossroads for the great caravans of central Asia carrying fabulous wares such as woollen rugs, *Pashmina* shawls, brass and silver, these exciting lost valleys in the **Karakoram Range**, circled by China, Tibet, Russia, Afghanistan and Pakistan, only opened to international tourism in 1980, and I organised and escorted the first group to be granted entry.

The impressive terrain must without doubt be amongst the most isolated and desolate on the planet. On our tours we encountered a monochrome environment of beige villages in stark mountains of beige, yellow and brown, their craggy tors and crevices accentuated by light and shadow. In this barren landscape, as old as time itself, people rely on melting snows to feed the rivers, and at the foot of rugged bare mountains we passed one churning watercourse introducing a slash of incredible blue. Ladakh is described more fully elsewhere.

The trip back to Srinagar was made by jeep, and this alone could provide material for an entire chapter. Renowned as the most treacherous mountain road in the world – there are many claims for the title, but this had to be one of the foremost contenders – I never came to terms with the terrifying conditions, especially if the surface was muddy from melting roadside glaciers, whereupon vehicles would slip and slide in an alarming manner, perilously close to the crumbling edge. In some sections the route is now one way on alternating time schedules, but when I made my first excursion, traffic used to pass on stretches so narrow that the big army trucks would ride with one of a pair of duel rear wheels over the brink. Constructed in 1962, when China encroached on half the territory in this northern state, the highway was primarily for the lumbering Indian army convoys, as many as three per day, each numbering up to one hundred vehicles, travelling in both directions. They had absolute priority and private transport had to be licensed to use the road. It was often necessary for the driver to get out and ascertain what was around a bend before progressing, and I vividly remember one occasion when, not doing so, we were suddenly confronted head on by the Indian army, which ground to a halt as we swerved onto a ledge (miraculously appearing at the precipice!) to avoid a collision. The officer in charge of the convoy alighted from the lead vehicle and berated our driver in no uncertain terms saying 'Don't you *ever* come around a corner like that again, and then turning to me he said 'Have a nice trip'! I and my passengers were extremely shaken (one hyperventilating), and it proved to be the last programme that I operated to Leh because on the next occasion the plane was cancelled; the logistics of getting in and out were becoming increasingly difficult.

By road it was an overnight trip with only one place to stay: very basic accommodation in the grim and depressing Shi'ite town of **Kargill**, second largest in Ladakh, at 2,740m (8,000ft) on the banks of the **Drass River**, a tributary of the 2,000-mile-long **Indus** – whence the country derived its name. The **Drass Pass**, and indeed the whole of Buddhist Ladakh, is said to be second only to Yakutska in Siberia as the coldest inhabited place on earth; Leh drops to minus 35°C in winter. Interestingly, the game of polo is believed to have originated here around 500 to 600 BC; the name, in a Tibetan dialect, means 'ball'. This extraordinary journey through mountains of granite and gravel, was also very dusty and dirty, leaving white circles (where protected by sunglasses) around eyes that peered from blackened faces, but it was certainly an adventure that most were pleased to have experienced.

Fatehpur Sikri

Returning to Delhi, we went to the fabulous deserted city of **Fatehpur Sikri** (described in the 1977 and 1984 chapters on India) built by Akbar the Great, but only inhabited for around 15 years and then abandoned due to lack of water. This time I only recorded a pool traversed by four narrow walkways leading to a central podium, and the **Hira Minar** (**Elephant Tower**) with stone tusks radiating from its sides. We passed fallow fields where large long-legged long-necked grey birds with crimson heads strutted gracefully through tall grass beside a stretch of murky water – in which a tanker lay half submerged as the result of a road accident. In a village street we came across a cow with highly decorative trappings. Baskets containing nuts, grains and lentils were displayed on the pavement or in open-fronted shops, and as we drove past in our coach I filmed food in a glass case, cooking fires in drums, piles of pottery, trishaws, and a pushbike carrying three people.

Jaipur

In **Jaipur**, I spent some time stalking the attractive striped hoopoe bird, a member of the kingfisher family, and we visited the **Jantar Mantar Observatory**. Built by astronomer-king Sawai Jai Singh II, and conceived before its time, it was full of huge astronomical instruments constructed from local stone and marble. I escorted my group to the airport where I saw them off, and headed back to Srinagar for my trek. Before undertaking the arduous trip, I relaxed in idyllic surroundings on a houseboat, this time with a view of the hilltop fort. I also appreciated early morning flower sellers quietly paddling past (no motorised craft were allowed on the lake), geese craning necks and flapping wings, lotus blooms on the water, gently gliding *shikaras*, and pretty flower gardens bordering the path to a houseboat moored beside the shore.

Trek

India is a vast country, with vast extremes in culture, scenery, and climatic conditions.

When the great Mogul emperor Shan Jehan, who built the Taj Mahal, spoke about Kashmir in the 17th century, he said: *If there is a heaven on earth, it is this, it is this, it is this*, and it is true. It is impossible to describe because no matter what I tell people they always say 'I wasn't prepared for this!' As well as the beauty of the surroundings, it is a sense of peace and tranquillity. For anyone not conversant with the concept, Kashmir was established by the British as one of the renowned Himalayan hill stations created to escape the sweltering heat of Delhi and the plains during the summer months. Purchase of land by non-Kashmiris was prohibited by the local maharajah, so demonstrating incredible ingenuity and perhaps typical of their arrogant treatment of the local populace, they circumvented the royal edict by building magnificent cedar houseboats on Dal Lake. After independence in 1948, these were left as a legacy to the Indian government, from which period, together with many new craft and totalling some 500 at the time of writing, they have been used for tourism.

It is worth a few words to describe them. At an average length of 150ft they are superbly carved inside and out. Each has a deck with a fretwork ornamented canopy and balustrades, where one can sip tea at any hour of the day and watch activity on the lake. This is accessed from a full-sized lounge room containing exquisitely crafted furniture, chandeliers, Kashmiri carpets, and drapes with hand-done crewelwork, which leads into a dining area, again with outstanding carved walnut furniture; an entire tabletop can portray a scene in relief some two inches deep. Behind this is a galley from where the food, three cooked meals a day, is served in true British tradition – even to heated plates! The boats usually have three bedrooms, each with private facilities including a bath, which is a luxury when one travels these days. They are redolent of sandalwood, fresh flowers and home cooking, and you can breakfast or sunbathe under an awning on the roof whilst watching the early morning flower sellers glide silently past. There is a staff of four (captain, two houseboys, and a cook) constantly at your beck and call to pamper and see to your every need, and unlike any other place in my experience they genuinely enjoy doing so. The Kashmiris are a very gentle and caring people. The only thing missing is the *punkah wallah* – because the fans are electric!

The boats are reached by *shikara*, a cross between a gondola and four-poster bed hung with silken curtains, with fanciful names like Haven of Love and Princess of Dreams, much like those adopted by the floating 'palaces': Gateway to Heaven and Sherazhe, to name a couple. Vendors with all manner of goods such as semi-precious stones, tailored coats and other garments, accessories like hats and scarves, papier-mâché articles, flowers, and even drinks and sweets ply the placid waters of the lake in these selfsame vessels. The hedonistic experience is guaranteed to convert one into a sybarite! Interestingly, the original boatpeople claim descent from the master boat builder, Noah.

The capital, Srinagar, founded by Emperor Ashoka in the third century BC, has a population of over seven million, essentially Muslim. Although situated only minutes from the shore, once on the lake there is no evidence of the noise, hustle, and bustle associated with a big city. And so began my trek.

As well as the idyllic lake, Kashmir is also a very popular trekking destination, and this year my friend Gulam and I completed a seven-day hike through what had to be some of the world's most incredible scenery. We came very close to glaciers and transcended the tree line into the realm of the clouds. It was a tremendous, breathtaking, and at times heart-stopping experience – a first and *last* for me!

Before we embarked upon this venture, I was asked to prepare a list of provisions for purchase, to which it was suggested that I add chicken. Without giving it much thought, I naïvely supposed that they had in mind chicken from a supermarket freezer, little did I imagine that we would carry them live. The first night we made camp, our guide-cum-'chef', Mohammed, prepared dinner in the cook tent with one of the birds perched on a saddle outside the flap! Not having had much experience with hens, I was surprised that they did not wander from the campsite. Obviously any fresh meat that we carried had to be eaten first so the chickens were the last to go; imagine how I felt after them having been our travelling companions for three days. At least Mohammed had the sensitivity to kill them whilst I was absent; I returned to be confronted with just a pile of feathers! Maybe because of the trauma of the trip, and even though Mohammed had a pressure cooker, they were tough. Although, considering our surroundings, the meals were surprisingly good, and on two occasions when we finished early we even had hot drop-scones for afternoon tea.

Along with the pack ponies, Gulam had hired one for me to ride, but feeling more secure on my own two feet I declined to do so. These incredible sturdy little animals can carry fantastic loads up impossible inclines, but even so, one had to be rescued when it became wedged between two enormous boulders. As we attained higher altitudes, and because he was aware of my fear, Mohammed took great delight in pointing out where even these sure-footed beasts of burden had slipped and fallen to their deaths over precipices. There was no path, only the occasional track made by wild goats.

On the first day, because the arranged ponies were late in arriving, we had a delayed start that necessitated extra time for the distance to be covered. By the end of a few hours my feet had blisters and I was ready to mount a horse, but because I had initially refused, the pony boy had gone well ahead – and there he remained all day. However, the river crossings we made were so cold that afterwards I could not feel my numbed feet anyway! On lower slopes, amongst the first things we encountered were men leading laden ponies, and a flock of vultures appearing to dance as they hopped with outspread wings across a grassy stretch.

Altogether, I was told that we climbed to almost 17,000ft, or nearly two-thirds the height of Everest, but in retrospect I doubt it was higher than 12,000. Nevertheless, coming from a part of the world that is almost totally flat, I am afraid fear got the better of me and I am not ashamed to admit that I was reduced to tears on about five occasions. At times, the trek involved some perpendicular climbing over loose rocks without so much as a clump of grass to break a fall. For someone apprehensive about ascending higher than the second rung of a ladder, it was like walking a 12-inch parapet on top of the world's tallest building. Normally, one is advised not to look down, but in these situations I could not even look up because there seemed to be no end in sight. Terrified that I would never make it, I just concentrated on carefully watching where I planted my foot at each step. One section was comprised of huge tumbled boulders from a previous landslide, between which it was impossible to see the bottom, so far below was it. Here, Mohammed related how on one occasion coming face to face with a bear he had nowhere to turn.

Although it was the end of the summer season, crests were still sheathed in snow; we were very lucky with the weather, had it rained conditions would have been extremely dangerous. As it was, on nearing the top of the first pass it started to hail, which stung and blew straight into our faces so that it was difficult to see. On reaching the top it started to snow, so because of the risk of dying of exposure by remaining up there, Mohammed instructed me to place my arms around his neck and he literally dragged me, slipping and sliding, off the summit. Being aware of the perilous terrain on the ascent, fortunately I could not see the ground over which I was hauled! It was bitterly cold, and all I was wearing was a T shirt.

At one stage, we sheltered overnight in one of a group of gypsy houses, which they vacate for the winter months, taking their livestock, goods and chattels to the low country. These were communal homes used by many families in their semi-nomadic lifestyle. They were built into the sides of mountains and constructed of clay and logs (even though we were well above the tree line), the roof thatched with grass. When planning my villa home, I remember being told that exposed beams would be beyond my means, and yet here we were, in a very primitive dwelling on top of the Himalayas, with massive joists supporting the ceiling, the inside even decorated with murals!

The only problem arose when Gulam and I went to investigate an ice bridge that we had to traverse the following morning and, turning to come back, saw gypsies descending from higher up – and we were in one of their houses! Because they can be very dangerous we were apprehensive and hesitated before returning. Meanwhile, to placate them, Mohammed had offered them tea – out of our cups. This did little to impress me because although very colourful and laden with turquoise and silver jewellery, they were exceedingly dirty. After studying me intently for some time, with what appeared to be an aggressive demeanour, one old woman finally approached accompanied by a tall willowy young girl. The latter, her eyes adorned with charcoal and very attractive, produced from behind her back, under the concealment of a multitude of shawls, an infant only days old. Sadly, it seemed to have an infection in its eyes, and I think they were hoping that I could help, but all I could offer was cotton wool and suggest (through an interpreter) bathing in warm boiled water. I doubt they acted on this advice.

It was extremely fascinating to watch this group unload, within minutes, their entire possessions from the backs of pack animals; they even carried an assortment of firewood that was unavailable at that altitude. The whole encounter was a fascinating interlude, which I was very reluctant to photograph in case I caused offence.

The crossing of the ice bridge was probably the most terrifying experience of the entire climb. It was virtually convex in shape, obviously exceedingly slippery, and barely six feet wide; there was nothing to prevent anyone who lost their footing from plummeting into the raging flood waters below. Being October and the last trek for the season, most of the ice connecting the slopes in winter had melted, and what remained was very precarious. For safety reasons, the ponies were sent across first to ascertain the strength, and we followed, single file, behind. The opposite wall was a sheer rock face – a daunting spectacle. In fact, I regretted having seen it the previous evening because the thought of what was to come prevented me from procuring a night's sleep! I did not envisage being able to scale it, but with considerable assistance (and bullying!) from above and below, I somehow made it to the top. In winter, the ice provides an avenue to facilitate movement between valleys for the populace.

However, it was not all bad; in crystal-clear glacial pools I witnessed some truly unbelievable reflections of mountains displaying colourful striations, and enjoyed the rare beauty of pure waters from the last melting ice of the season rushing over stony creek beds below tree-covered slopes with barren snowy peaks rising behind. We saw vultures squabbling over a morsel, a shepherd taking his sheep to lower pastures, and quaint marmots assuming their amusing upright stance to survey the territory. From inside my tent, pitched on a grassy plain, views of snow-capped ranges (framed by the flaps) were awesome, and I took film of the remaining chickens perched on a saddle next to a porter smoking a *hookah* outside his tent. I saw pink clouds at sunset, glaciers and rearing peaks mirrored in lakes cradled in craters normally only seen from the air and, as we climbed right into the cloud, incredibly blue glacial lakes from above. I have pictures of the gypsies rugged up and huddled together against the cold, their sheep and goats, another lakeshore camp, and more exquisite, absolutely perfect reflections.

Because of a morbid fear of heights, the trek was a traumatic and yet exhilarating experience that I felt an enormous sense of satisfaction in having accomplished; I wanted to yell it to the world when I arrived back at my houseboat, but there was nobody to tell. I only learned on completion that it was classified as an A-grade trek, which to this day remains the pinnacle of my achievements.

No description of India would be complete without mentioning the handcrafts. Each town and village seemed to have a cottage industry of some sort, but for Kashmir this was a major source of income. Every article produced was superb: from the world famous carpets to woodcarving, papier-mâché and embroideries, from gems to spices. Silk was woven in India earlier than written record, as attested by the murals at Ajanta. Indeed, Leh was one of the crossroads of the ancient silk road of the East. Laden with luxury goods like spices and indigo, caravans plied this fabled 6,000-mile route of antiquity to trade with China. Legend goes that the exotic fabric was introduced to India by Buddhist monks who carried the silkworm eggs and seeds of the mulberry concealed in hollow bamboo canes. Another story states that the items were secreted in the elaborate coiffure of a Chinese princess who came to wed and Indian prince. Natural colours used in the dying of silk included indigo leaves, turmeric roots, pomegranate skin, and iron rust. In the 1980s Kashmir was the last place in the world still creating hand-knotted carpets – Iran and Iraq having stopped production during the period of war – and I was informed that within a decade it would also be a dying art in Kashmir because it was so time consuming and therefore, cost wise, it was becoming prohibitive. Each carpet could take a family many years to create and was a genuine work of art. At the time of sale, the artisan would present the purchaser with a photograph of the family and a history of the carpet and request, in return, a photograph of where it was finally laid.

India still remains amongst my chosen destinations to revisit.

A couple of travellers' tales

On one of my tours, I graphically recall an entertaining incident (but not to the embarrassed individual concerned!) that occurred on a toilet (the Indians call it 'comfort') stop en route to Leh. Because of the barren terrain there were few places for privacy, but an amply proportioned member of my party managed to find a boulder and screened herself behind it. Out of nowhere, a Ladakhi woman appeared and squatted beside her to stare, unabashed and obviously intrigued, at the exposed huge white bottom; my flustered passenger had great difficulty replacing her slacks in her haste!

In the days when I went regularly to India, there was little advantage in staying at expensive hotels, so when travelling independently I used the economical government-run Ashok chain, but for my groups, in Delhi and Agra I used the five-star Sheraton. In these, as tour operator, a fruit basket was generally placed in my room, and on one occasion, I was woken in the night by rustling of the cellophane wrapping. Next thing I recall was being bitten on the finger by a rat, whereupon I rang reception to send someone to exterminate the offending rodent. It created a funny scene as I stood squealing in the centre of the king-sized bed draped only in a towel (I sleep naked) whilst the boy scurried around the floor in pursuit of my attacker. Finally evicting it (presumably), he then proceeded to roll up towels with which he blocked spaces such as the gap beneath the door. Adopting an attitude reflecting apparent ignorance at my state of undress, he bade me a courteous goodnight and I retired once again.

DECEMBER

India! One loves it or hates it, there is no in between, and with the combination of exotic sights, sounds and smells it is an assault on the senses.

Sights: From the incomparable Taj Mahal that is a testament to love created by man, to the world's highest mountains created by God; from the serenity and solitude of houseboats on picturesque Dal Lake in Kashmir, to the one-time opulence of maharajahs palaces and the starkness of mighty fortresses in the desert; from extravagantly carved temples to simple caves decorated with ancient paintings, and some of the finest handcrafts the world has to offer: marble, gold, silver, papier-mâché, embroideries, enamelware, brass, copper, ivory, elegant fabrics, furs, leather, gemstones, wood carvings and carpets.

Sounds: Streets bombarded with a cacophony of tooting horns, rowdy hawkers, bells, fireworks, the constant screech of traffic, and blaring radios.

Smells: Tantalizing curries, pungent spices, perfume – and the stench of refuse in the streets.

India is all this and more, and along with these immutable images it is a land of contrasts, where outstanding beauty and wealth sit side by side with grinding poverty, where ancient palaces and monuments mingle with modern architecture, and where the terrain varies from jungle to desert, beaches to snow-capped mountains. Mysterious, exotic, ebullient and alluring, it is where the unusual is commonplace. Added to the three 'S's' could be street stalls selling shorts, sandals, shoes, sunglasses, sweets and soft drinks, as well as fresh fruits, fish, flowers and fabrics. And there are shops where one can buy books, bronze, brass, bracelets and brooches amongst the wonderful assortment of jewellery, clothes, marble, enamel and ivory artefacts, gold, silver, precious gems, and of course carpets.

Altogether, I went to India 12 times, but because I never expected to return, the first was an in-depth discovery, and therefore subsequent trips (and not all) are only briefly described. In 1985, one of the three tours I conducted was different inasmuch as it concentrated on Rajasthan (see below), my second favourite destination in India, Kashmir being the first.

Jaipur

Our initial stop was the pink city of **Jaipur**, where we stayed at the beautiful Rambagh Palace Hotel with its marble corridors and domed rooftop pavilions. Built by Maharajah Sawai Jai Singh II in 1727, through its arches I obtained lovely views of a second royal residence in the lake. The first excursion was to **Amber**, the capital prior to Jaipur, with its magnificent palace inside the fortress. Flowering bougainvillea made a brilliant splash of colour in the foreground of stone walls built, like the Great Wall of China, along the crests of undulating hills. **Amber Palace** provided the option, taken by some of my members, of making the ascent in a *howdah* on the back of an elephant, the high gateways designed to accommodate it. The mighty beast was caparisoned in highly decorative trappings, its head and trunk painted with colourful patterns. The palace itself was a symphony of the dainty cupolas, stone screens, and delicately carved fretwork that epitomised much of Mogul architecture. From the fortress, one looked down on immaculate patterned gardens extending into the water of **Maota Lake** and the defensive wall climbing hills on the opposite bank. A wealth of stunning floral designs appeared in and around the arched vestibule, and in one spectacular section, which provided glimpses of cupolas through scalloped arches, the cornice and carved walls were inset with tiny mirrors that glowed in the dim interior, illuminating the patterned ceiling. Rich stained glass was also a feature, and a black and white flower-patterned wall was enhanced with marble panels bearing reliefs of vases holding a variety of floral arrangements. Painted figures under sculpted eaves included riders on horseback, an elephant, and large birds resembling ducks.

Our next venue, the **City Palace** and gardens (1728–32), featured many cupolas, scalloped arches, and embossed metal doors bearing images that included people on an elephant and the multi-armed Hindu god, Vishnu. Carved marble elephants flanked the entrance known as **Rajendra Pol** (**Gateway of Princes**), which was guarded by striking attendants in red turbans, long blue jackets and white trousers. A mass of intricate sculpting surrounded this access, viewed through which the decorated red façade of the **Diwan-i-Khas** (**Hall of Private Audiences**) was visible. To the left, topped by cupolas, a tall red gateway led to the white **Chandra Mahal** (**Palace of the Moon**, 1727), which could be seen rising beyond. The **Peacock Gate**, a scalloped entrance endowed with colourful figures and a floral frieze, had metal doors embossed with designs. Overhead, executed in the enamel for which Rajasthan is famous, lay a peacock with a spread tail. Above this again, and also featuring peacocks, was an elaborate stone balcony with small gilded spires on the canopy. I noted four sets of doors, each different: one embellished with floral bouquets and another featuring figures and feathers at the sides, the peacock again on top. This national bird of India was found everywhere, but at least these birds could not emit the unmistakable diabolical squawk!

My favourite attraction in Jaipur is the extraordinary pink sandstone **Hawa Mahal** (**Palace of the Winds**), built in 1799 by Maharaja Sawai Pratap Singh, the curvilinear top of its towering façade crowned by small pinnacles. It features a plethora of domed oriels and bay windows, behind the honeycombed screens of which, royal ladies would sit to survey the activities in the street below, now clogged with bicycles, cows, pedestrians that included tribal people in turbans, and street vendors making something like *samosas.* I saw purveyors of fresh flowers and a man cooking over the fire in a clay stove, his customer wearing a huge yellow turban.

The city was graced by a great number of pink buildings, many with fine cupolas, hence its appellation of the Pink City.

Sariska

Leaving the city, we passed through a village with old walls, rubble, cows, goats, and a well around which people in red robes were gathered. We were heading for **Sariska** in a valley of the **Aravalli Hills**, one of the country's wildlife sanctuaries. India's game reserves can never hold a candle to those of Africa, but we did see plenty of deer: some large and light coloured with big ears, some with impressive racks of antlers, and one with a spotted hide. We also saw small birds and silver-grey monkeys with very long tails, their faces and appendages black. Palm trees grew beside a small watercourse with a rocky bed, there were some interesting rock formations, and we entered a large cave. We saw a peacock displaying, two warthogs or wild boar, deer drinking from a pool, and a larger source of water affording beautiful reflections.

Udaipur

In **Udaipur**, the City Palace was another exquisite example of Mogul architecture, with an illustration of trees and Victorian-looking images on a façade facing a courtyard. Domed pavilions with scalloped arches appeared behind lacy balustrades above. Through a window, I photographed paintings of traditional figures and intricate web-like trees flanking a stone balcony with a green dome. Spires sat along the roofline. Many of the otherwise plain houses here were illustrated with people in elaborate garb riding fanciful elephants, a man on a prancing horse, and other flights of fantasy. Laden donkeys added to the congestion and clamour.

Vibrant bougainvillea and palm trees graced the entrance to the very lovely garden of **Saheliyon-ki-Bari**, which featured a large pool enclosed by pink and white buildings. In the centre of the pool, and reflected on its turquoise surface, stood a beautiful ornamental rotunda with water falling in a delicate veil from the edge of the dome. Black rotundas sat at the corners of the paved surround, and fine sprays of water arced into the centre from the rim. Watered by similar fine jets, an expanse of lawn was bordered by pots and palms.

Jodhpur

In **Jodhpur**, encompassed by a ten-kilometre wall with eight gates, we found a colourful street market with vendors sitting on the road. Displayed in large cane baskets, their prime-looking vegetables included cauliflowers, cabbages, carrots, tomatoes, peas, beans, garlic, leeks, and even aubergine.

Ladies dressed in saris, many favouring pink or red, made purchases that were weighed with the usual handheld scales, and goats mingled with the ubiquitous cows wandering through the middle. Other sellers stirred the contents of woks as they fried tempting foods over fires in old kerosene cans, and in front of one such, a hungry-looking dog lingered expectantly. One man was mixing dough with his right hand (the left is considered unclean because it is used for ablutions), whilst another piped shapes onto a griddle to create crispy pastry concoctions. A cart was piled high with red chillies, and surrounded by medicinal herbs and potions, a long-bearded man in red robes and a green turban sat cross-legged on a cloth.

In contrast, at **Jaswant Thara**, the cenotaphs of Jodhpur rulers, a stark white building with cupolas and a low central spire rose beyond red walls. Sitting cross-legged, a sword in a scabbard across his knees and smoking a *hookah*, we came across a turbaned man dressed entirely in white. The austere exterior of formidable 15th-century **Mehrangarh Fort** belied a rich interior that with its carved marble, mirrors, floral and latticework panels has been likened to poetry in stone. Views from its dramatic location on a rock escarpment showed a shining town of blue and white buildings cocooned in dry hills. We came upon another village market with tribal folk mainly in white, one leading a camel cart.

Jaisalmer

Jaisalmer, with its city walls and dominant fort, seemed to rise as if sprouting directly out of the desert sands from which it was created. Crenellated yellow sandstone walls protected what was originally the Oasis of Jaisal, founded by a prince of that name in 1156, and stone slabs inserted into these walls formed steps to ramparts now sealed off. It was like stepping back in time to be immersed in the Arabian Nights because there was no vehicular traffic in the narrow medieval streets, only cows, camels and carts. But the outstanding attraction in this city, once on the caravan route from West Asia and a place of great wealth, were the golden sandstone *havelis*. The carved façades of these breathtaking multistorey residences were a profusion of delicate lattice and intricate fretwork, their

sculpted stonework on a haveli

copious balconies sheltered by curved canopies, also of sculpted stone, supported by fine fluted pillars with elaborate capitals.

I took effective photographs of these wondrous houses framed by one of the elegant street arches. In glaring contrast, I came across a white wall with painting on a recessed blue panel. Cannon faced outwards from the ramparts, and from here I could look over flat roofs and down into a stone-walled enclosure where a bullock was steadily plodding in a circle to rotate some primitive contraption. Vaulted streets were lined with crumbling adobe walls, and the sky above was a clear blue. A man led a camel laden with bundles of sticks down an alleyway barely wide enough to contain it. Jaisalmer is described in more detail in the India 1984 chapter.

Khuri

We headed next for the highlight of my trip, a visit to **Khuri**. This was a small village that I had discovered on a previous journey when, alighting from the train at Jaisalmer, I was accosted by a man who had left his community to receive an education and returned to build the only substantial house, whilst nurturing visions of constructing a few units for tourists. He had appointed himself as ambassador to promote this totally unspoilt settlement in the **Thar Desert**. Entirely self-sufficient, the villagers produced their own pottery, tools, butter, cloth, blankets and bricks. Water was collected from a natural waterhole in bags made from animal skin, and loaded onto camels for transport back to the village. All vegetables were dehydrated, and I was prepared a sumptuous banquet cooked over an open fire in an unroofed walled space no larger than the average toilet! I felt very fortunate to have been the one selected for this privilege. Only 40km from Jaisalmer, it was a world away in ambience.

On this occasion, the brown adobe houses had been freshly decorated with white stepped patterns on walls and around doorways, a task repeated annually. In this parched earth of endless sand, few trees survived and camels were the main beasts of burden. A cow stood outside a group of thatched dwellings, and I saw goats and chickens. Women in long flowing saris, their arms adorned with rows of bracelets, walked past balancing pottery jars on their heads. Indian women have amazingly erect posture because they learn to carry items in this manner from early childhood. Kindling was piled against a fence, and brush was utilised to create cattle enclosures. Clay pots were everywhere: on stoops and in respective yards where a lady squatted to wind wool onto a wooden wheel and a woman toiled at scouring a metal container.

Seated on the ground, a potter worked amongst the finished product drying in the sun whilst his female assistant, bracelets up to her shoulders, turned jars by hand, adding a design around the top with the aid of a cloth dipped in dye. Nearby, crouching in the sand with an array of old cans, a man was engaged as a cobbler whilst a lady with a heavy gold anklet, also wearing bracelets to her shoulders, sat embroidering beside a wall.

We embarked on a short camel safari, whereby I came to the conclusion that they are the most uncomfortable creatures that God ever created. My capricious beast was determined to be the intrepid leader, and each time I stopped for a photograph it would race to be at the head of the team again. I am not well endowed but had to cross my arms under my breasts for support because the severe jolting was quite unpleasant! We sailed on these ships of the desert across a sea of sand, the city of Jaisalmer, in the far distance, standing out on its rocky mound rearing above the flat terrain.

On our way back to the city, we passed a village where red saris edged in green seemed to be the predominant colour, and barefoot women paraded in solid gold anklets. Drying on the brown earth, extensive fields of red chillies made a fascinating sight. A blood red sky at sunset was the precursor to a complete antithesis when, next morning, we flew over snow-covered mountains in a totally white world.

Kashmir

We arrived in **Srinagar**, **Kashmir**, to an unprecedented situation: for the first time in the memory of most, the lake was frozen solid and we were forced to stay onshore, at the Broadway Hotel overlooking the 'water'. It was not so much a matter of access – people were walking gingerly on the ice – but that the water in pipes had frozen and the plumbing was inoperable. Nevertheless, it was extremely picturesque to see the houseboats wearing their mantle of white. Although not snowing, it was a complete whiteout experience, with the demarcation line between white sky and earth totally obliterated; it was easy to understand how people and pilots could become disorientated. Gorgeous vistas revealed Christmas card scenes of snow-clad pines, and lacy bare trees appeared as if made of ice; even the famous poplars towered like giant feathery white plumes. People were still collecting the frigid water from a flowing section of river.

We managed a trip by jeep to **Gulmarg**, where people were skiing and the sun shone from a clear blue sky, illuminating gleaming mountain tops that peeked above cloud hanging in the valley. The road had been cleared to a carpet of white, leaving steep banks of snow on either side, but in some places the only indication of the route was half buried lampposts. A glimpse of the low-lying sun through snow-draped branches made a stunning picture to conclude the day – and the trip.

It was on this tour that one of my group members broke an arm from slipping on the ice. That story is related in the chapter titled Tour Leader in a following book.

I conducted my last group tour to India in 1986.

BRITAIN & EUROPE 1987

FRANCE

Paris

My second trip to Europe was with a couple who had travelled on two of my tours to India. We hired a new Citröen car with the intention of sharing the driving, but on my first attempt at negotiating the right hand side of the road I hit the kerb twice, and the husband, Don, threw up his hands in horror and refused to let either his wife or myself drive, which suited me just fine! We picked the vehicle up in Paris, and it was a nightmare navigating our way out of the city amongst the rapidly moving traffic on the *autostrada*; to begin with, thinking it was the slow lane, Don was travelling on the left but soon realised that it was, of course, the fastest!

Initially, we did not spend much time in **Paris**, just a couple of nights at a little establishment called Grand Hôtel des Balcons, which included a basic continental breakfast. After such a long time I have forgotten many of the places, but my first pictures show large buildings lining a canal, urns atop the walls of its embankment, and a sculpture in a recess at one end. Situated on the green lawn of a long median strip in an avenue of trees, a statue mounted on a pedestal formed the foreground to an edifice with a carved pediment above a pillared portico; columns circling its domed upper section made it appear much like the capitol buildings of the United States. In the opposite direction, clinched in an embrace, a naked couple headed a line of columns and pedestals surmounted by statues depicting scantily clad couples in various poses, with the impressive **Musée d'Orsay** beyond. Outside the museum, behind a fountain with prancing horses, stood a sculpture titled **Four Quarters of the World** (1867–72), with figures in the centre supporting a globe. Amongst its greenery, a lovely bonsai collection featured maple trees bearing the red foliage of autumn.

One of the highlights of any visit to Paris has to be the pale stone Gothic **Notre-Dame Cathedral** where kings of France were crowned, with its twin square towers, rose windows up to 13m in diameter, and 15m (50ft) flying buttresses. Begun in 1163 on the site of a Roman temple, it took almost two centuries to complete, but the 90m (295ft) contrasting black steeple was added in the 19th century. In the interior, roses in the arches of superb stained-glass windows showed, amongst other subjects, a lion with a saintly figure (St Mark?), a charger bearing an incongruous medieval knight wielding a sword and shield, and the Virgin surrounded (in the 'petals') by angels. Illustrations below were of intricate religious tableaux with haloed figures. Outside, an equestrian statue was surrounded by bare trees and old-fashioned three-branched lampposts. Much of the beauty of Notre-Dame lay in its location on the **Ile de la Cité** in the **Seine**; the river, bridge, and creeper trailing over the embankment wall completed the scene.

Called Le Montebello, a pretty restaurant had flowering window boxes above a green awning over the entrance, and I saw my first tulips in the formal garden of **Square John XXIII** behind the cathedral; a neo-Gothic fountain occupied its grassed centre. I photographed another of the many bridges over the Seine, the Conciergerie in the background, and city streets with traditional European buildings exhibiting tall chimneys, attic windows, spires, a clock, sculpted panels, and ornamental iron finials on wedge-shaped roofs, some with the addition of figures. The **Conciergerie** was built as a luxurious royal palace in the 14th century but served as a prison from 1391 to 1914. During the Revolution it was packed with over 4,000 prisoners, and it was where Marie Antoinette was held in a tiny cell until her execution by guillotine in 1793. Louis XVI and radical revolutionary Robespierre were also sent to their deaths from here. I found an arched tower straddling a narrow thoroughfare and, in a large square, street entertainment featuring performing dogs skipping a rope turned by two people and jumping through paper circles and flaming hoops, two men juggling skittles, and a fire-eater. A pavilion atop a stepped fountain stood in the background, and an al fresco coffee shop with red awnings made an attractive picture. An interesting hexagonal stone tower was surrounded by spires, one on each corner of its square base. An archway featured impressive groups of sculpted figures on the sides, and the **Arc de Triomphe du Carrousel**, erected by Napoleon in 1808 to celebrate military victories in 1805, had images in relief, statues above pilasters, and Victory, flanked by gilded figures, driving a chariot on top. The horses were copies of those on St Mark's in Venice; the originals were stolen by Napoleon, but he was subsequently forced to return them after his defeat at Waterloo in 1815.

I came across a large three-tiered fountain with metallic figures, a 3,300-year-old obelisk from the Temple of Luxor (Egypt) in front of long symmetrical columned buildings facing the **Place de la Concorde**, another charioteer on a roof, and the magnificent **Pont Alexandre III** (1896–1900), beyond which lay **Les Invalides**, built by Louis XIV as a hospital for veterans, and the gilded cupola of **L'Iglese du Dôme** (**Dome Church**, 1677–1735), containing the tomb of Napoleon in the crypt. The stunning bridge is one of my lasting memories of Paris and was named after Tsar Alexander III who laid the foundation stone. Its exuberant Art Nouveau decoration included gilt winged horses atop tall pedestals at each end and bronze figures of cupids, cherubs and nymphs entwined around ornate lamp standards. I stopped to observe a parade led by a band on horseback, the sun glinting off instruments and the plumed helmets of a corps of mounted troops following behind, which led a cavalcade of cars and motorcycles. Obviously some VIP, I was told it included the president. A church with symmetrical spires completed my initial Parisian experience.

BELGIUM

Bruges

We drove through countryside characterised by neat white stuccoed houses with shutters and tiled roofs, and the cobbled town of **Ypres** – with an avenue of cherry trees clothed in their full array of glorious pink blossom and a spired church at the end – to **Belgium** and the wonderful city of **Bruges**, enmeshed in picturesque canals. Boats were moored in front of façades rising directly from the water, and willows hung over vine-clad river walls with a photogenic steeple towering in the background. Many of the plain-fronted buildings featured stepped gables, and a light-coloured stone edifice with small spires abutted darker walls with white quoins. These faced an attractive square bordered on two sides by appealing 13th-century tall narrow-fronted buildings with dormer windows in steeply pitched roofs and figures on façades. Flags flew on poles, dainty wrought-iron decoration embellished lampposts, horses and carriages plied the roadways, people rode bicycles, and umbrellas sheltered tables at al fresco cafés.

In other streets, I found a wall bearing a sculpted head with a startled expression and gaping mouth, recessed semicircular panels with scenes in relief, and a statue in a corner niche. The skyline was penetrated by many towers, spires and stepped gables, and cheery checked cloths covered tables on the sidewalk. A series of narrow cobbled streets led to an arch with an image in a recess overhead and figures atop pillars either side. This opened onto a street with ancient buildings, old-style wall lamps, and lacy wrought-iron signs. Located above an archway, a room constructed of timber featured a gilded half moon hanging from an intricate iron-worked sign.

I strolled along the charming canals crossed by more than 50 humpbacked bridges and came across a small boat moored to a bollard outside a stone building, its creeper-adorned wall also enhanced with flowerboxes and wooden shutters. Further along, a white swan glided in front of stone façades opposite the tree-lined bank on which I was standing. Many people were enjoying the sunshine in a street café next to a lion-like image atop a tall pedestal, and I photographed a couple of lovely old stone bridges, overhanging trees, and a park with willows and a rotunda.

Brussels

I have film of a quaint building called Chalet d'Asse Kruenbourg, with red wagon wheels in front and white posts created from tree trunks, which retained a couple of lopped branches to act as brackets, but memory fails me as to whether this was our overnight accommodation en route to **Brussels**. Much the same as Bruges, buildings in this city were endowed with resplendent decoration but on a grander scale, and towers and spires were everywhere. Crowds ambled or sat in cafés around the 12th-century **Grand Place**, called by Victor Hugo the most beautiful square in the world and lined with wonderful old Baroque guild houses, colonnades, old-fashioned lampposts, and the Gothic **Hôtel de Ville de Bruxells** (**Town Hall**) from 1402, with four tiers of attic widows in its steeply pitched roof.

A flower stall was set up on the cobbled paving, a life-sized horse and rider crowned one gable, and façades and parapets were emblazoned with figures. The splendid tall narrow buildings were capped with cupolas, beautiful fancy-shaped gables, ornamental sculpting, and a host of spikes and spires, some gilded. On pedestals behind a balustrade, two robed female forms held gold objects, and hideous humanoid gargoyles with grotesque countenances leaned out from a structure in the foreground. In contrast, angelic faces were incorporated into floral designs.

A carriage drawn by sturdy horses passed me by, the driver in a light-coloured suit, top hat and long boots. One particularly fine gable was embossed with a black and gold insignia beneath a shield flanked by gold crouching lions; figures on horseback graced a ledge below. Beneath that again, I observed lovely gilded floral decoration and gilt urns on brackets. Adjacent, to the right, was an edifice with a carved pediment beneath the decorative gable. To the left, atop the peak of another ornate gable, stood a large statue with gilt trim; all three buildings had a wealth of images on the façades. A structure with elegant towers and a fancy finial made a striking picture framed by an arch.

The famous **Manneken Pis**, depicting a small boy urinating, surprised me because it was so tiny that I had difficulty locating it. A symbol of the city, which according to legend goes back to the eighth century, thieves have made several attempts to steal it over the years. One such, in 1817, shattered the statue and the criminal was sentenced to hard labour for life! The pieces were used to recast a replacement. The little lad has a vast wardrobe, part of which was on display in the **Musée Communal**.

I looked skyward at the towers of the town hall rearing above its muntined window panes and myriad medieval images in niches and on brackets. A stately classical building had figures atop the carved pediment and flanking the wide stone staircase leading to its columned portico. Another such structure stood near a contemporary fountain and a glorious bed of red flowers. Looming behind smaller structures, I noticed a church with intricate towers, spires, an onion dome and rose window; buildings with cupolas and spires were to be found all over the city.

Another captivating square, with a horde of people and large red-and-yellow banners on tall flagpoles, fronted buildings with beautiful gables bearing gilded figures and small spires. Standing in the centre of the square, a superb three-tiered monument, animal-like images in natural rock at its base, featured the heads and torsos of naked females supporting a structure on which stood a life-sized male in the act of hurling an object that I could not discern. Behind, the façade of a huge building incorporated an elaborate clock tower decorated with columns and statues in niches. Angels and saints graced the heavily carved arch of a church portal, life-sized figures flanked the doors, and a host of images adorned the tympanum. Gilt flowers surrounded a golden statue atop a tall pedestal. Back at a canal, another white swan floated by – stopping to look in a window at water level! A roof with lacy finials and spired gables on its attic windows provided the subject for my last picture of Belgium.

HOLLAND

Madurodam

We crossed into Holland, and our first stop, near **Den Haag** (**The Hague**), was the fascinating miniature town at **Madurodam**, portraying everything that is quintessential **Netherlands**, from a tiny harbour with shipping and a moving ferry, to a grey stone cathedral standing as tall as a man. The latter had a multitude of spires, a dome, cupolas, a red tower, and an ornate white entrance; in fact, everything was reproduced in infinite detail, even to people, cars and buses, street lamps, trees, flowers, and a fountain spurting in the middle of a lake. A church with a tower, stepped gable and rose window faced a huge colonnaded square that held a monument and a coach and horses. Other miniatures included a multi-arched bridge leading to a battlemented castle with towers and cone-topped turrets. There were bridges crossing canals, buildings with fancy gables, clusters of houses, towers, an obelisk in front of an edifice with a carved pediment, sails turning on a working windmill at the edge of a dyke, farmhouses, and animals. The large exhibition, from Middle Ages to modern, also included an airport with a taxiing aeroplane, a busy freeway, an electric railroad with a grand station and functioning trains, parterre gardens in the grounds of a large red building with towers, yachts on a canal, a park with a bandstand, and a second castle in a lake. A train crossed a steel bridge above a high waterfall dropping to a stony river. This ran through thick forest incorporating miniature yellow and green conifers (real), above which travelled a cable car. The final models I filmed were of ships entering a loch and a second working windmill. I took a photograph of beautiful pastel-toned flowers cascading below a wall lamp.

Lisse

We continued on to the glorious **Keukenhof Gardens**, the world's largest, at **Lisse**, which were a burst of radiant colour and one of the best displays that I have ever seen because we were fortunate enough to arrive at the height of the brief tulip season. Originally cultivated in Turkey, these were brought to Holland after being discovered in Constantinople. Flaunting their opulence, the magnificent blooms were displayed both in scattered beds in green lawns beneath spreading trees and in a conservatory containing a waterway. Amongst the many different varieties and colours were pinks, striking reds, pure white, yellow, and striped specimens such as red with yellow or white, pink and maroon, or purple and white. Some were such a deep purple as to be almost black, and they came in single or double blooms, with frilly or plain petals, and one variety like a spider orchid: very open, with long narrow petals in pink and white. However, although the highlight, tulips were not the only flowers, and I saw beautiful blue hyacinths, golden daffodils on the rim of a lake, white jonquils with bright yellow petticoats, sprays of orchids, and massed azaleas in pink, red and white.

Amsterdam

We crossed a lake and entered **Amsterdam**, the 17th-century world's most prosperous port, with its waterways and wonderful ornate gables on narrow multistorey burgher houses. One parapet featured white figures blowing horns or armed with tridents, sitting astride sea creatures. These stood out in stark contrast to the dark free-standing panels between which they were placed. There were myriad ornamental and stepped gables, a large edifice with a cupola and heavily carved pediment, attractive bridges over canals, a narrow archway with a distinctly lopsided pediment, and the usual spires. We did the obligatory canal cruise, but on the whole I was disappointed in this city because I found it dirty and full of dubious characters.

Ijsselmeer

We drove to the peninsula of the **Ijsselmeer** (old Zuiderzee), to delightful villages such as **Marken** and **Edam** (of cheese fame), where many launches and tall-masted yachts were anchored beside promenades lined with lovely old buildings. At **Enkhuizen** we visited the **Zuiderzee Outdoor Museum**. We found accommodation in a quaint houseboat with flowers flanking the gangway. The husband produced an album and regaled us with stories of WWII, which I am old enough to remember. The pictures showed ordinary soldiers relaxing in camp and could have depicted any army – but he was German. It left me somewhat depressed and with a sense of the futility and tragedy of such conflicts.

Angular buildings seemed in many cases to have a distinct lean and I noticed a tall, dark stepped gable with white statues on each level. A quaint café featured dormers in the steep roof and multi-paned windows, and the narrow streets displayed the now familiar gables and spires. A grey and white heron was perched on a pylon by the picture book harbour with its old-fashioned lamps, tall masts, a multi-tiered tower, and photogenic buildings with steeply pitched roofs and ornamental gables, one bearing relief of a cow. A feature of Dutch homes was the decorative use of lace curtains shaped to frame ornaments or plants proudly exhibited in windows. I came across a door with an elaborate metal knocker suspended from an angry-looking countenance, and window boxes even on sills below pavement level. In one section, the rough brick footpath was inlaid with an anchor and ship. Antiques were displayed behind the windows of a shop that, constructed of small bricks and leadlight glass, was itself an antique. A wall was adorned with an ancient embossed plaque, and in flat green terrain I saw my first genuine Dutch windmill. I photographed another through a window in the little community of **Zaanse Schans**, which was known for its windmills and centuries old wooden houses. These I photographed reflected in the still water of a canal. Other waterways also mirrored houses, along with a small bell tower built right on the edge. Buildings with steep roofs had false wooden gables, and an old set of stocks stood outside a café. Like the open-air museums of Scandinavia, several houses had been converted into traditional shops such as a bakery, pewter smith, grocery, and that with an antique clock display. One of the windmills produced mustard. In the fishing village of **Volendam**, a white wooden drawbridge, which appeared to be manually operated, made an attractive picture together with a clock tower and a building with a gambrel (inverted U-shaped) roof. Wearing the traditional dress of voluminous skirt and white cap, a lady was crossing a path lit by old-style lamps, which led to narrow alleyways. One of the neat houses had floral sprays painted on the inside of shutters.

GERMANY

Cologne

At that time, the country was still divided and it was difficult to enter the east. We crossed into **West Germany** via **Arnhem** – I have a picture of an army tank in the **Airborne Museum** in **Oosterbeek** – and **Aachen**, where an obvious Roman site contained free-standing fluted columns, their leafy capitals reaching for the blue sky. I also discovered deep relief on plinths, one showing a man working with a mallet and, abandoned on a patch of green grass, a white block carved with the strange scene of a human form bearing a horse and rider on its back. A more complete representation of the same fable appeared atop a solitary column with faces at the four corners of its capital.

By this stage, Don did not want to face driving in a city, so I took the train to **Köln** (**Cologne**, founded by Romans around 50 BC) to see the majestic Gothic **Cathedral**. Begun in 1208, building was suspended in 1560 for lack of funds and lay unfinished for nearly 300 years until completed in 1880. At one stage, it was used as a horse stable and prison by Napoleon's troops! It featured towering 157m (515ft) twin steeples, a forest of smaller spires, and carving on the multifaceted arches, in the tympanums, and on gables above. The splendid richly coloured 14th-century stained glass portrayed religious scenes including the adoration of the Holy Family and the removal of Christ's body from the cross. Other panels were predominantly blue and included contemporary designs. Behind the altar, in a richly bejewelled and gilded sarcophagus, lay what are believed to be the bones of the three kings who followed the star to Bethlehem. Luckily, even though the city was almost extirpated, the cathedral survived the heavy bombing of WWII practically intact and is now on the UNESCO World Cultural Heritage list.

On the pavement outside, street artists were creating chalk drawings that included portraits and the face of Jesus. Other nearby sights I managed to see in a brief space of time were half-timbered buildings, stepped gables, and the Romanesque **Gross St Martin**, consecrated in 1065, with austere stone walls and four slender turrets grouped around a central spire. An ornate façade was embellished with a clock, clusters of bells, coats of arms, a colourful embossed picture, and several small images. Again joining up with my travelling companions, we traversed countryside awash with blossoming almond trees and passed a large château-like structure in extensive grounds.

Rhine

We continued to **Koblenz**, which evolved from a Roman military camp established about 10 BC, where I have a record of the bridge and, 120m above the confluence of the **Rhine** and **Moselle** rivers, the massive **Ehrenbreitstein Castle**, with a square tower, a mass of spired turrets, and the town below. Picturesque **Boppard**, on a horseshoe-shaped bend 20km south, also began life as a Roman camp, and amongst its half-timbered buildings I perceived latticework, wall illustrations – and a sagging roof with a lopsided gable.

From here, we took a short Rhine cruise to St Goar, near the legendary **Loreley Rock**, passing hilltop castles, vineyards, and towers, which included the steeple of a white church rising above interesting houses on a grassy bank at the foot of a green hillside. The **Rhine Valley**, extending a distance of 130km (80mi) from Bingnen to Bonn, contains 50 castles. Some we saw were little more than ruins, but one imposing structure nestled in fertile environs had sturdy round towers and battlements. In **St Goar**, signs for cuckoo clocks had swinging pendulums, and atop a pole, the figure of a jouster on horseback pointed the way to the ruins of sprawling **Burg Rheinfels**, once the mightiest fortress on the Rhine. Another interesting sign featured a huge beer stein.

On the opposite bank, towering above the white sister town of **St Goarshausen**, the sombre imperious **Burg Katz** (**Cat Castle**) made a wonderful picture viewed through the lacy branches of bare trees on the grassy river foreshore, also planted with tulips. Extraordinary pink and white **Pfalz Castle**, with spired turrets and a domed hexagonal tower, stood in the centre of the river at **Kaub**. At 1,320km long, the Rhine is Europe's third largest river, and the castles, although romanticised today, have a less than idyllic history, having been erected by medieval robber barons to extort huge tolls from merchant ships by blocking their passage along the river with chains. From a height, one U-bend of the Rhine's constantly twisting course provided a panorama of vineyards on slopes behind a town that, from the distance, appeared like toy houses with tiny boats plying back and forth.

Heidelberg

Following the Rhine trip our itinerary becomes a bit vague, but my film shows yet another castle and a superb building with a shingled roof and half-timbered gables, its façades covered with illustrations of medieval figures. In **Wiesbaden**, the **Russian Church** (1847–55), modelled on the Church of Ascension in Moscow, had pictures of Jesus and Mary on the exterior and ornate spires topped with gold onion domes, which in turn were crowned with delicate tracery. Together with gold around eaves, these gleamed in the sunlight. In front was a huge pond with colonnades on three sides and yellow flowers along the fourth, all reflected in the blue water.

At **Zwingenberg**, the square clock tower of an attractive A-framed white church stood out above many half-timbered structures in green surrounds, and a profusion of wildflowers grew in grass encompassing lovely gardens belonging to stone buildings with half-timbered upper floors. **Heppenheim** was full of large half-timbered buildings, lacy wrought-iron signs (one with a gilt cherub), and spires. In the medieval market place, the half-timbered Renaissance **Town Hall** featured a square tower with automated gilt lions fencing above the clock, its chimes under a cupola overhead. The next town, **Weinham**, contained half-timbered houses and an interesting clock tower, its dark spire looming behind a white façade with red quoins. This had matching vertical projections on every level of its towering stepped gable, on the face of which were the gilt hands and numbers of a clock. Further along the street, a gilded statue graced a niche in the façade of a dark stone structure with a tall tower. It was then on to pretty **Schriesheim**, with a fountain in front of the half-timbered **Old Town Hall** (1674), gilt images in lacy metal-worked signs, wall illustrations, carved decoration on façades, and at least one statue in a recess.

Reaching our ultimate destination, romantic **Heidelberg** on the **Neckar River**, the castle ruins, bridge (1786), and a tower at the end appeared as apparitions, their ghostly forms emerging from dense fog. The 13th-century castle was devastated in 1622 during the Thirty Years War and its destruction almost totally completed by invading French troops of Louis XIV in 1693. Flags hung limply overhead as I walked the dark damp streets and came to the student tavern **Zum Sepp'l**, with a picture of the Student Prince between windows on the gable. Illuminated by an old-fashioned lamp, a wall bracket on the **Ritter Halle** (1592) held a knight in full armour wielding a medieval halberd (long-handled axe) and flaming torch, and a decorative arch was topped by recumbent lions. More knights, with swords and lances, flanked rampant lions atop the archway beneath a clock tower.

This lovely university town, which has long been the inspiration for artists and writers, was full of elegant buildings. Sky showed through the empty windows of a ruined structure with statues in niches and atop a wall. It was still foggy as I gazed down from a high vantage point and, once more at street level, up to spires reaching like pointed talons into the dull shroud. Founded in 1386, the university was the oldest in Germany. Heidelberg was documented for the first time in 1196, but the estimated age of the Heidelberg Man, whose jawbone was discovered in 1907, is 500,000 years. More recently, Mark Twain began his European travels here, his comical observations recounted in *A Tramp Abroad.*

Romantic Road

From Heidelberg, we continued east towards Würzburg and the beginning of the **Romantic Road**. A fountain and tables and chairs occupied a square in front of a structure with a tall tower, its upper floor extending over an open gallery. The half-timbered gable, inserted with windows and a clock, was flanked by two bay windows capped with red tiled spires. An outstanding half-timbered building was illustrated with, amongst other themes, flowers, pictures of pipers with children and cats (no rats!), maidens with birds, and the Brothers' Grimm fairy tale of the musical donkey, dog, cat and rooster. This was a most appealing half-timbered town, with window boxes, a gilt goblet in a sign on the Grüner Baum, and a stunning stone structure with half-timbered upper floors and a steep gable. I found fancy signs, cupolas, and a castle rising out of the mist on a hill beyond. A heraldic crest stating Stadt Freudenberg was surrounded by farm implements, fish, an anchor, shears and grapes, all industries of the area I guess.

Viewed from the opposite side of the **Main River**, another impressive castle was wrapped in verdant greenery, with the town below. Near a multi-arched stone bridge, people were fishing along an embankment planted with tulips, the turrets of a massive structure on high grey foundations standing out in the background. Old-fashioned lampposts and many Baroque statues of saints lined the parapets of the bridge. This was **Würzburg**, and the mighty edifice was the **Marienberg Citadel** (begun 1201), which I framed in prize-worthy style by one of the mitred clerics, his right arm extended, on the 15th-century **Alte Mainbrücke**. A beautiful garden was full of multihued pansy-like blooms in purple, red, white and yellow. A religious edifice featuring several spires and tall arched windows at its bowed end faced an exquisite building with intricate reliefs around windows on two upper storeys and dormers. A single statue was lodged in the centre of the façade. Formal gardens with lush lawn, clipped trees, flowerbeds and a pond, fronted symmetrical colonnaded structures with statues in front of balustrades forming the parapets. Our next stop was the **Palace of Weikersheim** on the **Tauber River**, again set in magnificent gardens, with statues on a mound in a large pool. Rising behind this light stone red-roofed building with its fancy gables and many small windows, a dark-topped tower added interest to photographs once again framed by a statue.

Other sights I filmed included a small chapel overshadowed by its tall tower, an onion dome on the pinnacle of a stepped gable containing a clock, a steep roof with three tiers of dormer windows, the twin square towers of Gothic **Jakobskirche** (**St Jacob's Church**, 1311–22; the nave 1373–1436), an ornate façade with a mounted St George battling the dragon amongst its sculpted decoration, and a golden animal head below a bay window in a half-timbered gable. Opposite stood a tall stepped gable and another with vertical projections like that at Weinham, a turret at its apex. All the latter were our introduction to charming **Rothenburg-ob-der-Tauber**, the most delightful of all the photogenic towns on the Romantic Route, which had its origins back in AD 960. It was still possible to follow 2.5km of the 3.5km sentinel's walkway on the city walls. The view from on high revealed many towers, stepped gables, and a monument in the centre of a road.

Horses and carriages stood outside Jakobskirche, its rounded end and tall windows almost identical to that described earlier, and there was enough light inside to film tableaux, angels and floral work on a superb wooden altarpiece executed between 1499 and 1505. Called the **Heilige Blut** (**Altar of the Holy Blood**), it contained a relic of the Blood of Christ in a crystal set in a reliquary cross circa 1270. The beautiful carvings portrayed Jesus' entry into Jerusalem, his prayer vigil in the Garden of Gethsemane, and The Last Supper, with Judas in the centre taking bread from Christ. The **High Altar** (1446) featured a crucifix flanked by four angels representing Faith, Prayer, Disbelief and Doubt, with six saints underneath. The wings of the altarpiece depicted scenes from the life of the Virgin Mary, as did one of the 56ft stained-glass windows from c. 1400. An earlier window (c. 1350) showed episodes of Christ's Life and Passion.

I came to one of the many stone clock towers arched across the narrow streets, this one with turrets on top. There were no cars, which made walking a pleasure. Another tower had steps leading to a wooden balcony that appeared to be part of the ancient covered ramparts, and from here I obtained excellent vistas over the city. Surrounded by attractive buildings, I discovered one of the fascinating clock towers featured in many promotional pictures for the town. Delicately wrought signs were plentiful, and the small wooden **Alter Keller** had tiny windows in gables, a window box, and plants climbing the façade. The most well-known scene of Rothenburg, that of a split-level Y-intersection with towers at the ends and a leaning half-timbered house at the junction, was every bit as atmospheric as pictures indicated.

Rothenburg-ob-der-Tauber

An interesting round tower abutted a squat square building, its sharply pointed tiled roof forming a spire. Both were mustard in colour, with contrasting frames and quoins suggested by paintwork. Whilst here, I also visited **St Wolfgang's** or **Shepherd's Church** (1475–93), built right into the battlements that fortified the **Klingentor** (Klingen Gate). It presented the usual church façade towards the city, but its outward facing walls revealed nothing except narrow slits for shooting. The inside featured three beautiful altars – and winding stairs to the sentinel's walk.

Other attractions were the **Doll and Toy Museum**, with exhibits dating from 1780 created from wood, wax, papier-mâché, china, cloth, celluloid and porcelain, and the macabre **Medieval Crime Museum** displaying instruments of torture from the 12th to 19th centuries. These included items such as a wooden ruff for women violating clothing regulations, a long tongue and big ears (symbolising gossip) on a mask of shame for women, a mask with a snout for men who acted like swine, a chastity belt, a ducking cage for bakers whose loaves were too small, a spiked chair, and even a shame flute for bad musicians! In 1631, Rothenburg was besieged, the lives of its councillors saved, and destruction of the city prevented when the ex-mayor succeeded in a challenge to drink a 3½ litre tankard of wine in one draught. The **Historical Vaults of Rothenburg-ob-der-Tauber** exhibited tableaux of life during the period of the Thirty Years War. The population was strictly divided into classes that even had their own dress regulations. Members of the upper class included the nobility, senators and the city physician. The second class was composed of academics, clergy and merchants. Strangely, goldsmiths, watchmakers, bookbinders, painters, stonemasons and clerks belonged to the third class.

Leaving Rothenburg, we continued south through a green valley, passing a stone bridge crossing to a village on the opposite bank of a river and a lovely garden with a pergola and bright beds of tulips and daffodils – also planted with statues on pedestals. A gateway with a portcullis overhead led to a half-timbered building beyond high stone walls that appeared to be part of a once moated castle. We drove through many towns, including **Dinkelsbühl**, **Wallerstein**, **Nördlingen**, 1,000-year-old **Donauworth**, and **Augsberg**, and my pictures show a church with an exquisitely sculpted altar, painted ceiling, and stained glass, a tower above an arched gateway flanked by spired turrets, an arched clock tower straddling a street, and figures on a tall fountain in the centre of a garden. This stood opposite gracious old buildings with ornate gables, dormers in one steeply pitched roof, and a statue on the corner of a wall. Lined faces were created from the weathered trunks of trees, and a lovely wall illustration pictured a lady and her swain under sheltering boughs. We were now in the area of the south with the odd name of **Pfaffenwinkel**, and I discovered a tall pole adorned with metal motifs, amongst them: rampant lions, a horse and foal, a goblet, the head of a cow, keys, and tools such as a mallet. Here, many buildings were decorated with paintings, which included floral sprays on the insides of shutters. In a fertile green valley ringed by grassy slopes, a small white church and steeple formed the foreground to our first sight of white-capped peaks.

We had come to the end of the Romantic Road and arrived at a corner of Germany near **Füssen** and the Austrian border renowned for its castles, namely: **Linderhof**, **Hohenschwangau**, and the famed fairy-tale **Neuschwanstein**, on which Disney based his Sleeping Beauty Castle. This fantastic monument, employing a variety of architectural styles, was begun in 1809 but never finished, and although lavish amounts of money were spent on it, King Ludwig II stayed only about 100 days in residence. It looked incredible with its majestic backdrop of snowy mountains, but we did not go inside, instead preferring to view it from the yellow ramparts of the much plainer – although still featuring turrets and towers – neo-Gothic Hohenschwangau where Ludwig lived as a child. Dubbed the 'Mad King', Ludwig ascended to the throne in 1864 at the age of 18 and was Bavaria's last ruling monarch. More interested in the arts, he was enamoured with Richard Wagner, who regularly entertained him with excerpts from his latest compositions. He was obsessed with building extraordinary castles at enormous expense, which ate up his personal fortune and a substantial amount of state funds. Finally committed to Schloss Berg, an asylum on Lake Starnberg, it was here, at age 41, that he and his doctor were found drowned.

We detoured briefly into **Austria** to see the classy ski resort of **St Anton**.

SWITZERLAND

Interestingly, Switzerland has no army or air force, but all citizens from the age of 20 to 50 undergo training and are detailed to a military unit that is 'on leave' to carry out civil occupations.

We crossed **Liechtenstein** (blink and you miss it!) into **Switzerland**, passing a lake circled by trees and green hills with snow-capped mountains beyond. Much of the attraction of this country was scenic. We found more painted façades (one showing a covered wagon and pioneers), a typical town with towers and, viewed from on high, another deep-blue lake encompassed by pine forest with a snow-clad mountain background. Horses grazed on a patch of green beside the water, a rustic shack stood nearby, and another small church, its bell and clock tower topped by a cupola, was dwarfed by the awesome environs. Coming to a town with yet more decorated buildings, nestled at the foot of mountains, men and women wearing black hats trimmed with white feathers, the men in long jackets and black trousers tucked into white hose, followed a band led by a flag bearer and a man carrying a baton as they paraded in a civil procession through the main street. In bright sunshine, with snow on peaks behind, people sat at the tables of a street café to enjoy the spectacle.

On a rare clear day, we drove past breathtaking mountain scenery with glistening snow, fields of flowers, pine forests, rocky terrain, and a church. Arriving at another small town, I took film of an onion-domed steeple with a red clock face rising against a snowy backdrop at the end of a narrow street. My next pictures show a lake, the pointed peaks of mountains emerging through enveloping mist, and a few rustic houses, followed by brilliant white, densely blanketed crests with a foreground of conifers and green slopes.

ITALY

In grassy surrounds, I found a photogenic well-maintained castle with battlements, a round turret and small drawbridge, past which I came to a lovely lakeside landscaped with lawns, trees, flowerbeds and old-style lamps at the water's edge. Bench seats were placed on a gravel pathway fenced by railing that was made attractive with plants in urns on its balusters. In the townsite, purple wisteria draped an iron-railed balcony, green creeper graced stone walls, tubs of flowers enhanced the pavements, and a narrow street was gay with striped awnings. Standing on the steps of one steep street, opposite a tall iron-worked gate, a rack held wide-brimmed hats for sale. Old-fashioned wall lamps adorned a stone building with a flowering vine trailing from a balcony. Alleyways were full of old-style lamps and overhead iron-railed balconies, the usual bell and clock tower often appearing at the end and glimpses of green environs visible between buildings. The whole place exuded charm.

We motored along a leafy road with bright pink flowers cascading down an embankment and were held up by a bus and caravan that had been endeavouring to pass and become stuck. We came to beautiful gardens with ducks on a lake and paths tracing a route between large trees encircled by massed flowers. Rounded bushes flanked a solitary pair of pillars supporting iron gates at the water's edge, and walks traversed lawns arrayed with colourful beds in pink, red, yellow and white. It was very relaxing, though somewhat misty. As far as I can ascertain, all these scenes were captured on a route through **Bellagio** on **Lake Como** in **Italy**, on to **Lugano**, thence to **Locarno**, and finally **Bellinzona**. Lying at the northern end of **Lake Maggiore**, Locarno had an interesting **Old Town** (**Citta' Vecchia**) full of 16th- and 17th-century buildings, including 14th-century **Visconti Castle** and **Chiesa Nuova** (New Church, 1630), richly decorated with lavishly inlaid and gilded wooden relics, Baroque stuccowork and frescoes.

SWITZERLAND

Arriving at an area of impressive layered waterfalls, we entered the tunnel of **St Gotthard Pass**, and on exiting the other end could not at first make out what had happened because we had no visibility, but soon realised that it was snowing heavily! Not being used to such conditions, we just had to make for the nearest accommodation, the Hotel Zum Weissen Rössli in **Göschenen**, where we spent the night. I took film as the snow dropped continuously in silent curtains of white, and flakes formed exquisite patterns on the window pane. Fortunately, next morning it had abated to a light dust still falling from a dull grey overcast sky, and we awakened to a picturesque white world with everything thickly blanketed in the frozen precipitation: cars, tops of walls, steps, lanterns, roofs, tables and chairs on a patio, and trees. Firs created scenes just like a Christmas card, and delicate branches looked like white lace. Nobody was about, but a St Bernard was romping and enjoying the conditions.

Lucerne

Still under cloudy skies, we reached **Luzern** (**Lucerne**), where large buildings lined the **Reuss River** with its wonderful 1333 **Kapellbrücke** (**Chapel Bridge**): a covered wooden bridge with 120 painted panels on the ceiling and a **Wasserturm** (**Water Tower**) at the end. Many of the 15th-century buildings were beautifully decorated, and looking back from the end of the bridge I could pick out **Zur-Gilgen-Haus** and the **Rathaus** (**Town Hall**), with dormers in the steep roof. White swans glided on the water, an attractive stone edifice had a square turret and tower, both crowned with fancy spires, and another featured a finely sculpted façade. A magnificent frontage was painted with floral patterns and figures, which included one on horseback, and another ornamented façade was complemented by attic windows and decorative roof tiles. Standing in **Kapell-Platz**, fronting a building illustrated with scenes and script, an impressive monument featured knights encircling a tall spire surmounted by a solitary figure. Other interesting sights included a spired oriel with a patterned frieze each side and artworks above; these included images beneath a tree with a serpent wound around the trunk.

There was a plethora of pointed spires and illustrated buildings, one with a picture panel on a white wall rising straight from the fast-flowing river and another with a figure resembling a cameo embossed on stone. Drooping willows formed a perfect foreground to the ornate gables, spires and cupolas of buildings on the opposite side of the river, including the **Jesuit Church** with its onion-domed towers. An extraordinary stone clock tower, with gilt hands and large painted images, could be seen from a distance looming above a partially half-timbered structure, its turret topped by a spire bearing the green patina of copper. Another extravagant façade was covered with figures and flowery designs, and in the evening, I took pictures of the bridge and tower under a sombre shroud of dark cloud.

Brienz

On the road again, we passed a wooden cabin in alpine meadows covered with wildflowers, behind which a high (but fine) waterfall plunged down a rock face between green pines. Unfortunately, the cloud closed in, as it did for much of our time in Switzerland; however, although the mountain tops were hidden, the green valleys were still very scenic.

En route to Brienz, we visited the open-air museum of **Ballenberg**, exhibiting a wooden mill with a working waterwheel and more than 50 large and small wooden farmhouses, all on stone foundations. From different cantons, they dated back to the 17th century and a granary had two animals, lettering, and the date 1656 inscribed above a wee window under the eaves. In **Brienz**, the **Burgerhaus** featured wooden balcony railing with carved figures and designs, flowering plants adorned the canopy of a tearoom, and pretty gardens enhanced a street corner, stone wall, and quaint shops. The town was full of potted plants outside stuccoed buildings, their upper floors constructed of wood. The usual church with its bell and clock tower was in evidence, and I noticed one illustrated building, antlers on a gable, and fretwork around eaves. In a scene that could have come directly from *The Sound of Music*, I filmed a house surrounded by green meadows, with tulips in front of its white picket fence and mountains in the background. We went to see the excellent **Geissbach Falls**, a turbulent multi-tiered cascade falling in a symphony of sound between verdant green growth and over rocks. It was possible to climb part of the way up for a view from above and to walk behind a curtain of spray, through which I observed a wonderful château.

Interlaken

By the time we reached **Interlaken**, wedged between lakes **Thun** and **Brienz** (hence the name), a wispy cloth of cloud had descended almost to the surface of the water and enveloped everything in an ethereal mist, which unfortunately precluded any views of the **Jungfrau**. Beautiful gardens, trees and houses fringed the lake, and at each end of one street, impressive monuments with figures atop tall pedestals stood silhouetted against the dull sky. An arched clock tower spanning a thoroughfare was topped by a lofty spire, and a stone turret was sandwiched between shop façades. A colonnaded building featured a spired clock tower and the striped shutters that were indicative of the area. I ascended for a view over rooftops and towers and, back in the centre, found a striking fountain with gilt decoration and figures.

Montreaux

We continued on to **Montreaux**, on the so-called **Swiss Riviera**, where elegant buildings included a grand edifice with a sculpted semicircular pediment above a clock and, visible behind, an ornate tower with a second clock. A stone château had a tearoom called, appropriately, Café du Château, and the old-world Montreaux Palace was imposing. Engulfed by tall buildings, some alleys were dark, but one opened to a light-coloured structure with bright red shutters and awning, appearing like a beacon at the end. Snowy peaks were evident once again, and from Montreaux we drove to see the chilling **Château de Chillon**, built right on **Lake Geneva**. The foundations were used in the Bronze Age and by the Romans, and parts of the current building were one thousand years old. The wine cellar was once a dungeon, near the entrance of which was the gallows, and after being hanged, prisoners were tossed, stones tied to their feet, through a window into the lake! More than 300 witches were tortured at a stake that still stands. Lord Byron wrote about this fortress and etched his name into one of the pillars; we did not go inside but it afforded very good photo opportunities. Also in the vicinity, but I do not recall exactly where, I have film of another castle atop a steep stony ridge.

Zermatt

Taking the Glacier Express from **Täsch**, we made a trip to one of the highlights of the entire journey: Zermatt and the spellbinding towering peak of the **Matterhorn** (4,478m/14,692ft), rearing its distinctive glistening white pyramid into the clearest of blue skies. We had taken a picnic lunch to a green hillside where, entranced, we just sat silently to absorb the splendour. Wildlife scampered at our feet, slate-roofed dwellings nestled in bucolic surroundings, and the Swiss flag flew overhead. In the town of **Zermatt** (5,302ft), right below the mountains, the Bristol Hotel featured a painted façade, and a large building with a clock tower had a green-tinged spire and roof. This typical alpine town also contained many wooden buildings on stone foundations and at least one impressive statue. There were no cars, but horses and buggies catered for tourists.

Underway again, we traversed a gorgeous alpine valley with a very blue river bubbling at the foot of green tree-clad slopes bearing just a hint of snow but with white crests apparent in the distance, eventually coming to a glacier melting right beside the road. At one stage, we boarded the open flatcars of a vehicular train, finishing up in a place with a large typical Swiss alpine hotel, a small white church, its steeple rearing into an all white environment, and a building dated 1947 with a quote in lovely lettering engraved below windows and a set of cow bells suspended from a beam above. Made even more outstanding by the clear air was a scene of wooden houses and horses by a stretch of teal-blue water with the gleaming white mountains rising behind.

Lucerne

Heading back to Lucerne, I took more photographs of the lake, framed by branches of white blossom, and distant snow. We passed the same high waterfall that I had filmed before, but this time with the summits of the wonderful white mountains (the melting snows from which created the cascade) now visible – what a difference! On this occasion, we took a cable car to the top of **Mt Titlus** (3,239m), which was covered in deep snow and provided a panorama over all the lower snow-capped peaks. This departed from the lakeside, where people were relaxing on green grass studded with wildflowers and ringed by trees to enjoy the sunshine, and musicians were playing stringed instruments in an orchestral shell.

The lake was somewhat misty again, but cleared for a round trip via steamer, cog-railway, and cable car to **Vitznau**, **Mt Rigi** (5,906ft), Weggis, and back to Lucerne. In the picturesque lakeside village of **Weggis**, a church steeple pointed to mountains high above, trees were heavy with pink blossom, and a house featured decorated shutters and a model schooner under full sail on a bracket beneath the gable. Cruising across jade-green water, I took pictures of rural houses, animals grazing on green hillsides, and a dwelling with flags flying, decoration under the eaves, and the striped ornamentation typical of the region. The now blue lake was crowded with white sailboats. Lucerne was also home to one of the world's most famous monuments, **The Dying Lion of Lucerne**. Hewn directly from natural pale grey rock in 1820, and dedicated to the 600 heroic Swiss guards of Louis XVI died in the French Revolution, it was described by Mark Twain as: *The saddest and most compassionate piece of rock on earth.* He wrote about the town in his *A Tramp Abroad*, and it was also home to Richard Wagner between 1866 and 1872.

Dying Lion of Lucerne

Schaffhausen

Leaving Lucerne, we headed north again, to the spectacular **Rheinfall** (**Rhine Falls**) at **Schaffhausen**. The largest fall in Europe, it dropped 23m with a tremendous roar as, every second, 600 cubic metres of water crashed down to rage over rocks. The **Old Town** was bursting with oriels, painted façades, and ornamental fountains. Attractive structures included an ornate clock tower, a steeple with a zigzag design on the spire, and metal doors embossed with biblical scenes, three of which showed Joseph leading Mary and the baby Jesus on a donkey, Adam and Eve under the apple tree, and a king with a detachment of spear-carrying soldiers. A second building featured a zigzag pattern on the spire of a turret, plaques adorned a façade, a sundial enhanced a wall, and a little white church had a single small arched window, tableaux of domestic scenes on beautifully carved wooden doors, and a steep slate roof topped by a tiny bell tower. A picture was lodged beneath the clock on an arched tower spanning the street.

GERMANY

Black Forest

We went from Schaffhausen through the **Schwarzwald** (**Black Forest**), where Hansel and Gretel encountered the wicked witch, and which was disappointing because there were hardly any trees left – but plenty of cuckoo clocks! The touristy town where we chose to stop was full of decorative wrought-iron signs (one with a gilt bear), painted shutters and façades, colourful flowerboxes, and ornately carved clocks (two crowned with antlered deer heads) both in- and outside the many shops. One wall illustration showed the industry in medieval times, even to a dog sitting in the midst of all the activity, and the window frames were surrounded by delicate designs. A large half-timbered house was ensconced amongst trees, a piece of driftwood with a whittled face was attached to a wall, and a life-sized bear balanced on top of a pole. Behind the bear, the steep gable on a pale façade was embellished with figures, crests and a clock. Oversized baskets reposed on the awning of a shop, whilst regular sizes were arranged on the pavement underneath. Also sitting on the sidewalk were cane chairs for sale, and other items hung on a rack or were strung like colourful garlands from rafters.

Europa Park

Whilst in Germany we also visited **Europa Park** in the town of **Rust**. The country's answer to Disneyland, it was introduced by a plot of yellow tulips near a small bridge and working windmills. Very 'Disneyesque', it included a Tea Cup Ride with cups radiating out from a large blue and white patterned teapot like Delftware, rafts floating gently on a willow-fringed lake with ducks, a Mountain Coaster, Pirates in Bavaria (very like Anaheim and Florida), a ride on a Mississippi paddle steamer past a waterfall tumbling down a rock face, where automated elephants, their large ears flapping, squirted passengers, and the Flume Ride akin to Splash Mountain. Animated tableaux behind glass featured a pretty girl with a head-nodding dog (Dorothy from the Wizard of Oz?), an old lady ironing outside a toadstool house with a mushroom merry-go-round in the background, and Gretel with Hansel, who was eating a pretzel, outside the gingerbread house: the walls completely inundated with confectionary, the wicked witch in the doorway, and animals on grass from which colourful toadstools sprouted. Also like Disneyland, there were different themed areas. Italy was represented by a bridge with a white balustrade, which led across water to a pink building with a yellow and white striped awning on its crenellated walls. A bell and cupola lay above the entrance, white statues inhabited the forecourt, and old-style lamps also made an appearance. There was a 75m sightseeing tower and, by the water's edge, patches of lawn with trees and benches for sitting.

Shows included performing seals that clapped or walked on flippers whilst balancing a ball on their nose, and leaping dolphins that 'walked' on water and teetered on the edge of the pool. More rides included bright yellow old-time cars that crossed a white bridge with jetting fountains in the water to one side, and the Palais de Cristal, a soothing boat trip through a white iron and glass gallery. This navigated its way past comical ducks, huge frogs, exotic artificial blooms, bright parrots, pelicans, vines, mushrooms, flamingos and toucans – all, except for a few fresh flowers, make believe. Lastly I partook of a toy train ride, and we finished up back at the carved entrance arch with a stone fountain in front.

Trier

We travelled past lush countryside with gently undulating green hills, farmhouses, and a large wooden cross bearing a crucified Christ beside the road. The next large town, **Trier**, was Germany's oldest, existing 1,300 years before Rome. It featured more shutters with painted patterns, attractive spires on tall buildings, fancy gables, turrets and towers, tables and chairs on the footpath, and an ornate metal fountain in front of a sculpted façade with a gilded image. The large **Hauptmarkt Square** was lined with tall narrow half-timbered and stuccoed buildings with many dormer windows and decorative Baroque gables. Its centre was occupied by three-branched lampposts, a flower market, a stone cross, a statue on a pedestal, and more tables and chairs for al fresco dining. Looming behind, a square clock tower had a steeple ringed by four smaller spires on tiny turrets, and an elaborate archway contained a figure in a niche. Another image adorned a corner of the Gothic **Steipe**, its decorated arches also a feature, and adjacent was the Renaissance **Rotes Haus** with an early Baroque gable. Rampant lions with gilded tails flanked French doors on the shingled upper storey of yet another grand building, and standing out in silhouette, a corner statue on a bracket below a canopy made an interesting study. The huge second-century blackened stone **Porta Nigra**, the city's chief landmark, looked out of place. An edifice with a green spire on a corner turret and unusual pyramidal gables above attic windows completed the town, which was also the birthplace of Karl Marx (1818). My next pictures show landscaped ruins and wooden houses.

Moselle Valley

On our homeward leg, we headed for France along the **Moselle Valley**, which I found much more enjoyable than the busy Rhine, a lot quieter and more intimate. We paused at **Leiwen** to photograph the panoramic scene below: a large river bend with vineyards in the foreground and a reflected bridge leading to **Trittenheim** on the tree-lined shore opposite. It was along the Moselle that we found the stunning 700-year-old double town of **Bernkastel-Kues**, which gets my vote for the most picturesque in all of Germany. Dominated by 13th-century **Landshut Castle**, it was a maze of narrow twisting streets and alleys lined with 400-year-old half-timbered buildings featuring filigree lamps, signs and weather vanes. Highlights were the **Markt** (**Market Square**) with its Renaissance **Town Hall** (1608), **St Michael's Fountain** (1606) with a filigree metal surround and, at the corner of converging streets on different levels, quaint **Spitzhäuschen** (1583), a tiny building with a tall peaked gable on an overhanging upper storey with a precarious lean. Other cobbled streets, such as **Römerstrasse,** contained myriad such gems in romantic ensembles of half-timbered buildings with window boxes, beautifully decorated gables, and oriels. A figure with gilded wings stood facing a building with an intricate wrought-iron and gilt weathervane on its rounded half-timbered gable. In sharp contrast was the 500-year-old **St Nicholas Hospice** or **Cusanus Convent**. White with red brick trim and a dark steeple, it was the heritage of the Moselle's greatest son, Cardinal Nicholas of Kues (1401–64), who was one of the first German humanists to suggest that the earth was not the centre of the universe. The dark 14th-century **Pfarrkirche St Michael**, its spired tower ringed by a crown of eight smaller spires, was originally part of the fortification walls and made an attractive picture next to a white façade with a rounded gable. Green forest cloaked steep hills in the background. The entire town was a sheer delight.

Spitzhäuschen
C. Arnoldi, Veldenz

LUXEMBOURG

Here again, I have forgotten our exact route, but staying away from big cities we went through **Luxembourg**, from where I have a pamphlet detailing two walking tours but do not recall undertaking either! We came across an imposing archway straddling the road, a spired turret one side and a steep sculpted gable the other. Deep relief and the name Brücken Schenke appeared on the front, and flowerboxes brightened the rear. Towers and buildings lined the opposite bank of the river at our next stop, and we found a castle-like structure with many spires, more half-timbered and stone buildings, a narrow street with a tall tower at one end, a fine square with a fountain and half-timbered gables, and a man in a red jacket and bowler hat turning the handle of a barrel organ on which reposed a toy monkey. Moving on, a castle sat on the crest of a hill beyond buildings along the edge of the river, purple wisteria draped a balcony, lopsided half-timbered buildings had tall gables that added to the illusion of toppling, and a sign on an *apotheke* indicated that we must have re-entered Germany. Wisteria graced an illustrated wall near an attractive lamppost, decorative painted panels appeared below a window box on a half-timbered façade, and an archaeological site, made inviting with pansies, had sculpted figures and faces on a series of square pillars supporting spired pediments.

FRANCE

Rheims and Paris

We came to mighty **Rheims Cathedral** with its host of spires, flying buttresses, copper canopies, tall arched windows, mythical beasts lining a balustrade, statues, a central rose window, and heavily carved tiered portals. We passed fields of glorious yellow rape and entered **Paris** again, where I made good use of the efficient and convenient Paris Metro to visit the 50m (164ft) **Arc de Triomphe**, featuring sculpted figures on horseback and scenes of battle. Built by Napoleon in 1806, it was located in **Place Charles de Gaulle** (formerly **Place de l'Etoile**) looking down the **Champs-Elysées**. The name Elysian Fields refers to a mythological Greek heaven for heroes and the renowned avenue began as a graceful tree-lined promenade. Commissioned by Queen Regent Marie de Médici in 1616, it was intended as a continuation of Tuileries Gardens, which were designed to provide a grandiose vista from the royal palace – the **Louvre**. From here, I took the Metro to the 324m (1,063ft) **Eiffel Tower**, inaugurated in 1889 by Edward VII, then Prince of Wales, which unfortunately lost the romance due to a young man jumping off and committing suicide shortly before I arrived. The covered body was still on the pavement and a multitude of police in attendance, so consequently I lost any desire to climb it. This monument, the world's tallest structure until the completion in 1931 of New York's Empire State Building, needs no explanation, but the surroundings were also impressive. Flanked by statues of a man and horse, the **Trocadéro Fountains** stood in the centre of the avenue leading to the curved colonnaded wings of the **Palais de Chaillot** opposite. **Pont d'Lena**, which joined the two sites, had images in relief between its arches and statues on pedestals and plinths, one showing figures on horseback, a second an angel blowing a long horn. I filmed the tree-lined **Parc du Champ de Mars** through the arch of the tower.

I found myself back at the opulent Pont Alexandre III with its flamboyant decoration, and filmed the Eiffel Tower in the distance, framed by an elaborate five-branched lamp with figures around the base. Another charioteer driving a team of four horses fanned out atop a building, and I passed a noteworthy edifice with statues around the roof. I took the Metro to **Sacré-Coeur** (1875–1914) atop **Montmartre**, one of its distinctive domes the highest point in Paris after the Eiffel Tower. From the grounds, I obtained a comprehensive but hazy panorama over Paris, with the Eiffel Tower off to the far right. Other sights included a wall clock in an ornately carved surround featuring the figure of Justice with the scales and, visible behind a bridge, interesting rooflines with a spire, dormers, and the typical French wedge-shaped roof flanked by tall chimneys.

On the Metro again, I proceeded to the area known as **The Left Bank**, an enclave of poets, philosophers and artists, one of whom was painting another engaged in the same pursuit. Behind ornate iron gates, I glimpsed the beautiful lacy 75m (245ft) spire of the **Sainte-Chapelle**. On the opposite side of the river, a gilded winged figure surmounted a tall column near the Gothic **Tour St-Jacques**. Dating from 1523, this was all that remained of a medieval church used as a rendezvous by pilgrims setting out for Compostela in Spain and destroyed by revolutionaries in 1797. An imposing building with a decorated façade had a clock tower between dormer windows in its steep roof, which was topped by figures and a finial. I saw many grand buildings, a statue on a pedestal with sculpted figures around the plinth, the **Genius of Liberty** on top of the **Colonne de Juilliet** and, once more making a statement against the sky: spires, tall chimneys, sculptures on a parapet, and iron embellishment on wedge-shaped roofs.

Calais

Having returned our vehicle in Paris, we set out for Calais and the ferry to Dover. As I remember, this was not as straightforward as anticipated because of misinformation on schedules, and we were shunted from one port to another more than once. In between, it was back to picturesque half-timbered buildings and a shop with the names of merchandise painted on the façade: vétements, cravates, chemises, confections, bonneterie, lingerie, corsets, chapellerie, mercerie, and so on. A beautiful church featured delicate stonework on towers, in and around the tympanum, and on pillars. A life-sized image adorned the upright between doors at the entrance, and at odds with the exquisite surrounds, hideous gargoyles encrusted with yellow lichen reached out overhead. Window boxes added allure to a small half-timbered building wedged between larger stuccoed structures, and another had shuttered windows displaying different colours of glass in their muntined panes; both had tiny attic windows. I came upon an extraordinary building, with many fine spires, a lacy iron finial on the roof, statues atop a turret and the point of a gable, and extravagant decoration on the façade, which even appeared around old-style lamps on stone pillars in the iron fence. A golden statue stood on a pedestal beneath an elaborate canopy formed by wrought-iron tracery of twisted vines and leaves with a gilded angel on top.

The coast was shrouded in mist, and waves washed up on the pebble shore and crashed against the sheer white cliffs. Delightful chocolate box scenes of a rill running alongside thatched half-timbered cottages with white fences were augmented by a half-timbered turret, a low wooden bridge, rustic brick-and-shingle buildings with gabled dormers, attic windows peeping from thick thatch, small gardens, window boxes, green meadows, brick and stone houses with shutters, and blooming wisteria on a stone wall. Old metal millwheels inhabited a small trilling stream beside a creeper-covered stone wall surrounded by dense greenery, which also enveloped a lovely flowering tree. Near sluice gates, glorious delicate pink maple-like leaves and a vine bearing a mass of pink flowers enhanced a second building with a rusted waterwheel. Ivy draped a façade with a spired turret, and I was now high on a hill where I could look down on the cliffs and sea below.

In **Calais**, the gracious Flemish Renaissance **Town Hall** (1927), with a finial, spires, tall chimneys, elaborate gables, and dormers in the steep roof, was dominated by a lofty spired clock tower and offset by gorgeous purple-and-yellow flowerbeds in green lawn. The channel ferry emerged out of the fog like some apparition in seafaring tales of ghostly ships. Calais has an interesting history too long to relate here, but it was where Lady Hamilton, wife of Admiral Lord Nelson died, and home between 1817 and 1830 to exiled English dandy George (Beau) Brummel.

ENGLAND

London

Back in England, my next pictures show an unusual cathedral-like edifice in two-toned brick, with a cupola crowning an exceptionally tall tower to one side and smaller symmetrical towers flanking its arched entrance. Lacy balconies enhanced a typical establishment called the Chef & Brewer at the corner of Buckingham Gate and Victoria Street, **London**. An ornate edifice featured stepped gables, crenellated turrets and tall chimneys, a square church tower with several spires stood behind, and a building with twin towers opposite. Behind this, and to the left, stood the elaborate spired clock tower of Big Ben. One of the famous red double-decker buses drove past a multistorey building with fancy free-standing gables, green-spired turrets, and iron-railed balconies. Strolling through one of the many parks, beneath large shady trees, I found a restaurant with hanging baskets on the façade and tables and chairs in the street. Creating three lanes of traffic, a tripartite arch with an inscription to Victoria Regina overhead lay beyond an equestrian statue. A similar statue stood facing impressive buildings with Big Ben in the background.

From **Trafalgar Square**, with its distinctive barbed quatrefoil fountain, I could see the tower of the Houses of Parliament, and even though it was raining people still flocked here undeterred – as did the pigeons. The square was laid out in 1841 in gratitude for (but 36 years after) Nelson's defeat of the French at Trafalgar, and his statue on top of the 56m column in the centre was five metres tall. Construction was supervised by an Australian engineer who had earlier explored mountainous country southwest of Sydney, during which time his party survived by eating snakes. I came to a domed edifice with a columned portico, afterwards finding myself outside a building that followed the curve of **Regent Street**, the Union Jack flying from many windows.

Azaleas made a show near a winged image on a heavily sculpted pedestal in a reserve, and people scurried under umbrellas as I made my way to **The Mall** and **Buckingham Palace**. Built in 1703 as a private residence, it was bought by George III in 1762 and has been the home of reigning monarchs since Queen Victoria in 1837. Wearing busbies and black trousers with a red stripe down each side, red-jacketed guards marched to and from a sentry box; I have seen the changing of the guard in many countries but never in the United Kingdom. In front of the palace gates, which bear the royal coat of arms, the imposing **Victoria Memorial**, surmounted by a golden winged figure, needs no explanation. The constant crowd outside the palace sheltered beneath umbrellas in the lee of a statue depicting a figure with a lion, which stood to one side of the monument. On the other side, mounted police were on duty near a similar portrayal. As I watched, guards wearing rain capes emerged to execute a contracted changing of the guard, whilst one wearing a long red coat sat astride a horse beneath an archway.

Nearby **Hyde Park**, where Henry VIII used to hunt deer, was well-known for **Rotton Row**, where fashionable Londoners used to exercise their horses, and its **Speakers Corner** where people of all political, religious and philosophical persuasions aired their views from soap boxes, engaging in verbal duets with interjectors. Thought by many to be an example of the West's tolerance of free speech, it actually came about several hundred years ago when condemned prisoners were allowed some final words before being hung on Tyburn gallows, which some say stood at the same spot.

Not so readily recognisable was **Kensington Palace**, used as a residence by many members of the royal family, including Prince Charles and Lady Diana, Princess Margaret, Prince Michael of Kent, and the Duke and Duchess of Gloucester. Queen Anne died in the palace in 1714, and Queen Victoria was born there in 1819.

In London's notorious foggy conditions, I took a city tour on one of the well-loved red buses, through the rain spattered windows of which, I photographed the Thames, Big Ben, and the Houses of Parliament (built in the 1880s but heavily restored after damage by German bombs) with one of the bridges in the background. The next sight was **St Paul's Cathedral** (1708), with its spire, figures atop a pediment, and columned dome, one of Christendom's largest. Designed by Christopher Wren, who reconstructed London after the Great Fire of 1666 and was buried in the crypt along with such names as military commanders Nelson and Wellington, the cross on top of the dome is 111m high. Nelson's coffin was made from the mast of a French warship sunk in the battle of the Nile, and his sarcophagus was originally made for Cardinal Wolsey, 800 years before him. Also interred here, were two of Britain's most renowned artists, Reynolds and Turner, and memorials with association to Australia included those of former Governor-General Sir William Slim and Prime Minister Billy Hughes. This was followed by views of shipping in the **Thames** and one of London's landmarks, **Tower Bridge**, which we crossed. The bridge was completed in 1894 and the two steel spans, each weighing 1,000 tonnes, can be raised in 90 seconds.

We now drove past an imposing edifice with spired cupolas, crenellated round towers and turrets to the multi-spired **Houses of Parliament**, officially the **Palace of Westminster**, with **Big Ben** – which is actually the name of the 13½-ton bell and not the clock or tower – rising above. Hung in 1858, it strikes each hour, and the enormous clock faces measure 6.8m in diameter, the minute hands are 4.3m long, and the figures 60cm tall. Nearby was a marvellous sculpture of a charioteer with a prancing horse. I saw a group of buildings incorporating decorative gables, wedge-shaped roofs topped by finials, tall chimneys and cupolas (much like I had seen in France), a statue of Churchill, and interesting twin towers with spires on the four corners. An ornate but delicate layered steeple denoted **St Bride's Church**; built by Wren in the 1670s, it was said to have been the inspiration for the first bridal cake. The diarist Samuel Pepys was baptised in St Bride's, and the poet Richard Lovelace, remembered for the lines *Stone walls do not a prison make, nor iron bars a cage*, was buried in the churchyard. The steeple was all that survived a

German bombing raid in 1940, but reconstruction was so successful that the church is known as the Phoenix of Fleet Street.

The twin towers mentioned above belonged to a religious edifice with a rose window between flying buttresses, a carved tympanum under the convoluted arches, and lacy spires on the northern aspect. This was **Westminster Abbey**, the interior of which, although it had the highest nave in Britain, I found surprisingly small because TV coverage of the pomp and ceremony within its walls always gave the illusion of far greater space. It has occupied the site since AD 750 when a Benedictine abbey housing a community of monks was called Westminster (West Monastery) because of its location west of the city. In 1050, Edward the Confessor enhanced the site and moved the palace next door, establishing the tradition of church and state. The present building, constructed between the 13th and 16th centuries, has been the setting for every coronation bar two since William I (the Conqueror) in 1066, and is the last resting place of many illustrious names, amongst them: Edward the Confessor, David Livingstone, Charles Dickens, Robert Stevenson (inventor of the steam engine), Queen Elizabeth I, Rudyard Kipling, William Pitt, Wilber Wilberforce (who spent his life fighting slavery), Mary Queen of Scots, Ben Jonson, Richard II, John Milton, Thomas Hardy, Isaac Newton, Henry V, Charles Darwin, and Dr Samuel Johnson. Oliver Cromwell was also interred here, but his body later dug up and put on public display after Charles II came to the throne. In poets corner was the tomb of Geoffrey Chaucer buried in 1400, a stylised statue of Shakespeare, and a bust of Australian Adam Lindsay Gordon, who committed suicide in Melbourne in 1870 at the age of 36. The most recent additions were those of T. S. Eliot, Dylan Thomas, and Lewis Carroll. The oak coronation chair, made for Edward I, was designed with a compartment to hold the **Stone of Scone**, said to have been used in the crowning of Scottish kings more than 1,000 years ago and seized from the Scots in 1296; it was subsequently returned to Edinburgh Castle in 1996. The **Abbey Treasures** contained such strange items as the 600-year-old funeral effigy of Edward III that shows his mouth drooping because of a stroke, a saddle thought to be the oldest in Europe and carried at the funeral of Henry V, a wax model of Nelson wearing his own clothes, and the oldest stuffed bird in Britain – a parrot that died in 1702! I also have film of life-sized images on a façade, and panels with crowned, mitred and helmeted medieval figures, but am not sure if these were part of the abbey.

Not to be confused with the abbey was **Westminster Cathedral**, the construction of which, completed in 1903, utilised 12 million handmade bricks. On view in a glass casket was the body of a newly canonised saint: a

Catholic priest hung, drawn and quartered during the reign of James I. I took a couple of close-up pictures of Tower Bridge and headed for the battlemented towers and walls of the **Tower of London**, under the care of the Beefeaters in their distinctive red and black uniform with its large flat hat. Built by William the Conqueror in 1078 (after the Norman Conquest in 1066), it has served several purposes, including those of arsenal, mint, zoo and prison; two young sons of Edward IV were murdered here in 1485, as was the second wife of Henry XIII, Anne Boleyn. Today it houses the **Crown Jewels**, which it was possible to see on a 'conveyor belt' tour. The world's biggest cut diamond, First Star of Africa (530.4 carats), was set in a sceptre. Two of Henry VIII's wives, Anne Boleyn and Katherine Howard, were buried before the altar of the **Royal Chapel of St Peter ad Vincula** in the tower precincts, and a paved plot just outside the church marks the place where the two queens were beheaded. To one side, a green common fronted quaint half-timbered buildings.

In **Covent Garden** (1830) I came across a young lady wearing a flowered hat and black shawl. Standing in the rain with a basket of blooms for sale, the scenario appeared straight out of *My Fair Lady*! Nearby were large monuments and the **Royal Opera House**, a columned building with a plain pediment and statues on the corners of the roof. London also had an arch with a winged image like Victory driving a chariot on top, which stood opposite yet another equestrian statue. In the vicinity of **Marble Arch** and its row of flags, I came again to Hyde Park, where azaleas made a bright splash of colour amongst grass and green trees, and a pedestal held a large image armed with a sword and shield. Originally erected outside Buckingham Palace in 1825 to commemorate the end of the Napoleonic wars, in 1851 Queen Victoria had Marble Arch moved to create a grand entrance to Hyde Park, where it supposedly occupies the site of the gallows described earlier. For 600 years, until 1783, the condemned were brought here in open carts, and executions were such a popular form of entertainment that tiered seating was set up; one hanging reported to have attracted 200,000 spectators! Close by was the famous **Dorchester Hotel** and a corner of **Park Lane**; I always consider London as the monopoly board come to life and find it an exciting city. I finished back at Trafalgar Square. I also saw **Number 10**, home of British Prime Ministers since 1735, but it was no longer possible to enter **Downing Street** because it was cordoned off by a barricade manned by police.

Cornwall

At this stage, I had left my companions and, investing in a four-day Britrail Pass, headed for the southwest corner of England. This was my first visit, and at that time I had no contacts in the country but was enthralled by this brief introduction to an area that still remains my favourite part of the United Kingdom. I particularly remember sitting on a stool behind a shop window eating a Cornish pasty and watching rain lash the beach, seaside buildings and walkway; it was very atmospheric.

From London, I went initially to **Cornwall**, where I recall wasting a considerable amount of time waiting for connections between **Redruth** and **Truro**, and the same on the return. Thinking that I was not taking full advantage of the pass, I went to a railway station and requested assistance to maximise its use. The helpful attendant mapped out a programme that took me from Land's End as far as (and even to) the Isle of Skye, across to Inverness, down the east coast via Edinburgh, and back to London. Although I experienced most of it through train windows, I certainly covered a lot of territory in three days and was full of praise for the much maligned Britrail service.

My first port of call was **Penzance**, from where I walked to one of the most photogenic of the many lovely villages, tiny Mousehole, and then continued on to **St Ives**, once Cornwall's busiest fishing port, with quaint old houses, narrow lanes, and a 500-year-old church. **Mousehole** (pronounced Mouzel) was so named because of the resemblance of a local sea cave to that of the rodent's habitat. In 1595, the Spanish made a hit-and-run raid, raping women and burning houses, and in 1891 the publican and eight villagers died in a vain sea rescue attempt.

This entire corner of England was a picturesque collection of communities with stone houses (many whitewashed) and flowers on narrow, sometimes steep streets leading to small sheltered coves, harbours, or shingle beaches. Climbing roses bloomed in profusion, hanging baskets flourished, and I saw a comical image in a tall red hat lying on his belly along the capping of a roof. The train passed a castle perched on a summit in the water; with the appearance of Mont St Michel in France, it was here called by the English equivalent, **St Michael's Mount**, and showed up almost as a shadow behind the glare of sunlit waves. It takes its name from Archangel St Michael who was said to have appeared to local fishermen in the year 495.

Topical names encountered were: Nelson's Bar (with a picture of the Admiral), Dolphin Cottage, Poldark Cottage, and Old Coastguard, with an illustration of a white-whiskered seafarer dressed in a cap and rollneck sweater and smoking a pipe. A sculpted façade featured the rope design that signified the occupation of a sailor, and a larger town contained a row of two-storey attached houses with bay windows, attics, and clusters of chimneys. A tiny whitewashed stone cottage with a slate roof had one small muntined window beside the door and two others below street level. Houses above a seawall faced a picturesque harbour protected by a long groin, where boats were lying high and dry at low tide. There were a few pretty gardens, cascading vines (one with a mass of bright purple flowers), and a stone wall enhanced with pink-blossoming creeper. A ship's figurehead adorned another stone wall, and sunlight glinted off the surface of the sea beyond whitewashed houses of rough stone with slate roofs and one half-timbered building.

The Union Jack was blowing proudly in a stiff breeze when I arrived at **Land's End**, where foaming white waves crashed at the base of rugged perpendicular cliffs and seagulls flew overhead. A white building bearing a sign stating First and Last House in England stood on the grassy verge. On a bright clear day, the deep-blue ocean and windswept green surrounds all made for spectacular pictures. At that time, it was free to wander around, but on my second visit it was necessary to pay – the price of progress?

SCOTLAND

I recollect arriving in **Glasgow**, located on the banks of the **River Clyde**, in the wee small hours of the morning and having time to spare before my connection. Because the bleak station was exposed and there was no waiting room, I took a brief excursion with a young soldier returning home on leave, who kindly offered to show me something of the city. I took pictures of a statue depicting a figure on a rearing horse, a towering obelisk in front of a building featuring a domed bell tower and cupolas, and a yellow flowerbed making a bright display in the dull light of dawn. Another imposing building had arched windows and dormers with elaborate gables. I filmed a mirrored wall showing the old reflected in the new, an exquisite pavement drawing of fluffy kittens secreted amongst white daisies in long grass to observe a butterfly and, framed by an arch, an elegant edifice with fancy capitals on fluted columns. A clock (reading 5.30am!) was set in an interesting stepped gable, flowers in tubs surrounded trees in the foreground, and in the dim foggy conditions of early morning, spires and cupolas were silhouetted against the sky. My fingers were almost too frozen to operate the camera and it was bitterly cold, so I went to a luxury hotel accessed from the station, curled up in one of their big cosy leather armchairs, and asked the concierge to wake me in time for the train! Known in the past for its shipyards (most now closed),

Glasgow has built more large liners than any other city in the world, amongst them the Queens Elizabeth and Mary.

Underway again, we passed miles of green meadows and hills, verdant forests, a tiny tree-covered islet, isolated dwellings, and plenty of water. At one stage, we went by **Loch Ness**, Britain's largest lake, of monster fame, but the other passengers did not tell me until it was almost out of sight. Reaching **Fort William**, begun as a 17th-century army fort, overshadowed by Britain's highest mountain, Ben Nevis (1,350m), and location for Mel Gibson's 1995 film *Braveheart*, I continued to **Mallaig** from where I caught a ferry to **Skye**. I took a bus to **Portree**, where I was supposed to have some time, but was informed that because the transport schedule was limited, in order to make the train to Inverness I had to leave on the return bus in an hour! This was the only fault that I found with the itinerary organised by Britrail. I had intended taking a tour of Skye but finished up just buying fish and chips (in the traditional newspaper!) and sitting on a rock on a grassy bank to eat them. In this idyllic location, I watched the fading light glinting off a colourful fishing boat reflected in the calm cove with mountains veiled in mist beyond the opposite shore. A short walk brought me to a vista of colourful houses facing small craft in a bay, and behind, on top of a hill, a church with a belfry atop a stone gable, the rose window of which was struck by the setting sun in a stunning burst of red and gold. I saw wild Scottish bluebells, ruins on a mound above a sparkling silver sea, and lonely cottages near a picturesque white lighthouse on a spit jutting into blue water. Flora Macdonald, who befriended the fugitive Bonny Prince Charlie, was buried on Skye, her body said to have been wrapped in a sheet on which the prince had slept.

The journey from Fort William to **Inverness** – where Macbeth probably lived in a castle long since built over, and near Culloden Moor where the last battle on British soil was fought between Bonnie Prince Charles and the Duke of Cumberland – is listed in the great train journeys of the world and was certainly outstanding: turquoise pools with water washed boulders, islets, forests, green swathes, and fields of brilliant yellow rape. At the small historic town of **Elgin**, I had an hour between trains, so I found the convenient tourist office in High Street and procured an excellent walking map, which albeit rushed, I managed to complete in my allotted time. Amongst the interesting sights were 13th-century **Cathedral** ruins viewed through the stepped arch of **Panns Port**, the only survivor of four gateways in its precinct wall, and the two-arched stone **Brewery Bridge** (1798) over the **Lossie River**, made even more appealing by lovely overhanging trees and white flowers in long grass on the bank. A mass of cascading pale pink blooms covered the stone wall of a house, and trees heavy with blossom stood on a green sward in front of the cathedral remains, one of the finest examples of medieval architecture in Scotland, evolved from an original 1224 simple cruciform building. **Greyfriars Street** was named after the medieval friary (1479), and the impressive **Town Hall**, with a clock tower rearing above its pillared portico and a three-tiered fountain in front, stood at one end of a large central square. As well as the **Muckle Cross** (1888), High Street contained many historically significant buildings with stepped gables, spired turrets, and arcades. The **Thunderton Hotel** was all that remained of Elgin's most splendid house, once a royal residence with orchards and a bowling green and where, in 1746, Bonnie Prince Charlie stayed on his way to Culloden. Finally, I took an attractive picture of the town with a bridge in the foreground and spires and chimneys silhouetted against the sky.

ENGLAND

London

Back in **London**, I came across a castle-like structure with battlemented octagonal towers, and the Egyptian obelisk and sphinx on **Victoria Embankment**, with bridges, Big Ben, and the Houses of Parliament in the distance. Figures graced the ornate plinth of a lamppost in front of St Paul's. I made a rushed visit to **Kew Gardens**, a beautiful park with flowers in urns on the bank of a lake and a large building sequestered in trees on the opposite side. Lawns beneath large spreading branches were enlivened by many colourful beds, a plump bronze pheasant and flocks of geese wandered freely, rhododendrons made a gorgeous display, and strange white statuary included a griffin and a spotted creature with hoofs. The interior of a church featured carving in colourful spandrels, and I bade farewell to England with a final picture of the Masons Arms (pub) draped with flowers.

YUGOSLAVIA

Belgrade

Now on the homeward leg of my travels, I spent a week in what was then Yugoslavia. Beginning in **Beograd** (Belgrade), at the confluence of the **Danube** and **Sava** rivers, and now capital of **Serbia** and **Montenegro**, where I stayed at the Metropol Hotel, I journeyed by train through the mountains of Montenegro, a fantastic feat of engineering with bridges spanning high chasms, to Bar (Serbia-Montenegro that is still called **Yugoslavia**), by bus along the coast to fabled Dubrovnik (**Croatia**), by ferry to the island of Hvar, and thence to Split, Zadar, Zagreb, the indescribably glorious Plitvice National Park (all in **Croatia-Herzegovina**), and back to the capital.

My introduction to **Belgrade** – a city that has been destroyed and rebuilt 40 times in its 2,300-year history, the first reference dating from 878 when it was called the White Town (Beli Grad) – was an impressive edifice with a dome, cupolas, and pillared portico, the sculpture of a figure with a rearing horse, and a church of Russian appearance with several domed towers. Passing other large buildings, I came to immaculate terraced gardens with cone-shaped bushes, flowerbeds emblazoning lawns, curtains of creeper on stone walls, tall trees, and views of a river beyond. Statues stood atop tall pedestals, a couple of attractive buildings sat at the lowest level, and much was situated in the shadow of a high stone wall with corner bastions, a tiered tower rising above, and large artillery at the base. Electric trams were an interesting form of transport. I located an ornate church spire, a second church of Eastern appearance, and a classical building with a window flanked by sculpted images on a ledge. Domes and spires punctuated the skyline, and I saw a pediment supported on the heads of four robed feminine figures, a sight that was to become familiar on subsequent trips to Europe.

Dubrovnik

Boarding the train, we crossed mountains with grey escarpments engulfed by forest, entered many tunnels, obtained glimpses of winding rivers at the bottom of ravines, and observed wisps of cloud on high crests – but few houses. From **Bar**, the bus followed the **Adriatic Coast** along what was referred to as Yugoslavia's Riviera, past picturesque **Sveti Stefan** – a settlement completely covering a small island joined by a narrow causeway to the mainland and once a pirate's nest – and small communities built along the shore below steep green slopes, to fabulous **Dubrovnik**. First revealed from a hilltop as the bus descended towards the town, I was made aware of daunting defensive walls, towers, congested buildings, and boats in the enclosed harbour. Here, my visit was made even more enjoyable by the company of two gay Jewish men with whom I spent a day, one insisting that he felt obliged to help me by carrying my camera and assisting me in climbing stairs. I find that homosexual men make good friends for women, in unthreatening relationships, and I corresponded with this young man for some time, his letters always concluding with love and shalom.

On the UNESCO World Heritage List, the ancient and unspoilt 16th-century **Stari Grad** (**Old Town**) was a warren of narrow, sometimes dark paved alleys, with stone arches and walls, statues in niches, and old-fashioned lamps, the whole constituting a living museum. In medieval times, it was second only to Venice as a centre of culture and economic power. Sitting in the centre of a square, **Velika Onofrijeva Česma** (**Onofrio's Fountain**) was a low, domed circular structure surrounded by columns. On one side, wedged between two flights of steep stone steps, was the small 16th-century **Crkva Sv. Spasa** (**Church of St Saviour**), with a rounded free-standing stone gable, a small rose window, and carving above the small pediment of its arched doorway. Adjacent was the 14th- to 16th-century **Franjevački Crkva** (**Franciscan Church**), with a tiered tower and a wonderful 15th-century depiction of the Pietà, sculpted in deep relief, between other figures above the portal. In the paved courtyard of the colonnaded cloister, tables and chairs were surrounded by trees, and the 15th-century **Minčeta Fortress** towered at the end of the street. The fortified walls loomed above narrow lanes across which washing was strung from windows, and the many small overhead balconies looked inviting with flowers and green plants. There were stepped streets, colonnaded buildings, old-style wall lamps, and sculpted armour on the corner of a wall. In the centre of another square I found the 18th-century **Crkva Sv. Vlaha** (**St Blaise's Church**), with figures around the roof, elaborate capitals on pilasters, an ornately carved entrance, and a pale dome in odd contrast to the ancient stone on all sides. Opposite another intricate doorway, people sat around 15th-century **Orlando's Pillar** portraying an armoured knight with a sword and shield, and members of a choir dressed in national costume made their way to the church where they performed on the steps. A large bell, part of the city clock, hung in the tower of the 16th-century **Sponza Palace**, with small pinnacles around the barrel-tiled roof and an image occupying a central niche above arched windows filled with lovely lacy stonework. Adjacent was an old stone building with dormer windows and wooden shutters, and also on the square was a small but elaborate fountain, again bearing the name Onofrio, with water spewing from the mouths of faces above crouching figures. I discovered an amusing pouting visage on a wall, and diagonally opposite the Baroque **Stolna Crkva** (cathedral) a colonnade with floral work and small figures on capitals, each one different, distinguished the Gothic **Rector's Palace** (1441).

Further afield, I found a belfry with three bells, a tiny tucked-away chapel with a small round window and belfry, and a façade with statues on the parapet and in a recess below a small pediment. Yet another square was ringed by old buildings and featured a large memorial with a statue on top. From outside the walls of the old town, I obtained views of coastal scenery and houses on a rocky limestone outcrop. Wearing headscarves, elderly ladies in traditional black walked the narrow alleys, one with a small church at the end. This appealing building had three bells in a belfry above a tiny round window, which in turn was above the decorative pediment of its portal. Abutting this was a structure with figures in relief above the carved stone lintel of its doorway. Many weathered walls featured elaborate sculpted decoration, and vines even sprouted from the stone. Another of the prolific chapels with a belfry had images above and below its round window. Amongst the many iron balconies was one with climbing roses and a second with intricate floral railing. At the end of another narrow passageway, I glimpsed the statues atop St Blaise's Church and its columned portico, in front of which an orchestra now performed, its members dressed in white shirts and trousers. Girdling the entire city, the perfectly intact 13th- to 16th-century walls were over 2km long, up to 25m high, and incorporated two round towers, two corner fortifications, and a large fortress.

Hvar

Departing Dubrovnik across vibrant blue water creating a stunning combination with green hillsides dropping to white limestone shores, I sailed to the idyllic island of **Hvar**. Here, I was greeted by the sight of a blue dome rising above red-roofed white houses secluded behind more massive 13th-century defensive walls, below which was an arched stone bridge and a harbour crowded with boats. In the streets, I found a profusion of red roses and a large paved square with tables and chairs (and pigeons) beneath coloured umbrellas at the foot of a wide staircase, its balustrades and ornately carved façade at the top putting me in mind of Rome's Spanish Steps. Two interesting doorways featured, respectively, a lion head knocker and a carved lintel with an intricate iron fanlight above. There were many belfries here also, and boats in the bay included a four-masted schooner under full sail. My euphoric room had shuttered windows opening to a vista worthy of the cover of a brochure: it revealed other small islands, boats in an indigo sea, laden orange trees, and pink roses.

Split

In **Split**, built around a fourth-century Roman palace of the Emperor Diocletian, I found carpets hanging on a wall and, fronting the harbour, a large square enclosed on one side by a structure with a huge arched entrance, and on another by a colonnaded building with a clock on the façade. Palm trees lined the promenade, and at the far end, viewed behind bobbing boats, stood a multi-tiered tower. Red roses cascaded from a tiny iron-railed balcony below a decoratively carved arched window in a weathered stone wall, and a succulent bearing a cluster of red flowers enhanced a second. Views from a height looked out over red roofs, a mass of white blossom, and islets in a turquoise ocean. Battlements above an archway were visible at the end of a narrow street enclosed by plain walls, which were nevertheless made appealing with trailing greenery and red roses climbing around shuttered windows. Lodged above a sundial, a bell hung beneath a cupola supported by slender columns, and near the tall tower seen earlier from afar, I discovered a delicate free-standing colonnade. At one end of this, an elevated columned portico had embellishment around the plain pediment. Tables and chairs sat in the court below, and others, under red-and-white umbrellas, lined the street on the other side of the colonnade, opposite which stood free-standing columns. At the other end of the street, remains of a wall, its windows open to the sky, were festooned with creepers. I also observed a sphinx-like statue.

Zadar

In **Zadar**, I filmed a large statue through a series of archways straddling a street, a five-storey spired tower behind the massive ninth-century circular **Sveti Donat Church** built over a Roman forum, and a busy square with an octagonal tower, a statue on a pedestal, and colourful umbrellas.

Plitvice

From Zadar, I went to pristine **Plitvice** (another UNESCO site), where even my arrival was an adventure. The bus did not go right to the park, but the driver dropped me off, after sunset, on a lonely stretch of road in the vicinity, with directions to cross a small bridge that I had difficulty locating in the dark. Not sure if I was on the right track, I left my heavy luggage (at that time I still persevered with a large suitcase) concealed in a deserted spot, ascertained that the rough rustic construction to which I eventually came was that which I sought, and was escorted back to retrieve my abandoned property.

However, the effort was all infinitely worthwhile because it was one of the most awesome venues of my travelling career: myriad large and small, high and low, wide and narrow, fierce and quiet waterfalls plunging through thick natural foliage and over moss-covered rock; foaming, thundering, rushing or just steadily trickling into vivid emerald lakes surrounded by shady trees, water plants, birdlife and bulrushes. Blending into the unspoilt environment, unfenced boardwalks revealed bridal veil cascades, perfectly mirrored images in quiet pools, and the sparkle of diamond lights off rippling waters. In all, 16 lakes (and a handful of lesser ones) on different levels, flowed from one to the other.

Zagreb

Plitvice was a glorious conclusion to my holiday, and I used up all my film so that I had none left for **Zagreb**, capital of Croatia since 1557. Here, I was given a city tour that included the **Kalemegdan Citadel**, the formidable **Cathedral**, the 18th-century **Church of St Marko**, and the old stone gates of the town, before kindly being deposited at the train station for my return to Belgrade. Although only from 1899, the cathedral contained 13th-century frescoes.

It was here that I first met my good friend Laurie as described in the Britain 1990 chapter.

In 1987, I also led another group to India.

HAWAII 1988

In 1988, I made a trip to the Hawaiian islands of Oahu and Kauai, and one of the highlights was a *luau* –with free-flowing blue mai tais!

Kauai

My first pictures show common but beautifully marked ducks beside a pool with giant lily pads, and an impressive waterfall in jungle surrounds that featured different varieties of the gorgeous red and yellow heliconia, waxy red ginger flowers, exotic white blooms, strelitzia, and clusters of red berries. I saw orange fungi on old brown bark, grey-and-white birds with vivid red heads, a shrub with pure white leaves and red flowers, a bright red bird, spathiphylums, climbing philodendrons, colourful decorative leaves, and lawns bordered by massed foliage in different shades of green. Views of a higher waterfall were followed by a cruise on the river, its wide course flowing swiftly between banks of tropical forest climbing to interesting mountain peaks. White birds stood out against the thick green canopy, and in this incredible land of water and dense rainforest a more tumultuous cascade tumbled to a narrow brown watercourse.

Along the surf-lashed rocky shore of the coast, I saw marvellous blowholes through which the sea erupted in clouds of foaming spray, and we continued past vistas of almost impenetrable jungle. The panorama from a high point overlooking 1,097m/3,600ft-deep **Waimea Canyon** showed stark and craggy red-hued rock at the rim, in sharp contrast to the green of a lush valley far below. Appearing like a tiny stream, a river ran between the precipitous walls of the narrow chasm. Called by Mark Twain the Grand Canyon of the Pacific, it is the largest in Oceania. This was **Kauai**, known as the garden island and location for the movie *South Pacific*, but I found it disappointing and not as verdant as imagined, maybe because of the season; light rain did nothing to enhance my impressions.

Oahu

From a lookout on **Oahu**, I have pictures over the city, with **Waikiki Beach** and **Diamond Head**, where Captain Cook first made landfall, in the background. An imposing symmetrical colonial-style stone building, with fine columns, a central clock tower, and a statue on a pedestal in the grassed forecourt, begins a series of pictures that includes the colourful **International Market**. Built around a 100-year-old banyan tree, this featured stalls, red totems, ferns and flowers amongst strangler figs, a macaw, and the tree house that was part of **Trader Vic's**.

Other photographs show attractive gardens with man-made falls, high-rise accommodation behind the palm-fringed beach, and people beneath coloured umbrellas on the strand, with Diamond Head looming to one side. Puffs of white cloud over the bay appeared painted on the canvas of an exceedingly blue sky. The very pink Royal Hawaiian Hotel on Waikiki opened in 1927, and amongst its illustrious guests were Shirley Temple-Black and Mary Pickford. The Moorish-Spanish mission design was inspired by the exotic movies of Rudolph Valentino. My film concludes with more thunderous surf crashing over pinnacles in the ocean and an enormous round balancing boulder under an eerie sky with silver light illuminating a gap between heavy grey clouds.

UNITED KINGDOM 1990

At one stage in its history, this small island was a mighty seafaring nation that ruled half the world's population and had a major impact on much of the rest.

The nine weeks of my second trip to Britain were spent in the company of a friend that I met and had lunch with on a city tour and transfer to the railway station in Zagreb, in the old Yugoslavia.

RUSSIA

Moscow

For the first and only time, I travelled with the Russian carrier Aeroflot (its bad reputation justly deserved!) on an aging Ilyushin aircraft, the journey necessitating a night (provided) in **Moscow** at a supposedly superior class hotel, which was an ugly concrete block with linoleum on the floors and ancient iron beds. On the flight, I had teamed up with an Indian girl, a fellow in the orange robes of a Buddhist monk, and a huge Maori with hair to his waist – who was gay! We made an incongruous group but interacted well and decided to eat together at dinner time. The Indian lass and I were sharing a room and, appearing in the dining room first, were shown to an allocated space where we attempted to reserve two more seats. However, the hefty and intimidating 'hostess' kept insisting, with pointed finger, that we 'Sit, sit' (all she needed was a whip!), and we caused great consternation endeavouring to achieve our purpose. As I remember, the food was terrible: cold *borsht* (beetroot soup) and half a hard-boiled egg amongst other unappetising fare.

On the whole, I did not find the Russians an attractive race, and at the terminal next day I again encountered extremely curt responses when trying to obtain information, virtually telling me to go away because they did not understand – and this a hospitality industry. Being a tour operator, I was at least given complimentary city sightseeing, which included the remarkable **Red Square**, site of the **Kremlin** and **St Basil's Cathedral** with its colourful multi-faceted onion domes. The monumental square was bordered by the massive **GUM Department Store**, a twin-spired church and gateway at the opposite end to St Basil's, and of course the Kremlin with its clock tower and turrets atop the high red walls, some crowned by red stars that were lit at night. A monument depicting two men, one with his right arm raised, the other bearing a shield, stood on a tall pedestal in front of the cathedral (see Eastern Europe 2000, book 2).

Spired onion domes (many gilded) featured widely amongst unappealing buildings around the city, and structures behind the Kremlin wall faced a waterway lined with bare trees. We stopped for an overview that revealed a large stadium and spires of a different type – tall twin smokestacks belching pollution into the atmosphere. A red flag flying in the breeze was the only colour in a drab environment. Snow lay on the ground between trees devoid of leaves, and the populace wore heavy coats and fur hats. I must have looked ridiculous dressed in pale green cotton slacks with white sandals and a light cardigan (because I was heading for a warmer climate); however, probably due to the excitement, I did not feel cold. My final picture was of the impressive university with its tiered tower.

ENGLAND

Before I left Perth, my friend Laurie wrote asking me what I would like to see, and thinking that it may be difficult to locate one, I responded with a request to visit a thatched village; I was mortified to find that the whole of England is full of such places, like a veritable picture book! Laurie picked me up from Heathrow and we drove straight to his home in **Fareham, Hampshire**. Our itinerary is a little vague in my memory because we covered so much territory in the ensuing time, and I do not recall the name of every small community; however, one that I shall never forget is the fetching village of **West Meon**, and I like to go there every time I visit. Here, we found quaint thatched wooden cottages with shutters, and adjoining thatched stone and red brick houses with bay windows, their tiny plots full of golden daffodils. An old-style hand-operated pump occupied a patch of grass in front, and a white half-timbered pub called the Golden Lion was resplendent with colourful window boxes and baskets. I saw red doors and shutters, and climbing roses on a whitewashed brick wall, its yellow door complemented by daffodils against the foundations. In the one main street, yellow blossoms overhung the path beside a small stream crossed by a stone bridge, and at the end of a row of blue, apple-green, and pale lemon cottages, daffodils bloomed in window boxes on a whitewashed half-timbered façade with blue window frames and a red door. This was located next to an elevated grassed stone embankment shaded by the bare branches of a big old tree. Daffodils also flourished beneath white railing on the grassy bank of the stream, and vines crept above doors and windows. Being early in the season, daffodils were the principal bloom, but later on roses took precedence. There were stone houses, stone fences, and a stone church with green hills in the background. An amusing sight was that of a ceramic Siamese cat crouched on a thatched roof. We enjoyed lunch at one of the local pubs, and the whole village exuded charm.

West Meon

We passed thatched red brick dwellings with muntined and bay windows, their shutters and picket fences painted white, and one portico covered in pink blossom, with flowers in tubs by the stoop. A house with steeply pitched thatch, tall chimneys, and flowers around the foundations sat in a very green meadow, and the Whitebread pub was a shingle and white-walled building with attic windows looking out from several gables; half barrels full of colourful flowers graced the entrance. Back in Fareham, I found a glorious almond, peach or cherry tree, its canopy of blossom resembling a gigantic snowball.

Next day, we went to **Southampton**, still displaying part of its old town walls, and the historic naval base of **Portsmouth** to see the house where Charles Dickens was born in 1812 and Nelson's flagship **Victory** (1765), its three masts a tangled web of rigging above three decks of gunports. Portsmouth was also the final resting place of the Tudor warship **Mary Rose**, which sank in the harbour in 1545. Housed in a special building, it was constantly sprayed with iced water to preserve its timbers, and the museum displayed a fascinating array of sailors' belongings including leather shoes, rosary beads, a jar of ointment (with a fingerprint!), a shovel, dice, a cut-throat razor, a longbow and arrows, and a 'pissing pot'. Ships were built at Portsmouth as long ago as 1194, and the first fleet to Australia sailed from there in 1787.

This was followed by a visit to **Stonehenge** on the green **Salisbury Plain** in **Wiltshire**. It was built in three stages from 2000 to 1400 BC, with some stones – up to ten metres tall but appearing lower because their bases were buried deep in the ground – brought from Wales! Although their purpose remains unclear, they were aligned with the winter solstice sunset (some disputed theories suggest also the midsummer sunrise), which indicated that Stonehenge was built for ceremonies. Unfortunately, one was no longer able to access the site, but I think we approached closer than is now possible, and I obtained excellent film of the enormous uprights with solid stone slabs across the top. In the background loomed the 123m (404ft) spire of **Salisbury Cathedral** (**St Mary's**), the tallest in Britain and visible for miles. The church was a favourite subject of artist Constable and it housed a copy of the original **Magna Carta**. The town of Salisbury was founded in 1219.

Stonehenge

Dainty white and yellow wildflowers raised their heads above lush green grass beneath a blue sky, across which white clouds scudded in a stiff breeze. In spite of the sunshine and clear weather it was cold, and I made considerable use of an old plastic raincoat (I had had it since I was 17!) that cut the wind; in fact, Laurie had to mend it for me with some very strong adhesive. A spire rearing beyond a stone arch bearing rampant lions supporting a shield was our introduction to a typical English town with the Union Jack flying, an elaborate stone rotunda at an intersection, half-timbered buildings with bay windows (and more daffodils in boxes), and the Pritchet Family Butcher shop with an old-fashioned lamp below a muntined bay window.

About this time, we visited **Winchester**. Founded in Roman times, it became capital of the Saxon Kingdom of Wessex under King Alfred the Great in the ninth century and later William the Conqueror. The 900-year-old **Cathedral**, immortalised by the Beetles, is one of the largest medieval churches in the world, with the longest nave in Europe. It contained the grave of Jane Austen, the body of King Canute, and a breathtakingly beautiful stone altar screen with tiers of carved figures. A green hill was crowned by the photogenic remains of a castle with several octagonal towers, and I utilised a tree of pink blossoms to frame a stone clock tower. A typical narrow street was bounded by white buildings, some with crooked walls, others half-timbered, and one featuring a green door and a tiny pink portico with matching window frames and dado. Green hills were apparent beyond a town with a tower, memorial column and equestrian statue visible through its arched stone gateway bearing two coats of arms. There was a large stone church in green surrounds, an impressive building with a clock tower, half-timbered structures, and a statue, one arm raised, of King Arthur; I seem to remember that there was even a replica of the round table thereabouts. A lovely old stone church with a square Norman tower had wildflowers, daffodils and ancient headstones in the grass behind its paling fence, and we passed large homes in immaculate gardens with impeccably manicured lawns. The British are very houseproud, and it was a common sight to see them carrying out annual renovations in spring. Everywhere, there were buildings of small bricks with muntined windows, half-timbered houses, and picturesque thatched cottages. Lodged behind a hedge, one overlooked a pond ringed by rushes and weeping willows in a swathe of green grass peppered with a mass of wildflowers.

half-timbered houses

Another stone church with a Norman tower preceded sighting of the enormous figure of a naked man etched into grass-covered chalk hills at **Cerne Abbas** in **Dorset**. This 60m figure, known as the **Giant of Cerne Abbas**, was possibly 2,000 years old and obviously played a role in some fertility rite because of its prominent reproductive organs! Situated near **Dorchester**, this enigmatic image has prompted theories ranging from Iron Age warrior, Saxon deity, Celtic figure, the Roman god Hercules or the Greek Heracles, to an invading Danish giant! The lovely stone and thatched Smith's Arms, with appropriate illustration, colourful flowers in barrels at the entrance, and surrounded by green lawns, willows and conifers, made an attractive picture as we travelled through countryside with abundant trees and rolling green hills divided into fields by low hedges.

Arriving at the south coast, still my favourite part of the United Kingdom, we entered a typical fishing village with pastel façades fronting narrow streets. In a by-way with little bridges crossing a small stream, I found a white building with pale blue shutters and a pink building with white. More tubs of flowers beneath bay windows brightened the sidewalk, and fanciful names such as The Mad Hatter and Barrel o' Beer caused comment. We spent a night here, and sunset produced pink-tinged clouds floating above white cliffs on the opposite shore of the bay. In the evening, we wandered along the seaside promenade past pink façades that had stood out amongst the cluster of buildings when viewed across the inlet earlier.

We visited a string of fishing villages in **Devon** and **Cornwall**, and it is impossible to pinpoint the exact locations after all this time, but amongst the places were **Lyme Regis**, **Exmouth**, **Dawlish**, **Teighmouth**, **Torquay**, **Paingnton**, **Brixham**, **Totnes**, **Looe**, picturesque Polperro with its small harbour and maze of narrow streets, **Mevagissey**, **Truro**, **Falmouth**, and **Bere Regis**, which was the setting for Hardy's *Tess of the d'Urbervilles*. The next I recorded was a tiny place with colourful fishing boats drawn up next to nets and floats on a pebble beach. Sheer cliffs rose to one side of the cove. A delightful stone cottage had lace curtains in the windows, baskets hanging on the façade, a statue in a paved courtyard gay with pots of daffodils, and tiny garden beds livened with red flowers. There were vines on the walls of a thatch-roofed house with a tiny thatched portico, and a stunning show was provided by daffodils surrounding trees heavy with deep pink blossom, the latter against the stone wall of a house with a shingled portico and a birdbath in the small patch of green lawn. I took some particularly attractive footage of sheep in green pasture with castle ruins, viewed through a network of lacy branches, on a slight rise behind. Adjoining pink and white thatched cottages featured doors and windows with unusual carved lintels, and another seaside scene was composed of fishing boats on a wide sandy shore, a village beyond, and cliffs in the background. From a high vantage point, the town unfolded below, and a carpet of emerald fields extended to distant red cliffs that fell to a bright blue sea beneath a cloudless blue sky, a rarity in this part of the world. A thatched pink dwelling with creepers, small multi-paned windows, a tiny thatched portico and a stone fence was called Rose Cottage. A paved courtyard contained red, white and yellow flowerbeds and a stone 'basket', its handle created with plants. A three-storey building had wooden wagon wheels propped against a wall and extensive lawns with daffodils in small beds. I took several series of thatched cottages, many with decorative capping on the ridge. A complex of stone structures included a mill with a waterwheel, and people rode by on sturdy Clydesdale horses.

thatched cottages

A larger town had narrow-fronted buildings and old-style lampposts, and the plaintive cries of seagulls could be heard as they wheeled above a large three-masted wooden galleon (enhanced with a colourful geometric design) berthed at the quay, overlooking which we partook in a Devonshire tea. Houses were terraced up both sides of the harbour, and names on white or shingled pubs included Smugglers Haunt and Sprat and Mackerel. A change of pace was provided by a humpbacked stone bridge over a gurgling river lined with trees and a peaceful church with a square tower, its green lawns containing colourful beds of mixed flowers and daffodils.

old galleon

More narrow streets revealed a stained-glass sign announcing The Smugglers Dungeon, vines growing on walls, and purple, red and yellow flowers in a barrel outside a restaurant. The latter had a ship's steering wheel and baskets on the façade and old-fashioned lanterns in the window. Some of the paved lanes were so narrow that one could reach out and touch both sides simultaneously, but they still had potted plants outside doors opening directly onto the street. Amongst the quaint names were Rock-a-bye and Fishermans Cottage, and a row of attached dwellings had pink, red and blue doors, jambs and window frames respectively – in some cases even matching downpipes! Window boxes and baskets were prevalent, and the Coachman Inn was denoted by a colourful sign depicting a top-hatted and caped driver with a whip. In early days, signs were used on English pubs so that illiterate people could identify buildings by looking at the illustration, for example, Hearty Sailor. I made a hobby of collecting interesting representations. Making our way down to the bay of this particular town, we found most boats high and dry at low tide. Gently curving hills appeared beyond the houses each side.

Moving on, the white vine-covered Crumplehorn Inn, with tables and chairs on a small patio, an old-style lamp and a waterwheel, was a source of pleasing pictures, as was a series of decorative bridges over a burbling brook in front of houses with pocket handkerchief lawns.

Crumplehorn Inn

Another excellent subject was The Old Forge Tearoom, with implements on its whitewashed façade and bright yellow daffodils in window boxes and on top of the stone wall. Photographs of **Polperro** consist of white stucco faces on a white wall of the Buccaneer Restaurant (indicated by a colourful sign portraying a peg leg pirate with a cutlass in his mouth), an establishment called Haunted House, walls of blue, pink, white or unadorned stone, and coloured doors. We looked out across the bay and down on a small harbour with boats beached between breakwaters. An entire wall of one house was decorated with pebbles and shells, and buildings on the wharf included the Blue Peter Inn and bright pink and blue premises with the ubiquitous gulls flying overhead. Appropriate names included Captain's Cabin, with red and white flowers hanging next to its blue sign and creeper surrounding the door, Wheelhouse Restaurant and Tearoom, The Old Barkhouse Fish and Chips, and the Three Pilchards pub with a sign depicting leaping fish.

Cornish fishing village

A pair of black and white cats sat on the black windowsills of whitewashed cottages, there were tiny shingled porticos, and I came across a cottage called Hope Cove. I also found the historic Noughts and Crosses Inn (c. 1595), a wall bearing a ship's figurehead in the form of a sailor, and a stone cross outside a stone and shingle building. Film taken overlooking white houses from behind a row of waving yellow daffodils is one of which I am particularly pleased. I hope my words help to convey some of the picturesqueness of these idyllic locations, made even more so without the intrusion of vehicles, for which they were almost completely unnegotiable!

Enclosed by hills with terraced houses, the natural harbour of our next destination contained a few yachts as well as the dories. A sign on the Fountain Inn showed fishermen in sou'-westers. We travelled through countryside with undulating green hills separated into fields by hedges and lacy trees, this early in the season still bare of leaves, and stopped briefly to watch the loading of china clay at a small port with pastel row houses. Of course, we went through **Plymouth**, well known as the start and finishing point of Sir Francis Drake's epic circumnavigation and where, in 1588, he was said to have finished a game of bowls before setting out to vanquish the Spanish Armada. It was from here too, that Raleigh departed on his great naval expeditions and the Pilgrim Fathers set out, in 1620, for the New World aboard the *Mayflower*.

We came to the **Lizard** and looked down on a rocky headland creating a protected cove. A sign in the parking area stated Please Park Prettily, and views from the top revealed rugged tors erupting from a green sea, the surf pounding at the base of cliffs. We found a stone building called (for obvious reasons) the Stocks Restaurant and one simply called Old Inn. We progressed to the north coast and the castle ruins of **Tintagel**, where we encountered photogenic buildings that included the 14th-century **Post Office** with its rustic stone walls and slate roof. Legend has it that King Arthur was born the son of a Celtic ruler at Tintagel Castle and immediately handed over to Merlin the Wizard at the mouth of a cave below, still called Merlin's Cave, but this Norman castle was built 600 years after Arthur's death in AD 537, and the ruins were a far cry from the popular conception of Camelot. The splendour was in its location above one of the wildest stretches of Cornish coast, and the site was no doubt occupied in Arthur's time because of remains of a fifth-century Celtic monastery.

Our next venue, via **Boscastle** and **Bude**, was **Clovelly** in **Devon**, one of the loveliest villages in the British Isles. Accessed via steep cobbled streets (up and down which residents transported purchases on sleds!), cars were not permitted to negotiate the impossible inclines and were obliged to park at the top. This was one of the few places to which I have returned and would never tire of visiting. We stayed at a delightful thatched cottage (referred to as a Family Farm B&B) just outside the village, which I went to great lengths to find again on a subsequent visit – described in a later chapter. After leaving the car in a field opposite our accommodation, we made our way to the steep gradient leading through the village and down to the 14th-century quay, a pebble beach and the sea, from where a man was laboriously climbing up with his collie dog, although later I spotted a girl running up on her hobby horse – oh to be youthful!

We wandered past many stone fences, behind one of which red blossoms made a splash against a pink wall with lace curtains behind white window frames. Clovelly was a sheer delight, because being early in the season there were no crowds, in comparison to the jostling wall to wall people that would clog the village's arteries later on. A pure white cat sat in the fork of a tree, bay windows and white walls (interspersed with pink) lined the thoroughfare, a church was tucked away behind a white stone wall with greenery over the top, and names noticed were Kingsley Cottage and New Inn – which was probably built in the1500s! Daffodils grew in tubs on a tiny patio with green vines over its shingled portico. They also climbed above muntined windows, and pots on steps held red-flowering plants, as did window boxes. Behind a whitewashed stone wall, pink blossoms made a show in the wee forecourt of a white craft shop with a white wagon wheel propped against the wall, and daffodils bloomed, together with a few red tulips, in minute beds along the foundations of buildings.

Proceeding down a stepped street with red-flowering creeper decking a wall, roses on lattice, ample greenery (and a cat), we finally reached the harbour, its entrance protected by a groin. A red-flowering tree appeared above one of the high stone walls between which steps led down to a house with a steeply pitched roof. Climbing back to the top of the village, other red blooms looked stunning against a whitewashed stone wall, and a creeper covered in white flowers formed the portico around a door. Tiny beds against the foundations of another whitewashed stone façade (with green downpipes) contained red flowers and green plants; stone steps led to its green door and massed red flowers on the stoop. The doorway to the **Chapel of St Peter** was also hidden behind greenery, and I found a clump of delicate English primroses. Another interesting name was Upalong Bar.

We drove through **Barnstaple** to **Lynton**, which was situated along the base of a gorge, the road plunging down steep tree-capped hills either side, and thence to another of my favourite places and one of the prettiest, also visited twice, the heritage listed thatched hamlet of **Selworthy**. Set in lush green surrounds with lawns, flowering bushes, trimmed hedges, trees, roses, ferns and daffodils, the white houses featured leadlight bay windows, picket fences, artificial birds on a thatched roof, and tall chimneys, from one of which smoke billowed. Ginger and tabby cats groomed themselves on a window sill beneath thatched eaves, a black and white feline sat on a step, and one cottage was even named Lorna Doone – of literary note. We found one tall narrow stone structure, a stone urn with yellow flowers, and beautiful blue hyacinths in the doorway of Selworthy Cottage. From the edge of the village, I looked towards the misty horizon across a graveyard with ancient leaning tombstones.

Three kilometres from **Minehead**, we came to the medieval town of **Dunster**, with a hexagonal stone and shingle yarn market (1609) in the centre of an intersection at one end and a château-like castle ensconced in dense foliage on a hill at the other. We drove through immaculate streets of stone and stuccoed buildings with white flowers cascading over stone fences and encountered ruins of a church atop a green hill. Topical names included Horse and Crook, The George and Pilgrims Hotel, and King William, with an image resplendent in the regalia of a royal personage. We continued through **Taunton** to **Glastonbury** (in **Somerset**) and the splendid **Abbey** ruins set in impressive surrounds of lawns, trees, and of course daffodils. This site of probably the oldest Christian establishment in Britain, featured remains of several buildings and imposing twin 'towers' (remnants of a doorway) filmed through an arch. It eventually suffered the fate of all abbeys under Henry VIII, but there remained a hint of its former size and grandeur. There were several legends associated with Glastonbury: Jesus travelled here with Joseph of Arimathea and the chalice from the Last Supper; about AD 60 Joseph of Arimathea built a small church of wattles and planted a thorn tree; St Patrick ended his days as abbot here (he died around 461), and it was the site of the grave of King Arthur of Camelot, which is generally placed about 11 miles southeast. The last abbot was hanged on **Tor Hill**, which was crowned by a tower and sat above the town.

Moving on to **Wells**, we visited the magnificent 12th-century **Cathedral**, with its many faceted façade holding myriad life-sized figures in recesses, tall stained-glass windows, square towers, small spires, roof balustrades, and a covered walkway above the road. The sculpted images, in excess of 300, included those of royalty, mitred clerics, prophets, saints, the apostles, the Virgin Mary and Christ, although many have been destroyed or damaged over the years. Small niches even contained figures of the dead emerging from their tombs on Judgement Day! With their tall chimneys, the mews of old **Alms Houses** made an interesting picture, and we proceeded to **Cheddar Gorge**, running through the **Mendip Hills** and near where, in the future, my son and grandchildren were to live. As gorges go, for someone from Australia it was singularly unimpressive, being only 113m (370ft) in depth (but still the largest in Britain), although the surrounding rural countryside was beautiful and included an enormous white horse emblazoned on a green hillside.

stone village

We motored via **Warminster** and a picturesque multi-arched stone bridge across a willow-lined river, to **Bath** in **Avon**, where Jane Austen spent some time and which was the setting for two of her novels. Here, the vista from a bridge revealed daffodils in grass on the banks, green and blossom-filled trees, the square tower of **Bath Abbey**, the covered **Pulteney Bridge** reminiscent of the Rialto in Venice, and boats on the river. The town end of the bridge overlooked pathways and green lawns, their circular beds displaying red tulips or yellow pansies together with pink hyacinths, the latter beneath the spreading branches of a tree festooned with red flowers. Square beds of alternating red, yellow and white thrived at the base of conifers opposite a tree covered in white blossoms. An obelisk stood in the centre of a large grassed circle ringed by yellow and white flowers in front of the cathedral, again with figures on the buttressed façade, tall windows, a square tower and spires, but not as ornate as that in Wells. A man in Elizabethan attire played a reed flute in front of the heavily embossed doors.

Before descending, we looked down on the extraordinary below ground baths, the water coloured a vibrant green by algae. Statues adorning the balustrade at street level depicted Roman governors of Britain, emperors and military leaders garbed in tunics. These were reputedly carved in 1894, but that of King Bladud was dated 1699, although its inclusion in earlier pictures indicates that it is much older. There is an interesting legend that credits the founding of Bath to Bladud, the father of King Lear, in 863 BC. As a young man he contracted leprosy and chose to become a swineherd. His pigs suffered from scurvy, but one day he observed one of the animals wallowing in hot black mud and when it emerged it was free of the disease. Bladud tried bathing in the mud and was cured of his leprosy; he returned to court, eventually became king, and built a temple at the site of the spring. Britons had built over the baths, which were rediscovered in 1879. I obtained excellent film of the cathedral through an arch bearing the long-moustachioed countenance of Poseidon, and nearby columns featured heads of a lion and horse respectively.

Our visit concluded with pictures of the covered stone bridge and the famed semicircle of 30 adjoining three-storey Georgian houses known as the **Royal Crescent**, facing a broad green swathe. Tall narrow-fronted juxtaposed houses with many chimneys, and on different levels, climbed a slope to one side. Number 15 was the fictional home of Sir Percy Blakeney, the Scarlet Pimpernel, and numbers 13 and 17, on **The Circus** nearby, were the homes of Dr Livingston and Gainsborough respectively, the latter said to have painted *Blue Boy* here. The Abbey, known for its angels climbing ladders to heaven on the façade, contained an Australian flag above a memorial to Governor Phillip, who lived in a house just off The Circus. I photographed a cheeky grey squirrel on the grass and, behind iron railing, a park featuring a memorial urn on a pedestal, massed yellow pansies, and branches with deep pink blossom amongst lacy trees.

Travelling through **Chippenham**, **Malmsbury** and **Cirencester**, a second octagonal stone market was topped with spires, we passed a church incorporating ancient remains, and negotiated narrow main roads bounded by thatched cottages, one with a strange stone tower. An attractive stone building had lace curtains at tiny attic windows in its sagging slate roof, and pot plants enhanced sills on a row of stone dwellings with dormer windows and coloured doors. I found a church with arched windows open to the sky and a pub called The Smoking Dog bearing an illustration of that canine with a pipe in its mouth. Although full of character, many an older abode had low doors (indicating that the populace were shorter in bygone days) that had dropped below street level, and with their tiny windows they must have been very dark inside. A picturesque stone village was accessed via a stone bridge and contained many red creeper- and ivy-draped walls with daffodils blooming along the foundations. We spent the night in a B&B with a white stag sign and bright yellow daffodils in wooden tubs at the entrance.

Our next destination was one of the most perfect villages in England, **Castle Combe** in **Wiltshire**. Used for the setting of the *Dr Dolittle* film, all 20th century intrusions such as television antennas had been removed. Creepers trailed over stone fences, tiny plots with daffodils and greenery flanked vine-covered porticos, there was a small stone church, a 13th-century canopied market cross, and a lovely old stone bridge spanning the river, from where I could see a beautiful cherry tree in full bloom.

Castle Combe

Arriving in the **Cotswolds**, we visited several villages with 17th- and 18th-century buildings (I noticed one wall inscribed with the date 1650) beginning with **Bourton-on-the-Water** where the **River Windrush** was crossed by arched stone bridges and a tiny runnel ran beside the main stream. Many had interesting names such as **Stow-on-the-Wold**, **Moreton-in-the-Marsh**, where Charles I stayed one night at the White Hart in 1643, **Chipping Campden**, **Shipston-on-Stour**, **Chipping Norton**, and **Broadway**, but my favourite, with the improbable name of **Lower Slaughter**, was another on my 'must see' list, also visited twice. An unpleasant title belied the delightful ambience of this small village, where tiny green commons held a stone well and geese, and rows of charming stone cottages had attic windows, vines over small porticos, and beds of red tulips, yellow daffodils, and tiny purple and white flowers along the foundations. An intriguing twisted tree stood in front of the church with its tall steeple, and a waterwheel turned beside a red brick mill on the stone embankment of the river. Most dwellings had white trim but a couple were enhanced with coloured doors and window frames, and daffodils bloomed around the base of trees on grassy verges. The entire village was captivating. **Upper Slaughter** was not nearly as attractive, consisting of solid stone houses, fences and chimneys, and fewer gardens – a scattering of jonquils in long grass – but set in lovely rural surroundings. **Broadway** had the Lygon Arms, built as long ago as the 1300s, where Cromwell was said to have slept before the battle of Worcester in 1651. Charles I was said to have spent a night here also.

Names observed in the various communities included The Duke of Wellington Inn (with the man himself on a rearing white charger), Kings Arms, The Curiosity Shop with crooked windows in its leaning gable, and The White Hart Royal, its sign portraying a white stag and shield. Larger plots were gay with tulips and daffodils, one incorporating a stone bird bath, and cottages lined grassy banks and pathways beside a river. We encountered a group of thatched stone cottages (one with a brilliant purple border around green lawn), a white half-timbered pub called The Horseshoe with window boxes, baskets, and planted barrels, The White Bear with an appropriate picture, and a stone B&B dated 1717 (where we spent the night) with bay windows, a strip of lawn beside the pavement, red tulips in a tub by the door, and yellow pansies in a basket above. On an evening walk, we found an interesting stone colonnade, many stone houses with dormer windows (one thatched) and a stone church. A rustic enclosed wooden overpass connected buildings bounding an alley, and sidewalks were bordered on one side by lawn and the other by walls with flowers at the base.

Driving further, we found an establishment called the Horse and Hound with the sign of a red-jacketed rider galloping behind a hunting dog. I also noted a steeply pitched thatched roof, a stone house with mixed maroon tulips and yellow pansies in window boxes beneath a large bay window, and a thatched half-timbered building with attic windows and crooked walls.

At **Stratford-upon-Avon** in **Warwickshire**, upon rounding a traffic circle with a glorious display of massed daffodils in the centre, we were confronted with many ancient dun-coloured half-timbered buildings and one red brick and tile, its window boxes glowing with bright yellow flowers. Stratford was of course synonymous with **Shakespeare**, and his old half-timbered Tudor birthplace in **Henley Street** was a centre of pilgrimage, second only to London, almost 500 years after the birth of the bard in 1564. The house featured a muntined bay window, a stone chimney, and iron railing that fenced a narrow strip planted with a hedge and flowers. Other places associated with Shakespeare were beautifully landscaped with hedges, colourful gardens (what else but tulips and daffodils!), trimmed trees, and lawns. They included the thatched cottage in **Shottery** containing the original bed, settle and other furniture of **Anne Hathaway,** the girl eight years his senior whom he married at the age of 18.

Anne Hathaway's cottage

I came across an amusing sign for my collection: called The Slug and Lettuce, the corner of the picture had been 'eaten' away. Of the town's half-timbered buildings, some featured excellent carved faces on solid beams and others had curved frames laid in decorative patterns. One long half-timbered building had a sagging upper storey, and a photogenic white dwelling had distinctly crooked walls and timbers. A pretty park containing a statue on a pedestal was enlivened with extremely colourful flowerbeds around trees thick with blossom.

We arrived next at **Warwick**, with city gates dating back to the 12th century and a castle on the banks of the **River Avon** at a site first fortified by William the Conqueror in 1068, its angular towers and crenellated ramparts surrounded by green embankments, trees and flowers. Oliver Cromwell's helmet was displayed in the arms and armour collection, and the reproduction of an actual Victorian house party in 1898, featuring a young Winston Churchill and future Edward VII, was created by Madame Tussaud. A resplendent peacock was sitting on extensive green lawns featuring a fountain, topiary trees, and garden beds enclosed by low hedges, landscaped by 'Capability' Brown. The dungeons of **Warwick Castle** told a different story from the gilded and carved halls and luxuriant furnishings in state apartments above. Down a narrow spiral staircase of worn steps, kept in a cavern drained only by an open gully in the stone-paved floor, and with only one small shaft of light, poor wretches suffered the torments of the damned under successive earls who used some of the most cruel and gruesome tortures devised by man.

From here, we visited one of the stately homes or palaces where, viewed through an arch, a gold orb surmounted a tiered archway on the opposite side of a large compound. The towering pillared portico was topped by a pediment, colonnades were crowned with decorative sculpture, and flat roofs encompassed by balustrades. Set amongst topiary bushes and hedges, statuary, and parterre gardens with low mazes, the river to one side, a series of blue pools contained fountains, and one featured an obelisk rising from a sculpture in the centre.

We proceeded through **Banbury** to **Oxford**, where my son was carrying out medical research at the time. This was a grand city, with ornate stonework decorating the many elegant university buildings (the oldest 13th century) and the tall steeple of **St Mary's church**. The round edifice of the **Sheldonian** was fenced by iron railings with busts on the concrete balusters, and there were spires, archways, heavy pillared porticos, and a covered stone overpass adorned with sculpted floral work and cherubs supporting a shield. A second round building, the reading room for the **Bodleian Library** bearing the odd name **Radcliffe Camera** (*camera* means room in Latin), had columns circling the upper floors and a balustrade around a central dome above. I used an arch to frame life-sized figures over the entry to one of the colleges fronting the green sward of a quadrangle. But I remember Oxford particularly for Queen's Lane Coffee House in **High Street**, which sold the best chocolate fudge brownies anywhere. I purchased a large box for £15 on both occasions I visited – and then had to carry the damn thing for weeks!

WALES

Making our way across the **Severn Bridge** to **Wales**, we visited **Tintern Abbey** (1131) in **Gwent**, made famous by a Wordsworth poem and a painting by Turner, and passed through **Cardiff** and **Swansea** to **The Mumbles**, the **Gower Peninsula** and Tenby. Amongst the sights that I was shown were a solitary fort-like structure on a rock in the ocean, a town with a battlemented dark stone arch across the roadway (making a dramatic statement against light-coloured buildings), the attractive Lord Nelson pub, and a wonderful panorama overlooking **Tenby** and boats in the bay, its unusual white sand beach protected by groins. Beyond the town, on the opposite side of the inlet, a grassy knoll held a large white statue, cannon, and a small building. Black-faced sheep grazed in green meadows on hills above the town, from where the view took in the sea and cliffs. We continued on through **St David's**, and I finished my film with shots of a brilliant blue ocean and rugged coastal scenery, which included a natural arch, the rock taking on different hues in the sun and shade.

IRELAND

The next part of our journey took us by car ferry to **Dublin** in **Ireland**, founded over 1,000 years ago by the Vikings and through which flowed the black waters of the **River Liffey** for which the city was named (*dubh linn* means dark pool in Norse), not a particularly pleasing place. Oscar Wilde was born in Dublin and Swift was buried in **St Patrick's Cathedral**. The first sight of interest was that of photogenic monastery ruins in lush green pasture where black cows browsed behind crumbling stone fences. Adjacent was a 'modern' (probably 16th century) stone church with symmetrical rose windows, which I filmed through the remains of an arch. A small rivulet crossed by a stone bridge flowed in front. Heading south, we went through **Wexford** and **Waterford**, but due to a strike the glass factory was closed. Wexford was the scene of one of Cromwell's worst atrocities in Ireland when, in 1649, he massacred about 2,000 of its inhabitants. In the **Franciscan Church** was a phial of blood said to belong to a boy martyr of Rome, killed by his pagan father with an axe on discovering that he had become a Christian.

Our next venue, past **Cork**, was 15th-century **Blarney Castle**, first viewed through trees at the edge of a babbling brook rippling through green meadows. It was interesting to note that the castle, with the fabled **Blarney Stone** supposed to endow the power of eloquence if kissed, added its name to the English language for posterity when Queen Elizabeth I, irritated by Lord Blarney's dissembling, exclaimed 'This is all Blarney, what he says he never means'. Another legend associated with the castle relates that a man born with a speech impediment saved a woman who fell into a swift and dangerous stream, she was revealed to be a witch and granted him one wish as a reward. Requesting the ability to speak properly, she instructed him to locate a particular stone that would cure him if kissed. Although partially ruined, the castle was still an impressive sight, with a bank of purple flowers at the base and a round corner tower. Ireland did not have the great castles, houses, and monuments of England, most of the attraction was in its scenic value, but of that there was plenty, and it certainly lived up to its name of The Emerald Isle. It was easy to see why it was so green because in the week that we spent it rained almost every day – and this in summer! On one of the few occasions it was sunny (albeit cloudy) I took film of white swans and a red boat on a blue lake surrounded by luxuriant greenery. We came to some spectacular coastal scenery of black crags and cliffs rising abruptly from the water, green slopes extending to the edge of the precipice, seagulls wheeling overhead, and white surf breaking over rock shelves at the shoreline of a very blue ocean.

Opening directly onto the pavement, we passed small cottages displaying no plants and unadorned except for colour – even chimneys were pink! Next, we headed to **Killarney**, from where we drove the **Ring of Kerry** and began to encounter mountains with white houses appearing like miniatures on the lower slopes and tiny toy-like white sheep standing out in very green fields divided by hedges. Water was also never very far away, and we descended to a river with creviced mountains beyond its rocky banks. The 'Ring', a road around the **Iveragh Peninsula**, also revealed lovely coastal scenery with stony shores and a strip of white beach directly bordering green fields. Just north, we navigated the **Dingle Peninsula**, setting for the movies *Ryan's Daughter* starring Robert Mitchum and *Far and Away* with Tom Cruise. At the commencement, the town of **Tralee** was an unattractive industrial centre worthy of mention only because of the song *Rose of Tralee*. Also disappointing was the tiny **Isle of Innisfree** in **Lough Gill** outside **Sligo**. An unkempt piece of real estate hardly bigger than a tennis court, it was made famous in a poem by Yeats, apparently simply because he liked the sound of it, and then immortalised by Bing Crosby's song of the same name in the early 1950s. Yeats is buried in Drumcliffe Churchyard, County Sligo. Six miles south of Tralee was the village of **Castlemain**, named in the song *Wild Colonial Boy* as the birthplace of Australian bushranger Jack Duggan. The beautiful panorama from a high vantage point looked out over black-faced sheep in green fields that resembled a patchwork quilt, with a rocky coastline and blue bay beyond.

We progressed through hamlets with subtle colour on plain-fronted dwellings facing the road, and passed more rushing rivers and unbelievably green meadows with yellow wildflowers. Adding to the enjoyment of this pastoral ambience were stone fences, cows in green pastures, and a stone bridge crossing a still stream with a rocky bed and overhanging trees. We visited a venue with crazy-paved paths between lawns laid out with red and yellow beds, the combination resembling floral squares in a huge carpet. A dense copse and well-tended gardens flourished in vast lawns extending to the edge of a lake with distant mountains beyond the opposite shore. The historic, austere grey stone house had a multitude of chimneys, gables, bay windows, and bare creepers on the walls. There was also an attractive natural high waterfall in an untamed part of the extensive grounds, and colourful boats were mirrored as picture perfect images in water without a ripple.

We entered **County Limerick** and came across the first thatched cottages, with tulips and daffodils bordering green lawns. More picturesque ruins were perched at the edge of an overflowing dam, and I obtained some very poor photographs of the stonework, stained glass, and decorative ceiling treatment in the dim interior of **Bunratty Castle**. This original 15th-century (c. 1450) edifice was a fairy-tale castle, not because it was pretty but because it epitomised every vision of gallant medieval knights and gorgeous delicate damsels. Accessed only by spiral staircases that made them impossible to conquer, impregnable towers in the four corners abutted the massive **Great Hall**, which was a scene of feasting and merriment even today. **Limerick**, at the mouth of the **River Shannon**, dated from the ninth century and was where the five line verse originated, but more recently it was home to Frank McCourt, author of the riveting and poignant Pulitzer Prize winning *Angela's Ashes*. Irish coffee was born when a barman at Shannon airport concocted it to comfort transiting passengers.

Prior to reaching the dramatic **Cliffs of Moher** in **County Clare**, my next film shows a pink thatch-roofed cottage in green lawn and a tiered cascade below an arched stone bridge. Up to 215m (705ft) high and rising sheer from a deep-blue sea, the cliffs completely overwhelmed the turreted **O'Brien's Watchtower** on one point, and with seagulls gliding over their green crests, and waves crashing far below, it was an awesome spectacle.

We continued to **Galway**, where Columbus was said to have prayed in the **Church of St Nicholas** on his way to the New World, and the wild windswept headland of **Connemara**, where dry-stone dividing fences became the norm. Ireland was the least populated country in Europe, a fact very evident here. I photographed scenes of a little isolated whitewashed cottage, sparse trees, fields, a rocky shore, and ruins on a tiny islet in a lake. *The Quiet Man* with John Wayne and Maureen O'Hara was filmed in County Galway in the early 1950s, and one also finds the ancient fishing village of **Claddagh** mentioned in the song *Galway Bay*. A less edifying tale attributes the origin of the word lynching to one James Lynch Fitzstephen, a fifth-century Galway magistrate who is said to have condemned his own son to hang for murder and, when no hangman could be found, carried out the execution himself.

The next point of interest, on the edge of a lake and enfolded by thick forest at the foot of a rise, was **Kylemore Abbey**, its white walls and square towers appearing grey under leaden skies. Viewed from the opposite shore, with tall waving grasses in the foreground, it made a striking picture. Far above, a white statue with upraised arms stood on a hillside, the top of which was hidden in mist. The next town extended along a stone-walled river with an arched stone bridge, and we continued on desolate roads, past more coastal scenery with surging whitecaps, stone fences sheltering sheep, their long fleeces blowing in a blustery wind, and lonely farmhouses in green fields with stony surrounds. Moving further inland, the terrain changed to a stand of pines and bare trees along a quiet river in green environs. We drove through a village with a steep street lined by plain façades showing just a little colour, and passed a thatched white farmhouse with many potted plants, stone fences, and cows in green pasture. A tiny settlement had a stone church located by a river, with an abbey on the hill behind. A tabletop mountain had sheep in the foreground, and a nearby stone church featured a small belfry. A fine mist was wafting in glens and veiling encompassing slopes as we continued past white houses and sheep in green fields on hills around a lake – I think we saw more sheep than people!

Eventually, we reached a fascinating area of prehistoric stone mounds like miniature versions of Stonehenge, for which nobody seemed to have an explanation. Several of these ancient monuments were set in stone-fenced green meadows, and nearby church ruins consisted of four intact stone walls with arched windows but no roof. Called *quoits*, the mysterious stone formations were plentiful in the United Kingdom. Driving past more rivers and hills, we came to a town with an impressive edifice featuring an Ionic-pillared portico, its pediment bearing relief of religious images and surmounted by sculpted figures. Rising above that again was a central tower with a cross at the apex. A stone steeple loomed above an isolated church in green surroundings, and more ruins occupied a nearby meadow. Passing ploughed fields and a river, with pink-tinged cloud lightening the sombre grey above, we arrived at an amazing corbelled 'cave' with rough crosses embossed on the solid stone slab above the entrance. This prehistoric construction was the 5,000-year-old passage grave at **Newgrange** in **County Meath**, which was penetrated by the sun at the winter solstice. With its grassed top, the mound created a mammoth artificial hill, and concentric circles decorated a massive rock at the site. There were gigantic standing stones nearby and a smaller grass-covered knoll visible in a fallow field.

Powerscourt in **County Wicklow** was our next destination, a gracious manor house set in extensive grounds behind intricate wrought-iron gates. We discovered formal terraces, ornamental Japanese and Italianate gardens, yellow and white flowers surrounding trees in green lawns dotted with a few statues, colourful circular beds containing red tulips, and a fountain that sparkled in the sunlight. A large lake with a statue in the water was surrounded by trees in multifarious shades of green, and a path climbed across manicured stepped lawns past trimmed conifers, flowerbeds and statuary to the stately mansion. A natural rock arch revealed a garden setting with blossom trees in red, pink and white amongst many tones of green, an unusual variety of palm, a three-tiered waterfall, and red wooden bridges beautifully mirrored in still waterways confined by grassy banks. A small gazebo completed the picture. At the lakeside, I found images of winged horses and a round stone tower ensconced amongst pines and pink blossom trees. Steps led to a long patio lined with statues and flowers in urns; a similar receptacle stood on a pedestal in a carpet of jonquils. From here, one looked over lawns, trees, the lake, and a couple of cannon to a pyramid-shaped mountain in the background. Closer to the lake, we encountered an interesting landing with an ornate metal balustrade where black and white pebbles had been utilised to create a pattern incorporating stars and the moon, also apparent on steps leading to it. These were bounded by urns, and statues at the top included a white lion. From this position I looked down towards the winged horses, which made a good frame for the image in the centre of the lake. In a wild undeveloped part of the property, we walked to a lovely 398ft natural waterfall created by the **River Dargle**.

Leaving here, we passed more lush fields and came to a stretch of bland white houses with grey slate roofs but colourful gardens, followed by a stony river and tree-studded hills where we found atmospheric ruins consisting of an old weathered church with crumbling walls, a lofty round tower with a cone-shaped top, an overgrown stone cross, and mouldering gravestones.

We went through **Letterkenny** in **Donegal** and as far as **Bloody Foreland** before crossing a corner of **Northern Ireland** (at that time unsafe to travel through) on our return to Dublin. My lasting memories of Ireland are of a delightful and endearing people but that all the jokes told about the Irish are true! When requesting directions they would respond with enquiries about your health, remark about the weather, ask if you were enjoying your stay in their country, and then proceed to give convoluted instructions that were all erroneous! We also found road signs turned in the wrong direction. After more pleasant travelling past rivers and green hills, we left on the car ferry to return to **Fishguard** in Wales, where our friendly host had remained up late at night on Easter Thursday and greeted us with hot chocolate. The couple had reluctantly accepted the booking prior to our departure for Ireland because they themselves were leaving to go on holiday the morning following our return. The cottage, with a split barn door painted red and flowerpots along the base of the white wall and on a window sill, was delightful, and our feminine room was decorated with dainty floral print wallpaper, floral bedspreads and curtains, a white cane chair, and a pink lamp on a small round table covered by a long pink cloth. They also possessed a menagerie of dogs and a cat. The waterfront of Lower Fishguard was used as a setting for the 1971 film of Dylan Thomas' *Under Milk Wood* starring Elizabeth Taylor and Richard Burton.

WALES

From Fishguard, we travelled north through a lot of towns with unpronounceable names, like **Aberystwyth**, including one with a red clock tower on a grey stone building with white accents. We encountered pretty harbours such as that with yachts and colourful fishing boats moored opposite red, blue, pink and green buildings facing the quay, and green fields on gently undulating slopes behind.

small Welsh harbour

Larger buildings fronting another bay, its strip of black sand beach broken by several breakwaters and jetties, made a nice picture, as did a round tower with spired turrets and murals depicting medieval figures. A second large stone edifice featured many towers, and one street had a series of bay windows, all with different-coloured woodwork. We came to a small cascade in verdant surrounds with a creeper-covered stone bridge, and a working waterwheel on a stone mill. At the next town, situated in the middle of a road we found an interesting stone market square (or cross) with an elaborate clock tower on top. Trees covered with pink blossom grew in the sidewalk opposite a pink façade. Similar to Ireland, we motored past green hills, rivers, and meadows dotted with very white sheep, as distinct from Australia's flocks, often dirty from dry dusty conditions. Across an old stone bridge, smoke curled lazily from a chimney in a row of white attached houses surrounded by trees that were a mass of pink and white blossom. They stood facing a river at the foot of a steep pine-clad rise. Even today, I remember stopping to photograph an emerald green glen with sheep contentedly browsing in fields that extended to the very edge of an inlet. Also like Ireland, Wales seemed sparsely populated, with isolated farmhouses in delightful locations.

Near the town of **Porthmadog** and overlooking the ocean, we discovered the whimsical Italianate village of **Portmeirion**, the product of one man's fantasy started in 1925 and one of the highlights of Wales. Enclosed by stone walls, admission was via a yellow gatehouse with a crest above the arch and a second rose-hued archway with muntined windows. Plants in white pottery urns capped pillars beside a gate, and a red-robed image stood on a balcony (from the turquoise iron railing of which a black ram was suspended!) facing a white building with an elaborate gable. This also featured an unusual arched entry with a figure in relief overhead, and cherubs flanked a shield above a bay window. Opposite, a figure with outstretched wings was perched on an orb atop a column. This was lodged in the centre of a circular flowerbed and faced a pink building with a fanlight, blue shutters, and shingled upper storeys painted white. Adjacent, in front of a tiered stone bell tower, was a lemon building with blue shutters. All these faced as area known as Battery Square.

In light rain, we followed cobbled paths to a pink and white octagonal structure with sculpting on the white porch and a blue dome. This stood next to a yellow building with a tower crowned by a blue cupola, which in turn was next to a white building with a red tiled roof. A colonnaded structure was located on a level below. Surrounded by large trees, a lovely grassed court featured colourful flowerbeds incorporating small conifers, a pond bordered by beds of yellow flowers, metal pillars surmounted by gold stars, and red blooms in pots flanking steps leading to a pool. Encompassed by yet more flower-filled garden plots, this had a fountain in the middle. Nearby, we found an ornate gazebo, a stone bridge and statue reflected in yet another pond, and a small shrine. Walking further, atop a pedestal opposite a pink and white building we came upon Hercules supporting a huge globe. The whole was a unique and refreshing interlude.

Caernarfon Castle (1285–1329) in **Gwynedd**, official seat of the Prince of Wales where Charles was invested in 1969, was an imposing edifice with battlemented walls and angular towers set in immaculate bowling green lawns. The castle overlooked houses in green fields and the boat harbour. Also in Gwynedd, the superb **Bodnant Garden** was one of the finest in Britain.

Conwy, with a great castle built by Edward I between the years of 1283–88, claimed to have the best preserved city walls in Europe, constructed the same time as the castle, and their round, dark stone crenellated turrets were certainly impressive. The walls spanned a roadway lined by narrow-fronted buildings with many chimneys, disappeared behind houses where they overlooked green fields, and were revealed again at the end of a busy street, this time with a square tower flanking the arch. Buildings in the thoroughfare included Ye Olde Mail Coach and a stone structure with a stepped gable. In the days when the sea reached the castle walls, sewerage was dumped down an open drain to be washed away by the tide. We followed the **River Conwy** past small white houses, fields and mountains to crowded **Betws-y-Coed** in the middle of **Snowdonia National Park**. In an interesting exercise, I took film in dull conditions of a lone house set in green surrounds, then the sun broke through and the sudden effulgence, just like a light having been switched on, transformed the scene to one of brilliant green with patterns of shadow. Arriving late, we had difficulty finding accommodation, so after taking a few photographs (in rain) of stone houses reflected in still water and a lovely stone church with a clock tower we decided to press on.

As it grew progressively darker, we became increasingly anxious about securing a place to stay when we came across a B&B in the middle of nowhere. Anticipating an expensive rate, I nevertheless knocked on the door and was agreeably surprised when they asked only £10 for a delightful room with soft-grey carpet and blue décor of drapes tied back with big bows, a chair cushion, the skirt around a table, dainty bedspreads and pillows – even to the frill on the wastebasket and blue pansies in a window box! Next morning, we awoke to a wonderful vista of trees and sheep in green meadows outside the window of our room in this cheery farmhouse. Underway again, I filmed a picture perfect scene of forested hills forming the backdrop to houses and a stone church in a grove at the edge of rapids racing over a stony creek bed. Another sylvan setting had sheep grazing on grass in front of substantial remains of a large stone church.

Our final destination in Wales was **Llangollen**, where the international music eisteddfod takes place. Here, we visited **Plas Newydd**, a manor with a decorative black and white exterior set amongst trees and facing a courtyard containing flowerbeds and clipped shrubs. It was inhabited in 1779 by two eccentric Irish spinsters known as the Ladies of Llangollen, who played host to a procession of celebrities including Scott, Sheridan, Wordsworth, and the Duke of Wellington. Their bizarre dress and lifestyle were a continuing source of gossip, and they lived together in the house for 50 years until Eleanor died in 1829, aged 90, followed two years later by Sarah at the age of 76. They were buried side by side in the parish churchyard with their lifelong maidservant Mary Caryll, also known as 'Mollie the Bruiser' because of her strapping physique and aggressive manner, whose money, saved from meagre wages, enabled them to purchase the freehold of their home. The house also featured muntined windows above intricately carved wooden porticos with slender posts.

ENGLAND

We crossed back into England and moved on to **Chester**, founded by the Romans around AD 70 as an army base, and another of Britain's highlights, with a wealth of half-timbered buildings displaying different designs and a spired stone clock tower. A chalk pavement portrait of Marilyn Monroe made a novel picture, and bay windows overlooked the street leading to **Eastgate** and its elaborate clock with a green dome. The multistorey gabled buildings featured different patterns on each level and no two were identical. Visible at the end of one street, a stone tower with turrets on the four corners belonged to the **Cathedral**, which also featured spires and a crenated parapet. A tall wedge-shaped metal roof topped a stone building between half-timbered edifices with projecting (jettied) upper levels; called **Rows**, these were thought to date from the late 1200s. I photographed more scenes with domed turrets, spires, gables, decorative façades and colonnades from the overhead walkway beneath the Eastgate clock, and from the ramparts of the ancient city walls I filmed Roman ruins, row houses, and a church steeple rising beyond a stone bridge crossing the river. A building called Tudor House exhibited particularly fine designs, and another had white fretwork around eaves above a bay window over an archway. This was flanked by taller structures, symmetrical but with different patterns of framework, one of which was emblazoned with the words: TO · GOD · MY · KING · and · MY · COUNTRY beneath carved images that included Jeremiah, Cain and Abel. Above these, a niche between leadlight windows held a statue bearing a gold orb and staff. The tracery of an intricate white metal sign completed the picture. My final film shows the image of Queen Victoria outside a building titled Old Queens Head and another picturesque stone bridge spanning blue water flowing between green banks.

From here, bypassing Liverpool and Manchester, we travelled north by way of **Morecambe** to the **Lakes District**, encountering green hills and our first glimpse of snow on distant mountain tops. **Lake Windermere**, the largest in England, was choppy and conditions overcast, but it still presented an attractive picture with overhanging trees, green surrounds, and high snow-capped mountains beyond. The following day saw a patch of blue peep through the cloud cover, which brought yachts and powerboats out on a more placid expanse of water broken up only by boat ramps and a jetty. Enjoying the inclement weather, a parade of ducks waddled along the foreshore planted with gay red, white and yellow flowers, whilst gulls flew overhead and white swans strutted or swam. In a rare burst of sunshine, bright yellow daffodils made a brilliant show, with red boats bobbing on the lake in the background. Again, we found a quaint B&B, called Fern Cottage, in a row with postage stamp gardens. These displayed climbing roses on a white wall, pot plants and window boxes on sills, vivid red tulips, shrubs, and daffodils mixed with other flowers.

This region had some of the prettiest scenery in England, with stone bridges over swiftly flowing rocky streams bounded by green banks and light sparkling off the dancing water like reflections from silver sequins. In one day we experienced all four seasons when, in pleasant sunshine, we motored past gurgling creeks and fenced emerald fields only to encounter, on climbing steep ridges, eddying cloud and a sudden hailstorm, which forced us to pull over because it was so severe. In spite of the dark clouds, whitewashed and stone farmhouses in idyllic surrounds provided subjects for beautiful pictures. Past **Ambleside**, in the pretty town of **Grasmere**, where Wordsworth lived in Dove Cottage from 1799 to 1808 and was buried in St Oswald's churchyard, we found a few half-timbered buildings, a photogenic stone mill with a river running underneath, and a wonderful display of daffodils and jonquils in the street. Beatrix Potter also lived and worked in the area.

We were heading for **Derwent Water** near the town of **Keswick**, where the Dam Busters of WWII fame practised dropping their bombs prior to their raid on German dams in 1943. They perfected the use of two spotlights under each plane for fixing its height, and dummy towers were erected for the purpose of gauging the correct moment to release their weapons. We were approaching much closer to the snowy mountains that ringed Keswick on three sides, the lake being on the other, and sheep appeared unaware of the cold as they grazed on very green pasture behind stone fences. Composing more perfect scenery, a river flowed between tree-lined banks below grassy slopes framing snow-covered peaks beyond. Jonquils flourished on a green verge with snow in the background, and whitewashed and stone houses with slate roofs were ensconced behind dry-stone walls. A few façades were still enhanced with creepers, and a sombre dark stone dwelling with small windows and a steeply pitched roof was enlivened by red tulips, daffodils, and green lawn. Jonquils were prevalent, and a house with smoke issuing from the chimney featured a dove cote in the yard. Continuing our excursion, fields were still a verdant green, and we passed a wider river with a waterfall cascading down a gully between mountains to one side. This area was quite densely forested, with many shades of green in the wide variety of trees. Back at the lake, indirect light filtering through heavy cloud silvered the water to beautiful effect. Small boats were moored to pylons or drawn up on a shallow beach where

picturesque stone bridge

ducks congregated. Colourful and bare flowerbeds combined with green lawn to create a patchwork effect surrounded by trees, and all the time snow-capped mountains appeared in the background. We passed fields of vivid green right at the foot of snowy slopes and a wild stretch of river bordered by a wooded area with many bare branches. Picturesque arched bridges of rough stone crossed streams rushing with melted snow, and a dusting of the white precipitation lay sprinkled for a brief period on the tops of fences and in patches on the ground.

SCOTLAND

Continuing through **Penrith** in **Cumbria**, we made a sojourn to **Scotland**, but did not venture far because I was running out of time. In **Edinburgh**, I discovered an impressive castle-like brownstone structure with many towers, turrets, gables and chimneys, a stone manor house on the crest of a hillock, and a stone edifice with a red door, stepped gables, and turrets with copper spires wearing the green of verdigris. A glorious display of massed red, white and yellow flowers marked the entrance, flanked by stone pillars, to civic gardens. **St Giles' Cathedral** (1385) was another imposing edifice with the usual arched windows and spires, but also a stonework addition resembling a royal crown (added in 1495) surmounting its square tower. Taken in dull conditions, dark photographs showed it silhouetted against the sky. The **Thistle Chapel** was added in 1911. Across the street stood a 15th-century building known as **John Knox's House** (1490), where the fiery leader of the Scottish Reformation was thought to have lived from 1561 to 1572, his small image adorning one corner. John Knox was a religious reformer who established the protestant religion in Scotland; he became minister of St Giles in 1560.

The statue of a rearing horse stood in front of a four-storey stone building with a carved pediment, and an edifice with many pilasters was constructed using two-toned brown stonework, a feature of 19th-century Edinburgh. **Princes Street Gardens**, separating the **Old Town** from the **New Town**, contained trees, colourful circular flowerbeds, and a 90-year-old floral clock. At the lower end of the **Royal Mile** stood **Holyrood House** (dating from 1671), the Queen's residence in Edinburgh and once home to Mary Queen of Scots, Bonnie Prince Charlie and Queen Victoria. From a high point, we looked down on the impressive Gothic black stone **Scott Memorial**, rising like a steeple more than 200ft from a grassed strip of the aforementioned Princes Street gardens. A large statue of a seated Sir Walter Scott with his dog Maida sat in the centre of the monument. Arriving at 1,000-year-old **Edinburgh**

Castle shortly before closing, I only managed to see a guard patrolling the perimeter, from where I filmed the view over the city. Situated on the crest of a green mound, the castle made an impressive sight when viewed from below. The roofline of another massive stone structure was punctuated with numerous towers, turrets and cupolas, and I photographed more attractive ruins and a lovely stretch of still water.

We left Edinburgh for a circuit of the peninsula jutting into the **Forth of Firth** in the **County of Fife**. Here, we found **St Andrews** – of golfing fame since the 1500s, and to where the bones of the apostle Andrew were supposed to have been brought in AD 347 – and several picturesque fishing communities, including Crail, once the haunt of smugglers, and **Anstruther**. An eye-catching street fronting stone houses had green lawns with gay flowerbeds shaded by trees displaying a mass of red blossom, and we paused to take a picture of still more ruins near water. We passed both whitewashed and stone houses with plain façades and dormer windows and a brownstone with a bright red door and narrow garden edging the pavement. This area also introduced red tiled roofs, which were unusual until now. A pretty stone church with a steeple stood on a slight rise opposite dwellings with creepers on walls and colourful plots of flowers. Tall narrow-fronted buildings with coloured doors were crowded together above a stone seawall, and we walked along a street with a stone tower and unadorned buildings with a host of chimneys, which caused me to speculate as to whether they served any practical purpose or were purely ornamental. My film of **Crail** shows tall stone and white houses with red roofs behind a seawall, the protected bay providing shelter for a fishing boat and birds.

Crail harbour

The beached red **North Carr** lighthouse boat made an interesting photograph, and an establishment appropriately called The Ship was located next to a building with a stepped gable. Further around the peninsular, a photogenic scene featured red-roofed houses on the curve of a bay, the steeple of a church towering above, and old gravestones on a grassy verge in the foreground.

Forth of Firth

We came across a building with one entire wall displaying decorative designs created with shells and overlooked a large stone house set in lawns terraced by rock walls. Red tiles seemed popular in this region and roofed an attractive rough stone cottage with a stepped gable and pink-framed windows, which adjoined a white dwelling with blue frames. We visited cathedral ruins with the steeple still standing proudly atop remains of the arched entry, two spires surmounting the portal at the opposite end, and a tower. Stone houses exhibited pretty gardens, including the usual tulips and daffodils, in small squares of lawn, and a large stone edifice with symmetrical turrets had coloured coats of arms above the entrance. Showing up in relief against a drab sky, spires and stepped gables were evident behind a stone monument with rearing red lions supporting shields on the corners, a central pillar, and water pouring from the mouth of a countenance at the base. Stone and whitewashed houses bounded narrow cobbled streets, and we spent that evening in a B&B with a view of the stone turrets mentioned above right outside our window. More church ruins, open to the sky, contained a square tower and a rose window in a gable above an arched entry; devoid of glass, its colour was provided by the heavens.

ENGLAND

Next, we reached extensive remains of **Hadrian's Wall**, set in bucolic surrounds of grass, trees, and a murmuring river. Begun in AD 122 as a defensive measure against barbarians (marauding Scots), it took the Romans 17 years to complete, stood four and a half to six metres high, was two and a half metres wide, and crossed 118 kilometres (80 miles) from coast to coast. Abandoned at the end of the fourth century, for the succeeding 1,400 years it was used as a source of stone for roads, churches, farmhouses, and even sheep pens. Yet today, long segments still survive, together with flagstones marking foundations of watchtowers and Roman forts; the wall originally incorporated observation posts and mini-forts called 'milecastles'. We visited a couple of the many sites, one of which was the **Cilurnum** (**Bath House**) at **Chesters**.

Staithes harbour

Bypassing Newcastle, we stopped at the towns of Staithes and Whitby, with both of which the young James Cook had an association. Leaving home at 16, he worked in the former at a shop (identified by a plaque) close to the harbour, and at the age of 17 moved to Whitby to join the crew of a coal ship. Apprenticed to

John Walker and living in his house, Cook sailed with Walker's fleet until 1755 when he joined the Royal Navy. In **Staithes**, houses on a narrow shelf at the base of steep cliffs faced a small inlet with several boats at anchor below the seawall, and white buildings along the seafront were lashed with spray. The interesting steep cobbled streets of **Whitby** were full of steps and stairs, a few small gardens, window boxes, buoys, boats, and an assortment of fishing paraphernalia. The main landmark was a ruined abbey built in 1078 on a cliff overlooking the harbour, and a dark stone house was effectively brightened by a yellow door, sills, and matching gay daffodils in a window box.

We encountered dense forest and a beautiful wild pheasant as we drove through **North Yorkshire** towards **Castle Howard** with its central dome and ornamentation on the balustrade forming the parapet. This was the location of the TV series *Brideshead Revisited*, and the delightful grounds featured urns and statues (including a wild boar!) on pedestals and a large pond, its central fountain adorned with naked images blowing horns, the water from which sprayed a central figure of Atlas supporting the world on his bowed neck and shoulders. There was a lake with a fountain in the centre, and a peacock stood on a sill – looking in the window.

We continued past stone houses with ivy- and vine-covered façades, flower gardens, and purple-flowering creeper cascading over a grey stone wall to historic **York**, another founded (in AD 71) as a Roman army base. Here, we were welcomed by an impressive turreted double archway across the road, ancient half-timbered buildings, and the beautiful **York Minster** (1220–1480), largest Gothic cathedral in England, with tall arched windows, large rose windows, square towers, and many spires. We saw quaint old buildings with crooked framework, and the famous narrow medieval butchers' street called **The Shambles** (featured in many pictures and where an artist was at work), with overhanging upper storeys that almost met overhead, and a view of the cathedral at the end. A tree heavy with blossom stood in front of one such, its windowless upper level extending over the sidewalk and supported by wooden posts; another had a bowed upper floor. York's 13th-century walls were amongst the most impressive surviving medieval fortifications in Europe, and another well-recognised aspect of the city and cathedral was that looking back from the ramparts. A small church and free-standing arched wall were beautified by trees laden with blossom, but many pictures were the same as described in the 1992 chapter. We visited the **Jorvik Viking Centre** with its tenth-century remains, also described later.

Travelling via picturesque **Knaresborough**, dominated by a church tower and its bridge on massive pylons spanning the **River Nidd**, we went to the **Yorkshire Dales**, where we visited the towns of **Burnsall**, on a slope above the **River Wharfe**, **Grassington**, 16th-century **Appletreewick**, and **Skipton**. A most interesting sight was that of a grotto church excavated from the face of a cliff. A large rock-hewn statue stood in a recess beside the arched doorway, and even muntined windows were set into framework carved out of the rock, with a pretty garden below.

grotto church

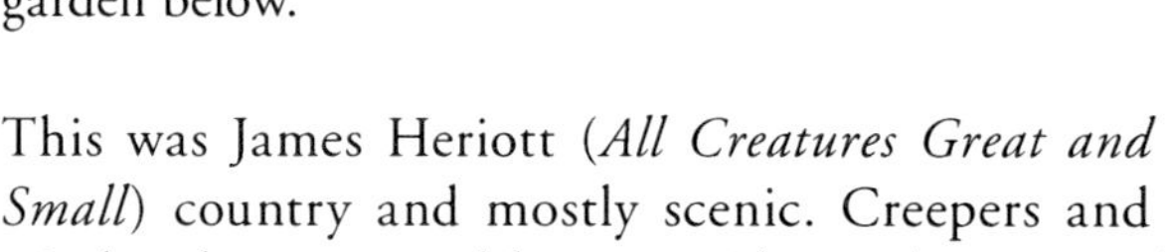

This was James Heriott (*All Creatures Great and Small*) country and mostly scenic. Creepers and window boxes graced houses with rough stone walls (the same material also used in generous proportions to create churches and bridges), and we saw green fields with sooty-faced sheep and pure white lambs. Purple and white flowers tumbled over a stone wall next to a white paling gate, and a stone cross stood in front of an interesting castle-like structure incorporating an elaborate half-timbered building. Perched on top of a turret-like corner with only slit apertures for archers, this unusual half-timbered section featured muntined glass and a slate roof.

We passed fields of glaring yellow rape, made even more intense by a dull sky, and came to a village with vines on thatched half-timbered cottages, a half-timbered building on tall wooden piles, and a multilevel half-timbered edifice with flags flying from windows – even the clock tower was half-timbered. It also had its share of leaning structures and bowed walls, and we found a lace-curtained tea room called Apple Charlotte. We made several attempts, to no avail, to locate a village by the name of **Eastnor**, and eventually deciding to give it a miss, booked in for the night at a historic Elizabethan B&B. Heavy beams braced the half-timbered walls of our room, and breakfast was served in a delightful conservatory full of

chocolate box cottages Eastnor

plants and overlooking green lawns, trees, frilly-petalled red roses, and alert grey squirrels. In a stroke of good fortune, our hostess knew of the village that we had been endeavouring to find, and we chose to give it one more try; a rewarding decision because it proved to be the most charming of all English villages. Literally a chocolate box picture, its cottages were used to illustrate same, as well as a variety of other merchandise such as jigsaw puzzles. Maintained all year, it consisted of barely half a dozen thatched half-timbered houses, but all were stunning in their magnificent surrounds of green lawns, garden beds, floral borders and pots of multihued flowers, trellised creepers, hanging baskets, blossom trees, and a single dove cote. Secluded behind a stone fence, one had a sign on the picket gate reading The Haven, which seemed very apt.

Starkly drawn by light and shadow, the perfect furrows of ploughed fields also made interesting photographs, and a vast field of yellow rape was dazzling to the eyes. Retracing our steps, on the homeward leg we went through the town of **Balfour**, with a mixture of stone and half-timbered buildings. An attractive rough stone structure had steps leading to an open gallery, arches around the perimeter of which supported a twin-gabled section overhead and a clock tower on top. A striking brown building with white quoins and dormer windows abutted a beige building with bay windows, and a half-timbered structure had carved figures on wooden uprights.

Next morning dawned very foggy, and we passed a river barely discernable through the mist, more pretty gardens, and cattle in luxuriant green pasture. In bucolic surroundings, we visited more majestic abbey ruins, with a large naked window rearing above others containing lovely stonework tracery. A settlement of neat thatched stone cottages with attic windows, conifers, creepers, blossom trees and flowers preceded another huge chalk etching on a green slope. This was the **Uffington White Horse**, west of **Wantage**, where King Alfred was born in 849 and who legend has it carved the image, but it actually extended to the Iron Age, 1,000 years before. Another source informed me that it was 100m from nose to tail and was the oldest British hillside art, estimated to be 3,000 years of age. We called in to see my son Michael who was, at that time, at Oxford University, the oldest in Britain with 36 colleges from the 13th century on. He was living in a flat at Adwell Manor House, set in extensive grounds containing a series of ponds with ducks and white swans, a little bridge, and a small waterfall in natural environs. In the vicinity, a red brick half-timbered building, the bricks in a gable forming a pattern, adjoined a white half-timbered structure with bowed beams. Also in **Oxfordshire** was **Blenheim Palace**, where Winston Churchill was born in 1874. We spent time at one of Britain's many magnificent gardens, **Exbury** near Fareham, with a blaze of brilliant red and pink rhododendrons, green trees, and carpets of purple bluebells, all of which provided exquisite reflections in a lake. I wasted considerable footage on a heron standing in the water before I realised that it was not real! However, it did not fool the fish, which swam all around it. A corner bed of bright yellow flowers was amongst many rendering the streets almost as colourful.

Laurie and I took a ferry to **Ryde** on the picturesque **Isle of Wight**, where we had to rely on public transport and 'shank's pony' so consequently did not see everything. An attractive stone and half-timbered building with decorative fretwork around gables had a garden fenced by a stone wall. Other ornate gables were perfectly mirrored in still water, and there were plenty of stone and white-walled thatched cottages, including a pretty corner tearoom with the unappealing name of The Bats Wing, which had lace curtains, flowering creepers and a narrow strip of garden bordering the road. Stone fences were prominent, and a wedding was in progress at a small stone church with a square tower.

Our next excursion took us east along the coast to **Brighton** in **Sussex**. Points of interest pictured en route were a shingle-walled covered overpass with a clock, a long wooden promenade, a parade of dignitaries in mayoral robes, a stone church with a tall steeple, and an elegant clock tower supported by flying buttresses at the end of a street with leafy trees overhanging garden beds. We made a stop at the **Bignor Roman Villa** in the village of **Fishbourne**, the largest Roman building so far discovered in Britain. Believed to be a palace going back to AD 75, its beautiful mosaic floors depicted Medusa, Venus, gladiators, horses with long curling fishtails, a boy on a dolphin, urns, flourishes and floral designs, and black and white geometric patterns with a three-dimensional effect. Six miles south of here, we came to imposing **Arundel Castle**, a grey mass with the usual towers and turrets looming above half-timbered buildings in the town.

At Brighton, the extraordinary incongruous **Brighton Pavilion**, with its numerous elaborate onion domes, spires, cupolas, and carved stone latticework, made striking film behind an expanse of green lawn with large beds of red tulips and a few daffodils. Looking more like a mosque, it was built in 1787 as a seaside palace for the Prince Regent, who later became

King George IV, and was redesigned and expanded between 1815 and 1822 to what we see today. After George's death in 1830, his successor, King William IV, stayed there on frequent visits; however, Queen Victoria decided it was not to her taste. The famous **Brighton Pier** (1899), with its domed pavilion, clock tower at one end and lighthouse the other, was draped with a huge banner advertising free deck chairs, an offer of which many people had taken advantage and which were lined up in perfect rows on the shingle beach. I found this very amusing, and it put me in mind of illustrations in old comic books! A street artist was creating a portrait on the pavement, and we returned to Fareham via the delightful town of West Meon once again. Along the way, I photographed a glorious solitary red tree in the middle of a field surrounded by green foliage, a white half-timbered cottage, a mass of wild bluebells in a copse of trees, a thatched grey clapboard house with a red door, shutters and cheerful garden and, beside a small stream, a stone house with muntined dormer windows and walls covered with ivy. One ancient building with leadlight windows was a combination of stone, brick and partially plastered half-timbered surfaces.

After a brief stay at home, we drove east again, through **Petworth** and rural scenery, past pretty plots behind white picket fences, and by houses gay with pot plants, baskets and window boxes to 14th-century **Bodiam Castle** (1385), also in Sussex. Standing in the middle of an artificial lake, it was one of the most photogenic in Britain, with round crenellated bastions at the corners, square towers, and battlemented turrets. It was accessed via a bridge leading from the grass verge (on which sheep browsed) to an archway protected by a portcullis. There was little to see inside because its attraction centred on the exterior aspect, but from one of the towers I looked across fields of yellow rape.

We continued on to **Rye**, yet another of my favourite places, with narrow cobbled streets and brick or half-timbered houses with muntined windows dating back to Tudor times. Once on the seafront and numbered amongst the Cinque Ports, since the harbour silted up 400 years ago and the ocean receded it was now two miles inland! In steep **Mermaid Street**, where most buildings were over 300 years old, we found the historic **Mermaid Inn** (1420), its façade overgrown with creeper. In the 1700s it was a haunt of smugglers. We also came across Simon the Pieman, considered one of the best teahouses in the United Kingdom. A lopsided half-timbered building, others facing a stone wall shaded by overhanging trees, narrow alleyways, a covered wooden overpass and, next to a belfry, a sign announcing Ye Olde Bell on a stone, half-timbered and shingle building with leadlight windows all served to make up charming pictures of this pleasant town. Other photographs I took at this time show an inn titled XVth Century White Horse, its white walls festooned with colourful flower baskets and a tall cross in front of crenated stone walls to one side. After driving through more towns in sylvan surrounds, we visited a manor house with many chimneys and gables, which was set amongst lawns featuring intricate topiary sculpture and a waterway lined with colourful flowerbeds.

Ultimately arriving in **Canterbury**, on the **River Stour**, an interesting old half-timbered building featured decorated gables, and at the end of a street the towers and spires of the imposing 11th-century **Cathedral** were visible, its façade adorned with escutcheons and small figures. It contained the shrine of the Archbishop of Canterbury, Thomas à Becket, murdered in the cathedral in 1170 by four knights of Henry II. The tomb was once studded with precious stones of every kind until ransacked by Henry VIII in 1538. Canterbury and the martyred Becket became the focus of one of the most important pilgrimages in Europe, immortalised by Geoffrey Chaucer in his *Canterbury Tales.*

Leeds Castle

We came to **Leeds Castle**, four miles out of **Maidstone** in **Kent**, referred to in brochures as 'The loveliest castle in the world', and certainly the oldest in Britain (1119). Transformed from a fortress by Henry VIII, and with angular turrets flanking the arched entry, this pale stone monument was also located in a lake. Water flowed beneath an arched section connecting the wings and it was surrounded by parkland. In the town, an embossed floral frieze embellished the woodwork of a half-timbered structure, and another was enhanced with animal images and the date 1585.

From Maidstone we took the ring road around London and headed for **Colchester** in **Essex**, and thence to **Suffolk** through **Braintree** and **Saffron Walden**. Suffolk was remarkable for the number of pink cottages and I think I must have photographed every one; in fact, the term 'Suffolk pink' has been coined! This beautiful part of the country was also filled with quaint towns, and looking across a red brick bridge we saw geese on the grassy bank of a river foreshore where white (and pink!) houses faced a green common. A pink dwelling with white fretwork around dormer windows also featured multiple chimneys exhibiting different patterns of brickwork, and a white thatched cottage had muntined windows. We passed a large manor house set in trees behind a field alive with wildflowers, and a wonderful old building in one small town had relief of large stork-like birds on its white stuccoed façade; tiny gabled rooms projected overhead. Small figures adorned a stone monument in front of a half-timbered building, and a church steeple towered above houses in a village seen across meadows covered with long grass.

Located amongst trees at the edge of an expanse of green, the delightful village of **Cavendish**, home of war hero Group-Captain Leonard Cheshire who died in 1992, featured white houses, a large thatched building painted pink, a stone church, and a pink half-timbered pub with dormer windows in the steeply pitched roof. In a picturesque scene at **Sudbury**, a couple of pink houses, a half-timbered white dwelling, and an ivy-draped brick façade faced a ford where water flowed across the road, beside which geese sat on a small patch of grass.

ford at Sudbury

This magical place was a picture book of colourful thatched cottages with tall chimneys, gay gardens, hedges, vines creeping up lamp poles and over paling fences, and grassy verges full of flowers. Suffolk was also an area overflowing with sagging and crooked half-timbered buildings leaning towards each other in narrow streets. A cream-coloured building with an old-fashioned multi-paned convex window faced a wider thoroughfare. Opposite stood a pink stuccoed structure with lovely white fretwork around twin gables on the half-timbered upper storey. Next to this, and sloping towards it, a white half-timbered building with muntined windows stood in turn next to a pink stuccoed façade with dormers in the steep roof. Yet another tall pink half-timbered building with bay windows, opposite a white structure with brown quoins, had a most distinct lopsided cant, and tubs of multihued flowers lined a sidewalk; it was all exceedingly photogenic. Nestled in green lawns with flowers circling the base of a large tree, a particularly beautiful pink cottage had a floral border along its foundations and roses climbing the walls and around attic windows in the decoratively capped thatch. Thomas Gainsborough was born in Sudbury in 1727, and it must have provided inspiration for his painting.

Having completed a circuit through Cavendish, Sudbury, **Kersey** – renowned for its cloth in medieval times and referred to in Shakespeare's *Measure for Measure* and *Love's Labour Lost* – and **Long Melford**, we continued to **Bury St Edmunds**, where we found the quaint Nutshell, Britain's smallest pub, with a floor space measuring 4.9m by 3.1m, an appropriate sign on the front, and the whole nearly hidden behind clusters of red blossoms on a tree! Bury St Edmunds was mentioned by Dickens in *Pickwick Papers* as a place where his character Mister Pickwick stayed, and Daniel Defoe also lived here for a time. The ruins of its abbey, once the greatest in England and where, in 1215, the barons made a vow to get King John to sign the Magna Carta, were the site of magnificent gardens entered through the old **Abbey Gate**. Large trees shaded lawns with brightly coloured flowerbeds in various geometric shapes. Predominantly tulips and daffodils, blue was introduced in the form of hyacinths and pansies. Flowers also grew in an urn on a pedestal in front of a vine-covered wall, and roses trailed up tree trunks; it was a whirlpool of colour. Ducks strutted across the grass, and a part of the old remains was reflected in a patch of water frequented by small birds. A delightful dwelling with attic windows in its thatched roof and white fretwork around the small portico had a gorgeous garden in pretty pinks, and we found a classical building, its columns and a carved pediment making a lovely picture behind the massed red flowers of a tree. The **Norman Tower** was one of the best preserved pieces of Norman architecture in the country. The town acquired its name from a king martyred in 870, and there have been local moves to have St Edmund replace St George as the patron saint of England.

Continuing to the city of **Norwich** in **Norfolk**, an embossed plaque showed a medieval interpretation of turreted towers flanking the arched city gate, and red stone panels featured scenes in relief. The **Norwich Cathedral** was renowned as the burial place of Nurse Edith Cavell, executed by the Germans during the First World War, and had fine stained glass illustrating typical religious themes. An interesting sign on the Cat and Fiddle pub portrayed the nursery rhyme: the dog laughing and the cow jumping over the moon. Suburban streets were a mixture of stone and half-timbered buildings; one of the latter, with old weathered brickwork and attic windows in its tiled roof, was covered with red roses. A tiny stone house with brick quoins and flowers around the foundations was further enhanced by white window frames and a blue door peeping through massed greenery. Two similar homes were graced, respectively, with pink blossoms around a window and white creeper around the door. Our next stop, in green surrounds, was the ancient ruins of **Castle Acre Priory**, which included carved stonework, arches, and a large picture window framing the sky.

Travelling as far north as **Walsingham** and **Wells-next-the-Sea**, we did a loop and again headed south, through **Kings Lynn**, to stately historic

Oxburgh Hall (1482), with its square tower, stepped gables, copious tall decorative chimneys (one with a spiral pattern), bay windows, and angular turrets. Set in the atmospheric surroundings of a water filled moat, an intricate parterre garden in a French design was laid out opposite. Accessed via a bridge, the perfect reflections even mirrored the blue of the sky and white clouds. Walls on three sides reared straight up from the water, whilst in front, a battlemented parapet and arched entrance faced a sward of green lawn planted with trees, also within the moat. Underway again, we stopped to film a twisting green-edged pathway leading to a picturesque small stone church, its central steeple towering above surrounding trees in a vast field of rape, creating the illusion of everything floating on a vibrant yellow ocean.

We made next for **Cambridge**, the name derives from the bridge over the **River Cam**, where our first sight was that of the towers and spires of wonderful **Ely Cathedral**. More half-timbered thatched white cottages displayed bright gardens, and in the vast grounds of a manor house, I photographed a beautiful white pheasant, a gazebo housing a large stone bowl, and a row of statues on pedestals arrayed down a grassed avenue between tall trees. I came upon another crooked half-timbered building, a classical edifice with Corinthian columns and a sculpted pediment, a long three-storey structure with a large monument on the lawn in front, and a red building with angular turrets, which was further distinguished by beige quoins on the arched entry and relief of a figure with gilded rampant animals overhead. The crenellations of its red brick ramparts were outlined with beige masonry, and once again tall chimneys adorned the roofline. Cambridge University, founded in 1209, has numbered amongst its students such names as Marlowe, Milton, Spencer, Coleridge and Wordsworth, and we must have visited on a weekend because quite a few people were punting on the river. Nowhere in the city seemed very far from water, associated with which were lovely bridges, green banks (called **The Backs**), colourful plants and drooping willows. Surrounded by yellow flowers, a decorative stone rotunda stood in a large grassed quadrangle enclosed by gracious college buildings. These featured dormer windows and arched portals flanked by turrets, one with figures overhead; another, a clock. The spired dome of **Johns College** was prominent from many vantage points. Installed amongst plants behind white paling, the half-timbered Ye Olde Fighting Cocks (and its sign) made an attractive picture, as did ancient stone walls, a sagging half-timbered façade, and a leaning gable next to a building with planter boxes in every window.

In another area of chalk engravings on green hillsides, Australia was represented by a map of the country and the army insignia, together with that of the YMCA and others. We came to a stone church with a square Norman tower and more stone houses with thatched and slate roofs, creeper-covered walls and pretty gardens. One large home behind a low stone wall had blooming wisteria on the façade and a bird bath on lawn in the centre of a circular driveway. However, even after all that I had seen in this land of fairy-tale villages, I was enchanted by the beauty of a roadside rill running at the foot of ivy-draped stone walls, meandering under little stone bridges, and murmuring past creeper-adorned thatched stone cottages (one with red doors) and clumps of multihued flowers beside a narrow pathway at the water's edge.

rill beside stone cottages

A market cross made an interesting picture in front of a half-timbered building, and ten miles from **Frome**, in **Wiltshire**, we visited the world famous **Stourhead Gardens** in the village of **Stourton**, with blue wildflowers in green lawns, a scalloped hedge, and a glass conservatory encapsulated by a mass of flowering wisteria. These breathtaking surrounds, landscaped from medieval fish ponds dammed in the 1740s to create one big lake, also featured colourful creepers climbing rustic pergolas, a 1720s manor house, and both cultivated and natural foliage on wide expanses of lawn and undulating hills. Massed trees were combined with brilliant displays of azaleas, rhododendrons and camellias. Scattered structures included the **Temple of Apollo** (1765), **The Grotto** (1748), the **Pantheon** (1753), with images of Hercules, Flora and other classical figures, the **Bristol High Cross**, acquired in 1765, and the **Temple of Flora** (1744) with busts of Marcus Aurelius and (possibly) Alexander the Great. The **Gothic Cottage** and stone bridge were beautifully reflected in the lake, together with surrounding trees and a fantastic array of multihued blooms; a family of geese and goslings wandered on the grassy bank. Bright yellow blossoms made a stunning splash of colour, and there was also the little **Church of St Peter** on a grass-covered rise in front of a stand of tall timber. As we stood facing the lake, with ducks swimming on the unruffled surface and colourful flowers on the verge, flawless reflections created twice the impact; in every direction we looked it was a magnificent display of greenery and colour.

Shaftesbury in **Dorset** was the location of **Gold Hill**, a particularly steep cobbled thoroughfare lined with thatch- and tile-roofed houses, one side shorter than the other! I took photographs of nondescript stone and stuccoed houses at the edge of green fields (a single red door making a stark statement) and a small church dominated by a square tower. Summer was now in full swing, and a vine with gorgeous large pink blooms decked a stone wall above vibrant yellow flowers. A stone and half-timbered building viewed through an arch, bay windows and interesting streets with a stone church and belfry, a castle beyond sheep in a meadow, and green fields to the sea made up the following pictures. At our next stop, a peacock with vivid blue and green plumage proudly spread its fan-like tail, and there was a beautiful burnished copper pheasant, a lake surrounded by ferns and lush undergrowth, a glorious show of azaleas, and a pure white peacock (that I had never seen before), displaying its tail above rear feathers that quivered in a courtship ritual.

Gold Hill

Passing more creeper-draped thatched stone cottages with shutters, we came to **Poole**, the narrow neck of its cove forming a natural harbour with fishing boats and dories in the water or drawn up on a shingle beach next to a little wooden shack. The photogenic ruins of a castle crowned a crest, and we stopped to film a sheltered bay with chalk cliffs on the opposite shore. Near Poole we found **Compton Acres**, another of Britain's entrancing gardens, on a smaller scale and more intimate than Stourhead but no less appealing. Considered one of the world's finest, it covered an area of 15 acres and contained water features and themed gardens such as Italianate and Japanese. The former was exquisite and had 'the works': bronze statues of athletic figures at one end of a long pool, a white marble statue in a gazebo at the other, and a three-tiered fountain, statue and water lilies in the middle, reflected on the still surface. White figures (sans gazebos) also stood at each side of the pool, which was bordered by a walkway between strips of lawn bearing white urns on pedestals and flowering shrubs, the whole enclosed by a high hedge. Floral displays included tulips, rhododendrons and azaleas, all shown to advantage amongst dense green foliage and reflected in ponds. It was all outstanding, but most exceptional was the awe-inspiring Japanese garden, probably the best in Europe, the beauty of which

I could have revelled in for hours. Set around a large pond with ducks and koi, water lilies, a fine fountain, stepping stones, a cascade, and artificial long-legged water birds, it also contained a red pavilion with red railing and a two-tiered red roof blanketed by a splendid canopy of cascading wisteria with a profusion of delicate mauve flowers. Amongst the verdant variegated greenery were arum lilies and an overwhelming burst of colour in flowering trees, all mirrored in the water. It was enchanting, and at first sight literally left me speechless.

Japanese garden

I have pictures of another three-masted schooner and an exhibition of iris, which surprised me with the number of varieties. We visited the **Worldwide Butterflies and Lullingstone Silk Farm** in **Compton House** near **Sherborne** in Dorset, exhibiting yellow, orange, and gorgeous blue-and-black specimens. Frustrating and difficult to photograph because they rarely obliged by resting for long, these ephemeral insects made a beautiful sight fluttering gently from flower to flower. Gravitating to like-coloured blooms, they were well camouflaged: orange admirals alighting on orange lantana, black, red and white landing on bright red flowers, a black and red on black-spotted deep orange tiger lilies, and black and yellow on yellow lantana. There were spotted and striped varieties and moths with big 'eyes' on their wings. The setting was also very attractive, with tiny bright yellow birds, tropical and long-leaved plants, vines, and water lilies in a pond that also held a small turtle. The silk farm provided said delicate fabric for the last two coronations, the Queen's wedding dress, and that of Diana, Princess of Wales. My next pictures show a neat village with narrow cobbled streets winding between white buildings, a thatched cottage with a steeply pitched roof, and another garden with masses of blooming rhododendrons and a pond covered with water lilies. The picturesque ruins of **Corfe Castle** crowned a green hill in Dorset.

A few hours in **London** introduced me to a picturesque free-standing half-timbered wee pub called the Coach and Horses with a lacy green tree in front – both surely a rarity amongst the tall buildings in the heart of the city – and one of the famous red double-decker buses passing an arch bridging a narrow street.

My itinerary included other towns, such as tiny **Tichborne** with a handful of thatched cottages, beautiful **Bolingey** with a 17th-century stone inn, one mile from pretty **Perranporth** on the south coast, and innumerable other small hamlets that I cannot put a name to. Tichborne claimed world attention as the location of one of the most remarkable hoaxes of all time when, in 1866, a Wapping butcher's son who had immigrated to Australia in 1852, claimed to be the heir to the Tichborne estates who had disappeared at sea in 1853. Although speaking with an east London accent and barely literate, he managed to convince many people, including Sir Roger's mother, but was convicted of perjury and jailed, maintaining his bluff to the end.

On one of my visits with Laurie, because it was in his home county of Hampshire, we went to the ruins of **Beaulieu Abbey** (founded 1204) and the **Palace House**, incorporating an extensive motor museum with over 200 exhibits. I was presented with a lovely booklet detailing the history of the house. The actual running of the household read like a chapter from *Upstairs, Downstairs*, documenting amongst the duties of a footman, the cleaning of silver coins carried by the ladies! Servants' hours were from 6am to 10.30pm or when the master retired. One evening a week, a half day on Sunday, and one full day a month was allocated as free time, and wages ranged from £25 a year earned by the butler to £5 for the scullery maid, out of which the cost of a uniform was deducted if that issued wore out before time. One candle a week was provided. The staff of this manor house numbered 20.

SULAWESI 1990

This was my first visit to **Sulawesi**, once known as the **Celebes**, but much is described in a subsequent chapter.

En route, I spent a night in **Bali,** at a hotel with the usual immaculate tropical gardens, a stone fountain with traditional figures, and a pool bounded by statues and palm trees. Enclosed by a rough stone wall topped with a sculpture, the unique annex to my room featured a private courtyard with an open-air bathroom, plants, and a stone lantern.

Flying above the crater of **Gunung Agung** volcano, I took identical pictures to those of the following year, and on arrival in **Ujung Pandang**, formerly **Makassar**, I was greeted by the same scenes of reflections in water-filled paddies, cultivated fields, wooden and bamboo houses, and boats on a river outlet. However, the countryside was greener, and more growth flourished on the interesting limestone formations. Containing large fish traps, another estuary was fringed with banana plants and palm trees, and on this occasion I entered a **Bugis** dwelling where the lady of the house was tending a smoky open fire next to a large pottery jar. I stopped at the same store with huge dried fish (not the same!) hanging beneath the corrugated iron canopy and also to film the *pinisi*: schooners of the Bugis fishermen constructed, as they have been for centuries, without any nails. These were anchored near a solitary fish trap in a calm inlet enclosed by palms and a stand of the delicate drooping bamboo that always puts me in mind of the Prince of Wales feathers. In bygone days, when Makassar was the gateway to the Spice Islands, the daring exploits of pirates in these tall-masted vessels struck terror into the hearts of merchant ships and spice traders on this crossroads of well-plied sea lanes. To this day, the schooners still sail the seas, trading between islands.

After a lunch stop in **Pare-Pare**, at a restaurant with views over the town, ocean, and abundant plant life that included exotic red flowers and bananas, I took a boat ride to a small neighbouring island. Here, I found a rustic village of thatched wooden and woven bamboo houses, tall palm trees, washing on bamboo poles – and a lot of children. Underway again, we passed roadside stalls predominantly displaying yellow bananas and green melons, a man riding a donkey, and the fascinating sight of another herding ducks along the verge with the aid of a long flexible bamboo rod. This time from a lower vantage point, I photographed the same beautiful river bend with palm trees and other foliage dropping to green banks and white sands, mountains in the background, and sculpted clouds in an overcast sky. On either side of the road, beds of bright red impatiens and multihued nemesias bordered houses nestled in dense green jungle. Sadly, due to the widening of the highway, these had all disappeared on my next visit. I came to the same pyramid-shaped mountain, which again provided the backdrop for excellent photographs, and other grey peaks wearing skirts of green added interest as they loomed above traditional houses set amongst red bougainvillea and palms; it was all extremely picturesque. We passed stands of wood stacked for sale and a man in the traditional long sarong, shawl and black cap. We arrived at the mythological **Erotic Mountain** (explained later), which was also much greener than on subsequent visits. Blue sky made an appearance through puffy white cloud, and the metal dome of a mosque stood out. In a palm-shaded valley, watched over by the rearing craggy grey tors, sunlight glinted off the silver roofs of houses surrounded by banana plants and other tropical vegetation.

Surmounting the gateway to **Tana Toraja**, a typical bow-roofed structure was complete with carved buffalo head and decorative designs; the words *Selamat Datang* (Welcome) were engraved below. The first stop was made at a cattle market, where men were carrying a pig on a litter and I got my first look at the valuable spotted buffalo, a pink and grey beast at ten times the value of the common variety. This was followed by the **Hanging Graves**, excavated from a cliff face, with a row of whitened skulls lined up on a wooden casket at the bottom and miniature replicas of houses – vessels for bearing the bodies – lying askew. One intricately engraved hollow tree trunk had a skull exposed in the centre and a decorated wedge-shaped lid on top. Other open wooden coffins displayed skeletal remains, and it all seemed unkempt and neglected, as did even an undamaged casket. There were a few *tau-taus* (effigies) on a wooden shelf above.

Entering a nearby traditional village, there were signs of the growing season in pretty ferns that sprouted from the thickly thatched saddle-shaped roofs of the houses, which were decorated with sculpted spotted buffalo heads and delicate designs incorporating roosters and floral patterns in blue, beige and sienna. Horns were attached to tall poles erected in front, and one façade was adorned with an eagle bearing a shield. Weaverbird nests hung from bamboo fronds. Some of the best scenery that I have encountered anywhere included a stony stream flowing between verdant vegetation that cocooned isolated prow-roofed dwellings. Mountains and whisper-soft cotton wool clouds were reflected in water-filled rice fields awaiting planting, and rising above emerald paddies, clusters of houses stood on hillocks also accommodating tall bending bamboo, palms, and trees in different shades of green. From my room at the Marannu City Hotel, I looked out over fertile terrain with mist hanging below mountain tops.

Passing terraced rice fields and contentedly grazing cows, I visited the hanging graves at **Londa**, where effigies wearing white costumes and turbans or headscarves stood on stone galleries cut into the rock face. These images were also to guard valuables interred with the dead for use in the afterlife. Their clothes were changed annually in a ceremony called *Ma'nene*. Another site featured old intact caskets (no longer evident on later trips), and colourful portrayals of the deceased sheltered beneath a rock overhang. All the sites were surrounded by superb panoramas. At **Suaya**, I saw the lonely grave of a tiny baby strapped to the trunk of a tree hung with dangling lianas. At **Lemo**, effigies with staring white eyes appeared a lot newer and introduced a little more colour, some wearing gold caps that gleamed in the sunlight. The square graves were sealed with wooden doors, and as distinct from later visits, the rock face was draped with greenery trailing from luxuriant growth above. More houses set in a dense thicket of bamboo and various tones of green foliage lined a muddy brown river, and a village with lawns and striking red cordylines formed the basis of exceptional pictures. Later trips included visits to **Batu Tumonga**, **Lempo**, **Deri**, **Marante**, **Nanggala**, **Ke'Te Kesu'**, **Buntao**, **Pallawa**, **Sangalla** and **Siguntu**.

Armed with gifts of cigarettes, I experienced my first **Rambu Solo** (funeral ceremony). People, many in the conical coolie hats, were lined up along the roadway to the venue with pigs trussed to bamboo poles. In the central arena, a circle of men in black sarongs and white T-shirts was chanting and swaying around animals in the middle, whilst a procession bearing offerings paraded behind them. Mourners dressed in black carried brass urns and jars, but family members of the deceased were beautifully attired in ornate and colourful costumes, with elaborate hairstyles, makeup and jewellery. In order to greet people coming and going, they stood under multihued sunshades at the foot of steps leading into the family pavilion, which had colourful cloth draped around the exterior; others of these temporary bamboo constructions, erected for friends and visitors, many who had travelled long distances, were arrayed in red. When the chanters dispersed, butchering commenced in the large compound. Held in the same period each year, funerals were often delayed days, months or even years, and until such time as the burial took place the deceased person was referred to as 'sick'.

Following scenes echoed the appeal of those above, and I could not resist copious footage of houses on lush mounds, like islands literally adrift in a sea of green.

Leaving Toraja with fond memories, I journeyed back to Ujung Pandang, passing a small mosque enveloped by palms and massed foliage at the end of a murky stream, only its dome visible and verdant mountains in the distance. In front of just such a backdrop, vendors sat beside the road with baskets containing chickens, fruits and vegetables. The onion dome of another mosque appeared above dense greenery, neat hedges, small houses, and flowers growing on the verge of the road.

Returning past flooded paddies (enjoyed by ducks and buffalo!), the golden glow of sunlight filtering through clouds was reflected, together with houses, in the water, and a busy market sold common commodities such as vegetables and eggs.

BALI & SULAWESI 1991

Indonesia is composed of over 13,000 islands, of which I have visited just four. The world's largest flower, rafflesia, with a bloom measuring almost one metre in diameter, grows in Indonesia.

In 1991, I conducted my first group tour to the island of **Sulawesi**, spending a night in **Bali** on the way, at the friendly family owned and operated Bumi Ayu Bungalows set in exquisite tropical gardens with red coleus, frangipani, palm trees, hibiscus, bananas, and other large-leaved plants.

Flying above Bali's active **Gunung Agung** volcano next day, we could see right into the crater, with **Lake Batur** in a second (extinct) caldera beyond. Directly after landing we began our ascent to **Tanah Toraja**, journeying past paddies, water buffalo wallowing in mud, leaf-thatched or tin-roofed small wooden houses on stilts over (or near) water, and fishing boats of the **Bugis** people. Interesting limestone formations were reminiscent of Guilin in China, and splendid scenery was unfolded at a river inlet. We paused to photograph a man who posed with gigantic dried fish hanging in his rustic stall, and as we began to climb, bends of the **Saddong River**, confined by green banks, palm trees and other foliage, were laid out below us. Framed by waving leaves of a banana plant, one pyramid-shaped peak made an attractive picture as we ascended into the increasingly rugged **Latimojong Mountains**, on two of which, **Kandora** and **Gandang**, according to Toraja mythology the first human beings descended to earth. With some embarrassment, our guide pointed out a barren beige-coloured group of creviced hills near **Mt Bamba Puang** (Gate of God) in the **Enrekang Valley**: specifically, bare **Batu Kabobong** that folklore believed to be female pudenda, with the appropriate male counterpart opposite. The terrain exhibited colours varying from the white of limestone cliffs to brown ridges and a few grey tors, with pines making an appearance amongst the greenery. Enmeshed in flowering plants, which included the exotic heliconia, our delightful accommodation was sited in the middle of dry paddy fields with mist-draped mountains in the distance. The people survived on agriculture, which consisted mainly of rice, maize, cassava, vegetables, fruits, coffee and cloves, and most families kept their own livestock such as chickens, ducks, pigs and buffaloes.

Next day, we visited the villages of **Siguntu** and **Kete-Kesu** (Ke'Te Kesu'), where the highly decorated traditional wood and bamboo houses, called *tongkonans*, had roofs shaped like the prows of sailing ships, believed by some to signify the vessels that brought their ancestors, and even the granaries were enhanced with colourful geometric designs. Greenery sprouted from many of the roofs, which were thatched with banana leaves. We followed this with a visit to the 'hanging' graves at **Londa**, which were actually tombs chipped out of cliff faces with rows of effigies arrayed on wooden shelves or in niches beneath a rock overhang standing guard. These fascinating representations of the deceased were dressed in white or beige garb worn with sashes, the ladies donned in conical hats and male figures wearing turbans. Small carriages with the traditional bowed top, used to transport bodies, lay at the base of cliffs. Londa was one of the oldest sites, belonging to the nobility.

Our next stop was at a cattle market offering many buffalo and trussed pigs, whence we ventured to a second group of graves with effigies attired in colourful costumes. These stood in a natural recess in a towering rock face surrounded on three sides by lush vegetation and fronted by bright green rice fields. Our route along a precarious road was marked by stunning scenery incorporating water, mountains, fields, verdant forest, and terraced paddies, in some of which workers were bending as they toiled to plant a crop. We were on our way to see the elaborate structures of a temporary bamboo village on stilts, built to house mourners at a funeral ceremony – described more fully in the 1994 chapter on Sulawesi. This was also ensconced in a thick cluster of trees and palms with rice paddies in the foreground.

The villages of **Nanggala** and **Maranta** possessed the same rice barns and houses with saddle-shaped or 'horned' roofs, a second explanation being that the shape of the roof resembles the horns of buffalo. Symbolising fertility, strength, and protection from evil spirits, many displayed the carved head of a buffalo on the façade and tiers of buffalo horns attached to the towering pole supporting the prow of the roof. Red cordylines made a colourful show in the green surrounds. We visited a site with tall granite-like *stelae* and, at **Suaya**, a baby grave distinguished by a multihued long-handled umbrella.

One of the prime reasons for a visit to Sulawesi was to experience a funeral ceremony (*rambu solo*). Progressing to a second community, with flags and streamers on the temporary shelters, we were confronted with a pile of bloody slaughtered and skinned buffalo that were in the process of being butchered, the heavy hides carried on bamboo poles braced between the shoulders of two men and stretched on nearby racks to dry. In spite of the macabre events being enacted around us, the view across paddies, feathery bamboo and palm trees from this high vantage point was superb. Most of my group were reluctant to watch the actual killing of the animals, and I must confess that I was more than pleased just to view it through the small viewfinder of the camera! It made no difference that I was using silent film, because with their throats slashed the buffalo made no sound except for thrashing around in the undergrowth. A variety of containers, including lengths of bamboo, were employed to collect blood from the neck for religious and superstitious purposes. After performing sacrifices to appease the spirits of the dead, the meat was distributed to all present and used to feed families that had travelled long distances, often on foot, to attend.

In the afternoon, we went to **Tondon**, **Makale** (county capital), and **Tampangallo**, typical villages with lawn, colourful potted plants, and beautiful river scenery. A half day tour took us to **Barana** and **Palawa**, the latter the oldest village in Toraja, still featuring the carved heads and painted decoration but displaying a greater number of buffalo horns. Free-range chickens scraped around in dry surroundings, and here we were able to see inside a home.

At **Lemo**, I filmed my group lined up like the effigies in front of which they stood. Graves were hewn into a sheer cliff face, the bodies lowered by people attached to ropes, and houses were lodged in luxuriant environs of palms, flame trees, banana plants and bamboo on the banks of a river with a mountain backdrop.

Men staggering under the weight of a pig were the introduction to a second day of funeral celebrations. Slaughtered pigs were tossed onto fires in order to burn off the bristles before butchering, and there were dead and live pigs everywhere: being transported strung on lengths of bamboo or trussed and lying in piles. Men hacked en masse with long-handled knives and hatchets, and boys carried off portions of meat on bamboo poles, one man bearing an entire haunch on his shoulder. People came and went all day. We witnessed a small procession of mourners in black, and others filed past me carrying bundles or with baskets slung from the forehead on their backs as they laboured up a steep incline. Most were in peasant garb, but some were well dressed, with jewellery and the large cone-shaped hats. Ladies wore sarongs, the men lap-laps, but more often the invidious T-shirt and jeans. One man was attired in an elegant kaftan. More special scenery followed: an ethereal effect created by mist wafting on the stunning mountains, cattle in fields, graceful palms, and roadsides lined with feathery plants alternating between flaming red and bright yellow.

Back in Bali, we visited **Lake Bratan** at **Bedugal**, with its beautifully landscaped surrounds and the multi-tiered pagodas of **Ulun Danu Temple**. This was located on a dot of land in the shimmering blue water that filled the ancient crater of **Mt Bratan**. We were lucky to encounter a procession, the participants bearing baskets or offerings of bamboo creations on their heads and carrying long-handled fringed sunshades. En route to the picturesque 16th-century temple of **Tanah Lot**, we passed myriad rich green rice terraces, neat houses with colourful plants and thatched shrines in their courtyards, and elaborate free-standing gateways of red brick and carved stone leading to open temples. Situated on the hilltop of a tiny island, this popular subject for pictures was now almost hidden behind vegetation. People were wading in the water, exotic plants such as ginger grew nearby, and a large colourful kite flew overhead. In Bali, motorised transport was provided by minibuses called *bemos*; horse-drawn carts were known as *dokars*.

CHINA 1991

China has the oldest continuous civilisation in the world, with a recorded history of 4,000 years. The famous Peking Man, *Homo erectus*, direct ancestor of modern man, whose relics were found in caves near Beijing, lived about 500,000 years ago.

En route to **Guangzhou**, with a 2,000-year history, I spent a night in **Hong Kong**, where tall buildings formed the backdrop to a market with purveyors of everything from flowers to fresh eggs, and to one of the world's busiest harbours, which always made interesting pictures.

Guilin

Flying from Guangzhou, I began my escapade in **China** with one of the most beautiful trips in the country, or indeed the world: a cruise on the **Li River** in **Guilin**, also known as 'The best sight under heaven'. But first I experienced a scene that epitomised my concept of this land, gleaned from copious illustrations, that of jagged mountains beyond a little humpbacked wooden bridge crossing a peaceful lake, its banks lined with drooping willows, a rotunda with curled corners on the roof, and a few flowerbeds. A high lookout revealed the range of rugged peaks receding into the misty distance, the river and town in the foreground, and a typical pavilion on the edge of a cliff towering behind me. Poetic names given to these spires included Wave Curbing Hill, Solitary Beauty Peak, Piled Silk Hill, Folded Brocade, Five Tigers Catching a Goat, Yellow Cloth in Water, and Peak of Unique Beauty. The highest point, at 120m (400ft), was Piled Festoon Hill. My hotel in Guilin, on the façade of which neon lights resembling beaded and swagged curtains made a great display, also had the delightful flower name of

Osmanthus, and another I stayed in was called Inner Magnolia. Guilin means Osmanthus Forest, and the fragrance of these trees pervades the warm air in summer. But the titles were not always complimentary: two sites near Wuxi were called Foolish Man Valley and Big Dustpan Hill!

A march of workers carrying red banners included two colourful Chinese dragons wreathed in smoke; I do not know if it was a protest or celebration. And so began my river journey. From its rocky bed, people were gathering pebbles or sand, which they placed in containers at the ends of a pole slung across the shoulder before walking gingerly across the stony river bottom and back to shore. Like fingers of rock, the unique karst mountains pointed skywards from gentle green slopes and sheer white walls. In places, the spires reared from a line of verdant trees and delicate fronds of feathery bamboo, the series of sculpted ranges appearing one behind the other, their mist-shrouded tops in the background blending into a dull sky. On waters that fluctuated from quiet stretches to low rapids, we passed people poling rafts and a couple of larger vessels ferrying passengers. The former included the famed cormorant fishermen, with their birds and baskets to hold the catch, on shallow craft constructed of bamboo poles lashed together. We passed isolated houses, a huge natural cave, towering cliff faces, myriad needles of rock reaching for the sky, and many fascinating creations of a wondrous nature featuring incredible shapes like those exhibited by icebergs. Soaring peaks in the distance were framed by valleys, and closer formations erupted from hills in many shades of green; it was very dramatic scenery. Low-lying cloud added to the ethereal effect of this strange, but extremely beautiful, magical terrain. In keeping with Chinese tradition, a rock in the river was titled Yearning for Husband. Resembling a European skyline punctured by the spires of many cathedrals, one could easily imagine the surroundings as God's own house of worship.

Li River

Approaching the village of **Yangshuo**, we came to stone houses with black tiled roofs, the houseboats of fishermen, cattle contentedly grazing, a two-tiered pagoda with red roofs, and many of the cormorants roosting on rafts. Yangshuo itself was an uninteresting much commercialised place, with fields behind the stone buildings, vegetables for sale beneath umbrellas, and another pagoda on a hill overlooking the river.

Back in Guilin (where I stayed at the Ronghu Wintersweet Hotel), I witnessed a poor panda relentlessly pacing with its awkward pigeon-toed gait in a concrete compound with only a tiny patch of grass and a small pool, whilst the pretty surrounds of rocks, topiary trees and red flowers were reflected in a large pond. I visited the much photographed **Elephant Trunk Hill**, a rock formation resembling that particular appendage immersed in water and said to be the elephant on which the King of Heaven travelled the country. When it fell ill, a local farmer nursed it back to health, in return for which the elephant helped in the fields. The angry king turned the animal into stone and its trunk dipped into the river at Moon in the Water Arch, so called because the full moon reflected on the surface seemed to float within. Another view of the wonderful lake featured a marble and stone 'moon' bridge, so named because the reflection of the rounded overpass made it appear as a full moon.

My second meal in China was quite an event. Expressing the desire to experience genuine local cuisine, my guide nominated a few dishes that I might care to try, including duck with water chestnuts that I selected. He wrote the appropriate words in Chinese on a scrap of paper and directed me to a shop with tables and tiny stools in the street. I was ushered in and a cloth ceremoniously produced as I handed over my written request. Whilst waiting, an elderly man in the traditional blue Mao suit, most commonly worn at that time, sat down beside me with a cage holding a live snake and proceeded to slit its belly to extract both blood and bile, which he drained into two small glasses containing rice wine. The poor creature was left to writhe whilst the man used chopsticks to beat the mixtures, which he then drank. In the meantime, my meal was served, and my stomach was heaving up and down like the snake as I attempted to consume the toughest meat of my life! Not to be outdone, I returned next evening and tried the bloody drink, but stopped short of the brilliant green bile. Another reptile having sacrificed its life, I completed the experiment with snake soup.

Whilst in Guilin, I also visited **Ludi Yan** (**Reed Flute Hill**), its limestone caverns bearing romantic names such as Dragon King's Crystal Palace, but unfortunately I was not equipped to be able to film them. One of the stalagmites was known as The Old Scholar because whilst sitting and attempting to write about the grottos, a poet was unable to find words to adequately describe the splendour of the formations and pondered for so long that he eventually turned to stone. The Chinese have colourful names and stories for just about everything. The **Reed Flute Cave** was named for the reeds that once grew near the entrance and were cut and fashioned into flutes by local people. During WWII the local populace hid in the caves for protection from Japanese bombing raids.

Kunming

In **Kunming**, 1,895m above sea level and also called City of Eternal Spring or Capital of Flowers, the main mode of transport, even for army personnel, was the ubiquitous bicycle. A street market set up under umbrellas outside ramshackle buildings furnished many subjects for my camera: fruits, a man weighing tomatoes on handheld scales, dried goods, cooked items in covered pottery containers, and a man standing to eat from a bowl with chopsticks. One lady carried a babe in a shawl on her back, and another had lemons in baskets at each end of a pole across her shoulders.

Entry to the **Longmen Grottos** (**Dragon Gate**) was marked by a decorated pavilion containing a shrine, and the venue consisted of a series of such structures and excavated caverns ascending the face of a high cliff, with panoramic views of **Lake Dianchi**, also known as Pearl of the Plateau, from the top. The path and caves took 72 years to hack out of the rock, and a second pavilion, engulfed in greenery, was circled by auspicious red pillars and inscribed with gilded Chinese characters. Various images and script adorned rock walls, and the whole was a source of extremely good pictures, the most impressive taken gazing up at the overhanging tree-lined precipice above and looking from the interior of a cave, the entrance of which framed a small pagoda on a higher level. With colourful elaborately carved eaves, floral decoration that included a large red lotus flower on a gable, and bamboo-tiled roofs, the structures held great appeal. Climbing the staircase, which overlooked the red rooftops, I found a stone lion at the foot of steps to the side and a beautiful circular window screen showing a white peacock on the branch of a tree.

Surrounded by trees, a three-tiered pagoda created superb reflections in a lily-covered pond, its lights twinkling in the water, and I was taken to lunch at a building with more stone lions at the base of stairs. Here, I was served my own banquet of numerous (about 20) unfamiliar dishes, the origins of which I had no idea. I considered that I would be safe with one crinkly white substance appearing like cabbage, but it turned out to be the webs of ducks feet! Disparaging themselves, the Chinese jest that they eat everything on four legs except the table and everything that flies except aeroplanes. Other dishes that I became aware of included: hot candied fish slices, soft-shelled turtles, fish balls wrapped in lotus leaf, braised snake with shredded chicken, fried shrimp balls and eight-jewel crisp duck, braised camel's paw, and roasted bones with sweet-scented osmanthus chicken wings and necks! Actually, the menu read 'sweat-scented' but I am sure that was a mistake! My meal was followed up by more film of decorative roofs on structures enmeshed in lush foliage.

My next tour was to a village of the **Sani** people and the Stone Forest. The former was a collection of primitive adobe dwellings with tiny windows and roofs of bamboo tiles or thatch in dirt streets at the entrance to the Stone Forest, which could not have provided more of a contrast with gorgeous mirror images of its monoliths and overhead clouds in a perfectly still lake. Wandering the village streets, I noticed an abundance of corn drying in trees (and together with chillies on walls and roofs), stacks of wood and sticks, a woman winnowing grain, chickens, washing, stone fences, wooden carts, a pile of pumpkins, moss on a thatched roof, ladders against walls, one horse, and pigs, the latter including a big sow with a dragging belly and a litter of piglets – one peering in an open doorway. I came across illustrations on a door, a man herding goats along the street, a woman spreading grain with a long-handled wooden implement, a white dog hesitantly wagging its tail, a lady carrying buckets on a pole across one shoulder, and a red blanket hanging on a line, complemented by chillies on a wicker platter in the foreground. In spite of the obvious poverty and crumbling walls, the people were dressed in the colourful costume of this minority tribe.

Leaving the village via more wonderful reflections, I entered the **Stone Forest** and walked to a high vantage point where I could see over the formations, which loomed above dense trees that included many pines, before making my tortuous way along narrow chasms between towering pinnacles, strange eroded shapes, balancing rocks, and jagged peaks up to 30m (100ft) tall. One section of still green water vaguely reflected walls and fingers of rock erupting perpendicularly from the surface. Some were smooth, others weathered into furrows and fantastic formations in shades of grey with splashes of white and brown, but they were clustered so closely together that it was difficult to find an aspect incorporating the entire scene. Throughout the park, various formations had also been given poetic names such as Layered Waterfall and Phoenix Preening its Feathers. Legend stated that Ashima Rock was named for a young girl kidnapped by a wealthy aristocrat. Her lover tried to rescue her but she died and was turned into stone. China abounded with such tales. It was said that Chinese Immortals created the stone labyrinth to provide a place where courting couples could have privacy. Attempting to sell handcrafts, gaily dressed girls carrying multihued sunshades shadowed visitors heels.

On the road back to Kunming, my guide and I drove past more photogenic thatch-roofed stone houses ensconced behind stone fences, buffaloes, a man toting baskets on a pole, and a quaint white cottage with long garlands of corn suspended under its eaves, smoke curling from the chimney, and green hills behind. In a fascinating market full of colourful caged birds and parrots on perches, I saw an old man in the blue suit and cap smoking a traditional pipe. I toured a venue featuring a series of tiered pavilions with curved roofs and decorated eaves (one with the proverbial dragon), bright flowerbeds, and a lake with a rotunda and willows. An elaborate gateway led to a path lined with flowers and lacy green shade trees, and fir-fringed walkways were connected by small humpbacked bridges across water.

Outside old wooden buildings with latticed windows, a street market congested with bicycles had produce in baskets and lemons in crates on the roadway, cooked foods in basins beneath red umbrellas, steaming cauldrons, a man with a large basket containing some green vegetable on his back, a youth struggling through the crowd with yellow chrysanthemums for sale, and a cart carrying both sacks of goods and children. Pot plants enhanced a couple of shophouses, and an open gateway revealed a tiny yard containing a hen.

At **Emeishan**, I visited a small zoo where I got my second look at the magnificent black and white panda, one of which slid on its belly, its four legs extended, down a kiddie slide – a feat that I managed to capture on film. A second stood on hind legs to reach for saplings, from which it stripped leaves with its teeth. Another exhibit featured the appealing red panda; small, more like a racoon, with russet fur, a striped tail, and white-tipped ears and face, it was totally different from its namesake. I came to another market with people humping large baskets on their backs and lemons everywhere. Men were playing dominoes or checkers, people stood to read the daily paper hung on walls, and a bus drove through with a great number of ducks – just sitting on the roof!

Chengdu

My next destination (where I stayed at the Swan Hotel) was **Chengdu**, City of Hibiscus or City of Brocade, also 2,000 years old, from where I travelled 165km (102mi) to see the mammoth **Dafu** (**Grand Buddha**) in the sleepy backwater town of **Leshan**. Carved from the face of **Mount Lingyun** at the confluence of the **Min**, **Qingyi** and **Dadu Rivers**, this 71m (233ft) image, begun in AD 713 and seated with hands on knees, was so immense that 100 people could congregate on its head, and one toe alone measured 24ft long.

Originally covered with gold leaf and protected by a 13-storey pavilion that was destroyed in the Ming reign, it was now totally exposed but guarded against serious erosion by an ingenious internal drainage system.

Viewing it first from beside the gigantic head, which looked out over river and plain, I then descended to where people clambered all over its toes, each of which would also accommodate numerous people. On my film they project the illusion of a crowd of Lilliputians on a foot of the fabled Gulliver! More street scenes included ducks in panniers on a bicycle, other birds in cane baskets hanging from a pole across a shoulder – and more lemons! I visited one of the many elaborate temples, this one in a lovely setting of flowerbeds and dense trees with a verdant mountain backdrop. Framed by an arch, it produced perfect pictures. Unfortunately, with the old super 8 movie film I could not record the interior of any of the attractions.

Employing an old-fashioned wooden implement drawn by a buffalo, a man was ploughing next to newly planted paddies with a flock of white birds in the background. Another venue had restful water gardens with lotus and pavilions. Leaves from overhanging trees fell gently onto the green surface crossed by wooden walkways and a stone bridge. In Asia, similar traders always seemed to be assembled together, and bicycles, an oxcart, trishaw and bicycle cart, as well as pedestrians carrying loads, all stirred up dust in front of a row of open cooking stalls with carcasses hanging outside. I actually ate a meal here and seem to remember that it was quite good. On the road again, I saw enormous lengths of bamboo being transported on the inevitable bicycle, people stripping and selling bamboo, items displayed on the verge of the road, and live pigs, some wrapped in matting, strapped onto carriers.

Yangtze River

Chongqing was the headquarters of Chiang Kaishek and his forces during Japan's campaign to occupy all of China in the 1930's, and Zhou Enlai also lived here, but at the time of my visit it had little relevance for the tourist except as a ferry departure point.

From **Chongqing**, with its 2,000-year history, I travelled 1,300km to **Wuhan** on the famed **Changjiang** (**Yangtze River**), at 6,300km the world's third largest. Many people have been relocated and much of what I saw now submerged in the making of a colossal dam. Barges were a common sight on the opaque brown water, and we stopped to visit a complex of exquisite pavilions and pagodas showcasing wonderful traditional art. A large monastery with many curling eaves was apparent on a slope behind. On foot, we crossed a long suspension bridge that led to the ancient village destined to be lost to the world forever. In the centre, two people wheeled a trolley with huge baskets containing flowers of all colours, others toted poles from which large woven platters of vegetables were suspended, hens just sat on the pavement, and a man carried two by the legs. Plenty of tempting fresh greens were on display.

Back on board, we steamed past large ugly buildings like concrete blocks, barges, and a tall white pagoda that stood out on a hilltop. At times, the Yangtze was quite narrow and hemmed in by the high cliffs of three successive gorges (Qutang, Wuxia and Xiling), which allowed little light to penetrate. One section contained dwellings beneath a natural overhang in the looming mountains. As we proceeded, the enveloping high peaks and sharp ridges covered with low green scrub were almost lost in mist, layers of interesting shale-like rock formed part of the shoreline, and it took four men rowing with long-handled oars and poling to propel one small craft against the strong current. Scenically, the journey was awesome.

Gently rounded hills introduced our second stop, the ancient town of **Fenjie**, where I found old men with white beards wearing white turbans and carrying long sticks. All the towns along the river were situated at the top of steep stairways, I assumed because of the risk of flooding, and here a few people sold produce on the steps leading from the landing. I do not know if every day was market day, but one was certainly in full swing in this town. Many people were walking around with handcarts and the baskets on poles, and others sold a white commodity (perhaps rice) whilst seated on the paved street outside stone buildings.

After **Qutang Gorge**, near Fenjie, we took a detour up three of the **Danning River** gorges: **Loncmenxia**, **Bawuxia** and **Dicuixia** or, in English, **Dragon Gate**, **Misty Gorge** and **Emerald Gorge** respectively, passing beneath a high overhead bridge spanning the narrow entrance of the first. We had transferred to a smaller vessel, which at times had to be poled through fast moving rapids, the stout rod actually bending with the pressure exerted to propel our boat forward. Here, the water was a beautiful blue-green at the base of abruptly rising perpendicular white cliffs, their summits also greener in appearance. We veered around many rocky shoals and only passed a few other craft. People were washing their laundry on stony banks, an area of low hills encouraged the planting of crops, and the tops of mountains again disappeared into the haze. In one region, where I noted a lone tree with red foliage, people seemed to be panning on the rocky shoreline. Small boats drawn up on the beach in front of fields were used by farmers who had to travel in order to tend their crops, and white goats grazed on rocky slopes behind. People with loads of goods sat on rocks at the water's edge waiting for river transport, and we came to a still section with enchanting mirror images and white pebble banks. We sailed past a large natural cavern with Chinese characters on a boulder in front and a sprinkling of autumn hues above. In places, the white cliffs were tiered, like gigantic steps with green carpet on the treads. Again, lyrical names abounded: Tortoise Aiming High, Fairy Peach Peak, Ox Turning Around Cave Curtained by Waterfall, and Monkeys Reaching for Moon in the Water. It took three men to pole us the last turbulent stretch to the uninteresting town at the end, where people were washing at the foot of steps that accommodated many more vendors, and I seem to recall that we had lunch.

Returning to the murky brown Yangtze, we continued through **Wuxia** and **Xiling** gorges, passing an area of taller trees. It was interesting to learn that at one time only *junks* plied the Xiling, each having to be hauled through the rapids against the swiftly flowing current by 400 men on the riverbank. Pines formed the foreground to stark white cliff faces with jagged ridges, and we progressed past a couple of isolated houses, rock tors, rounded stone outcrops resembling turrets, and a red and white pagoda. In an interesting encounter, we entered a loch with all manner of smaller vessels – two piled high with oranges. At a final stop, trees and a pagoda were beautifully reflected in a quiet patch of water, and another active market sold garlic, ginger, greens, potatoes, cauliflowers, tomatoes, celery and lettuce. Large burlap sacks contained a variety of goods, and a row of bright red chillies in neatly stacked pyramids made a colourful splash. Meat hung in the open alongside 100-year-old eggs and other most unappetising-looking speckled and coated specimens. I saw a lovely white pagoda with bells on delicately carved curled corners; these monuments sprouted everywhere, like cathedrals and castles in Europe or temples in the rest of Asia. Approaching Wuhan, the setting sun was a red orb in a polluted sky, and a fishing smack had a net on long bowed poles extending out one side, making it appear as if listing.

Wuhan

I disembarked at **Wuhan**, which was actually made up of three cities clustered on both sides of the Changjiang and its largest tributary, the **Hanshui**. The first was **Hankou** where we docked, the second **Hanyang**, where I visited the **Zhongyue Temple** with a pavilion above the red gateway, much like a miniature Tiananmen Square. On entering, I found a bridge lined with a lion and other stone figures, and doors containing beautiful panels with gilded relief of stork-like birds, willows, lotus, mountains, flowers, smaller birds, and branches. Metal urns stood in courtyards, and overlooking the river, its tongue protruding, was the head of a dragon that constituted the coping on a wall. A row of shops featured interesting rooflines, and I went to a demonstration of tea in a building with ornate wooden railing and trees in tubs. Another market, with fresh fruits including oranges, bananas and apples, piles of red and green chillies, ginger, Chinese cabbage, radishes, leeks, dried sardines, and numerous other dried and packaged products, most of which I did not recognise, made for colourful pictures. Purchases were weighed on handheld scales and meat, which included kidneys, chopped in the open. I came across fish traps in the river and, close to the waterfront, the Ming and Qing dynasty **Guiyuan Monastery**. This featured fretwork around moon gates, more metal urns, bamboo tiles, and sculpted eaves, their corners bearing dragons and hung with temple bells. Carved brackets bracing red pillars also depicted dragons, and door panels with gilded embossing portrayed classical figures, one holding a hair whisk. Bamboo featured amongst other greenery visible behind openings inset with beautiful leaves, fruits and flowers.

From here, I went to the **Yellow Crane Mansion** in **Wuchang**, the third city, with a crane sculpture in the forecourt. In reality, this was a five-storey pagoda (with upturned eaves) replacing the Ming dynasty (1368–1644) structure that burnt down in 1884. Originally built as a watchtower in AD 223, in the time of the Three Kingdoms, it was repeatedly reconstructed throughout history after being destroyed by fires and war. The pagoda was situated between two smaller pavilions: Kanchuan (Overlooking the Land) and Lanhong (Taking Hold of the Rainbow), and the complex also contained a massive three-arched gateway flanked by white stone lions. This framed a white *stupa* in one direction, the pagoda in the other. Circular multihued flowerbeds, hedges, and topiary trees graced the courtyard. From upper balconies, the stunning panorama encompassed the gateway and pavilions, the river, bridge and city to one side, trees and gardens on the other. There is a fascinating story of how the pagoda received its name. Briefly: An innkeeper met a sick old man lying in the snow and carried him home on his back, where he treated him with food and drink. After six months the old man left, but before doing so drew a crane on the wall with a piece of orange peel. Fulfilling the old man's prophecy, following the clapping of hands the bird descended from the wall, and the news spread far and wide, attracting much business. After ten years the old man returned and played a jade flute, causing plum blossoms to bloom and the crane to dance. At the end of the performance, the man mounted the crane and flew off into the sky, whereupon the innkeeper built the tower and decorated it with yellow cranes.

Attractive railing lined a walkway where rotundas, pleasure craft, a stone bridge, fish traps and boats were all mirrored in still water, a lack of air creating not even the slightest movement. Trees included autumn foliage, pines, and weeping willows, viewed through the fine trailing branches of which, pavilions made a lovely scene. The large white statue of a classical Chinese figure stood in front of a pagoda, and elsewhere glorious red flowers made a superb foreground, providing the only colour in pictures of pavilions enveloped in mist and surrounded by tall trees on the opposite shore of **East Lake**. Comprised of several lakes, this was six times the size of West Lake in Hangzhou. Amongst the poetic names associated with it were Flute Playing Hill, Wave Stones, Falling Wild Goose, Listening to the Wave Chamber, Moon Enjoyment Pavilion, Multifarious Scenery Platform, Water Cloud Pavilion, Poem Chanting Pavilion, White Horse, Lake Reflection Pavilion, Nine Girl Mound, and Painted Lakeside Corridor.

In 1911, the people of Wuhan staged an uprising that overthrew the last feudal dynasty in China.

Shanghai

I moved on to **Shanghai** (the name means On the Sea) and **The Bund**, with its tall colonial buildings and a multihued display of flowers arrayed around a monument. As distinct from India, with respect to colour I found China monotonous, and rain added to the impression, spoiling my appreciation of a market, sheltered by awnings, where most were dressed in the traditional blue and even umbrellas were black, with the occasional addition of red or pink. However, in the city centre, the dull conditions could not detract from the outstanding **Yu Yuan Mandarin Garden**, entered via a zigzag bridge across water. Panels featuring black birds and trees, appearing like silhouettes, enhanced white walls enclosing a tiny courtyard containing rock gardens. Pavilions and delicate pale green willows were reflected in man-made lakes, and lovely scenes of lacy bare branches and Taihu Lake rock were framed by a moon gate. Taihu Lake rock was a significant feature of Chinese gardens, and its origin is explained later. Also featured were wooden balconies ornamented with fretwork, rotundas, more zigzag pathways, a few flowers including an exhibition of chrysanthemums, and covered walkways. Dragons were manifest on the corners of roofs and undulated atop a wall, with the inevitable lion amongst stone images beneath its bared fangs. Being winter, I obtained an entirely different perspective of gardens in China than on my subsequent visit (in summer) when they were alive with blossom. On this occasion, a man in a bright red shirt stood out in stark contrast to the monochrome surrounds.

Back in the streets, an impressive stone archway spanned a busy road and I came to the **Friendship Store and Exhibition Centre**, the star atop its towering spire reaching 106m into a murky sky. I do not recall the name of my next fascinating venue but it featured many images of Buddha in rock-hewn niches, one laughing representation, with a fat tummy, holding beads and flanked by smaller figures of acolytes. This particular image seems to be one favoured in the West but seldom seen in China. The garden also contained an old stone pagoda and an excellent relief of horsemen. It was in the grounds of a large red temple with flaming torches in the forecourt and round windows with beautiful metal-worked screens portraying dragons, birds and trees. Flowers and bamboo grew in front of screens depicting dragons and a white wall enhanced with graceful leaping gazelles executed in stone. A young girl played a traditional stringed instrument, and rotundas were encapsulated in dense greenery. Red lanterns hung from the corners of a pavilion overlooking a lake, and behind a large slab of Taihu rock, a waterfall cascaded from the mouth of a fearsome-looking mythical beast almost hidden in lush growth.

Still outdoors, painted cranes and auspicious red furnishings formed the backdrop to a stage for Chinese opera. By the woebegone face of the performer, exhibiting an elaborate hairstyle and dressed entirely in white, it was obviously a tragedy. This is *not* my favourite form of entertainment, and for once I could be grateful for the lack of sound in old movies! An elderly man in the blue suit and cap sat entranced, a young child, her hair adorned with red pompoms, on his knee.

On a paved area of the city, in front of a statue in the centre of greenery and bright red salvia, a woman wielding a sword was gracefully executing slow-motion *tai chi* movements.

Hangzhou

Moving on to 2,000-year-old **Hangzhou** (Gateway to Heaven), described by Marco Polo in the 13th century as *One of the most beautiful and most splendid cities on earth*, I stayed at the Wanghu Hotel, which boasted an incredible carved wooden panel depicting traditional Chinese life filling an entire wall of the foyer. They would not allow me to photograph it so I 'acquired' a compendium with the appropriate illustration from my room.

The Song dynasty established its capital in Hangzhou, and it was here that the most refined age of China was born. It lasted until the Mongol armies of Kublai Khan put it to the sword and destroyed it in a campaign to bring the whole country under their heel.

Today Hangzhou has nothing to recommend it apart from the huge serene **West Lake**, created in the eighth century, which alone made the visit worthwhile. Dragon boats waiting for custom lined the tree-shaded paved pathway around the shore, and I photographed a young lady in traditional costume with an ornate headdress. A sculpted horse reared atop an upright floral clock, and hordes of bicycles, including a trishaw laden with flowers, travelled the road circling the lake. The photogenic scenes included the usual pavilions, birds, willows, a stone bridge, and a background of hills.

Taking a boat ride, we puttered past an island with a small rotunda in the midst of trees, to another with a zigzag walkway leading across water to pavilions and rotundas surrounded by willows and other foliage, all beautifully reflected amongst lotus on the surface. Chinese people honour the lotus flower because it retains its purity even though it grows in mud. Behind one of the apertures in a white wall, a young lady with a cheery smile waved for the camera, and a stone lantern stood in the lake. Altogether there were three islets, one bearing the enchanting name of Three Pools Mirroring the Moon. Scenic spots had names like: Viewing Fish in Huangang Pond, Listening to Orieles Among the Willow, and Autumn Moon on the Calm Lake. Hangzhou was the beginning (or end) of the **Grand Canal**, which travelled 1,794km to Beijing in the north and was one of China's ancient wonders. Begun 2,400 years ago, it was the earliest and longest man-made river in the world and linked five water systems, including the Yellow and Yangtze rivers.

Suzhou

Suzhou, with a history of 2,500 years, was the Venice of the Orient, and tiny houses lined both sides of a maze of narrow but dirty canals where a lady stood on steps between buildings to scour her night pail. Little bridges crossed the waterways where street signs were attached to buildings, and stone steps led directly to the water from doorways of dwellings. Some greenery was evident in a few pot plants on ledges and trees that overhung walls. Behind the canals, bicycles were almost the sole source of transport in tree-lined streets full of shops with living quarters above and ancient tea houses with bamboo-tiled roofs. A bicycle inundated with woven mats was wheeled past, and another, with ducks hanging from the carrier and handlebars, was ridden by. Washing hung on buildings, and colourful birds sat in cages outside an open window above a canal; some were still there four years later and I think they were for sale from a shop, the front of which faced the street. If one could turn a blind eye to the filth and dilapidation, it was all very picturesque.

Suzhou was also renowned for its gardens, in four of which I spent considerable time and never tired. The first featured creeper-covered stone bridges, lotus, pavilions with a chain of red lanterns hanging from a corner, willows, intricately carved eaves with a floral design above small tableaux underneath, a moon gate in a white wall, which was the perfect foil for an autumn tree in front, and of course magnificent reflections; I even filmed a self-portrait in a large mirror. More photographs of the calm canals with their stone bridges (one with a stone lion), white houses and weeping willows followed. In interesting side streets, I found an old man sitting on a stool in front of a round gateway with a small garden in the street, and I had a fascinating encounter with three ladies. Rarely was any English spoken, but I managed nine weeks in China with just 'Hello', 'Thank you' and 'Goodbye' in Mandarin, all of which I used on this occasion. The only other phrases I mastered in this extraordinarily difficult language, where the inflection makes a difference to the meaning, were the very important: 'How much is it?', 'That is too much', and 'Can you make it cheaper?'!

Pausing to film the round entrance near where the three women sat, one offered me a piece of bread from which she had been eating. Not wanting to appear rude (they were quite dirty) I accepted, putting my faith in inoculations, and found it freshly baked and surprisingly delicious. Indicating that I would like to purchase some, I was pointed in the direction of a stall with few items left but returned later when the baker had a new supply. Seated outside his home, which opened directly onto the street, a second man was smoking a cigarette. Washing hung overhead on a line strung from the front wall to the edge of a canopy above the door, and red flowers sprouted between the foundations and brick-paved road. Holding an infant, a smiling mother stood on a balcony (an attempt at beautification provided by bonsai plants in tins) overlooking a canal, a man staggered by under a heavy load that weighed down the pole across his shoulder, and others sat with items for sale on the pavement. Washing was strung on poles (bamboo had an infinite number of uses!), a washing machine sat *outside* a house, a man cycled by with a laden cart, and more washing stretched overhead across the narrow street.

With the aid of long-handled tongs, a man was baking bread in an outdoor clay oven, another was reading whilst seated on a chair in front of his door, where more red flowers emerged from the street, a woman washed vegetables at a well, and another scrubbed a large container. A barge made its way towards me as I stood on a bridge, and yet more red flowers (in pots) lined a parapet opposite white houses mirrored in the waterway. In a courtyard with washing hanging on the line, a duck nestled beneath a table holding utensils, a corner store sold fruits, and a lady pegged socks on cord strung under the roof of her tiny patio. In confined space beyond an open doorway, a man was industriously chopping food on a wooden block beside a blackened cast-iron boiler, which sat on top of a clay oven surfaced with cracked white tiles, and on the steps of a canal, a woman washed a bucket with a straw brush.

Investigating the delights of a second garden, I strolled along vine-covered zigzag walkways connecting rotundas and pavilions with upturned corners on their bamboo-tiled roofs. This one exhibited a plethora of white stone, decorative balustrades, reflections and a stone lantern in the water, figures of fish and birds etched into a pebble pathway, willows, a glorious display of colourful flowers around a Taihu rock monolith, and a lovely scene captured through a rectangular window. From another bridge, I photographed more houses with steps leading to the water of a canal, and a complete circle formed by the perfect mirror image of a humpbacked stone bridge. A third garden featured beautifully reflected strings of blue and red lanterns, with willows and a tall pagoda in the distance. Red lanterns also added colour and dimension to the picture, framed by a moon gate, of a zigzag bridge, trees and pavilions. It was extremely peaceful, with few other patrons to disturb the tranquillity, no breeze to stir the leaves, ducks drifting on the water, covered walkways, a small courtyard with the artistic white stone, and a little humpbacked bridge. Walking past shops and a yard with the usual washing and utensils, I came to the fourth garden, but because my ticket stubs were all in Chinese I have no recollection of which was which. Delicate trees stood in front of a white wall with tracery insets, which were also given names such as Dragon Playing with Pearls and Phoenix Playing Among Peonies, and again there were beautiful reflections in this landscaped work of art. All the venues made extensive use of water.

More intriguing street scenes included the bakery shop where I had purchased my bread, a person chopping with a cleaver just inside a doorway, and a cat on a high windowsill, obviously disinterested in food on woven platters below! These were followed by pictures of a vendor wheeling a bicycle almost buried beneath the exceedingly colourful large round congratulatory tributes and a cart full of freshly slaughtered meat with a person weighing vegetables in the background. Boats loaded with vegetables were moored in a narrow waterway (their occupants emptying containers overboard!), and people cooked in a large steaming boiler on steps behind. On other boats, draped with the eternal washing and lined up beside a wall, people were eating their midday meal – although Chinese ate all the time! At a street market, fish lay in basins of water aerated by hoses, and chickens sat under a large net whilst others, trussed by the legs, were being weighed on the handheld scales.

My next stops were to photograph one of the elegant multi-tiered **Twin Pagodas** erected in the Song dynasty and two men poling a barge under a bridge. One of my most memorable and heart-warming encounters was with an elderly gentleman who sat eating his noonday meal in a minute front yard created by the Y-junction of two streets. With china bowls on a table to one side and his slippers on the sill behind, he contemplated the passing parade (including me) as he consumed his food. I must confess that I attempted to obtain a candid shot without his notice, but when he became aware of me, I requested his permission, which to my surprise was freely given. This delightful old man insisted on posing (with a beaming toothless smile above a greasy chin!), and when I passed by later in the day he greeted me with a cheery wave; although seemingly engrossed in his newspaper, he never missed a thing!

I thoroughly enjoyed ambling along the narrow twisting streets of this charming town, past a vine-draped moon bridge, sacks of grains or lentils, and the preparation of fascinating foods, which people ate in the street. Two types of *dim sum* snacks were produced: one by selecting small portions of meat with chopsticks and wrapping it in rounds of flattened dough, the second by spooning batter over grated potato in a ladle, which was then plunged into boiling oil in a wok on a metal drum containing a coal fire fanned by hand. An old man in the blue suit and cap, a burning taper in hand, sat smoking a long-handled pipe, and a meat cart, partially covered with cloth, stood in an open market where vegetables were also sold and a lady sat using chopsticks to stuff balls with a filling. Another weighed fish taken from a wooden container filled with water, and two people made sweet concoctions from rolled pastry cut into strips, twisted, and deep fried in lard using a large slotted spoon. Willows, people poling and carrying loads, a small garden outside white walls, a more affluent home with a moon gate, reflections of yet another bridge, and the inevitable washing completed my sightseeing.

Wuxi

Travelling by boat on the main canal (a journey described in detail in a later chapter), I left Suzhou for **Wuxi**, with a long history going back 6,000 years. The present city was built in the second century BC when tin was discovered in a nearby hill. It was named Yauxi meaning Has Tin, but was later changed to Wuxi (No Tin) when the metal was mined out. Nowadays, because of rich natural produce, it is called by the equally unromantic name of A Land of Rice and Fish. I stayed at the Hubin Hotel, with a magnificent panorama from my window of the **Spring Lingering Pagoda** in the water, willows, and a lovely curved bridge in **Liyuan Garden** at **Lake Lihu**, made up of five smaller lakes. The covered **Thousand Step Corridor**, its wall decorated with around 100 flower-shaped windows, led to the **Four Season Pavilions**. Symbolising spring, summer, autumn and winter, they were named Flowing Red Pavilion, Green Dripping Pavilion, Drunken Yellow Pavilion and Chanting White Pavilion respectively, and were represented by spring plum, oleander, osmanthus and wintersweet. Going down for closer inspection, I found a sublime garden in an idyllic setting, with perfectly mirrored images in still water, ornamental bridges, graceful trees, and decorative rooflines, all of which comprised some of the most beautiful film that I had ever taken, particularly in the glow of sunset. A tank contained white 'goldfish' with red topknots, which glistened in the sunlight, and flowerbeds in the hotel grounds featured flawless blooms of enormous dahlias in pink, white and yellow. Beds of this same flower, in mixed colours, were also an attraction in yet another garden, along with trailing blossoms reflected in water, large white birds gliding over a lake, pavilions, and a variety of massed blooms in front of a triple-arched gateway.

Seated on the ground, I encountered a group of young girls dressed in colourful garb with elaborate hair adornment. Because of the edict that allows only one child, each was gaily attired (in contrast to the adult population), indulged, pampered, and inclined to be precocious. Thousands of bicycles negotiated streets where I found freshly baked buns and, along canals, small houses with wooden upper stories and tiny attics. I also came across an ornate multi-tiered pagoda, men playing cards on the sidewalk, and fishing *junks* on a sparkling sea. Wuxi, also called Radiant Pearl in the Lake, was a major centre for the production of silk, and it was from nearby **Taihu Lake** that the ornamental stone was procured; the fourth largest lake in China, it was no more than ten feet deep at any part.

Nanjing

The history of **Nanjing** (**Nanking**) can be traced back to 4000 BC, featuring most significantly in the first Opium War, the Taiping Rebellion, as a brief capital (in 1911) under Sun Yat Sen's provisional government, as the 1937 headquarters of Chiang Kaishek's government, and in 1949 when the communist forces of Mao Zedong took the city. But I came for one reason: to visit the **Memorial of Sun Yat Sen**. Surrounded by thick forest, it was entered via a triple-arched gateway leading to a mammoth staircase. Wide and 323m long, it ascended a series of hills with a pavilion at the top of each level, the main monument concealed until the last rise. It was a lengthy and arduous climb (392 steps), but the views made the effort worthwhile. The Revolution of 1911, led by Dr Sun Yat Sen, overthrew the Qing dynasty and founded the Republic of China.

Nanjing also had an avenue of fanciful life-sized stone images facing each other in pairs on a tree-lined median strip: the **Sacred Avenue of the Filial Tomb** of the Ming dynasty, or **Avenue of the Spirits**, leading to the tomb of the first Ming Emperor, Hong Wu. Beginning with ancient warriors, it progressed through squat-looking horses, elephants – both standing and kneeling, as were stubby-legged camels – and the ubiquitous lion, finishing with warriors again. The 35-mile Ming city wall, two-thirds of which still stands, was the longest the world had ever seen. Nanjing lies between the Crouching Tiger (mountains) and Curling Dragon (Yangtze River).

Luoyang

I continued on to **Luoyang** and one of four sets of amazing grottoes that I was to see on my trip. These awesome venues contained literally thousands of Buddha images carved into rock-hewn niches and recesses. Ranging in size from a mere few centimetres to many metres in height, the largest, a seated **Vairocana** (meaning illuminating all things in sutra) **Buddha** in **Fengxian Cave**, was 17.14m (59ft) high, the head 4m and the ears 1.9m. He was flanked by disciples Kasyapa and Ananda. Holding a pagoda in the palm of his right hand and crushing a demon underfoot, an image with a serene face stood next to one carrying a weapon and wearing an angry countenance. These **Longmen Buddhist Grottos** were carved around the year 488 and added to in the Tang dynasty, leaving a magnificent heritage that had taken 400 years to accomplish. More than 2,100 grottos containing 100,000 images covered a cliff face overlooking the **Yi River**. The figures were either seated or standing and some had a hand upraised as if in benediction.

A couple wore elaborate headdresses, and most had elongated earlobes. Several, having suffered the ravages of time, were without arms or heads. Unfortunately, some had also been lost to overseas museums. Sculpted relief lay above excavated archways and around a few of the heads. The gigantic façade dwarfed tall trees on top.

The principal image in the **Cave of Ten Thousand Buddhas**, a 4m-high **Amitabha** (Buddha of Infinite Light), was seated on a lotus flower throne (*sumeru*) shouldered by four muscular warriors carved into the sides. On the walls, 15,000 tiny (4cm) Buddhas appeared to be representations of the main figure, and sitting on lotus leaves above lay 54 *bodhisattvas* (enlightened beings) in long flowing skirts, their poses as vivid as life, their visages displaying a variety of moods: grave, reserved, naïve, and joyful. According to the period created, the Buddhas reflected severe, benign, or kindly countenances. Perhaps the most extraordinary was the sixth-century **Medical Prescription Cave**, with 140-odd ancient remedies inscribed on its stone walls, including both herbal – pills, powders, potions and ointments – and acupuncture treatments for a wide variety of ailments and injuries. Sculptures in the oldest cave, **Guyang**, tell of how Prince Siddhartha, founder of Buddhism, attained enlightenment. They show the entry of the white elephant into the womb of the prince's mother, her excursion into a park and the birth of the prince under a tree, his baptism by nine dragons, and other events that form a complete story in stone.

Passing donkeys pulling carts with the appearance of enormous cane baskets, I was taken to an extremely interesting underground village. Consisting of rooms leading off an excavated square pit with trees in the centre, the individual dwellings were entered through doorways in the tile-capped sides of the cavity, which was accessed, like the tombs of Egypt, via steps down a sloping ramp between high walls. From above, I could see a cat on a cane chair, chickens (some on a doorstep) with a basin of feed, a straw broom, a wooden bed, and a bucket and bowls in the communal yard. Nowadays, people lived mostly above ground, and in a bucolic setting I found many chickens and pigs, one absolutely immense like a small pony, wandering amongst the dwellings, and old ladies in blue, who seemed very surprised to see a stranger. One was tending a black cast-iron pot on her outdoor clay oven, another sorting grain on a mat. Here also, I saw bicycles and a cart, a cane basket, washing on lines, a wagon pulled by a cow, piles of kindling and wood, corncobs hanging to dry – one string with a hen on top, pecking at kernels and flapping its wings to maintain balance – and the sun setting behind a curled roof.

Zhengzhou

From **Zhengzhou**, en route to Xi'an, I took a tour 80km to see the **Shaolin Monastery** (AD 495), considered to be the birthplace of Zen Buddhism and the martial art of *kung fu*. The main four red buildings were no different from dozens of others, with carved eaves, guardian lions, and metal urns in the courtyard, but were surrounded by a fantastic forest of 220 tiered yellow brick pagodas: a cemetery dating back 300 to 1,000 years, where remains of eminent monks in the history of the temple were interred. A few were bulbous with ringed spires (like *stupas*), one was adorned with fine embossing, and a couple slightly overgrown, but all blended well with yellow autumn trees against a background of dry hills. A forecourt containing *stelae* was sheltered by an enormous shade tree with delicate pale green leaves, a sculpted stone gateway led to another courtyard, and an entrance featured a wonderful polychrome guardian with a benign face. Scenes in the rural village included the usual chickens and washing.

I was particularly fortunate inasmuch as a festival was in progress at one of the temples, where stone lions guarded the tripartite entrance with an elaborate pavilion on top, again like that in Beijing. A large congested crowd carried flags, and offerings were for sale by vendors seated on the ground. Also sitting cross-legged on the pavement, devotees sold sheets from stacks of paper bearing Chinese characters and weighted down with stones or bamboo. A metal image that had the appearance of a martial arts exponent was the focus of attention, with people touching it for luck and rubbing its tummy – one lady holding up a baby to kiss the protuberance! Huge fierce temple guardians flanked the doorway, people carried balloons, and one bearded man sold some item in metal bowls to a man carrying a sheepskin bundle. Quite a few representatives of the Chinese army were in evidence. Fine artwork decorated the gateway and temples, life-sized statues were lined up inside, and beyond one doorway I observed red lanterns and a huge gaudy figure with eyes on the wrist. One man in a black robe had long hair wound into a topknot, and people selling fruits sat back to back in a row, whilst others, their clothing nearby and obviously pilgrims, squatted with chopsticks to eat noodles from portable containers, one man drinking from a bucket. Along the road, I saw a donkey pulling a cart concealed by a load of hay as big as a house.

The Chinese also conduct festivals at the drop of a hat; two such celebrations included the traditions of 'enjoying looking at the moon' during the Mid Autumn Festival, and 'enjoying looking at chrysanthemums' on the Double Ninth Festival – ninth day of the ninth lunar month. Operatic arias included Weep Over the Ancestral Temple and Kill the Son at the Outer Gate of the

Government Office! Even the beautiful azalea is given inappropriate names: Green Dressing and Crown, Broken Pieces, Horse Ribbon, Monkey Head, and Deer Horn!

Xian

Xi'an, the 3,000-year-old **Chang'an** (Everlasting Peace), capital of ancient **Cathay** in the Han dynasty (206 BC–AD 220), once the largest city in the world and now capital of **Shaanxi** province, was a depressing city and the most polluted that I had ever experienced; in fact, for the first time I was forced to spend a day in bed because of it, but once it was the start of the fabled silk road that drew merchants trading in porcelains, precious stones, silks and spices. The capital of China for 11 dynasties, at that time it was an imposing city rivalling Baghdad, Constantinople and Rome. It was renamed Xi'an (Peace in the West) in 1369.

The first things that I saw were pavilions atop the 12m/40ft-high **Old City Wall** – best preserved in China, constructed in the Ming dynasty to defend the city against marauding barbarians – the tall Tang dynasty (618–907) **Pagoda of Xiaoyan** (**Small Wild Goose**), a bridge spanning a fairly dry river outside the crenellated grey walls, and a colourful archway across a street of dull grey buildings with the occasional decorative doorway. The brown 45m-high 15-storey pagoda was built in the **Bliss Proffering Monastery** in AD 707, and one could not miss the mighty **Drum** (1308) and **Bell** (1384) towers, which as the names suggest, once contained a huge drum and cast-iron bell respectively, both used to toll the hour. A variety of cooked foods were on offer in proximity to large round loaves of flat unleavened bread stacked near a metal drum belching black smoke.

A visit to the **Qin Shi Huang Mausoleum**, with its over 8,000-strong terracotta army, horses, chariots and weapons, was also a disappointment because the serried ranks appeared just like all the pictures that I had seen, filming was strictly forbidden, and they stood to attention in a covered enclosure viewed from an elevated catwalk along which one was continually urged to keep moving. I believe that restrictions on photography have now been relaxed, but at the time I could only film one warrior – behind glass. The most interesting fact was that each bore the distinctive features of the man on whom it was modelled. 700,000 workers took 36 years to build the tomb, the main chamber of which, with its repository of riches, was yet to be uncovered. Qin Shi Huang was a ruthless dictator, the unifier of China, who standardised the written language, linked the Great Wall, and founded the

Qin dynasty (221–206 BC). Opposed to education, culture and commerce as non-productive, the Qin society was a harsh warring regime with sophisticated weapons, which ruled through fear. It used such methods of punishment as flogging, cutting in two at the waist, and boiling in a cauldron. The Great Wall was achieved using forced labour. In earlier dynasties, servants, slaves and attendants had been entombed with their master, a tradition later replaced with wood or straw effigies. Qin's was the first tomb where life-sized realistic figures appeared. Carrying bronze swords, spears and crossbows, which did not feature in Western European warfare until the 14th century, the army of fierce, grave, earnest, smiling and kindly countenances stood row upon row, followed by horses hitched to wooden chariots, which together with their leather harness no longer existed.

Even the lake was a dirty grey, but still reflected pavilions, rotundas, willows, a white dragon, a stone walkway, and green slopes beyond. Viewed one behind the other, a couple of round grey gates surmounted by dragons made an attractive picture, as did two smiling children, the boy in army uniform, on the steps of a pavilion. I also visited the Tang dynasty **Dayan** or **Big Wild Goose Pagoda** (AD 652) in the **Monastery of Great Benevolence**, and in the vicinity of a large mosque with cupolas and decorated arches, I was surprised to see a man turning kebabs over a coal brazier next to hanging carcasses. Donkey carts were driven down the main streets, as was a herd of cattle, sheep and goats! Round flat bread was stamped with a pattern of circles and glaze applied with a brush before being placed, by means of a long skewer, into a deep open-topped adobe oven.

The weather had turned very cold, and snow lay on the ground when I visited an interesting pastoral area with a small mosque, flat-roofed stone houses, cattle, a rustic ladder leaning against stables and/or storage huts with straw on top, log fences, outdoor clay ovens, horses (two with feedbags), chickens, and more dogs than I had seen to date, all with a mountain backdrop. Taking a short walk, I found that the white precipitation had beautified a sombre grey landscape. It blanketed the fir forest and a frozen stream, coated rocks, and enveloped a scintillating frozen cascade; a rabbit even scampered across my line of sight. I photographed a family group, two of whom wore red cardigans that brightened the picture. A cow was tethered to an enclosure fenced with bamboo, a tractor-drawn cart sat in a yard, and a woman was gathering something in a pail. Accompanied by his dog, a man was riding one sturdy mountain pony whilst leading another, and a man on a horse led a shaggy long-haired camel, the like of which I had not seen before but was common in this part of the world. Known as the Bactrian, they were the lifeblood of the ancient Silk Route because they could go months without water and carry 270kg loads for nearly 200km at a stretch. They tolerated temperatures from freezing cold to blistering heat, and their long eyelashes and scalable nostrils helped protect them from blowing sands. Stopping for pictures of another community, I observed a small mosque, flat-roofed dwellings with straw on top, cows, barking dogs, tiny birds in a tree, and a mud-brick wall with gateways leading to individual yards. I was invited in by a smiling mother holding an apprehensive serious-faced infant with very ruddy cheeks, warmly dressed in an orange woollen hat, thick black-mottled yellow coat, and blue pants. In another area, bread was being baked in front of a small mosque, and men in black congregated in a wide street where stallholders were preparing food surrounded by flocks of sheep and both donkey and bicycle carts. In the evening, I attended a Tang dynasty Dinner Show at the Lido.

Kashi

I flew to Urümqi, and from there over snowy mountains to **Kashi** in the extreme west of this vast country, known as **Kashgar** on the other side of the border, where my principal purpose was to experience the Sunday market. By now the reader will be aware of my penchant for markets, but this had to be the most amazing spectacle that I have ever witnessed. I spent considerable time on the verge of a long straight road lined with bare poplars, filming the influx of thousands of people arriving in a constant stream by foot, on bicycle and horseback, riding donkeys, in donkey carts and drays, and by the occasional car or truck. In fact, every conceivable conveyance was piled with goods to trade, which included sacks of produce, huge ornate red boxes, and a load of square baskets, stacked higher than the man standing on the front of a wagon to urge his small donkey forward! A tethered cow plodded behind a cart. Mostly rural people – desert nomads and tribal Uygurs, Tajiks, Kerghez and Uzbeks – the long-bearded men were dressed in fur or woollen caps and long coats, and the women wore woollen hats or headscarves, but the Muslim women were completely covered by veils. Amongst the walkers were two leading, respectively, a cow and four sheep (three black and one white) by ropes. People were perched on top of goods, a man cycled whilst holding hens by the legs in one hand, another rode past on a frisky horse, tossing its head as it trotted in front of two horse-drawn carriages and a tractor-drawn cart, and a donkey trailed behind yet another cart. I filmed amusing vision of a small donkey ferrying a large bearded man whose feet nearly touched the ground. There were loads consisting of long poles, piles of melons or gilt boxes, and carts laden simply with people.

Adjourning to the huge market arena, I found people bartering for sheep, wagons lined up with donkeys still in the traces, baskets of greens and fruits, loads of hay and melons, men in turbans gathered around woolly sheep, trays of eggs on a handcart, a man leading a big black bull, doughnuts on a stall, carpets in a donkey-drawn cart, and a young boy cradling a puppy but wary about the camera. All was perpetual motion in front of flat-roofed buildings with colourful traditional patterns on doorways. My film of the constant hustle and bustle continued with a man weighing meat cut from suspended carcasses, two old men with grey beards sitting quietly talking in the midst of the organised (I assumed) chaos, heaps of what looked like sugarcane and a type of grass, a parade of carts piled high with cabbages, and a woman, her head swathed in a woollen scarf and wearing long gumboots, carrying poultry. An elderly bearded man sat cross-legged on a wagon, and a cart hauled lengths of trimmed branches that trailed on the ground behind. I saw a small herd of long-haired white goats and a man stuffing pastry to create fancy-shaped snacks, which were cooked in a huge clay oven. Nearby, people were drinking from bowls and more butchers were in evidence.

I took a brief respite from the overwhelming turmoil to see a tiny pavilion decorated with a small amount of patterned brickwork and reflected, along with drab adobe houses, in a patch of water, the only colour provided by laundry. The **Abakh Hoja Tomb**, with its green tiled dome and minarets (tiled in many colours) like towers at the four corners was, by contrast, outstanding. Surrounded by cone-shaped graves, the main tomb contained 72 burial places, most decorated with mosaic tiles, and it was said that wealthy Muslims wanted to lie beside the central sarcophagus, which according to legend held the costumes of Xiangfai (Fragrant Concubine), a renowned beauty from the region kidnapped by a Qing dynasty ruler and taken to the Forbidden City in Beijing.

Back into the fray, I saw women in shawls, the inevitable buckets carried on the ends of poles, more butchers, hessian sacks filled to the brim with nuts, dried goods, spices and herbs, and even grapes in tubs and baskets. Raisins were a big industry in Turpan (see below). Along one wall, a row of barbers was fully employed shaving heads and faces, and I arrived at the cattle market, where I noticed an unusual black and white spotted cow. Here, food was being cooked in large enamel and cast-iron basins on top of clay ovens with roaring open flames. Amongst this hotch-potch of scruffy humanity, I came across cattle, braying donkeys, sheep, the haughty two-humped furry camels, and horses in colourful beautifully crafted saddles and blankets, which were being put through their paces by riders urging them up and down to show them off.

One of the most intriguing things that I observed was the making of fresh noodles, which entailed quite a bit of showmanship. Rolled strips of dough were stretched by swinging like a skipping rope until long enough to loop and twist automatically together, a process repeated until a desired thickness was achieved. The resultant mass was then banged on a floured table and magically separated into copious strands! The end of the whole was then stuck to edge of the table, stretched again, and the threads broken off for immersion into boiling water. A man sat eating the finished product (or porridge) from a bowl with his fingers. In another area, where food was being prepared and cooked in steaming cauldrons or kebabs fanned over naked coals, people were eating at long tables covered with red plastic.

I found prospective buyers gathered around a fleece on the ground and two men with long white beards sitting with jars of potions under an international Red Cross sign; an adjacent stallholder was selling powders or some such from small hessian bags. Bright carpets with traditional patterns hung on a line, money changed hands, and used clothing was for sale. According to my guide book, even in the 19th century it was a great bazaar in which Indian, Afghan and Russian traders jostled and rubbed shoulders with Muslim and Mongolian tribesmen, Chinese settlers and exiles, bandits, tomb and temple robbers, and some of the scurviest most dangerous human flotsam of Central Asia, even Russian spies. And nothing much seemed to have changed! It was said to be further from the sea than any other town on earth and was a vital watering hole, trading post, and supply depot for Silk Route camel caravans – and a prime target for nomad attack.

Outside the market, a cow running down the main street was leading its owner a merry dance, and narrow back alleys had covered overpasses. A man was weighing grapes taken from a cane basket on his cart, and another, hammering a horseshoe, sat on a small stool near a small fire in front of a shop with musical instruments on a sign above the door and a caged bird hanging from a bare tree. An elderly man sat on the pavement with his kettle, a few bright red tomatoes on a mat, and some white product in baskets.

But there were other sights in this dusty isolated desert town, namely, the large yellow brick **Id Kah Mosque**, with colourful tiles on the arched entry, elegantly carved and coloured wooden pillars, and stone tracery in the windows of its minarets, two three-storey structures with sculpted arched balconies, and a large building with a dome and two cupolas on top. The entire time I spent in Kashi provided subjects and opportunities for superb footage – and I did not see one other European!

Urümqi and Turpan

I flew back to **Urümqi** where, sadly, because of the wintry conditions, I could not get to see its most splendid attraction: **Sky** or **Heavenly Lake**. I was amazed that in a region accustomed to snow and ice, vehiles were not equipped with chains to handle it and slipped and slid every which way; it was the same in Hohhot, where even walking was treacherous. From here, I set out to travel overland, passing cattle being herded across the treeless expanse of flat desert plain with snowy mountains in the far distance, and then traversing a waterless sea of dunes leading to **Turpan**. Once an important stop on the southern and central Silk Roads, this was situated right in the middle of the **Turpan Depression**, where the desert floor sank 154.43m (492ft) below sea level to form a piteously hot furnace. Turpan means Lowland, and it was the second lowest spot on earth after the Dead Sea. The daytime temperature on the slopes of **Huoyan Shan** (**Flaming Mountains**) often reached 70°C, and the rock and red soil flared into shimmering 'fire' when struck by the sun, hence the name. With multi-creviced sides, their topography also took on the appearance of myriad flames. However, my accommodation in the Turpan Hotel, with decorated balconies and cupolas on the roof, was delightful.

From here, I visited the two ruined cities of Jiaohe and Gaochang. The former, founded in the second century and a Tang dynasty garrison in the wars against the Turkic tribes, was razed by Genghis Khan in the 14th century, and the latter, established by the Uygurs when they migrated from Mongolia in the ninth century, was mysteriously abandoned in the 14th century. Although derelict, their ancient mud-brick and rammed-earth buildings appearing more like weathered stone monoliths or monuments, the aura was incredible, because apart from my guide, I was the only person at both venues. In the utter stillness, one could almost hear the cries and commotion of people and carts in the deserted once paved streets of these prior important hubs, where relatively sophisticated communities even had underground chambers dug below each dwelling to give shelter from the fierce daytime heat. With the permission of my guide, I collected a couple of shards of ancient pottery, which was a thrill. **Jiaohe** stood at the edge of a sheer deep ravine, with fields, a few bare poplars, horses and water far below. Windows like empty eye sockets stared sightlessly from lone walls, and I took photographs of more-recognisable structures framed by gaping holes, whilst other remains appeared as rock tors against the light. One building still retained some decorative brickwork, but much was hidden by time and sand.

Leaving here, we paused at a house where a man was sorting sultanas on a mat beneath bare vines covering a pergola, and I was shown wells and the ingenious Karez system of irrigation that travelled a considerable distance relying on gravity for the flow of underground water. Famous for this particular fruit, Turpan was also called the City of Grapes and consequently known as the hottest, lowest, driest and *sweetest* place in China! It earned the name Fiery Land in the Yuan Period because of the heat, the highest recorded temperature being 49.6°C.

Back in town, I filmed the exquisite exterior of the new mosque, with six fine minarets and intricate decoration above the entrance, startling white against its grey façade. This was very different from the nearby older and plainer green-domed place of worship with crescents on top of its two minarets.

Following a dun-coloured canyon with smooth windblown sides, craggy ridges, and a winding waterway divided into several streams criss-crossing an almost dry bed we came to the ancient burial complex of the **Atsana Tombs**, their walled entries, again like Egypt, sloping into the earth, and many as yet unopened. I was taken to see a body amazingly well preserved in the dry atmosphere of this arid, stark, but surprisingly arresting countryside. We drove through a village beside an irrigation canal, where mud bricks were used to create an open pattern on fences, and goats 'climbed' trees to reach sparse dry leaves. **Gaochang**, with some homes resembling cave dwellings, seemed to have withstood the rigors of time even less, and it was remarkable how both cities had utterly cohered to become part of the landscape from which they were originally forged.

On the return journey, I saw an attractive mosque constructed with dun-coloured bricks, and donkey carts trotting down the highway between adobe walls the same colour as the earth. Large logs were stacked on a verge, and small bridges crossing a culvert provided access to a village where I found another small mosque, carts with green vegetables, bicycles, pumpkins and root vegetables placed on jute bags on the ground, donkeys, a lone sheep, a tethered goat, and a population mainly of men – all of whom stopped to stare. As a foreigner in China, at times I found it very disconcerting when people, quite unabashed, openly pointed at things like my nail polish, and laughed outright at my feet clad only in sandals, which was not the done thing, I gathered, in the filthy streets where spitting was a constant expectation and animals fouled the pavements. Whenever I heard the sound of someone (men *and* women) clearing their throat, I was apprehensive as to where the resultant mass would lodge! At no time did I feel threatened, but it could be embarrassing.

We made our way back past the monotonous incised slopes of the 'flaming' mountains, and once again in town, I saw vendors with meat hanging in a stall near a mosque, donkey carts being driven along dusty thoroughfares, people unloading hay from a wagon, a man walking a cow down a narrow alley bounded by adobe walls, a cow in a byre made from the clay bricks, a lady washing clothes in an irrigation canal and, in front of the very colourful façade of yet another small mosque, a man driving a dray carrying long trimmed branches. A donkey cart carrying cabbages was followed down the main road by sheep and running children (one small boy having great sport chasing the sheep!), and ducks waddled off to the side. I spent a most enjoyable time ambling along dirt streets where empty wagons lay outside doorways, and donkey carts stood patiently beside dilapidated adobe walls (a few with open brickwork decoration) or were driven through the narrow lanes. One carried greens covered by a carpet, the donkey with red adornment on its nose. I also saw a mosque enhanced with a colourful diamond design and script, a dray carrying a family, and a baker using tongs and a long-handled wire basket to remove fat crusty loaves from the inside walls of a clay oven onto which they had been stuck to cook. I came to a market devoted solely to the sale of green and brown raisins, which were displayed in heaps on matting on the ground, weighed by handheld scales, and tipped loose into customer's bags. One man was wearing an interesting embroidered cap.

Crossing a vast salt pan, I visited a mosque that, except for open brickwork on the balustrade of its flat roof, had a plain façade but featured a conical mud minaret beautifully decorated with engraved flowers, lattice and zigzag patterns. A bucket with a long rope attached stood at the edge of a brick-lined well in the compound. Set amid arid terrain, it was the subject of excellent pictures. Amongst interesting alleys, I found a food market where, next to piles of bamboo and heaps of apples, a man was cooking large lumps of lard and a goat's head, its teeth bared in a rictus of death, in a boiler over flames! Minarets of a mosque reared above mud-brick walls with vegetation placed on top to dry, pure white ducks waddled down the street and across a canal, a cow stood tethered to one of the old walls, a herd of goats came towards me in the roadway, a wooden bed stood in a yard, and I filmed the sunset behind the dome and crescent topped minarets of another mosque.

Train travel in China was interesting to say the least. On one occasion, fellow passengers in my carriage requested (with sign language) to look at my ticket, which they passed amongst themselves with great hilarity, for the obvious reason that I had paid at least twice the going rate, always the case for foreigners. I also found it extremely difficult, after sharing a sleeping compartment with all men, when I was scheduled to alight in the early hours one morning; nobody was awake, none spoke English anyway, and all the signs were in Chinese characters. I had to rely on the conductor being conscientious enough to notify me when we reached my destination, which brings me to two more interesting, but again heart-warming episodes, this time illustrating the language problem. The first was on this same trip when the lady conductor patiently attempted to convey something to me and finally, in desperation and frustration, resorted to writing it on paper – in Chinese! Retaining the slip, I later enquired what it read and was informed that she had been asking me if I required anything to eat; hot water was always provided in a thermos for people to brew their own tea from leaves carried in screw top jars.

The second incident occurred when I caught a train on the final leg of my exciting journey tracing the ancient silk route to the far west of China on the border with Afghanistan. Heading for **Dunhuang** (City if Sands, founded 11 BC), in **Gansu Province** and traversed by the **Silk Road**, I was put off at a station that appeared to be in the middle of nowhere. Aimlessly wandering the platform, I just kept repeating the name of my destination to anyone who would listen, but to no avail. Finally, a female guard came along and, without a word, took me by the arm, led me towards another disembarking passenger, and put me in her care; neither spoke a word of English. Much to my consternation, this young lady, hustled me to a bus station. Anticipating a train connection, I kept saying 'Dunhuang', but she insisted that I purchase a bus ticket and wrote the amount on the palm of my hand. I ultimately understood that we had arrived at **Liuyuan**, a siding three and half hours from Dunhuang across the **Gobi Desert**, which we traversed in an ancient, decrepit and filthy bus that bounced, lurched and jolted over rough roads in a most uncomfortable ride! I managed to achieve some very jerky film of dry scrub on a flat plain with black mountains in the distance.

The young lady was very proud to be in charge of my welfare and chatted to me incessantly throughout the entire journey, not one word of which I understood! I just kept smiling at her and saying 'I wish I could understand you but I don't'. Finally arriving at the town, where I had a reservation, I tried to tell the bus driver the name of my hotel, but he did not comprehend. Passing an establishment with 'Hotel' in the title, I tried once again to indicate what I wanted by using the Chinese word, but he deposited me at an alternative hostelry. Also dismounting, my kind companion engaged me the one and only taxi in town, which eventually transferred me to the correct establishment, where yet another problem arose – the hotel had rooms but no dining facilities because it was partially closed for the winter. However, opposite was a hotel with food service but no rooms, so it was arranged that I eat there, which proved an inconvenience in the freezing conditions! Next morning, out of the blue, the young lady turned up (of course she knew where I was staying) and began to harangue me with questions again. In the foyer of the hotel I met a German-speaking guide leading a group, so I took her inside and asked him to translate. He told me she wanted to take me to the **Mogao Grottos**, 25km southwest, but I had a tour already arranged so had to decline her generous offer. She contented herself with a picture of the two of us and left, but it was a special encounter.

Mogao Grottos

Carved into **Singing Sand Mountain**, the grottos themselves had a strict prohibition on photography because so much had been ransacked by foreigners over a period of years from the late 1800s. Similar to those described earlier and dating from the year 336, there were only 492 out of more than 1,000 caves left. As well as the 2,315 clay figures, the largest standing 33m (108ft), the grottos were adorned with 45,000 square metres of detailed murals, bas-reliefs and three-dimensional wall sculptures, and several thousand pillars were decorated with the lotus motif. The spectacular murals, if placed side by side, would measure 25km. The caves were abandoned in the 12th century when Dunhuang was no longer part of the trade route.

This journey was also an adventure: crossing stony terrain with a few bare poplars, and passing perfect light-coloured sand dunes with knife-sharp ridges and windblown hollows accentuated by light and shade. Other sections were sculpted by wind into fine ripples, and the only thing to mar the surface was a set of camel tracks. A couple of these odd shaggy beasts were resting near where I alighted to take pictures, and far off, others were slowly plodding across the desert floor. Nestled at the base of a high dune, my guide and I came to a waterhole shaped like a crescent moon, and indeed called **Crescent Moon Spring**, with two horses standing near a solitary dead tree, a few rocks, and an endless tract of smooth sand etched into fascinating shapes, where the only foreign intrusion was my own shadow as I filmed the panorama. This was the real Gobi. It also made stunning photographs looking towards the sun, which split into rays of many hues. The only community we passed consisted of white row houses lining both sides of the road.

At the site, because there were no people around, I did manage to sneak some forbidden pictures of the mostly red-and-green murals (a touch of blue in one section) depicting patterns, people, and bird-like figures. I also filmed the striking seven-storey wooden pavilion built into the cliff face (much like at Datong, described later) and illustrations around the fretwork of its window grilles. The difference here was in the use of concrete to create some alcoves and recesses. As with the Longmen Grottoes at Luoyang, the complex was situated beside a wide (but only partially full) river, with *stupa*-like structures and a small rotunda containing statues near the banks. Pictures of the site from the opposite side of the waterway, with dry poplars in the foreground and sandhills towering behind, showed how extensive it was. I also saw some ancient mud-brick mileage towers.

Lanzhou

From Dunhuang, I flew to Lanzhou, over cracked and creviced, sometimes red-hued, but mostly dun-coloured stony outcrops and hills with a little black relief. A river snaking away from a large incredibly blue lake provided an extreme contradiction as I filmed the landscape through the scratched windows of an ancient two-engine twin-propeller China Airlines aircraft (CAAC) – known in the trade as China Airlines Always Crashing! The environment changed to a patch of paddy fields as we landed briefly before continuing over miles and miles of barren wasteland, with fantastic sculpted sandhills, rounded wind-scoured rock, and patches of ice around small blue lakes, which appeared incongruous in desert terrain.

Lanzhou again presented stark scenery, with deep gullies and sharply etched hills into which the adobe houses seemed to be absorbed. It was still cold, and en route to the city I visited a village cloaked in early morning mist, where men led donkeys beside a frozen stream and bare trees; the only other inhabitants I saw were a black pig, a dog and chickens. The waterway widened to a captivating vista of shining ice 'flowing' between sheer amber-coloured canyon walls with hills beyond. Surrounded by a few pines, a hilltop pavilion was an attractive sight, and my first view of the city was across the wide swiftly moving **Yellow River** – second longest after the Yangtze, travelling an incredible 5,464km (3,395miles) – with the curled eaves of pavilions amongst the mud-brick and stuccoed buildings and a monument on a hill behind. As I paused to take photographs from a bridge, a man crossed with a pole bearing baskets laden with bright red chillies – a startlingly colourful intrusion on the drab surroundings.

In the streets of the town, I found carcasses on a cart and hanging from hooks, fretwork around windows looking onto narrow alleys with wooden balconies overhead, and a beautiful stone carving depicting various plants, including the fruits and leaves of the grapevine. A group of people, all wearing gloves, was executing tai chi outside a red-pillared temple overlooking the dome and minarets of a mosque, the bridge, and the city sprawling on both sides of the river. I was taken to an extremely atmospheric ancient site built on a hillside and shrouded in fog, which added an air of mystery. Along with the usual attractive rooflines, moon gates, and bare trees, it featured a paved court containing red pillars, walls with open brickwork, and fine old art on ancient wooden panels. These portrayed birds on leafy branches, a rooster with a hen, flowering long-leaved plants, and traditional Chinese mountain scenery. One entrance was illustrated with camels. Restored pavilions featured colourful patterns on ornately carved eaves, and ancient sculpted roof capping incorporated small floral spires. From higher up, I obtained a lovely view over these same rooftops, and even the trees were ancient. At the lower level again, a frozen pond with a dragon wall to one side and surrounded by bare trees, willows and pavilions, was crossed by a bridge and zigzag walkway. The entire scene was like something from an old sepia picture, the bland colour even repeated on hills beyond. A newer temple, with a metal urn in the forecourt, was draped in red banners.

I went next to the amazing pyramid-shaped hill of **Maiji Shan** (Wheat Stack), containing a series of Tang dynasty grottos and Buddhist sculptures cut into the cliff in AD 384–417 but buried, along with the treasures therein, by a violent earthquake in 734. However, although some 194 grottos had survived, a survey by Chinese archaeologists in 1952 found the site too dangerous to excavate and it was no longer possible to climb the precarious stairway up the face of the cliff. Nevertheless, from below I could easily distinguish guardians outside doorways and murals beneath overhanging ledges. A large sombre-faced Buddha was flanked by two with inscrutable countenances, and higher up, one of another group of three had been destroyed.

At a nearby village, with views of a very green valley, I saw paddy fields, cattle and a white pig beside a rivulet, crumbling adobe walls, contented cows munching on dried material in a yard, ladders against walls, a compound with a donkey and haystack, wooden doors in gateways adorned with tiles and Chinese characters, and everywhere corn hanging to dry. Larger beasts of burden (possibly mules) were tethered in a line beside a grey brick wall, a long-bearded man carried a large basket on his back, carts displayed twists of sweet-looking bread, and people were eating and drinking tea. Lying on the roadside, wares for sale included cane baskets, twig brooms, and some unrecognisable food product. Horses were labouring to pull wagons inundated by enormous haystacks, which brushed the road surface and appeared to be moving under their own steam, without the benefit of wheels underneath! Caged birds hung on a number of walls, and a man sat outside his front entrance together with a small child on a tiny chair, a pig snuffling around their feet. I saw another set of ancient pavilions, where old men accompanied by birds in cages were playing a Chinese card game. It became a common sight to see people carrying these feathered companions and congregating in parks to converse. Approached via an avenue of shady trees, another pavilion featured a panel showing deer amid foliage, an intricate carving incorporating a dragon, and screens depicting long-legged birds. In a street market devoted to fruits (mainly mandarins and apples), a man carried many chickens by the legs, others occupied the pannier of a bicycle, and carts, on one of which an old gentleman was seated, were pulled and pushed by hand. The roadway was lined by small open-fronted food stalls under sagging grey tiled roofs.

Travelling past extremely high rock precipices and across a wide river, I was taken to yet another temple, with a yellowish pagoda similar in style the those of the Wild Goose in Xi'an and extraordinary trees that I always identify with China, their twisted tracery of trunks and bare branches creating absorbing silhouettes. A monument in a large square sat opposite a massive pavilion, its red doors embossed with elegant Chinese figures in traditional scenes. I came across another exponent of the art of noodle making by the stretch and double method, the resultant strands plunged into boiling water and served almost immediately, and a man was preparing delicious-looking pancakes by spreading batter on a hot plate, breaking and spreading an egg in the centre, flipping, adding what appeared to be precooked fish, and applying sauce with a brush before folding. Another vendor was spooning meat chopped on a wooden block into a type of pita bread, and a surprisingly neat mall, patronised by pedestrians and cyclists, was hung with Chinese paper lanterns. Many buildings had red pillars and signs in Chinese, but a modicum of decoration.

Lanzhou, on the south bank of the Yellow River, had more than its share of pavilions, but on the north bank, the complex of **Baita Shan (White Pagoda Hill**; *baita* means white), with Ming and Qing dynasty pavilions and a tall multilevel Buddhist pagoda, had artistry even on roof capping. This took the form of dragons and large glossy orange ceramic flowers. Viewed between carved eaves of pavilions in the foreground, the pagoda made a fine picture, as did a striking bright red circular window screen, the only other source of colour on grey walls amongst bare trees. In the forecourt, reddish wooden doors and a few red lanterns graced the main temple, and the same colour was used on the eaves of small pavilions housing the enormous bell and drum, normally familiar inclusions that I had not seen since Xi'an. A large *stele*, metal urn, and stone lantern completed the picture, and metal lions stood outside the red-walled entrance to another temple, which featured gold-studded red doors. Standing on a porch beneath heavily sculpted eaves, impressive larger-than-life guardians with ferocious faces and carrying weapons were enough to strike terror into the heart of many a wayward miscreant!

Extensive walls still encompassed part of the city, and from the ramparts I looked down on people riding through one of the gates and another of the many incongruous sights in this amazing country: at least ten billiard tables set up in the street, with people playing snooker as carts rumbled by, along with the constant procession of bicycles. Rural houses with uniquely shaped roofs had yards containing chickens, strings of chillies hanging to dry, carts, stacked saplings, baskets, and a donkey in a stable. Dried material like sugarcane or maize, used for fodder, was piled in a street. Hung with red lanterns, a tidy narrow lane led to sculpted panels, intricately carved doorways, fretwork on overhead balconies, and a serene pool reflecting a rotunda and humpbacked bridge; the scene was one of refined beauty mellowed with age.

Outside the walls, in a pastoral setting with a tethered cow sitting in the foreground, I stopped to film another isolated ancient structure having the appearance of a stage for itinerate actors. Back in the centre, I photographed the ornate entrance to a paved mall, and a brick façade with openwork panels depicting birds and red-and-white flowers. With snow now lying on the ground, yet another of the many ancient wooden temples featured stone lions, gnarled and twisted trees, *stelae*, enormous metal warriors, pavilions with carving on the curled corners of their tiered roofs (even on the ends of blue bamboo struts from which dried grass sprouted), and dragons winding around the wooden poles from which they were executed. Again, I composed a beautiful picture utilising a gateway for a frame. Except for the touch of blue and a few red pillars, all was the same dull grey as the overcast sky. I saw some delicate decoration beneath sagging eaves, a pond in an octagonal stone enclosure, bare trees, metal lions outside an entrance, a rotunda – and not a sole anywhere around.

Datong

Boarding the train for **Datong**, we passed houses and stacked logs covered with snow, one man shovelling, another pushing a bicycle (but few venturing out), and a white landscape that included bare trees and shrubs literally appearing as if made of lace. To my mind, the **Yungang Grottoes** of Datong were the best of the four that I visited. Carved into the perpendicular northern face of **Mount Wuzhou** more than 1,500 years ago (AD 460–524), the 53 caves stretched one kilometre and contained 51,000 Buddhist statues and bas-reliefs, the largest being the 17m (another source said 13.7m/44ft) seated **Sakyamuni Buddha**, with the familiar inscrutable but slightly amused expression. Lions graced the entrance to an ornate multilevel wooden pavilion built right into the cliff, its intricate eaves supported by verandah posts adorned with the antlered heads of gruesome mythical creatures. Snow lay on the ground, the curved roofs, and the mountaintop, and an attendant was clearing the latest fall from pathways to the caverns as I approached the most impressive, its entrance defined by substantial rock-hewn pillars. This contained a wealth of images on a red and blue background; larger figures with beautiful turquoise headdresses and sashes occupied recesses. Amongst the small figures were many-armed images like the Hindu god Shiva, and other caves housed several towering Buddhas with elongated earlobes, a couple with faint blue colouring on the dress. Smaller more-exposed unadorned niches and the statues they contained were without any colour but looked awesome against the lovely azure hue of the sky above. Altogether, the grottoes were an outstanding demonstration of devotion.

Yungang Grottos

En route to visit a monastery, I stopped to photograph a blue tiled three dragon wall, a glaring addition to the drab surroundings. Considered to bring good fortune, these were also a familiar part of Chinese culture and varied in size, but always with an odd number of dragons. Surrounded by snow and bare trees, a red-walled temple complex contained a blue wall with seven gilt dragons, which I filmed through a circular opening. Sadly, again I was unable to film any of the opulent interiors.

Hohhot

Arriving in **Hohhot** (Green Town in Mongolian), capital of the autonomous region of **Inner Mongolia**, interesting streets scenes included people rugged up against the intense cold, food stalls, and a jumble of hardware, with a light dusting of snow, completely obstructing the footpath: pipes, brooms, basins and baskets being amongst the clutter. Hovering overhead, a red, white and blue hot air balloon released showers of paper, a man was chopping meat, a tall red temple stood in the midst of shops, and a convoy of bicycles loaded with brooms was wheeled past. A monastery containing another large dragon wall also featured curled eaves adorned with the legendary beasts, as well as small decorative spires. Tall metal lanterns, their tops white with snow, stood in the courtyard.

In other street scenes, smoke plumed from chimney pipes and vapour from the mouths of people, and a row of carts sold, amongst other items, fruits, strings of garlic, and some type of green tied in bundles and covered with a cloth. Indicative of the industry of the region, one man (with earflaps on his fur hat) stood with a basket of coal, and snow cloaked the woodpiles and sagging roofs of derelict-looking buildings, from a couple of which dry grass still sprouted. People stamped their feet against the cold, and most wore gloves. It was amusing to see puffed up chickens on window sills and huddled together for warmth on the bar, seat and pillion of a bicycle! Decorative window treatment consisting of colourful patterns inserted behind wooden grilles was a common feature of the town, and red washing on a line brightened the scene in a compound where a dog surveyed me with interest – but was too cold to bark! I saw sheep penned in one yard and loose in another, a big black sow in a sty, geese, metal drums, sacks of potatoes, heaps of snow-covered coal, bundles of saplings, and a donkey in an enclosure with crumbling brick walls. More geese strutted near a man drawing water from a well in the street, and I filmed many deserted alleyways. Snow lying everywhere even beautified mounds of rubble, making the depressing conditions appear pretty. I came upon more vendor carts, these stocked with strange greens, root vegetables, cauliflowers protected from the cold by a blanket, bread, and fish including a large red variety, which people carried threaded on string. A man wearing the familiar fur hat (the earmuffs sticking out) was marketing citrus fruits, another hardware outlet, with pans and copper articles amongst the brooms and so on had ceramic bowls stored on the roof, and a man puffing at a smoking pipe stood selling produce from sacks beside the fire in a drum, the flu also belching smoke.

The **Huayan Sutra Pagoda**, also known as the **Ten Thousand Volumes of Avatamasake Sutra Pagoda**, but more simply **White Tower** because of its light colour, was an impressive eight-sided 45m (147ft) wood and brick structure. Built between 983 and 1031, it had embossed images around two lower levels, and with snow gently falling in a delicate white curtain onto the white environs from a white sky, it made a wonderful subject for pictures. A group of men were gathered beneath bare trees to trade sheepskins loaded onto bicycles, and from my hotel window I looked down on a garden with snow blanketing marble-railed stone bridges, covered walkways, rotundas, a frozen stream, and trees. These included a few evergreen firs but the remainder, even the willows, were denuded of leaves. I ventured into it but was soon forced back by the bitter cold; my numb fingers could not even operate the camera so I beat a hasty retreat indoors. It was actually the last time that I was to use the movie camera because conditions caused something inside to crack.

An attractive temple with an unusual cupola made a nice backdrop to breads and biscuits being displayed on upended baskets, and a couple of people sold oranges and bananas outside shops with smoking chimneys, artwork under eaves, and red woodwork. A grey brick wall was illustrated with large paintings of a tiger, a man on horseback, a warrior figure, and traditional Chinese scenery. I found a complex of single-storey pavilions with simple roof decoration, and even shops featured the red pillars and roofs with curled corners. Bicycles and carts were prevalent, but I saw no cars in the icy conditions. Another unusual temple, guardians in relief around its base, had several tiered spires adorned with myriad Buddha images.

Beijing

Flying over a sea of white, with mountains completely enveloped in snow, I finally reached **Beijing**. With a history dating back 3,000 years, and China's capital since the reign of Genghis Khan in 1215, it was the last port of call in this huge country. My first visit was to the vast **Tiananmen Square**, largest city square in the world, with pavilions atop the monstrous red walls of the **Forbidden City** or **Palace Museum**. Commenced in 1406, this Imperial Palace of the Ming and Qing dynasties had 9,999 rooms in 800 buildings and covered an area of 180 acres. On top of an unusual carved column, a dragon stood guard before a bridge to the main **Gate of Heavenly Peace**, still with a portrait of Chairman Mao overhead. Inside the gate, I photographed the buildings through arches and the beautiful lacework of bare branches. A series of white marble bridges led to pavilions in front of which sat large metal lions wearing the green patina of aged copper. As distinct from summer, when crowds flew kites in the main square outside the walls, there were few people in the immense snow-carpeted courtyard. Steps flanking a mammoth sculpted panel featuring dragons in high relief, led to more pavilions, and other large metal objects included a crane or heron, a turtle, lanterns, and huge gleaming bowls. Doors were embossed with delicate gilding, and carving beautified tops of marble railing. A red wall with green enamelwork was located behind a golden lion, the claws of its right paw clutching a gold orb, and tiny animals decorated roof ridges, but for such an enormous and important venue it was surprisingly simple. The white *stupa* of Beihai Park was visible over rooftops, and gnarled trees surrounded pavilions that graced the city's gardens at the rear. Flowers, animals and leaves were etched into paving, and a kneeling copper or brass elephant guarded the exit. The Palace Museum is described more fully in the later chapter on China.

The frozen moat, a venue for pleasure craft in summer, made marvellous pictures with the green willows, now just a network of fine branches, framing the high walls and pavilions. This brought me back to Tiananmen Square with the 36m (118ft) **Obelisk** and massive **Monument to the People's Heroes**, depicting figures of soldiers, peasants, workers and women from the 1949 Communist Revolution.

My next visit took me to the Qing dynasty **Summer Palace**, now a public recreational area on the shores of **Lake Kunming**, with pavilions, temples, rotundas and bridges set in splendid gardens. Being winter, the lake was frozen, a fact of which the populace took advantage to ice skate. I was greeted by a dragon-like folkloric beast with antlers, and a stone bridge led to a small island from which a gleaming golden path, created by the lowering sun, crossed the ice. Skaters in front of hills with pavilions lodged amongst bare trees were the subject of more good pictures. Snow lay on roofs, a number of which were enhanced with tiny animals, and traditional art graced a few walls. Filmed behind naked branches, an elaborate pagoda and a pavilion with decorated eaves and roof capping made stunning pictures, as did a small humpbacked bridge with a rotunda on top, in the middle of the lake. The 7,228m (7,655 yard) **Long Corridor** was a covered gallery full of frescoes with mythical themes, and the ultimate in kitsch was the Empress Dowager's white marble paddle steamboat 'marooned' in the ice beside a pathway bordered by lotus-topped pillars, its vibrant stained-glass panels striking when lit by the rays of the setting sun. More lovely bridges, pavilions with red posts, and bare but still graceful willows made for excellent photography. Twenty-four emperors ruled from here, each of their imperial edicts concluding with the traditional exhortation 'Tremble and obey'! The turbulent history of the capital makes fascinating reading but is too long to relate in these pages.

My next destination necessitated a train trip from the city, but unfortunately I have forgotten the name, although it was obviously another palace, with pavilions, pagodas and bridges in an ocean of white. Ice crystals on glass created amazing patterns that glittered in the dim light. There were a few evergreens, but in the main, except for the orange orb of the low-lying sun, the environment was a monochrome shade of grey. Beautiful reflections, which were missing at the Summer Palace, appeared in a patch of motionless unfrozen water.

I visited two mammoth monasteries in a built-up area, the first with a multilevel red temple, tall metal lanterns, many *stupa*-like structures on rooftops, red-and-white buildings, a monk in maroon robes, and fretwork screens. From afar, the enormous lamasery looked like a miniature Potala Palace in Lhasa and was obviously Tibetan in origin. Shining green tiles decorated a red wall with elaborate pavilions above its arched gateway and a stone lion in front. Wearing a crown, a life-sized stone elephant with long tusks knelt in a court, its forelegs bent forwards in an impossible angle at the knees. The roof of one pavilion was adorned with the undulating serpentine bodies of slender dragons, and there were tiny animal figures and temple bells on the corners of eaves. A towering green pagoda completed the excursion. The return journey passed rural housing, high mountains, a partially frozen river running through a gorge, and many fields spread with a cloth of low-hanging mist.

I went next to the remarkable **Temple of Heaven** (also described later), where I entered through a series of carved stone gates and filmed the various round pavilions through successive arches, the final ascent to the **Temple of Prayer for Good Harvests** reached via steps between tiered railings. The smaller of two ornate halls, the **Imperial Vault of Heaven**, contained tablets of the gods of the firmament and elements: sun, moon, stars, rain, wind, thunder and lightning. Built in 1530, it also had a **Whispering** or **Echo Wall** where, by speaking to the stonework, one could telegraph their voice to a person some distance around it.

I visited a pet market, where I saw birds in a cage suspended from the handlebars of a bicycle, people inspecting and haggling over goldfish in plastic bags of water, other fish in basins or jars, and grey or white rabbits just sitting on top of a basket. I went to **Beihai Park**, begun in the tenth century, with its **White Dagoba** (*stupa*) and **Temple of Everlasting Peace** (both built in 1651), pavilions, bridges and willows, but the foggy conditions prohibited good photography. A Chinese opera was performed in an open pavilion, the artists in red and pink costumes with ornate headdresses, and on the frozen lake, a large group of skaters executed professional-looking manoeuvres that included impressive spins.

One could not visit China without seeing the **Great Wall**. Constructed more than 2,600 years ago, it stretched over 5,400km, with watchtowers at strategic points. Being winter, it was comparatively devoid of the summer crowds and exuded a wonderful ambience, with views of the wall snaking over undulating hills and mountain tops before disappearing into the distance. It was wide enough for four horsemen to ride abreast, and in places I was surprised at how steep it was. The impact of its concept and achievement was made even more remarkable by the terrain; set in a landscape of snow, bare trees, and austere mountains, it projected an even more daunting spectacle. My last tour was to the **Ming Tombs**, with impressive larger-than-life statues lining the **Triumphal Route** or **Sacred Way**, their job being to guard and advise the emperor in the afterlife.

On the banks of a great river in the province of Cathay there is an ancient city of great size and splendour so wrote Marco Polo, the first 'tourist' in Beijing.

Interesting facts: the remains of the first known human settlement, dating back to 700,000 BC, were found southwest of Beijing; Mandarin is the world's most commonly spoken language, followed by Spanish, English and Hindi; China gave the world gunpowder, paper, printing, and the compass, and despite being the largest country on earth, there is only one time zone; chopsticks are the oldest form of eating utensil and China manufactures 60 billion disposable pairs each year, the equivalent of some 25 million trees!

In conclusion, I found travel in China to be challenging and frustrating, yet enlightening, exciting, and at times even amusing.

BALI 1992

In 1992, I operated my second group tour to Bali and Sulawesi in Indonesia.

My main memories of this trip are of cultural shows in **Bali**. Graceful Balinese dancers with long curved fingers, dressed in beautiful costumes with frangipani tiaras atop cascading jet-black tresses, performed to a tinny gamelan orchestra made up of metal xylophones, *trompongs*, huge tuned gongs, flutes and drums. Another act introduced a god or demon attired in an elaborate outfit with beaded fringes and the glitter of sequins. This was followed by bird figures with 'wings' and gilded bird headdresses, even the toes of their bare feet curling like talons. A girl wearing a tall golden crown, gold necklace and gold armlets, which augmented her colourful costume of bright yellow and shimmering green, executed jerky side to side head movements and rolled large expressive dark eyes. She was joined by a male dancer waving a fan and garbed in exotic tones of purple and gold. Unfortunately, I have no information about the meaning of these dances.

At a second venue, two girls in floral headdresses and elaborate multihued costumes performed the **Legong Dance**, which told stories from the *Ramayana*. The hero of this Hindu epic is Rama, the eighth reincarnation of Lord Vishnu. In the **Barong Dance** (described in Asia 1974), a comedy routine was followed by the fierce masked figure of Kalika wearing a costume of feathers and flaring bands of colourful cloth and a performer on stilts with the Monkey King. The dance tells of the eternal battle between good and evil, and the extremely fanciful Barong (representing good) and mythological monster Rangda (representing evil) entered in the final act. The show concluded with the **Kris Dance**: men 'spearing' their chests with the lethal *krises*. The stage was set with bamboo decorations and statues of gods in typical Balinese black and white checked sarongs. I have an explanation for the Barong play and Kris dance, but it is long and complicated and can be picked up in Bali. Another popular form of entertainment in Indonesia was the *wayang kulit* (shadow play), in which a puppeteer manipulated fretwork figures silhouetted by lamps onto a screen.

As part of the tour we visited a village with thatched cottages, ducks on cobbled pathways, a pig in a brick pen, thatched shrines, and neat gardens with colourful crotons; few places in the world can rival Bali for lush tropical plants in immaculate surrounds. At the conclusion, we stopped at a viewpoint overlooking **Lake Batur**, surrounded by jagged green mountains and a distant volcano. The lake itself was located in an old caldera with **Mt Batur** in the middle.

Displayed for sale, quilts in gay hues lined the roadside.

I have no pictorial record of the **Sulawesi** portion of this trip.

ENGLAND, GREECE, PORTUGAL & SPAIN 1992

ENGLAND

I began my holiday in the living picture book that is **England**, in a typical town with tubs and baskets of flowers outside red brick and stuccoed walls, lace curtains in bay and multi-paned windows, and moss-covered tiled roofs. Small patches of bright green lawn fronted creeper-bedecked walls of houses with gabled attic windows and tiny porticos, one with a vivid green door in a white wall. Carriageways led into courtyards, and there were white half-timbered walls, lanterns, flower boxes, and colourful street beds. Standing outside the white façade of the George Hotel was an ancient yellow carriage; a brick building, painted white, had a red shingled roof and muntined windows, and the XVIIth Century Royal Inn was a picture with a mass of flowers, ivy-adorned stone walls, and tall brick chimneys on its slate roof. A yellow stone edifice had a pediment with carved figures, a red vine enhanced another wall, and I observed a square Norman tower. White woolly sheep grazed on incredibly green grass on the banks of a lake, crossed by a stone bridge, which afforded stunning reflections. The next village revealed a white house with cobalt blue trim, multihued baskets and red pot plants, an old-fashioned hand-operated pump on a grassy common, and half-timbered houses in plaster- or brickwork with thatched roofs and shutters, one in a chocolate box garden setting.

thatched cottage

The promenade at **Brighton** exhibited trees and colourful flowerbeds in extensive green lawns. Travelling through **Bodmin Moor**, we came to **Jamaica Inn**, which featured in the novel of the same name by Daphne du Maurier. Lying in a bleak cobbled courtyard and shrouded in brooding mist off the moor, it projected a forbidding atmosphere; one could almost imagine the smugglers still lurking thereabouts. An attractive white adobe cottage near a rocky headland had tiny windows in its walls and an eyebrow window in the thickly thatched roof.

I was travelling with an English friend from Perth, and we drove to a fantastic attraction of which, regrettably, I have forgotten the name, portraying scale models of famous landmarks from around the world in outstanding botanical surrounds. Mt Rushmore reposed on green lawns with a brilliant red floral display; the Statue of Liberty, with an authentic green copper tone, stood amid massed blossoms of red, white and yellow; Easter Island *moai* were arrayed on a swathe of green planted with blue, orange, yellow, bright pink and white flowers interspersed with clipped bushes; native huts on stilts were lodged behind pampas; a miniature English half-timbered white manor house was also surrounded by pleasant gardens; a Scandinavian stave church was located next to an image of Buddha; the Taj Mahal was complete even to the reflecting pool lined with shrubs trimmed to represent the pencil pines; a Japanese temple stood in a lake bordered by rock and typical trees, and the Sphinx and Pyramids looked out of place in a green setting with a glorious burst of azaleas in the foreground! France was represented by the Eiffel Tower; Stonehenge sat atop a green mound; Greek-themed balalaika music played at a white Parthenon with a sculpted pediment, which looked striking on green lawn with vibrant red flowers; a copper replica of Denmark's Little Mermaid sat on a rock beside a pool; a red, white and green Dutch windmill nestled in blooms of red and yellow was reflected in a pond, and a helmeted statue with a trident and shield bearing the Union Jack in her right hand, an olive branch in the left, was Britannia. Italy's contribution was the Leaning Tower of Pisa and Michelangelo's *David*, the latter standing in flowers near a red maple. The superb gardens were just as enticing as the monuments, and a bed of red flowers in the shape of a cross lay at the foot of Christ the Redeemer, his arms outspread, from Corcovado, Argentina. Music was piped throughout the venue.

Cornwall

We moved on to one of Cornwall's picturesque enclosed harbours, its stone quays and fishing boats overlooked by quaint houses on slopes above. By boasting a beach, this one was a little different, and a couple of homes perched on an outcrop of rock surrounded by crashing breakers were connected to the mainland by a small bridge.

The next places of interest were a typical street of shops with at least one inn, a coastal walk past tiny houses on a windy grass-covered rocky promontory, and a barren point with black stone formations erupting from the ocean like Victoria's Twelve Apostles along the Great Ocean Road in Australia. Another delightful small harbour, providing moorage for sail- and fishing boats, had bells of a carillon tolling to vie with the call of seagulls flying overhead.

English harbour

Here, I found both coloured and stone walls, candy-striped awnings, and a building with entrances on parallel streets at different levels. The Clipper Restaurant had pots of flowers on the pavement and an appropriate anchor on the façade, whilst an attractive stone structure was beautified with a mass of blossom around the door. A sign reading Please Do Not Tap On The Window was taped to the glass of a shopfront, behind which slept a contented ginger cat (real) beside white ceramic felines painted with flowers.

two cats

Also on display were a chess set, an equestrian statue, model boats and a picture of sailing ships, an illustration of an owl in an ornate frame, telescopes, books, and figurines. A man walked down the street wearing a large pink corsage, top hat and tails. Investigating interesting thoroughfares lined with coloured façades, I found alms houses dated 1875 in a cul-de-sac, a stone half-timbered pub called The London Inn, and other stone and shingled buildings with bay windows.

A second charming harbour, with fishing boats anchored on extremely blue water and houses on encompassing green hills, was approached down a steep street lined with little stone or whitewashed dwellings having shingled roofs and colourful doors.

Cornish fishing village

Old-fashioned lamps and plants in tubs enhanced alleys narrow even by English standards, and with its distinctly crooked upper storey, the white shingled (with black trim) Harbour Café presented a wonderful subject for pictures. Seagulls floated near the pebble shore, and a red rowing boat was pulled up on the beach below houses with mossy roofs, one with a stone wall painted pink, a white balcony, and white window frames. More wandering revealed an old-style hand pump in the street, multi-paned windows – behind one of which another ginger cat sat sunning itself – creepers hanging over leaning stone walls and, above an alley, a wooden structure with windows and a shingled roof connecting buildings either side. In an anomaly, The Golden Lion was also painted pink! Narrow cobbled lanes led past cottages with quaint names such as The Sail Loft and Smugglers Rest, and Frank and I took tea in the sunshine, sitting at tables and chairs outside the Slipway Hotel.

village streets

Continuing our walk up and down steep streets, we came to a white house with attic windows and a gorgeous display of pink, yellow and red roses behind its iron fence. Creeper surrounded the doorway of another dwelling, and I found white walls with blue doors and window frames – even blue downpipes. Cannon reposed on ramparts with incredible views of the water, which was deep blue but green in the shallows, the town, and green hills beyond. Boats were hauled up in the centre near the crooked café, which had window boxes on one side.

village centre

Retracing my steps down the narrow passageway with the overhead structure and hanging baskets, the ginger cat behind the window now sat gazing with interest at the passing parade, and all the while the haunting sounds of seagulls were carried on the air.

quaint alley

We enjoyed a second Cornish tea in a tiny courtyard in front of the Old School Hotel with its spired clock tower. Other sights included a gaudy pink and blue stone building and the XIV Century Cornish Fudge Shop, with attic windows in its bowed slate roof.

Devon

Pausing just for pictures of stone buildings on the bank of a swiftly flowing estuary at the foot of hills, we progressed to one of the most picturesque villages in the whole of Britain: **Clovelly**, on the north coast of **Devon**. I had stayed in a delightful whitewashed thatched cottage in this captivating hamlet on a previous visit, and the elderly landlady professed to remember me. It was the first time that I had seen an antique pottery hot water bottle, produced by my hostess to warm my bed! No cars were allowed in the town, which in any event would have proved impossible; visitors and locals alike parked at the top and negotiated steep cobbled streets by foot, some transporting goods on wooden sleds! Prolific plants and flowers beautified the pastel and whitewashed houses all year round but particularly in spring. I observed a small store called The Donkey Shop, tiny porches, hanging baskets, tubs in every nook and cranny, vines on walls, minute garden plots, colourful window boxes, red creeper on a stone façade (painted white) with a green door, pots mounting moss-covered steps, and vistas of the harbour far below, the boats high and dry behind a solid seawall. Outside Clovelly I found a stunning cottage called Disneys Olde Thatched Inn, with all but the fan shaped attic window hidden by a blaze of blossom and low fir trees.

estuary houses and Clovelly

Lining the main road of a bigger town was a row of attached Edwardian houses with bay windows on upper and lower levels. We attended a water display featuring fountains illuminated by coloured lights, erupting in different patterns of spray that moved to music. We came to a rocky bay with emerald slopes and turquoise water, but it had begun to rain quite steadily as we arrived at a town ascending a hillside, its narrow streets on different levels. Attractive buildings faced a stone quay sheltering small boats, at the end of which stood a lighthouse.

stone quay and lighthouse

I think it was the location for scenes from the film *The French Lieutenant's Woman*.

We moved on to another of my favourite villages, also visited for the second time: a charming and photogenic cluster of thatched cottages called **Selworthy**, with muntined windows, tiny thatched porticos, and a profusion of beautiful plants and flowers. Rain was still falling continuously and dripping from my umbrella as I attempted to take photographs, but nothing could spoil the ambience of this idyllic special place.

Avon and Cheshire

Continuing through **Bristol** – with row houses featuring groups of chimney pots and iron-railed balconies, an impressive building with Ionic pilasters and a sculpted crest on the pediment, hanging baskets on lampposts, and the **Clifton Suspension Bridge** over the densely wooded gorge of the **River Avon** – we came to the unique town of **Chester**. Distinctive streets in the shopping district, called **Rows**, were thought to date back to the late 1200s. The half-timbering on the wonderful old buildings came in a multitude of different designs. One façade, with a decorated gable and carved eaves, also featured rosettes in squares formed by the wooden framework, itself bearing embossed anchors; the words GODS · PROVIDENCE · IS · MINE · INHERITANCE inscribed underneath. Two red brick clock towers with attractive spires appeared one behind the other, and the 1897 clock above **Eastgate** was enhanced with delicate iron filigree and a copper cupola. A red brick building was accented by white quoins, and there was a plethora of black and white half-timbered structures, one with carved figures embellishing the timber arches of its windows and coats of arms adorning the façade below. I came across arcades and lighted windows with tiny panes, and the skyline was broken by a maze of tall chimneys, towers and cupolas. Ye Olde Boot Inn featured decorative carving on brackets.

We climbed for a view of the bustling street from under the Eastgate clock, and followed the medieval ramparts around the city to where they overlooked Roman relics. The Romans established the city as an army base in AD 70, and the remnants included plinths, a few columns, building ruins, and a colourful mosaic set in lawn, all surrounded by lovely green and plum-coloured trees. Also visible from the wall was a row of elaborate shingle-roofed half-timbered houses adjoining a larger building of similar structure bearing the words THE : FEAR : OF : THE : LORD : IS : A : FOUNTAIN : OF : LIFE. Further on, I obtained a view of the river crossed by a stone bridge with a prominent church spire in the background. Unusual illustrated signs to add to my collection included the Bear & Billet, Cross Foxes, with the red antagonists challenging each other, one simply called Ye Olde Inn bearing a head from the Shakespearean era and, on Ye Olde Custom House Inn, a colourful scene appearing to incorporate a gallows. Window boxes and baskets were once again prevalent, a light-coloured brick church stood behind a decorative iron fence, and a striking building in a combination of red brick and black and white half-timbering featured a cluster of chimneys and both round and angular turrets, the latter with gabled windows in the conical shingled roof. Large trees, low conifers, and multihued flowerbeds lay in spacious lawns near a multi-spired stone church, and the plaque on a stone tower commemorated the place where King Charles stood to witness the defeat of his army on **Rowton Moor** in 1645. Back on the ramparts, lit at night with old-fashioned lamps, more river vistas and birdlife were revealed. Chester was the only English city with its medieval walls wholly intact, and its **Cathedral** was built between 1250 and 1540.

Chester

Cumbria: Lake District

Country roads with rolling green hills, tall trees with autumn tones amongst the green on the banks of a quiet stream crossed by a little stone bridge, grazing sheep in fields delineated by timber fences, low stone walls or trees, white farmhouses, the **Pennine Hills** and mountains beyond – this was the **Lake District**, where birds and sailboats floated on the water, and pretty towns were massed with flowers. Smoke wafted lazily from chimneys of whitewashed and stone houses lining a narrow rural lane with coloured trees. An exceptional dwelling, one entire wall covered with hanging baskets and red-flowering tubs along the foundations, stood opposite a colourful garden established on the green roadside verge. The fine weather had changed, and in the ensuing (temporary) foggy conditions, we drove over cobbled roads past stone buildings and white façades, crossed a second stone bridge, and observed pastoral scenes of very white sheep on startling green meadows. The next village we arrived at was the stuff of dreams: a collection of slate-roofed stone houses with tiny white-framed windows set amid gardens and verdant greenery; a vine, its leaves turning red, covered one wall. They were situated on the banks of a swiftly running river falling in boisterous cascades and flowing under a stone bridge; however, even the roar of the water could not drown the birdsong. Herriots Hotel (of *All Creatures Great and Small* fame) was located here, the village church visible behind high moss-topped stone walls to one side. Another wall was adorned with a red and green vine, window boxes containing bright blue, lemon and white flowers, and a lantern.

stone houses and bridge

Following yellow-green fields, we came to a church with a Norman tower, a small grassed square outside its stone fence almost entirely taken up by a lichen-covered stone cross. Within the village, a stone house set on a pocket handkerchief green lawn with rich blue flowers in pots was almost completely hidden beneath creeper, only its white door and window frames exposed. The Riverdale Country Lane Hotel, with colourful flowerbeds at the base of its stone walls, provided picnic tables and benches on the narrow green verge. A stone bridge afforded views of thickly grouped green and yellow trees on the banks of a river and stone houses surrounded by lush lawns. A series of small communities presented peaceful postcard scenes, including a row of attached houses opposite a grassy median strip, a horse grazing on a village green, a little church with a tall steeple, and a two-storey house with white windows peeping out from red vines inundating its walls and chimney. We stopped on another bridge to film forest with moss-covered trees beside a rowdy river tumbling in stepped falls.

pretty river

Conditions were again foggy, and behind stone fences, ruins on a distant hillside emerged from the mist. It was a thrill to see a pheasant amongst bleating long-tailed black-faced sheep browsing in a meadow. At one stage, we had to stop for a flock of these sooty-faced animals running along the road.

Yorkshire

Approaching historic **York**, we came to a tower gate embellished with crests and flanked by bastions. Viewed from a height, the imposing Gothic **Cathedral** (1220–1480) loomed behind impressive buildings set in beautiful gardens and green lawns. On an evening stroll, we found leaning shops and, flanked by red brick buildings, a half-timbered structure with muntined windows, twin gables, and a distinct bow in the centre. In narrow pedestrian streets, creepers formed a green umbrella overhead and the Minster was visible at the end. Shading the alleys, jutting upper levels (a technique called jettying) were a feature, and the surrounds of a busy outdoor produce market were a mix of half-timbered and brick buildings with red tiled roofs, bay windows, and bright flower baskets. Also enhanced with a colourful hanging basket, a particularly memorable half-timbered structure had attic windows in the red tiled roof and a sagging black and white upper storey. This protruded above multi-paned bay windows in half-timbered walls with red bricks laid in a decorative pattern. A high point offered another view of the pale-toned Minster behind lawns and trees, and from a bridge I saw stone buildings and a red brick edifice with many chimneys, gabled attic windows, and a rounded corner. A team of eight was rowing a single-masted boat on the river.

old half-timbered building

We moved to the site of a ruined abbey reminiscent of Glastonbury, with arched windows standing aloof and open to the sky. Remains of the 13th-century two-storey quatrefoil **Clifford's Tower**, built by Henry III as the keep of York Castle, stood on a mound in the heart of the city. In a square encompassed by substantial but boring constructions, the ringing of a bell alerted us to the town crier, splendidly arrayed in a tricorn hat, white shirt (a jabot at the throat), red waistcoat, long blue jacket, black pants, white leggings and black shoes, who read news of 'This twenty-fifth day of September in the year of Our Lord 1992' from a scroll that included items about the then Prime Minister, John Major, and 'this day in history', which saw the first blood transfusion in 1880.

York Castle Museum

The **York Castle Museum** presented glimpses of past everyday life in reproductions of ancient shops back to 1580, some possibly still standing today, the William IV pub in Edwardian Half Moon Court, and a Victorian Police Station on faithfully recreated lamp-lit **Kirkgate**, also exhibiting a horse-drawn hansom cab.

York was also home to the fascinating **Yorvik Viking Centre**, built over the site of an authentic dig where remains were unearthed when the city demolished existing buildings in order to undertake an agenda of redevelopment. Complete houses, utensils and clothing, and workshops still containing tools from a civilisation buried for a thousand years, were uncovered beneath **Coppergate** (a Viking street) by archaeologists. One could board a time capsule to be whisked from WW11 back through the centuries to Norman times and experience the sounds, sights and smells of a bustling market, craftsmen working in antler and wood, smoky houses with the family gathered around a hearth, and a busy river wharf, recreated in accurate detail with a rowing boat and fully rigged sailing ship, in the city of Yorvik (the Viking name for York) in Viking Britain. The ride finished at the reconstructed dig and a display of delicate objects found, including woollen socks, oriental silk, coins, and even blackberry seeds, all remarkably preserved by the waterlogged soil. Sounds were recorded in Old Norse, and the smells that would have permeated the ancient streets, from fresh fruits in the market and a tasty stew for an evening meal to less appetising odours of pig styes and backyards, were created by heating various aromatic oils. York, founded by the Romans in AD 71 as an army post, was England's second largest city when seized by the Vikings. Losing the settlement when King Eric Bloodaxe was expelled in 954, the Scandinavians retained influence under the rule of Anglo-Saxon Earls until the Norman Conquest in 1066.

Leaving York, we came to the fairy-tale village of **Great Tew** where, set in tiny patches of green grass with hedges, trees, coloured foliage, and a few flowers, we found an avenue of yellowing stone cottages with steeply pitched thatched roofs, red and green vines on walls, and muntined windows. The Union Jack flew from a flagpole and a red vine covered the façade of the Falkland Arms, which also sported a sign bearing a shield flanked by a lion and unicorn. Containing a dovecote with white feathered inhabitants, a garden overlooked fields and trees displaying a multitude of greens from yellowish-lime to rich emerald. Iron gates between solid stone pillars provided entrance to a large yellow stone manor with white quoins, its façade beautified by brilliant red creeper on free-standing stone gables crowned with small spires. An attractive stone building with a tall chimney on its red tiled roof and a porch with an arched door had the appearance of a church and stood on green turf behind a roughly laid stone fence.

Great Tew

Church bells rang out over the streets of **Wootton**, and baskets hung on the stone wall of the Post Office Store, which had a tea room at the back that we entered for a light meal. A large collection of embossed ceramic plates picturing cottages and country scenes such as a mill and waterwheel decorated the walls, whilst a clock, pottery ducks and other sundry items stood on a buffet and old dolls on shelves. Narrow roads between stone houses led to green fields, and we found ancient half-timbered buildings and a stone structure with a turret and square clock tower. Two inquisitive terriers sat behind a window, and a well-tended churchyard had perfectly shaped conical trees surrounding gravestones on green grass.

Gloucestershire: Cotswolds

Progressing to another of my favourite destinations, **Lower Slaughter** in the **Cotswolds**, I filmed the two-storey stone cottages with attics in their steep shingled roofs, tiny porticos, coloured creepers climbing above doors and enhancing walls, flowers and shrubs along foundations, and a strip of green grass in front, all reflected, together with ducks, in a small trilling stream crossed by little white wooden bridges. This enchanting waterway ran through the village to a red brick mill and working waterwheel at the end. The yellowing stone shone golden in the sunlight as two riders went past on horseback, and geese commandeered another patch of lawn.

Lower Slaughter

Our next stop was a busy wide thoroughfare featuring a mixture of brick, stone and half-timbered buildings, one of the latter with three matching gables and the familiar sag in the middle. A Celtic cross stood at the top of the road leading down to fields beyond the town. One stone building, with an archway leading to a courtyard, had glass panes in decidedly crooked frames. Stone fences enclosed a colourful garden, and a village pond mirrored white houses, a cross on the green common, geese, and ducks with ducklings. The images were so clear that the ducks appeared to be walking upside down. Roses were planted around yet another cross on a village green and also climbed walls of white thatched houses behind. My final pictures were of a pale-toned cathedral beyond a park with birds and a lake.

village green with swans

I also recall visiting **Oxford**, a seat of learning since the 12th century with 28 collages, and **Woodstock**, site of **Blenheim Palace**, where Sir Winston Churchill was born in 1874, its grounds landscaped by Capability Brown.

GREECE

The history of **Greece** is complicated, but interesting, and involves, amongst others, the Minoan civilisation, the Mycenaeans, Dorians, Spartans, Persians, Peloponnese, Macedonians, Romans, Goths, Vandals and Huns in quick succession. It then became the Byzantine Empire until Constantinople was captured by the Turks in 1453. The Crusaders also featured, as did of course the highly educated Alexander the Great, who was tutored by Aristotle. Greece was the complete antithesis of the leafy highways and byways of England.

Athens

My introduction to **Athens** was a large cathedral with symmetrical tall slender bell towers flanking its dome and a colourful mosaic on the façade above the triple-arched entrance. Outside, I found a strange character with a white beard, a sign (in Greek) around his neck, holding a cross, and seated astride a dappled white horse. From a rooftop with tubs of red geraniums, I caught my first sight of the Parthenon, sacred temple of Athena, atop its sheer rock plateau towering above the city and, to one side below, temple ruins surrounded by trees. In the centre of the famed Plaka district, oldest in Athens, I procured a tiny bare room in the hotel of the same name but with a stunning view of the **Acropolis**. A powerful Mycenaean city in 1400 BC, declared province of the gods by the Delphic oracle in 510 BC, and the most important ancient monument in the Western world, I could lie in bed and watch as its Parthenon changed colour in the sound and light show at night! This old Turkish quarter with its narrow labyrinthine streets was the centre of the ancient capital. Nearby, was the appealing stone structure of the **Monastiraki Church**, with a red tiled dome and roof.

view with Parthenon in the background

That evening, I watched the sunset at the archaeological site of **Cape Sounion**, where the **Temple of Poseidon** (444 BC) and a few remains of the sanctuary of **Athena Sounias** stood on a craggy spur that plunged 65m to the sea. Of the original 34 broadly fluted Doric columns of the temple, 15 remained, with lintels balanced on top, to take on a warm glow against a vivid blue sky. Silhouetted against the sun with the ocean as a backdrop, the rays burst between like gleaming golden stars. That night, I wandered an alley with goods from shops displayed outside. In the background, the whole Acropolis was lit by red light, the monument on top standing starkly white against an inky black sky.

Next morning, I reached the huge **Plateia Syntagmatos** (**Syntagma Square**), surrounded by ugly concrete blocks of modern edifices and full of pigeons, in time for the changing of the guard at the **Tomb of the Unknown Soldier** in front of the **Parliament Building**, prior palace of Greece's first king, Otto. Dressed in red caps with long tassels, belted khaki tunics above white leggings with black tassels behind the knees, and comical red shoes with large black pompoms, these very tall guardsmen (*evzones*) stood at attention and then executed an ungainly ritual. This consisted of raising one leg horizontal, bending at the knee, lifting again, and then scuffing the foot before marching in hesitant goose steps whilst raising and lowering the right arm in salute, the left holding a rifle over the shoulder.

I made the long worthwhile climb up 277m (1,000ft) **Lykavittos** (a.k.a. **Lycabettus**, Hill of Wolves), the highest of eight hills around Athens and crowned with the small white **Chapel of Agios Georgios** (St George), for extensive vistas of the enormous sprawling city and environs. I could identify the Parthenon and remains of the **Temple of Olympian Zeus** in a dry dusty compound surrounded by many trees. This latter, largest in Greece, was begun in the sixth century BC and finally completed by Hadrian in AD 131, over 700 years later. Returning to the interesting streets of the **Plaka**, from many of which the Acropolis was visible, I came across a man turning the handle of a barrel organ, and looking back at the hill that I had just descended, the white cupolas of the chapel stood out. The interior of the **Cathedral** was typical of the richly ornamented Greek churches: paintings of angels and saints, Christ in the dome, and elaborate scenes on walls. At the foot of the 156m-high Acropolis I found a six-sided structure with well-preserved deep relief of winged images. Ruins of the **Roman Agora** included a pediment atop fluted columns, remains of slender white pillars, a scattering of carved blocks, and a stone jar behind remnants of low walls. It was at the **Ancient Agora** to the west, that Socrates spent many hours expounding his philosophy; Greece was credited with inventing this science, along with classical music, drama, logic, physics and the Olympics.

My next destination was the famous **Parthenon**, which I found, disappointingly, to be in a state of disrepair. Built of marble between 447 and 438 BC, and consisting of 46 fluted columns supporting pediments and sculpted friezes, this was the largest Doric temple, attesting to the glory of Greece. It was commissioned by Pericles to serve as a treasury and to house the giant statue of Athena, considered one of the wonders of the ancient world. Finished in 432 BC, this image was made of gold plate over a wooden frame and stood 12m tall on its pedestal. The face, hands and feet were of ivory, and jewels fashioned the eyes. Many of the pieces that once adorned the exterior of the Parthenon were on show in the on-site museum, but I did see three (probably replicas) that remained in situ. Two small headless figures lay in an embrace under the solitary capping stone of a pediment, and a second pediment held a figure reclining on an elbow, one knee bent, with remnants of a frieze below. Under corner eaves, a protected tile portrayed a man battling with a centaur, its arm strangling his neck. The hill that I had recently vacated was visible in the distance behind the **Erechtheion** with its **Caryatids**: six robed maidens, their arms missing, supporting the stone portico on their heads. These images were plaster casts; the originals, except for one taken by Lord Elgin along with the famous Marbles, were in the **Acropolis Museum**. Decorative patterns on lintels were much deteriorated.

caryatids and lintel

Items in the museum included a lion with kill and two others straddling a horse, which were difficult to discern except for an explanatory picture panel. Heads and torsos embellished a pediment along with a figure riding a serpent-like image with a fishtail. Little also survived of a horse and rider, but a female figure with a serene face, long braided locks, and a dove in hand was almost complete. Remains of a frieze depicted more riders on horseback, and a stone block featuring a charioteer was flanked by robed figures on pedestals. Good views were obtained of the **Herod Atticus Odeon** (AD 161) and the **Theatre of Dionysus** (342–326 BC), where dramas by Sophocles, Euripides and others were performed, both on the slopes of the Acropolis. I could also pick out the Temple of Zeus with its ornate capitals (as seen earlier from the hilltop), and **Hadrian's Arch** topped by columns and a pediment.

The **Tower of Winds**, built in the first century by Syrian astronomer Andronicus, stood on the summit of a hill with other remains in the foreground, and a reddish temple complex had carved remnants scattered around. The **Academy** and **National Library** were imposing traditional buildings, the former flanked by tall pillars with statues on top depicting, respectively, a helmeted figure in flowing robes with a spear and shield and an image, naked except for a cape, holding a lyre.

Supported by fluted Ionic columns, the pediment had heavy relief with similar figures, and winged lions with female heads and torsos stood atop the corners. Robed scholars were seated on pedestals in the well-tended lawns and gardens. At another venue, an equestrian statue portrayed a warrior, his right arm extended and index finger pointing. My final picture of Athens was of another small stone chapel with a red dome like that described earlier.

figure with lyre

THE GREEK ISLANDS

Samos

I headed for the port of **Piraeus** to embark on one of the most exciting and enjoyable journeys that I had ever undertaken. Armed with an extremely good value ferry pass, I caught an overnight boat to Samos in the **Aegean Sea**, the first of 19 Greek islands visited and birthplace of philosopher Pythagoras in the sixth century BC. Young backpackers were cheating the system by purchasing a ticket for the closest destination and remaining on board.

The islands epitomised the meaning of the word idyllic and Samos was no exception. However, I rushed around most of them like the proverbial scalded cat and envied people relaxing with a drink at quayside cafés and *tavernas*, vowing to one day return with more time at my disposal. Even before leaving the mainland, views of the sunset across the water, houses below a white church on the crest of a hill, and the harbour lined with yachts and launches were beautiful. We cruised past the long breakwater, uninteresting tall buildings lit by the fading sunlight, blue domes and towers of churches, which were to become a common sight, and cliffs with dull green vegetation. Misty mountains formed a backdrop, and low-lying cloud drifted across closer peaks with white villages at the base.

Rising above buildings on the waterfront, the dome and spires of a church welcomed us to stunning **Samos**, where my first photograph was of a lady lifting a bag from the pannier of a donkey in a narrow street with shops lining the pavement and palm trees at the end. Thick vines formed a canopy over the door and windows of a white dwelling on a stepped street where a red-flowering plant seemed to flourish in the pavement to one side. Houses covered barren hills behind the picturesque harbour, where tall-masted vessels and colourful fishing boats bobbed gently at the wharf.

Samos harbour

Mounting a slope behind the settlement, **Varthy**, I looked across a clock tower, the red dome of a white church, and a crenellated stone structure to the sparkling blue ocean beyond. Set in conifers, I found a chapel with the usual clutter of pictures and icons, a candelabrum, lace drapes in front of the white *iconostasis* (altar screen), and incense burners, lamps and gilt chandeliers hanging from the high curved ceiling, where a colourful painting of Christ looked down from the centre. A small grotto containing potted plants, a picture of the Mother and Child on an altar draped in red cloth, and crosses leaning against the rough-hewn wall led to a dark cave lit solely by votive lights, which led in turn to a blue sanctuary. Climbing higher still, I again looked down on the scene described above, with a boat chugging past on the indigo sea. A clock tower with a green cupola was tolling five o'clock as I came to atmospheric ruins above the windswept coast, with remnants of fluted pillars and a plinth ornamented with a deeply carved flower. White stone took on a golden hue in the setting sun, or turned black as the crumbling walls were silhouetted against the sky. I wandered back through an avenue of flowering oleander to the lovely sight of coloured lights reflected in the black water of the bay at night.

Next day, my first impressions were of a lolly-pink and white façade with bright green shutters and an iron-railed balcony. I proceeded to the archaeological site of **Heraion**, where the goddess Hera (Roman Juno) is said to have been born, an unspoilt location with only foundations and low walls, a decorated circular plinth, and a column of stacked round blocks, all ensconced amid tall grasses and a few stunted trees. Another cluttered stone church featured an intricately crafted pulpit and an *iconostasis* surmounted by angels and secular figures, its small pictures surrounded by elaborately carved floral work. A crystal chandelier was suspended from a blue dome painted with stars and an image of Our Lord, and paintings occupied the spandrels below. Pillars with carved capitals supported arches leading to a second altar, its *iconostasis* containing larger illustrations. In front of a third, even bigger altarpiece, silver candelabra stood on a black and white marble floor featuring a star design.

Streets winding up from the village into the old quarter of Vathy revealed a drinking fountain with a coat of arms above hideous faces, their mouths gushing water. An elderly man rode sideways on a spotted donkey, coloured gourds hung from vines trailing over a stone wall, and an old lady dressed in black filleted fish in her yard, with an opportunistic cat feeding on the scraps. A man led a donkey down a narrow alley between old stone houses with wooden doors and little overhead balconies, and a lime-green wall had white trim and darker green shutters.

man with donkey

Steps painted in the same hue led to a red door in a white wall also enhanced with green shutters. A crooked street, barely wide enough for a loaded donkey, had a white drain down the centre and was confined by mustard-coloured walls and whitewashed façades with yet more green shutters. At the top, I obtained a view over rooftops with red barrel tiles, the familiar blue dome of a church, and rocky hills covered with scrub, to which the light gave a bronze sheen. A photogenic stone house (painted white) had a rustic porch with red flowers; terraced vineyards crept down a hillside, and on slopes cloaked in thick forest with limestone outcrops I observed a couple of slate-roofed houses.

Back at sea level, I relished vistas of a white township at the foot of hills across the incredibly blue water of the bay. Harbour-side cafés, one with red and white checked cloths, music and a resident cat, the other with tables and chairs right at the water's edge, projected a wonderful aura. In a light breeze, boats rocked gently at anchor on a surface with scarcely a ripple.

harbour-side café

Crazy-paved streets with tables and chairs and little overhead balconies also presented a line of trees in white tubs, a yellow hexagonal tower visible through an arch, and yellow roses climbing a white wall with a yellow awning. On the quayside promenade, lined with blue and white buildings, a third café had umbrellas shading tables, and a black and white cat slept on the olive-green windowsill of a white cottage, its door and meter box a matching green. Steps led to dwellings clustered close together, their balconies draped with vines. Towards evening, I came to a magnificent panorama above an almost enclosed marina: boats and red-roofed white houses all bathed in the glow from the sun as it set behind distant hills.

sunset over the marina

Patmos

Patmos, called Jerusalem of the Aegean, and first of the **Dodecanese**, was next on my island agenda. It was famous for the massive **Monastery of St John the Devine** (1088), its sombre crenellated grey stone walls giving the edifice an appearance more of a formidable fortress, and it did indeed once serve as a refuge from pirates in the island's history. It was visible from many vantage points as it loomed above the town of **Hora**, a two kilometre climb from the port of **Skala**. Banished from Ephesus by pagan Roman Emperor Domitian (AD 81–96), St John spent two years on Patmos, where he wrote down the *Book of Revelations* (*Apocalypse*) from God. Subjected, like the rest, to many invasions, the Dodecanese were the first to become Christian, and it was the Knights of St John of Jerusalem (or Knights Hospitallers) who, in the 14th century, built the mighty fortifications that eventually fell to the Turks in 1522. In 1912, they in turn were ousted by the Italians who, in 1943, during WWII, surrendered to the British, after which the islands became a battleground for British and German forces, resulting in one of the last major victories for the Germans. They were finally returned to Greece in 1947.

Approaching the harbour, we passed white houses mounting hillsides devoid of vegetation; it was a surprise to realise that the Greek islands lacked the lush growth of those with which I was more familiar. I was struck by the glaring white of Patmos, with little of the colour of other settlements. A white church with a white cross on the rounded gable was startling against a vivid blue sky, three bells were set in the arches of a square brownstone belfry, and rocky mountains towering behind were cloaked in low rust-coloured scrub, making them appear red. Purple bougainvillea served to accentuate a white courtyard in a steep street that I climbed for a view of the brilliant blue harbour, its fishing boats, and the occasional red tiles amongst the mostly flat roofs and white domes. I wandered down narrow alleys enclosed by high stark white walls with wooden doors (one in a striking indigo recess) and glimpses of the monastery. I continued past a large all white church crowned by a dome and cross, a bright blue and white vine-shaded patio, and a lonely white house in russet hills over which people were leading heavily laden donkeys. A solitary white dwelling at the bottom was surrounded by a few cultivated trees, its bare compound divided by low stone walls.

At sea level again, I waved to a fisherman in the blue bay and photographed an isolated tiny white chapel beside a solitary tree. Climbing once more (the islands were all up and down!), I came to a church doorway with a fine metal cross above a wonderful fresco. The old rough-hewn stone walls and the tiles of its conical dome were all painted white; I assumed that originally whitewash was applied, but paint was obviously more durable. The belfry, with the usual grouping of three bells, was in contrasting brownstone, and the view beyond the walls was of the ubiquitous olive trees in a valley far below, a townsite on dry brown hills in the distance, and of course the water, which was never very far away. White buildings, some with brownstone quoins and old-style wall lanterns, lined streets so narrow that it was possible to reach out and touch both sides simultaneously.

typical narrow street

Arriving at the 11th-century **Holy Monastery of the Theologian**, I was confronted with a high rough-hewn stone wall relieved above the gateway by the painting of a blue-robed haloed figure holding an open book. Inside, slender but wide-spanned arches interlocked with a belfry, and there were more white chapels, including that of **Panagia** dating from 1210 to 1220; they seemed to breed like churches in the United Kingdom, cathedrals and castles in Europe, and temples in Asia! Frescoes on the undersides of arches showed colourful figures with scrolls, others completely covered a vaulted ceiling, and pictures of Greek clerics (some badly eroded) decorated walls. A brass lantern hung from the ceiling, and a brass urn was the repository for votive candles. On an end wall, a remarkable fresco of the **40 Martyrs of Sebaste** showed Christ with arms outstretched over a crowd of semi-naked emaciated figures and crowns floating in the ether between. Entering an embossed stone doorway, the dark interior revealed a variety of silver objects suspended overhead, candelabra, a wealth of pictures and icons in elaborate carved surrounds, and remnants of artwork on the ceiling. The most exquisitely sculpted *iconostasis* that I had seen, with images on top and a Crucifixion scene in the central panel, was located beneath the illustrated dome. There were paintings of saints on walls, and a second altar screen featured a seated Virgin nursing the baby Jesus and a miniature of Christ in the ornate gilded doors. An intricate gold cross on top of the screen obscured a clear view of frescoes behind, but a graphic picture painted directly onto the stone wall depicted men leaning from a boat to haul on a net that had snared a figure, dressed only in a loin cloth, attempting to swim in the waves. Other images lay above, and all were in vivid colours of red, rich blue, yellow and pink. On the rooftop, I found a stone chapel, exterior paintings around a walkway, two belfries, and steps leading to ramparts.

wall illustration

Returning to narrow streets with overhead vaults, I came across a carved wooden door, another with a fan-shaped transom, and rough unadorned stone walls surrounding gnarled trees with a goat tethered underneath and the monastery on a summit beyond. I saw a vivid red door standing out against white walls, a white belfry, flowers (now dried) sprouting from the stonework of a parapet, white walls ornamented with stone quoins, stepped streets, an all white chapel, and white houses superimposed on an unbelievably blue sky.

Lipsi

A large yacht called *Zeus* lay at anchor as I arrived at little **Lipsi**, with a blue dome dominating the white town and a backdrop of low brown hills. Fishermen onboard one of the gaily coloured boats moored beside a wharf were shaking out their nets, and many of the unpretentious white houses had wooden doors and shutters in recesses outlined in bright blue. The twin towers of the stone church were topped with blue cupolas, an almost gaudy blue wall had a green picket gate, and a girl played with a dog outside a half blue, half white house as I traced the hilly streets up to the church, the interior of which was comparatively simple. The *iconostasis* contained the usual paintings and had winged animal images on top. There

Lipsi island

were gold candelabra, crystal and gold chandeliers hanging beneath the blue vaulted ceiling, and murals adorning white walls and spandrels. A half green house, its doors and windows framed in blue, had a bare vine over the porch, and an old lady dressed in black from headscarf to shoes sat on a step outside her blue-framed white house with plants hanging over a wall. Two black and white kittens were playing on an unguarded blue concrete staircase with yellow edges, which led up the side of a wall bearing the same colours, and the vine-covered courtyard of yet another blue and white house was enclosed by a white fence with a blue balustrade.

Leros

One hour (albeit rushed) was sufficient time to devote to the tiny islet of Lipsi, and I caught the next ferry, which sailed past white cliffs remarkably like those of legendary Dover fame, to the island of **Leros**. This was a much larger harbour, fronting a wide square on which several cars were parked. Buildings climbing hills to one side introduced more colour, but there were fewer boats.

Leros

Kos

At night, lamps and lights strung across the stepped streets in busy carefree **Kos**, on the island of the same name, created a lot of atmosphere. Boats were also lit up, I found a restaurant called Zorbas, and there was a great deal of laughter and gaiety; I enjoyed the nightlife here. Kos was the birthplace of Hippocrates, father of medicine; the **Sanctuary of Asclepius** (god of healing) and medical school were built in the fourth century BC to perpetuate his teaching, and he is said to have taught beneath a huge plane tree in **Freedom Square**. Ptolemy II of Egypt was also born here.

I visited extensive ruins, which included the **Castle** built circa 1450–78 by the Knights of St John. Here, amongst scattered palm trees, I found crenellated round stone towers, walls, remnants of white pillars, an overgrown arch, a coat of arms featuring a crown and the fleur de lis, carved blocks, and a distant blue-domed mosque. The latter I framed, with the spire of its minaret, between stone walls on one side of the site; the ocean lay below on the other. A second location, the **Ancient Agora**, had more-complete columns with leafy Corinthian capitals, low walls – and a glorious red tree.

Pleasure craft and multistorey hotels lined the wharf, and I spent a magic couple of hours climbing quickly above the town. The sound of singing lured me to an open-air restaurant with pot plants on low walls and a patio covered by a thick vine. A cook was attending chickens on a rotisserie and turning meat on a flaming grill whilst serenading with Greek arias, which he interrupted to sing 'Do you like, mademoiselle, the Greece?'! A pretty pastel-accented restaurant had rustic blue wooden posts, plants in pink and pale blue tubs against a white wall with an inbuilt wood-fired oven, and coloured gourds hanging from vines overhead. A board out front listed Greek specialities such as souvlaki, moussaka, dolmades, *tzatziki*, stuffed tomatoes, and feta cheese. In this solitary street of **Zia**, I saw many of the small motorbikes that zipped around the islands, a garden with more pink pots and a scarecrow-like figure, and a live tortoise on the ground.

A church contained vivid wall paintings, brass chandeliers and candelabra (all tied with bows of white ribbon, possibly for a wedding), and a comparatively plain altarpiece with life-sized pictures on the lower level. The principal of the *iconostasis* (literally, stand for icons) is explained in the chapter on Latvia in book 2.

Bazoukia music played in the background as I stood on a patio, its crude log railing painted blue, and looked over tree tops to a blue-domed church near olive groves, a townsite surrounded by sparsely vegetated fields, and infinitely blue water beyond. A small restaurant with blue and white checked cloths was set up in front of a belfry, and bare peaks loomed behind yet another café set amongst trees. Pottery displayed on tables outside a store included a gorgeous purple tea set, the pot decorated with ceramic flowers, as was a purple vase and an indigo jug placed in a bowl with a fluted edge. I returned to the small restaurant with pink and blue pots, where it had been recommended that I eat, and in delightful surroundings beneath the vines of the shady patio, I partook of one of the most delicious meals in which I have ever indulged. Leaving the choice to the discretion of the congenial owner, who was grilling over a fire in the oven, I was served a meal commencing with fried cheese and followed by goat and other local delicacies.

Making my way down again, past a blue dome and cross just visible above trees shining yellow in the sunlight, I appreciated a panorama across more domes and the water to white houses on the far shore – which was Turkey. Undergrowth on the verges of a road leading to white houses half way up a stark stony slope was turned a glowing bronze colour by the light, and I stopped to talk with a man cuddling his playful donkey – clouds of dust flying up when he patted it! More ruins contained toppled columns beside a stone wall with the minaret of a mosque in the background, which was also viewed through the one standing arch with a sculpted visage on the capping stone of its lintel. Tiny chirping birds made use of this gateway for a resting place as they flitted to and fro. Fallen blocks were carved with scrolls and squares, a couple of ginger and white cats sat atop an abandoned white stone plinth ornamented with flowers, an elaborate carved capital lay on the ground by low walls, and a partially destroyed floor mosaic pictured birds in faded red, black and white squares. A rough stone tunnel framed some of the lush surroundings of palms and trees. Back at the harbour, colourful fishing boats created the foreground to yellowed stone fortifications on one side.

Rhodes

Sailing across an indigo sea on the approach to remarkable **Rhodes**, largest of the Dodecanese islands with a history paralleling the other islands plus involvement in the war with Sparta, I was aware of the castle and extensive battlements from the entrance to **Mandraki Port**, which was marked by a bronze doe and a stag with large antlers atop tall pedestals, one either side. This was where one of the original wonders of the world, the Colossus of Rhodes, was believed to have straddled the harbour entrance in 290 BC, until toppled by an earthquake 65 years later. As with much of Greece, the origin of the island was interwoven with mythology and the 35m bronze statue, torch in hand, was supposedly that of the sun god Helios who chose Rhodes as his bride and bestowed light, warmth and vegetation upon her. A second reference named the giant statue as Apollo, built between 292 and 280 BC.

Large buildings, a clock tower, three windmills, the tower of **St Nicholas Lighthouse**, and many boats including luxury yachts and catamarans also greeted the arrival of the ferry. Crenellated grey stone walls and towers, a statue in a niche above an arched gateway, turrets, a round tower bestowed with a crest, and a series of arches all served to make up the impressive 12m-thick walls. Considered one of the best surviving examples of medieval fortifications, they were erected, along with the finest buildings, by the Knights of St John who captured Rhodes in 1309 after being ousted from the Holy Land. These religious warriors held the island until expelled by the Turks in 1522. The few hundred that remained marched with honour to their final home in Malta.

Following the **Knight's Road** past the **Inns of the Knights of Seven Languages**, I came to the 14th-century **Palace of the Grand Masters** or **Knights' Palace**, which was rebuilt by the Italians in the 1940s as a summer palace for King Victor Emanuel and Mussolini. Entering the stone-paved inner courtyard, I found a series of arched recesses containing statues of Roman emperors on pedestals and, inside the palace, excellent ancient floor mosaics from Kos. Within a patterned border, one portrayed a man in a laurel wreath and blue tunic using a spear to confront a leaping tiger; another showed a naked man and maiden together with a winged figure, a tree, and a warrior with a shield. Two more pictured the head of Medusa in an elaborate surround and peacocks and ducks circling a vine in an urn. The vast interior, with solid walls and vaulted ceilings of multihued stone, contained paintings, decorative metal chandeliers, a few pieces of dark and ponderous 16th- and 17th-century wooden furniture from the West, and a stone staircase lined with sconces leading to the upper level.

mosaics

Narrow cobbled streets were hemmed in by heavy stone structures, often connected by vaulted buttresses (on top of one of which I filmed two sleeping cats) or arches with rooms overhead. The severe façades were relieved by wooden shutters and doors, and I noted coats of arms and a statue on a bracket. A massive red church was enhanced with white accents, and I came to a marketplace with a tower, plants draping a stone wall with an ornamental iron door, and an extremely narrow lane with austere walls supported by numerous stone vaults. In the **Old Town**, a market square with a fountain in the centre was bounded by old stone buildings, pigeons roosted on a dome, a seafood restaurant was situated in front of imposing broad stone towers, and a second fountain featured three large metallic seahorses. Creepers hung overhead as I strolled down a narrow street towards the port and viewed, through an arch, a yacht with furled sails gliding past the lighthouse.

Knight's Road

Back at the market square, I photographed a strange face painted on tiles, old ruins, iron-railed balconies, a minaret and clock tower rising behind an arcade, and a bow-fronted entrance with a sculpted plaque and delicately carved window treatment. A gorgeous display of brilliant purple bougainvillea covered crenellated steel-grey stone walls facing a square containing a small trickling fountain. Tables and chairs, one group with red cloths, were placed in cobbled and vaulted alleys with vines overhead; others, with yellow cloths, were set in front of a vine-covered building with a squat six-sided structure appearing behind.

picturesque restaurant

Symi

Departing the marina, I looked back at sleek craft and crenellated ramparts beyond. The wind whistled loudly as we sailed over incredibly blue sea, past barren rock and a white windmill, to **Symi**, made prosperous in Ottoman times by sponge diving and boat building. As we entered the small harbour, bells on the tall church clock tower that we had come to see pealed in response to a long blast of the ship's horn. The ornate five-tiered coloured stone structure was abutted each side by white walls of the **Archangel Michael Monastery** on the tree-lined wharf. With a crowd of local pilgrims, I approached the chapel via steps and a black and white zigzag-paved courtyard with old twisted vines climbing the white pillars of its arched colonnade. The interior was breathtaking: a gleaming golden chandelier and myriad gilt and silver lamps and/or incense burners strung overhead, elaborate decoration on the vaulted ceiling, wall paintings (one showing a red-cloaked haloed figure on horseback), an abundance of carving – including a pulpit with gold trim, inset pictures, and a gilded eagle on the rim – and a life-sized icon portraying a winged figure with an outstretched arm, only the painted face visible behind the embossed silver veneer. This revered treasure, similar to those found in Russia, was surrounded by intricate sculpting and further embellished with a cross, flowers and prayer offerings. Yellow flames of votive candles flaring in front endowed the silver with the appearance of gold. Large colourful illustrations of a winged figure with a scroll, saints, and the Virgin with Christ Child were set in the richly carved *iconostasis*, the ornate cross and figures on top almost hidden behind the plethora of hanging objects. Portrayed standing beneath arches, other haloed images were painted directly onto the wall next to a second horseman, with drawn sword, rearing above a man underneath.

A picture was mounted in an ornate frame beneath a colourful delicately carved canopy, and another embossed silver icon stood beneath a carved wooden arch supported by elaborately sculpted pillars.

Back on board, we passed other towns tucked into hillsides and a lonely white monastery with a red dome set amongst a few cultivated trees in the rocky terrain. A second white monastery, with a tall tiered bell tower and red dome, sat behind white walls above a scattering of homes on a red rocky outcrop, and a tiered clock tower stood on the waterfront near fishing dories and a few buildings presenting a harmonious medley of colours. We moored in the natural port of **Egialo** (**Aigialos**) in **Gialos** town, from where I climbed to **Hora** (Horio, Chora or Ano Symi, by all of which the capital can be referred), built up a slope with the **Church of Panagia**, biggest in the island, on top, and towards which I headed for vistas of steep streets with many vines and red roofs descending to indigo water. A priest in a long black cassock and traditional hat was making his way down one of the many stepped streets. In a narrow alley I found bright blue steps leading to a white house, a cat sitting on a stone ledge, and just the black tail of another hanging through a hole in a white wall! As I wandered up and down, I also observed a church with red cupolas on symmetrical white towers and ruins evident on the barren mountain backdrop. A blue dome appeared above houses with vine-draped white walls, and on the summit, the large church loomed behind a classical statue, one arm missing, atop on old wall. I did not make it to the top but still obtained magnificent views of the picturesque harbour and dry hills.

Monastery of Archangel Michael

A warning siren signalled the departure of the ferry, and back on the wharf barrows of fruits and vegetables formed the foreground to boats and pastel houses climbing the hill to one side. I filmed the entrance to the quaint pension where I spent the night, and a Dalmatian dog with one blue eye and one yellow! This town was renowned for its natural sea sponge, a great variety of which were displayed in baskets beneath umbrellas and awnings in the street, or sold directly from some of the blue-and-white boats tied to the promenade lined with ornate three-branched streetlamps, where band music was playing. Crooked steps led to a white house on a street bounded by mustard-yellow walls, and on a walk to the five-tiered clock tower I found two cats grooming themselves on white steps in front of a pale blue door in a lemon-coloured wall. In a poorer section, a rough stone façade half painted in blue and yellow had green shutters, a rooster crowed in the unkempt yard, and a toddler waved a greeting. Green, white and blue pots sat on the small porch beneath red and yellow washing on a line strung from the balcony. It all combined to make a splash of colour against the stark grey rock behind, which matched the undecorated upper storey that appeared derelict and uninhabited. Three old windmills stood on a breakwater behind a boat displaying large shells, corals, starfish and sea urchins along with the sponges. Towards evening, I photographed the moon framed by a circular opening in a stepped arch, shields on a tower, a plaque on an old wall, and a marble drinking fountain on an ancient grey stone structure.

Next morning, I toured a venue with Moorish appearance: a gypsum rotunda with a central well and a fountain in the middle of a paved courtyard circled by concentric colonnades. Beautiful purple bougainvillea spread above wide arches through which the ocean was visible. Ornamented columns of a pergola were interspersed with greenery, and the whole was well maintained and interesting. Invited inside a home, I filmed many decorative plates displayed on a shelf covered with an embroidered valance and hanging below photographs and pictures on a wall. Log beams overlaid with strips of bamboo or saplings formed the ceiling, and a bed and cloth-covered table stood on a patterned rug. The lady of the house was obviously very houseproud but reluctant to be photographed.

Rhodes

Back on Rhodes, on a day tour to lovely Lindos – established around 2000 BC; St. Paul landed here on his way to Rome – kindly provided by Ialyssos Travel, we stopped first at **Kalithea Thermi** (spa) and a pottery outlet where an artisan was creating vases on a wheel. Finished pieces were painted with traditional designs and legendary images that included winged horses. Ornaments with richly coloured peacocks and flowers had the appearance of cloisonné, and black items were decorated with classical figures in gold.

The ruins of the **Sanctuary of Lindian Athena**, older than the Acropolis of Athens, were situated in dramatic surrounds above sheer cliffs, the azure of the sky and cobalt blue water acting as a canvas for the fourth-century fluted columns supporting a few lintels. Ancient walls were also abundant, and far below, the stunning view showed a protected, almost totally enclosed, natural stony harbour where several boats were moored and sunlight sparkled on the water. At the base of the sanctuary, the prow of a full-sized Lindian Hellenistic *trireme** was carved into the granite.

Approaching the present day **Lindos**, we obtained incredible views of white buildings on slopes below the massive overpowering **Acropolis** (a Crusader castle) and a belt of green trees between the town and stony shores of the teal-blue and turquoise bay ringed by rocky outcrops.

Features of this charming town included steps bearing designs created by different-coloured pebbles and white walls with brownstone doorways, one with Ionic pilasters and a classical sculpted face. I found a similar visage constituting a brass door knocker, white painted steps on steep ladder streets with purple bougainvillea overhead, the vine-shaded patio of a restaurant, a courtyard full of flowering plants, unframed paintings (for sale) pegged to lines stretched across a wall, and a second courtyard with green plants and tables with red cloths enclosed within sculpted walls. A kitten sat in a narrow white paved street, a passageway led beneath an arched stone tower, and a heavy iron gate revealed a view of the castle ramparts on a precipice behind, also visible above vines forming an arch over a narrow white lane.

Crete

We come now to **Crete**, Greece's largest and most southerly island, and my first destination was **Knossos** with its famous frescoes. Capital of the Minoan kingdom, built in 1700 BC, it was destroyed by the eruption of the volcano of Santorini in 1500 BC, which vulcanologists believe to be the most cataclysmic on record. Vivid illustrations, of which only fragments remained, included tall narrow-waisted red figures wearing a type of lap-lap in blue or yellow with different designs and others in white loin cloths with elaborate headdresses. The former, on a wall beneath a canopy supported by square white pillars, were carrying beautiful jars as part of a procession bearing gifts to the king.

frescoes

Large pottery amphorae with decorative relief were prevalent here, and the extensive site was

* The trireme was an ancient Greek galley with three rows of oars on each side.

a maze of solid blocks and rough stone walls; a set of steps with remains of columns on one side led simply to empty space! I have forgotten the significance of a pair of colossal 'horns' found at the venue, and one highly decorated interior featured floral patterns and designs in bright colours on a mustard-hued background. Red columns with black and white capitals lined steps leading to the astonishing 4,000-year-old **Queen's Bathroom**. This featured a painting (copy) on alabaster of almost life-sized blue-and-white dolphins swimming amongst small pink and green fish, the original heralded as one of the most exquisite Minoan artworks. I also noticed a floral frieze around a window and a decorative maroon and white panel on the wall above a terracotta bathtub, which was the same shape as modern-day conveniences. There was also a water closet, purportedly the first ever to work on the flush principal, the water poured down by hand. In the **Throne Room**, with original gypsum benches, an outstanding red wall had a white fresco of plants surrounding a mythical creature symbolising heaven. It was explained that the body of a lion indicated the power of the ground, and the head of a snake was the underground divinity. I have since learned that the creature was actually the earliest depiction of a griffin, with the head of an eagle. In this room, black columns were topped with red-and-white capitals.

mythical creature

Crete was the birthplace of Minoan culture, Europe's first advanced civilisation that flourished from 2800 to 1450 BC. The Roman occupation lasted from AD 69 to 330; it fell to the Arabs in 824, Venetians in 1204, Muslims in 1645, and the Turks in 1669. It united with Greece in 1913. Knossos was named after King Minos, legendary son of Zeus, said to have been born here on the slopes of Mt Dikti. Given a bull to sacrifice to the god Poseidon, the king decided to keep it, which enraged the god who punished him by causing his wife, Pasiphae, to fall in love with the animal, the result of the union being the Minotaur (half man, half bull) that lived in a labyrinth beneath the palace, feeding on youths and maidens.

The museum at **Herakleion/Iraklio** exhibited stone containers with lids, ornate jugs and jars with interesting decoration (one showing an octopus; another cattle), figurines with upraised arms, a charioteer driving three bulls, a sarcophagus with deep relief, and marble busts and statues, including one without arms or head dressed in a tunic. A second depicted a naked male with a cloak draped over his left shoulder and arm. Also on show were amphorae, a floor mosaic, and two sculpted friezes, one portraying small images on the backs of extremely long-legged horses, the other, heads of open-mouthed lions interspersed with floral designs. Carving on a stone block represented naked female forms with braided hair and tall headdresses, and a large decorated jar had handles and a bull or cow embossed on the neck.

An ancient stone church had tiered domes and a plain façade with only a single round window above the sculpted architrave of the entrance. A modern cathedral featured ornamented bell and clock towers and a highly decorated interior, with paintings on the vaulted ceiling, beneath the curves of arches, in spandrels, and under the dome, where a large representation of Christ looked down from above a row of saints. Extremely colourful picture panels portrayed contemporary interpretations of bible stories, including the Crucifixion, baptism of Jesus by John, and the Ascension.

modern cathedral art

An elaborate filigree chandelier incorporating miniature portraits was suspended beneath the dome. White fluted pillars, a white pulpit with a white dove on the rim, a white *iconostasis* and white balconies emphasized the colour overhead. A silver-covered icon showed a mounted figure with a cross, and a beautifully carved receptacle for votive candles featured peacocks in recesses defined by tiny spiral pillars.

Anyone for pork?

Leaving this inspiring venue, I came upon meat, tripe and bloody pigs' heads hung on hooks in the street!

In contrast, opposite a small white church, bracts of bright pink bougainvillea, lit by the sun to glorious effect, were blowing in a welcome breeze as they reached over a wall. Black cats sat beside a white doorway in a narrow lane, and a tiny chapel with a whitewashed vaulted ceiling had many framed pictures, a simple chandelier, two gold lamps, and a golden stand for candles on the rough stone floor. With a small belfry on top, it stood in a restful paved courtyard carpeted with fallen leaves from overhead trees, and white benches were placed beneath their spreading branches. Colourful scenes included an enclosure shaded by thick green grapevines laden with purple fruit and, leading off it, bright blue, yellow and green doors in white walls. Behind the last was a small courtyard filled with plants, and a tabby cat expressing obvious curiosity at my approach. A yard with a mass of bougainvillea and white flowers also held large terracotta jars and an old wooden press, whilst a colourful street had vines over a pumpkin-yellow wall and cats outside an olive door in an apple-green façade at the end. Another yard had a striped mat hanging on a line, plants in pots and tins painted lolly pink, and a red bench seat under shady vines. At the old port, pleasure craft and white fishing boats decorated with red, blue or yellow provided the foreground to the imposing **Koulés** (1523–40). This 16th-century fortress guarding the harbour had battlements and a sculpted panel above its arched entrance.

Santorini

Next destination, where I spent three days, was undoubtedly my favourite in the Aegean: sensational **Santorini**, or **Thira**, in the **Cyclades** group, with dazzling white houses built above sheer red cliffs rising abruptly from the sea. The island is part of the rim of a dormant volcano that forms a ring of islands jutting from the deep-blue ocean. Inhabited since at least 7000BC, the Cyclades have undergone a tremendous upheaval over the centuries, being ruled in stages by the Minoans (2000–1500 BC), Myceneans (1500–1100 BC), Dorians (eighth century BC), and the Ptolemy's of Egypt in the era between 323 and 146 BC. Rome made an entrance in 146 BC, and in AD 395 handed control to Byzantium (Constantinople). In 1204, the islands belonged to Venice; Turkish dominance followed in 1537, and they fell briefly to the Russians in 1771, before reverting back to the Ottomans. During the Second World War they were occupied by the Italians.

From the top, the main town of **Fira**, a jumble of blue domes and white buildings connected by white steps and winding paths, tumbled abruptly towards the sea, with the more-original less-touristy Oia visible on a far point. Flat roofs created patios for tables and chairs, where I obtained vistas across domes and clustered buildings to a ship anchored offshore and white structures, far below, built into the cliff face at the harbour of **Skala**. A large crystal and gold chandelier hung in the richly hued interior of a church with modern illustrations and the usual image of Christ in the dome, executed in brilliant blue and red with angels and saints below. Again, paintings adorned spandrels and the undersides of arches and depicted, amongst other themes, the baptism of Jesus and disciples manning a boat whilst Simon Peter swam towards Christ onshore. Mary and the child Jesus reposed in a half dome above the *iconostasis.*

It seemed that every street produced magnificent views as they twisted and turned down vaulted alleys and past paintings next to a colourful fruit and vegetable stand displaying fresh greens, luscious ripe tomatoes, apples, melons, zucchini, oranges and grapes beneath a green awning. Rugs were hung on a wall, others folded and stacked on the cobbled lane, and a large terracotta jar was placed at the foot of steps in a courtyard containing tables with blue cloths. Four bells constituting a belfry began to toll, whilst another cast its shadow on the wall of a white church with a white cross crowning stepped domes. A narrow white walkway led between high white walls and stone buildings to a blue dome and clock tower at the end. An open rooftop restaurant with palms, pink mats on white tables shaded by umbrellas, and music in the background provided a magical panorama over the expanse of blue bay from where people and donkeys climbed laboriously up hundreds of zigzag steps to the town, also accessed by cable car. A flock of white birds flew over buildings and boats almost directly below – it was an awe-inspiring sight. The occasional pale pink, blue or ochre wall introduced a little colour.

typical Santorini streets

From a distance, the white-capped red cliffs appeared covered with snow or as an iced cake. Continuing my walk, I found a cute tabby kitten sitting in the protection of a drainage hole in a wall, and another sitting on a chair on a blue and white porch. I encountered many blue gates, a view to the blue sea through a white arch with a filigree wrought-iron gate, a large white house with lilac trim and a plaster pelican perched on the balustrade, and a smaller house trimmed in pale blue with an ornamental seagull. The wind was so strong that at times it was impossible to hold the camera steady. A brown dome proved different, red hibiscus made an impact against a blue wall overlooking a sheltered red paved courtyard with potted plants, and at the top of a stepped section of the cobbled cliff path I saw a bright blue dome near a free-standing multi-tiered bell tower.

There were plenty of cats; I took a picture of an old lady wearing the traditional headscarf, smiling broadly, and cradling a tortoiseshell as she rested on the step in front of a purple door, but I only saw three dogs. Potted plants stood at the top of a flight of stairs braced by a vault spanning the street, and a tiny white courtyard with a white table and chairs and a few pot plants was highlighted by deep blue accents provided by the gate, the frame of its single window, a small shutter, and the lace-curtained door. A stone arch with a cross on top framed an all white church with a belfry and barrel-shaped roof, and ladder-like steps led to an isolated white chapel with a blue door, its crazy-paved courtyard emphasised in white, and whence a second path led to a rocky tor on a promontory jutting into the ocean. Vines crept up the white wall of a house with jars scattered on its flat roof, and a belfry with a single bell was superimposed on a blue ocean. Appearing like a shadow, a black cat sat beside a white wall, and another lay absorbing the warmth on a white roof.

there were many domes

Behind a cobalt blue gate, an amphora stood at the top of steps beside a door of the same colour in a stark white wall, and white stones bordered the narrow path at the edge of the steep cliff with its multihued strata of lava and pumice. Cherubs, one with pan pipes, stood atop the stout concrete pillars of a wooden gate leading to steps with an urn on the solid stone newel post, and the sun shone tantalizingly on the water. Two men sat having a discussion on the seawall, purple bougainvillea cascaded over a white fence, and a fancy clock tower stood beside an apricot-toned church (with a white dome) viewed behind a series of similarly coloured arches. I came across a star created with pebbles in a path constructed from the same materials, rugs in strong hues on a stone wall, and a narrow cobbled street of shops introducing yellow alongside the pink and blue. I filmed a lonely church on a mountainside with a cloud-shrouded peak. Tucked into a recess, it was accessed via a steep zigzag path. A somewhat different picture of Santorini was presented by the statue of a female at the foot of dark-coloured steps, a copy of Michelangelo's *David* on top, and a lantern on the white balustrade.

Taking a bus to the east coast of the island, which by contrast shelved to a black volcanic shore, I found chairs and sunshades placed near scant trees lining the black sand and pebble beach, which was lightly lapped by gentle surf. A sheer wall of grey rock formed the opposite side of the bay. From here, I could see an attractive blue and white church, and a red rowing boat was one of few pulled up on the strand. Loud music issued from a utility, where I spoke with a man selling home-made food products as he sat on the tailboard, and a large brown and white dog romped with a black and white puppy in a yard.

Back on the western side, I climbed down the steep winding staircase between high enclosing walls, wary of the dozens of donkeys that left little space to pass. Most, with colourful patterned saddle blankets, tinkling bells, twitching ears and swishing tails, were standing patiently with their owners, waiting for customers. One man was curled up on steps – fast asleep! Further down, buildings were clinging to the sheer cliff like the hanging monasteries of Asia, and yachts were anchored below on an indigo sea; it was an extraordinary sight.

At the bottom, I took a *caique* (small Turkish skiff) to the black **Kamenes** (**Palia** and **Nea Kameni**), part of the bleak and barren opposite rim of the volcano forming its own still volcanically active islands. This also provided a different aspect of Fira on the massive coloured cliffs rearing above an incredibly blue ocean. Approaching our destination, glistening jagged black lava erupted from the surface of water that was teal blue in the shallows; the continually changing hues of the seas were astonishing. A brief onshore excursion revealed slopes of grey stone and shale, and typical colours associated with volcanic activity: yellow from sulphur, and the red and greenish tinges of other elements, probably iron and copper. The wind was still howling and fumes issued from vents; it was very atmospheric. There was one clump of grass in this otherwise forbidding, desolate and arid area, and from every vantage point the ocean appeared like an enormous vivid blue lake, with Fira always in the background.

Leaving here, we anchored in a small bay with a tiny white chapel on the shore, one house, a rowing boat, and a couple of goats. Underway again, we headed for a different landing on Santorini: a shelf beneath craggy tors. Here, we found rowing boats, restaurants on the waterfront, a cluster of rundown low white buildings with blue, red and green doors, a few trees, and donkeys and mules waiting to transport people to the top – I walked. This path led to the shabby traditional village of **Oia**, with prickly pear plants and paint peeling off walls but more character than the more pristine Fira. There was also more variation in colour: green instead of the usual blue on some of the houses and one gaudy two-storey bright pink residence with blue trim. A white chapel with a small yellow belfry was located above houses built into a natural rock face. The skyline was punctuated with domes, and there were the same magnificent views to startling blue water far below. A particularly attractive white church favoured blue trim with pink motifs above its blue door, over which were four bells. The panels of its pink octagonal tower were delineated in white and its blue dome topped by a white cross. It was attached to a building with pink borders around its green wall and shutters. Similarly, a brilliant red façade, its corners and frames defined by dark green, formed one side of a small courtyard, the other fenced by a low white wall topped by blue railing between light green pillars. White steps led to a blue door in the white wall at one end, which had a green shutter in the side abutting the street. There appeared to be a greater incidence of rounded roofs here, to which rustic ladders provided access. I saw numerous cats, and walking to find a stepped tower glimpsed behind the red wall, I heard the tinkling of a bell and the clip-clop of hooves as a man led his horse, adorned with a tassel on its forehead and a colourful blanket, along the narrow street.

Oia

I came across another bright green wall, steps leading to a tiny patio looking directly down to the distant water, and an old lady, all in black, sitting behind the green iron fence of a small red courtyard outside the blue-framed green doors and shutters of her white house! Before making my way back to the port, I paused briefly at a café in a stepped alley with characteristic red and white checked cloths on the tables and blue and white striped jars at the entrance for a drink with acquaintances that I had met on my walk. Pulling away from the shore, I obtained a good view of the steep winding staircase, buildings above and below, and colourful tables at the waterside. Arriving at Fira, I again faced the long ascent, with donkeys coming towards me as they descended – a lot faster!

I took a tour to the ancient site of **Akrotiri**, ruins of a Minoan city destroyed by a mighty eruption of the island's volcano, on the opposite end of the island from Oia. Found buried under ash like a prehistoric Pompeii, many of its treasures, including marvellous wall paintings, are now in the National Archaeological Museum in Athens. However, amongst the unearthed buildings, walls and tumbled stairs stood a pottery dish on legs and many restored decorated jars with handles; other remains were still lodged in the earthworks of the excavations. The cataclysmic explosion was believed to have caused the demise of not only Akrotiri but the whole Minoan civilisation as well, although an absence of skeletons and treasure led scientist to believe that people escaped the city. It has been claimed that the island was part of the lost continent of Atlantis. The panorama from the site, one of the highest points on the island, was fantastic and looked across dry fields and communities to Oia in the far distance. Our group stopped at a venue with Greek music, where everyone toasted me with wishes for happy and safe travelling.

Back at Fira, an unexplored area displayed a glaring red roof atop yellow walls in the midst of bright blue domes. This section was a maze of stairways leading off in tangents. A dog slept on a roof, a belfry was outlined against a now purple sea, pink doors appeared behind pink flowers, which peeped through pink pickets topping a white wall with a blue gate, and I saw mustard-coloured buildings. Here again were peeling walls, and a solitary thatched windmill with rigging for sails – now absent. Behind iron railing, an exceptional yellow mansion was enhanced with a small pediment above the door, sculpted lintels and pilasters, and a parapet around the roof, the whole accented in blue, white, and grey. It also boasted a rare garden. I spotted many belfries and a man rowing far below.

windmill Santorini

With their rounded roofs and surfaces, some houses appeared almost to have been moulded from clay and some were hewn from soft rock. One presented a rose-hued façade in otherwise all white surroundings, ruins stood next to a white chapel on a point, and the soft glow of twilight descended upon the scene, making the pale blue and white walls almost phosphorescent. A cat was curled up in the hollow of a block reinforcing the corner of two walls, atop one of which sat a dog that surveyed me with interest, whilst another stood wagging its tail down below. A striking pink wall was inset with a sculpted figure and tiles portraying a face and two headless naked male bodies. Lights began to illuminate the houses and tiny courtyards, whilst soothing orchestral and piano music played in the background; it was another peaceful and magical moment.

Next morning, as I headed out of town to the port for the embarkation of larger vessels, dawn sunlight broke through a few greyish clouds to strike the white crests above striated cliffs rising from the already very blue water, their base washed by gentle surf. Rowing boats were pulled up on the black rocky shore, and as we drew away the white terrain above the brown horizontal strata appeared like chalk cliffs that at times seemed to bleed into crevices, giving them the appearance of glaciers. We sailed past the jagged black lava of the Kamenes where yachts were berthed in a protected cove, the windmill on the point, and many blue domes. And so I bade farewell to superb Santorini.

harbour for large boats

Ios

The first sight to welcome me to enchanting **Ios** was a bell and cross on the white dome of an isolated below ground chapel, the backdrop consisting of a few houses climbing a stony slope. In the town of **Hora**, I noticed a number of rough stone fences with rustic blue posts and gates, and bazoukia music was emanating from a small shaded pergola. From a high point, I saw a beautiful church with two belfries at the entrance to **Ormos Harbour**, boats, buildings, and the small chapel seen earlier. Another grand church stood on an open space, again surrounded by rough stone walls, and the interesting houses, looking like square boxes, were relieved by domes, a tower, and a windmill. Another windmill graced a less populated part, but I paid only the briefest of visits.

Paros

I was then on my way again, to perfect **Paros**, past black and pink-toned rock monoliths protruding perpendicularly from the ocean: one with a lone building perched on top and one sculpted by wind and sea to appear like a granite iceberg. Set apart from the rest, two formations like twin pillars of a gigantic gateway were standing opposite a long rocky promontory with a church, flat-roofed matchbox buildings, a windmill, and a stone breakwater; the thing that struck me most was that it was totally flat. A fishing boat chugged by on the choppy cobalt blue water. Approaching the harbour, **Parikia**, terraced hills formed the background to the usual settlement and church, and I found a room in a delightful *pensione* with a view from my window of a crazy-paved courtyard fringed by plants, which overlooked a deep-blue sea and a small chapel on a distant point. The intensity of colours displayed by the ocean never ceased to amaze me.

A leisurely walk took me to a windmill next to a stone church (painted white) with a belfry in its stepped gable. Three pretty kittens were grooming themselves on a garden wall adjacent to a small brownstone chapel, which in turn was attached to a white wall draped in bright pink bougainvillea and inset with a sculpted drinking fountain. With its colourful boats, the tranquil harbour was a picture, and narrow alleys with tiny overhead balconies were enhanced with potted plants and red, green and blue shutters, doors and frames. Crazy-paving outlined in white was a feature of this town, and a most unusual sight was that of dried octopi hung on a line by means of wooden clothes pegs! Many buildings had stairs, either with coloured railing or unguarded, leading directly from the path to colourful doors. One such set of unprotected steps climbed the white façade of a church to a belfry with an ornate iron cross on top; another cross was embossed on the lintel of its stone doorway. Red hibiscus made a startling addition to an adjacent white wall.

A rooster was crowing as I entered a crazy-paved alley barely wide enough for even a donkey to pass. Steep white steps each side were guarded by blue, red and green wooden balustrades, and overhead, pink-flowering creeper hung down a white wall.

narrow alleyways

Other colourful observations included lime-green shutters, vibrant pink bougainvillea growing in front of a vivid blue door, and a tiny alley with green and red shutters (and a complementary red plant), which led to another blue door, all adding interest to white walls. Three mischievous kittens frolicked amongst a group of pot plants on a low wall entered via a blue gate beneath a blue arch leading to a blue door. These were complemented by a blue pot (with a red geranium) placed on the pavement. I found a narrow stepped street and a red door with a matching red hibiscus at the side, the stems of which had been painted white to blend with the wall!

three playful kittens

At dusk, I arrived at a place with a windmill silhouetted against the sky and the golden glow of sunset lighting the white town across a shallow bay, a fishing boat drawn up onshore in the foreground. Further along, tinted clouds and colourful boats were mirrored in perfectly still water; it was a gorgeous scene pre-empting a brilliant sunset that flooded the horizon, creating a red path across the sea and filling the entire camera lens with vibrant colour. As darkness fell, streets were lit, tables and chairs appeared under vines, rugs were displayed on a wall, music played, and three arched recesses beneath a set of steps were illuminated to highlight a carved figure with a sword.

reflections

Next morning, beside a crazy-paved path, I found a windmill outlined against a cerulean sky and a second behind coloured boats reflected in calm conditions, creating yet another superlative scene. A man was leading his laden donkey, another squatted on the ground engaged in tending fishing lines, and there were more cats, trees with trunks painted white and, at the junction of a Y-intersection, a white building with a wide teal-blue dado. I came across a pink door and frames, and even the red, blue, green and yellow plastic crates containing vegetables made a colour statement stacked in front of green and blue doors in white surrounds. I saw a lady in black entering her doorway with shopping, but the streets were surprisingly quiet. Other snatches of colour were provided by balconies in pastels and darker shades, a bright flowering creeper, a vibrant red door, pink geraniums in front of a pale blue door and railing, red pots on worn white steps, and a decidedly crooked blue dome. Following a donkey with loaded panniers, I came to a street with tables beneath vines, coloured shutters, and an arch at the end through which I could see the sea. There were myriad steps and stairs and, also finishing in an arch, another crazy-paved passageway, this time with flowering oleander. The donkey had halted before a doorway where the vendor was selling to an occupant.

vendor with donkey

Situated in the centre of the old town was the semi-ruined **Venetian Kastro** (castle), built on the remains of a temple to Athena in 1260. Circular fragments from these earlier ruins were embedded in its massive walls, which enclosed a round tower. Pale blue tables and chairs sat under a pergola on a paved area enhanced with greenery. I was heading for the inspirational old stone church of **Panagia Ekatondapyliani** (**Katapoliani** for short), or **A Hundred Doors**, dating from AD 326 and one of three most important monuments from the Byzantine period in Greece. According to tradition it was built by Saint Helen, mother of Emperor Constantine the Great, on her way back from the Holy Land where she found the true Cross of Christ. A cat sat amongst fallen pieces outside, and the interior dome, vaulted ceiling and walls were constructed with different textures and shades of stone but offered little in the way of sculpting. It was hung with large crystal and ornate gilded chandeliers, and simply furnished with carved wooden pews, an elaborate pulpit, candelabra on the altar, and an *iconostasis* with a large crucifix on top. I also noted a copper or brass incense burner, silver icons, and a stained-glass panel that infused a stone wall and pillar with red, green, blue and yellow squares. Led by the deep voice of a priest, the monotone chanting of prayers resonated in the vast space and added to the overwhelming aura of being in a holy place. The **Baptisti Rio**, in the form of a cross, was the only one of this type to have survived in Greece. Its minimal sculpted decoration, dome constructed with different colours of stone, and vaults (except one restored) survived an earthquake in 1733. Broken panels in the courtyard dated from Early Christian and Archaic Greek times, and plinths were adorned with strange but comical portly images seeming to represent See no Evil and Speak no Evil.

I stopped for lunch at the single table beside a huge pottery jar in a narrow paved alley terminating in a belfry and a view of the ocean, and also containing geraniums in a tub, other plants in pots, and creepers.

A black and white cat with four kittens of different colours interacted on a step, and back at the Kastro, which was visible at the end of many streets, tiny birds flitted on and off a dead branch protruding from the wall, whilst doves roosted in niches created by missing masonry. In daylight, I observed that the illuminated arches I had filmed the previous evening were festooned with greenery, and the steps led to a bright yellow door. Oleander with white painted trunks made an attractive sight against the white walls and steps of a church, its belfry and blue dome blending into a correspondingly blue sky.

two restaurants

Naxos

Next stop was notable **Naxos**, largest and most fertile of the Cyclades where, according to mythology, the god Dionysus, god of wine, also called Bacchus, was born from the thigh of Zeus. Its capital, **Hora**, was dominated by a **Venetian Castle**, and I stayed in a modern motel-like edifice called Mathiassos Village, with purple bougainvillea over white walls, an Olympic-size swimming pool, and individual bungalows. Mine overlooked a somewhat overgrown garden that surrounded a blue-domed white chapel and belfry, its almost gaudy, recently restored interior featuring a dome containing a sombre-looking Jesus holding a book, with coloured angels and saints on a blue background below. One spandrel featured a figure with an unfurled scroll, and a painting of the face of Jesus on a shroud appeared beneath a half dome. Under this again, a severe-looking Mary with the Holy Child was located above a plain mustard surface with a small blue-framed window. Richly coloured wall paintings included a modernistic manger scene and Christ's baptism. A crystal chandelier hung from the centre of the dome.

Many tables and chairs with checked cloths lined the waterfront promenade, and Naxos was a maze of the narrowest twisting and turning crazy-paved alleys with white stuccoed walls.

Naxos waterfront

I saw plenty of potted plants, a plethora of stairs to houses on different levels, coloured shutters, steep and stepped streets, numerous passageways with stone or wood-beamed vaults – and cats. Doors opened directly onto the street, and I found a gorgeous pink geranium cascading down a white wall, black-and-white cats on white steps with red geraniums at the foot, and an elderly grey-haired lady sitting crocheting in her doorway.

I came to an elevated spot, where I looked towards ruins on an islet connected to the mainland by a short stone causeway. A solitary gateway, a remnant of the **Temple of Apollo**, stood in defiance of time amid remains of foundations and scattered blocks, with a view of the sea behind.

streets of Naxos

Yet more cats, unguarded steps, paved paths beneath arches, and a steep narrow access way with an ancient twisted vine clinging to an unrendered wall led to a church wedged between other buildings; a small statue stood in a niche above the door and a relief lay above grey shutters opposite. Other narrow thoroughfares had recessed doorways, one with shields embossed on the stone lintel. Bougainvillea hung overhead, and the ends of many streets enclosed by high walls revealed glimpses of the sea beyond. Ancient terracotta tiles on a façade bore the date 1688, pink flowers lined a steep stepped street outside a house built on different levels, and greenery adorned an arch.

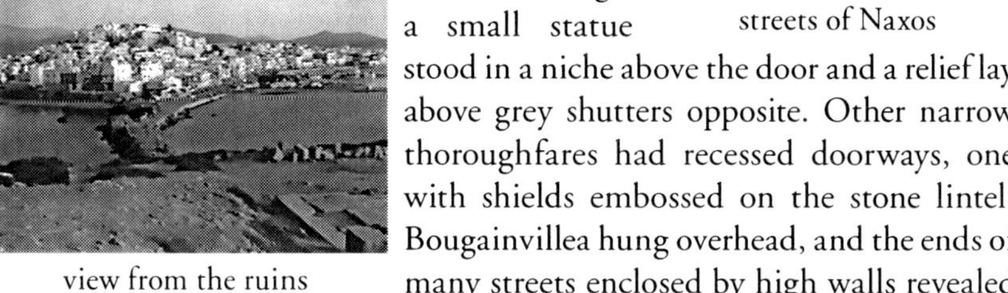
view from the ruins

Coming to the ruins described earlier, the sunset was a vermilion band on the horizon, which was stunning seen through the silhouetted arch. In the other direction, framed by the tall square pillars and lintel, the town looked like a white pyramid as it climbed the hill to crumbling 13th-century castle walls. Music wafted on the evening air as, from another point, I looked down on the harbour promenade and rugged mountains behind. On the mainland again, I gazed across the bay at the gate standing like a lone black sentinel on its spit of land above placid water and birds flying to and fro in the last remaining vestiges of daylight. I came across a night wedding with the priest in elaborate robes and the bride, attendant, and two flower girls all in white.

Naxos was where Theseus deserted Ariadne after she helped him slay the Minotaur on the island of Crete.

Mykonos

Next morning, I again set out on the ferry, passing a lonely church on a rocky outcrop to enter a harbour with gleaming white buildings situated above the bluest of oceans (even a solitary cruise vessel was all white), and so I arrived at one of the loveliest, although commercialised, of the islands, that of mystical **Mykonos**. The row of thatched windmills, identified from many photographs, rose above the cubic buildings and a white-domed chapel in the capital, also called **Hora**.

Mykonos windmills

A strong wind was blowing, and as we drew near, I observed tall-masted vessels and patches of blue on buildings so close to the water's edge that small boats appeared to be moored directly in front. I found accommodation in a *pansion* with a wonderful view that evening of a lighted ship just outside the harbour, a chapel on the point, the windmills on their crest, and fishing boats pulled up on the sheltered shore of a small cove below. I took a familiarisation walk and discovered a crazy-paved courtyard with vines on a white wall, tables with pink cloths and blue chairs, and waiters dressed in pink shirts and black trousers, the sky creating a black ceiling overhead. The narrow crazy-paved streets, their slabs outlined with regularly applied white paint, were well maintained and full of creepers, steps, many little coloured balconies (a cat, washing, and a pottery urn filling one), boutiques and *tavernas*. Even at night, a vivid blue door and red shutters stood out, as did a scene combining green, yellow, purple and blue on doors, walls and shutters, augmented by red garments displayed for sale on a line. A couple of stepped white belfries made an impact against a midnight-black sky.

Early next morning, I filmed two ladies conversing beside a muzzled donkey carrying several panniers of vegetables and standing under a tree next to white steps with a pale blue balustrade. The active wharf with its old-fashioned lamps was the venue for a flower market, where long-stemmed gladioli were prevalent, and I looked down on a scene made famous by the film *Zorba the Greek* starring Anthony Quinn: water lapping the foundations of picturesque coloured houses belonging to sea captains in the area known as Little Venice, with rowing boats pulled up on the shore in front.

A lady in black was arranging flowers on the crazy-paved courtyard outside a chapel with a white belfry and purple bougainvillea making a show over a red gate. Red flowers bloomed in white pots on white unrailed steps leading to elevated doorways, some opposing stairways so close together that there was only the width of two paving slabs between them, and vines reached across the intervening space overhead. Walking towards the cluster of buildings featured in the movie, I found several restaurants. Tables with red cloths were set beside the seawall, and blue boats occupied a narrow strip of beach on the seaward side, where low whitecaps rolled onto yellow sand. Further along, I found green tables and more with red cloths (and blue chairs), from where one looked across at the five windmills, one without its wooden arms. A red boat sat on the walkway, over which waves splashed as I wended my way past a blue wall, overhead balconies, and white plaster horses flanking the base of crazy-paved steps. I was greatly amused by the antics of an Alsatian puppy romping with playful waves, barking at them and retreating as they washed over steps; it was a venue full of undeniable charm, and an artist's delight.

Little Venice

No less charming was the appealing story of the island's resident pink pelican named Petros and his scruffy white mate Irini, both substitutes for the originals that called the town home in the 1950s. Arriving during a storm, the first Petros was regarded as a good omen because the island began to prosper, and the population, out of respect and concern, introduced a 'friend' from France. Petros I met a tragic end when hit by a car on his beloved harbour front on November 29, 1985. Irini II was sent from Louisiana in the US in the late 1960s, and the villagers held an actual marriage ceremony complete with crowns and priests. Unfortunately, the original Petros totally ignored her after the 'wedding', but a subsequent Petros from Germany (welcomed at the airport with a basket of fish and driven to town in the mayoral Mercedes!) took to this bird with mean temperament immediately, and a big festival with dancing and music ensued, attended by the mayor. At the time of my visit, after a large breakfast of fish provided by local fishermen, they spent their time taking a leisurely swim before sauntering up and down the port and posing for countless pictures. Mykonos also had over 5,000 cats, one of which was sitting unconcernedly with the pelicans when I first saw them. I enquired if the ill-natured white bird was safe to pat and was assured in the affirmative, only to be rewarded when I attempted it with a loud and vicious snapping of the large beak. In a stroke of luck, I managed to frame a red-domed white church and its brilliant blue shutters with the open mandibles.

A ginger and white cat sat on a blue windowsill as I progressed to the most photogenic, totally white, Byzantine church of **Panagia Paraportiani** that, with its dome, rounded roofs, ruined walls, and belfry (minus its bell), had the appearance of being created out of frosting. Regrettably, it was no longer possible to enter its one doorway.

Petros

Panagia Paraportiani

Back at the waterfront, the fish market was in full swing, with hundreds of fish arrayed on a concrete slab in the hot sun. I went inside the small blue-domed white chapel on the end of the quay, where I found a comparatively unadorned interior. A crystal chandelier hung from the centre of a blue dome with simple decoration of stars and plain white spandrels underneath. Coloured glass panes lit their surrounds with squares of red, blue and yellow that were reflected on a mirrored surface, a single votive candle stood flickering in a glass on the sill, gold lamps were suspended on the white *iconostasis* with its obligatory images, and there were a couple of other framed pictures. An ornate gold stand for candles stood in front of

fish market

the altarpiece, which in turn stood before a black half dome. Outside, blue, red and yellow fishing smacks, trawlers and the masts of larger vessels, reflected and rocking in the gentle swell, made a colourful background to the activity.

Vegetables were being sold from the back of a truck near two red rowing boats high and dry on the ground. Also facing the promenade, a glaring white church with a startling red dome and roof was superimposed on a deep blue sky. Four cats sat atop a wall, a donkey laden with wicker baskets and greens in wooden containers, from one of which hung a set of scales, stood patiently, whilst a dog ran around the legs a woman holding a painting depicting a local scene. Dressed in the traditional hat and long black robes, a cleric with a white beard was seated at a table with other patrons, and a vendor was placing four crayfish into a plastic bag for weighing.

patient donkey at the wharf

A building down a none-too-salubrious-looking tiny alley had a sign announcing Veterinary Surgeon, and a brilliant blue sky outlined the belfry of a white church, its stone lintel above the red door embossed with angels flanking a cross. The white pelican made a wonderful subject for my film as it spread its wings and opened and closed its large bill with a resounding clap. In a superb picture, I managed to frame a red-domed white church with the open mandibles. Making an ungainly descent down steps, Irini waddled unconcerned along one of the narrow streets to the harbour, whilst pink Petro lay without moving. Following it to the waterfront, I saw more donkeys, and watched a lady repacking the produce on one carrying a few flowers, vegetables, and swinging scales. Bearing baskets filled mainly with floral offerings, a second slowly made its way between the tables and chairs of outdoor cafes, the purple and yellow blooms, orange marigolds and white daisies making a striking picture on the back of the dark-coloured beast as it stood swishing its tail when stopped in front of a door. I walked behind the third, with amongst the orange flowers, as it negotiated the winding alleys (one with an enormous jar outside a door) and halted for customers, each time taking the opportunity to scratch its forehead on stone steps!

Sunset produced an extraordinary display of changing colours as I filmed the Paraportiani church with a starburst of rays on the roof and a series of belfries and crosses in the background, all silhouetted against the setting sun. Zooming in to a belfry and cross on a pale blue sky with bands of yellow and orange on the horizon, the black monument was suddenly superimposed on an intense yellow and orange screen. I do not know if it was an effect seen solely by the camera lens, but the colours moved and mingled in an amazing display like a polar aurora. Across the ocean the red orb of the sun dropped behind black hills rearing into a brilliant orange heaven. I took my evening meal at one of the colourful tables, now set with a small vase of yellow flowers, at the edge of water resembling a sea of ink, the sky infused with a red glow above the opposite shore. My final photographs of Mykonos were of the pink pelican preening the feathers of its wings.

there were many donkey vendors

According to legend, Mykonos was a huge rock flung into the Aegean by Poseidon during a battle with the gods.

Delos

I took a day excursion to dramatic **Delos**, its stony brown hillsides covered with extensive ruins from the third century BC; seen from the ocean, pillars appeared like a coppice of white trees. This uninhabited sacred island of antiquity where, according to mythology, the sun god Apollo and his sister Artemis, the beautiful huntress and goddess of marriage and fertility were born, was for centuries regarded as a religious sanctuary ranked with Olympia and Delphi. Another source named Apollo as the god of light, poetry, music, healing and prophecy.

The archaeological site, with temples, altars, and all the buildings associated with a large population, extended almost the entire length of the island (6km × 1km), but many of the remains consisted only of low walls and sections of fluted pillars. A circular white marble funeral altar was endowed with some carving, and there were foundations and uprights of what were obviously once houses and shops. Square plinths stood on the perimeter of a large paved area, and I observed stone jars and many empty pedestals. Higher walls provided a good illustration of how grey or brown stones of all sizes were roughly shaped and fitted together, and paved paths on well-defined streets were laid with different sized slabs. The sapphire sea provided a stunning backdrop to the partially overgrown site, which extended to the water's edge.

Well-preserved mosaics, some almost complete, graced the floors of more-substantial remains, which obviously protected them to a certain extent in spite of exposure to the elements. Almost three-dimensional in effect, a cleverly executed cubic pattern in white, grey and red had a border of blue scrolls and an anchor to one side. Similar flourishes surrounding other panels could have represented waves because of the setting in which the city was located. One design depicted a flower enclosed in a circle within a diamond, but the most impressive was a remarkable panel with remnants of a still discernable snarling tiger, a winged figure with a spear, and an urn with handles. Surrounding the floor, tall glaringly white columns reached into a clear blue sky.

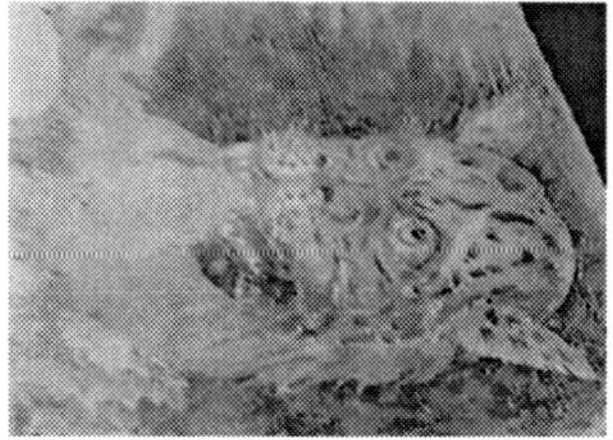
House of Dionysus

Anchored on the incredibly blue sea, beyond a headless white statue ensconced amongst pillars, our modern boat was an incongruous addition to the picture. An almost intact building, its roof supported by white columns, was visible between high walls, and a hillside was covered with toppled pillars and other remains of a barely recognisable theatre. Statues of a male and female, beautifully draped but also both headless, stood together on a rectangular white marble pedestal, and a series of below ground arches could have been part of an ancient cistern.

House of Cleopatra

Looking down paved streets, the white of columns was accentuated by the brown walls, and I found another colourful mosaic floor, the scrolled edge surrounding a flower in the centre of concentric circles within squares, and an anchor entwined with fish to one side. An open-mouthed lion's head adorned a sculpted lintel, the life-sized head of a bull sat under eaves, and like the legendary sphinxes and rams in Egypt, a row of emaciated-looking animals with gaping jaws guarded the **Lions** or **Sacred Way** leading to three temples.

Terrace of Lions

Also like Egypt, a palm tree was viewed through a free-standing arch, and a semicircular marble structure appeared like an elaborate bench seat. There was a figure in a Roman toga, again headless, and a birdlike image embossed on a square pedestal topped by a huge scrotum and broken penis!

Steps led to a well that still held water, yet another floor mosaic pictured a two-toned flower in a red circle, the heads of bulls with garlands of fruits made up heavy relief on pedestals, and a tablet was inscribed with a dedication in ancient Greek script. From the ninth century, for approximately one thousand years, Delos was the religious centre of the Aegean, where no one was allowed to be born, fall sick or die.

sculpture

Tinos

I sailed back to Mykonos and on to terrific **Tinos**, which even before landing presented a different face, built as it was on red hills, with towers instead of domes the prominent feature. At the head of a broad avenue leading from the quay, the large and beautiful **Church of Panagia Evangelistria** – in cream and white marble with a multi-tiered bell tower, ornate parapet, colonnaded balcony, old-style lamps, and a clock on the façade – dominated the town. The interior was hung with so many silver objects such as elaborate chandeliers and ships that it was difficult to see the ornately carved *iconostasis*; even the pulpit, with miniature paintings around the top, appeared wrought in silver. Tall gold candelabra stood behind a white marble divider in front of the altarpiece, and a silver-coated icon with several figures was housed under a most ornate gilded canopy with angels on the corners. Bells began to toll as I took a closer look at the *iconostasis*, above which I saw a painting that I took to represent Jesus with an open book seated at the right hand of God, who was holding a globe (the world?) on his knee. Painted angels appeared on the wall overhead. There was a mass of other delicately detailed carving, stained glass, a silver icon in a gold frame with a carved wooden surround, and a gold-covered icon. The church occupies the site where was discovered an icon of the Virgin to which miraculous properties are attributed.

Church of Panagia Evangelistria

Besides the elaborately decorated dovecotes for which the island was known, I also came across this same 'cut-out' work in walls and above windows, one of the latter in the shape of a leaf inset with tiny flowers. Colourful houses in blue, pink and yellow stood on a red hill, and a white church with a four-tiered tower was perched overlooking the water where, at sunset, silhouetted black boats bobbed beneath an orange sky. A sculpted drinking fountain was recessed into a marble wall next to purple bougainvillea, and the red, yellow and green of vegetables and fruits such as apples, squash and grapes made a colourful picture in front of blue doors on a paved street leading to the water; one was never far from the sea on the islands.

Other street scenes included a bell tower with a silver icon of Mary and Jesus in a niche, a small painting portraying the face of Jesus inserted above perforations in an otherwise plain white wall with a single bell on top, flowers on a sill and the tops of walls, and a small chapel. The view from a rooftop, also exulting in an incised pattern, looked beyond the bell tower to fields and a distant settlement. In general, Tinos was an exceedingly white town, with archways, stairs and at least one steep stepped street. Uneven surfaces of the stuccoed buildings looked as if they had accumulated years of whitewash, and a black and white cat sat atop one glaringly white wall near a little red shutter. Catching a local bus, I ventured into the countryside, where I took a picture of a man mounted on a donkey and obtained a close encounter with the famous dovecotes. The size of a small house and even having steps and chimney-like protrusions on the roof, these elaborate constructions were intricately ornamented with the cut-out work in a wealth of geometric designs.

dovecote

Before returning to the mainland, I spent a night at one more destination of which the name escapes me but where I stayed in the pretty red and white Argo Hotel with stunning views from my balcony of massive hilltop churches and towers, which dominated even this large town. In the street outside stood a tree covered with butterflies, appearing like a mass of orange-and-white blossom.

CENTRAL GREECE

Meteora

Back at the Plaka Hotel in Athens, I obtained my room with the view of the Acropolis, bathed at night in an effulgent red glow below the white Parthenon, which next morning showed up with great clarity atop its now grey mountain retreat. I took a four-day tour that included another of the highlights of my travelling career: the awesome mountaintop monasteries of **Meteora** in the northwest corner of **Thessely**, first established in the 14th century and a World Heritage Site. The name was derived from the Greek word *meteoros*, which means 'suspended in air' and aptly describes the monasteries.

monastery Meteora

Driving through countryside with houses on fairly dry hillsides, summits wearing white villages like crowns, and wayside shops, we ascended the mountains to look down on a fertile valley with a river winding like a ribbon towards a stretch of blue water, and a large white structure shrouded in haze on the opposite shore. The sky cleared to a beautiful blue with puffy white clouds, and the terrain became greener, with thick bush and small conifers at the base of pale rocky mountains into which white villages on their slopes blended. It was nearing night as we approached our destination, and the fantastic peaks showed up in silhouette against a darkening overcast sky. I saw my first monastery cradled atop a sheer ridge as if enveloped in a nest of stone, and below, the twinkling lights of **Kalambaka** were reflected in the inky water of a lake.

Next day, the white town lay nestled beneath brooding umber walls under sombre grey cloud, the forbidding monasteries and towers just visible. Perched on top of the overpowering perpendicular cliffs they appeared impossible to access; indeed, in bygone days apparently the monks were hauled up in nets or baskets at the end of a rope. Later, from my balcony, this same scene took on a grey hue, the dome and towers of a large church glimpsed behind very green trees below, but still with a dull sky overhead. When the sun temporarily broke through, the mountains were transformed to glowing gold as if magically altered by the rainbow that touched one crest like a wand. It started to rain as we left to visit the monasteries, and in the depressing conditions one built directly into the rock looked more like a fortress. The extraordinary shapes and pinnacles towered above, and almost defying gravity, other sanctuaries were constructed right at the edges of chasms up to 1,000m (3,300ft) deep. Of the 24 monasteries, only six remained inhabited. Eventually arriving at a high vantage point, we gazed down on a river far below, looked towards a monastery cocooned in a peak opposite, and peered straight upwards at another, which almost appeared part of the formidable immense cliff face onto which it seemingly precariously clung. A white cross stood on a rock ledge below a third, bare except for turrets and a couple of trees in the compound. It was raining heavily at this stage, which added to the gloomy, even malevolent atmosphere.

Inside, the austere stone walls were no less daunting, but the view across a sheer narrow ravine showed a lighter-toned edifice with red tiled roofs roosting on its precipitous perch opposite. Various shades of greenery, vivid in the wet, clothed flat jutting surfaces of the rock. Farming implements, harness, and large cow bells hung on the solid stone walls, and a wooden wheel and stone jars sat on the floor. A long rope ladder with wooden steps was coiled below the parapet, and the dark kitchen contained utensils that included huge pans; kettles hung above the open fireplace. Wonderful ancient murals adorned a peeling rendered brick surface, some in rich reds and others in faded pastel tones. Outside again, the rain had ceased and left in its wake an almost ethereal scene with soft cloud suspended in valleys below the monasteries. Trapped by the abyss walls, it hung like cotton candy or blew in fine wisps above the very green floor; it was truly beautiful, and the whole experience, although somewhat surreal, was uplifting. The tolling of a distant bell was muted by the mist as it wafted across, obliterating the monastery on an opposite outcrop.

monasteries Meteora

Set in a lovely garden, our second venue was a magnificent ancient church with patterned stonework, an octagonal dome and barrel tiles. Inside the dark living quarters were a large wooden wheel, a wicker basket, pottery jars, wooden containers, a metal cauldron, an enormous wooden barrel, and many indeterminate objects. Yolks for oxen hung on a wall below a walkway in front of an alcove with a holy picture overhead. Its locked door had six skulls arrayed on shelves in an opening, their black empty eye sockets staring for eternity with an unearthly red glow that lit them from behind. A small shrine lay beneath protruding rock, and I peered straight up at the gantry on a tower looming overhead.

More exhilarating panoramas, towns glimpsed between tors, and lush growth on canyon floors marked our departure past many monasteries: some very large, others totally covering smaller peaks on which they resided. Smoke curling from the chimney of one such indicated that it was inhabited but many were now deserted. In the late Byzantine period and during Ottoman rule they became sanctuaries for the persecuted. At our next stop, white birds flew across a distant vertical rock face with a cavity containing remains of **Agios Georgios Monastery**, which must have necessitated its occupants being lowered from the top, but unfortunately all that could be distinguished were coloured scarves, replaced each year on the day of St George. We drove past gigantic isolated fingers of dark grey stone wearing verdant green skirts and soaring above still low-lying cloud; it was an incredible, almost bizarre encounter.

PELOPONNESE

Corinth Canal

Heading for the **Peloponnese**, we went through rocky terrain to **Thermopylae**, where I photographed the statue of Leonidas, naked except for a helmet and carrying a spear and shield.

From the window of my room, I filmed a vendor selling doughnuts and bagels from a cart in front of an haute couture dress shop, and feeding pigeons between customers. Onward to the impressive **Corinth Canal**, an exceptional feat of engineering that carved a 6km-long 23m-wide 90m-deep channel barely the width of the ships that passed through. From the metal pedestrian bridge on which I stood, one could look along the entire length of the canal. In one direction the water was a brilliant blue, on the other, a sparkling silver stream that fed into a scintillating sea. The concept to cut through the isthmus and link the Ionian and Aegean Seas was first visualised by the tyrant founder of Corinth in the sixth century BC who, when the project proved too daunting, opted for a paved slipway across which sailors dragged small ships on rollers, a method used until the 13th century. Many, including Alexander the Great and Caligula, considered the vision, and in AD 67 Nero, using a golden pickaxe, actually struck the first blow before leaving the task to 6,000 Jewish prisoners. Halted by the invasion of the Gauls, it took a French firm to bring it to fruition in the 19th century (1883–93).

In ancient Corinth, Peirene was transformed into a spring by the tears she shed for her son killed by Artemis. Greece abounds in legends.

Mycenae

Our next destination was the impressive ruins of **Mycenae**, the walls of which, according to myth, were built by descendants of the Cyclops, giant of Homer's *Iliad* and *Odyssey*. In his epic poems Homer told of *well-built Mycenae rich in gold* founded by Perseus, son of Danae and Zeus. Perseus' greatest claim to fame was the killing of the hideous snake-haired Medusa whose looks literally petrified the beholder. Mycenae was the most powerful sovereign influence in Greece until 1100 BC, when it was destroyed by fire; it was revisited in the tragic verses of Sophocles. There was evidence to support the claim that it was inhabited from 3000 BC.

Entry was through the **Lion Gate**, the oldest example of monumental sculpture in Europe, a stone inserted above the lintel bearing worn relief of a pillar flanked by two rampant lions.

Lion Gate

Walls and extensive excavated foundations dotted the site, and a deep grave circle containing six royal tombs was surrounded by concentric circles of upright slabs. Unearthed rough stonework of a whitish hue mingled with the grey of the earth and the few green bushes, whilst the reddish-brown of houses blended with russet grasses in the rocky environment. On the nearby hill of **Panayitsa**, archaeologists brought to light the most significant edifice of Mycenaean construction, the **Treasury of Atreus** also known as the beehive **Tomb of Agamemnon**. Resembling those in the Valley of Kings in Egypt, it consisted of a mound with a walled approach, a single solid stone slab creating the lintel, an open triangle above, and a corbelled dome inside.

Epidaurus

On the road again, we stopped to photograph an interesting church constructed from different colours of stone and featuring an octagonal dome, a bell tower, and a beautiful mural over the door. Our next venue was the theatre at **Epidaurus** (third century BC), the most famous, largest, and best preserved in Greece. Built of limestone and seating 14,000 spectators, the acoustics were so perfect that even the merest whisper could be heard in the last row, from where the view of surrounding trees and mountains in the background was amazing. Nearby, were the foundations of the fourth-century Doric **Sanctuary of Asclepius**, god of healing, said to have been born in Epidaurus. It was believed to have contained a huge statue of the god made of gold and ivory. **Mt Arahneo**, mentioned in the tragedy *Agamemnon*, rose directly behind the sanctuary. Another wonderful vista was obtained overlooking the town of **Nafplio**, first capital of Greece, reputedly created by Palamides, son of Poseidon, and situated on a perfect, seemingly painted, deep-blue bay ringed by mountains. In the centre of the bay lay the fortified islet of **Bourtzi**, with its battlements, octagonal tower, and foundations washed by waves.

We spent the night in this picturesque place featuring elegant houses, steep stepped streets, cascading flowers and creepers, iron-railed balconies, Turkish fountains, and thoroughfares containing orange trees laden with the brightly coloured fruit. Bells chimed as I wandered along a street with tables and chairs in front of vine-covered walls to the paved **Syntagma** (constitution) **Square**, where café tables lined one side and interesting buildings included a mosque. I passed a stone house with tendrils of red bougainvillea above blue shutters, and came to a narrow alley where plants and white tables with pink and green chairs were placed at the top of (and below) steps descending to a creeper-adorned stone wall bearing an ornately sculpted drinking fountain with the moss-covered tiles of a dome looming above.

On a stony hill overlooking the town, the well-preserved fortifications of the **Palamidi Fortress** (1711–14) wended their way down to a shabby area of crumbling stucco walls and one large pink building with blue shutters. Towards dusk, lights came on in a wide avenue with trees in the median strip and the symmetrical towers of a white church at the end. Tables and chairs seemed to materialize everywhere: on pavements and the roadway. One row was set up in a laneway with vines overhead and potted plants between folds of cloth draped over the wall opposite. There were checked cloths, pink cloths, green cloths, and more tables with white cloths and pink or green chairs. In the light from streetlamps it was all very festive. At one *taverna*, a ginger and white cat sat washing itself on top of a glass display cabinet containing fish! The clock tower behind heavy stone walls on a rise above the town indicated the time at ten minutes to six. Tables and chairs were also placed beneath an awning on the seafront, where palms swayed and the rippling water danced silver in the last light of day. The now dark castle in the centre looked mournful and melancholy.

Olympia

Departing next morning, we passed several small roadside shrines with holy pictures inside and a cross on top as we ascended the **Arcadian Mountains**, in very windy conditions, to **Tripolis** and thence to **Olympia**. Here, amongst its many exhibits, the remarkable **Archaeological Museum** featured a plaque depicting a scaly mythical creature appearing to have both hooves and the tail of a fish, remnants of an intricately patterned pottery plate, a small pediment with remains of figures, and amazing life-sized images from the much larger western pediment of the **Temple of Zeus**. The theme of this was the fight between the Centaurs and Lapiths, its figures ranging from a central standing image of Apollo to those, gradually decreasing in height, in positions of kneeling, crouching and, at the ends, lying. The eastern pediment showed the chariot race between Pelops and Oinomaos, and a *metope* (sculpted frieze) portrayed the *Twelve Labours of Heracles*. Pelops, after whom the Peloponnese was named, defeated king Oinomaos in a chariot race and married his daughter, Hippodamia. Also on display were sculptures of women and horses, statues of naked and scantily dressed men, including the winged Nike of Paionois, and a black Grecian urn decorated with traditional images. The exquisite marble sculpture of **Praxiteles' Hermes** (330 BC) depicted a naked Hermes minus his left arm, his right cradling the infant Dionysus, also minus an arm, swathed in flowing fabric. There were other semi-clad images, yet others in capes, tunics and breastplates embossed with figures, a large bull, a stylised bronze horse, pottery figurines, and a clay head of Athena from 490 BC.

Although with few substantial structures, the actual site of the original Olympics was awe-inspiring because of its connotations. Indications are that the games were held as early as 1000 BC to honour Pelops and Hippodamia. Exclusively local at the start, they gradually attracted the interest of other towns, and in the year of the first Olympiad (776 BC) they were dedicated to the honour of Zeus. During the games, an Olympian truce was in force and all hostilities suspended. The victor's prize, a crown made from a wild olive branch, was always cut from the same tree, which still survived in the grounds! The initial games, which included foot races, wrestling, the *pankration* (a vicious form of boxing), a pentathlon, chariot and horse racing, as well as artistic and literary competitions, came to an end in AD 393 when Theodosius I banned them by decree at the advent of Christianity. They were revived in 1896, where they had been born, by a French historian. Theodosius II ordered the total destruction of the sanctuary's temples, and sixth-century earthquakes completed the ravages of time. Slaves and women, either as participants or spectators, were not permitted to enter the sanctuary, and those caught trying were thrown from a nearby rock.

Situated in lovely grassed surrounds with many shady trees, the majority of remains consisted of rows of broken columns (the **Gymnasium**), low walls constructed with large stone blocks, and steps. Complete fluted pillars with square capitals made the usual attractive picture against a blue sky. The still impressive 30,000-capacity **Stadium** was entered via a stone arch, its huge arena, on which we were invited to run, surrounded by a sloping green sward but no seating. Large stone discs were places of sacrifice or offering, and one area was scattered with tumbled fragments of fluted columns. More-complete structures included a wall with an arched opening and, located behind stone lattice, pillars sculpted with floral patterns.

CENTRAL GREECE

Nafpaktos

The dark interior of a church was adorned with wall murals, elaborate chandeliers, a white *iconostasis* with large pictures, and a silver icon depicting Mary and the Holy Child. A pretty white house with a bright blue door had massed pot plants along the foundations and up steps. We stopped at **Patras**, where I photographed the **Church of Agios Andreas**, a massive edifice with a green dome, many cupolas, and a triple-arched entry. The apostle Andrew preached and was martyred in Patras. Even low-lying cloud over the fortified harbour entrance, where fishing boats were drawn up on a small patch of beach to one side, could not disguise the turquoise colour of the water as we boarded a ferry for **Nafpaktos** on the mainland. A series of mountains was almost hidden by mist from the ceiling of heavy cloud as we approached another harbour enclosed by battlements, with the obligatory church behind. Sheltering colourful fishing boats, this small protected anchorage was most picturesque, its narrow entry guarded by crenellated stone walls with round fortifications at the ends: a statue atop one, a turret on the other. Trees and Stuccoed houses lined the seawall between these arms, the smooth surface of languidly undulating teal-blue water below. Fortifications were also visible above a paved square holding tables and chairs, trees, and a bust atop the Ionic capital of a fluted column.

Nafpaktos harbour

We proceeded past rugged coastal scenery with frightening drops and stopped to film a church on a summit, which dominated red-roofed white houses climbing the hill at its feet. Below us, a small natural harbour with a rocky shoreline was a haven for a few tall-masted vessels, and white villages dotted the shore and hillsides opposite the extremely blue bay.

Delphi

Arriving at **Delphi**, our first stop was the **Museum**, where interesting exhibits included a frieze depicting a battle between the Greeks and Trojans from 525 BC and the winged figure of a squatting lion with a human head, braided hair, and the sublime face of a woman: the 550 BC **Sphinx of the Naxians**. A fire-blackened ivory head with shimmering gold tresses dated back to the sixth century BC. A pair of identical male nudes (c. 590 BC) portrayed brothers **Kleobis and Biton**, given the gift of eternal sleep by Hera after yoking themselves to a chariot to convey their mother to her temple. Another naked male was without arms, and a marble column featured three dancing females back to back. A fifth-century BC scholarly figure called the **Bronze Charioteer** commemorated a victory in the Pythian games of 478 or 474 BC. A black and white mosaic floor with a patterned edge showed birds in circles within squares. Another featured an intricate design around images of a figure in a laurel wreath and blue tunic and one carrying a bowl of fruits, which included grapes and an unusually bright green melon – most colours were subdued. This also featured octagonal shapes holding birds and animals, amongst them a large eagle and blue peacock, a camel, horse, and a creature with a bushy tail like a fox.

frieze Delphi Museum

Outside, sarcophagi were carved respectively with griffins flanking a flaming torch and a naked man leading a horse. Another had much deteriorated figures, and the courtyard was enmeshed in trees with stony white mountains rearing beyond.

sarcophagus

Looking down on Delphi, I could discern the **Sanctuary of Athena** and the imposing three-columned gateway of the **Tholos**, a marble rotunda built in the fourth century BC in a dramatic setting on a precipice of **Mt Parnassos**. Juniper trees flourished below, majestic mountains rose opposite, and the **Gulf of Corinth** was visible in the distance. This was the domain of the oracle, and one prophecy to Nero resulted in her death. In retribution for shouting: *Your presence outrages me. Begone matricide! Beware 73* at his approach, the furious Nero condemned her to be buried alive and, after cutting off their hands and feet, her priests with her. She was vindicated one year later when Nero died and was succeeded by a 73-year-old emperor. It was also prophesied that Homer: *Shall be deathless and ageless forever.* The world was richer for the philosophy of the priests, endorsed by Plato, who preached reverence for women and honouring one's word, condemned cruelty, encouraged self-control, and advocated compassion for the afflicted.

Large blocks of stone marked foundations of other buildings, and as the sun's rays broke through enveloping dark cloud, questing fingers of light fanned out to strike the monument, illuminating it in semblance of some divine proclamation or revelation. Descending to the site, I looked back at the lofty red walls from where we had surveyed it, standing in sharp contrast to the white ruins. The carved lintel of the Tholos gateway featured a rearing horse and floral design, and pencil pines stood out amongst broken columns around an amphitheatre in the distance. From above the site once again, I looked to one side at terraced ruins surrounded by thick vegetation. With stark mountains beyond, waving grasses in the foreground, and framed by a tree displaying a brilliant burst of glorious red blossom, they made a great picture. A round stone-lined excavation appeared below the red stone of the terraced walls, and priceless white blocks lay around like so much rubble.

Above the water, more rays transformed the edges of thunderous cloud to gold as we stopped for a view of the town where we were to spend the night. This was one of the prettiest places yet, with copious flowers and plants enhancing stepped streets, trailing over walls, and hanging from iron-railed balconies overhead. One colourful street also had fruits and vegetables displayed on the steps, and a table with a checked cloth on a landing halfway up. The thoroughfares were immaculate, and old-fashioned two-branched lampposts hung with baskets paraded down the centre of a wider set of paved steps with mountains visible beyond the top. Beautiful flowers grew opposite an old white stuccoed cottage, its turquoise door and window frame an enigma amongst the mainly red-roofed white houses. One was built on the edge of a ravine with a winding river in the valley below and a view of the gulf, where heavy black cloud was once more lit from underneath. A plain stone house was enhanced with clusters of purple, white and yellow flowers. It was very windy, and clouds turned to pink as lights came on in colourful shops and an outdoor café, which was also surrounded by gay flowers.

Next morning, we returned to the archaeological site, pausing first for photographs of a panorama that took in the entire verdant green valley: the river, rugged ranges, and the distant sea. Visiting another section of the ruins, I noted free-standing white columns, and a sculpted pedestal occupying a recess in a wall constructed from reddish rocks below a similarly hued escarpment. Additional red walls constituted what was once a row of merchants' shops, and solid stone blocks exhibiting different textures and colours made up remains of yet other structures. The more substantial **Treasury of the Athenians**, from the end of the sixth century BC, still had three walls – the fourth side being the entrance consisting of a pediment and carved lintel supported by two central columns – but no roof. As we strolled along ancient paving, more pillars and a solitary Ionic capital placed on a fluted segment stood in dynamic defiance of the mammoth mountains behind. The extensive site included a fourth-century BC **Theatre** that, ensconced as it was in a belt of green trees at the foot of rearing mountains, revelled in a setting equalling any drama that would have been enacted upon its stage. From the top of the theatre, I could see far below to the site visited the previous afternoon. Also encompassed by trees was the **Stadium**, best preserved in Greece, with seating down one side of the arena and always the mountains behind. Roughly restored pillars on an elevated paved platform were all that remained of the sixth-century BC **Temple of Apollo**, where the oracle supposedly sat. Zeus released two eagles, one from the East, the other the West, and at the point where they met he threw the sacred stone marking the centre of the earth. It was here that the oracle was developed. The first prophesies were uttered by the earth goddess Gaia; her son Python, guardian of the oracle, was killed by Apollo who took over.

On the return journey to Athens, we stopped again at the old village of **Arachova** seen on the way up. Known for its handmade rugs, many of which hung outside shops, it sat in the lee of mountains and consisted of a collection of red-roofed houses below a lone tower occupying the top of a remarkable pinnacle of rock.

Arachova village

Our passage was marked by churches dominating towns clinging to hillsides and by a series of mountains with glimpses of the gulf, now far away. In just such a setting we visited the magnificent 11th-century Byzantine **Monastery of Ossios Loukas**, overlooking orchards or olive groves, fields and the ever-present mountains. Constructed of different sizes and colours of stone reinforced with buttresses, and with obvious later additions in white, it was surrounded by gardens and cobbled paving. A niche above an arched gateway contained an illustration of the head and shoulders of a bearded man in a gold surround, and windows had carved stone insets. Lovely flowerbeds brightened the base of a white stone façade with a square bell and clock tower on top. Inside, the theme of many different types and hues of stone continued in the corbelled dome, arched windows, and sculpted pedestals. In the second of these interconnecting churches, circles containing coloured portraits were entangled in elaborate black-and-white patterns on groins overhead. There was a small altar and ancient worn murals on the stone walls, two appearing to portray the removal of Jesus' body from the cross and interment in the tomb.

Monastery of Ossios Loukas

Designs also decorated the undersides of arches supported by stone pillars. A semicircular recess on the façade contained a mural depicting a crowd scene. In the main place of worship, a huge octagonal building, Jesus holding a book resided in the dome, the omnipresent angels and saints were depicted below, and tiny birds darted and swooped up and down. Here, the marble-veneer walls were of much finer quality, with Arabic-like two-toned striped arches above niches, embossed patterns, gilded surfaces, and many 11th-century paintings. Yet another part featured rough stone walls, a dome, carved capitals, a barrel-vaulted ceiling over the altar, framed paintings, and a fresco of Jesus washing the feet of his disciples.

Jesus washing disciples' feet

En route again, I filmed one more small white chapel and red and green foliage lining the road. We stopped for lunch at a restaurant with a gobbling turkey strutting in the car park, and arriving back in bustling Athens, I visited a market square. Food carts in the middle were selling everything from confectionary, peanuts and bagels to meat dishes and drinks from a bubbling fountain. A lovely domed building with an arcaded balcony sat on the perimeter, and an old stone structure was visible above colourful souvenir shops. Accompanying his own vocals, a violinist was seated near café tables in the lee of the Acropolis. Remains in the vicinity included a multi-columned edifice with a plain pediment and indistinguishable figures under the eaves, pedestals holding sculpted images without arms and/or heads, and scattered blocks. Pink clouds heralding the sunset lay over the hexagonal structure described on my second day in the city, with the Parthenon atop its perch behind. Domes on a stone church made a striking picture silhouetted against a blue sky patterned with apricot-hued clouds. Also in silhouette, pillars topped by a pediment framed a distant hilltop where a dome was superimposed on orange cloud (that faded as I watched), whilst the haunting sounds of a flute floated on the still air. Mats were draped for display down the centre of a set of stone steps, with other items arrayed on the pavement or hanging above. It was a lively and colourful area at night: café tables with bright cloths, vendor carts, and a glass case containing an octopus on top of a mound of crushed ice. The latter next to an upmarket store with a fur coat in the window! That night, I could hear the sounds of the son-et-lumiere from my room.

SARONIC ISLANDS

Next morning, bells tolled loudly from the Monastiraki Church in the square near the hotel as I made my way once more to Piraeus for a day cruise to the three closest **Saronic Islands**: Aegina, Poros and Hydra. Sailing over calm, inevitably brilliant blue sea with rock erupting from the surface, we passed a large modern stadium, hills white with the towns that covered them, more 'Dover' cliffs, mountains, and yachts in a sheltered cove.

Poros

The approach to **Poros** presented a somewhat different face to the usual blue and white, inasmuch as some pastel-toned buildings rose up behind the waterfront and the only prominent feature was a single tower. However, the narrow twisting streets were the same, and I saw scarlet bougainvillea cascading over blue shutters in a pink wall, roses growing on a roof, and blue tables and chairs on the pavement. White steps led to a ledge that accommodated a boat with oars in rowlocks and flags fluttering from its rigging. Many small craft were lined up at the harbour, where I also saw a white church with a hexagonal red dome, a monument, and Greek flags flying. My brief visit coincided with a ceremony, and I was lucky to witness a parade of sailors marching to band music, followed by excited children in traditional costume waving the national flag. Bystanders, including officers in naval uniform, were dressed up for the occasion, and the happy event, which I think was an annual celebration for the navy, was presided over by the bell tower. Unfortunately, because I was attempting to see three islands in limited time, my photography was very rushed and consequently poor.

Hydra

Sunlight glinted like mirrors on the surface of the water as we approached **Hydra**, its more protected harbour displaying colourful buildings, the usual donkeys, an impressive square bell and clock tower on the waterfront – and no vehicular traffic!

Hydra

Narrow cobbled lanes led past thick white stuccoed walls, one with a bright blue picket gate and a curtain of purple bougainvillea. A second façade featured yellow window frames and royal blue steps leading to a yellow door, and another had red shutters. Music accompanied my progress, tables and chairs with green and yellow cloths sat under spreading trees, a tortoiseshell cat looked expectantly into an open doorway, and I came across shady courtyards. Large red pottery jars reposed outside green gates in the white wall of a church with a burnt-orange belfry, and stepped streets led upwards to red-and-grey mountains. A stone house with pale green shutters abutted a stark white residence with indigo and white tubs beneath blue framed windows. Overhead, more were lined up on the parapet of a balcony with a blue and white striped awning. White walls had colourful doors and shutters opening directly onto narrow alleys, one with pink geraniums outside a pale blue door, another with red plants flanking green steps leading to a blue door; white pots occupied a small ledge overhead. A citrus tree flourished in the narrow space behind a wall, and back at the harbour I saw a five-tiered bell tower, two donkeys (one black and one white) standing head to tail, a wide paved promenade, the square tower mentioned above, shops and cafés, two cats sitting one above the other on steps, and masses of bright pink bougainvillea spanning streets and draping balconies. A building with an arcaded frontage and balcony featured a carved marble crest with the double-headed eagle, hanging lanterns, and busts on pedestals in the courtyard. Like Aegina, it was once a great sea-going force, but the populace made their fortune by running the British blockade of French ports during the Napolionic Wars. The island was used as a location for the 1950s film *Boy on a Dolphin*.

Aegina

Aegina lacked the mountain backdrop, and from the ferry I could see a red-domed church, symmetrical square clock towers, white and pastel buildings sitting beyond a cobalt blue sea, and luxury boats riding at anchor in the harbour. By the seventh century Aegina was the premier maritime power in the region, amassing great wealth through trade with Egypt and Phoenicia, but today is solely Greece's prime producer of Pistachio nuts. Mythology relates that the island was named after the daughter of river god Asopus, who was abducted there by Zeus. Her son Aeacus, who became one of the three judges of the underworld, was the father of Achilles of the Trojan War.

A tiny white chapel on the quay, a painted image in a niche beneath its single bell, was simply furnished with a cut-glass chandelier suspended from the dome, portraits on the low curved ceiling of an alcove housing a small *iconostasis*, votive candles, a table with a lace cloth, an icon on a stand and, on one bare white wall, a framed picture of a cleric or saint appearing the same as that on the exterior. Harnessed to buggies, decoratively adorned horses were waiting patiently, their owners ringing bells to attract the attention of tourists. Fruits and vegetables such as cauliflowers, bananas and apples in crates and bunches of garlic hanging from rigging were being sold from boats. Restaurants lining the wharf included a yellow building with red and green awnings and blue al fresco tables and chairs. Streets behind had vine-covered patios, a ginger cat sat on a white ledge above a vivid blue doorway, and squid or octopus hung outdoors above a charcoal grill on which they were being cooked. They were then chopped and served with lemon at a tiny table and two chairs standing nearby. Other produce was hung on walls, stacked on tables, displayed in sacks or baskets, and preserved in glass jars on shelves. Heading back to Piraeus, the ferry passed small fishing boats pulled up on the beach below a hillock crowned with ancient ruins. The lingering sunset melting into the west was one of the best that I had experienced. Once again, I watched the changing lights on the Parthenon atop a black Acropolis – a fitting finale to Greece.

SPAIN

Separated by the **Pyrenees** from the rest of Europe, Spain stands out in my memory for some of the most superlative architecture the world has produced. Influenced by 700 years of Moorish rule (from 711 to 1492), it echoed of splendours past. I also remember it as a place where I was the victim of two robbery attempts.

London

Staying overnight in London before journeying to Spain, I took a walk around **St James's Park**, the oldest in the city and close to **Buckingham Palace**, so named because it was built by the first Duke of Buckingham. Here, from the **Blue Bridge**, I observed a winged figure atop an elaborate monument across **St James's Park Lake**, trees clothed in the vibrant tones of autumn, ducks with bright orange heads, drooping willows, green lawns, a fountain in the water, and gulls. Through the trees, a forest of grey spires and white cupolas looked like some English Disneyland, whilst russet, plum, yellow and orange foliage created carpets of colour on the ground. **Big Ben** was also visible above treetops. Outside the park, a metallic memorial with heavy relief was inserted in a brick wall, and I filmed the Grenadier Guards in their Busby's and long grey coats in front of **St James Palace**. This proffered an elaborate clock face and battlemented towers, and was the royal residence from 1660 to 1837, after which it was considered insufficiently impressive. It was on the train between England and France that I saw my first skyscraper; standing amongst much lower buildings, it assumed an even greater impression of height.

Madrid

Beginning in **Madrid**, I took photographs of magnificent buildings with as much interest on rooflines as façades. A three-tiered white cupola had the appearance of a wedding cake, and white figures appeared below a metallic winged image at the apex of a decorated dome that capped the turret-like front of a building called Metropolis. Life-sized figures also stood atop columns between windows below. Prevailed over by spired towers, the cathedral-like **City Hall** fronted **Plaza de**

Cibeles Fountain

Cibeles, where the goddess Cybele, driving a chariot drawn by two lions, occupied the centre of a large fountain surrounded by flowers and flags. This was very near the convenient accommodation that I had managed to obtain with the help of the obliging tourist office, which also provided information on how to get there on the Metro.

I observed images below a figure with prancing horses atop a dome, cupolas, towers, and more fountains with flowers and flags – always accompanied by the constant traffic roar of a busy major city. With its sculpted flags and figures, the five-arched **Puerta de Alcalá** put me in mind of the Brandenburg Gate in Berlin. Being the weekend, popular **El Buen Retiro Park** was full of crowds taking advantage of a glorious day. A tall two-tiered fountain had life-sized figures frolicking around the centre and a magician performing tricks with a cane in front. People were rowing boats on the large lake from where steps led to a tall pedestal holding an equestrian statue of King Alfonso XII crafted by 32 sculptors. Embossed panels were inserted in the plinth and clusters of figures arrayed above. Behind the monument stood a semicircular colonnade with a balustrade on top and solid carved pillars at either end. A series of lions stood on low pedestals above other images at the water's edge. A band in colourful red and purple attire (even to their hats) entertained with jazz music played on a saxophone, clarinet, trombone, and two types of drum. The **Paseo de las Estatuas** was lined with images originally from the **Palacio Real** (Royal Palace).

Detailed carving over a doorway depicted an angel and other images below an arch with floral relief, a flower stall brightened a tree-lined street, and a carved pediment, pillars with Corinthian capitals, and lions flanking the staircase, marked the traditional grey stone **Congreso de los Diputados** (Parliament Building). Antiquated five-branched lampposts stood in the street outside. Another dome was adorned with figures, and sculpture enhanced the parapet of an edifice with iron railing on carved stone balconies. This also possessed a colourful illustration in a recess below a turret with decorative ironwork on top. Approaching **Plaza Mayor**, old-fashioned lampposts in the street added character to the square red brick towers topped by tall spires on the **Santa Cruz Palace**. The plaza was entered via a three-storey arcade, the arch at the end revealing another equestrian statue, the spires of twin clock towers, tables and chairs with music playing in the background, and the inevitable pigeons. The enormous edifice surrounding the square had bright red walls with white shutters, iron-railed balconies, and a colonnade at street level. Part of the stunning façade featured colourful paintings of larger-than-life naked men and women, which included one climbing to escape a charging bull, another riding a leopard, and an archer, all between windows with ornately sculpted lintels.

A line of spires was silhouetted against the sun, and I saw the old **Convent of las Descalzas Reales** (founded 1559) constructed in different mediums, but was not permitted to film its gorgeous interior furnished in the period of the 16th century and containing paintings by Titian and Rubens.

illustrated façade

A row of classical statues stood on pedestals amongst trees in a nature strip by the sidewalk of a wide boulevard. This was the approach to **Plaza de Oriente**, a broad avenue of gardens and trees with a statue of King Felipe IV on a rearing horse, again with images and a sculpted panel on the pedestal, standing in front of an imposing building. Interestingly, the balance of the horse proved technically too difficult for the artist until his friend Galileo recommended making the rear legs solid and leaving those in the front hollow. I noticed a head and torso in the centre of a finely embossed façade beneath carved eaves, and a face also appeared underneath a circular window below a turret. A clock chimed in the tower of a plain building, its foreground beautified by a two-tiered fountain surrounded by red flowers, beside which a man was feeding pigeons. Viewed from the opposite side, the flowers complemented red awnings behind, and atop buildings down a neighbouring street a charioteer and glowing copper cupola resembling a flame could be seen. The former turned out to be one of twin drivers standing astride identical chariots, each pulled by four horses. Other figures stood on the parapet below.

A sight seen all over the world was that of a person acting as a statue until prompted by donations to move; this one stood in front of a metallic bear climbing a metallic tree. A monument surmounted by a globe stood in a large reflecting pool, to one side of which crouched a naked female form shielding her eyes with a hand as she gazed out. I reached the Royal Palace in time for the brief changing of the guard. Carrying rifles, soldiers in white caps with red feathers, black shirts with red epaulets, and black trousers with a red stripe down each side, marched to drums and flutes. The fairly ordinary façade had fluted columns with Ionic capitals, statues on the parapet, and carved triangular and semicircular pediments above windows. Nearby, a dome in the background was effectively framed by a tri-level fountain with figures around the base. Later in the day, another ceremony was being enacted at the palace, with guards in white-plumed helmets on horseback, military personnel standing at ease on the pavement, and band members in tricorn hats, sashes across long-tailed jackets, white leggings and black boots. An official black Rolls Royce was parked to one side. Presenting arms, all came to attention and music played as a police motorcycle escort led a cavalcade of three gleaming cars out of the entrance, whereupon the music abruptly ceased – all that pomp and circumstance for a few seconds! The car that had been parked at the side then entered followed by the soldiers, three more vehicles, and police. There must have been more activity anticipated because sirens blared and motorcycle patrolmen lined both sides of the roadway. Opposite the palace, I climbed to see the beautiful Renaissance-type **Sabatini Gardens**, with maze-like hedges, ornamental and trimmed trees, walkways, and white statues.

The first part of Cervantes' immortal work, *Don Quixote*, was published in Madrid in 1605, and magnificent Goya paintings portrayed the famous revolt when Napoleon put his brother Joseph on the Spanish throne.

Ávila

After this brief introduction to Madrid, I boarded a train travelling alongside the banks of the **Adaja River** to the historic walled town of **Ávila**, at 1,127m the highest city in Spain and birthplace of St Theresa, the 16th-century reformer of the Carmelite order. It was also the place of the most brutal phase of the Spanish Inquisition, where 2,000 people were burnt at the stake in the late 15th century.

The first attractions were ancient stone buildings with tiny windows. A grey stone church had a small belfry, the figures of a man and boy on a bracket, and coats of arms on the otherwise plain façade above its triple-arched entry. Another figure stood atop a tall pedestal in the centre of the wide, dry and dusty **Plaza de Santa Teresa** lined with trees and streetlamps. At one end stood the umber stone **San Pedro Church** with its unadorned façade, large rose window flanked by two tiny round windows, and a portal with conjoined arches decreasing in size. However, the outstanding thing about Ávila de los Caballeros (knights) was the amazingly well-preserved 11th- and 12th-century *muralla*, the crenellated dark stone wall, appropriately called **Curtain Wall**, which surrounded the city, making it the most complete walled enclosure from the Spanish Middle Ages and best of its type in the world. Rectangular in shape, it was 2½ kilometres in length and 3 metres broad with 9 gates and 88 stout towers averaging 12m in height at intervals of roughly 25 metres.

Opposite the church of San Pedro, at the other end of the plaza, lay the massive **Alcázar Gate**. Stone figures appeared above another entrance at the top of steps, and an arched wall of warm-coloured stone framed a medieval building in the background as I made my way through the main gate to the 12th- to 14th-century **Cathedral**, oldest is Spain, guarded by lions reclining on pedestals in the street. The entrance of serried arches, each with a larger-than-life sculpted figure, was itself under a stone canopy with a carved balustrade. Small images graced the tympanum above the embossed wooden door. A second arched entry was flanked by only two figures, but a number of smaller male and female images stood on brackets overhead. Life-sized faces, each different, adorned these consoles, and dainty embossed canopies sheltered each figure, one of which, wearing a mitre and portrayed with crossed keys, probably represented St Peter.

Ávila Cathedral

Apart from these doorways, the façade was once again comparatively unadorned, except for fancy-topped fluted pilasters, a square bell and clock tower, cone-shaped spires, and a figure in a niche on top. Built into the defensive enclosure (the apse formed part of the wall), the cathedral was also a fortress. As opposed to its arid location on a treeless tableland strewn with immense boulders, outside one section of the wall a very green slope rolled down from its hilltop position. Stone houses, old-fashioned lampposts, cobbled streets, numerous belfries, and some sagging tiled roofs above colourful walls with crumbling stucco all made for interesting pictures.

old houses

La Granja

As a guest of Julia Tours I visited the palace of **La Granja de San Ildefonso**, modelled after Versailles, its typical square towers culminating in pyramid-shaped roofs with metal spires. The classical garden had white pottery urns containing sculpted fruits, statues on pedestals, some simple topiary, hedges in concentric squares or circles with a dusting of snow, and the most glorious autumn foliage lit by the sun. A gilded crown and fleur-de-lis (French imperial insignia) decorated a wrought-iron gate, white sphinx-like creatures and cupids with arrow-filled quivers were placed around the grounds, and a forest of naked black trees revealed snow on mountains beyond. Urns also lined a set of steps, and green lampposts had gold relief on the base. Aside from the spires, arched windows, and round windows in decorative surrounds, the exterior of this huge palace built around a bare courtyard was uninspiring and belied the wonders to confront me within.

The Rococo interior took my breath away with its almost garish mixtures of colour and crystal chandeliers hanging from illustrated ceilings. The first, encased in a border of multihued stuccowork incorporating flowers and garlands, depicted a bearded man in red holding a laurel wreath, a woman in green and cherubs, all reclining on cloud. Two seraphs supported an open book between them whilst in flight.

La Granja

The second, framed in elaborate highly coloured stuccowork extending to the cornice, portrayed cherubs, a chariot pulled by white doves, and a woman in blue lying on cloud and reaching down to a warrior, flames flaring behind him as he looked up at her whilst resting on boulders, his right arm supporting a shield and cradling a sword.

Surrounded by gold filigree, a third celestial scene showed two cherubs holding a blue sphere and a woman embracing a child. A marble bust sat on a pedestal in a niche of brown-toned marble radiating a high sheen; white relief appeared above and faces on a ruby red panel below. This room had marble flooring and another beautiful ceiling painting, which depicted ladies reclining on rocks, their jars spilling water. It also featured dogs, horses, a man hoisting a woman, and cherubs on cloud overhead, the whole surrounded by gold filigree on a white background.

ceiling painting

ceiling painting

Once again enclosed by flamboyant gold stuccowork, the next ceiling pictured ladies in red, blue and yellow respectively, the latter seated sideways on a pony, and cherubs holding aloft a length of green cloth.

An ornate gilt-framed mirror on a marble wall reflected multiple images, creating the illusion of an avenue of mirrors. Standing in front of one such reflective surface, a black marble half table with elaborate gilded legs held two black candelabra flanking a porcelain vase with a frilled edge. Making the décor even more striking, mirrors reflected the marbled pillars, paintings and wealth of gold decoration.

the impact was augmented by gilt framed mirrors

A second black marble console with ornate gold legs, this one bearing two blue candelabra in the form of vases containing gilt flowers, which were placed either side of a vase showing a gentleman and two elegant ladies, stood in front of a mirror with a gilded floral surround. Another heavenly vista depicted a lady in green and red, a second in blue and yellow clutching a sprig, cherubs, a horse, and a solitary camel, all on cloud. There was no gold, or even much colour framing this painting; instead, white alabaster figures were enmeshed in white embossing. Below the portrait of a child in formal dress, a gilt clock featuring a mother nursing an infant stood on a reddish marble half table with gilded legs. The second to last exceptional ceiling portrayed a naked female with a bow and arrow, a man holding a scorpion, a large lizard, snakes, and a dog. These looked down on a brown marble and gilt half table holding two black and white Chinese figurines standing either side of a white marble clock with small images; other ornaments included tall vases flanking a black clock decorated in gold. A sumptuous room, its ceiling picture in an irregular surround forming the deep colourful cornice, displayed an exquisite white statue of a lady holding a goblet, the veiled face so finely crafted that there was a perception of features visible through transparent fabric.

A tapestry depicted Cupid with his bow and a blindfolded Justice with scales and a sword, and a room with walls covered in red fabric had matching red drapes, an elaborate chandelier, period chairs and, on a highly polished long wooden table, gold compote dishes with figures around the stem. The walls also held gold-framed paintings and mirrors. Containing a tall blue and white lidded vase and an ivory inlaid box with a mirror and tiny drawers, the next room was lined with paintings and oriental-looking floral panels. One picture depicted a cool restful scene of blue water and a figure praying in a green glade; faces featured in gilded motifs on top of the panels, and the dado was formed with pink, blue and white marble. In another salon, below a still-life painting and next to rich red Regency chairs, a mottled marble console incorporating faces in its gold legs held a gilded ornament between blue vases with gilt handles. Another red-walled chamber, with a large painting of bewigged gentlemen and refined ladies in a drawing room, had views of the garden with snowy mountains in the background. A gilt clock with ebony images on the sides was placed below the painting, and flags together with a shield and crown constituted part of a heavy gold frame containing a portrait.

Reflected in a mirror, tapestries such as that of a hunting scene with a floral border announced the **Throne Room** with its red walls, stunning chandelier, more rich red chairs, a red marble table top, black and white marble floor, and red carpet on the dais and steps leading to it. A simple chair sat on the dais under a canopy, the wall-hanging behind featuring a crown and coat of arms. A clock lay between vases on a rose-hued half table with solid gold legs, and another garish cornice and framed equestrian picture completed the room. There was a small simple chapel, and the **Royal Bedroom** featured a delicately carved oriental screen inlaid with mother-of-pearl, its panels depicting birds on flowered branches, horses and, strangely, monkeys. A small tapestry portraying an ancient theme hung above an unornamented half table, and other items included a crystal chandelier, a four-poster bed with spiral posts, floral wallpaper and drapes, a ceiling painting, and embossed figures in gilt surrounds on the cornice. Lit by a single chandelier, a large sombre room had dark-toned traditional tapestries completely covering two walls, and a table and chairs on patterned carpet. A tall vase, Regency chairs and a half table lined the walls. Lighter décor showed several tapestries to advantage, amongst them two ladies and a figure with a spear, two men accompanied by a youth, a crowd scene that included men carrying spears, and a group of people in colourful attire. Spanish and Flemish creations in wool, silk, silver and gold were exhibited in the **Tapestry Museum**, its walls hidden from top to bottom behind the enormous works of art. Completely covering one end wall, a picture showed angels amongst the occupants of a room and a red-robed figure kneeling before a vision of the Virgin.

tapestry

Outside, vibrant golden trees with black trunks made a superb display against yellow walls, and snow lay on the roof beneath a blue and white sky. The grounds also contained a beautiful **Neptune's Fountain**, but we did not see it.

Segovia

From La Granja (literally, The Farmhouse), the tour progressed to **Segovia**, its magnificent **Cathedral** (1525) on **Plaza Mayor** topped by numerous spiky spires. Fluted columns supporting the lofty vaulted ceiling branched at the top to form a criss-cross pattern. Created by the splayed tops, arched recesses in the walls were filled with stained glass. The main altar lay beneath a dome with similar stonework, and elaborate small chapels were seen through metal screens with delicate gilt tracery along the top. There were paintings on chapel walls, a white marble pulpit with figures in deep relief, coats of arms in the floor, and a cool and inviting green cloister surrounded by arches featuring sculpted openwork.

The narrow streets of the city were enclosed by high dark-walled buildings allowing little light to penetrate as we made our way to the majestic 15th-century **Alcázar**. Here, we obtained a view over the entire surrounding countryside: a belt of thick golden trees following the line of a river, a stone bridge, houses and a tower, a few green fields amongst the brown, and distant defensive walls. On closer inspection, this castle with its ornamental stonework, round towers topped by conical black spires, and a rectangular section surrounded by turrets, looked like something straight out of the life and times of King Arthur. Inside was no exception, with a mounted figure carrying a lance (both horse and rider in suits of armour), a few paintings, and just a little decoration on mostly austere walls lined with suits of armour; even a small stained-glass window featured a knight on horseback. However, ceilings were another story, with highly decorative woodwork reminiscent of Arabic designs: one with small partitions studded with rosettes, and a second with an octagonal 'dome' inlaid with the typical flower pattern and surrounded by a deep ornate gilded cornice that contained tiny round stained-glass windows. Carpeted steps led to elegant carved chairs beneath a canopy, the wall behind bearing a banner depicting an eagle holding a heraldic shield. A huge empty room with suits of armour and stained-glass windows (featuring knights) preceded others with armour and a large dark tapestry. Two smaller rooms followed: one with carved flowers on the gold ceiling, the other with a honeycomb pattern created from gilded strips of wood, both with deep carved cornices. The first of these was inset with stained glass, the second, above portraits on a red wall, presented a row of colourful ceramic figures with crowns and swords.

ceramic figures on the cornice

A painting portrayed villagers greeting crusaders outside the city walls, and a dark rendition of the adoration by the Magi was located near a particularly elaborate gilt altarpiece set with figures and pictures. A lighter illustration on a triptych showed a horseman in the predella and four figures in the wings.

Segovia was perhaps best known for its splendid bi-level extremely high (up to 28.5m) 728m long Roman **Aqueduct** crossing the roadway. Built without mortar around AD 50, it had 163 arches and still carried water to the city. Battlemented ramparts rose behind buildings at one end, and it was an extraordinary sight looking up at the blue sky through its many arches. Other buildings, one with filigree sculpture in windows, featured similar ornamental stonework to that of the Alcázar. In a small square, the statue of a figure holding a flag and sword stood on a tall pedestal next to an interesting pale stone edifice with the now familiar spired pyramid atop its square bell tower. This building also featured a colonnade and a doorway with figures on the convoluted arches; a turret and the domes of the cathedral appeared behind. A grey stone structure had a shield on the façade and a colonnaded balcony with a stone balustrade; many buildings featured iron railings. Standing in this same old quarter was a sad-looking white sphinx with the head and draped bust of a woman. A large edifice diagonally opposite the multi-spired cathedral was crowned by a clock between twin square turrets with the pyramidal roofs and spires. I observed crooked tiled roofs with tiny dormer windows, a black and white sgraffito wall with the three-dimensional effect, the aqueduct visible at the end of a street, and a metallic Romulus and Remus feeding from the wolf.

El Escorial and Valley of the Fallen

Returning to Madrid in the evening, I found myself once again at the **Cervantes Monument** on **Plaza le España**, a group of life-like figures at the base and the man himself, astride his horse, reflected in the still pool.

Cervantes Monument

Again with Julia Tours, I went to the **Monastery of El Escorial**, or **San Lorenzo** (1563–84), and the inspirational Valley of the Fallen. The 207m-long grey façade of the monastery had solid pilasters, a statue in a niche below the plain pediment above the entrance, and spires on each of the square towers at the corners. Viewed through an arch, a building opening onto a courtyard and flanked by symmetrical clock towers had a ledge on the façade lined with statues on pedestals. This was the entrance to the **Pantheon** (1617–54), the elaborate octagonal room below the main altar of the basilica where, except for two, all the Kings and Queens of Spain are interred. Passing a large painting behind glass, we descended steep steps in a tunnel-like arched passage of highly polished reddish-brown marble. The room itself was entirely of red-hued marble with gleaming bronze decoration on the domed ceiling, cornice and capitals of pilasters. Lit by a central chandelier, the walls were lined with niches holding ornate marble caskets with bronze plaques nominating the royal personages therein. Bronze angels bearing sconces (also bronze) lined the walls and stood either side of a bronze crucified Christ.

By contrast, the **Pantheon of the Infants** was of stone and white marble with different cubicles holding members of Spain's royal families. The first vault contained a white marble coffin with a gold image on top and one with a full-sized white marble reproduction of a lady clasping flowers whilst in the repose of eternal sleep. Above the altar, a picture showed Christ's body being lowered from the cross. In the centre of a second sepulchre, a three-tiered white circular tomb with elaborate ornamentation around the top of each layer resembled a wedding cake, a term by which it was in fact known. This contained 60 niches for male infants and had images holding crests around the second tier. Yet another simple crypt contained full-sized coffins, unadorned except for crosses, and coats of arms were all that relieved the wall behind. At the entrance to one chamber, marble representations of poised macebearers stood guard.

Entering the **Austrias Palace** section, beautiful vistas of an immaculate parterre garden with trimmed hedges creating decorative designs and a pond with a central fountain could be seen from windows. Beyond a wall, the outlook revealed trees, grass and mountains in the distance. In total, the monastery had 89 fountains, 86 staircases, 300 cells for monks, 1,200 doors, 2,593 windows, 16 patios, and 1,600 paintings by names such as Goya, Velázcuez, Titian, Tintoretto and El Greco. The library alone contained 40,000 volumes, in addition to manuscripts and so on. It was built by Philip II who wanted to control the entire Spanish Empire from here. An intricate ceiling was composed of small stucco figures (mostly white) within a variety of moulded shapes surrounding a painting of colourful winged figures in a small gilt-edged central panel. This led into a chamber with a black and white checked marble floor, the statue of an angel in the centre, and artworks including the Last Supper lining the walls. The vaulted ceiling had painted patterns in black, grey, white and brown separated by beige stuccowork. We traversed a corridor lined with beautifully coloured paintings portraying

Jesus' trial, the Way of the Cross, and his ultimate Crucifixion framed by pilasters that flared at the top to support the barrel-vaulted ceiling. Now in the **Basilica**, the ceiling frescoes depicted scenes of heaven with hosts of colourful figures and angels. One was located above the intricate high altar that was almost as brightly coloured. The theme was continued, combined with some earthly scenes, above side altars and the organ, but the central dome was an incongruous plain stone affair.

We left the monastery to journey to the **Valle de los Caídos (Valley of the Fallen)**, commemorating those who died in the Spanish Civil war', which was apparent long before reaching it by the enormous cross situated on top of a stark stony hill. Measuring 150m in height, it had a cross beam so wide that two cars could pass along it. Figures at the base represented the four evangelists and their attributes: bull, angel, eagle and lion. Even though located below ground, the bunker-like entrance was imposing. Approached via a wide set of steps between low creeper-covered walls and pencil pines, its semicircular colonnade faced a broad courtyard with a view over mountains, low-lying cloud, and a village in a distant valley. A relief of the now familiar eagle and shield adorned each end of the colonnade, and a black stone Pietà (carving of Mary cradling the body of Jesus) reposed on a ledge above the arched door. In spite of the austere exterior and terrain, the monument was strangely moving, with windswept cloud across blue sky behind the cross.

The bronze doors were comprised of embossed panels depicting stories in the life of Jesus and included the stable scene in Bethlehem, his scourging, and the crowning with thorns. The gigantic cross lay above an enormous interior dome, which in turn lay above the main altar in the rock-hewn church. At each end of an internal grille, a bronze archangel bearing a sword stood in a lighted niche, the only illumination in the entrance tunnel except for wall sconces. Accompanying a service officiated by many priests, the sound of singing reached us clearly due to the remarkable acoustics. Alabaster statues of virgin patrons of different military bodies stood above the entrances to side chapels housed in alcoves, one containing a painted reredos (altar screen), a second with a white figure lying below a cloth-draped cross and a bleak red and black interpretation of Calvary on the ceiling. Woven in gold, silver and silk, eight Flemish tapestries between the chapels, purchased in Brussels by Philip II in 1553, depicted the Apocalypse. In the monstrous central dome, a mosaic made up of six million pieces featured saints and characters from Spain's military and political history ascending towards Mary and a seated Jesus. The plain altar held a Christ by the sculptor Zumaya on a cross created by two branches cut from a juniper tree by General Franco, founder of the institution formed to look after the valley. The reredos above the altar contained 8 paintings and 15 sculptures between small jasper columns. At the conclusion of the service, to the accompaniment of loud organ music, priests filed out between two more huge bronze angels.

The route back took us to the very photogenic village of **San Lorenzo de El Escorial**, accessed via an old stone bridge across the river.

San Lorenzo de El Escorial

Ascending a hillside behind crenellated walls, the town, its towers and spires, and another large cross standing alone on the crest of a hill, were a source of great pictures. Views from the road overlooked the dun-coloured buildings blending into their rocky loft, green verges on the riverbanks below, and magnificent mirror images in a still section leading to a dam and rapids. The keyhole arch in the roadside tower of the bridge framed the walled village and coats of arms above its portal at the end of the lamp-lit walkway.

keyhole arch

On crossing this and entering the portal, I was rewarded with the sight of twin towers, their spires showing the green patina of copper, rising above crenellated walls surrounded by grass-covered slopes with pencil pines, red foliage, hedges, shaped bushes and pampas. A monotonous-looking grey building occupied the top of a hill. The symmetrical towers belonged to an edifice bearing, once again, the eagle and shield. A long narrow building called Casa Pedro divided a street, and a pair of red brick turrets added interest to a façade that featured solid stone quoins, a statue in a recess, and stone pinnacles atop columns either side of the arched entrance. Passing steep narrow streets, I headed for an octagonal tower with fancy spires just visible through trees. Up close, the multi-faceted structure had figures on brackets, and I found a recess containing images on pedestals flanking an elaborate cross on which pigeons roosted.

octagonal tower

Toledo

Another tour took me to **Toledo** in **Castilla-La Mancha**. More than 18 centuries old, it was surrounded on three sides by the gorge of the **Tagus River**. My first pictures were of bright yellow façades and tables and chairs around a square bordered by five-storey buildings. Beautiful sculpted archways – one incorporating a face, another sacrilegiously plastered with paper advertisements including one for *La Boheme* – and Moorish architecture seemed to be a feature of this town, which was a National Monument. Dark narrow streets provided glimpses of a pink and white building with Venetian-type windows and the asymmetrical **Cathedral**. Connected by an enclosed overhead passageway to buildings opposite, this featured a dome, bell tower, and images on the façade and multi-arched entry. Plain brick pillars, a vaulted brick ceiling, and a lacy screen offset the extraordinary altarpiece with its host of small subtly coloured images enacting various scenarios in delicately fashioned compartments. Figures framing a round window were silhouetted against the incoming light to great effect. Shown to advantage against a red background was a fabulous gleaming gold monstrance crafted by Arfe, and amongst the paintings were some by El Greco (who lived here), Valázquez and Goya.

exceptional altarpiece

In the streets, I noted a second overhead passageway spanning a road, bay windows, iron-railed balconies, old-style lamps, and a row of half-timbered buildings with a bell tower at the end.

A good example of the 500-year coexistence of Jews, Muslims and Christians in this area was the 12th-century **Santa María la Blanca Synagogue** with its Arab influence. The interior produced rows of typical round arches supported by fancy-topped columns to create a keyhole effect, embossed designs appeared in the spandrels, and there was a shell-like fluted half dome. The **Santa Tomé Church**, again with a painting by El Greco (*El Entierro del Conde de Orgaz*, depicting the burial of the Count of Orgaz by Ss. Stephen and Augustine in 1322), also had a fine gold altarpiece with pictures in small panels. The restful garden of the cloister was viewed

I am always fascinated by narrow alleys

through lacy stonework in arches, the pillars of which were adorned with sculpted figures and flared to support the vaulted ceiling. Everything was very rushed, as was almost always the case on tours.

Next visit was to the exceptional 18th-century **Royal Palace** in Madrid. Outwardly, this immense structure, its sombre grey façade unadorned except for pilasters and an ornamental parapet, varied little from any other, and faced a mammoth courtyard with a single multi-branched lamppost in the centre. Indeed, initially the inside was not very inspiring either, until we ventured further. Paintings, filigree brass or copper sconces, white walls and columns, interesting window treatments, and a white marble statue constituted my first impressions, but I found the central works of art on ceilings to have the most appeal. Located above a stairwell, the first depicted a dark celestial vista surrounded by smaller artworks, gold garlands, and white stucco faces and flowers. A lighter heavenly scene in an elaborate gold surround enhanced a pink and white room. Apart from patterned carpet, sconces, a tapestry, and paintings on walls, practically the only objects in the next room were items on a long table and ornaments on a simple side table. A second pink and white room featured another dark view of heaven framed by white alabaster cherubs lifting gilded garlands. Also supported by cherubs, plaques bearing relief of gilded figures enhanced the corners. This unique ceiling reigned over black statues, a bust on a pedestal, gold and crystal chandeliers, tapestries, and a stunning table with large golden griffins, their wings spread, forming the legs.

Lining walls in the **Throne Room**, mirrors with extremely elaborate gilt frames incorporating gold cherubs reflected pairs of candelabra and a gold clock on intricately carved tables below.

Throne Room

The entire ceiling was covered by a scene in predominantly pastel tones, painted in the 1700s when the artist was 68 years old. Flanked by four golden lions playing with marble balls, two gold thrones with filigree decoration sat on a red dais at the top of four steps.

thrones flanked by golden lions

The room was furnished in the mid 1800s in the style of Charles III, but the thrones were changed with every reigning monarch. Walls were covered with red velvet embroidered in silver, and a highly polished reddish marble doorway, flanked by naked black figures holding weapons and with white cherubs, gold sprays and a mural above the architrave, had heavy maroon drapes tied back to reveal a painting and an enormous brilliant chandelier in the next room. Entering this salon, I caught my breath at the sight of a four-tiered glittering gold candelabrum, the like of which I had never seen, reflected in shining gilt-framed mirrors on ochre-coloured walls. A deep cornice with relief of gold flowers, birds with spread wings, and white fluted ornamentation like the shells of molluscs served to frame a painting of heaven and earth executed in rich hues on the ceiling. In the following room my senses were once again assailed by the vision of a superb crystal and gold chandelier suspended from a ceiling covered with cavorting naked and semi-clothed bodies, a bearded figure with a trident, and an angel blowing a horn. Figures on large golden medallions in the corners were bracketed by alabaster images. Illuminated by a glowing candelabrum, a jewelled clock borne on the back of a white figure was displayed in an open case, its black-domed top supported by fine black columns entwined with gold leaves.

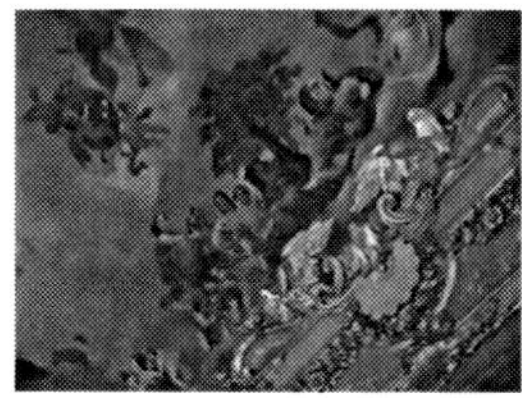

wall and ceiling detail

There are not enough superlatives to describe the opulence of the **Porcelain Room**, its white ceiling completely covered with coloured ceramic sprays, flowers, leaves and, in corners, Japanese figures beneath trees. Hanging from the centre, an exquisite gold chandelier with strings of crystals like miniature prisms split light into colours. Reflected light also shone from the intricately patterned flooring and high sheen of a round table with a solid central support featuring large golden birds, but all focus was on the magnificent ceiling, which was reflected in ornate mirrors on all four walls, one above a mottled marble fireplace with a gold clock and candelabra on the mantel.

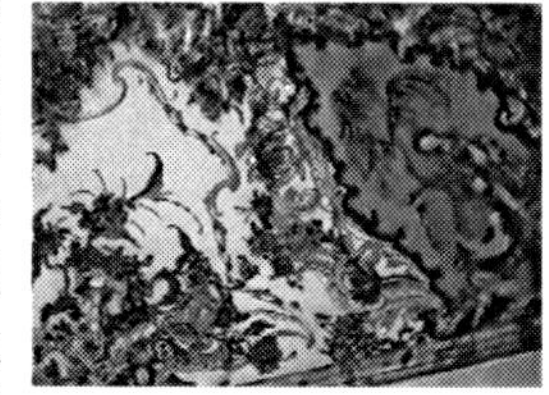

ceramic decoration

The décor was completed by a deep dado of dappled marble, period tapestry-upholstered chairs, and a table holding intricate gold candelabra and an ornament. Similar patterns appeared in the floor of a room with a gold chandelier suspended from the ceiling, white figures circling the central leg of a round table, a framed painting, gilt mirrors, a gold clock and ornaments, gold and crystal sconces, and a tall lidded vase. A richly coloured scene of earthly events on the ceiling was augmented by a gilt crown on the cornice and white cherubs holding wreaths above the heads of gilt lions in corners.

The **Dressing Room** of King Charles III was another astounding revelation: walls adorned with large flesh-toned ceramic cherubs (some presenting bare bottoms!) surrounded by swirls of dark green 'fabric' and holding aloft white vases trimmed with gold and containing greenery. Fruits and flowers, green garlands, and plaques bearing white images continued this fantasy. Faces on green 'cloth' appeared in the elaborate corner decoration of this small narrow room, and a crystal chandelier like cascading raindrops hung from the centre of the ornate ceiling. But most of the detail was on the walls, reflected in mirrors with ceramic frames also incorporating floral enhancement. It was interesting to note that the porcelain pieces could be removed and placed in other locations. Amongst the benign countenances in this jovial room, I noticed a scowling face with long moustachios in a corner and a pair of malevolent-looking visages with pointed ears on the dado. A pair of pink porcelain vases stood on a plain marble table with a chair either side. Tied back with gold tassels, dark green velvet curtains separated this chamber from the bathroom.

dressing room

The next salon featured a table with spindly outer legs and a filigreed central support. Belonging to Charles IV, it incorporated the signs of the zodiac and was also a clock telling the time, day of the week, and month. Elaborately patterned walls and carpet set off furniture with gilded embossing, a white floral bouquet on the lid of an urn, crystal sconces, and a chandelier hanging from a ceiling painting framed by gold squares and circles with carved flowers in the centre. Candelabra in corners of the **Gala Dining Room** did not detract from black panels with scrollwork, leaves, and large figures in different poses, all in gold, which lay behind them. Tapestries between doors with swagged pelmets above tied-back heavy red curtains completed the wall decoration in this long room, which was divided by an archway supported by marble columns; gold figures featured in the spandrels thus formed. The two recessed ceilings possessed paintings surrounded by ornate gilded cornices with, in the first instance, rosettes in squares, in the second, faces above figures in plaques. Large chandeliers hung over the enormous table with seating for one hundred and fifty people.

Heading down a corridor lit only by a single brass lantern, with recesses housing white statues of a king and queen, we came to the masterpiece of the **Royal Chapel**, used on only two or three occasions during the year. The plain iron-railed pulpit seemed out of place beneath the magnificent high dome portraying the Coronation of the Virgin Mary, in rich blues and purples, by an Italian artist. White alabaster cherubs adorned panels and circular windows around the base. These also appeared above a side altar and beneath four broad arches with gold flowers in coffers. Paintings graced spandrels created by the arches. Gold-decorated panels adorned walls with a veneer of grey marble, and black marble pillars with gold capitals were striking. Below an altar, with large figures flanking a painting by a German artist, a crystal case contained the body, covered with wax, of Spanish martyr St Phillip, gifted by a pope to Queen Elizabeth II. Another huge painting lay behind the main altar set with a gold crucifix and six tall gold candlesticks. A second ceiling illustration and bright carpet completed my observations.

dome

Because I had a new appreciation of art, my one regret in leaving Madrid was not having seen the **Museo del Prado**, one of the world's great museums with an incomparable collection including works by Goya, Velázquez and El Greco, and masterpieces by Rubens.

Santiago de Compostela

Taking the train past hills, castles, and across a wide river to **Santiago de Compostela**, revered place of pilgrimage in the Middle Ages (as even to this day), I came to the conclusion that nearly every hilltop in Spain must be crowned with a fortress. The first building of note that I photographed, in the paved **Praza do Toural**, was the 18th-century **Pazo de Bendaña** with lacy iron balconies and a statue on the roofline. The centre was a maze of narrow streets bounded by colonnades as I walked down the **Rúa do Vilar**, the ornate tiered bell and clock tower of the **Cathedral of St James** (Sant Iago), to which all roads eventually led, at the end. The discovery of the Apostle's tomb in this place around AD 813 was the raison d'être of the city, and the stunning Romanesque cathedral of the 11th to 13th centuries on the **Praza do Obradoiro** was why I had come. One side of the massive square was bordered by the **Pazo de Raxoi**, a neoclassical mansion housing the President's Office and City Council, with balustrades forming a parapet, Ionic pilasters, rounded pediments at the ends, and a central pediment depicting men on horseback waging a battle armed with swords and shields. Atop the apex, a figure sat astride a rearing horse, a cross in one hand and sword in the other, raised to strike a supine figure with his left arm upheld to fend it off. An arcade extended the width of the front at street level.

To the left stood the **Hostal dos Reis Católicos**, bearing a host of small images around the imposing doorway. The wonderful cathedral, its ancient weathered stone façade encrusted with yellow lichen, was adorned with many images, cupolas, twin bell towers, pilasters with fancy capitals, figures on balustrades, and a wealth of carved ornamentation. Between the looming bell towers with their spired cupolas, a towering central section featured elaborate decoration including cherubs (one holding an unfurled scroll), niches containing clerical figures with scrolls, and one with a staff standing beneath a small arch through which the sky was visible.

Pazo de Raxoi

central tower

The tolling of a bell added to the spiritual aura as I approached the amazing **Pórtico de Gloria** (1188), with figures beneath the curve of its deep arch and in the tympanum. At both sides of the door, life-sized apostles and prophets holding scrolls occupied ornate pedestals. A beautiful rendition of a seated apostle made up the central supporting column of the giant portal, whilst another was seated in the tympanum directly above.

Through this door, I glimpsed the dark multi-arched interior with the shining candlelit gold altar of the **Capela Major**, the figures cavorting on top of its elaborate canopy cast into silhouette by light from behind. Suspended from the dome, this mammoth work was supported below by larger-than-life angels and ornately decorated pillars. A huge filigree chandelier was suspended in front, again only showing up as a silhouette in the dim interior. Bare vaulted ceilings, stone pillars, and plain walls provided a

Pórtico de Gloria

perfect backdrop for the multitude of sculpted and carved works of art. The many elaborate side altars were very different in style: one with fine statuary, another displaying intricate wood carving, and a third with a sculpted stone altarpiece containing many small figures. There were all the usual attributes of great cathedrals (stained-glass windows, decorative capitals), but the craftsmanship in the proliferation of carving was outstanding. In an ornate recess, a large delicately coloured tableau representing the removal of Christ's body from the cross portrayed obvious compassion, reverence and anguish on the beautifully executed faces.

tableau

A series of carved wooden columns with figures on top was decorated with the fruits and leaves of the grapevine. It was possible to walk to a place of veneration behind the lavishly decorated principal figure on the main altar, from where I obtained a good view of the central nave with a rose window emitting a purple glow at the end. A plain dome covered a side altar with less carving but a stunning floral chandelier hanging in front, and in another, a crucified Christ hung between elaborately sculpted stone pillars. Spiral columns framed expertly crafted life-sized figures beneath a date palm. Unfortunately, due to the lack of adequate lighting, it was virtually impossible to capture the superb detail of most pieces.

Outside once again, I studied the façade more closely and observed that the studded metal doors at the head of the steps had lion's head handles and huge hinges, whilst figures around the balustrades bore various objects: a sword, monstrance and snake, scroll, goblet and jug, and a staff. Another of the four squares surrounding the cathedral, the **Praza dos Praterías**, featured the Baroque fountain of **Los Caballos**, with horses spewing water from their mouths and surmounted by a seated figure facing one of the clock towers. Faces protruded from a wall behind.

tableau

Los Caballos

Amongst the outstanding doorways, also an attraction of the town, were several with free-standing carved granite gables. One of these elaborate creations portrayed a horseman together with pedestrian figures. A booming bell and chiming clock rang out in unison as I gazed in awe at heavy stone structures topped with bell towers, cupolas, and sculpting around rooflines.

Wandering past the little **Calle Tras de Salome**, with figures in relief on the corner, I came to a simple chapel inside which a crucifix on the bare stone wall was directly illuminated by a shaft of sunlight slanting through a tiny window to one side. The streets were a succession of colonnaded thoroughfares broken up by interesting paved squares with fountains, monuments, and solid stone buildings adorned with lacy iron balconies, coats of arms and lanterns. Views through arches included that of a building with a small bell tower and delicate carving of figures and floral arrangements on the façade. Another bell tower appeared behind the sagging tiled roof of a white stuccoed structure. I walked past a saxophonist, and the penetrating soulful sounds of a flautist permeated nearby streets. Near where the Rúa do Vilar divided to form the stepped **Rúa do Franco**, a hungry dog was scavenging amongst tables on the footpath, and a couple of yellow autumn trees in the vicinity of another of the magnificent doorways created a beautiful picture. Between fluted columns with Ionic capitals, this one featured figures on brackets under decorative stone canopies, all of which, together with a small pediment over the window, a shield, an array of small figures and roof ornamentation, was duplicated above.

doorway on the square

Finding myself back at the cathedral, I took more footage of the yellowed façade, greenery lodged in crevices, and the iron cross above the gate leading to the stone staircase that zigzagged to the entrance. Finally tearing myself away from this hard to resist venue, I came to **San Francisco Church**, with spired cupolas on its twin bell towers, small windows, and carving on the façade. A tall stone monument stood in the forecourt. Always seeming to revert to the cathedral, the ancient weathered surface of its **Acibechería** face had a mottled appearance. Twisting alleys revealed interesting streets with columns, crests, and figures in niches at every turn. Via the **Via Sacra**, I reached the huge **Praza de Quintana** behind the cathedral. Steps led up to the **Casa da Parra**, which displayed heavy relief of fruits beside doors above and below a long iron-railed balcony reinforced underneath by the heads of ten lions. Gargoyles projected overhead and there was even delicate ornamentation on the large chimney. Also facing this square was the **Torre de Reloxio** and a green lichen-spotted face of the cathedral with three tiers of spired balustrades and the beautiful **Porta Santa**. This also featured large bunches of fruits, one each side of a scrolled ledge above life-sized figures in niches over the door. Smaller figures occupied banks of squares between pilasters.

I found a lovely stone carving, its colour badly faded, portraying Joseph leading a donkey carrying Mary and the baby Jesus beneath a green tree with cherubs overhead.

Holy Family

On the **Calle del Castro**, the peeling walls of a white stuccoed building with green window frames and a dip in the roof made a good picture, and zinnias were prominent amongst bunches of flowers for sale. A lacy ironwork gate was erected between solid stone pillars with sculpted metal urns on top, a lady in black bore a long load on her head and another yellowing façade, facing an iron-railed balcony full of plants, had greenery sprouting from its surface, a coat of arms in a divided pediment, a figure in a recess above the doorway, small windows, and a squat square bell tower. An agitated Alsatian dog, issuing a shrill mewling sound in response to a deeper bark in the street below, looked as if it was about to jump out of a first floor window above a shop. Sculpted relief on panels beneath windows of a nearby large edifice depicted children with grapevines.

My forays concluded with more towers, cupolas, and narrow lamp-lit alleys, one of which, at the end, revealed a tiny round window below a pediment with a cross and birds (stone) on top. Ionic columns flanked a group of carved figures in a panel above the door. A large coat of arms adorned the corner of a building with growth shooting from the parapet, and a red roof stood out against all the ancient granite. I came to the wonderful 16th- to 18th-century **Church of San Martiño Pinario**, with three tiers of sculpted figures in recesses between ornate columns and, below street level, heavy metal doors with embossed faces. Finally, I came across more twin towers, white buildings around the **Calle de las Campanas de San Juan**, and a man with a bright red and black smoking 'train engine' in which he was roasting chestnuts.

PORTUGAL

Oporto

I would be returning to Spain at a later date, but for now I rode a rattling train over a wide river with a number of tiny islands, and past neat green plots separated by hedges, little white houses dotting hillsides, and the inevitable battlemented castles. We progressed past towns, sparkling tree-lined waterways, spires behind fortress-like walls, small white boats moored near riverbanks, green fields, symmetrical white towers, mountains, a cluster of white buildings with red roofs, and the dome, cupolas and huge rose window of a cathedral visible above trees on a hilltop. At one stage, I rode in the engine and filmed through filthy windows as we sped through a town, past a horde of white churches with steeples, across an enclosed rail bridge, past villages and people waiting at crossings, under an overpass, and past green meadows to finally arrive in **Oporto**, Portugal.

Oporto, or Porto, the second city, was said to have given its name to the country and was probably best known for the drink that originated here, but nowhere could I find reference to the astonishing façades decorated with blue-and-white tiles like delftware and incorporating picture panels. The first was a church labelled Edificada en 1810 (built in 1810) with a clock in the pediment and a tiled bell tower and façade, the latter integrating pictures that included the Crucifixion; the second was a house with identical floral tiles and an iron-railed balcony below a picture of the Virgin. A third had a combination of tiled and red walls, muntined glass with different-coloured panes, a filigree-iron balcony, and lace-like trim under eaves. A lolly-pink façade with arched windows was also enhanced with a lacy balcony; intricate iron fanlights appeared above doors, and ornamental gables added character to attached row houses. A yellow tree overhanging an iron-railed balcony contributed to a multihued effect achieved by the use of different-coloured tiles. Another had a delicate design painted above black and white diamond-patterned tiles, and a floral grille hid a small window. The entire front of one three-storey building was covered with the blue tiles, and the extraordinary façade of a stone church had an illustration depicting Jesus, his arms outstretched over a basilica, accompanied by angels. This was one of several panels; another, with an elaborate border of urns, flowers, birds and a winged face, portrayed Christ ministering to the people. A small figure stood in a niche between the tiled bell towers, from which pigeons flew in and out.

church façade and detail

These wonderful painted tin-glazed ceramic tiles, called *azulejos* and predominantly blue, were a legacy from the Moors who conquered Portugal in 711, then known as Lusitania and occupied by the Romans under Julius Caesar. In 1147 the great stronghold of Lisbon was recaptured by Alfonso I and the Christian Crusaders, but it was one hundred years before Alfonso III completed the ousting of the Moors.

In the centre of town, declared a UNESCO World Heritage Site, yellow awnings adorned a shop called Reis Filhos with a female bust above deeply carved relief over the doorway. From a prominent position, I overlooked the high bi-level steel bridge, built by Gustave Eiffel, crossing the **Douro River**. On the opposite bank, in smoggy conditions, sat a little white church, and houses were built on streets that climbed like a set of giant steps up the hillside beneath a looming cliff. Wandering up and down the steep stepped streets of the depressed **Ribeira** district along the waterfront, I was confronted by mildew on damp dirty walls, litter, carpets hanging outdoors, rubbish bins, a barking Pekinese dog, a cat, a crying baby, children playing with a top on the stairway, and a man sitting on his stoop. All the doors of the conjoined houses opened directly onto the street, a solitary bright yellow wall (and washing on others!) providing colour. It was probably quite a foolhardy thing to do, but there were many people around and most seemed friendly enough.

Ribeira

Reaching the promenade beneath the **Maria Pia Bridge**, I looked up at five-storey buildings also with washing on walls. Walking further, situated below battlements and a tower I found a ramshackle cluster of colourful shacks: blue-and-white tiled, yellow stucco, green corrugated iron, and one, with a red tin roof, constructed of rusted iron so that it too appeared red, an illusion augmented by red laundry on the front, above which hung a cage inhabited by a yellow bird. A large white edifice on a hilltop dominated the city from all points. Perfectly still water reflected even the gulls flying above fishing boats with long prows, fishermen were casting rods, and market stalls were set up along the embankment. Descending steps to the river walk, the bridge towered overhead, and on the upper level tables and chairs sat beneath red-and-white umbrellas in front of a yellow building with a red awning and sunlight glinting off its windows. This stood next to a tiled façade with bright red shutters. Tall narrow frontages featured the tracery of iron balconies, and in the bustling noisy street a woman was feeding something into a naked flame below a memorial adorned with fresh flowers.

Portraying Christ looking down from heaven on a battle scene of foot soldiers charging with bayonets and a mounted soldier wielding a sword, this in turn was next to a clothing store with dresses hanging in the street. Boxes of carrots, potatoes, garlic, apples, peas, lettuce and onions sat on the brick-paved roadway in front, and an awning and bright pink sunshade protected bolts of fabric and other fruits and vegetables in crates and baskets, whilst vendors competed in crying out their wares. I saw potted plants and flowers, a puppy curled up on a pile of clippie mats for sale, live crabs, bivalve molluscs and other shellfish displayed in the sun, bread, black and green olives, and nuts including walnuts, chestnuts and unshelled peanuts, all with the arch of the bridge in the background, the river on one side, and multistorey tiled and coloured façades draped with washing, flapping like curtains in the breeze, on the other.

houses along the embankment

Colourful striped mats and woven baskets hung beside a stone archway, a dog peered through washing on a balcony, a fat speckled hen lay under makeshift benches holding greens, and a bucket of white chrysanthemums was placed next to oranges, lemons and other produce. A team of oarsmen sat in a stationary longboat, and onlookers clapped as two rowed past in a skiff. Green tables and chairs under red-and-white umbrellas occupied the space in front of a decorated stone wall on the end of a building that divided a street to create a narrow lane, with washing suspended overhead, down one side. An interesting monument in the crowded square consisted of a metal bird on the side of a huge cube balanced on one corner.

Oporto streets

I strolled back from the waterfront up steep winding alleys, their tiled façades mixed with red, orange and yellow walls, all with iron-railed balconies. At the end of one street, the clock tower of a church reared behind a historic figure adorning a monument. Another large stone church, with entrance gained via a zigzag stairway, had little enhancement other than a few figures on top, but nearby buildings featured decorative windows, coloured glass panels, arches and columns. A small square was surrounded by narrow-fronted buildings with little or no decoration (apart from the eternal washing!) but with the inevitable church tower rising behind. Cobbled streets, iron-railed balconies, images under eaves, an elaborate many-tiered bell and clock tower, an interesting roofline in silhouette, a dainty carved cameo below heavy stone struts, and a fountain with winged lions all made good pictures.

One entire wall of a large religious institution was devoted to a massive tile illustration portraying an angelic haloed figure standing at the top of steps and appearing to address a large crowd that had gathered beneath a tree, many carrying crosses and one with a mitre and shepherd's crook. A second group of people congregated on cloud, and the whole was bordered by an elaborate design, as were the windows and doors.

wall illustration and detail

Wedged between taller buildings, a tiny church with a white tiled façade had a delicate red pattern defining the gable, corners, a tiny round window, and arches. Red cannas made a striking foreground to a row of dull narrow-fronted buildings visible behind the bare branches of lacy trees. A guard stood at ease in a blue and white striped sentry box outside an official residence, probably a palace, but I did not carry a guide book and because nobody spoke English it was often difficult to ascertain what things were. Surrounded by lawns and flowerbeds, an impressive memorial had a winged image on top and graphic metal sculptures of a cannon, soldiers with guns, a flag bearer and fallen horse around the base. The detail was excellent, even to the realistic expression of fear on the face of a woman clutching a terrified child in a sinking boat.

memorial

I came to a section of very narrow cobbled alleyways bounded by whitewashed and rough stone walls, the latter with greenery on top. A tortoiseshell cat sat on a sill above lines of washing, and I found pale blue and green walls, red walls, glaring yellow walls, and a house with turquoise doors and window frames in a pink wall! A plain grey façade had plants on the porch roof, and a salmon-pink residence had a coloured plaque on the front and statues on the edge of its flat roof. A church with a lilac tiled façade also featured an elaborate door surround, ornamented windows, and clocks below its symmetrical square bell towers. The use of so much colour in poor areas possibly helped to brighten a dull or deprived existence. Even autumn leaves created colourful carpets on the cobbles. Back at the river, a pumpkin-yellow shingled wall, a teal façade bearing a small picture, bright red roofs and walls, green and blue frontages, green iron railing, and a few yellow buildings stood out amongst the colourful array of old houses climbing the hill, with the omnipresent washing hanging over balconies. Rugs were draped over the stone wall along the waterfront. Drawn as if by magnet to the market again, I saw bananas and other fruits displayed next to women cooking chestnuts in smoking drums (even *I* succumbed to the temptation to buy), and finding myself once more at the stepped alley described above, I now encountered laundry strung like banners from one side to the other overhead – it must have been washing day for the entire city! From a high position, I looked down on red rooftops, a few tiled surfaces, washing, shouting people, flying seagulls, and the ornate clock tower mentioned earlier, standing like a beacon in the distance.

view from an elevation

Coimbra

My next destination was the 13th-century university town of **Coimbra**, which possessed more-substantial multistorey stone buildings, including a beautifully decorated façade with a cross and small spires on top. A broad boulevard with an equestrian statue at one end and a tower the other had, in fact, many structures with spires, including a tiered bell and clock tower rising above naked figures. Opposite stood a Bank of Portugal building, its pediment containing images in deep relief with statues overhead. Pigeons flew around and landed in the lap of a naked amply proportioned lady seated on top of a fountain located on the wide grassed median strip, which led to steps accessing the ornate edifice with its clock tower at the far end of the thoroughfare. Obscuring the beautiful building behind, smoke billowed from a cart where a man was roasting chestnuts. Pigeons also roosted above a figure and coats of arms on the entrance to a vaulted alleyway with rough stone walls. The interior of an ancient church with small images either side of the arched doorway had an intricately carved wooden reredos and two rows of life-sized figures below a sculpted dome.

From a balcony, I obtained tremendous views over roofs, the river, and a dome on top of a formidable stone structure with slit windows in battlemented walls.

A long white edifice had a clock tower and a serries of turrets, and a yellowing stone archway had figures in niches flanked by fluted pillars with decorative capitals and plinths. A large mosaic embellished the pavement in front. I came to another elaborate church façade, an ancient cobbled lane brightened by green and yellow walls, an austere dark stone building with crenellated ramparts, and a split-level path, the lower level leading to a pink-hued façade – it must have been washday here also! I took fascinating film of a dog behind a window, avidly watching pigeons flying back and forth, rapidly turning its head to follow their movements, and demonstrating obvious frustration at not being able to give chase. A view of the foggy river showed perfect reflections and smoke drifting lazily from a chimney. Birds in cages sat outside first floor windows, from one of which a man hung over the sill to converse with a neighbour (likewise leaning) and friends in the street below. The passage beneath a decorated overhead vault led to the **Porto do Castilano**, where a cat sat on worn steps between faded and peeling red walls, and a pure white feline, its tail cut, emerged from a crack in foundations. A tall wedge-shaped building formed a Y-junction dividing streets, the upper level featuring a sculpted head above a doorway. Generally, there was nothing to compare with the rest of Europe in ornamentation, but this lack was made up for in colour.

old church

Coming to another high point, I obtained a wonderful view over the marvellous **Fonte da Manga** in the **Jardim da Manga** off Avenida Sá da Bandeira. The fountain was covered by a dome supported by slender columns and connected by struts to four free-standing turrets with spired cupolas. Steps and a path across a channel filled with murky green water led to the centre, and parterre gardens enhanced the outer corners. Sellers displayed wares on the steep cobbled street to my left, and bells rang out from a church visible over rooftops – but I could not get away from washing! Next, I came to a beautiful church portal with a number of small figures surrounded by delicate sculpting, all at one time white, on the pale brick façade. Pigeons and a snow-white dove perched on the stone carving, from which weeds emerged.

The interior featured a vaulted ceiling with bosses, fine woodwork beneath the organ, small statues, gold objects on one of several altars, a wooden pulpit with relief of seated images, a beautiful carved altar screen, and exquisite blue-and-white tile work. Bordered by an elaborate design incorporating cherubs, this depicted, amongst other things, a crowd scene including soldiers and a figure holding a cross.

tiled wall and wooden pulpit

In a large square, two ladies operated steaming chestnut carts set up at the foot of steps beside a plain yellow stone church with a multi-faceted arched entrance. Finally, I found an ancient aqueduct and a gorgeous garden with box hedges, autumn foliage in reds, yellow and orange amongst the green, cone-shaped bushes, a large three-tiered fountain, and an ivy-covered memorial wall with a sculpted head. It was very peaceful, just the sounds of running water and birds chirping. Two impressive buildings featured in turn a decorated dome and the natural tones of carved stone superimposed on a red surface.

An interesting fable tells of a man declared innocent of a crime after a slaughtered and roasted cock had crowed. The bird has become a popular folk symbol.

Fátima

I left Oporto to journey to the quiet town of **Fátima** for one of the most moving experiences of my life, and where I stayed at the delightful Pensão D. Maria. A statue on a pedestal was all that stood in the enormous forecourt of the modern **Basilica**, its 65m-high central tower surmounted by a bronze crown weighing seven tons and a crystal cross that is lit during night services. The basilica was flanked by long curved colonnades with figures on top, and the walls behind contained 14 mosaic Stations of the Cross. The statue of Our Lady in the **Little Chapel of Apparitions**, the heart of the sanctuary, marks the exact site of the appearances to the three children in 1916. A white column indicates the site of the holm oak over which the Virgin appeared. Actually, I find this very confusing because all my research nominates two alternate locations for the revelations. On three different occasions in 1916 Lucia Santos and Francisco and Jacinta Marto saw an angel who taught them to pray, and on May 13th in 1917 the little shepherds from Aljustrel, then aged 10, nearly 9 and 7 respectively, saw what they described as 'A lady all of light' above a small oak tree in the **Cova da Iria**. Her message was a plea for sinners to stop offending God, seek forgiveness, and amend their lives, and she asked the children to return on the 13th of each month for five months. From the second appearance onwards the apparitions were witnessed by increasing numbers of people, 70,000 bearing witness to the great miracle of the sun, a startling spectacle of light that occurred immediately after the sixth and final appearance.

Different scenes of the apparitions were depicted in contemporary stained-glass panels in the church. But all this – the stark square capable of accommodating millions of pilgrims, the austere colonnades, and the plain pristine interior – was as nothing compared to the simple site in the ferny grotto where the supposedly original gnarled and moss-covered tree, now supported by a stout stake, stood amongst ancient white rocks, and where the translucent pure white life-sized marble images of the three children knelt before the Blessed Virgin.

the appearance in the grotto

A stone-paved pathway, where many crawled on knees, followed carved tableaux of the Stations to the **Chapel of St Stephen**, with Calvary reproduced on top, which stood on the hill where the angel appeared. The remains of Francisco and Jacinta reposed in the Basilica. The whole place projected an aura of peace and serenity.

Lisboa

On to the capital, **Lisboa** (**Lisbon**), founded according to legend by Ulysses, but recorded history gives the honour to Rome in the third century BC. I stayed in the Pansão Sevilha, approached via a grotty entrance with broken steps, an elaborate but dirty tiled floor, grimy yellow doors, and peeling red walls. However, it was very central and near a huge broad thoroughfare where an obelisk stood in front of a long three-storey red and white building with many attic rooms and figures in and above pediments supported by columns at both ends. Trams ran uphill between this building and another red and white structure; Lisbon was another city built on seven notable hills – and many lesser ones. Chestnuts were being cooked over braziers on the footpath at the terminus of the tram.

In the **Baixa** district, an amazing 147ft decorated concrete tower housed the **Elevador** (elevator) **de Santa Justa**, designed by an apprentice of Gustave Eiffel in 1902, which transported people from one street level to the next. At the base, red-and-white umbrellas sheltered tables with red and white checked cloths, and a man was shaking armfuls of coloured scarves onto the pavement for selection by prospective buyers. Flower sellers and vendors of roasted chestnuts stood in a pedestrian mall bounded by tall buildings, Christmas decorations were strung overhead, and a statue on a pedestal was visible through an arch (and smoke!) at the end.

Looking through another arch, above which were rooms with iron-railed balconies, I could see a figure atop a column and a three-tiered fountain with sculpted images. Passing underneath, I was confronted by a mammoth square containing two large complementary circles patterned with pebbles. The first was occupied by the fountain in a pool with water spurting upwards from figures at the rim to the centre, the other by people feeding a huge flock of pigeons around the column, which also had life-sized figures on the plinth. At one end, a large white building with red banners between Ionic pillars supporting a carved pediment with figures on top was obviously a theatre, museum or the Opera House. Buckets of flowers including small roses, baby's breath, tiger lilies, zinnias, and plumes of pampas in vibrant blues, purple, red, yellow and green were massed by the fountain, the noise of traffic blaring all around. A black equestrian statue, also covered with pigeons, gave rise to the name **Black Horse Square** and was photographed against the background of imposing battlements around the **Castelo de São Joege** (St George) atop a hill. An edifice with rounded arches and an ornate clock was Moorish in appearance. A black winged image and white armoured figure ornamented the base of an obelisk with hordes of birds winging their way overhead, and moving on, I looked down on a garden and pond with muted traffic sounds in the background. Bordered by patterned paths where people were sitting on bench seats, the grassed median strip in a wide avenue held tall trees and a statue of some stern-looking dignitary. In the centre of a busy highway fronting an inordinately wide boulevard well laid out with roses, hedges and lawns, the top of another elaborate monument had a bewigged figure in a frock coat standing with a lion, both wearing the greenish patina of copper. White images beneath included Neptune in the waves and a figurehead on the prow of a boat.

A tour with Gray Line, which has looked after me in many places the world over, included the sensational **Coach Museum**, exhibiting many of the most ornate vehicles that I had ever seen, endowed with sculpture and heavy gold embossing. The first, red with elaborate gold trim, was one of several with pictures painted on the sides, a couple were decorated entirely with embossed gold, and

carriages

three featured large golden figures and horses. All were extremely ornate, even to decoration on the roof and gold trim on elaborately carved wooden wheels. They were lined with blue brocade or plush velvet in red or black. The building itself was a museum piece, the pink ceiling featuring a central picture depicting a group of people below the usual cloud, this time occupied by an equestrian figure and angels. This was encompassed by smaller paintings and decoration in moulded surrounds, whilst illustrated panels and designs enhanced the cornice.

The dim interior of the huge **Jerónimos Monastery** (1496) was embellished with dark wall paintings around a gold altarpiece, bosses on the vaulted ceiling, and stained glass, including a large rose window that did little to lighten the heavy stone walls. There was sculpted ornamentation around arched windows, and flared pillars were each carved with a different design. The embossed tomb of **Vasco da Gama** had a supine figure on top, and a white arch, also demonstrating different patterns, revealed a heavily embossed gold ceiling beyond.

Next on the agenda was the **Belém Tower** (1521), a former watchtower built as protection against pirates, and the starting point for intrepid explorers, which guarded the entrance to the estuary of the **Tagus River**. This much photographed grey stone structure, a drawbridge at the entrance and standing in water that lapped at its foundations, had numerous bastions and carved stone oriels on its crenellated walls.

The **Navigator Monument** to Prince Henry, whose discoveries in West Africa made Portugal the 15th-century mistress of the seas, was a plain light-coloured vertical slab with a crowd of larger-than-life figures climbing slopes on the sides and, I assumed, Henry himself at the fore. Henry led expeditions to pioneer a route to spice rich India[*], but it took Vasco de Gama, rounding the southern

* Spices were a highly prized commodity in ancient times. The only way to preserve perishable goods was to salt them heavily, and spices made salted food palatable. Transporting them across the long and dusty desert routes was expensive, and by the time they reached their destination prices had increased by 600%.

tip of Africa, to reach India's Calicut in 1498. We stopped for a fantastic panorama over the city, laid out like a town in miniature, where I could pick out the concrete elevator and the equestrian statue in Black Horse Square.

Further investigation of the centre brought me to a vista, familiar from pictures, of lush palms in the foreground of buildings ascending a hill. A rose window appeared behind a small bright red building standing adjacent to a sgraffito façade, which juxtaposed a yellow frontage with a red roof and white columns. A green-tinged equestrian statue crowned a pedestal with white figures and a horse at the base. It also stood in Black Horse Square, entered on one side through an arch reminiscent of the Arc de Triumph in Paris but surmounted by images. This was the same arch at the end of the pedestrian mall described earlier, and on this occasion the street contained a human 'statue' with a clown face, and a vagrant wearing a shaggy blue woollen hat, sitting on the pavement, his dog curled up beside him, and a large pink panther hanging from the handle of his shopping trolley!

Passing an aqueduct en route, another full day tour began at the sumptuous 18th-century **Queluz Palace**. Amongst the wonders unveiled were the large **Ballroom** featuring small illustrations in gold embossed surrounds on the cornice, life-sized golden heads and torsos on pilasters and, above mirrored doors, latticework and gilded garlands framing paintings of vases containing beautiful flower arrangements. Shining crystal chandeliers added the finishing touch.

the ballroom

The **Music Room** held a grand piano with a portrait of Queen Dona Maria I on the wall above, a satin-upholstered couch on a beautiful rug, and an old piano with floral inlay. A salon endowed with a large wall mirror, its deep gilt frame incorporating an image, also had an ornate cut-glass chandelier suspended from the centre of a simple design on the white wooden ceiling. The stunning **Sala de Mangas**, containing elaborate urns, an antiquated carriage, crystal chandeliers, and bird panels above doors, was lined with pictures in predominantly yellows and greens, painted on tiles. These included a rotund lady seated sideways on a reclining cow, both wearing garlands of flowers.

The plain ceiling of the **Throne room**, with painting of historical figures around the edge, was not as ornate as some, but small pictures ornamented the cornice. At one end, in front of a mirrored surface with brighter ceiling illustrations overhead, this room contained two thrones on a dais raised above a black and white tiled floor. Crystal chandeliers and a pair of tall lidded vases flanking French doors leading to the outside completed the décor.

Cherubs and a winged warrior decorated the ceiling of a room with a parquetry floor and a gilt table below a picture of ruins. An exquisite coloured glass chandelier from Murano in Venice hung from a copper-toned filigree pattern in the centre of the plain ceiling in a small room with a blue dado on white walls, one of which was hung with a picture in a small but elaborate dark metal frame. It also contained a desk with myriad tiny drawers and wood inlay of flowers. The many mirrors of the next room, with pictures in ornamental gilt stuccowork between (and even on) the glass and around the cornice, reflected a crystal chandelier and ornate filigree on the ceiling. Similar mirrored walls reflected a pink and white cut-glass chandelier hanging from a fancy bronze-coloured rosette in the centre of a beige wooden ceiling.

Located between paintings in elaborate surrounds above mirrored doors, gold heads and torsos served to augment the gold canopy of a four-poster bed residing in the **King's Bedroom**. Painted cherubs flanked pictures around the base of a central dome. A room with gold flowers in sections of a honeycombed ceiling, gold decoration on the cornice, and pictures in elaborate gilt frames completed the tour.

In front of a pink and white façade of the palace, the magnificent parterre gardens featured shaped bushes, hedges in circles, squares and triangles with glorious plum-red foliage in the middle, and pedestals holding potted urns and statues. Poseidon with his trident was amongst figures occupying the centre and around the rims of large ponds fronting white and yellow buildings, the latter with white pilasters, a solid pediment, sculpted figures on the roof balustrade, delicate trim around windows, and green woodwork. The pools were dispersed amongst more hedges in various shapes, their centres alternating between blue-tinged plants and the red. I walked back through a large empty room containing just chairs around the walls and a vase on an ornate table below a painting. Light from its crystal chandeliers gleamed on the highly polished surface of the floor, which led to the first mirrored room.

Our next stop took in the imposing **Monastery of Mafra**, with pink marble walls and pilasters but an otherwise comparatively plain interior. The floors, also of marble, were elaborately patterned in pastel colours of pink, white, yellow and blue. There was a large painting behind the main altar, but others featured panels containing beautifully executed tableaux in white Italian marble, even to the delicate carving of lace on vestments. The huge dome was unadorned, but below it were decorated pediments, carved capitals, and the fine filigree of suspended ecclesiastical objects. The massive exterior had twin bell and clock towers, a carved pediment, statues, and columns.

Arriving at the seaside resort of **Ericeira** for lunch, I filmed a white working windmill, its sails spinning with a rowdy clatter, and the scene from a promenade overlooking the town and deep-blue ocean, which turned turquoise near the shallow shore where it broke in wide gentle surf like white sheets. Hills covered by spray appeared beyond a lonely house standing on a promontory. After lunch we proceeded to **Sintra**, the westernmost town of the European continent. Backed by a chain of hills and the ruins of a Moorish castle, it was one of the oldest towns in Portugal and had inspired many great writers and poets, amongst them Lord Byron. Interesting sights included a square tower with a spire ringed by four pointed turrets, a monument in a cobbled square, a pink façade with white stucco decoration and an elaborate doorway, narrow streets with iron-railed balconies overhead, and conical towers appearing above a structure with ornate sculpted windows, plain arches, and a fountain in the courtyard. However, the pièce de résistance, 1,300ft up a mountain, was the incredible fairy-tale **Palácio da Pena** (**Pena Palace**, 1839), which would have to be Portugal's answer to Disneyland.

First glimpses through trees revealed a green dome, yellow cupola, and two square red towers with turrets and white parapets. These abutted round yellow towers with white trim and open arches, but the remainder of the fortifications consisted of plain grey crenellated stone walls and towers. Approaching closer, creeper-covered façades, turrets and arches formed the ground level, and we entered through stone archways adorned with colourful tiles. The ramparts of a hexagonal tower loomed above spiked turrets flanking a sculpted gateway, and in isolated splendour atop a corner, one attractive stone cupola was very reminiscent of India. Above an arched entrance, the most amazing oriel, festooned with sculpted leaves, was supported on the back of a bearded figure wearing an angry countenance as he strained under the effort, his mouth drooping at the corners. This grotesque creature, his legs terminating in scaly fishtails, was squatting in a large clam shell, his private parts covered by stone flowers in the scalloped edge!

oriel

Seen against an azure sky, one aspect revealed a black and white zigzag-patterned spire, bright yellow walls, and vivid red surfaces with white accents. Viewed Through arches, panoramas extending all the way to the sea were comprised of forest and large buildings below, fields beyond, and the town in the distance. Finally, a tiled archway was ornamented by a heavily carved window.

Passing several coastal resorts, including **Cascais** and **Estoril**, with colourful boats bobbing in an incredibly blue harbour, we arrived back in Lisbon (and the cacophony of traffic!), where I found more patterned pavements and interesting buildings. One displayed Moorish-style arched windows with carved surrounds and coloured glass, which appeared almost iridescent when caught by the sun. Another had an ornate façade with the tracery of iron balconies, heavy stone relief, and windows displaying innovative shapes of glass. I photographed the green dome of the **Tivoli** and, flanked by overhanging trees in the sidewalk, a soothing restful canal with lush greenery and a long-bearded figure reclining on the plant-covered rock of a waterfall at one end. A black swan and large white birds seemed content to call this green oasis in the middle of the busy city home.

Lisbon street

Altogether, I took three tours from Lisbon, the last beginning at the charming walled town of **Óbidos**, one of the prettiest villages that it has been my privilege to experience. Full of tile-roofed whitewashed houses ascending up and down higgledy-piggledy narrow cobbled streets with greenery and white flowers outside every door, it also featured colourful wide dados and corners in red, ochre and vivid indigo. Creepers climbed walls, pots enhanced many windows, one façade had a small panel of the blue-and-white *azulejos*, and each of two lovely white churches was outlined in black and had carving above the door and a spire on a small square bell tower. There were old-fashioned streetlamps and, at the top of most streets, the crenellated walls of the old fortifications, with some houses built right onto

Óbidos

them. Stone and stuccoed archways spanning streets had rooms with tiny windows and tiled roofs overhead.

One bright blue door stood at the top of steps, and a heavily sculpted stone doorway faced a tiny square with a couple of trees. I observed one decorative gable, small-paned windows, stone quoins, a building dated 1773, potted plants lining a parapet, and another on a bracket in front of a predominantly blue mural of Our Lady. Lawn was visible through the iron gate of a larger dwelling, and a great view of fields surrounding the lower town was obtained from the crest of the hill. A special surprise was a vaulted stone archway with wall lamps both sides of an extensive blue and white tile picture showing soldiers and a winged image. This was set around a stone-framed window opening onto a small balcony under the vault, and a polychrome flowery design decorated the ceiling.

balcony and detail

Tile work inside a dim church gleamed in the light from a small chandelier, but because it was time to return to the bus I had to content myself with a series of quick pictures. Dividing two levels of cobbled laneways, an interesting tower of rough stone had a tiny balcony above an arched window and door. It was connected to a white wall with a yellow dado and trailing creepers by an overhead vault with a small room on top. My final film shows a white building with stone quoins and a multi-arched stone doorway, a small statue beneath a canopy flanked by tiny windows with pots each side, and a cross on top of an elaborate white doorway in front of the ivy-draped crenellated fortifications. Outside the walls, I saw a local market with fish and vegetables under moss-covered shelters in a compound formed by white walls with vibrant yellow dados.

The 12th-century abbey at **Alcobaça** was immense. A white structure but with walls streaked brown by the elements, it had long wings flanking a taller central section with a rose window and a figure in the niche of a free-standing gable between symmetrical square bell towers. The stark stone interior, its vaulted nave supported by heavy pillars, had little adornment but contained the tombs of two Portuguese nobles. Beautifully crafted from white marble, one had a full-sized bearded figure lying on top, his head on pillows, feet on a dog, and surrounded by small ministering angels. Lacy carving and miniature figures engaged in various activities adorned the sides of the tomb, which had a rosette at one end and was standing on the backs of lions. Sculpted from stone, a group of people stood below a colourful rendition of the Virgin Mary in deep relief on a wall. I photographed one of the bell towers through an arch, and a fountain in a carved hexagonal surround in the centre of a circular chamber with open arched windows. A stepped colonnade mounted one wall of a large warm-toned solid stone hall, its flared pillars lit at the top by concealed lighting, and arches allowed glimpses of an inviting cloister with box hedges and trees. In another section, white stuccoed walls featured statues on brackets – one in armour, holding a shield and brandishing a sword – and blue-and-white tile pictures portraying scenes with armoured soldiers, men on horseback, a castle and angels. I saw one small round window with coloured glass.

Moving on to the picturesque 17th-century fishing village of **Nazaré** for lunch, I found an attractively designed black and white cobbled promenade beside a strip of yellow beach. Gulls lined the shore, and spray blew from flat surf beneath an overcast sky. To one side of the bay, houses on top of sheer cliffs, some built right on jutting rock ledges, were reached by funicular railway. At the foot of steps, a stallholder sold an assortment of goodies including olives; ladies in black walked the narrow streets leading from the waterfront, and another stall had nuts and dried apricots amongst its wares. There were a couple of colourful façades, blue and red awnings and, sandwiched between red roofs, a black spire on a bright turret the colour of turmeric.

Batalha Monastery

Proceeding on, we came to 14th-century **Batalha Monastery**, one of the finest buildings that I saw in Portugal. An equestrian statue stood in the wet forecourt, which reflected it and the many small spiked spires of the church, making it appear as if both structures were standing in water. The exterior featured ornamental flying buttresses, decorative roof capping, turrets, and an elaborately sculpted recess above the successive arches of the entrance. The interior was endowed with an abundance of stained-glass windows in ornately carved stone recesses and a beautifully sculpted white marble piece incorporating small tableaux. The walls were plain, but fluted pillars supported a lofty octagonal dome ornamented with bosses, and the cloister was surrounded by a colonnade, the tops of its arches filled with intricate stonework. A memorial was protected by a perpetual guard, and an unfinished section contained superb examples of the stonemasons craft in filigree carving like fine lace beneath arches and on delicate bosses. Pilasters were ornamented with leaves, latticework, flowers and interwoven branches.

The last port of call was a return (for me) to Fátima where, whilst the group visited the main sanctuary, I ran like the proverbial wind, one mile through the **Way of the Cross**, to the old village of **Aljustrel** to find the houses of the children. I photographed an old lady in her yard with a goat, chickens, a cat, food scraps – and flies. She spoke no English but indicated the direction I should take when I mentioned the names. I was able to enter the home of Lucia, who became a Carmelite nun, and the kitchen of the simple dwelling was equipped with a small table, a bench seat, utensils above an open fireplace, and crude shelves holding wooden bowls, pottery jars and other articles. Another room contained a wooden dresser and a small table and chairs, and the bedrooms were furnished with plain iron beds and pegs for hanging clothes. The ceilings were wood, the white walls unadorned except for crosses and religious pictures, and it was kept very neat by an elderly lady in black, but I do not know if anything was original because she also spoke no English. Outside, the red-roofed white house was enhanced with greenery and white flowers, but the home of Francisco and Jacinta, where both were born and Francisco died from Spanish influenza at the age of 10, and which I had difficulty locating, was a plainer stuccoed building, again attended by an old lady in black who spoke no English. This was also the case at the tile-roofed stone building in the backyard of the Santos home, where I returned to find the well that was the site of the second appearance of the angel in 1916. Here, in a very emotional moment because I was the only other person in the vicinity, the old lady drew a bucket of water from the well and gave me a drink. This peaceful site also featured exquisite white statues of the three children kneeling before the angel and marked the end of a wonderful visit to an impoverished but lovely country full of warm friendly people – a distinct difference from those that I found in Spain. Jacinta passed away, also from influenza, aged 9, but Lucia attained the age of 97.

well at Fátima

SPAIN

Sevilla

I journeyed to **Sevilla** (**Seville**), for centuries the capital of Europe, where my first film was of a huge red building with two corner towers. This faced an impressive square, where branched lampposts were surrounded by tall narrow-fronted buildings with interesting stone, white and yellow façades; one massive ornately decorated stone structure occupied the centre. Another interesting building had a turret-like section at one end, its first storey circled by the open arches of a colonnade, but Seville's pride was the Gothic and Baroque **Cathedral**, begun in 1401 and taking four centuries to complete. With over 40 chapels and altars, and containing two famous Murillo paintings, it was the supposed burial place of Christopher Columbus. The dome was impregnated with figures, and statues stood in niches on both sides of the dazzling gold and silver altar, which was flanked by carved columns supporting a sculpted pediment. Vaulted ceilings, stone balconies and stained glass completed the picture; I could not investigate too closely because a service was in progress. Girls in colourful flamenco costume with very full sleeves and flounced skirts paraded outside the carved façade of the cathedral, beneath trees laden with oranges – which I found were sour when I was tempted to pick them! In fact, this is a variety known as the Seville orange, and used mainly for marmalade. A huge rose window lay above the multi-arched entry, which had figures in each facet and in the tympanum above the green-tinged metal doors. The roofline was punctuated with flying buttresses and spires, palm trees lined the footpath, and another highly ornamented entry also had a rose window overhead.

Waiting to catch tourists, buggies with tinkling bells stood beneath crenellated city walls, and I saw an elegant five-branched lamppost with filigree on top and hideous faces around the plinth. This stood in the centre of a traffic circle surrounded on three sides by a wedge-shaped lemon and brown building, a pink-toned edifice with an ornate stone entrance, and a white building with open brickwork and a belfry. The ornate 93.82m **Giralda Tower**, with its many bells, latticework, spire and small windows, abutted another elegant cathedral entrance featuring elaborate carving and figures around the arched portal. Once the leading Muslim city in Spain, many Arabic influences remained, and the 12th-century tower (1172–98) was the minaret of the main Almohad Mosque, on the site of which the current cathedral – supposedly the third largest of its kind, although in 1999 the *Guinness Book of Records* called it the biggest – was constructed between 1401 and 1507. Giralda has been imitated the world over and rivals the Kutubiyya Mosque in Marrakesh and the Hassan Tower in Rabat, both in Morocco and both of which I have seen.

Arabic archway

Elsewhere, patterned wooden doors were enclosed by a round Arabic archway of intricately carved stone, with statues on brackets each side and a sculpted tableau overhead.

It seemed that every city had an **Alcázar**, and Seville was no exception. I visited this 12th-century Mudéjar-style* royal palace next. Begun by Pedro the Cruel in the 11th century as a fortress, a tantalizing glimpse of Moorish patterns was afforded through an arch in the ancient stone wall. Entering the compound, I was surrounded by typical Moorish arches bearing a tracery of delicate stonework in a variety of designs incorporating leaves and lacework. The immaculate walled gardens contained trimmed hedges, purple bougainvillea, palms, creepers, and glorious trees with a mass of vibrant pink blossom. Sculpting enriched colonnaded balconies sheltering doorways with diverse carving, thus producing elaborate arches behind arches – and this was just the outside!

Inside, I found delicate stone filigree in windows, and decorative sculpted panels featuring leaves, flowers and myriad designs. There was also an exposition of gold and other ancient objects.

I continued my sightseeing with the discovery of a yellow bell tower with a metal spire above the multi-faceted portal in a plain stone wall, a view of the Giralda Tower at the end of an alley, and great pictures through an arch of intricate carving on the cathedral, including a row of small figures below a third round window.

Seville Cathedral

Narrow streets had glass-enclosed balconies overhead, and a pet market displayed three puppies in a tiny cage, colourful birds, white mice, guinea pigs, baby turtles and goldfish. Picture panels on walls included one, flanked by sconces, showing angels herding naked people gathered below cloud on which, surrounded by a crowd and holding a cross, stood Christ – perhaps a depiction of heaven and hell.

* Mudéjar refers to a Muslim who remained in Spain after it had been reconquered by the Christians in the Middle Ages.

Abutting a beige and khaki building, lacy black balconies enhanced a dusty-pink façade with white pilasters, shutters and pediments, and a striking red and yellow church had symmetrical tiered towers, but a long plain white edifice was decorated solely with rows of pigeons!

I saw decorative windows and gables, a traffic circle with a figure in the centre of a large fountain surrounded by flowerbeds, a square colonnaded turret through palm trees, and the round **Torre del Oro** (**Golden Tower** – looking anything but!) behind another fountain. The attractive wide black and white paved **Paseo de Cristóbal Colón** followed the **Rio Guadalquivir** and provided benches for seating amongst potted plants, orange trees and palms. Changing its name to the **Paseo de las Delicias**, I followed this to the **Jardines de San Telmo**, passing a pool with high-gushing fountains, the spray from different types of jets enveloping a black figure in front of a map of Spain. A carved obelisk also stood in the water, and flowerbeds brightened the grassed surrounds. An imposing building composed of horizontal bands of pink, beige and grey stone incorporated turrets at the four corners, a crenated parapet, and Moorish-style arched windows. The serene gardens featured a series of pools and fountains, a magnet for white birds, in lawns with creeper-covered pergolas, hedges, palms, and trees with green and yellow foliage.

the horse and buggy is popular with tourists

As I mentioned in my introduction, Seville was one of the places where an attempt was made to rob me. Filming beside the road, I had my video camera clasped in both hands when a scooter cyclist roared past and grabbed my bag. Because my hands were joined the bag would not yield, and I screamed abuse at him so loudly that he let go and hastily accelerated away. I later learned that a fellow tourist had not been so fortunate and had been dragged by a bike rider, resulting in a broken collar bone.

One of Seville's many highlights was the truly remarkable **Plaza de España**, containing a massive semicircular structure with a watercourse spanned by bridges separating it from the mammoth paved concourse in front. The four-storey central section, graced with beautiful panels of blue, yellow and green tiles set in the brickwork, was further enhanced by symmetrical towers at the sides. These in turn were flanked by enormous colonnades, each with a smaller three-storey building halfway along and terminating at each end in a lofty seven-tiered tower with columns, turrets and spired cupolas, all perfectly reflected on the mirrored surface of the still water.

The central portion faced a huge fountain with many jets, and the square was bordered by hedges and trees. Blue-and-white tiles were also used in the construction of bridge balustrades. Even with an overcast sky, the whole was the subject of stunning pictures, and white ducks were amongst birds enjoying the ambience. Opposite, only the clip-clop of a horse-drawn carriage broke the silence in a tree-lined avenue where I came upon a semicircular white mansion with plaques on the exterior, ornamental wrought iron above a door, colonnades, and towers with glistening yellow domes. On the other side, the **Parque de Maria Luisa** was another delightful venue with a series of ponds: one with water spewing from the beak of a stone bird in the middle, a second with white birds flitting in and out of sprays arcing from the rim to the centre, and a third ornamented with ceramic tiles. It also featured hedges, parterre gardens, a small structure like a mosque, at least one statue on a pedestal, and leaves falling in showers from branches drooping over pathways equipped with tiled bench seats. A few more pictures of the cathedral, appearing like a lacework silhouette, completed my film, and I caught the train to Córdoba. We passed many hilltop castles, one with a white town at its foot, showing up black, austere and formidable beneath sombre clouds.

Córdoba

Córdoba, also on the Guadalquivir River, had its share of fine structures, including a white edifice with a winged figure on top of an elaborate round tower. A carved pediment above a pillared portico was visible at the end of an alley, a square stone tower stood behind a winged statue atop a column, studded metal doors with large decorative hinges barred a stone doorway with fluted Ionic pilasters and a carved pediment, and I caught sight, through trailing creepers and lamps, of a tall slender tower at the end of a narrow street. Thoroughfares barely the width of a doorway were lined by white-walled buildings with balconies overhead, and Moorish architecture was obvious in the patterned wooden doors of a sculpted stone keyhole arch with faded paintings in three small arched recesses above.

another narrow alley

But I had come here to see the magnificent **Mezquita**, begun in the year 784 by Islamic Arab caliph Abd al-Raham I, on the World Heritage List, and ensconced behind solid stone walls opposite the towers of the **Palace of Exhibitions and Congresses**. This building alone made the city the most important in Spain for around 200 years, after which time it was overshadowed by Seville, and in the 13th century both cities fell to the Christians. For a period it was the largest mosque in the entire Islamic world, but in 1236 it was converted to a church, and in the 16th century (1525–1766) the stunning cathedral was built into its centre. On entering the main 14th-century Mudéjar portal, **El Perdón**, at first impression, even though lit by 4,000 bronze and copper lamps, the dark interior seemed rather a nonentity. I was confronted with 19 rows of arched aisles like tunnels, the two-tiered rounded red and white striped tops arcing from 850 pillars with fancy capitals and meant to resemble palm trees. Wending through this forest of marble, jasper and onyx, I found deeply carved vaulted ceilings, figures above arches, recessed lighting, window grilles in lattice and flower designs, and embossed ceiling beams, each with a different pattern and all lead to a mosaic Muslim tabernacle.

forest of pillars Mezquita

cathedral and ceiling

With its brightly illuminated and heavily carved altarpiece and surrounds, the amazing inner sanctum of the **Cathedral** provided a dramatic change. There was also a remarkable change in colour as the simply patterned russet stone overhead gave way to deep relief on the grey stone ceiling.

Behind the gleaming gold and silver altar, the elaborate warm-toned marble reredos, with a golden statue in a small recess, was framed by pillars supporting a pediment with life-sized images atop each end, one holding a cross. A large painting was located above. A finely carved black pulpit stood on the back of a sculpted white figure, but there was minimal stained glass. Huge pale stone columns flared to support a decorated dome and ceilings with circular embellishment from which hung silver lamps. Hidden behind a dark sculpture with a host of figures, a side chapel had small paintings above the altar and an early Baroque ceiling featuring cherubs, faces, figures, and intricate designs.

Back in the dim interior of the main body of the Mezquita surrounding the cathedral, I found terracotta-coloured reliefs in arches formed by the splayed tops of pilasters, a coffered ceiling with designs in the centre of its small squares, and small windows with coloured panes. Large flowers adorned groins in the ceiling above striped scalloped arches. A recess held a small bronze figure below gilded relief of lions flanking a single flower. As I approached the Muslim sanctuary, I was forced to eat my words because this also was extraordinary. Three shining round arches – the striped effect created by a multitude of small panels that, on close inspection, revealed different minute designs in complementary earthy colours – had intricately carved surrounds and small ornate (but shallow) arched recesses above. Overhead lay an exquisite dome with the subtle introduction of blue in the floral and lattice-like pattern, which was repeated in the variety of designs in groins and around skylights below. Another section featured a deeply sculpted dome above intricately carved walls bearing a mass of diverse designs with a lustre imparted by the subdued lighting.

Muslim sanctuary

Once more wending through this confusing maze, I finally came to the **Cathedral Treasury** that contained, in a glass case trimmed with gilt leaves and flowers, the sumptuous 2.63m gold monstrance by Enrique d'Arfe, shown for the first time in a Corpus Christi procession in 1518. It completely overshadowed the works of art, statues, other gold objects – which included a second monstrance, gold candlesticks and plates – and a finely carved wooden piece incorporating a picture and statue. The floor was inlaid with coats of arms, a large rose window displayed a kaleidoscope pattern, and a painted dome resided above an elaborate side altar. The exterior walls of the Mezquita had several entrances: the main one with statues on brackets above a typical rounded black and white striped archway, another with studded red doors beneath a red and white striped arch, and a third with a belfry and cross on top.

The nearby **Plaza Vallinas** exhibited a sculpted façade, juxtaposed red and white buildings with Moorish arches, and a large free-standing stone arch, to the right of which I could see an octagonal tower of the Mezquita and through which I filmed paintings beneath arches on the **Palacio**. There were arches everywhere. An elaborate Moorish façade with a crenated parapet also featured a wealth of diverse red-and-white sculpted patterns around the arched doorway.

A fountain was lit up in the evening, and I passed a group of Latin American musicians performing in the street. Córdoba was also a jungle of narrow white-walled streets with creeper-draped arches overhead, and I found an enclosed courtyard full of greenery, one wall decorated with colourful ceramic plaques in delicate metal filigree surrounds.

The **Alcázar de los Reyes Cristianes** (**Fortress of the Christian Monarchs**, 1328) boasted a splendid collection of Roman mosaics that included a pair of embracing cherubs, the bearded face of Poseidon surrounded by fish, a large geometrically patterned panel, an angelic countenance in a frame of scrollwork and interlocking chains, designs like mazes with dolphins at the corners, a fanciful figure with a cane, and a large depiction of a man and woman, both semi-clad and portrayed with a mythical creature.

Roman mosaic

Looking down from above a high crenellated wall, the gardens were spread out below. These featured a series of long pools descending in tiers, with fountains arcing from the edge to the centre and a couple of statues at the sides. Parterre gardens had rose bushes within the hedged shapes, trimmed shrubs, and different shades of foliage such as plum and yellow mingled with the green. Additional reflecting pools were flanked by an avenue of stately lopped pencil pines interspersed with white statues on pedestals, a group of three at one end. The whole was a veritable oasis with the low city skyline beyond. From the opposite end, the towers of the fortress rising up behind the arcs of spray composed an excellent picture. In other parts of the extensive gardens, I came across round ponds with fountains and a courtyard formed by the outer wall and a white colonnaded building. This contained citrus trees in hedged squares and a clear aquamarine pool with a channel gently trickling through the paved surrounds.

More narrow cobbled streets, with a man walking his dog, the tile picture of a horseman in red (advertising the Restaurante Bandolero), artefacts hanging on walls, and lighted lamps, brought me to a building featuring scalloped arches and the intricate webs of typical Arabic patterns. A lush *cármene* (indoor garden) in a tiled courtyard had a palm in the centre and vines creeping over colonnades. This was the **Viana Palace**, with 11 patios and a garden. A fountain bubbled within a bed of ferns and, circled by potted plants, another was visible through an arch. Pot plants, together with a red-flowering creeper and blue-tinged shrubs, also encompassed a wishing well filled with foliage. Other attractions of the garden were hedges, a small pond containing a fountain and statue, trees, roses and palms. Roses also flourished amongst orange and lemon trees. Surrounded by colonnades, a pattern-paved patio contained fountains in a long tiled pool bordered by the blue-tinged plants. A third court featured a checked design created with cobbles, a round fountain also encapsulated by the unique blue foliage, and more citrus trees; a fourth, again graced with a fountain, was enhanced by trees in circular beds containing agapanthus amongst their luxuriant display, all surrounded by paving. Yet another had a high-spurting fountain, philodendrons, trees, and vine-bedecked walls. Each patio led one into the other, and two could be seen through a blue door with orange-laden branches either side. There were fountains everywhere: one behind an iron grille with a bell tower in the background, another in a colonnaded courtyard with blue plants, bamboo, and ivy climbing up walls, and finally, one in a tiled pond with potted geraniums around the rim and orange trees ringed by hedges on one side. The visit was completed by a red and white tiled bench set into a stuccoed wall, pictures above an old Spanish settee of carved wood, and a white wall with a heavy stone gateway bearing figures and a coat of arms. The plain yellowed façade of an ancient stone church and its square bell tower contrasted greatly with the white portal ornamented with spiral pillars, a statue in a niche, and other decoration on a building with twin bell towers.

Córdoba was designated the City of the Three Cultures, namely Christian, Muslim and Jewish because it was here that the three denominations lived side by side for several centuries.

Grenada

Spain's world famous **Alhambra** in **Grenada**, crossed by the rivers **Darro** and **Genil**, was where I headed next, passing haciendas on dry plains, white towns with turrets and towers, orchards, farm houses, green fields, and a remarkable mountain looking exactly like the features of a sleeping giant. At one stage, we travelled at the foot of a stony grey range, which soon disappeared to be replaced by distant snow-capped peaks of the **Sierra Nevada** with many more orchards, ploughed fields, crops and white villages in the foreground. Arriving late in the evening, for the first time I had difficulty in obtaining accommodation. Carrying my entire complement of luggage up and down the extremely narrow alleys around the cathedral (where I had been told that there were many rooms) and attracting quite a bit of unwelcome attention and comments, I felt quite threatened. However, I eventually found something and took a hurried look at the square with its attractive three-branched lampposts, a tall lighted fountain, and a *floristeria* selling colourful flowers such as gladioli, roses and zinnias.

Next morning, I encountered a Moorish arch, a huge circular edifice with two tiers of colonnades, and autumn foliage behind a wall bearing an elaborate fountain adorned with cherubs, strange faces, and a coat of arms. I have experienced Islamic architecture the world over but Granada's Alhambra (the name means Red Castle), begun in 1238 and one of the most magnificent structures on the continent, was absolutely breathtaking in the sheer proportions of its intricately carved stonework and 30 towers. But first of all we (I had taken a tour) stopped for excellent panoramas of the city from the fortifications of the **Alcazaba**, Alhambra's fortress dating from the 11th to 12th centuries.

Built for Granada's rulers in the 14th and 15th centuries, the **Casa Real** (**Royal Palace**) was the Alhambra's centrepiece. Located near a green pool enclosed by high squared hedges entered via a clipped arch, the introduction was a series of stone arches with intricately carved lacework and Arabic script.

intricate stonework

Inside, entire walls were covered with delicate and varied patterns that included tiny flowers, the only light coming from open arched windows below small apertures with stonework screens.

stone screens

Another small marble-paved patio, with tiled doorframes and dados on carved walls protected by heavy eaves, contained a central fountain, the tinkle of water the only sound. Room after room featured walls of sculpted tracery in unbelievable detail, and wooden ceilings were endowed with typical Arabic embellishment that included the traditional rose motif. Inset with tiles or mirrors, one dark ceiling glittered as if studded with stars. Every panel portrayed a different pattern, and even the balustrade around a balcony featured a variety of designs. Muslim architecture is distinguished by what I term miniature stalactites, which I later learned was called pendentive work, very evident here in spandrels and domes, on a cornice, and under arches. More aptly described as prisms on a concave base, they are also known as *mocárabe*, and the decorative stucco vegetal motif characteristic of Caliphal art is called *ataurique.*

example of mocárabe

stone lace

One room contained lacy window screens, tiles on the dado, and panels of lattice, script, and the large rose design mostly seen on woodwork. Every nook and cranny in the high-ceilinged rooms was filled with sculpted filigree like Spanish lace, some even three dimensional with minute carving within carving, and arched doorways were incredibly elaborate.

Standing in another courtyard, one could see arches beyond arches beyond arches, and surrounded by delicate arched colonnades, the **Patio de los Leones** (lions) contained a fountain supported by a dozen of these predators executed in marble, with water issuing from their mouths. This I have seen replicated more than once. Representing rivers, four channels flowed from the central structure to the sides of the courtyard, each terminating in an additional small fountain. If possible, the decoration here became even more elaborate, with internal arches bearing the white pendentive work hanging like icicles overhead. Pillars were mostly unadorned but everything above was carved, and the fine detail was so perfect that it was almost impossible to comprehend that it was achieved by hand.

Lion Fountain

Two rooms worthy of note featured, respectively, star shaped and octagonal ceilings; the former was the **Chamber of Abencerrajes** with windows of lace and 'stalactites' in the central dome and hanging from angles between the points of the star. The latter gloried in pendentive work radiating from the centre of a huge piece looming overhead like some hovering entity from outer space. Connected by arches featuring this *mocárabe* decoration, a series of small antechambers also featured this ceiling ornamentation above high (but small) patterned window screens, the walls enhanced with delicate carving and tiled dados. As a relief from all the overwhelming stone sculpture we came to a pleasant fountain gracing an inner courtyard with trees and plants bordered by hedges. Finally, I found the famous picture by which the Alhambra is recognised: palm trees reflected in a large pool forming the foreground to an arcaded pavilion topped by the square **Damas Tower**. Water poured from the mouths of lions at the near end, and hills formed the background. All the accolades showered on this monument were justly deserved, and mere words are inadequate to describe its wonders.

From here, we headed to the equally stunning **Generalife**, summer palace of the sultans, but in this case the attraction was the soul-soothing gardens. In the first section, steps mounted tiered terraces created by stone walls, and a bell tower was visible behind trees that included beautiful autumn foliage, again surrounded by hedges. Amongst the plum-coloured hues and variety of greens, the soft shade of a willow, drooping over a long pool, stood out against dark green ivy engulfing a sculpture on the wall at the end. Slender pencil pines formed the backdrop to more terraced gardens, and a marmalade cat walked on white paving enclosed by a two-tiered hedge. This pathway circled a single plume of water pulsing from a pool in the middle of hedged flowerbeds and trees. The next refined garden was entered via arches cut into high hedges, giving access to paths either side of long reflecting pools connected by fountains and bordered by roses behind box hedges. At one point, I obtained great views of the white city below massed autumn foliage around the yellow stone fortified walls and towers of the Alhambra.

Generalife

A rectangular pool connected two circular ponds, from the rims of which sprays splashed to scallop-edged fountains in the centre, also emitting a forceful stream of water. In a walled courtyard with trees surrounded by yet more hedges, quieter bubbling fountains erupted from the edge of a barbed quatrefoil pool. But the most superb, oft-photographed aspect was that of gorgeous flowerbeds in a blaze of colour (and one tree a mass of stunning pink blossom) flanking rectangular pools lined with inward arcing jets;

circular pools containing scallop-edged fountains in the centre and at the ends. Arcaded pavilions faced the length of the pools, which were bounded on the sides by a colonnade and vine-covered wall respectively.

Walking around the outside, past banks of hedges, autumn trees, and an ivy-draped wall surrounding a small patio containing roses, hedged flowerbeds and a single fountain, I ascended one of the pavilions for an overview of the inspiring display. This encompassed not only the row of fountains, pools, and tremendous colours in the flowerbeds, but a panorama over the walls to other immaculate gardens, the Alhambra, surrounding countryside, and the city beyond. It also pinpointed a maze and tall trees, and going down for a closer look, I discovered a cobble-paved avenue lined by more high hedges into which openings had been cut. Rose bushes filled these spaces, a large fountain played in the middle of the pathway, and greenery also created bowers overhead.

Small courtyards, interconnected by arches cut into tall perfectly squared enveloping hedges, brought me back to an earlier idyllic pool with water lilies and fountains. Twisting paths wended between trees and interestingly shaped hedged flowerbeds with a high crenated hedge on the perimeter. I encountered a palm-shaded pool, a tower reflected in a pond, and a view overlooking a stepped courtyard with trees and trimmed shrubbery, but no flowers. This was obtained just within the battlements, over which I could see the town, now directly below. I could distinguish colonnaded courtyards and plazas, towers, and the green dome, solid buttresses and square tower of a mammoth cathedral. More-natural environs contained pines and a blaze of autumn colours, and a series of ponds covered with water lilies lay in pebble-patterned surrounds also featuring trees, shaped hedges and flowers. Sitting in the fork of a tree, three cats (a tabby, black, and black-and-white) comprised my last picture. Both the Alhambra and Generalife are on the World Heritage List, Spain being one of the countries with the most number of sites on the register.

Abutting a bright blue building in the city's streets, I encountered a brick façade with iron-railed balconies, lamps flanking a sculpted window frame, a painted design, and a large illustration of a figure with a bow and arrow doing battle with a dragon.

wall illustration

Ancient stone bridges crossed a tree-lined stream, a church had a tall square bell tower on one side and three statues in niches above the sculpted stone entrance, and more Moorish architecture featured a carved façade containing small arched windows above an arched entrance with pendentive decoration. Known as keyhole arches, I have also seen the round Moorish arches described as horseshoe shaped. Perched on an ornate rounded gable, a huge sculpted bird with outspread wings reigned over iron and stone balustrades on curved balconies below. At the end of a narrow street, the first glimpse of the early 16th-century **Cathedral** revealed typical lacy parapets and spiked spires, and a nearby large grey stone edifice was endowed with elaborately sculpted window frames and ornamental decoration. Next to the cathedral, the **Capilla Real** (**Royal Chapel**) housed the tombs of Fernando and Isabel, the Christian conquerors of Granada in 1492. In front of the altar, behind an elaborate filigree grille with small figures and a crucifix on top, I found four white marble tombs with representations of the interred, their heads on marble pillows and surrounded by sculpted images, cherubs, and a shield in the claws of an eagle. That of the queen had an animal at her feet and a pig amongst the images around the sides! Ornamented by bosses, ribs reinforced the dome above the main altar, its screen beautifully carved with tableaux including Christ's Passion and a graphic portrayal of the beheading of John the Baptist. It also depicted a girl in a large metal urn attended by two scantily attired black men, one pouring from a long-handled ladle! On the walls, two more savage-looking eagles bearing shields were in sharp contrast to a small gold altar and an elaborate gold piece nearby. Viewed through heavy bars, the gleaming deep relief of a stunning gold reredos filled the wall and extended almost to the vaulted ceiling of a side chapel.

altarpiece and detail

Again in stark contrast, I came to an Arabic structure with a coloured dome like glowing crystals set into a decorative wooden ceiling above small lacy stone window screens. These in turn were lodged in the elaborate walls of an octagonal room with *mocárabe* enhancing recesses in each segment. A plain building served to emphasise its elegant wrought-iron gate, and I encountered another large church. The fascinating narrow streets of the bazaar, with hanging lamps, trailing plants overhead, and terminating in archways, had rows of bright yellow,

beheading of st. john

pink, green, blue and red Flamenco dresses with copious frills and voluminous sleeves hanging outside stores, together with colourful scarves, bags and other accessories. A novel exhibition featuring a miniature world of adobe buildings around a marketplace depicted a horse turning a grindstone, people dancing to a tambourine and drum, the firing of pottery, vendors selling handcrafted wares, a man tilling with an ox, a pile of vegetables and a flower garden, two donkeys with panniers, nobles on horseback, a waterfall, a dog with a group of musicians around a fire, and a shepherd with his sheep.

It is said that when the last king surrendered to the Catholic Monarchs in 1492, on looking back at the city for the final time he burst into tears. His mother reproached him with the famous sentence: *You weep like a woman over what you failed to defend like a man.*

Alicante

The next stage in my circuit of Spain was **Alicante** on the east coast (**Costa Blanca**, White Coast), with the usual collection of churches, one with split pediments, large figures between columns on its dark stone façade, and spires atop twin square towers. Except for a winged image on a dome, uninteresting buildings lined a busy boulevard with a long row of launches and yachts moored opposite. Further along, perched on a rocky tor, the 16th-century Moorish **Castillo de Santa Bárbara** overlooked fountains in a large traffic circle and the promenade beside a wide strip of beach with the city skyline at the far end. Five-branched lampposts stood outside a long light-coloured stone building with three towers, a dome, and modest window decoration. In an attractive street with palms, plants and old-fashioned lampposts, a grey stone building was enhanced with extravagantly decorated doorways and blue shutters behind iron-railed balconies (also blue). An ornate but badly cracked façade, again in the shadow of the overwhelming castle, featured symmetrical bell towers, large figures, spiral pillars, and delicate sculpting incorporating cherubs – favoured by white doves as a resting place.

Climbing a stepped alley with a precipice rearing at the end, I reached the Castillo, which provided a superb panorama across the bay to the city, with the mountains to the left, the marina and palm-fringed beach to the right. There was nothing exceptional about the castle with its stone ceiling, walls and floor, the latter inset with a large coat of arms. Suits of armour, banners, shields, flags, lances and sconces lined walls with tiny windows. From an outside courtyard, with carving on one wall, a more comprehensive view of the city revealed the huge stadium, a red dome amongst ugly colourless high-rise buildings, and the ranges beyond. A vista past a corner bastion extended to a rowing boat like a dot on the sea. The ocean and city were also visible from the castle's **Plaza de la Torreta**, accessed through an arch with an interesting face painted overhead. Back in the narrow streets, I encountered plenty of plants: in pots, on walls and ledges, beside steps, and enhancing lacy iron balconies. A sculpted head, water issuing from its mouth, was lodged below a picture on a plain white wall. Wide blue dados added colour to some façades, and a street artist was reproducing the striking scene of a plaza with a tower rising above blue, red, tan and white buildings, the castle in its eyrie looming over all. Men were playing bocce to the thud of the heavy metal balls, and a large fountain played in front of a memorial and tall buildings.

Murcia

From Alicante I backtracked to Murcia. The train sped past rugged red mountains sharply etched against a blue sky, with white towns at the base and greenery in the foreground. A castle perched on a peak loomed above even lofty the bell tower of a white church below. **Murcia** itself, standing on both sides of the **Segura River**, contained a wide well-laid-out boulevard with tall buildings, palms, old-style streetlamps, and a grassed median strip with fountains and trees. Standing in a square, diagonally opposite a warm-toned building with elaborate sculpting and iron-railed balconies, the magnificent similarly coloured stone **Cathedral** was a total surprise. Begun in the 14th century, this Baroque edifice featured life-sized images on balustrades and in recesses on the ornately shaped gable, which was also endowed with extensive carving and fluted columns with Corinthian capitals, as was the façade. It also had a dome and one lofty tower with spired turrets and a cupola. It made a fantastic picture looking upwards against a brilliant blue sky.

cathedral façade

Almost as impressive were a side entrance with a rose window above a faceted arched doorway, and highly ornamented rounded and angular sections, the latter sporting coats of arms and chains wrought in stone. Other things of interest included small figures on a weathered grey façade surmounted by a cross, the attractive pink and white **Teatro de Romea**, and substantial tall buildings with cupolas. In front of the theatre, an impressive monument dedicated to Al Maestro Fernandez Caballero portrayed that gentleman below the black figure of a naked woman holding aloft a wreath.

Approaching Murcia, I had seen another photogenic castle atop a hill and decided to alight on the return journey for closer inspection – a decision that nearly turned into a disaster. I do not remember the name of the town, but as I walked from the station towards a blue-domed white church in the lee of tall misty grey mountains, I was immediately aware that it was a lot less affluent than any I had visited to date. Drab concrete houses with minimal colour stood at the foot of craggy peaks that took on an ochre hue in the waning daylight. Steep streets featured a second dome and one dwelling with a door, window treatment and pots, all in vivid blue, highlighting the bare cement façade. The only things worthy of comment were chalk drawings on the roadway: one with the word *Hola* surrounded by flowers and another showing a huge face of Jesus. From the top, near the castle, I obtained panoramic views across the flat or red tiled roofs of clustered houses with the occasional green or blue door, yellow or blue wall, crammed together in higgledy-piggledy fashion beneath the grim and foreboding stony mountains. Washing decorated many of the flat rooftops, two painted bright blue and red respectively. A white chapel was sequestered amongst greenery in a crevice at the foot of the range, and dogs barked incessantly.

I have no record of the castle because it turned out to be occupied by families of gypsies. On passing a group of youths, one of them followed me demanding money. Using my limited Spanish I informed him that I did not have any (it was under my clothing) and kept walking, unfortunately into a blind alley whereupon, my being cornered, he accosted me and grabbed my camera bag. This contained no money but, to me, my films were worth risking my life, so we both jostled for possession. During the ensuing struggle I kept moving back towards the entrance with the knowledge that when the gang saw what was happening they would either join in the mugging or let me go. To my eternal gratitude, the obvious leader decided on the latter course and told his friend to desist. I walked as fast as I could (without running) back to the first train and Alicante. An analogous situation was to occur exactly ten years later in Cuba.

Alicante

Arriving in the evening, I came across a group of Latin American musicians wearing striped ponchos. Next day, this time in the safety of a tour, I visited a wonderful picturesque town dominated by a photogenic castle completely covering the summit of a

hilltop castle

reinforced hillside. With round battlemented turrets on corners, crenellated ramparts, and a square tower, the light-coloured stone structure was the epitome of a medieval fortress. Red-roofed white houses surrounded the base of the hill, and the whole made a great sight across the furrowed fields of an empty landscape. The homes were in shadow, whilst sun struck the castle with dramatic effect.

The narrow streets all looked up towards the fortress, as did a lovely square bordered by beautifully sculpted doorways. These included that of a yellow stone church with a tall bell tower capped by a combination delicate iron cross and weather vane. Water issued from the beaks of metallic swans occupying a fountain in the centre. The fetching square was the subject of perfect pictures, but unfortunately I cannot put a name to this place.

At the next stop, interesting sights included the **Plaza de la Constitucion** with its white bell and clock tower, a pattern-paved pedestrian mall where an accordionist was performing, and a busy street market (*mercado*) selling enormous dried fungi, fruits such as oranges and bananas, vegetables, flowers including gladioli and carnations, confectionary, items of clothing, and colourful caged birds.

castle from the village

Continuing through dry terrain to a white town at the foot of a tabletop mountain, I had the opportunity to rapidly investigate the deserted narrow streets with their bell towers and colourful doors before resuming our journey past palm trees, crops, orchards and mountains. At another stop, I appreciated the splendid carving, golden altar, decorated dome, stained glass and stuccowork inside a dark church, silent except for the tolling of a bell. Flags and draped balconies marked an official building, and a tall white tower proved to be a dove cote set in beautiful gardens. This extensive site featured crimson plants around the base of palm trees, pathways circling beds featuring trees dressed in plum-coloured foliage amongst the green, and steps mounting grassed slopes bordered by beds of scarlet. Ponds, roses and philodendrons added to the attraction, one of the white roses having the merest hint of delicate pink on the edge of its petals.

In Alicante again, I found a palm-lined avenue with urns on stone pillars at the entrance and a tower at the end, steep narrow streets, an archway with a room overhead, and an antique fair in front of the long pale stone building described earlier. Amongst items for sale were a silver candelabrum and an old-time gramophone with a horn. The dark interior of a church was relieved by colourful images in a lighted tableau beneath a gleaming golden dome, its coffered depths ornamented with carved flowers.

Barcelona

I headed for **Barcelona**, passing the tabletop mountain again and another castle on an impossible pinnacle of rock. With no help available, I found the massive railway station daunting, so made my way to one of the first class hotels, where I was able to get assistance and a map. I secured a room at the central two-star Hotel Condestable and my first pictures were of large buildings, one featuring a rooftop pillared portico with figures surmounting the pediment and a dome topped by a figure riding on the back of a bird with an enormous wingspan. Another had a winged image above a clock and massive corner towers; because it was also adorned with flags and large red stars, I wondered if it was Russian. The city was endowed with numerous *plaças*, domes, towers, beautiful façades – and a four-storey red brick colosseum. Between symmetrical box-like structures crowning one building, I admired a tall clock tower with images atop its cupola. This faced a large paved square with trees and a huge fountain ringed by grass and yellow flowers, the sun creating a rainbow in the changing patterns of its many jets. Grand buildings included one with two figures and a horse in a recess above the doorway and the ornate façade of a huge church with two octagonal towers, viewed between palm trees set in lawn with extensive flowerbeds. Jutting into a marketplace, a tall hexagonal clock tower had decorated slit windows.

A market was also set up around the church, where a family group sat with a cute white puppy. Blowing in a stiff breeze, Christmas decorations with a metallic sheen formed scintillating colours of cerise, red, pale and dark blue, green, gold and silver; colourful paper windmills on sticks spun and whirled furiously, and a man with a drooping moustache, long hair, and dressed in a bright pink hat, striped vest and multihued shirt sold crocodile teeth necklaces. Other items for sale included trees created from semiprecious gemstones, handmade pottery and peculiar figurines, black masks painted with iridescent colours, wall plaques of black ceramic faces swathed in vibrant scarves made from leather, and exotic flowers such as bromeliads next to common red geraniums, snake plant (mother-in-law's tongue) and ferns. There was a service in progress, so I did not see much more of the church interior than the ornate gilded altar in an equally elaborate alcove with stained glass, paintings, numerous images, and crystal chandeliers. The exterior featured an interestingly shaped gable, beautiful sculpting, pillars with decorative capitals, and a multi-arched doorway with figures in the facets and tympanum. It was possible to walk through the church from one crowded square to the next; the second, with a mass of people (and pigeons), boasting an enormous fountain exhibiting a large reclining figure surrounded by smaller images. Emitting a roar competing with the noise of the crowd, water flowed from urns held by these images, as it did from the middle of the structure and a ring of jets around the outside. This was greatly appreciated by birds that roosted all over the central figure.

Gaudí's Batlló House

Points of interest around this plaza included overhead vaults, the two octagonal towers of the church – one with a spire and lacy parapet – and painted floral decoration (in pink) on the façade of a building with iron-railed balconies. A man was selling quaint bird puppets that looked like two yellow pompoms with a yellow beak and spindly black legs, one of which, by manipulating strings, he 'walked' across the pavement – where it stopped to peck! Further out, I came to an old multi-arched stone bridge and a russet tree in front of a similarly coloured brick gateway with crenellated towers. Away from the hustle and bustle, the inevitable narrow streets hemmed in by high stone buildings with wall lamps and plants on balconies were very quiet. The old **Mercado** made an attractive picture with its tile work and ornamental wrought iron – which included a green parrot and gold crown – on the dome, cupola, and peaks of gables. Interesting buildings around the market included a red and white structure with a spire on the steeply pitched roof, its façade featuring a crown above a sculpted crest supported by lions. An ornamented beige stone façade also had gargoyles and a crenated parapet, and a grey stone building featured deep relief, decorative pilasters, and a slim ornate clock tower between life-sized images on top. All of these, together with oranges on a tree in front, made up the scene being painted by a street artist. There was yet another large fountain, and a fascinating skyline in silhouette showing a majestic lion (its head erect), domes, small spires, and a clock tower with a filigree cupola.

I took a tour to see Antoni Gaudí's work, passing a suburb of flat box-like buildings, yellow in the light of the sun, forming narrow streets with a single dome and tower in the centre. Twin towers topped by cupolas, another lovely fountain with figures in lawn around the edge, ornately decorated metal-and-glass turrets with wrought-iron railing and weathervanes, and a view of hilltop towers and a castle greeted me as I approached Gaudí's **Batlló House** with a brilliant bed of orange marigolds around palm trees in front. The incredible avant-garde work of this master architect, son of a boiler maker, eclipsed all other buildings, even the beautiful traditional **Casa Amatller** with its stepped gable and sculpted façade that stood next door. Fantastic, innovative, mostly rounded shapes epitomised Gaudí's art, this one with an erratic roofline, a single turret with a double cross on top (a signature of the artist), oddly shaped balconies almost appearing like the jaws of sharp-toothed fish, balustrades and columns simulating bones, an exquisitely tiled façade in contemporary patterns and hues, gorgeous circles of glass in mauves and blues in the irregularly shaped windows, and gold decoration at street level, all contrasting with the old-style lampposts in front and columned porticos to one side.

Visible above rooftops, an elaborate dome presaged the futuristic **Loewe Building**, with deep relief including griffins on ornate rounded balconies, flowers on spandrels between arched windows, sculpting around latticework railing between fluted pillars with Corinthian capitals, and a mini-spired parapet. Even the white paving slabs exhibited a lace-like pattern.

Loewe Building

Other fine buildings in this eclectic mix of styles included one with stone- and iron-railed balconies in different shapes, underneath which were heavy carvings of birds with spread wings. Another exhibited obvious Arabic influence in the arched windows, and a third, a circular cascade of water in front, had domes and a round colonnaded structure behind the parapet. Traditional statues lined the balustrade of a pedestrian bridge with high-spurting fountains each side. Water trickled from the pedestal of a statue outside the classical Hotel Ritz, and a lacy cupola enhanced yet another rooftop with a spired parapet. The unmistakable stamp of Gaudí was on an extraordinary structure that put me in mind of the excavated cave dwellings of Cappadocia in Turkey. With the clover-like double cross on top, the **Milá House** or **La Pedrera** was all rounded corners and shapes, with balcony railings resembling networks of vines, and tiny windows in the curved roof. Our next destination was the church of **La Sagrada Familia**, Gaudí's triumphant masterpiece that was left to the family to complete following his death when hit by a tram in 1926. Begun in 1882, less than half the task was achieved by 1999. On the intricate façade, perfect small figures were enmeshed in a mass of concrete moulding, which also overlapped the beautiful coloured glass windows.

From this angle I could see four of the eight existing towers, all over one hundred metres, of the projected eighteen on completion. These tapering round openwork structures were crowned by a flower or sunburst decoration, each in itself a work of art. Capped by a cross, a lower central tower was decorated with sculpted greenery on which roosted 'fluttering' white birds, and spiky ornamentation like huge holly leaves was arranged on the summit of a white pedestal. A partially constructed wall contained rose windows open to the sky. Walking around this edifice, the remaining towers, exhibiting different ceramic tops, loomed with a towering crane against the sky. Through an iron fence I could see another rose window and a shorter angular tower with pinnacles on top and glazed arched windows made up of multiple panes. In contrast to the fussy round towers, the pyramid-shaped entry was all angles, with script under the point above a crucifix bearing a naked Christ, and a skull and figures, hands covering their faces, at the foot of the cross. Below, a tableau depicting the Way of the Cross had soldiers intimated by gaunt suits of armour and a figure (without a face) holding the shroud imprinted with Jesus' countenance. To the left and right, other niches contained haloed images on the back of a donkey and sorrowful figures placing the body in the tomb. An amusing addition was a gargoyle in the form of a large snail.

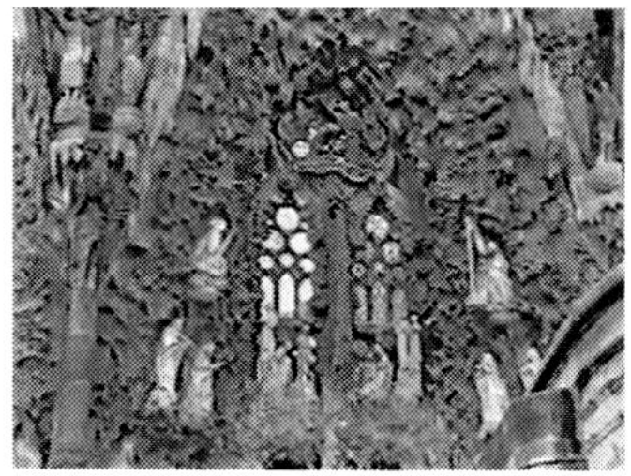

La Sagrada Familia

the Way of the Cross

From here, we proceeded to **Parc Güell**, another Gaudí attraction, with flights of fancy creating a Spanish fantasy world. Greenery surrounded pillars created from natural stones, and two adobe-like structures had whimsical towers on the roof.

fantasy house

Inset with ceramics, these reared above treetops, in contrast to plain concrete buildings beyond. Red cannas composed the foreground to a mosaic parapet inset with pieces of white tile, pottery, glass and/or mirror, which curved around the top of a colonnade. Sturdy brownstone archways leading to circular cave-like recesses were inlaid with tiles in a checked pattern, each individual tile constructed with tiny pieces. These recesses flanked a wide staircase with a larger-than-life lurid polychrome iguana, water trickling from its mouth, in the centre of the steps. In front of this, also on the steps, was a garden with a fine fall dripping from the mouth of another weird beastie onto lush greenery that included ferns, philodendrons, small yellow flowers, moss and trailing creepers, all in a white tiled surround. In close proximity were the two fascinating buildings mentioned above. With a rough brown texture and rounded eaves, its pillars, roof, checked tower (with the double cross) and cupola in blue and white, the first resembled a frosted chocolate cake, the other featured a studded cupola on a roof patterned with mosaic chips. Giving the appearance of smoke curling up from flames, white plumes of pampas in a red garden bed stood out in very green lawn in an area of green trees, palms, flowers, and a pergola draped with red, green and pale blue foliage.

Outside the park, silhouetted against a lilac, palest blue and lemon evening sky, a sculpture representing giant-sized broken matches made a somewhat different picture. Above its multi-faceted arched entrance, the red-tinged exterior of another church featured a beautiful rendition of the Sacred Heart of Jesus surrounded by a multitude of people and angels. Rising behind, a contrasting grey stone façade with a rose window had Christ with outstretched arms on top of a central tower. This was flanked by life-sized images below spires surmounted by crosses. We stopped for a superb view over a chapel on a hilltop, the lights of the city spread out at the foot. Inside the chapel, the dome and walls were painted with numerous figures and Spanish galleons under a flaming sky. Finally, my film shows ornate sconces, a carved ceiling, and spandrels with the heads of various animals, their mouths agape, below ceramic flowers.

Montserrat

The following day, I joined a tour to the 1,236m mountaintop monastery of **Montserrat**, founded in 1065 to commemorate an apparition of the Virgin Mary at the site. En route, we passed a 17th-century Romany château a unique pyramid-shaped stone bridge, its wide central span flanked by two arches, and craggy grey mountains with green foothills. A building nestled near the top gave an indication of what was to eventually confront us. The incredible peaks looked like towers of God's own cathedral reaching to heaven. We looked down on one monastery at the rim of a high plateau, the red-roofed light-coloured stone buildings forming a quadrangle with a tall bell tower at one corner. At first sight, Montserrat was a forbidding-looking place, with austere, heavy stone outer walls congregated below the looming tors. However, when lit by the sun and with a brilliant blue sky above, the towering grey peaks turned a reddish shade, matched by walls within the compound, and assumed a less daunting aura. Viewed through the grey stone and red brick entrance, these remarkable formations changed again to take on a yellow hue.

Montserrat

The archway led to an enormous courtyard with a line of trimmed trees in tubs, lampposts crowned with crosses, and steps leading to four-storey buildings in the shadow of the overpowering stone cliffs. Scant shrubs in the soaring rock provided green relief, as did plants on the sills of arched windows, a small patch of lawn, and a few pencil pines, but the main attraction was in the setting; in almost every direction one was overwhelmed by the surroundings, around which a church bell reverberated with the call to prayer. A small chapel was sited on top of a monolith to one side, and through a free-standing arched wall with statues in niches on the front, I observed a lonely cross standing on the opposite point. The angular free-standing gable of the church, with sculpted decoration and a row figures below its clock and circular window, made a striking contrast to the plain façades of the monastic buildings.

In the dimly illuminated cavernous interior, many priests participated in a service being offered to sung responses. It was difficult to appreciate the vaulted ceiling, but the suspended cross and gleaming gold altarpiece showed up to effect in the meagre lighting, only supplemented by that filtering through high stained-glass windows augmented by the tiny flames of multicoloured votive candles. The fabulous acoustics were further demonstrated when we were invited back later for a choral performance, with organ accompaniment, by the glorious voices of a large mixed choir with a 700-year-old history. This, along with the **Black Virgin** purportedly carved by St Luke and brought to monastery by St Peter in AD 50, was the pride of Montserrat. Another legend states that St Ignatius of Loyola reputedly laid down his sword here, discovered his religious vocation, and went on to found the Jesuits.

The peace was shattered by a horde of schoolchildren, so I walked to a viewpoint overlooking houses amongst distant trees, one large edifice in landscaped grounds, and hazy mountains – and where I was made aware of the dizzying height! Another vista revealed a walkway to a point where a building opposite, smoke wafting from its chimney, abutted the rock. From this platform, I obtained a wonderful panorama of a river, winding roads, wooded slopes, a town with several large structures and a tower, reflected bridges, snow on crests in the far distance, and a view back to the first monastery mentioned. The topography of the region put me in mind of America's Grand Canyon, and mist shrouded the mountains like a gossamer veil. On the return trip, rays of the setting sun burst like stars behind the questing fingers of rock.

Barcelona

Further investigation of the city next day produced façades with lacy balconies, a turret at the point of a wedge-shaped building, a church with a heavily sculpted façade, and octagonal towers on the roof of a building with angels flanking a clock. This brought me to Barcelona's famed walking street, the tree-shaded **Rambla**, which was a rainbow of colours created by numerous flower stalls selling every conceivable bloom: gerberas, hippeastrum, both red and white anthuriums with their shiny plastic-looking petals (or bracts), perfect roses in red, yellow, white and pink, snapdragons, orchids, red and yellow lilies, cyclamen, carnations, gladioli, strelitzia, and exotics such as ginger and red or pink bromeliads, all arrayed amongst decorative leaves (including mottled maroon-and-yellow), ferns and the epiphytic bird's nest plant. There were baskets filled solely with vibrant pinks or reds, and floral arrangements containing gerberas, roses and gladioli in a combination of colours: red, yellow, orange and white. Even the common white daisy was represented in bouquets, and there were some glorious blue blooms. I wandered down a narrow pedestrian mall with decorative bells hanging overhead and found five-branched lampposts in front of two imposing buildings with columns and statues. At the end of another narrow street I could see a tower with tall arched windows, a lacy parapet, and bells in filigree ironwork on top. Closer inspection revealed a spiked spire, gargoyles, and unusual treatment with walls protruding like buttresses from the angular rear section, also containing tall arched windows. This was the 14th-century Gothic **Cathedral** that was also depressingly dark inside, although evening had now closed in. The low light only enabled me to film some stained glass, the central boss on a ribbed ceiling, and tall brick pillars. An extraordinary sight was a gaggle of noisy honking geese in the dark cloister.

Back in the street, the fretwork pattern of an intricately carved stone vault was outlined by lamps, coloured figures stood on a wall bracket beneath a canopy, and a group of musicians, playing accordion, guitar, flute and tambourine, were busking beneath the many spires and solemn walls of the cathedral. My filming was not very successful in the night streets, but I did capture a wall plaque, a fountain at the end of a narrow alley and, approaching the front of the cathedral, a network of pinnacles circling the base of a particularly beautiful central spire that was lit from within. Walking beneath an archway with a chandelier illuminating a figure overhead, I came to an edifice with a horseman in a recess on the façade, its lighted windows showing off the superb illustrated and carved walls and ceiling of an elegant interior. On a wider brighter street, another band featured bass, guitars, trumpet and saxophone. Illuminations included a globe atop a turret, a façade with gables highlighted by pink and blue lighting, the four faces of another turret containing glowing panes in different colours, and two large lighted fountains with statues standing between them and well-lit buildings behind, one with a gleaming red clock face. Blowing sad strains, a lone trumpeter leaned against a wall as unheeding crowds hurried by.

Next day's highlights included juxtaposed narrow four-storey frontages, one with shuttered windows and iron-railed balconies surrounded by a pink floral design and another, barely the width of one room, with attractive iron balconies. Flanked by figures atop tall slender poles, a silhouetted triumphal arch, cupolas at each end, made excellent pictures with the yellow sky of early morning framed in the opening and a blue and grey firmament above. Up close, this red brick structure featured rampant lions supporting a shield and crown, below which was a frieze with a classical theme flanked by angels, two blowing horns and two holding aloft wreaths.

triumphal arch

Looking through the arch from the other side, palm trees and figures around a monument stood out against the yellow sky. A statue depicting a mother and child surmounted an ornate pedestal near an impressive red brick building with a beautiful spire of iron and glass on a hexagonal turret and a line of white plaques with blue figures below the indented parapet.

statue and building

In front of the building, a large pool surrounded by modernistic chameleons was the antithesis of a traditional fountain comprised of white figures on the rim of a bowl in the background.

A row of elaborate metal sculptures with a mythical theme crowned the balusters of a low wall, a cupola added interest to ornate gables on the corner of a building, a family group occupied a wall bracket, and an equestrian statue stood out in black relief against the pink-toned façade of a seven-storey edifice with a decorative gable and cupolas.

Back at the cathedral, flanked by similar but lower spires inserted with coloured glass, the central spire seen the previous evening sat above a multi-arched doorway with sculpting suggesting a large flower overhead. Intricately carved openwork triangles with angels at the apex topped the arches of windows each side. The bell tower with the filigree top mentioned earlier was visible behind, but other walls were unadorned. A tour of the inside showed me arches, fluted pillars with splayed tops, and rib-vaulted ceilings, all in brick. It also contained stained-glass windows, a fantastic gold altarpiece behind a screen, marble panels with deep relief, elaborate choir stalls bearing coats of arms, and bosses with figures or delicate designs, but the highlight, as on the previous evening, was the cloister. By daylight, two fountains became evident, the first consisting of a horse and rider mounted on a rock over which water fell into a many sided bowl. Water also flowed from heads around the base of the pedestal holding the rock, and sprays erupted from a greenery-bedecked fountain in a pool behind railing that confined the geese – now quiet and peacefully swimming. The 12 birds were kept in memory of the first Christian martyr of the town who was a shepherd of geese. I discovered a reclining figure in an ornately carved niche and looked up at a gargoyle and one of the 47m bell towers.

lovely arch

In a narrow street beside the cathedral an artist was creating a dramatic black and white picture that highlighted the tracery (noted the previous evening) of the overhead passageway between heavy stone walls.

Through an arch I observed a multi-paned window displaying antiques, and walking down an alley with cascading white flowers, old-fashioned lamps, ancient stone walls, and a tower at the end, I came to a structure with plain walls but beautiful Gothic stained-glass windows. Lovely piano music emanated from nearby. A historic grey stone building had hideous countenances beneath a balustrade and, inside, an extensively carved angular 'dome'. A bi-level colonnade enclosed a courtyard containing a pond and trees. Outside, a flautist and his partner, strumming a stringed instrument whilst clapping foot-operated cymbals, performed beneath an elaborate arched doorway. Opposite stood the equally impressive entrance of a museum and a building with a corner bastion.

Joining a bus tour, we drove past the **Monument a Colom**: a statue of Columbus atop a tall pedestal with figures on the plinth and lions around the perimeter. It stood at the end of La Rambla and opposite an edifice with an elaborate roofline. We were heading for the **Parc de la Ciutadella**, with an amazing panorama and the outstanding **Cascada** created, with the young Gaudí lending a hand, in the 1870s. Surrounded by lawn and trees, this monumental water display consisted of high-leaping fountains in a large crystal clear blue pool flowing across a series of stepped pools containing more spurting fountains, one with a green garden in the centre. At the bottom, beyond yellow flowers and green bushes, the city unfolded below me, and I had no difficulty picking out the Columbus Column at the end of the tree-lined Rambla, **Port Vell** harbour, the spires and hexagonal towers of the massive cathedral, and the haze-covered Sagrada Familia, its eight towers pointing like needles into the firmament. Next, we drove to the hill called **Montjuïc**, site of the ultramodern stadium erected for the games. Barcelona '92, a sword, and the Olympic circles were the only decoration on the soaring stainless steel torch that, in contrast, stood opposite the ornate towers of an aged traditional church. The inside of the former, with seating around a grassed arena surrounded by athletic tracks, was no different from any other stadium worldwide except for the figures of riders on rearing horses flanking the clock in an old-type mounting.

Moving on, we came to **Poble Español**, a picturesque collection of buildings in different styles from various regions of Spain. Entry was via an ornate carved archway bearing the eagle holding the coat of arms, which led to a street spanned by a white arch connecting stone buildings either side.

Poble Español

Cobbled and stepped side alleys had old-fashioned wall lamps, potted plants, arched doorways, and little wooden or iron-railed balconies. At the end of one such street, a bright yellow building stood opposite a white tower, its ascending levels decreasing in size. A tiny square accommodated trees and a monument, and one wall was decorated with a design of petals. A statue stood on a pedestal ringed by lanterns, and tables with pink cloths sat in a cobbled street next to a small fountain. This was located in front of an elegant entrance with a sculpted lintel flanked by marble columns. The ornate gable resided above spiral pillars, sculpting, and a lacework iron balcony. The adjacent façade was graced with decoration above windows and under eaves. The village was full of craft shops, and we paused to watch a glass blower at work. We came to an area with plants on tiny overhead balconies of whitewashed houses bordering narrow lanes, and from a stone bridge, I looked along the street, past a building with a creeper-covered stone wall, iron-fenced balconies with trailing plants, carved pediments above windows, and old-style lamps, to a colonnaded square. Entering the large plaza bounded by three-storey buildings, I took a series of quick pictures that included a figure on a bracket, a stone rotunda in one corner, tables and chairs outside cafés, and tiled, brick, stone and stuccoed façades.

Gerona

I left Barcelona behind and travelled to one of the most photogenic towns in Spain, **Gerona**, ensconced between mountain massifs in the **Ter Valley**, although first impressions from a bridge, with waste water pouring into a river lined with squalid housing, left a lot to be desired. In spite of this, reflections of yellow and ochre-coloured buildings and a white tower were stunning. These houses, right on the very edge of the **Oñar River**, were constructed towards the end of the Middle Ages and were attached to walls enclosing the ancient quarter. The yellow façades continued, along with plain stone walls and recessed doorways, in a steep stepped alley with old-style lamps and flourishing plants on a balcony at the end.

stepped alley

Another narrow street featuring balconies with copious plants terminated in a view of a white octagonal tower. A maze of impossibly narrow (and at times dark) cobbled lanes, bounded by rough walls with overhead arches, old-style lamps, hanging vines, and greenery sprouting from the ancient stone, marked the old Jewish sector or ghetto named **The Call**. Within this quarter, which dated back to the year 890 and was a thriving community until the expulsion of the Jews in 1492, I visited the **Isaac el Cec** building. Surrounded by vine covered stone walls, its lovely courtyard, emblazoned with a large Star of David, also had an alcove full of plants and a stone trough of which I have forgotten the significance. As in the time of the Nazis, Jews were forbidden to leave the Call without wearing traditional clothing in order to guarantee their identification.

The Call

A thoroughfare with a low ivy-draped wall and trees on one side led to a church with an attractive belfry, and latticed windows were a feature in the streets or *pias*. A scene often depicted in paintings was that of a large skew arch with a coat of arms between windows on top, which stood at the junction of stairs on different levels, one set leading to the 14th- to 17th-century Baroque area containing the **Palace of the Agullana Family** and the ornate façade of **Sant Marti Sacosta**. Here, the buildings were all brown or grey stone. At the summit of a steep flight of steps with a stone balustrade, the unusual box-like **Cathedral**, a hexagonal belfry standing incongruously on one corner of its flat roof, nevertheless had a beautiful façade. A large circular window in a sculpted surround lay above eight statues in niches, each bordered by fine columns. The cloister and part of the tower were the only sections of the original 1038 Romanesque building to have been preserved. A bell rang out as I entered the treasure-filled interior. This exhibited rose windows, a shining silver 14th-century reredos with myriad small figures, larger images on a glistening carved altarpiece, an exquisite gilded main altarpiece reflecting sufficient light to make it also glow, and the widest (22.9m) Gothic nave in the world. Baroque paintings on the principal altarpiece featured two portraits, and its colourful ceramic figures included Christ in an elaborate surround supported by cherubs. The last two screens reached to vaulted ceilings. The **Chapter Museum** contained a tenth-century manuscript of the *Apocalypse* and a 12th-century embroidery called *The Creation*.

Outside again, I came to unguarded weed-enveloped steps leading to ramparts, old creeper-draped stone walls, and the bell tower of the 13th- to 16th-century **Ex-Collegiate Church of Sant Feliu,** seen reflected in the river on arrival. This was located at the foot of the original city walls, approached down cobbled steps with a carpet of autumn leaves and across a stone overpass. This route brought me back to the river, with more perfect mirror images of the ochre-coloured houses, and I took pictures through the solid stone arches of the colonnaded **Rambla de la Llibertat** behind the waterfront. I discovered another obvious Gaudí construction, with a turret topped by the double cross and a cluster of eight coloured 'spires' on an odd-shaped tiled roof, its ridges bearing ornamentation like green mushrooms.

Zaragosa

Moving on to **Zaragosa**, capital of **Aragón** and City of the Four Cultures, which began as a Roman colony between the years 19 and 15 BC, I was immediately struck by the Moorish influence again. This was apparent in battlemented turrets, a carved arch, lacy stone window screens, square towers, and the lace-like scalloped arches of the **Palacio de la Aljafería**. These beautiful arches surrounded two adjoining courtyards: one with trees in red flowerbeds, the other with a gleaming red marble floor. On certain arches the white tracery was superimposed on rust-coloured stone, itself delicately carved. Patterned red wooden doors in a keyhole arch were surrounded by fragile carving that continued, along with script, on inside walls.

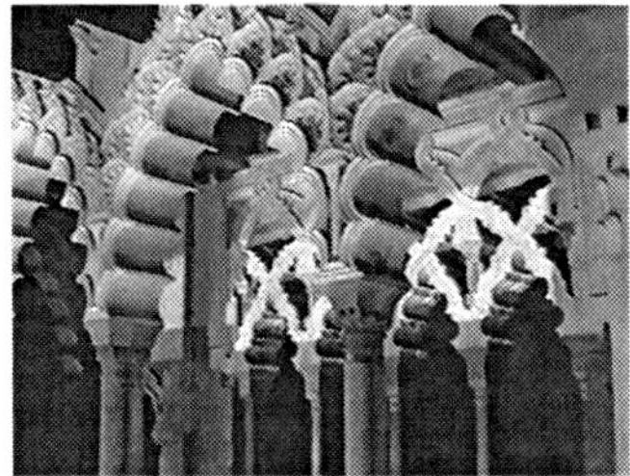

Palacio de la Aljaferia

However, Zaragosa's masterpiece was the multi-spired 17th-century **Basilica of El Pilar**, not the best but certainly the biggest that I had ever seen. The roof was a forest of towers, spired cupolas and colourful tile-patterned domes.

Basilica of El Pilar

Situated by the **Ebro River** near the **Puente de Pradera**, it was bounded on the other side by the 500m-long **Plaza du Nuestra Señora del Pilar**, with an immense waterfall cascading over huge basalt-type crystals into a zigzag stream running between concrete banks incised into the pavement. There was also a monumental globe (and thousands of birds) in the forecourt, and from every angle the Basilica (full title: **Basilica de Nuestra Señora del Pilar**), abutting the **City Hall** and **Episcopal Palace**, made incredible pictures. It was in Zaragosa that Goya served his apprenticeship and painted his first works, some of which were in the Basilica. The city also possessed some old overgrown walls with steps to ramparts, and an imposing angular tower with a decided lean, which loomed above **La Sao**, the 12th- to 16th-century cathedral with a lovely carved Mudéjar portal. This stood at the south-eastern end of the plaza, where I also found fountains, an attractive old-style covered market, and

Roman ruins marked by a series of trapeziums in different colours and mediums.

But everything centred on the Basilica that with all its towers and comparatively plain walls was wonderfully reflected in the water flowing from the cascade through the square. The white interior was also breathtaking, with shining marble floors, carved woodwork, ornamental pilasters, a network of domes with skylights, coloured glass chandeliers, patterns under and above arches, an intricate altarpiece with tiny figures and tableaux, sculpting around a circular window above an arch leading to a second altar, illustrated domes, and sculpted and painted spandrels. But the most amazing aspect was the central altar beneath an enormous red marble baldachin (canopy), with figures in deep relief on a white marble panel and images atop its dome and pediment. This dome within a dome housed the most spectacular gold altarpiece with white figures, but I could not approach very near because of a service, the beautiful singing resounding in this chamber of epic proportions. The basilica also contained a revered piece of marble pillar believed to have been left by the Virgin Mary when she appeared to Santiago (St James) in a vision here in AD 40. Further inspection of the exterior revealed figures on the rooftop balustrade, an impressive doorway, a white panel with heavy relief, and the flags, colonnade and iron-railed balconies of the adjacent building.

My last photographs were of the lovely ornate stonework towers of the **Church of San Pablo**, and the incongruous red and white **Bullring**. Blockaded by Napoleon's troops during the War of Independence, Zaragosa was practically reduced to nothing, with heavy loss of life, buildings and art, but a new city arose from the ruins.

Burgos

I caught the train once again, past a pyramid-shaped mountain, to my last but not least destination, **Burgos**. Entrance was via the striking turreted **Arch of Santa Maria** at the end of a bridge over the **Rio Arlanzón**, with the steeple of the cathedral towering behind. Houses, drooping willows, and bare trees lined the river on both sides of the archway. The outstanding **Cathedral**, on the World Heritage List, dated from the year 1221, and it was here that the remains of legendary **El Cid**, hero of Burgos, were interred. It was a feast of ornate spires, angles and curves, rose windows, flying buttresses, and openwork in symmetrical towers. Figures reposed on walls, in the tracery of a square tower, beside the simple arched door, and in delicate arched recesses above the central rose window. There were balustrades on different levels, a sculpted tableau in a recess, and life-sized images on a side entrance.

Burgos cathedral

In other streets, I found two arches: one of red stone, the other free-standing and facing a row of tall colourful narrow-fronted buildings and old-style streetlamps. A beautiful façade had turrets and regal-looking figures in niches, and a lovely willow-shaded river walk had iron railing and patterned paving beside green grassy banks. A large building topped a hill on the opposite side.

A thoroughfare with decorative paving, a fountain, trees, interesting topiary bushes, and garden beds led me to the huge **Plaza Mayor**, where I found a central statue on a pedestal, five-branched lampposts – and scores of birds. The square, surrounded by umbrella-shaped trees and tall colonnaded buildings, offered a glimpse of the cathedral spires in the background. A building of rough stone with small heavily carved balconies was the 15th-century **El Cordón House**, where the Catholic Monarchs received Columbus after his return from the second voyage.

Situated between two bridges, opposite a red and white edifice and with a memorial to one side, the **San Lesmes Church** with its splendid three-tiered belfry made a wonderful picture looking along the canal. A two-storey structure was built above a broad archway, and an appealing wide avenue had bare trees, a fountain surrounded by russet plants, and a paved path containing a wide green median strip with large pines. More colourful narrow frontages, twin spires on a long grey building with angelic figures on a gilt background within the portico, striking pictures of the bland grey cathedral behind deep red roses, detail of a boy astride a beast on a trickling moss-covered fountain surmounted by a statue in front of the main entrance, and a magnificent view of the edifice from steps overlooking narrow coloured façades on a colonnaded plaza, completed another series of photographs. Burgos played an important role on the pilgrimage to Santiago de Compostela. In 1542, Andrew Brooke, physician and former bishop of Chichester, wrote: *By land it is the greatest journey an Englishman may go.*

In the early 1500s, Spain could boast the largest European empire since Rome, but a succession of wars, domestic inflation, famine and pestilence, internal turmoil and the loss of several colonies eroded her power. In an analogous situation, Portugal was once a mighty seafaring nation with many colonies but degenerated into Western Europe's poorest country.

I saw the white cliffs of Dover on the channel crossing en route to London for my flight home.

AFRICA: OVERLAND EXPEDITION 1993

In 1993, I participated in a ten week African overland expedition from Nairobi to Harare organised by Tracks, a company so badly operated that in addition to our own bad experiences, I heard numerous horror stories. At $3,335 the journey was cheap, but they did not last in the industry. This was the first of three such trips undertaken, and they were challenging endeavours, traversing primitive areas where roads, communication and other services taken for granted in Western society were either very poor or even non-existent. All chores such as cooking, marketing, collecting and chopping firewood, and digging the truck out of sand or mud were performed by group members. The truck was stocked with water, often our only source of supply and tasting foul because of the high content of added chlorine. However, except for meat, which was hung in the open and susceptible to insects, produce from markets was on most occasions exceedingly good and full of flavour, being picked at the optimum time.

MAURITIUS

I had a pleasant surprise even before leaving Perth (with Air Mauritius) when, paged at the airport and expecting to be offloaded because of my agents discount fare, I was invited to sit in the cockpit for takeoff and landing.

En route to Africa, I spent a couple of days on a second visit to the island nation of **Mauritius**, at the nicely landscaped Island View Club Hotel in **Grand Gaube**. Rattan furniture contributed to the tropical ambience in an open dining area (shared by cheeky sparrows!) overlooking the pool and ocean. Ladies in richly hued saris patronised village food stalls, and I caught a local bus through cane fields to **Gran Baie**, where boats bobbed at anchor on the blue water and far mountains rose in the background. Bright yellow birds made a striking picture amid red foliage, and I came across two unusual mosques surrounded by palm trees. I made a brief stop at **Le Jardin des Pamplemousses**, where I filmed pink and blue water lilies and weaver birds flitting around their nests, but I found it run down since my first visit.

AFRICA

KENYA

Kenya straddles the equator and yet the terrain ranges from desert to rainforest, with a wide variety of bird and animal life. Here also 1,750,000-year-old relics of the earliest toolmakers were found. The infamous *Mau Mau* rebellion was propagated when much of the land was allocated to white settlers, creating a shortage for Africans.

Nairobi

I flew to **Nairobi**, a dirty and dangerous city, over turquoise sea, green fields, and jagged mountain ridges. My first sights were of vintage vehicles and, outside the large covered market, a more-familiar style of mosque with minarets and domes. Inside the market, flowers, vegetables and fruits were mingled with hand-woven baskets, and a mezzanine floor was stocked with crafts. Pottery, African dolls, and more cane wares were arrayed outside.

wooden effigies

The city was more modern than I had anticipated, with towering skyscrapers and traditional statues of indigenous dignitaries. Located beside a winding pathway bordered by brilliant red-leafed plants, water spilled over the top of a contemporary S-shaped work of art decorated with a native design of men and cattle. Situated beside the road, I came across a solitary tin shed with the grandiose name of Friendly Bargain Curios where a lady was selling an assortment of merchandise.

Mombassa

With a few days to spare before joining the expedition, I caught the vintage overnight train to historic **Mombassa**, where my first recollection is of a white colonial-looking building with a square clock tower. Begun in 1593 by the Portuguese, **Fort Jesus** had weathered stone walls, heavy studded wooden doors with carved surrounds, others of embossed metal with spikes, and cannon facing the sea. The **Western Wall** was decorated with crude engravings, mostly of sailing ships, one room contained drums and chairs, cannon balls were piled in a corner of the courtyard, and I came across a deep stone lintel bearing chiselled relief. A view from the top showed a row of cannon in front of a white arched colonnade roofed with red tiles, and a tower and palm trees were prominent in the **Old Town** beyond. In spite of the fort, which changed hands nine times between 1631 and 1875, the Portuguese were massacred to a person in an uprising by the townspeople. It was later reoccupied without a fight when the Mombassan ruler, deciding further resistance was useless, reduced the town to rubble, cut down all the palms and fruit trees, and withdrew to the mainland. Driven out again by the Omanis in 1698, it was retaken once more, but the end finally came in 1729 following an Arab invasion and revolt by the population. In 1832, the Sultan of Oman, Seyyid Said, moved his capital and court, including one hundred concubines and eunuchs, from Muscat to Zanzibar, and the Omani flag flew over Fort Jesus until Kenya's independence in 1963.

Outside, below the walls, with more cannon and a bright splash of purple flowers at the base, a man was wielding a scythe to cut grass. In the narrow but atmospheric streets, I found old stone-walled and stuccoed houses with wooden balconies (some enclosed) jutting from upper levels. One whitewashed wall was illustrated with animals that included a green crocodile, pink pig, and yellow elephant! In the harbour, fishing boats lay at anchor whilst men unloaded the catch from nets. Wooden butterflies were mounted above an intricately carved door, and I saw a stone rotunda.

Lamu and Malindi

I caught public transport north to the tenth-century Arab towns of **Lamu** and **Malindi**, the former, Kenya's oldest. Already a thriving port in the early 1500s, it was little changed over the centuries. The Portuguese, who had established trading stations in these old coastal towns, were ousted by the Arabs in 1729. Traditionally, buildings were constructed from local materials: coral-rag blocks, wooden floors supported by mangrove poles, *makuti* (palm leaf) roofs, and intricately carved wooden shutters, doors and lintels. Lamu had a slave-based economy until its abolition in 1907, and as a result of the cheap labour, traders grew rich exporting ivory, cowries, tortoiseshell, mangrove poles, oil seeds and grains; importing oriental linen, silks, spices and porcelain.

People were cooking in a market set up on the sidewalk by the busy bus station, others selling to the buses from trays or toting loads wrapped in coloured cloth on their heads, and babes were borne on the backs of women (this became a common sight) as they wended between wooden carts. One woman leading two girls by the hand, another on her back, carried green fronds at least ten feet in length on her head as she walked past clothing for sale in shelters roofed with dried plant material. Goods and a cooking fire occupied the pavement in front of adjacent dilapidated shops in different hues, and small Arab dhows skittered past in a stiff breeze as I strolled to the end of a long jetty to look back at the settlement.

Bicycles were the preferred mode of travel in the dusty streets, and I saw mounds of what appeared to be a root product, a crate of chickens covered by a sheet of cardboard heaped with bananas, and young men with painted faces, shell necklaces on their bare torsos, and dressed in colourful costume sitting beneath macramé hangings, with discarded cardboard boxes blowing in the wind in front. An area devoted to craft shops displayed carvings of animals, birds, and people with grotesque visages, their hair made from tufts of fibre. Amongst squalid housing in the dirt lanes, I saw food cooking and several men in the red robes of the Masai. Back at the noisy congested bus station, I encountered impossibly overloaded vehicles around a solitary tree of immense girth, and stalls displaying second-hand clothing. Also to become a familiar sight, these usually contained articles donated by the Red Cross and other charitable organisations; meant for distribution to the needy, they had found their way into the hands of vendors.

Returning to Mombassa, I found that the bus could not enter the city due to rioting, and I was deposited some distance away. Thanks to the assistance of a local man who knew his way around, I made it back to the centre, where I was nearly mowed down by a truck full of soldiers, their weapons at the ready, standing on the tray at the back. Police in helmets controlled crowds milling in the roads. I concluded my short stay in Nairobi with pictures of a snow-white round minaret and streets so narrow that the balconies of whitewashed buildings nearly met overhead.

Masai Mara

And so we embarked on our adventure, across plains dotted with cattle and the typical flat-topped acacia trees. The initial surprise came with the introduction to our four-wheel-drive Bedford truck, which was painted shocking pink – hardly conducive to blending with the African veldt! The meeting with our tour leader was no less dramatic when she emerged, covered in black grease, from underneath the vehicle.

As usually transpired, at 54 (I had my 55th birthday en route) I was the 'grandmother' of the group, the remainder all being in their 20s. Our first halt was at a nondescript place for supplies, the truck parking opposite a basic concrete construction that sat behind a pile of rubble and housed the New Blue Hotel, Holiday Bar, and a shop with the ubiquitous Coca-Cola sign on the front. A donkey cart stood in the petrol station. We stopped at a historic shrine and for photographs overlooking the **Great Rift Valley**, a deep trench in the earth's crust extending some 6,400km (3,976mi) from the Dead Sea. Formed by the pulling apart of the earth's plates, it advanced through the Red Sea to Mozambique and separated East Africa from the rest of the continent.

Heading towards the **Masai Mara**, we saw a beautiful blue, russet, white and black bird and our first giraffe, towering over a low acacia to which it bent its long neck to browse. At one of the isolated convenience stores, a woman dressed in red robes, a babe and basket on her back, wore bracelets, long earrings, a wide choker around the neck, and anklets above bare feet, all created with tiny beads. Traversing dusty dirt streets, we passed a mosque with a green dome, its white minaret topped by a green cupola. Surrounded by battered vehicles, a large cattle market was patronised by many of the red-blanketed **Masai**. We filmed a pair of ostrich and stopped for a group of *morani* (adolescent warriors) wearing extraordinary headgear created from sticks and natural materials. They demanded payment for pictures, which did not come out well because the sun was behind them.

morani

Entering the nature reserve, we came across long-horned deer, a group of three giraffe seeking shade in the meagre shelter offered by a spindly tree, and two zebra in the background. These were followed by larger antelope, a herd of elephant with babies, more zebra, secretary birds with tufted feathers either side of their heads, and close proximity to an ungainly hyena expressing obvious curiosity. At our first campsite, we attracted the usual audience as we erected makeshift tents; the equipment was appalling, with many parts missing. The truck soon let us down and had to be replaced, which necessitated wasting an entire day.

We saw large birds, more elephant with young, and approached very close to one big old buffalo with impressive horns and boss. Vultures in a lone acacia made for good photography against a sullen sky, as did a solitary bird on a bare branch of a dead tree. Yet more giraffe and elephant, their giant ears flapping, stood in flat terrain with mountains beyond.

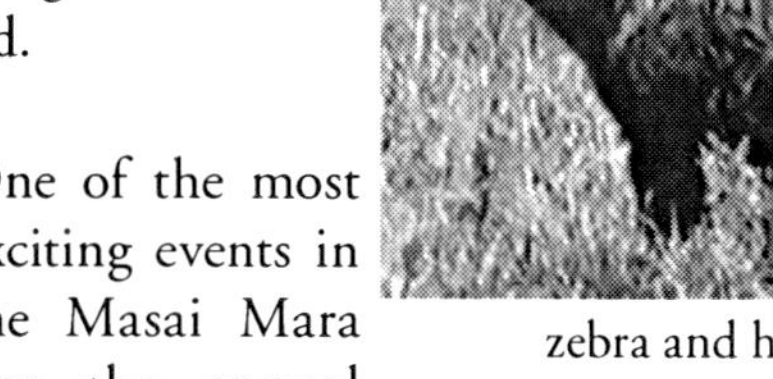

zebra and hyena

One of the most exciting events in the Masai Mara was the annual migration of enormous herds (more than 1.5 million) of wildebeest (gnus) to greener pastures on Tanzania's contiguous Serengeti. We were fortunate to coincide with the end of this ritual, witnessing large numbers of these awkward-looking beasts purposefully plodding in a slow but steadfast line towards the **Mara River**, where knowledgeable crocodiles lay patiently in wait. Aware of the danger, it was fascinating to watch the frenzy of activity as the gnus made a panicky plunge to cross.

buffalo and elephants

keeping a wary watch

We came upon a spotted hyena and our first lions, lying lethargically in the heat, flicking ears and tails to ward off insects, and seemingly unconcerned by our presence – they appeared deceptively cuddly! We were excited to find a whole pride lying on and around a cracked clay pan, the male a rather scruffy specimen. A panting mother was suckling her offspring,

wildebeest

and others seemed almost docile as they stretched out to relax, even the cubs were subdued. I was pleased with close-up film as one stared with interest directly into the camera and of another performing ablutions: licking its paws to wash its face just like a domestic cat and finishing with a gigantic yawn exposing long lethal fangs.

lions

A cub rolled onto its back, its legs spreadeagled, and endeavoured to play with the tails of two adults that, except to raise a head, barely responded. Joined by a second, the pair nipped and tumbled in a listless manner. I took pictures of a beautifully hued roller bird, but it only showed up in silhouette. We saw more hyenas, this time with a kill, another large herd of gnus, a lone lion blending with dried grasses as it walked across the plain and, as a finale, experienced a vivid African sunset – before having to dig the truck out of a bog!

king of the beasts

Next day produced a secretary bird strutting around, whilst vultures perched atop a small tree on branches seemingly too flimsy to support their colossal weight. We parked beside a male lion with a magnificent mane, which turned piercing yellow eyes in our direction before resuming his sleepy pose. We could see others of the large pride roving further afield.

Accompanied by three babies, a trio of adult elephants provided wonderful footage drinking at a waterhole; few of the animals we saw had tusks, and of those that did, they were short.

the pause that refreshes

We encountered more ostrich, a roller, deer, gnus, one scrawny monkey, giraffe and buffalo, the latter annoyed by small birds pecking insects from their heads and nostrils. A highlight was the discovery of three sleek and beautiful cheetah, nature's fastest animal, resting in the sparse shade of a small tree, their distinctive markings distinguished by lines like the paths of black tears either side of the nose.

I made a third unsuccessful attempt to photograph a roller, obligingly perched on a dead limb, and we saw a herd of larger antelope with twisted horns, possibly Grant's gazelle, but I could not positively identify them. A vervet monkey, its black face surrounded by white fur, and with black hands and feet, a white underbelly, and a brown topknot and back, displayed an incredibly bright blue scrotum as it sat in our campsite clutching a stolen pancake!

antelope and monkey with stolen pancake

Setting out next morning, on another excellent day of game viewing, zebra, deer and wildebeest ran from the truck, and scavenging vultures were disturbed from a rotting carcass. The vulture is one of the largest raptors, with a wingspan of almost three meters, but it is a poor flyer and glides. Feeding only on carrion, it can consume huge quantities at once but is capable of going without food for six days. Presaged by a tree inundated with vultures, we came upon a recently deceased elephant covered with these hideous birds and noticed a few long-legged jabiru storks on the fringe of the fracas. It was amazing to observe these scavengers as they attacked the remains: squabbling with each other, tearing meat from the rear, stomach and throat, screeching and squawking, and flapping their huge pinions. Tugging in all directions, one group tore strips to shreds in seconds, and others perched on or walked across the carcass, striped white with their excreta, as they entered the fray to gorge themselves. Their ferocious beaks ripped the thick hide with comparative ease. As we started up, the noise of the engine caused two hyenas, which had been waiting in the wings for their turn, to run from protective shelter. It was an outstanding but confronting event.

ostrich, deer and cheetah

vultures on elephant carcass

Passing ugly warthogs and attractively marked copper-toned topi with smooth beige-coloured rumps, we arrived at a muddy brown river, home to a pod that congregated en masse in the middle. Huge bloated bodies lay motionless atop each other, only the occasional movement indicating that they were alive, whilst equally motionless crocodiles basked on the bank absorbing the sun. Birds pecking at insects walked without fear across the broad backs of these 'river horses' (interestingly related to the pig), but the sleepy appearance belied an extremely aggressive nature; considered the most dangerous creature in Africa, more people have been killed by the hippopotamus than any other animal. All at once, possibly due to the sound of our horn, there was an upheaval amongst the entire group. It soon settled, and one glistening black body walked almost imperceptibly in the shallow water.

hippopotami

alert mother with cobs

On the road again, we passed river rapids, baboons and, by lucky chance, a cheetah feeding on the body of a deer as large as itself, which it dragged a safe distance by the neck before resuming its feast, tackling the area below the still intact head with its horns and glassy eyes. Disturbed by the sound of the truck, it stood guard over the remains as it surveyed the area.

cheetah with kill

More elephants included one enormous old bull with long tusks, which much to our alarm executed a mock charge, flapping its huge ears and trumpeting, before turning and ponderously walking parallel to our vehicle. A male lion was well camouflaged in dry grass, and vervet monkeys presented their brilliant blue 'balls'.

Visiting a Masai village, I observed wattle and daub houses with crumbling walls and skinny cattle in a corral constructed from branches. The cluster of homes was encompassed by a brush fence. Goats and a cow with a calf stood outside one dwelling, the only light in its interior provided by an open fire. Brightly attired women adorned with copious beaded chokers, necklaces, bracelets, and dangling earrings in elongated lobes, were selling similar jewellery; the tinkle of cowbells accompanying negotiations. I noticed that their heads were either shaved or close cropped, possibly for hygienic reasons. A hen and chickens foraged in the compound, whilst a man squatted with a staff to guard his herd. Even this tiny community boasted a bar. Children waved as we departed, but unless endeavouring to sell trinkets, I found the proud Masai to be aloof and generally unfriendly. As nomadic cattle herders they despised farming and had traditionally always been in conflict with their **Kikuyu** neighbours who were settled agriculturalists. In order to enter manhood, at one time a youth was required to kill a lion. In preparation for his final journey, when a Masai dies he is not buried but laid out in the open, a clump of grass in one hand and a pair of sandals and cattle stick in the other.

Masai kraal and cow/ Masai ladies

We made another stop near a garish red-roofed blue, green and yellow concrete structure called Exodus, and one titled Jambo Paradise Mall incorporating Café de Paradise! Natives (and chickens) congregated around the truck, which was always a source of fascination. We passed more simple housing hidden behind high brush fences and became bogged for the second time. On this occasion, we had willing locals to assist us push; Westerners always provided entertainment, and our antics caused much hilarity. Entering a small townsite, I saw men carrying spears, a cart laden with dried matter, and children playing the perennial games found worldwide.

pushing the truck

Lake Naivasha

We awoke next morning to the sight of a cumbersome hippopotamus in our lakeside camp, which had obviously lumbered between the tents! I followed it some distance as it carried its massive bulk on squat stubby legs, chomping and browsing on grass before loping off.

hippopotamus in camp

This was freshwater **Lake Naivasha**, a delightful spot teeming with birdlife. I saw white ibis with their long curved beaks, preening spoonbills on the marshy edge, and cormorants in rushes, one perched on a stake, its wings characteristically spread to dry. Poised as still as a statue, a large blue heron was reflected in the water, kingfishers roosted on posts, a long-legged wading bird foraged in a pool, and I observed a larger variety of kingfisher, ducks and, gleaming in the sunlight, the blue, rust, black and white bird that had been our first sighting on heading for the Mara. Fishermen sat in a small boat offshore.

ibis and blue heron

Lake Nakuru

Our first glimpse of **Lake Nakuru** revealed the pure white soda edges with sun sparkling off the surface of the water. A few scattered houses were located nearby, low mountains enveloped in heat haze rose beyond the far shore, and fluffy white clouds appeared in a blue sky. The soda was sodium carbonate, or 'washing soda', that came from local volcanoes. The lakes could be a death trap for most living things, the exception being flamingos. In order to purchase supplies, we went first to the market in **Nakuru** where, amongst other things, friendly people sold fruits (including papayas), vegetables, and a black product like dried fish. Stalls and drink stands were set up in the shade of a large tree, women wove rope baskets, others carried babes in shawls on their backs, and there was more noise and colour here than at any previous stop. Outside the market, a group in brightly hued robes jumped up and down and chanted to the beat of a drum. Dilapidated cars were parked in front of ramshackle stores; called Tiger Shoes, one sported a black, brown and yellow diamond pattern on the façade.

I particularly remember the congeniality of this place because it was here that I was successfully robbed for the first time. Being the last to board the truck and deliberately jostled by several people, the zips on my camera bag were opened and the contents removed. They were not able to take the actual VCR, but because the tapes and all the accessories were stolen, I was unable to recharge the battery and desperately tried to conserve what power remained for the gorilla trek. It was very upsetting because no warnings had been forthcoming until after the event. Thereafter, I tied the zips together with string, and was constantly apprehensive of people approaching too close

– a lesson well learnt. I was informed that had we been able to stay a couple of days it would have been possible to buy the equipment back at the market! On that occasion, I carried a less common brand of camera, and in a strange twist of fate, prior to joining the trip the only other member of our party to have the same make and model also had her charger stolen.

On the way to the lake, we came across a beautiful long-horned waterbuck lying in open grassland. The incredible sight of literally thousands of flamingos (around two million) greeted us as we approached over the crusty salt plain to the white-rimmed water where they were wading, preening, feeding in shallows at the edge, and flying above. Floating feathers and dead carcasses also littered the area, but if one could tolerate the diabolical smell, the absorbing display would intrigue for hours. A sombre purplish sky could not disguise the pink tinge of the mass of birds, backed by scrub, near the opposite shore. More deer stood in a grassy patch, gulls and a few marabou storks with long red wattles mingled with the flamingos, and there was a large colony of pelicans, many of which took flight in their unwieldy manner as I drew near. Amongst the 400 species that lived around the lake, waddling cormorants were also in evidence, and I identified noisy geese. Approaching closer to this amazing performance, it appeared congested but must have involved a semblance of order because flamingos around the outside seemed to be marching in line.

Ringed by a deep band of pink (the birds!), a larger expanse of water superbly duplicated even the bruised colour of the sky. A glorious effect was created when rays of the hidden sun pierced cloud to radiate in fanlike formation and touch the scorched earth. Moving to another position, we found more deer, warthogs with their cruel-looking curved tusks, and other large birds perched in a tree. I was lucky to film the tiny dikdik, smallest of the antelope species. Lovely light-coloured hartebeest inhabited an area of sparse trees and low scrub, and an alert jackal ran across open savannah. A shimmering pink hue in the distance announced our approach to a second part of the lake, the flamingos appearing upside down as they were perfectly mirrored in still water.

fine sets of horns

Leaving this fascinating location, we were fortunate to catch sight of an elusive cheetah approaching a wary giraffe across open grassland, but it was obviously not interested in the quarry. We spotted two large birds with long pale blue tails and paused for giraffe crossing the track, their graceful undulating movement resembling that of a camel.

Their side to side masticating motion was also similar to that of the 'ship of the desert'. Stopping at a height for an overview of the lake with its pink and white perimeter and clouds reflected on the quiet surface of the centre, we found a bright blue lizard with a red head sunning itself on a rock, and rodent-like hyrax, also known as dassie. Astoundingly, by virtue of common physical traits, the hyrax is more closely related to the elephant than any other creature!

stalking cheetah and giraffe

blue lizard and hyrax

We entered another busy market, where people were climbing over a huge mound of some dried product to select their choice. We took our lunch break in a compound, where we accumulated a bemused group of sober-faced children, some of the older ones holding babies, for which they were often delegated to take care.

The favoured method of transport in Kenya was the ubiquitous *matatu*, described by Lonely Planet as 'A minibus with mega-decibel sound system, seemingly unlimited carrying capacity and two speeds – stationary and flat out'.

captivated audience

interesting faces

UGANDA

Kampala

Storks roosted on trees displaying a gorgeous show of pink blossom in the city of **Kampala, Uganda,** once labelled Pearl of Africa by Winston Churchill. A strange mix of old and new, the city featured an imposing white civic building in the vicinity of adobe huts, barbers working in the street (one lad in our party was brave enough to risk a haircut!), dirt thoroughfares with thatched shelters, sacks of produce, bicycles, and a square tower looming behind an edifice with the Ugandan coat of arms: spears behind a shield bearing waves (representing Lake Victoria), the sun and a drum, flanked by a rampant kob (deer) and crested crane.

barbershop

Black and white colobus monkeys frequented our campsite. A disturbing incident (for me) occurred when a few of us entered a shop to find the shelves almost bare of goods for sale. In a country still recovering from the repressive regime of despotic Idi Amin, there was little finance to buy, even if wares had been available to replenish stock. I found it extremely embarrassing when the other members of the group laughed openly at the situation; admittedly they were young, but I considered it highly insensitive and it caused discomfort to the owners. Many stores with dirty and broken windows were vacated altogether.

I made an independent visit to the tombs of the royal family of **Buganda** at **Kasubi** and was presented with an informative booklet. Except for those of the last five rulers, each tomb had a shrine to house the jawbone of the king, which was believed to contain his spirit. The last four to reign began with Muteesa I (born around 1835–38), who was so afraid of rebellion that he imprisoned all his brothers in a great trench, where many of them died from the insanitary conditions. A powerful king, he had 84 official wives and many hundreds of women in his harem. His successor, Mwanga, had 32 Christians burnt to death because they refused to obey him on matters that conflicted with their religious beliefs. These Catholics were canonised and became known as the Uganda Martyrs. A rebellion against the British failed, and Mwanga was exiled to the Seychelles, where he died in 1903. The rule of his son, Daudi Chwa, saw great changes, including the building of the railroad between Kampala and Mombassa in Kenya to promote trade with Europe. When he died in 1939, one of his many sons was chosen to succeed him at the age of 15. Muteesa II attended the best English language schools and spent two years at Cambridge University in England. He became the country's first president when it attained independence in 1962 but was forced into exile and died in England in 1969.

The traditional architecture of the **Great House** or **Palace**, utilised poles, reeds and grass; rings of palm tree leaves, supported by upright posts, comprised the large roof. The king's subjects were divided into clans, each of which had a specific task to perform: the Ngeye (Colobus Monkey) Clan was responsible for thatching and the Ngo (Leopard) Clan the decoration. The mother of Muteesa I was from the Elephant Clan. Certain prohibitions had to be observed during construction. For example, thatchers had to abstain from sexual activity and no women were allowed to enter at this time; if violated it was believed that the roof would leak! Cloth was made from the bark of a variety of fig tree, the stripped trunk of which was then wrapped in banana leaves to protect it from the sun. This was later replaced with cow dung or mud, which dried and fell away to reveal new bark, a process that could be used several times before the tree became too old to produce satisfactory results. In a lengthy complicated procedure, the material was created by a succession of beatings with mallets, stretching, folding, rubbing and kneading. Cloth makers were of the Ngonge (Otter) Clan. The Buganda used drums and masks in both sacred rituals and public festivals, and cowries were used as a form of decoration and a medium of exchange. Today, coffee beans have taken the place of the shells as ritual gifts, and coins have replaced their monetary value. The people also believed in the power of fetishes or charms made by skilled local healers for use in rituals, illness, childbearing, hunting and warfare.

Bushman dance

The African Bushman

On the red dirt road again, we passed long-horned African cattle on the verge, under the watchful eye of a figure in purple robes, and goats gathered near people sitting on wooden chairs outside thatched log shacks. Diverting to a narrow track bordered by tall green grass and trees, the peak of a mountain emerging through cloud at the end, we came across a solitary figure in the middle of nowhere; Africans often walked extremely long distances to get from place to place. We eventually arrived at a site of steaming mud pools and geysers located in lush tropical growth that included a great many palm trees.

A visit to see the pygmy bushman was an interesting but depressing experience because they had been adversely affected by the introduction to drugs and alcohol, a means of degradation for many coloured races. These people, who spoke a strange type of 'click' language, were dirty, unkempt, and living in squalid conditions. A couple carrying loads wrapped in cloth on their heads endeavoured to sell crude artefacts, and bare-breasted women were surrounded by naked children, their distended stomachs indicative of malnutrition. Our presence caused a great deal of commotion, and in our honour they formed a circle to perform a primitive shuffling dance to the sounds of drums and wooden whistles. A number carried bows and arrows, and one man presented a pipe for smoking and an ethnic stringed instrument. The atmosphere began to get strained, and we were glad to leave this community and its degenerate populace behind.

a mother's love

Ruwenzori and Volcans National Parks

After a market stop in another dusty town, we made a halt at a concrete ring marking the equator before continuing on to **Ruwenzori National Park**. Here, a game drive revealed large numbers of impala; one of the most common antelopes, these gracefully creatures have the prodigious ability to leap ten metres in length or three metres in height at a single bound. The **Ruwenzoris** or **Mountains of the Moon** were named by Ptolemy 2,000 years ago. Driving through mountainous country, past thatched *rondavels* and square log houses in the midst of maize crops, we reached an old blackened lava field that glistened in the sun. Part of **Parc National des Volcans**, this was actually in northern Rwanda, where it met the borders of Uganda and Zaire. Grey parrots with red tails frequented this desolate area surrounded by lush vegetation.

local market

ZAIRE

Gorilla Trek

Crossing into **Zaire**, we were confronted by a dramatic change in conditions: muddy, barely existent roads made for very difficult driving. Shortly after entering, we were held to ransom by an armed adversary demanding that we purchase insurance. This was an illegal scam, so we returned to the border to pick up an official who accompanied us back without further problems arising. On another occasion, in **Kinshasa**, when only our guide was in the rear of the truck, an assailant leapt on board and tried to rob him at knife point.

We had come here to experience another of those once in a lifetime events: a gorilla trek in **Kahuzi Biega National Park**. We were fortunate in that it took little more than an hour to locate our quarry, following trackers who hacked through the jungle with machetes, the trees meeting overhead to create an arboreal tunnel. The group we found was foraging for food and consequently kept slowly on the move, which was a disappointment because apparently if they are at rest they will often approach and interact with humans. It was quite a large family, ruled over by a big silverback that issued a throaty warning sound on becoming aware of our presence.

silverback

handsome profile

Almost appearing pensive, one reclined casually against a tree trunk in a human-like attitude, and others picked bamboo, peeling it by hand to eat the tender white shoots.

dinnertime

Again resembling a human activity, one scratched its head, whilst another ran a vine through its teeth, stripping it of the leaves in order to eat them. Two interacted with each other, and an adolescent beat its chest in a brief display of challenge.

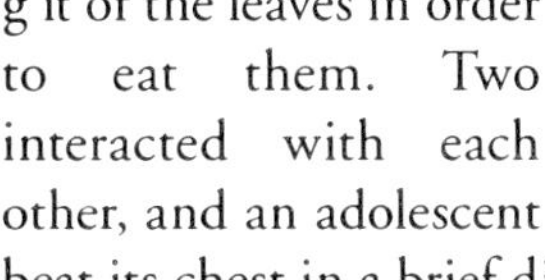

beating his chest

This same gregarious juvenile, obviously showing off, held onto a narrow trunk, swung around it at arm's length, and then moved to a larger tree to drum with its palms against the bark.

The big blue-black beasts, their coats glossy in the sun, attracted many bothersome insects. A mother with a baby clinging to her back stopped to eat, another adolescent lay sprawled along a branch, dangling its arms and legs in an ungainly manner, others swung from limb to limb or climbed, and one scratched an armpit!

juvenile behaviour

nothing like a good scratch

Sadly, much of my film is very poor quality because at times thick foliage made it impossible to focus on the subject. We were so overawed at such proximity to these marvellous creatures that except for the sounds of teeth biting into bamboo and the rustle of trees as the group moved there was almost total silence.

I managed to obtain film of an infant crawling over the supine body of an adult, and there was more beating of chests, swinging from vines, and scratching of faces. Tragically, one had lost a hand to poachers, but thankfully this insidious trade was on the decline because the large amount paid by tourists for the privilege of partaking in these strictly supervised encounters was more lucrative. At that time, both the mountain and plains gorillas were an endangered species; I do not know the current status, but Dian Fossey did much to help preserve their numbers.

Much of Zaire was explored by Stanley (after he found Livingston) and became the Belgian Congo. Not long after our visit, the country was embroiled in civil war, a conflict not soon resolved.

RWANDA

and only one headlight

Leaving the park, we came across more of the ridiculously overloaded conveyances so common in many Third World countries, one utility with people and goods extending several feet on three sides and a cart carrying saplings approximately 30ft in length.

Heading for **Kigali**, capital of **Rwanda**, we passed iron-roofed timber houses in a shanty town where the voices of excited children followed our progress. We suffered another breakdown; from memory we had a total of nine punctures, but the forced halt provided an opportunity to film women in colourful dresses and the *tignon* (African headscarf) as they walked past bearing loads on their heads. One was using a sunshade, two ladies strolled by with a cow, and boys herded a few long-horned cattle.

capacity load

local restaurant

BURUNDI

Underway again, we traversed a mountain road past primitive dwellings, banana plants, and a wide river (with little water) on the plain below, before crossing into **Burundi**. Recollections of the capital, **Bujumbura**, were of yawning hippos in **Lake Tanganyika**, boats on a canal, and a neat reserve containing a memorial with coloured illustrations of natives engaged in various occupations.

At the roadside, a group waiting for transport carried whole hands of bananas or goods in bowls and baskets on their heads. One lady, a baby on her back, balanced long canes. It was a colourful scene.

bearing all manner of goods and even the baby

We attended a performance of the renowned Burundi dancers who have entertained in many places overseas, including Australia. Clothed in the national colours of green, white and red, and led by a man with a spear and shield, they entered in a high-stepping march to the beat of long drums carried on the head and beaten in unison with sticks. Upending the drums on the ground, they executed energetic antics accompanied by some singing. Individual dances involved a lot of leaping and whirling, and the show was produced on a high dusty plateau.

We left via rural surroundings of furrowed fields, neatly swept compounds, and waving children; it was an idyllic place with peaceful people, giving no indication of the violent bloodbath brewing, and we were astounded to hear of hostilities breaking out between Rwanda and Burundi just two days after we moved on to Tanzania; in fact, we were fortunate not to have been caught up in the turmoil.

Burundi dancers

In 1994, Rwanda was plunged into another bloody episode following the shooting down of a plane carrying both the nation's president and that of neighbouring Burundi. Led by the army, a period of genocide began, with death squads ranging at will, killing, looting and burning. Half the population went on the rampage and within four months up to two million people were hacked to death with *pangas* (machetes), shot through the head, or otherwise butchered with anything to hand. The streets of Kigale were littered with disembodied corpses, and the stench of rotting flesh prevailed.

TANZANIA

Tanzania has Africa's highest mountain, **Kilimanjaro** (5,895m/19,340ft), its deepest and longest freshwater lake, **Tanganyika**, and **Selous Game Reserve**, at 54,600 sq km the world's largest; the Serengeti covers 14,763 sq km.

Serengeti

On the southern shore of **Lake Victoria**, the world's second largest freshwater lake, where cormorants roosted amid huge balancing boulders, we stayed at the little visited port of **Mwanza**. These same rock formations looked stunning silhouetted against a burst of the sun's rays, which also cast a silver glow on the surface of the water. Game viewing in the **Serengeti** – Siringitu to the Masai (meaning Endless Plains or The Place Where the Land Goes on Forever) – showed us animals on the savannah beyond a large flock of vultures, two adult giraffes with a couple of cute babies, and a pair of ostrich herding young. Here again was the steady straggling line of wildebeest, and more vultures stood guard over a zebra carcass whilst others perched on the branches of a dead tree. A crocodile swam below us as we stood near the brink of a body of water accommodating another mass of hippopotami clambering clumsily over each other in that close proximity they seemed to enjoy. Four lions sat in the shade of a tree whilst elephants, all with respectable tusks, indulged in a ritual dust bath nearby, and one could not mistake the distinctive gait of baboons in the distance.

As the dun-coloured track changed to red, attractive trees reared into clear air beneath a blue sky with puffs of white cloud, and zebras ran across in front of our vehicle. We saw more waterbuck, a male lion hopefully stalking an intended victim, and a group of cheetah camouflaged in long dry grass under a tree. It was fascinating to watch as one dragged the remains of a deer into forked branches. The blue plumage of the now common glossy starling (the multihued bird with glaring white eyes) shimmered in the sun, and one resembling a hoopoe was found near interesting rock formations.

Ngorongoro

From the rim, we surveyed the incomparable **Ngorongoro Crater** and the lake on its floor. This microcosm of the continent contained representatives of the Big Five (elephant, lion, hippopotamus, rhinoceros and buffalo) and most other animals, with the exception of giraffe, captured in a natural 22.5km-wide 610m/2,001ft-deep enclosure covering 160 sq km (62 sq mi). Known as Big Hole to the Masai, the caldera was 2.5 million years old and its unbroken rim the largest in the world. We encountered zebra, jackals (including three cubs), hyena, grunting hippopotami in a pleasant pool ringed by tall green grasses, and rhinoceros still retaining excellent horns and well hidden in high undergrowth.

Olduvai Gorge

Leaving the crater, we made a visit to **Olduvai Gorge**, famed because of the Leakey's discovery of the skull of *Zinjanthropus man*, one of the earliest ancestors of modern man. Unearthed two years later and estimated to be

2,500,000 years old, the skull of *Homo habilis* established the Rift Valley as the 'cradle of humanity' and radically altered accepted theories of the origin of the species.

Because of the numerous breakdowns and delays we ran out of time to see **Manyara National Park**, known for its tree-climbing lions. Again, my film is of poor quality; in an endeavour to conserve what little life remained in the battery I was only recording snatches of the various attractions: a second hyrax, colourful lizards, an eagle, and hundreds of black and white striped fish mingling with blue in a clear pool. The dry landscape, with bare branches making lacy patterns against a cerulean sky, rustic houses, grain storage huts, and chickens running free, was relieved by the introduction of vibrant red flame trees.

Arusha

The countryside became lusher as we neared **Arusha**, at the foot of 4,556m **Mt Meru** in northern Tanzania, where we made a fuel and supply stop. The wide median strip in the main boulevard, boasting one skyscraper, was planted with an avenue of flamboyant trees in full flower, and a man walked by supporting a large tray of fruits on his head.

Dar es Salaam

Our next stop was the administrative capital, **Dar es Salaam** (Haven of Peace), which started out as a humble fishing village, where we camped on a surprisingly clean beach with white sand and turquoise water. It was here that my battery finally gave out, and I was offered the loan of a still camera to take a few pictures.

Utilising local materials, a circular bar/restaurant in our campsite was built around a tree that reared up in the middle, its huge canopy spreading over the thatched roof. In a nearby settlement of mud-brick and grass-thatched houses with chickens and ducks ranging underfoot, women pounded grain in tall cylindrical mortars created from hollowed trunks. A man mended nets whilst his wife, seated on the ground, prepared vegetables. A couple of small stores provided necessities, and a woman displayed a few bright red tomatoes and a local green, which she spread for sale on a cloth on the bare earth. There were bundles of straw, sapling fences, and rush-covered windbreaks screening outdoor cooking fires. Others of the happy industrious populace in this small community were engaged in activities like chopping wood and winnowing, and one mother gladly agreed to photographs whilst breastfeeding her baby.

Cattle foraged on a rubbish heap in a local market, and once again we had to resort to digging the truck out of loose sand. In combination with quaint housing on parched earth, glorious red flame trees made stunning pictures, even flourishing right on the seashore with a backdrop of blue ocean and sky. Another section of beach featured palm trees, and small pleasure boats rocked in a slight swell.

Zanzibar

Armed with a second borrowed camera, I went by ferry from the picturesque port of Dar es Salaam to the magical spice island of **Zanzibar**, once the most important town on the coast and notorious for being the largest slave trading centre in East Africa. An early Arab and Persian trading post, in the 12th century goods such as ivory, tortoiseshell and leopard skins were exchanged for items like glass beads from India and porcelain from China. It came under Portuguese control in the 16th and 17th centuries and Arab domination later. In the 18th century, insidious slavers in pursuit of their human cargo were the first to penetrate the interior of Tanzania, venturing as far as Lake Tanganyika. This sordid trade decimated the tribes of Africa to the tune of nearly 50,000 per year through Zanzibar alone, where a duty of two dollars was charged for each. Originally, Britain did not want any involvement in East Africa, but having committed itself to ending the slave trade, persuaded the Sultan of Oman, who prospered by it, to sign a treaty forbidding their export. Known as the Island of Cloves, at one time it produced 75% of the world's supply, even though only introduced from the Moluccas in 1818.

The name conjured up visions of Arabian nights. I found palm-fringed beaches, little shops selling everything from Panadol to pawpaws opening directly onto narrow paved streets, houses with wooden shutters, overhead balconies with fretwork trim, and heavy studded Arabic-style doors featuring intricately carved lintels, often portraying the lotus motif. Whilst most of the group who made the trip headed for an overnight stay at the beach on the opposite shore, I was content to

Old Stone Town

get a room in the UNESCO classified **Old Stone Town** and spend my time wandering and investigating the photogenic twisting alleyways.

shop in the Old Town

Tomatoes and Brussels sprouts were amongst produce displayed below bananas suspended from an elaborate lintel. Another store sold pottery cups, metal woks, cane items, plastic wares, and other assorted paraphernalia.

It was a change to see people in Muslim dress, bicycles were plentiful, and youths lounged on carts for hire. Making a splash of colour on the pavement, a row of vendors sold bright red tomatoes mixed with a few lemons, onions and aubergines. Approached via tiled steps, one particularly fine carved entrance featured exquisite floral fretwork above massive doors with spiked iron studs.

ancient doorway

Enclosed as it was by the confines of narrow streets, the imposing **Anglican Cathedral** (1877), standing on the site of the Old Slave Market, seemed incongruous. Straddling the road, an impressive stone building had Venetian-type arched windows behind a stone lattice balcony.

Zanzibar architecture

wooden architecture Zanzibar

The most prominent building, **Beit-el-Ajaib (House of Wonders**, 1883), formerly the Sultan's Palace, was an elegant four-storey colonial-looking white edifice with wide verandahs on each level and a square tower. Next to it sat **Beit-al-Sahel**, begun in 1828, which served as residence to the Al-Busaid Sultans until the dynasty was overthrown in 1964. Both structures were rebuilt after being damaged by British bombardment in 1896. The latter was now a museum displaying the period of the Zanzibar sultanate. One magnificent three-storey building had overhead verandahs supported by pillars carved with typical Arabic pendentive work.

Other pictures I took show a dry well in the **Persian Baths**, night time food preparation by lamplight in the **Jamituri Gardens** outside the fort, where I bought cheap but extremely good spicy local curry, and the old fort itself: a massive crenellated and bastioned structure built by the Portuguese in 1700. A memorial incorporated stained glass with an African theme, the interior of one of the cathedrals possessed ancient artworks, picturesque ruins were situated amid palm trees, and outrigger canoes were stranded at low tide on the flotsam-riddled beach. Apparently, there was a mosque dated 1107, but I did not see it.

MALAWI and ZAMBIA

From Dar es Salaam we turned inland and drove southwest to **Malawi** (meaning Flames of Fire), where our first camp was on the edge of 570km-long **Lake Malawi** (**Nyasa**), which makes up about 20% of the country's total area. Next morning revealed a less welcome aspect of this supposedly idyllic location. I was on cooking detail and breakfast consisted of fresh fruits (including pawpaw and watermelon), which it was impossible to keep free of the millions of minute marauding insects that stuck to everything. They also invaded hair, eyes, nose and mouth unless constantly waving hands and arms, a feat that I was not able to achieve whilst preparing food. However, many disadvantages were compensated for by the friendliness of the people.

Travelling alongside the lake we, continued to the capital, **Lilongwe**, from where we drove to the capital of **Zambia**, **Lusaka**. Bush camping on the way meant that we did not have to contend with the substandard conditions and facilities of designated sites, but it was often difficult to find shade; we lunched one day beneath a small clump of palm trees. I have no record of our brief stay in Zambia as we transited the country and crossed into Zimbabwe.

ZIMBABWE

Victoria Falls

We made our way to the grandeur of mighty **Victoria Falls**. Twice the height (108m/354ft) and, at 1,700m, one and a half times the width of Niagara, they are one of the natural wonders of the world and its widest uninterrupted fall. Seen from afar as mist rising 500m (1,640ft) from a plateau, they are known to the natives as Mosi-oa-Tunya, The Smoke that Thunders. From the 2,800km-long 1.6km/1 mile-wide **Zambezi River** the water plunged in a series of tumultuous cascades down sheer rock walls – at an estimated rate of 545 million litres (120 million gallons!) per minute in the rainy season – and flowed along narrow chasms (60m/195ft) forming the zigzag path of the river. The whole was comprised of five falls: Main, Horseshoe and Rainbow Falls and Devil's and Eastern Cataracts.

awesome Victoria Falls

The jungle surrounds of this spray-generated rainforest provided a sharp contrast to roads recently travelled, and bright red flowers resembling protea bloomed in dryer patches. Although green, it was not as lush, nor was there as much water as on my previous visit. A bronze statue of Livingstone, the first white man to view the astonishing sight in 1855, sat amongst foliage by the falls, and there were rainbows in lesser drops at one end. It was awesome from every angle, and water dripped from leaves as I wandered the unfenced pathway along the rim. In quieter sections, away from the roar, perpendicular rock faces loomed above green pools at the bottom. At the campsite, a monkey was digging furiously whilst its offspring clung precariously to its chest, and a large incredibly ugly warthog with three babies ferreted around our tents.

I was fortunate to be given a seat on the **Flight of Angels**, which provided a better appreciation of the size of the river – fluctuating between green and blue depending on the light and surroundings – and its twisting course as it cut deep into the gorge. It was easy to distinguish individual cascades making up the whole as we flew above the bridge to Zambia; it was an incredible spectacle.

Victoria Falls from the air

We explored the legendary **Victoria Falls Hotel** (1904), its landscaped gardens featuring extensive lawns, coloured foliage, strelitzia and bougainvillea, a lily pond, and a large swimming pool. Moth-eaten monkeys inhabited the grounds, and it was entertaining to watch the comical antics of their young, with the wizened faces of old men and outsized bare pink ears, playing around a cyclone wire gate: one vigorously scratching its backside, another being reprimanded and hauled along by an adult, and a couple soundly chastised by elders.

Walking across the bridge to the Zambian side, I bartered with a group of men for a stunning African face carved from a root of ebony and polished to a high sheen but with the 'hair' left in the natural state of the wood. It was purchased for one United States dollar and a tartan shirt – which they all coveted!

In the evening, we attended a cultural show where figures in striped costumes of knitted wool (even to sagging female breasts!) and fearsome patterned masks with straw hair performed a comedy routine, which included an energetic wiggling of bustles. Announced by the call of a horn and executed to the beat of clapping sticks, chants and drums, other dancers, their brown bodies gleaming, wearing skirts of animal pelts and with fur tied around their calves, performed a song and dance act using shields and sticks with knobs on the end like an Irish shillelagh. Also entertaining was a figure on stilts wearing a peaked mask, a second in a voluminous woven straw costume, another wearing a tall hat, and a fourth with a horned headdress, maracas and a whisk.

tribal dance costumes

Next evening, a twilight cruise on the Zambezi River produced beautiful vistas and plentiful birdlife, including ibis, egrets and cormorants amongst reeds at the edge. To our unbridled joy, an elephant with the best tusks that we had seen suddenly emerged from rushes to cross in front of our craft from one bank to the other, where it stood gently flapping its huge ears and swishing a long tail. We also saw the noses of two submerged hippopotami protruding above the surface. The water fluctuated between still reflective passages and choppy sections, and birds flew in silhouette across a sky awash with the red glow of a brilliant sunset. As the sun dipped below the horizon, windswept clouds changed to purple and pink. With an unlimited supply of alcohol, the party became very animated and noisy! As before, I did not imbibe but simply appreciated my surroundings.

BOTSWANA

Chobe National Park

Leaving Zimbabwe, we headed for **Botswana** (known as Bechuanaland under the British) and the **Chobe National Park**, where I pitched my tent in an isolated spot overlooking the water and from where, later in the day, I observed a striking sunset laying a golden path across the surface. Accompanied by an armed guard, a walking tour in the park brought close encounters with two elephants, long-horned deer barely visible in tall dry grass, birds, two giraffe – and a green scorpion.

Okavango Delta

Back on the road, an ostrich paced for some time beside the truck. Our final week began at **Maun**, from where we experienced another of the trip's highlights: Ngamiland's **Okavango Delta**, which fed into the Kalahari Desert instead of an ocean. Here, we travelled by *mokoro* (dugout canoe) to observe rich displays of wildlife including many elephants. Negotiating narrow channels bounded by tall reeds, papyrus and palms, and passing patches of water lilies, the only sound was the soft lapping of water on the sides of our small craft. Amongst others, we encountered colourful wading birds, kingfishers, white birds in a lone tree, and egrets, but even the slow motion of our gentle gliding disturbed the skittish creatures. Perfectly mirrored images of white clouds, like cotton wool balls in a blue sky, seemed to float on the still surface of the water.

ZIMBABWE

Great Zimbabwe and Matopos

Returning to Zimbabwe along the northern fringe of the **Kalahari**, we stopped at **Bulawayo** to see the mysterious ruins of **Great Zimbabwe**: remains of a large city, home to an Iron Age African empire founded about AD 1200 and later (about 1450) abandoned due to overpopulation and the depletion of natural resources. Extremely narrow passageways wound between rough stone walls constructed, without mortar, below, above and around colossal boulders. Strange chimney-like formations capped one wall, and a truncated conical tower built from uneven handmade bricks rose 10.3m, its diameter tapering from 5m at the base to 2.4m at the top. Its purpose was unknown. Another source named the ruins as Khami, an important site of the Rozwi Empire, inhabited from the 17th century until 1820, but there seemed to be much conjecture as to their true origin.

Taking a private tour of **Matopos National Park** with its massive wind-sculpted granite hills and balancing boulders, I was lucky enough to see nine rhinoceros. It was also the site of Cecil Rhodes grave.

Harare

Moving on to **Harare** (founded in 1590 by Rhodes' British South Africa Company), where our journey ended, I found a great deal of amusement on the last day when I adjourned to a local park where, pegged on lines, women displayed lovely crocheted items for sale. Squatting with them on the grass, I produced all my discarded belongings from the expedition: a torn plastic shower curtain used as a ground sheet, a dirty towel, tatty magazines, old clothes (including sexy red knickers snatched by one old lady!), playing cards, and even wooden clothes pegs, the latter causing much hilarity. In exchange, I obtained an elegant black blouse. On asking the lady who grabbed the briefs what her husband would think, the entire group burst into hearty laughter.

Fothergill Island

At the conclusion of the truck trip, I was hosted for a few days at fantastic **Fothergill Island**, a complete contrast in conditions, providing comparative luxury, a pool, and elaborate meals. My unique bathroom was a stone-walled annex open to the stars – with fallen leaves around the toilet bowl! For part of the year connected to the mainland, when the water dropped this land mass was isolated and the animals trapped. The reserve was created in the 1950s when Rupert Fothergill initiated Operation Noah, which rescued thousands of animals from the rising waters of the world's largest man-made lake, **Kariba**. On jeep safaris I encountered many elephant, the largest imaginable congregation of buffalo, reminiscent of the tales of huge herds that once roamed the vast plains in the American west, and most exciting of all, on a 'sundowner' jaunt I witnessed several lions charging their prey.

This African safari was an undertaking with few opportunities other than a basin behind a bush for adequate washing, and dirt became ingrained into my skin; I had never been so filthy and dishevelled in my entire life. I particularly recall one occasion when, several of the group wanting to make telephone calls home, we trooped into the foyer of a leading hotel. I found it extremely embarrassing and cringed into a corner of one of the big plush armchairs, where I remained until they were ready to leave.

It was on this trip that I realised for the first time just how selfish and self-centred young people can be. After a forced 'march' to make up time, we arrived at a bush camp very late, and as I prepared the evening meal (being on cooking roster) the others erected their tents. Not a sole offered to assist with mine, so after all had retired I had to perform this chore alone.

It was on this same extended drive that, being unable to sleep in a sitting position, I stretched out on the floor of the truck beneath legs reaching across the middle from seats lining the sides. All night I was disturbed by a diabolical smell. Assuming it to be the odour of feet, I attempted to dismiss it. Only in the morning did I discover that I had slept with my head next to the cooler box, the ice had melted, and all the contents were rotten!

At one stage, when camped in a reserve, we set out in two groups to search for chimpanzees, but unfortunately, whilst the first group saw quite a few, ours was unsuccessful.

And so I survived my most gruelling adventure until then and (almost!) since.

BALI & SULAWESI 1994

In 1994, I returned to **Indonesia** as escort for another of my group tours.

SULAWESI

Ujung Pandang and the Bugis

After two nights at the Bumi Ayu Bungalows in **Sanur**, **Bali**, we flew to **Ujung Pandang** (the old **Makassar**) in **Sulawesi**, where we were greeted at the airport by a banner reading:

Selamat Datang/Welcome
Faye Day Group

This was accompanied by two adorable serious-faced children wearing vibrant pink costumes with elaborate designs in gold and bearing trays of pink orchids. An interesting snippet of trivia: Makassar was known for its Macassar oil, from which evolved the English word antimacassar referring to small covers to protect upholstery.

Transferring to a coach, we set out on a fascinating eight-hour 328km drive to Toraja in the highlands. Our first stop was at a coastal fishing village of the **Bugis** people, where chickens roamed around iron-roofed wooden shacks built on stilts for circulation of air. Surprisingly comfortable inside, rooms were open for the breeze, and one contained an elaborately carved wardrobe with mirrored doors that reflected the interior. Magazine pictures decorated walls. In the kitchen, basins hung above the bare flame of the stove, and a baby lay in a cloth cradle suspended from the ceiling. A little roadside stall of split bamboo and corrugated iron sold produce in packets. We stopped for photographs of traditional tall-masted *pinisi* (schooners) anchored in an estuary lined with jungle growth. Arriving at a venue where we were greeted by smiling children dancing to the beat of drums, we found two sombre-faced couples richly adorned in shimmering emerald and gold respectively, their guests in colourful robes.

Toraja

The perfect pyramid of a solitary peak rising from the plain heralded our approach to the misty blue mountains of **Toraja**. As we climbed higher, vegetation became sparser, and a pause at scenic **Puncak Lakawan** revealed the **Erotic Mountain** (see Sulawesi 1991) framed in the foreground by long swaying grasses. Rustic houses sat amid the thick foliage of banana plants, palm trees and bamboo on a riverbank, and we began to encounter terraced rice paddies. Cloud covered the mountaintops before we reached our destination and checked into Rantepao Lodge, romantically situated in the middle of a rice paddy.

The following morning we visited a village where the traditional houses (*tongkonans*) were decorated with carvings of animals and/or geometric designs; copious buffalo horns on uprights in front indicated status and wealth. Thatched with banana leaf, the concave-shaped roofs boasted prows, and the homes indeed appeared like ships on a green sea of rice. It is thought that centuries ago the original settlers came from South Asia by boats, which they converted to houses, thus setting the style for the present day. Construction conformed to age-old traditions, which insisted that materials used (wood, bamboo, rattan) must come from the vicinity; iron nails and hinges were taboo. Motifs were coloured red and white to represent human life (blood and flesh), yellow for God's blessing and glory, and black for death and darkness.

We went to see the unique and fascinating ancient hanging graves at **Lemo** and **Londa**, where bodies were interred in looming cliff faces, and rows of life-sized wooden effigies depicting the deceased were arrayed on ledges in front, gazing for eternity with sightless eyes over jungle and paddy fields below. In an annual ceremony, these representations were lovingly dressed in new clothes. At the base of the cliffs, and sporting curved lids in the same manner as the houses, sat several structures used to convey the corpses. In the vicinity we found beautiful heliconias and a man in a field with his buffalo.

Next day, saw our exciting trip to an absorbing funeral ceremony, which sounds macabre but was actually an amazing spectacle accompanied by feasting and dancing. Lasting from four to ten days, these rituals culminated in the sacrifice of large numbers of buffalo and pigs to appease the spirits and pave the way for the soul's entry into the hereafter. Following a way of life based on ancestor worship and animistic principles, the people of Toraja originally believed that some twenty generations ago their ancestors descended from heaven onto a mountain to create this Land of Heavenly Kings, although with 20th-century exposure to the outside world, these once isolated communities were turning to Christianity and Islam.

Complexes of temporary shelters, constructed entirely of bamboo and draped with red cloth, were erected to accommodate family groups that travelled long distances to attend. They were arranged around a large compound, in the centre of which slaughtered animals lay for butchering. One façade was decorated with the head, created from wood, of a spotted white buffalo. The bereaved women were elegantly attired in royal blue and red, one man wore a red suit with a white sash over his right shoulder, and many mourners milled around simply dressed in T-shirts and shorts or slacks. A long procession led by a man wearing a decorative hat, white cloth draped across a magenta shirt, and pink shorts, wended past the butchering that was being actively carried out with cleavers and machetes. Directly behind him, one of the ladies in royal blue preceded women wearing long black sarongs and pink blouses, each carrying a thick bamboo pole. Also in the line was an enormous black and white pig trussed on two poles borne on the shoulders of four men. A row of ladies in bright pink with tall elaborate multihued headdresses paraded to the bereaved family's enclosure, in front of which they moved in rhythmic motions accompanied by strident singing. On the opposite side of the arena, men clothed in vivid orange shirts and long black wrap-around sarongs formed a chanting circle. Lastly came friends and the elderly, most dressed in black, a couple wearing the peasant coolie hat, and a few bearing offerings. They were followed by a line of buffalo, which included one of the valuable spotted beasts with decorated horns and a garland around its neck. It was led by a stout stick attached to the nose ring, the man executing hopping steps to the beat of a drum. In the midst of it all, still bound to poles, squealing pigs were deposited in the centre for slaughter. As the heap of butchered meat grew, a dog ferreted amongst the carcasses, and the orange-clad men squatted around the perimeter. It was a scene of organised confusion!

BALI

Lake Bratan

Back in **Bali**, we passed a temple with the ornate Balinese carved stone gateway and a house with several thatched altars behind a brick fence and a shrine in the courtyard. Enclosed by verdant surrounds, we ultimately arrived at a gorgeous waterfall plunging down a sheer cliff face to tumble over boulders below. Leaving here, we visited **Lake Bratan** with its appealing multi-tiered thatched pagodas in the water and landscaped with lawns, pathways, hedges and trees. On the return, we came across a street procession; mostly dressed in bright yellow and white, its participants carried long-handled umbrellas and flags on bamboo poles. The leader was flicking fluid from a whisk dipped into a silver container, many carried baskets with offerings on their heads, and they marched to clapping hands, bamboo flutes, kettle drums, brass cymbals, and gongs suspended on poles braced across the shoulders of two men. Heading for a service, they proceeded to a religious venue featuring a forest of coloured umbrellas and the artistic bamboo creations for which Balinese are well known. The people were Hindu and their gods: Brahma (creator), Vishnu (preserver), and Shiva (destroyer), were represented by the colours red, black and white respectively.

AMERICA, CANADA, MEXICO & HAWAII 1994

Australia and America: two young countries sharing a British heritage and both massive in size, featuring everything from big cities to vast empty spaces, diverse cultures contributed by immigrants the world over, and a wealth of resources.

America had always been low on my list of priorities, basically because I considered that it had the same relaxed easy-going outdoor lifestyle as our own and therefore nothing to offer – how wrong I was!

CALIFORNIA

Los Angeles

After a long exhausting flight, and courtesy of the international dateline, I arrived in the **United States** shortly after leaving Perth! Los Angeles International Airport (LAX) must surely be one of the most chaotic in the world and one to be avoided; however, it had an excellent service for tourists: the Travellers Aid Society would find and book accommodation in any price category. I caught a local bus from the terminal but spent only one night in the city. A fellow passenger pointed out a bridge that had just reopened after having collapsed in a recent earthquake. As distinct from their reputation for being loud and brash (probably deserved overseas), I generally found the American people to be friendly and generous, with empathy for Australians.

Santa Barbara

I had purchased three 30-day Amtrak passes and on the first sector of my journey, to Santa Barbara, I was approached by a young lady requesting information. When I explained that I was a visitor, we chatted until its arrival and then boarded the same train. She was travelling first class and made her way through the carriages to find me and insist that I stay with her when I reached my second destination.

Another short anecdote to illustrate their outgoing and generous nature: On one Amtrak sector I was engrossed in a crossword when a young man passing through the carriage commented 'You like puzzles do you?' Replying in the affirmative, I gave it no further thought until he came by again and dumped a pile of books in my lap saying 'You may be able to use these, my brother has a newsagency'. He continued on and I never saw him again. However, Americans do tend to believe that there is no place like the United States and are often very ignorant about the rest of the world.

We passed scenery that had featured in countless movies and television series, and **Santa Barbara** was delightful, presaging better things to be unfolded. A lovely fountain featured leaping dolphins, and a long wooden boardwalk extended into a beautiful blue ocean from a line of tall palm trees along the clean sandy shore. Low stuccoed buildings exuded Spanish or Mediterranean ambience; in fact, much of the original architecture was built by the Spanish. I came across red tiled roofs with cupolas, and the **County Courthouse** (1929), a white edifice with figures and columns enhancing the stone doorway, its square clock tower reaching to a deep blue sky. It was surrounded by palm trees and landscaped gardens, which I looked down upon and across to distant hills from a building opposite. A fountain stood in a courtyard containing blue and white striped umbrellas shading blue tables and chairs, and paved streets with overhead arches were enhanced with flowering plants in pots. A curved pink wall, greenery visible through openings at the top, bordered one side of a square, banners hung in tree-lined streets, and I found a round white turret and a roofless arcade with flags, cafés and trees; it was an attractive tidy town.

I took a bus to the **Old Mission Santa Barbara** (Queen of the Missions), founded by Spanish Franciscans in 1786 as part of a chain of 21 extending 600 miles up the west coast from San Diego to Sonoma, each one day's horseback journey from the next, although the current church, completed in 1820, was the fourth on the site, the previous one having been destroyed by an earthquake in 1812. It was established to teach and minister to the

Indians; originally hunters, fishers and gatherers of seed, they were taught to raise crops of wheat, barley, corn, beans and peas. They established vines, orange and olive groves, and tended cattle, sheep, goats, pigs, mules and horses. They also made adobe tiles, shoes and woollen garments, learned the trades of carpentry and masonry, and discovered the arts of playing musical instruments and singing.

The mission was approached via neat white houses and a swathe of green lawn with colourful flowerbeds. The austere interior displayed a monk's room with a switch for self-flagellation hanging next to a robe, rope girdle and cowl on a wall, the only other adornment being a sacred painting and crucifix. The room also contained a desk holding a quill, candlestick and books, a chair, telescope, basin and ewer, and a rug on the otherwise bare floor. The kitchen had a simple cross above a recess containing a whitewashed but blackened brick oven with pans on top, a kettle and grill to one side, and bunches of garlic and herbs hanging overhead. A wooden table held produce, and utensils were suspended on a wall. In the chapel, a small altar held statues and a gold monstrance, and workshops displayed a trolley, a rustic cart, implements, tools and a ladder. The peaceful arcaded cloister surrounded a garden with lawn, palm trees, and a Moorish fountain built in 1808, its large basin acting as a *lavendaria* used by Indian women to wash clothes. There was also a small cactus garden. Skulls and crossbones on a stone wall denoted the entrance to the cemetery, where approximately 4,000 Indians were buried.

From outside the walls, I took a final photograph of the squat, square, red-domed twin towers behind blossoming trees. I wandered back to the bus past picture book wooden houses with white picket fences, gables, brick chimneys, coloured shutters, green lawns, and flowering gardens. It was a revelation to realise that most American homes were constructed from wood, and I did not consider their average standard of living as affluent as our own. I passed a couple of well-to-do houses (one with a belvedere), a mansion in extensive landscaped grounds, and a white church. A lovely grassy park, with red trees reflected amongst the green in a pond covered with lilies, made nice pictures, as did a second white church with a tower and rose window.

Back in the centre, I returned for a look inside the courthouse, which was another eye-opener with its decorated ceiling and cornice, chandeliers, and walls entirely covered with paintings. The massive scenes depicted stony outcrops where Indian warriors, dressed in loin cloths and carrying spears and shields, watched the landing of a sailing ship and the raising of a flag. Men on horseback, cannon, and monks supervising the construction of Santa Barbara

Mission continued this pictorial record of historical events. Interestingly, they were done on cloth so that they could be removed in event of a severe earthquake. The building also featured a rose window and decoration in and below a high octagonal dome.

The interesting **El Presidio de Santa Barbara** (1782) was like something transposed from the Old West. Again with Spanish influence, it was the last in a line of four military fortresses built by Spain along the wilderness frontier of Alta California to protect the missions and settlers against Indian attack. They also served as a seat of government and guarded against foreign invasion. Constructed from sun-dried adobe blocks laid on foundations of sandstone boulders, the whitewashed buildings, which included a chapel, enclosed a central parade ground and were surrounded by an outer defence wall with two bastions for cannon. Tiled roofs were supported by timber joists, and verandahs had wooden posts. As with the mission, the Presidio was extensively damaged by successive earthquakes in 1806 and 1812, but its final death knoll was sounded with the American occupation of California in 1846, and today only two sections remain. **El Cuartel**, the family residence of the soldier assigned to guard the western gate into the **Plaza de Armas**, was the oldest building owned by the state. One room, its ceiling consisting of split bamboo laid over exposed wooden beams, featured a metal trunk, a statue and candles on a small wooden table, a crude bed with a striped blanket, and a crucifix, rosary and holy picture of the Mother and Child on whitewashed walls. A niche in an outside wall contained a tile picture portraying a ship with the Maltese cross on its sails.

At the Amtrak station, a Moreton Bay Fig (native to Australia) planted in 1877 had a canopy of 160ft, and it was said that at noon more than 10,000 people could shelter in its shade.

San Luis Obispo and San Simeon

Rejoining the train, I headed north, through dry yellow earth below blue skies but with a thick mantle of white cloud draping barren brown hills. Shortly after Santa Barbara the train passed **Point Arguello**, scene of one of the greatest peacetime naval disasters when seven destroyers, mistaking a turn in thick fog, were wrecked with a loss of 23 sailors.

At **San Luis Obispo**, founded as a mission in 1772, an impressive street fountain outside the **Chamber Building** featured a metallic figure and a life-sized grizzly bear, its paw deflecting the spray of water. I was picked up from here by my new found friend Linda, who had driven a considerable distance to collect me. On the way to her home we pulled into **Morro Bay**, but it was too late for photographs of the 576ft rock in the water, the last in a chain of extinct volcanoes.

Next morning, from her house in Cambria, Linda drove me to the fabulous **Hearst Castle** at **San Simeon**. Built in 1919 by publisher William Randolph Hearst on a hill he called Cuesta Encantada (Enchanted Hill), this magnificent estate, now a California historical monument, was comprised of 165 rooms with a vast collection of art and antiques. These included 16th-century Spanish and 18th-century Italian ceilings, Renaissance paintings, French silver, a third-century BC Etruscan bronze *cista* (chest), a 16th-century Florentine bedstead and that in black walnut of Cardinal Richelieu, lamps from Spain and Genoa, classical pottery from the eighth century BC, a 15th-century Madonna and Child from the school of Bellini, Flemish tapestries, Spanish columns, ancient Egyptian statues, and 15th-century Gothic fireplaces. The grounds contained two enormous pools and acres of gardens with terraces and walkways. At one time, the estate even had the largest private zoo in the world, but now all that remained were a few deer, zebra – and cattle. A double staircase with stone balustrades, urns on newels, and an alabaster panel with deep relief of naked female forms led to one of the elegant buildings, its balcony almost obscured by pines, palms, and other large trees. A second flight of steps was flanked by busts on pedestals, which acted as pillars for lighting. A figure stood atop a tall fanciful fountain, and strands of mist from the sea wafted eerily, offering further tantalising glimpses in a game of hide and seek with the environs.

We came to the fabled oval-shaped **Neptune Pool**, its incredible blue tiles incorporating a typical Grecian pattern in black. It also featured semi-elliptical colonnades, alabaster statues of cherubs astride swans and mermaids with long flowing hair, classical sylph-like images bearing lamps, and a structure in imitation of a Greek temple with Corinthian columns and beautifully sculpted figures on the pediment.

Hearst Castle

Even copious solid stone balustrades and stairways could not overpower the various attractions, and lamp standards fashioned like Grecian goddesses were everywhere. Amongst the smooth, glaring white statuary of naked forms scattered around the grounds was a metallic winged figure with a shield.

A naked lady, a parrot in her left hand, sat in the garden fronting a white façade with arched windows, its intricately carved enclosed balcony of dark wood reminiscent of Spain or the Middle East. A figure mounted on a white horse stood beside a path bordered by purple and white flowers, hedges and decorative trees.

One entrance featured sculpting above the ornate door and a beautiful coloured mosaic depicting an oriental scene inserted in the white wall; even the chimneys were decorated. Moving inside, all the ceilings that I managed to film displayed elaborate relief, reminiscent of Arabic designs. One bedroom had rich yellow drapes behind the heavily carved bedhead, a mirror in a carved frame hanging above an inlaid cabinet, and a fine sculpted cornice; a second had a wall tapestry, and the third another carved bedhead, this time backed by maroon drapes. A relief hung above Persian vases on a mantel with an ornate mirror to one side, and the décor was completed by silver light fittings, an interesting iconic woodcut standing on a polished surface, and ornamental treatment of cornice and windows, but no curtains only Holland blinds. Yet another bedroom, furnished in similar manner to the first, also contained an old painting in an elaborate gilded frame.

In the grounds once more, a fantastic statue of **The Three Graces** embracing was endowed with a pearly sheen and mounted on a pedestal behind, of all things, a sarcophagus bearing relief of elegant figures! In keeping with the international flavour, the oldest works of art, dating from 1350 to 1200 BC, were four granite statues of Sekhemet, the lion-headed Egyptian goddess of war, flanked by steps with two free-standing Ionic pillars at the top.

The Three Graces

Mist was still floating silently, creating an ethereal atmosphere as we approached the elaborate main entrance, a fantasy of figures and carved stone surmounted by symmetrical towers with crosses at the apex. Life-sized images flanked the doorway, a man rode a charger directly above, and a statue inhabited an ornate niche overhead. Above that again, armed horsemen advancing towards each other were the subject of a frieze, which lay below a balcony with tiny figures underneath. Located in a pool reflecting palm trees and an urn, a naked nymph, her long hair blowing, reclined on a long-tailed

reclining nymph

sea creature atop a dark pedestal with birds at the corners and shells adorning the sides. Spiral lampposts were twined with embossed flowers, and coats of arms were lodged under eaves braced by carved creatures.

The **Assembly Room** was the repository for several magnificent tapestries full of vitality. These included a religious picture with a mêlée of figures – one in a chariot brandishing a cross – and a 17th-century Flemish work titled *Neptune Creating the Horse*, which showed the sea god with his trident and a rearing horse, surrounded by near-naked figures. This 'busy' room also contained busts on pedestals, gilt-framed white wall plaques with images in bas-relief, other art and statues, solid chairs, and a coffered ceiling from the 1600s, its rectangular sections heavily embossed with floral work. Other items of note were a painting of the Crucifixion beside a mantel holding two alabaster busts. This was supported by carved images between which a shield was flanked by naked male figures wielding clubs. Fussy decoration above the mantel extended to the cornice. Beneath another incredibly intricate cornice and ceiling, a kissing couple occupied a nook partially lit by a fanlight installed beneath a stone lintel with a frieze above.

mural behind arches

The **Dining Room** featured one huge tapestry with an Elizabethan theme, banners, and sculpted stone arches, behind which a lighted illustration depicted mounted protagonists, their swords drawn, in a scene of battle.

On the opposite wall was a solid carved stone fireplace. Elaborate lanterns were suspended from high ceilings with panels bearing deeply embossed figures including St George and the Dragon, and a long table was set with serving dishes and solid candlesticks, all in silver. There was a slate floor and carved wainscot (wooden panelling) on the stone walls.

deep ceiling relief

tapestry

More magnificent tapestries featured in the **Billiard Room**, including a rare Gothic *mille fleurs* circa 1500 from Flanders, the name derived from a carpet of flowers worked into the background of the pictures, this one a hunting scene. This room also contained sculpted stone, a heavy wooden ceiling with patterns painted on the beams and cornice, and colourful panels of ceramic tiles on the stone walls.

The castle even had its own full-sized **Theatre**, where we watched home movies showing Hollywood identities such as Charlie Chaplin who were regular guests. Subdued lighting was achieved by sconces in the form of figures holding globes. The final attraction was the extraordinary indoor **Roman Pool** (actually beneath the tennis courts) with solid gold tiles, ornate standard lamps, statuary of naked and draped gods, goddesses and Roman heroes, rich blue walls, and yellow-patterned beams, all reflected in the water. Hearst's collection of objéts d'art was assessed as the largest and most valuable held by a private individual. The estate also had a landing strip, and amongst the trivia I gleaned from the tour was the fact that Hearst owned the world's first private jet in the 1940s.

Cambria

Next morning, before driving into the quaint colonial-looking town of **Cambria**, I took pictures of Linda in front of her lovely two-storey pink and white wooden home ensconced behind a white paling fence. With indulgence, I would like to describe several of the buildings. Juxtaposed were: a pretty pink shingled shop with a pink awning, a stone store with an oriel in the steep half-timbered gable, a yellow half-timbered structure with a shingled roof, and a white half-timbered façade with blue awnings. Streets presented gay umbrellas, bay and multi-paned windows, old-fashioned signs, and orange butterflies hovering over pink blossoms amongst massed flowers in planters and beds on the pavement. Americans are very patriotic and the flag featured prominently. A stone shop with a shingled roof had a brick chimney, dormers, and bay windows. An attractive blue and white house, appropriately called Victoriana, featured lacy fretwork, a turret, tiny attic windows, and a red shingled roof. A grey building with pink trim had a belvedere, a shingled roof, and a window box with white flowers. A delightful blue and white garden shop was almost inundated with vines and honeysuckle or jasmine creeping up verandah posts, whilst bushes and flowers flourished in beds and tubs. A notice behind flowering agapanthus read: A little bit of 19th century New England…Herbs, Spices & all manner of natural creations & Pleasantries. At the back was an English country garden with white butterflies flitting over lavender, daisies and other blooms. The entire small town was immaculate.

Monterey

We enjoyed an alfresco lunch by the river before Linda deposited me back at the station for the train to **Monterey**, capital of California under Spanish and Mexican rule in 1777, the streets of which were lined with lamps and hanging baskets in full bloom. Pulitzer Prize winning author John Steinbeck put Monterey's Fisherman's Wharf on the map. Born in Salinas Valley in 1902, many of his books, which included *Cannery Row*, *Sweet Thursday*, *East of Eden* and *The Grapes of Wrath*, were set in Monterey. In 1879, Robert Louis Stevenson spent time here gathering impressions for his classic *Treasure Island*, it was the site of California's first theatre, and it was also possible to walk on a footpath made of whalebone! The state was proclaimed part of the United States in Monterey.

White columned buildings were fronted by spacious lawns, and one corner residence was beautified by an alluring sidewalk garden. A picture postcard white house had a colourful display including tall blue and white agapanthus behind its white picket fence. Another had hanging baskets under the eaves of its balcony and pink plants in urns atop pillars in the stone fence. A small bright crimson dwelling with tiny white-framed windows was almost submerged by a burst of white flowers, and white daisies also added balance to a red and white house with an old-fashioned well in the yard. A friend of Linda's kindly gave me a folding trolley for my increasing volume of luggage.

Carmel

From Monterey, I received a sticker stating 'I Rode the Wave' – referring to the bus. This took me to one of California's gems, **Carmel**, where Clint Eastwood once presided as mayor and still owned the Hog's Breath Inn. The route along **Pacific Coast Highway** followed the rugged **Big Sur** coastline, with rocky outcrops in a cobalt blue sea on one side, the **San Lucia Mountains** the other. The obliging driver stopped for me to photograph the sheer cliffs with their sparse mantle of low vegetation, which loomed above the indented shoreline where frothing white surf pounded rocks in the water. On the opposite side of the road, misty pine-clad hills veered off into the distance, and a mighty bridge spanned one inlet.

At Carmel, I visited historic old **Mission San Carlos Borromeo del Rio Carmelo** (1770), with a fountain in the large quadrangle bordered by red-roofed verandahs. Coloured creeper graced old stone walls below the bell tower, and in addition to flowers and trees, the garden was planted with cactus. From the front, the lovely asymmetrical yellow and white building made a wonderful picture. In the dark interior, I found crockery on shelves, jars on a blackened stove, a basket of produce, and various implements; garlic and herbs hung on walls that were coated with lime plaster made from burnt seashells.

Houses in high-priced Carmel included one with a deep red vine on its white stuccoed façade above stone foundations and a green wooden building with white trim and a pretty garden. This stood next to a red adobe dwelling with dormers, spherical-shaped trees in pots flanking the white door, and vines on the picket fence. Whenever I refer to adobe it is usually rendered with stucco. Streets and arcades were gay with hanging baskets, trees and flowerbeds; brilliantly coloured flowers bloomed around the base of an old tree, and even the fire hydrants were yellow. Benches were located beneath shading branches, coloured canopies enhanced stone, stuccoed and wooden shops with shingled or tiled roofs, and one called White Rabbit, with a planter box under the display window and a garden bed containing a white pottery bunny in front, looked like a converted house. Creepers climbed walls, one stone store had a bright yellow door, and there were bay and multi-paned windows, steep half-timbered gables, and one half-timbered complex with a sagging upper storey. A lovely forecourt contained a garden, a fountain, and a bird bath complete with occupants – albeit ceramic!

pretty Carmel

Monterey

Returning to Monterey, I went to the aforementioned **Fisherman's Wharf**, with the eye-catching pink **Harbor House** and its blue lighthouse at the entrance. From an elevated position, I could survey the busy boardwalk lined with colourful shops, which included a shingle-roofed turquoise and yellow wooden building with white railing. Flags flapped merrily in a stiff breeze, and on the seaward side, barking seals cavorted in the water, on rocks, and on a raft near a buoy. Crying seagulls wheeled over a fishing boat, yacht and launch. Overlooked by a restaurant on pylons in the water, a protected anchorage harboured a forest of masts.

On **Cannery Row** I visited the **Aquarium**, a showcase for the marine life off Monterey's coast. The foul-smelling canneries were long gone, their place taken by upmarket restaurants and shops. Sea otters entertained with their ever-fascinating antics, and shinning silver shoals swam around larger fish in the world's tallest tank filled with different colours of gently waving weed. Amongst the many fish were a black species with thick white lips, a red 'saddle' and white-edged tail, varieties in pale and deep blue, a spotted shark, and ugly grouper-like specimens. Another exhibit featured vibrant red starfish, coloured corals, and delicate anemones. The latter, their long spidery tentacles swaying, came in pink, white, yellow or orange.

anemones

At the imitation **Elkhorn Slough**, seabirds such as long-legged sandpipers probed for food in sand hills and amongst plants and driftwood, others, with long fine upturned beaks, foraged in weed washed to and fro by the swell of artificial waves on the shore. A display of massed corals in different shades of pink from almost white to magenta made a marvellous show, and rusted metal was encrusted with red and pink growth. As they dived with the fish in a large glass tank, I watched the lovable otters from below, then again from above, where they performed human-like actions of scratching, floating on their back, bobbing up and down through an opening in the rock, rolling, and interacting with each other. I went by bus to a position opposite the wharf, where I watched the westering sun illuminate a scene of colourful shops reflected in the water, with pink cloud and the call of gulls overhead.

Next morning, I came across a yellow fountain, a lovely garden that contained tall brilliant blue delphiniums in a wooden tub, and a quaint historic theatre (1844), California's first. Inside was a saloon with the framed picture of a naked lady above shelves displaying an amazing collection of bottles, which included comical characters. More visions of colour were provided by gardens and hanging baskets.

San Francisco

Moving on to **San Francisco** by bus, we crossed the **Bay Bridge**, which provided good views of the city skyline, and continued past skyscrapers into the centre. From my window, I observed a 'street person', complete with shopping trolley, feeding the myriad pigeons. Taking my first exploratory stroll, I saw the famous cable car, a statue atop a column in a neat square with hedgerows, trimmed trees and palms, and an exclusive upmarket store that I entered just to see how the other half lives – to be confronted by snooty salespersons, labels such as Yves St Laurent, and a magnificent floral arrangement incorporating orchids and bromeliads in a big bowl.

Joining a tour, we were first taken back across the bridge to a vantage point on the opposite side of the bay. The panorama included tremendous vistas of the city with the prominent needle-like spire of the **Transamerica Pyramid**, at 853ft its tallest structure. This was built on the site once occupied by the Montgomery Block, the in-house bar of which lured patrons like Mark Twain and Robert Louis Stevenson and where, in one of the apartments, Chinese revolutionary Sun Yat-Sen plotted the overthrow of the Manchu dynasty and wrote the 1911 Chinese constitution. A legendary blanket of thick fog lay in the background, with hills peeping above and formidable **Alcatraz** (regrettably, I did not have time to visit) sitting at the edge of the concealing cloudy bank, which contributed to its austere forbidding profile. A large white cruise vessel was berthed in the harbour.

In an area of plain four-storey terrace houses with bay windows on upper floors, we entered a church with ornate stonework on the façade. Unusual ceiling treatment consisted of exposed beams decorated with autumn-toned zigzag stripes, and the elaborate altarpiece contained five images. These included one with feminine features in a short skirt, long boots, and wielding a sword. Dark life-sized statues stood on brackets between pairs of brown marble pillars supporting the pediments of side altars. Located in a garden setting, the cemetery with its ancient headstones was full of appeal.

Next stop was the **Chinese Garden** in **Golden Gate Park**. Always enjoyable, this one featured pavilions, a towering red pagoda surrounded by topiary and tall trees, a steeply rounded wooden bridge, and tranquil pools with rocks, rushes and ferns. There was extensive use of intricate topiary beside walkways lined with stone lanterns, a statue of Buddha, waterfalls, and both plum-coloured and gorgeous pink foliage amongst the variety of greens. The latter included a beautiful pale creeper rambling across the roof of an open-sided pavilion overlooking a pond containing turtles.

We stopped in the vicinity of **Cliff House**, which provided more rugged coastal vistas – and more fog. The 745ft towers of the famed 1.7mile **Golden Gate Bridge** were emerging from the mist like some leviathan, and many sailboats dotted the choppy bay near a marina with Alcatraz in the background. This notorious prison, labelled 'The Rock', closed in 1963 and served as home to such infamous identities as John Dillinger, 'Pretty Boy' Floyd, Robert 'Birdman' Stroud, and Al Capone. In 30 attempts, no escape was ever recorded, although five were never captured and presumed drowned. Named Isla de los Alcatraces (pelicans) after the birds that were the islands sole inhabitants, the penitentiary was the only one in the federal system to have hot showers – designed to prevent the inmates acclimatising to cold water!

Historic **Fort Point**, a three-tiered brick structure tucked beneath the southern end of the bridge, was built to fortify the bay during the Civil War, but its 150 cannon were never used for defence. A few statistics on the bridge: built between 1933 and 1937, the engineer erected the nation's first safety nets, saving 19 lives; 11 men fell to their deaths. The bridge sways 27ft to withstand winds of up to 100mph, annual maintenance requires more than 2,000 gallons of orange paint and takes four years to complete, the two great cables contain 80,000 miles of wire (enough to encircle the equator three times), and the concrete in its piles would pave a five-foot-wide path from New York to San Francisco.

Here, we also encountered the **Musée Méchanique**, a penny arcade museum displaying, amongst other interesting items, a laughing machine with an automated gap-toothed figure producing lusty belly laughs, which could not fail to engender a reciprocal response! Driving further, we came to a mooring with a three-masted barque, and I left the tour to return to the Chinese Garden, where I took more footage of the artistic topiary trees, and birdlife around a lake.

I availed myself of a complimentary ticket on the **Cable Car**, operating since 1873 and declared a national monument in 1964, which progressed (at 16km per hour!) to a location called **Alamo Square Park** on a hilltop overlooking the well-known street of Victorian houses referred to as **Postcard Row**, of which innumerable pictures have been taken. In fact, on the grass of the park they were taking photographs of a new model car for advertising purposes, using the houses and city skyline as a backdrop. These examples of 19th-century Victorian architecture, in Italianate, Stick, and Queen Anne classifications, had been preserved and were known as the **Painted Ladies**. The first style, fashioned after Roman Classical ornamentation, featured a flat roof (often hidden behind a false façade), slim pillars flanking the front door, and bay windows, the second added ornate woodwork and gables, the last included turrets, towers, steep roofs, arches, stained-glass windows, and shingles.

Back in the city centre, the imposing Beaux-Arts **City Hall** featured doorways decorated with gold and an ornate dome looming above the carved pediment on its columned façade. Another edifice had interesting sculpting and a corner dome, but most buildings were like unattractive utilitarian concrete blocks. In contrast, the lobby of the exclusive **Stanford Court Hotel** on **Nob Hill** (the word comes from *nabob*, a wealthy man or Indian ruler), still one of the nation's most prestigious addresses, contained beautiful subtly shaded Tiffany-inspired stained-glass domes. One was located above a fountain with flowers in urns around the perimeter, the second above an exotic floral bouquet with a mural enhancing the wall behind. Also on Nob Hill, the **Fremont** was one of only two survivors of the disastrous 1906 earthquake, the other being the Pacific Union Club. In a square with ornamental fountains, I saw another unkempt street dweller shuffling along with all his worldly possessions in a shopping cart. Riding the trolley as it negotiated its way up and down San Francisco's hilly streets was like seeing the Monopoly board come to life in London, with scenes familiar from countless movies. It was interesting to watch it change direction at the terminus, physically manhandled with the aid of a revolving turntable. As we trundled our way along, the bell clanging loudly, there were glimpses of the Transamerica spire and Bay Bridge at the end of narrow ravines formed by the tall buildings, and I took photographs of photographers lining the route of this famous San Francisco landmark. A gift from Taiwan in 1969, the gaudy pagoda-like entrance to **Chinatown** was visible above rooftops when the trolley chugged laboriously up hills. Gathering speed as it free-wheeled down, it was checked by continual use of the long-handled brake operated by the aptly called gripman – accompanied by squeals and screams at the steepest inclines. This method of transport was introduced by a Scottish wire cable manufacturer after witnessing a horse-drawn carriage rolling backwards and dragging the animals behind.

I disembarked at the top of **Russian Hill**, named for Russian sailors buried there in the early 1800s, to see intriguing **Lombard Street**. Known as 'The crookedest street in the world', it was laid out in the 1920s because the almost 40° slope was too severe for both pedestrians and horses. With eight hairpin turns, the paved roadway wound around beds of massed hydrangeas and white, pink and blue roses enclosed by low hedges. From the top, the view extended as far as the Bay Bridge, and I made my way down the steps past high-priced real estate, which included a four-storey blue half-timbered house covered in coloured creeper and a pink Mediterranean-style home with white shutters and barrel tiles on the roof. At the bottom, it was fascinating to watch the steady stream of vehicles slowly wending their way like a coloured snake with sun glinting off scales of glass. It was a pleasure to wander around the vicinity, also endowed with its fair share of Victorian architecture: turrets, gables, bay windows, balconies, white fretwork, and one house draped with deep blue morning glory.

A paved mall had coloured awnings, planter boxes, and tables and chairs beneath trees. I continued on to the hub of San Francisco's entertainment area and the second most visited venue in California, renowned **Fisherman's Wharf**. Although one of San Francisco's top tourist attractions, it was still a working harbour and the centre of the city's fishing industry. It was a beautiful sunny day and a Negro dressed in overalls sporting the red, white and blue stars and stripes of the American flag was playing jazz on a saxophone beneath the symbol of the wharf: an outsized boat wheel with a huge red crab in the centre. From this gay locale with happy noisy crowds, I watched a ferry sailing past a sombre Alcatraz and, from the upper level of **Pier 39**, enhanced with tubs of yellow and white daisies, surveyed the throngs on the boardwalk below. The pier had over 110 shops and restaurants, and my viewpoint encompassed wooden buildings, a colourful fruit stall, attractive lampposts, planters with red flowers defining an area for al fresco dining beneath red umbrellas, fluttering flags and screeching gulls, with yachts beyond in one direction, the city skyline the other. Creepers climbed posts and clung beneath a wooden overpass, baskets were suspended from beams, and attractive dried arrangements hung on the wall of a blue restaurant. A sign pointed the way to Handcocks Wind Chimes & Bells, tables and chairs were set up for luncheon, and other shops included: Casa de Fruta Orchard Outlet shaded by bright red bougainvillea, Nature's Own, Leather Blues, Wound About, and a speciality chocolate store. There were things like clam chowder to try, but I am not partial to shellfish, although I found the sourdough bread delicious. Music played, frisky seals sported in the bay with the bridge in the distance, soap bubbles floated on the air, and there was even a merry-go-round. Buskers performed opposite the entrance to the pier: one, his face painted as a clown, was tying balloons to create animals, and a second adroitly imitated a mechanical man that executed stilted movements when given a donation. I came across more live jazz and a square containing small stalls, flower barrows, and a fountain featuring a metallic mermaid. People were literally hanging out the sides of the now crowded cable cars. The Transamerica Pyramid, its windows like stacked boxes, was built on enormous pylons, as was at least one other building that I saw; possibly a measure to provide resilience to counteract the effects of earthquake. Amongst the skyscrapers, one had distinctive mullioned walls and many were glass fronted, reflecting the surrounds. A forecourt was beautifully landscaped with flowerbeds that included bright orange marigolds, hedges, and a pool with a small waterfall. Statues stood in a traffic circus opposite a French-style building.

Between the years of 1923 and 1993, at least 60 movies were filmed in San Francisco, amongst them: *The Jazz Singer*, *The Maltese Falcon*, Alfred Hitchcock's *The Birds*, *Guess Who's Coming to Dinner* with Sidney Poitier, *The Graduate*, *Dirty Harry* starring Clint Eastwood, *Towering Inferno*, the James Bond thriller *A View to Kill*, *Star Trek IV*, *Sister Act* with Whoopie Goldberg, and Robin Williams as *Mrs. Doubtfire.*

A piece of culinary trivia: San Francisco has a garlic restaurant that advertises 'Follow your nose to The Stinking Rose'!

Sausalito

Travelling by bus, I crossed the Golden Gate Bridge, still with clutching fingers of enveloping mist, to **Sausalito**. With a quaint nautical ambience and Bohemian attitude, Sausalito (meaning Little Grove of Willows) was as pretty as its name. A corner florist, its blue awnings sheltering blooms spilling onto the pavement, was a blaze of colour, and I saw an interesting six-sided belvedere, shingled facades, colourful buildings with barrel-tiled roofs, small wooden houses, plants and trees, all with misty hills in the background. Even a bright yellow convertible parked in front of a red establishment contributed to the colour. I discovered pretty gardens, flowerboxes and planters, and a lilac clapboard house with a hexagonal brown shingled belvedere. Also in this lively community were free-standing gables, a store called Crazy Shirts, a pink wooden building with a green canopy and, situated over the water, a blue and white harbour restaurant with flowers on the decking. But most outstanding was a dainty pink structure with small round windows in symmetrical gables and covered in fancy white fretwork like icing on a wedding cake, even the slender twisted poles looked like candy sticks. Old-fashioned streetlamps tied with colourful balloons stood on the sidewalk in front.

Sausalito

Returning to San Francisco on the ferry afforded a different aspect of the town and its houses climbing up hillsides. Sailing over teal-blue water, we passed the Golden Gate Bridge, now with a thick fog bank behind and lying like a cloth of cloud above the city. As we came close to Alcatraz and its lighthouse, the fog miraculously lifted, revealing marvellous vistas of the Bay Bridge, city and port. Constructed in 1895, the **Ferry Building** at the foot of **Market Street** was a San Francisco landmark, its 73m clock tower modelled on the Giralda Bell Tower in Seville, Spain. It was one of the few downtown structures to survive the 1906 earthquake, which measured 7.9 on the Richter scale.

Haight-Ashbury

My next excursion was to **Haight-Ashbury**, flower-power haven of the 1960s hippies with their counter culture of free love, drugs and antiwar demonstrations and now a punk yuppie area, its funky stores filled with kitsch, antiques, and second-hand clothes. Two hundred thousand people descended on the area for the 'Summer of Love' with its love-ins and free concerts by names such as the Grateful Dead and drug-addicted Janis Joplin. Three- and four-storey red and pink houses stood near powder blue, yellow and pale green, and there were still flowers in the street, albeit in buckets outside a florist. Victorian turrets featured along with fretwork, and a classic building dated 1883 had a tiny portico with a pediment that was duplicated above windows. Flags were flying, and a small red structure with white trim and a green roof was wedged between larger buildings. I realise that there is considerable repetition involved here, but I am attempting to convey a thumbnail sketch of several similar locations. San Francisco's **Chinatown** has the largest Chinese community outside Asia, and famous faces that called the city home included Nicholas Cage, Francis Ford Coppola, Jerry Garcia, Danny Glover, George Lucas, Boz Scaggs, Linda Ronstadt and Robin Williams. At the time of my visit I observed no small cars, only huge gas-guzzling American monsters.

San Jose

I left San Francisco for Sacramento, with a stop on the way at **San Jose**, founded in 1777 as Pueblo de San Jose de Guadalupe, to see the absolutely astonishing **Winchester Mystery House**. This bizarre $5.5 million 160-room mansion was built over a period of 37 years, from 1884 to 1922, by the eccentric Sarah Winchester, widow of the arms manufacturer, on the advice of a psychic who told her that she must appease spirits of people and animals killed with Winchester repeater rifles: 'The gun that won the West'. I heard a wealth of interesting tales and statistics too long to relate here, but the house was a rambling maze of corridors, stairways that ended abruptly at ceilings or rose only to descend, and doors that opened onto solid walls; one on an upper floor, complete with handle, opened directly into space! It was all meant to confuse and disorientate unwelcome evil spirits, but was made inviting to kind ghostly guests, and altogether there were 41 stairways (one with 44 steps only two and a half inches high and seven turns, ascending just nine feet!), 40 bedrooms, 13 bathrooms, 6 kitchens, 47 fireplaces, 2,000 doors and 10,000 windows, but only two mirrors because these did not please poltergeists! A $1,500 Tiffany window was installed inside, skylights emerged from floors, shingles appeared indoors, one hallway was two feet wide, one door only four feet ten inches high, and a storage cupboard opened to half an inch of space! A brick chimney rose up four storeys and stopped one and a half feet short of the ceiling!

Winchester House

The number 13 in fixtures and fittings abounded throughout, and contorted shadows lent an eerie aura. One story recounts how, on finding a handprint that she regarded as the sign of a malevolent presence in the cellar, Sarah had it closed off – wine and all. Sarah herself always wore a veil, dined on a $30,000 gold service, and at midnight donned a gown with occult designs for a nightly séance in the Blue Room, reached via a secret panel, a window onto a flight of steps, and a maze. She was highly educated, extremely cultured, and an accomplished musician. Building continued around the clock until the day she died at 85, and it was a remarkable legacy that required 13,000 gallons of paint to restore. It has become a California Historical Landmark, and to this day there remain accounts of haunting, in the form of a baby crying, organ music, strange lights, cold spots and footsteps. It was also very beautiful, with stained glass, Carrara marble, sculpted French wallpaper, heavy drapes, and the rich hues of carved mahogany, rosewood and teak in banisters, fireplaces and wall panels. There were ornately carved canopied beds, gold and silver chandeliers, parquetry floors, doors with inlaid silver, a piano, and period furniture.

The estate spread over six acres, and a piped commentary followed the visitor around extensive grounds that featured statuary, trees, herbs, flowers and shrubs from more than 110 countries. Plants included roses, hedges, palms with floral borders, a magnificent white flowering tree, flax, and conifers. A Cupid fountain with water spraying from the mouths of frogs and a long-necked bird was located on the lawn, and there were multiple views of the extraordinary exterior with its towers and turrets, tiny windows, lattice, turned posts, decorative panels, and half-timbered, clapboard and shingled walls. Shutters opened to a small balcony set in the centre of a shingled porch roof. President Roosevelt visited the reclusive owner in 1903, but left in a huff because servants instructed him to use a side door, the front entrance being permanently locked. I was presented with a press kit that even contained a Dennis the Menace comic book devoted, in part, to the weird house!

Cupid fountain

Sacramento

I continued to **Old Sacramento**, and anything less like a capital I have yet to see, even the **Supreme Court** building was provincial and unimposing. A small white trap stood outside, and horses seemed to be a favoured mode of transport. A white horse hitched to a white carriage was standing patiently in front of red brick buildings with white façades, their balconies, supported by wooden posts, creating cover for wide plank footpaths with old-style street lamps and a jungle of advertising signs overhead, one even reading American West. An amusing business was titled Baker and Ham, another, Fanny Ann's Saloon, and there was The Vicar's Cottage, Fulton's Prime Rib, and Gran's Café. The whole ambience was like that of the Old West, and indeed it was a faithful restoration of the city during the 19th-century Gold Rush. Two horses drawing a large wagon trotted past the old white **Firehouse** (dated 1853) and adjacent **Assay Office** (1872). The **California State Railway Museum**, largest in the world, housed resplendent vintage steam locomotives with gleaming brass lanterns and fittings on top; even the huge black funnels were sparkling, and the wooden carriages pristine. There were 21 engines in total, replica streets, and a miner's or railway worker's camp. Sacramento was the western terminus for Pony Express riders in 1860. Constantly plagued by flooding, in 1875 the streets of the city were raised 12ft with dirt dredged from the **American River**.

In the 'new' area of the city, a Warner Brothers Studio Store had larger than life cartoon characters Bugs Bunny and Daffy Duck above the entrance, Tweety and long-moustachioed Sam in a covered wagon out front, and the Roadrunner and Coyote nearby.

Warner Brothers Store

A paved arcade containing a fountain and outdoor elevator was furnished with tables and chairs under red or blue umbrellas, and trams consisted of four long carriages. Bordered by palm- and tree-lined streets, the **Capitol Building** was in the same style as most states: a huge Ionic-pillared portico, a deeply sculpted pediment with figures on horseback atop each end, two tiers of columns circling the dome, and a cupola at the apex. Side entrances featured similar porticos with depictions of people, a bison, bull and horses on respective pediments; a motto below one read *Bring Me Men to Match My Mountains.*

Capitol pediment

Placed there in 1883, a larger than life Carrara marble statue beneath a dome in the interior was titled *Columbus' Last Appeal to Queen Isabella.* Other statues stood near the foundations outside. The building made tremendous pictures viewed behind a green pool with a fountain in the middle and red and white roses in the foreground. Alert squirrels hopped about the lawn.

The old paddle wheeler **Delta King**, now a floating hotel, was moored with other riverboats on the **Sacramento River** waterfront, and the **Central Pacific Rail Road Depot** (1876) was located on **Front Street**; city blocks were logically divided by Front, 2nd and 3rd streets, with cross streets being named I, J, K and L. The rear of a working steam locomotive was loaded with wood. A cobbled road passed the United States Hotel with its typical wooden balcony; modern buildings reared behind. A small yellow and white wooden structure had a bell tower in the centre of its roof, and a 12ft-high bronze statue commemorated the 1,960 mile Pony Express mail run from Sacramento to Missouri in 1860, a feat performed by 80 riders in just ten days. The Express was finally disbanded in 1861 at the completion of the transcontinental telegraph. Other relics of a bygone era were a painted advertisement picturing a bulldog and promoting Boss of the Road Overalls on a brick wall of the Morelos Hotel and a sign on a balcony that read San Francisco Cordage Agency …rope at manufacturers' prices…

Queen Isabella

OREGON

Portland

Leaving Sacramento, my route took me to **Portland**, **Oregon**, the light of early dawn touching tops of shrubs and turning them to gold, which spread like a carpet before distant snow-capped peaks and finally, with full break of day, developed into scenery composed of dense pine forest with glimpses of a river. On this section of the route, snowsheds were built over the tracks to protect them from snow accumulation and avalanches, and we went through **Martinez**, home of the martini.

A friend had given me the name of a contact in Portland who took me sightseeing along part of the 55mi-long 1,219m/3,999ft-high **Columbia River Gorge**, once the most treacherous leg of the Oregon Trail, where we stopped to survey a panorama of the waterway traversing a green valley between mountains rearing into a cloudy blue sky. We progressed to the fabulous two-tiered 189m (620ft) **Multnomah Falls**, second highest in the United States and the world's fourth highest, plummeting from a precipice on **Larch Mountain** and surrounded by rock and lush greenery, with **Benson Bridge** (1914) spanning a small pool between the two drops. There were several cataracts in this impressive area of granite, which was nevertheless softened by a vast range of growth that included pines and, at variance with the many shades of green, a few autumn tones of red and yellow. We stopped at **Horsetail**, **Latourell**, **Bridal Veil Falls** and one other before making our way back through excellent mountain scenery bordering the river.

Multnomah Falls

Investigating Portland, situated on the **Willamette River**, I found a classical building with hideous faces flanking a benign countenance below a small pediment, mounted police patrolling the streets, rows of bright flower baskets on lampposts, long colourful trams with oak interiors, a fountain in a square shaded by large leafy trees, a bridge with small turrets, and the **Convention Centre** with 150ft steel-and-glass spires on its twin glass pyramids. My discoveries continued with an isolated multistorey rectangular structure that stood out like the proverbial sore thumb, glass-fronted buildings, and two enormous bronze lions flanking the tiered gate with its 64 dragons at the entrance to **Chinatown** – next to a shocking-pink wall! Concealed behind solid fluted columns with Corinthian capitals, a flower-decorated stone doorway, with carving incorporating an eagle above the lintel, enclosed a superb embossed metal door, its panels depicting scenes from everyday life. Finally I encountered a bridge like that across Sydney's harbour.

heritage building

Given a complimentary bus tour, I found myself back at the valley viewpoint described earlier, now hidden to a certain extent by cloud. We stopped at different falls, the first narrow but very high, falling past bright green ferns clinging to remarkable formations like clusters of long many-sided crystals onto rocks below. The next fall was lower and not so steep, but cascaded in a raging torrent over boulders and between thick greenery. Revisiting Multnomah Falls, this time I climbed as far as the bridge from where I could follow the course of their passage to a calm crater pool. In a beautiful setting of water, rocks and gardens surrounded by lawn and a hedgerow with an undulating top, we visited a stone-and-timber Forestry Department building with dormers in its steep shingled roof and a stone chimney. Cloud hung very low over a covered wagon in the yard, and we returned to Portland beneath a dramatic blue to purple sky with windswept cloud.

Next day, I spent more time in the centre, where I discovered tubs of flowers, horse-drawn carriages, and a stunning contemporary fountain in **Pioneer Courthouse Square**. Having the appearance of a Roman theatre, a broad curved red brick stairway had free-standing white columns at the top and was bordered on one side by a stepped cascade with water issuing from the sides of individual blocks rather than running over the top; it was a popular place to cool off. This city was also a nice blend of old and new. Lofty trees created a canopy above a lovely wide median strip with lighting, a memorial, and statues that included a sombre Abraham Lincoln. Benches for seating lined pathways bordered by grassed strips with tall cannas forming the centrepiece in red, white and blue flowerbeds. A brownstone church had beautiful stained glass, and the **History Centre** was deceptively painted with two pillared structures and four giant figures, which included Lewis and Clark, projecting a striking three-dimensional effect. A mural on the brickwork at the rear portrayed wagon trains, settlers, cattle, merchants and workers. Created with a

History Centre

combination of rocks and layers of slate, a landscaped water feature was enveloped in foliage of different hues.

The exceptional **Japanese Garden** was a haven of peace and tranquillity, with lawns, hedges, stone lanterns, walkways, delicate willows bending to a pond, numerous small waterfalls, and striking trees with pale green foliage on black branches. I saw perfectly rounded shrubs, a gorgeous red tree with a black trunk, banks with rich mossy carpets, little bridges, iris, ferns, water plants and conifers. Lawn reached right to the edge of a rock-lined pool in the **Strolling Pond Garden** (*Chisen-kaiyui-shiki*), others were ringed by plants, and one had pebbles providing a landing place for metallic cranes. Every direction composed fantastic pictures, and the water was full of colourful koi or carp – what pond would be complete without them? There was a veritable arboretum of different plants, and a stone lantern in a delightful dell was silhouetted against soft green light just penetrating the delicate leafy cavern like illumination through coloured glass. There was a small stone pagoda, a tea house, and a **Sand and Stone Garden** (*Karesansui* or *Sekitei*), a typical Japanese arrangement of large brown rocks surrounded by swirls of raked white gravel, which I believe represented islands or continents in an ocean. There was a second garden created with pebbles, a poetry stone engraved with a *haiku* (traditional Japanese verse), and a glorious coloured maple. The **Flat Garden** (*Hiraniwa*) had the white chips arrayed in a pattern of squares around islands of lawn depicting a saki cup and gourd bottle, signifying pleasure and a wish for happiness, and I came across an exquisite pink-leafed tree. The **Natural Garden** (*Shukeiyen*) had trimmed plants mixed with natural growth of different colours in pleasing displays and the foggy city skyline as a backdrop. Designed in 1963 by Professor Takuma Tono, an internationally renowned authority on Japanese landscaping, the garden has been acclaimed as one of the most authentic outside Japan. It was an idyllic place of devastating beauty.

Back in town, I went to the Saturday open-air craft market located in a square with flowering baskets on lampposts and a colonnade on one side. It was a lively venue with continuous entertainment provided by buskers; a man paraded with a bundle of balloons attached to the hat on his head and another, holding a guitar, sat on the rim of a fountain. The blowing of a horn announced one of the funniest performances that I have ever witnessed, enacted by a man wearing a costume representing a horse, his head and torso emerging from the middle as if seated in a saddle, false limbs dangling at the sides, and long cloth hiding his legs. He proceeded to put the animal through its paces: sidestepping, trotting – with appropriate head movements and exaggerated sway of the horse's rump – and finally, in simulated slow motion, jumping a tiny hurdle. It was all accompanied by comical quips and was clever, extraordinarily realistic, and extremely funny. Items for sale included carvings, clothes, and a striking painting of cacti silhouetted against a red and purple sky cleaved by white lightning. A woman was nursing a black and white cat (real) decked out in a similarly toned cap adorned with stars, and there were hot food stalls. In a tent set up nearby, a long-haired individual with a husky voice was singing and belting out rock on an electric guitar. Another act featured a lady in a red wig, green coat, and matching handbag in the shape of a fish, interacting with a toy dog.

I followed this entertaining episode with a visit to the lovely **International Rose Test Garden** in **Washington Park**, providing splendid views across the city and 500 varieties of this queen of flowers. Portland was known as the **City of Roses**. Another of my favourite hobbies, which I indulged here, is taking close-up photographs of individual blooms; every shade from silver to all the reds was represented, many with drops of water clinging to petals and glinting like diamonds in the sun.

Pittock Mansion (1914) was built in French Renaissance style and set in immaculate grounds with trees, rolling lawns, and colourful flowerbeds. The interior featured a curved staircase reflected in a huge ornate mirror, which was flanked by tall candelabra created to resemble branches bearing gilt flowers. The dining room contained an old screen, a sideboard with crockery, carved chairs, plates on the mantel of the fireplace, and a side table holding candlesticks and an Italianate coloured glass ornament. Woodwork, even on the ceiling, gleamed with a rich red hue. Another room featured a decorated domed ceiling and bright blue walls. Containing a grand piano and harp, the music room had a picture window overlooking the gardens, city, and five mountains beyond, a wooden floor with a carpet square in the centre, a chandelier and sconces, and beige drapes to tone with the patterned wallpaper. Another mantel held decorative plates, a pair of blue and gilt ornaments flanking a gilded clock with graceful images, and matching brass candelabra, their bases also endowed with figures. A room containing many books was furnished with a wooden inlaid table, tapestry-upholstered chairs, and familiar white china dogs (recalled from my youth) on the mantel of a fireplace with embossed decoration. A brass coal shuttle sat beside the brass fire screen. A silver jug occupied a dresser against a papered wall featuring large floral sprays, and a semicircular nook containing chairs and a period lounge upholstered in rich burgundy velvet also held a small table set for tea. A novel alabaster statue beside the stairway in the foyer depicted a boy intently inspecting his foot.

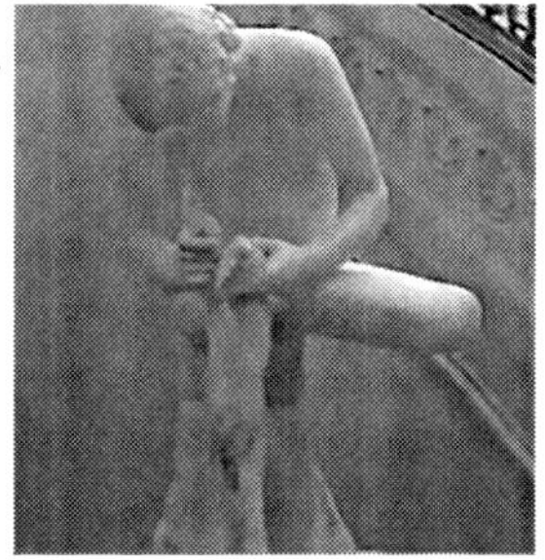
boy examining his foot

A walk in the pleasant grounds revealed more of the exterior, where the red shingled roof and orange flowers in carved stone window boxes relieved the sombre look of the immense grey structure with its heavy balustrades and twin turrets, one either side of the picture window. Bright yellow beds and massed colours including a vivid blue also lifted the tone and were favoured by birds.

At the age of 17, English born Henry Pittock journeyed 'barefoot and penniless' from Pennsylvania to Oregon on a wagon train. He began working for the Weekly Oregonian newspaper, which he eventually owned, and in 1860, at the age of 25, married his 15-year-old bride. He went on to build an empire incorporating real estate, banking, railroads, steamboats, sheep ranching, silver mining, and the pulp and paper industry. He died in 1919 aged 83.

Leaving here, we passed more upper class housing to arrive at the unique attraction of the **National Sanctuary of Our Sorrowful Mother**, known simply as **The Grotto**. Perched on top of a 130ft cliff, a tiny red and white chapel, surrounded by acres of vivid green lawn, garden beds, groves of towering fir trees with flower baskets attached to their trunks, and rhododendrons amongst plants around the base, was an inspirational setting for meditation. At the bottom of the overgrown cliff, a pure white Crucifixion tableau occupied the summit of a mound of rocks planted with greenery. Making my way up, I passed another statue in a secluded ferny dell beneath the looming rock and a 'candlelit' sanctuary in a stone cavern surrounded by flowers and trees. This one contained a copy of Michelangelo's Pietà atop rocks draped with luxuriant growth and flanked by two dark angels.

The Grotto

At the top I found myself alone with only butterflies for company, the total silence imparting a truly wonderful, totally serene atmosphere, which seemed far from the bustle of the city just at the foot of the escarpment. As well as the delightful picturesque wooden chapel with its simple interior, which put me in mind of the song *Little Brown Church in the Wildwood*, I found a figure holding a child, and two plaques portraying, respectively, the sorrow of Joseph on the flight to Egypt and his joy at safe deliverance.

Other holy statues were placed in a garden bed and in the centre of a pond beyond a vine-covered arbour with the grey stone convent in the background. A sparkling winding waterway reflected overhanging trees, rocks, and a floral presentation in the middle of a path. Whereas most were alabaster or marble, a group of images worked in wood depicted Joseph, a bundle on his back, leading Mary and Jesus on a donkey.

wooden sculpture

Executed in bronze, St Francis of Assisi stood with a couple of furry friends on a pedestal amongst the pines, palms and blue firs, and another wooden tableau showed one of the Stations of the Cross: Jesus meeting his Mother. From the upper level, panoramas of the **Columbia River Valley**, **Cascade Range**, and **Mount St Helens** opened up. I looked down through branches onto the copper dome of a tower with sculpted and painted figures on the side and, making my way back to street level, came to ethereal shining white images, which I took to be the Virgin appearing to Bernadette, in another grotto filled with ferns, lush growth, and mosses on the rock wall; the sacred aura would even have charmed and restored the flagging spirits of an atheist. In the main church below, the impressive dome above the altar was illustrated with the crowning of Christ surrounded by angelic figures, and the story of Christ's Passion was the subject of a frieze painted in rich glowing colours above white sculpted Stations. A stunning mosaic was created with chips of glass.

Back in 'civilisation', a huge kneeling figure holding a trident was located in front of a contemporary building with a glass façade, and I came across a fountain issuing from below a pedestal surmounted by a regal-looking metal stag and a second large artificial fall in front of another modern structure. Cascading noisily in three directions, its enormous volume of water flowed over tall staggered blocks and beneath slabs. That evening, as I made my way to the station – an attractive building with a clock tower and colourful hanging baskets – for the trip to Seattle, Washington, I noticed a large lamp-lit fountain with many high-spurting jets. Amongst its list of attractions, Portland had the world's smallest dedicated park: **Mill Ends** at just 24 inches! It consisted of flowers planted in a posthole and boasted a resident leprechaun!

WASHINGTON

Seattle

The first sights to greet me in **Seattle**, on **Puget Sound**, were the well-recognised Space Needle and white window boxes with red flowers on a blue stone façade with yellow pilasters flanking a pink door! I stayed conveniently near **Pike Place Market** next to the waterfront, where bunches of large red peppers were suspended above displays on the footpath outside a greengrocery, and a man played a piano in the street. Across the road, flowers decked the roof of a verandah, above which was a restaurant where I ate overlooking the scene. The most fascinating aspect was the entertaining fish market, where I encountered species of all sizes packed in ice and a fishmonger wearing a T-shirt emblazoned with the words Caution! Low Flying Fish – I soon found out why! When a customer made his selection, even up to several kilos in weight, it was thrown by this man and deftly caught in paper by another behind the counter – fish were flying every which way! I guess it was an everyday occurrence for them and just another boring job, but as he was bagging what looked like yabbies or marron he said to me 'If this is exciting for you ma'am, you really need to get out more often', then yelled his intent to toss the crustaceans, the piano belting out a tune in competition. There was also a large array of Dungeness crabs.

I left for a while and returned to try and capture the antics on film without bystanders in the way, and the vendor turned to me with the comment 'Are you *still* here?'! It was a large popular market, with bouquets in baskets, dahlias, daisies and gerberas in buckets, and colourful displays of excellent produce. This included fruits such as apples, pineapples, honeydew and watermelons, and chillies hanging with garlic above bright red tomatoes, shiny green cucumbers, glossy purple eggplant, butternut pumpkin, marrows, carrots, red and green cabbage, spinach, and sweet potatoes.

Vintage Australian trolleys, which I remembered from my childhood, made their way alongside an extensive boardwalk following the waterfront, but this was marred by an ugly bi-level traffic overpass: a massive concrete construction running parallel between the harbour and high-rise of the city, where sun glinted off glass and an amazing blue sky reigned overhead. Nevertheless, the promenade was a pleasant place to stroll, with benches for seating and red and white flowers in planters. I came to a large red and yellow wooden structure, tables and chairs for outdoor eating, and touristy horse and carriage transports.

Leaving the waterfront for the centre, interesting sights included a wall of water in a tree-lined square, a tall narrow skyscraper with a tapering base, a modern fountain, and everywhere flowers in tubs. A small tree-filled square displayed a tall colourful totem portraying the head of an eagle, in an unusual position at the bottom, topped in order by a shark with a victim in its jaws and a gaping-mouthed visage below the horizontally protruding dorsal fin, a second bird, a red racoon-like animal with rings around the eyes, a frog, a humanoid figure holding the head of a creature with long ears and, at the apex, a bird with a long beak.

A character wearing a tall striped top hat like that of Dr Zeus' cat was operating a hot dog stand in the street beside a glass roofed lacy iron gallery sheltering tables and chairs, and another shaded area contained carved wooden images. A special little oasis in the urban rush was the self-enclosed **Waterfall Garden** in **Pioneer Square**. With its plants, flowers, and a 22ft-high drop plunging over a granite wall and boulders, it was uncannily remote from the busy streets around. In another stand of totems (not as colourful), one depicted, from top to bottom, a bird with the face of the sun below its bill, a figure with bulging eyes and a broad nose, its arms enfolding smaller images, another bird, and a second face. The other simply had a single figure on the top.

totem

I joined one of the strangest tours ever offered, almost macabre inasmuch as it documented the death of a city. The 90-minute underground walk below Pioneer Square, accompanied by stories of colourful characters and events narrated by our guide, begun from **Doc Maynard's Public House** (a restored pub), meandered along spooky, musty, dusty passageways, and traced a route beneath a city that was literally rebuilt more than 80 years later on its own ruins. On an ancient bare brick wall of this subterranean metropolis was a sign reading HOTEL, and thick cobwebs congregated beneath pebble-glass panes of overhead pavement skylights with weeds taking hold in cracks. A network of antiquated pipes lay below the reinforced wooden 'ceiling', and we passed a teller's cage before entering the fascinating location of a former department store, with a counter, pictures of old street scenes on wooden panelling behind, and once-polished wood-turned posts. Another area had painted decoration on a wall and cornice (also adorned with cobwebs), and we were confronted by a rusty stained sink, bath and toilet exposed to all who passed by. 'Streets' were littered with rubble, scattered beams, a workman's saw, and a board bearing the words MEETING TONIGHT upended against a wall; there were holes knocked through surfaces, old doors, and some ceramic decoration on brickwork. In sections it was pitch black, the type of eerie environs one would consider agreeable to a scary ghostly presence.

Back in the light of day, making my way to a high point for stunning vistas of Seattle and Puget Sound, I came across interesting housing and a talented violinist performing in the street. From the elevation, it was easy to pick out the intricate white ironwork arches of the **Pacific Science Centre** and, looming above all else, the Space Needle. On the way back, I found a partially half-timbered brick house with manicured lawns and immaculate red and yellow flowerbeds and a wooden residence with a shingled belvedere, attic window, and a delightfully haphazard multicoloured English country garden. Another had an eyebrow window in the roof above the entrance and a cat sunning itself behind the glass of a shingled turret. A closer encounter with the **Space Needle** revealed an outside elevator, and gazing up it had all the appearance of a flying saucer overhead, outlined by a very blue sky. A large pool outside the Science Centre featured a couple of fountains and was home to prehistoric dinosaurs including a woolly mammoth and triceratops.

My next visit was to the **Aquarium**, where fantastic fish included a neon-blue variety with a yellow tail and tropical vertically striped black-and-yellow fish swimming sedately in and out of weeds and corals. A black-and-white-striped species with a yellow tail looked like they were wearing football jerseys, and a spotted exhibit hovered motionless near the bottom. Small black fish with white spots flitted and darted amongst orange anemones. It was intriguing to watch a large crab walk slowly on four spindly hind appendages, looking all moving legs and arms like an ungainly stick creature. Also featured were pink and brilliant red starfish, sea urchins with red, white or purple spines, bright green and delicate pink or white anemones with waving tentacles, and a white variety with a frilled edge on a stalk. Showing only slight movement of tails, a shoal of red fish appeared suspended, and I watched from below as seals gracefully turned and revolved in the water; cute cuddly looking sea otters performed the same manoeuvres as they floated in typical fashion on their backs.

Jimi Hendrix was a native of Seattle.

MONTANA

Glacier Park

I rejoined the train for a journey to the Big Sky Country of **Montana**, past clear green rivers with beds of white stone, thick forest, jagged mountains, and waterfalls. It was an overnight trip and sunset produced vermilion-and-grey cloud reflected in a steel-grey lake. The following morning introduced some yellow foliage, blue water, rapids, white cliffs and pale pines. Affording remarkable reflections in still sections, the river changed to an emerald ribbon flowing between walls of grey rock, which appeared like white marble at the waterline. I was travelling on regular rail routes but many still provided a host who went from carriage to carriage with a commentary. Amtrak also provided excellent route maps with descriptions of all the towns and points of interest along the way. The line travelled up and down gradients beside a river fluctuating from narrow to comparatively dry flood plain. Sunlit sections of yellow growth appeared on banks backed by rugged ranges with high pink-tinged cloud above, one grey patch lying over the crater-like top of a solitary perpendicular tor like smoke billowing from a chimney. With a deep-blue lake below and the prevailing dull conditions creating sharply etched summits, the scene looked like a painting on an artist's easel, and an Indian tepee appeared in a small clearing on the far bank. By this time I was in Montana, and disembarked at **Glacier Park** station with a couple of friendly Canadians who were heading across the border to their home in **Pincher Creek**, Canada. They extended an invitation to join them, which I gratefully accepted, and we motored past scorched earth with patches of low green scrub and huge rocky outcrops like flat-topped mesas. It was a constantly changing vista that also presented fir forests with a mountain backdrop, the cloud settling like snow on ridges below blue sky and forming elevated cover overhead. In the distance, an exceedingly blue lake lay at the foot of stony white slopes.

CANADA

ALBERTA

Waterton Lake

Crossing the border, we came to a windblown teal-blue **Waterton Lake** surrounded by majestic mountains with the exposed Prince of Wales Hotel perched on a windswept plateau at the foot. I took a boat cruise on the lake, and from different angles the water alternated from shades of indigo to turquoise, and mountains varied from thickly vegetated to limestone slopes with pockets of pines and other trees. It was still extremely windy, and light filtering through intermittent gaps in heavy clouds with sombre grey underbellies silvered the surface of the lake. This was the world's first **International Peace Park** (1932), called **Waterton Lakes National Park** on the Canadian side of the boundary – a line cleared in the growth – which we crossed to **Glacier National Park** on the United States side. We sailed past mighty mountains covered in green conifers interspersed with yellow foliage, rock faces of red, white and grey, and saw two bald eagles, at that time a threatened species. Close in shore, the water took on the green hue of the tall trees, and the edges of grey clouds were silvered by light emerging from the centre of the canopy. As we neared the end of the cruise, the cover finally cleared to reveal a blue sky, and we passed by the green-roofed **Prince of Wales Hotel** sitting on its perch above brilliant blue water, with the mountains looming behind. It was an imposing six-storey structure with gables, dormers, and a spire in the middle of the roof, but completely dwarfed by its magnificent surroundings. A plate glass wall in the front afforded stunning views over the fiord-like lake and its encompassing peaks.

In the small alpine village, I came across two beautiful shy deer, their white backsides uppermost as they grazed on grass between trees. On the roadway opposite housing, a group of bighorn sheep included two lambs. A short walk brought me to an interesting waterfall flowing down slanting rock strata into a clear but shallow emerald pool. Trees lined the crest and mountains rose up behind. From the top of the fall I could see across to the lake.

Early next morning, I decided to take a solo walk in the park, which could well have had disastrous consequences because I could easily have become a bear's breakfast. Without the benefit of prior warnings (issued at ranger stations) to create noise by clapping hands or ringing bells, and thereby alerting any bears in the vicinity of your approach, I was doing the exact opposite, moving with the utmost stealth in the hope of spotting deer. My mistake was only pointed out to me by another early morning hiker, a very apprehensive man who had turned back but then asked if he could accompany me for security – and duly placed me in front! Nevertheless, it was a worthwhile exercise because although I saw no wildlife the scenery was tremendous, with the deepest of blue water, mountains, parallel threads of white cloud appearing as if swept across a blue sky, and **Waterton** village far below. Other summits had dense cloud above, and I passed a stream tumbling and gurgling through fir trees to plunge over stepped red rock. A higher fall cascaded down a steep escarpment.

Below a distant pyramid peak, I caught sight of two patches of blue like crater lakes. Emerging from between stands of tall timber, a green inlet emptied into a turquoise body of water enclosed by an immense flat-topped natural amphitheatre, and golden autumn leaves blowing on branches in the foreground framed the blue stretch of Waterton Lake, its surface silvered in the distance by reflections of cloud. Patches of yellow stood out amongst the green clothing hillsides. In winter this area was subject to avalanches, which could be triggered by rain, sudden changes in temperature, or a fresh snowfall, and with a rumbling roar reach speeds of over 200km/h. The interlude left me with an ambition to return to the Canadian Rockies, which I did in a subsequent heli-hiking trip (refer Canada 1996, book 2).

My kind friends transferred me back to Glacier Park, passing picture perfect scenes composed of a sparkling clear stream running over rocks between banks lined with green and yellow trees in a valley surrounded by mountains. In the small village of **Essex**, we stopped at the rustic half-timbered **Izaac Walton Inn**, the yard containing a tepee fastened with sticks and decorated with the moon and stars, triangles, and paw prints. We also paused at two lakes: one a rich blue with a white pebble beach and mountains beyond, the other, also surrounded by peaks, green and quiet with lovely reflections. Glacier Park, in an area of 50 'living' glaciers and 9,000 to 10,466ft mountains, had an interesting lodge partially constructed with trees estimated to be 600 years old. In the large lobby, stuffed eagles hung overhead and a white bearskin was draped across a balcony. Other examples of the taxidermist's craft included two white long-haired mountain goats and the heads of bighorn sheep and deer (represented by elk and caribou) mounted on rough-hewn timber columns. Ochre-coloured walls held paintings of the park, and lanterns hung from the rough log ceiling, their shades, made from hide, bearing Indian motifs of animals, people in canoes, tepees, trees, fish, Indians hunting buffalo with spears, men firing guns, and mountains. A moose head was mounted above a large fireplace, its stone lintel engraved with cattle or donkeys, a decorated tepee, a bird, stick figures with feathers in their hair, and one on horseback wearing a full headdress and carrying a spear. The central image depicted a snake coiled around arrows, and to the right was a sailing ship, men wearing hats and carrying guns, a bullock-drawn wagon, and women in long dresses. A more sophisticated rendition of a peace pipe was painted on one side.

I was given a tour along the **Going-to-the-Sun Road** in a big old red bus with a canvas top, which was rolled back in favourable weather. Traversing narrow tracks lined by tall conifers, we passed a brown creek with stony white banks and massive mountains with green skirts and creviced grey granite tops with greenery in pockets. Our route climbed to a high place providing panoramas of a twisting thread of water flowing through a narrow valley between pale green slopes and clumps of yellow mingled with thick darker green foliage. Rising above all, the grey mountains were predominantly flat on top, and we turned one corner to be confronted by a sheer rock wall towering directly in front of us. Another viewpoint showed us alpine flowers in the grassy meadows of a valley between pine-clad slopes that framed a peak with lingering snow in crevices. We caught the glimpse of a river looking very small far below. Here, I saw my only wild mountain goat, its shaggy coat a pristine white. We made another stop at a nice waterfall, its individual drops falling like scintillating gemstones and a lovely rainbow arcing across the middle. At ground level again, and by the river, all the wondrous pinnacles and jagged ridges loomed overhead, and more snow and a glacier were visible.

Going-to-the-Sun Road

At teal-blue **St Mary Lake**, its pine-fringed banks surrounded by monolithic mountains, a perfect cone of pale grey stood out, assuming the appearance of a snow-covered peak. As the day lengthened, the lake turned indigo, which changed to a charcoal shade like polished steel cut by a shining silver path, and copper-coloured leaves on the foreshore were lit from a cloud swept sky. The black ridgeback spine of silhouetted mountains lay beyond the lake, and minute **St Mary's Island**, supporting a few pines, sat in the middle. More superb scenery followed.

AMERICA

IDAHO

Lewiston and the Snake River

From the park, I crossed into **Idaho**, native state of Ernest Hemingway and famous for potatoes; in fact, I even brought a couple home – in the form of badges! I made my first stop at **Lewiston** with its quaint adobe Trailhead Saloon, and embarked upon an exciting speedboat trip up the **Snake River** in **Hell's Canyon**, the deepest gorge in North America, its twisting course carved by the river. Passing first an old riverboat, perfectly mirrored even to the sun winking off its funnels, we came to an astounding mountain composed of long grey-and-brown rock 'crystals', their multi-faceted vertical formations appearing behind yellow trees at the base. The ever-changing terrain then displayed a stepped area like huge mounds of mud stacked one atop another, followed by smooth, softly rounded reddish monuments of nature's creation. The high-water mark was denoted by a line of white rock, and there were some fantastic formations on boulder-strewn banks.

We negotiated some of the best white water in the northwest (churning class IV and V rapids) but still found quiet sections producing beautiful reflections in the narrow waterway with its towering, creviced and craggy sides. There was little growth, and colours of the rugged rock fluctuated between black, red, grey, white and brown. The hues of the water also varied from green to blue depending on the depth, and for a change we experienced brilliant blue sky with just a few white clouds. Intriguing sections featured a single band of green trees between grey boulders on the shore and a backdrop of both smooth and rough-textured dun-coloured mountains. We came to a solitary pine tree and a flight of ducks escaping the roar of our engine, whilst near a sandy beach, another bird kept pace with our craft. Rising beyond banks covered with dried grasses, we began to encounter massive rounded and pyramid-shaped yellow hills with red summits, and we came across one large isolated homestead. This area also included a wall of 'organ pipes' and it was fascinating to watch as we rapidly approached those boiling parts of the river. Nearing the end, we passed beneath looming rust-coloured mountains with black-and-white boulders at the base, and I was amazed by the surprise revelation of a protected rock surface covered with 2,000-year-old petroglyphs depicting bighorn sheep and stick figures with weapons.

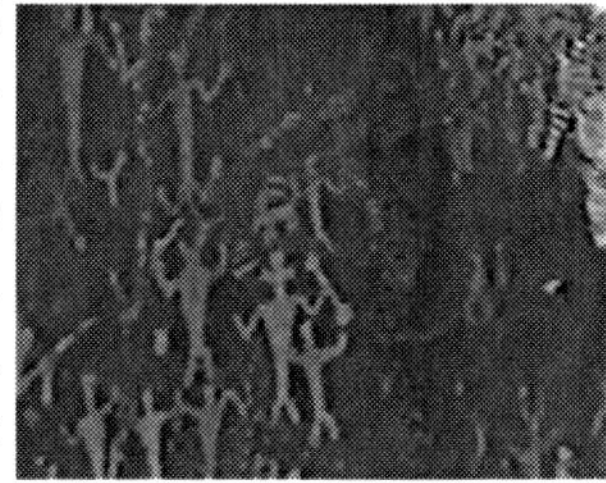

primitive rock art

Boise

Moving on to the capital, **Boise**, I captured more river scenery with the golden tones of autumn amongst the green, a lake with Canada Geese, perfect pictures of a bubbling brook bordered by pines and lacy yellow trees with black trunks, and of course mountains. Bounded by pine-dressed slopes, the highway followed a watercourse that raced, raged and roiled in stepped cascades alongside.

My initial film in the city was of a particularly attractive huge paved plaza with red, white and purple petunias in concrete tubs, a many-jetted fountain, trees, a bronze tableau of three boys playing marbles, and river-washed stones in a shallow pond with a metal stork, its wings spread, perched on sculpted metal logs, whilst umbrellas of different colours shaded tables and chairs behind. The grey stone **Capitol Building** was approached via a vibrant multihued flowerbed set in green lawn. Shrubs planted in symmetry filled a grassed circle located before the entrance, which had a scale replica of the Liberty Bell at the base of its staircase. Pathways were flanked by mixed red and yellow blooms. Because it was early evening the windows were lighted, and I observed a draped headless statue and marble columns within.

Trees and flowers in another lovely landscaped area provided the foreground to an edifice with a needle spire on top, and I walked along a street featuring different-coloured neat wooden houses with lawns, flowerbeds, and weeping trees. Pink pelargonium, even on the verge, grew in front of a grey dwelling with white trim next to a yellow house, and a white façade with grey shutters was enhanced with mauve and purple pelargonium. A bright garden beautified a street corner, and a bird bath graced the middle of a bed in lawn beneath a spreading peppermint tree.

WYOMING

Yellowstone

Two sisters provided an excellent tour, the first stops being a picturesque log church called **The Little Church in the Pines** with a low bell tower on the roof, followed by a log mill-house in dense forest beside a weed-filled river in which, together with its waterwheel, it was reflected. Making an early start in anticipation of a long day, it was extremely cold, and sculpted clouds of grey, apricot and white made a striking picture as we came to log farm buildings with horses in a corral. Our ultimate destination was **Yellowstone National Park** in **Wyoming** (the world's first, established in 1872), and on first entering I was excited to see a large herd of elk, the male with a massive rack (they can have a spread of six feet), browsing on a vast flat plain covered with dry grasses through which flowed a blue river with blackened trees, the result of fire, standing sentinel on slopes behind. I was even lucky enough to record the reedy high-pitched sound of their call (bugle), strange for such a large majestic animal.

elk

Sheer rock walls tinged with yellow lichen, pines miraculously clinging to their sides, confined a fast-flowing river with a rock tor in the rapids, and we came to a tumultuous fall tumbling over massive boulders and through a narrow cleft to the sometimes mossy-edged waterway.

Nearby, a striped squirrel hopped with agitated movements, and I was thrilled to have my first close-up encounter with a bison, its body looking disproportionate with the huge woolly head and hump, solid shoulders, and slender hindquarters. They weigh up to 2,000lbs and can sprint at 30mph.

falls in Yellowstone

I have been privileged to experience the mighty thermal areas in both New Zealand and Iceland, but nothing compared to those in Yellowstone, which contained 10,000 hot springs and geysers, two thirds of the world's total. Our first sight was of a river with steam rising from a pool behind. Filming towards the light, my pictures show a silver river in front of white mist rising to a sky covered by grey cloud above blackened hills and trees – striking black and white vistas. This was followed by an area of yellow grasses and scant trees beyond a rapidly boiling blue pool, its grey edges rimmed with lime and a herd of bison in the distance. The thermal area was composed of a series of such pools, but streams provided abundant water to support the animal inhabitants, although the grass was dry and dead trees were still prominent. Also in the distance were a series of plumes rising like smoke from unseen chimneys, and we came to a gaggle of Canada Geese strutting in an area of red-and-yellow groundcover near a patch of water with a geyser erupting in the middle, almost obscured by dense steam that blew towards it, competing with pink, purple and grey cloud overhead. A grotesquely picturesque scene consisted of light vapour wafting across stark dead trees standing and reflected in shallow still water lying on grey-and-reddish mud, with yellowed grasses and green firs in the distance.

thermal area

The colours, created by deposits from the mineral laden water, heat resistant algae, or bacteria, were incredible; bubbles rose lazily from a turquoise pool with a white rim, and there was a hint of green in red-and-yellow travertine (calcium carbonate) banks from which issued clouds of billowing steam. From one large crater, camouflaged by its thick vapour, I could hear the faint plip-plop and just discern the spurting mud forming grey banks. Surrounded by white rocks (with evidence of sulphur) and yellow vegetation, gases noisily burst forth from fumaroles (vents) in the ground – it was also extremely smelly!

The area was accessed via a network of boardwalks with green trees in the background. A particularly beautiful quiet aqua-coloured pool with a gentle veil of mist reflected its surroundings. Enclosed by mounds of red-and-grey cracked earth like a moonscape, a larger steaming cauldron of bubbling liquid had tiny fumaroles alongside. The molten core of the earth was close to the surface here, and the entire site was a boiling seething mass of primeval force. The heavy grey cloud canopy overhead added to the feeling of awesome power, whilst steam billowed everywhere in gentle or fierce jets. Relieved by red and white, an extensive expanse of grey contained an extremely active yellow-rimmed blue pool continuously spouting high into the air, with yellow grass, low hills, and steam blowing across another pool in the background. A pristine patch of white set off a deep-blue stretch of quiet water, and twisted branches made a good foreground to another vapour-covered and perfectly rounded pool. White calcified trunks and exposed root systems lay like skeletons in shallow rust-coloured and mottled yellow sections.

thermal area

Presenting a different face, a rushing blue fresh watercourse had fuming rivulets running into it, creating additional clouds of steam where the two collided at the base of silica-like terraces coloured brown, green and ochre. Originally called Yellow Rock by the Indians, it was these terraces that gave the park its name, but of these I missed the best, **Mammoth Hot Springs**. In a comparatively subdued section where rainbow colours lay in patches on the surface, the oft-repeated phrase 'like an artist's palette' definitely applied; in fact, this area was called **Fountain Paint Pots**. Another perfectly rounded red-ringed blue pool appeared painted on a grey and white canvas with yellow and green plant life as a backdrop. A larger area reflected pines and, different again, a wide expanse of ridged mud in shades of brown, sienna and vibrant vermilion, partially covered by water, reflected trees and was in places silvered by both the light and mirrored grey cloud as vapour drifted gently across from a vigorous area behind. The swirls of faint and bold intermingled colours were like modern paintings and extraordinarily beautiful.

Another hill arrayed in burnt trees was fronted by steam, turquoise water, brown boulders, and calcified white trunks on red earth. A vivid blue pool, orange at the edges, was located right beside a deep-blue freshwater stream crossing a white, yellow, russet and green plain covered with belching steam vents. In the distance, towering eruptions reached for the firmament above, and a second herd of shaggy bison with a few calves roamed at the foot of the blackened hillsides as they grazed.

bison

Just when I thought I had seen it all, I came to a green pool with an emerald edge abutting an almost purple lightly steaming patch, the two separated by a narrow strip of red and white earth from a calm sapphire-blue pond reflecting a few small white clouds; the river and green pines lay just beyond. Surrounded by dry grass, a large flat field of white contained petrified roots and deep holes with green and red lichens around their rims, which emitted gurgling sounds and small puffs of steam. One was enclosed by vibrantly hued rings of red, orange and yellow like a rainbow. Others were filled with water that splashed and splattered whilst steam and noise erupted from their depths, and a brilliant patch of red lay dramatically on the white; it was both fascinating and frightening at the same time. Water surging upwards from one opening in the earth spilled over rock yellowed by the minerals it contained. In contrast, an eerily silent scene had steam floating like fog across upright black trunks and fallen white logs on a white, yellow and orange scorched land. Apart from the unfenced boardwalks, there were no safety precautions to prevent people approaching these numerous manifestations of Mother Nature's terrifying force.

The enormous **Old Faithful Inn**, with its shingles and gables, high log ceiling and walls, and huge 500-ton stone fireplace in the galleried lobby, was originally constructed in 1885 but destroyed by fire in 1894 and rebuilt utilising local materials in 1903. After investigating the inn it was time to explore more of the park. Nearby, stark white petrified trees, remnants of forest buried by volcanic ash, were reflected in a large but placid rich blue waterhole with a wide, vivid orange rim surrounded by a swathe of white. Sporadic wisps of vapour rose against another backdrop of dead trees, clouds of steam issued from a continuously spouting geyser that was separated from the river only by its rim, and there was a small amount of dry vegetation.

Another turquoise pool was enclosed by wide bands of brilliant yellow and orange, which was divided from a belt of green trees by a narrow strip of white. More burnt forest was the backdrop for a clearing with swirls of red and orange interspersed with white, like snow on a Martian landscape. An unruffled but steaming emerald pool had a mustard-coloured rim bordered by white. I felt compelled to describe so many because each was different and they appealed to me tremendously.

We finally came to one of the highlights of the park, **Old Faithful**, putting on a spectacular show every 90 minutes. Spurting a powerful plume up to 60m (200ft) into the air, it formed a mushroom cloud that rapidly dispersed, greyed, and became confused with clouds in the very blue heavens, completely obliterating the view of pine-clad hills behind. We enjoyed a delicious lunch prepared and set out on a red and white checked cloth by the ladies, before continuing on to thundering **Yellowstone Falls**, dropping into 2,100ft-deep **Yellowstone River Canyon** and churning between stark rock walls similar to those at the falls described earlier. The indigo **Yellowstone Lake** was also surrounded by activity, which included smoking fumaroles and a milky blue pool bounded by red grasses and white lime, all with the brilliant lake just beyond, its surface broken by whitecaps in the continuing windy conditions. Waves lapped the white shore covered with bleached timber debris, vermilion patches, and a glistening lime-green rill, almost like liquid gold, called **Lakeside Spring**, which trickled from a patch of blue water. Nearby, more small boiling mud pots and steaming orange and blue holes were so close that the waves almost washed over them. Also on the edge, I observed a perfect white cone with a small crater like a miniature volcano and a rippling deep-blue but clear pool with a yellow and white rim. Like a river of molten lava, mixed colours of rust and yellow spread with stunning effect across the white shore right to the blue lake, and quiet sienna-coloured pools were separated from a steaming sapphire cauldron by its white rim. An elevated platform overlooked a multihued surface with green grass and stunted trees, a channel connecting two small olive-green pools, and an array of ponds in various tones of blue. It was a peculiar phenomenon that even with the proximity of these adjacent pools ranging from pale to dark blue, some were milky, some clear, some steaming, and some still. In this desolate but incredibly beautiful place, I even saw a startling red waterhole encased in its white cocoon. Finally, an area with the white trunks of dead trees emerging from white ground looked uncannily like a snowy landscape.

In summary: The thermal theatre that is Yellowstone had its origins in a cataclysmic eruption that covered most of North America in ash around 600,000 years ago. It left this giant caldera that features the most extensive area of geothermal activity in the world. A multitude of hot springs dot thermal basins, geysers hurl thousands of gallons of boiling water skyward, hissing steam vents punctuate valley floors, and petrified tree stumps, remnants of a primeval forest buried by the volcanic ash, stand starkly on the eroded terrain.

The Tetons

Leaving the park, we passed a shimmering blue watercourse winding between and around banks of grasses that glowed red in the sun and powerful **Lewis Falls** gushing down a cleft between steep slopes, their sides coated with yellow growth, dropping to the **Lewis River**. A great amount of dead timber had washed down and was piled up near the foot of the falls. From the top of a cliff one could follow the course of the river between blackened slopes with naked dead trees, the yellow now only at the waterline.

The day was drawing to a close as we neared the **Grand Teton National Park**, its sawtooth range featuring ten mile-high summits. Striking the scene, the waning sun transformed leaves and grass to copper, silvered the lake, cloaked the mountains with a filmy veil, and turned aspens to gold and bronze. We stopped at a rustic wooden church with this magnificent panorama visible through the chancel window. I walked down to the blue lake where yellow and green trees grew right to the stony grey shore, and struck by the light, a grey mountain opposite appeared almost white. Deep crevices held remains of winter snow, and I filmed the vista framed by the trunk and a spreading branch of a gnarled old pine. Except for the gentle lap of the water and slight rustle of leaves in the wind, it was totally quiet and peaceful, the trees, lake and mountains shining in the last rays of the sun.

the Tetons

Further on, we came to a herd of browsing deer in a dry open field, which later took flight and raced away. A few final pictures of a scintillating blue river in front of an orderly row of upright yellow and golden aspens, with glimpses of snow on peaked crests behind, concluded the scenic aspect of my day.

Jackson Hole

We pulled into photogenic **Jackson Hole**, sheltered in the lee of mountains and featuring unique archways composed entirely of antlers, many false-fronted timber, shingle, and log buildings with covered verandahs, a wooden clock tower – and a real Wild West feeling. The saloon had a cowboy riding a bucking horse (in neon) on top of the Million Dollar Cowboy Bar (boasting stools created from genuine saddles!), and names of stores included Ralph Lauren, Ride Out, and Jackson Depot Stage Stop. Houses were also constructed of timber and logs. Continuing on, past more jagged ridges and cattle contentedly grazing in a yellow field with a lone golden aspen, I was finally deposited back in Idaho, this time at Idaho Falls, at the conclusion of a very long but totally exhilarating day.

Standrod House

IDAHO

Idaho Falls

Idaho Falls was memorable for its central dam with a low but wide fall spilling over a wall onto boulders, one section occupied by a long line of geese all standing and facing the same direction. The dam confined the blue Snake River, creating a vast, perfectly still stretch, which reflected the impressive white **Mormon Temple**, its stepped pillars forming a central spire with the white figure of Angel Moroni on top, standing out against a clear blue sky. A lovely landscaped greenbelt alongside the river had colourful garden beds, one encompassing a native Indian carving, and rivulets ran over rocks into the main watercourse. I admired more amazing mirror images as I strolled, with just birds and butterflies for company, on a glorious summer morning. A large number of white and Canada Geese were swimming (disturbing the perfect reflections), waddling, or lying in the shade of a tree.

Idaho Falls

Idaho Falls façade

Pocatello

As a guest of Cart Transportation, I made a visit to historic **Standrod House** in **Pocatello**, a large grey mansion constructed from rough-textured stone blocks, with a shingled roof, turrets, gables, a spacious covered portico, and a verandah with wood-turned balustrades and posts. Inside, it displayed lacy ironwork, swagged drapes, an ornate metal fireguard, carved chairs, and walls papered with Regency stripes, a checked pattern, and fussy floral on a dark background.

The townsite was rustic, featuring false-fronted timber and brick buildings and a sorry-looking zoo with most inmates in austere concrete-floored cages. A sad-looking grizzly was constrained in a small wire enclosure with water running over boulders, a pretty puma (cougar) paced from one side to the other on the cement floor of a similar cage, a fox-like coyote with its bushy tail and long muzzle had a box-like den, and a spotted lynx, tufts of fur on the tips of its pointed ears, was housed in the same conditions. A couple of dainty but bedraggled, extremely miserable-looking red foxes were sitting and standing respectively on tree stumps – with painted greenery in the background! A solitary rotund raccoon with a striped tail was actively foraging with human-like hands in a creek flowing from a thin fall of water and channelled along the concrete floor of its enclosure. The creature seemed intently engaged in the aimless pursuit of picking up pebbles, rubbing them vigorously together between its palms, and depositing them elsewhere – amusing to watch.

raccoon washing pebbles

After this diversion, the fat furry critter straddled the artificial stream on all fours and then laboriously climbed a log propped against a tree, this latter providing some degree of comfort in its compound. The animals all appeared healthy, and I like to think that they had better or at least adequate accommodation for the night.

raccoon

Oregon Trail

I moved on to the replica of **Old Fort Hall** trading post (1834) on the route of the massive migration of the Great Trek West – the **Oregon Trail**. Inside its whitewashed stone walls, I found a well (complete with bucket), a covered wagon and scattered wheels, a corral, shingle-roofed log workshops, and similar living quarters shaded by a canvas awning. A tepee was also set up in the compound. Besides its stone fireplace, the interior of the blacksmith's shop exhibited a bellows operated by rope attached to a long wooden handle, horseshoes, a leather apron, harness such as bridles, a vice, grindstone, and other accoutrements of the trade. The actual trading store held stone jars, a wooden crate labelled Best Procurable Scotch Whisky, mugs, knives in scabbards, a chest, traps, clothing, furs and pelts, beads, books, blankets, barrels and bolts of cloth.

A single man's sleeping quarters were adorned with a mounted deer head, the complete skin of a cougar on the pallet, candles, harness, a steer skull, and a bear skin and other hides on log walls, possibly assisting to keep out draughts through chinks. The only other furnishings were a table, a trunk with a pelt on top, a wooden barrel, cane chair, and one fashioned from saplings. A second room had the heads of a glassy-eyed moose, deer and a bison mounted on its timber walls, a crude chair (with a fur seat) made from branches tied with twine, a wooden chest, lantern, skull, and a skin on the bed. A slaughter house contained a chopping block with a cleaver and knives, a metal box, hurricane lantern, stone jars, cast-iron boilers, and a shelf with metal plates.

The kitchen of more-elaborate living quarters featured a wooden table and bench seat, a cabinet and shelves with crockery and glass jars, a broom, barrel, wooden chairs, a lantern, copper kettle, butter churn, tin trunk, and a fur on the floor. A skin, rifle and powder horn, and the picture of a rider hung on the whitewashed stone walls of another room, whilst books and candlesticks lay on a small table. Pegs hung with a fringed garment and dresses, a bed, two chairs, dressers (one with basin and ewer, the other bottles), hides on the floor, a wooden cradle, chests, a mirror, lantern, and two pictures – one of a rider, the second of Indians with tepees – comprised the bedroom. Lastly, a second kitchen was equipped with a split-log table and benches, utensils were suspended from a log beam above the stone fireplace, a long-handled pan hung on the front, an iron was placed on the mantel, a

fort kitchen

cauldron sat on a rack over coals, and boilers and a ladle were suspended at the sides. Herbs and corn hung from rafters.

The Oregon Trail was the most important wagon route. The longest in history, it stretched around 2,000 miles over plains, mountains and deserts. In the greatest peacetime migration of the world, between 1842 and 1860 some 300,000 people travelled the trail, a gruelling journey battling the fury of suffocating dust storms, intense heat, pounding rain, freezing snow and physical hardships.

Idaho Falls

Here, I would like to insert another story about the kindness of Americans. I had filmed a beautiful display of roses outside the Tourist Information Office in Idaho Falls, which was some distance from the centre, and was making my way back to town along the road verge. There were few footpaths in the United States because Americans did not seem to walk anywhere; in fact, it was such a strange sight to see that a vehicle stopped beside me to inquire if I was OK. When I replied in the affirmative they drove off, only to return on the other side of a median strip because they had been travelling in the opposite direction to me. The family insisted on giving me a lift and invited me to their home, eventually going out of their way to drive me many miles to Craters of the Moon National Monument. My onward bus trip to Rapid City in South Dakota being a very late departure, I checked out of my accommodation (again at their urging), spent the evening with them, slept, and was awakened by the husband who transferred me to the bus depot. This was my first encounter with Mormons, and I must stress that I found them to be a genuine and loving family that never once mentioned their faith, let alone tried to convert me; it did more to further an appreciation of the beliefs by which they actually lived than any sermon.

Craters of the Moon

Craters of the Moon

The wilderness called **Craters of the Moon** was a vast (75 sq km) bleak swathe of stark black lava and boulders, with whitened dead trees and exposed root systems providing a graphic contrast; it was a weird moonscape traditionally avoided by Indians, pioneers, ranchers and miners alike. A deathly silence also pervaded and hung over this plain of black crazed lava, sharp edged pillars of cinder crags, sponge-like pumice, and smooth rounded slopes. The fissures, volcanic cones and lava flows began erupting 15,000 years ago and ceased only 2,000 years ago. Over the millennia a few clumps of green and dry grasses had taken hold, and surveyed from a hill it was easy to trace the original paths of the rivers of molten rock, with sparse vegetation on dull brown sandy wastes between. The parched and burnt landscape stretched in every direction, almost as far as the eye could see, and one outcrop was coloured red with mineral content. The desolate black terrain was thrown into even more dramatic relief against a blue sky, and sun glinted off particles (probably obsidian) in the ancient lava.

The area featured expanses of *A'a* (sharp and jagged) lava, *Pahoehoe* (relatively smooth), and lava tubes, formed when the surface cooled and hardened, thus protecting the molten lava underneath and enabling it to keep moving, eventually leaving a tunnel. Some contained stalactites created by the dripping of the molten rock before cooling. More diverse scenery was apparent on the return as we drove past brown rocky outcrops on red and yellow earth confining a small blue lake. This changed to an area of red formations, tumbled in places like huge devil's marbles, which was transformed yet again to hills with a smattering of pine trees.

SOUTH DAKOTA

Dakota is an alternative name for the **Sioux** Indian, who counts amongst his illustrious forebears Sitting Bull, Crazy Horse, Red Cloud, Little Crow and Big Foot. Tepee (*tipi*) is a Sioux word meaning dwelling, and their beautiful artwork featured stunning geometrical patterns created with porcupine quills.

Rapid City

First sights in **Rapid City**, situated at an altitude of 3,240ft and where I stayed at the Tip Top Motor Hotel, were the **Capitol Building**, a store with the delightful name of Prairie Rose, timber structures, flowers in tubs, and the bronze statue of a miner's donkeys laden with a pack, pickaxe and shovel. Not a particularly interesting city, the most elaborate structure was a three-storey red edifice with a turret, gables, dormers, tall chimneys, and an iron-railed balcony. Colourful scenic art decorated a wall, an onion dome topped the turret of the

Buell Building (1889), and the historic multistorey **Hotel Alex Johnson** (1927) featured a combination of classic European architecture and Lakota Sioux Indian art. Amongst signs in the lobby was a swastika, a symbol used (like the Hindus) by Native Americans since prehistoric times. The **Buell Building** had housed a variety of stores and offices over the years, including the Weather Bureau when flags indicating the forecast flew from the top of the 'onion'.

Situated on green lawns but having few gardens, lovely wooden houses with many gables and small porches lined a wide tree-filled boulevard. One was red but most were white or pastel shades, including a pretty pink house with white trim, a dormer window in its steeply pitched grey roof, and an unusual platform fenced with wrought iron balanced on top. The roof of a rounded section created a balcony accessed from the first floor. Making a striking picture behind scarlet plants, a large two-storey all white home on a corner block featured a belvedere and several gables. An attractive yellow and white dwelling was enhanced with a large spray of artificial sunflowers beside the front door, and another had a tiny window behind delicate trim at the apex of a steep gable. As I was to find in Salt Lake City, streets were planned wide enough for a horse- or ox-drawn wagon to turn easily. In the **Sioux Museum**, a primitive decorated hide featured myriad small images depicting feathered Indians and black-hatted white men, horses, bison, a dog or wolf, houses and a log cabin, tepees, a smoking railway engine, a wagon, flag, boots, a sword, drums, a horsehair switch, a rider, and a bear.

illustrated hide

Mount Rushmore

I was given a seat on a Gray Line bus tour to the splendid site of **Mt Rushmore National Monument**. We went through the appealing gold town of **Keystone** (9,300ft) with its low but colourful false-fronted wooden buildings, their awnings forming covered sidewalks. They featured quaint names such as Rattlesnake Jakes, Readers Mine (a bookstore), Reds Export Outpost, Candy Pantry, Indian Den, The Critters House, Rosewood Gallery, Dakota Originals, Black Hills Gifts & Gold, and Historic Ruby House.

Originally a gold mining town, the first important discovery occurred in 1894 when William Franklin found a large gold nugget and staked his claim. The trend was to name mines after wives, so Franklin called his Holy Terror! Keystone's other claim to fame was as the home of Carrie Ingalls Wilder of *Little House on the Prairie.*

The four gigantic, incredibly realistic faces of George Washington, Thomas Jefferson, Theodore Roosevelt and Abraham Lincoln, visible for 60km, were an engineering as well as artistic feat. Begun in 1927 and taking 14 years to complete, each stood 60ft from forehead to chin, a man appearing like a speck against them. Had the work been carried out full scale, each figure in relation to the size of the head would have stood 465ft tall. They appeared white against the brown rock from which they had been carved, and a rubble slope below was host to scattered pines, which also lay thick in the foreground. Through a gap in the mountains, a good view of the profile of Washington was visible from the road.

Mount Rushmore

Our next stop was the venue for an astounding undertaking to create a stupendous likeness of **Chief Crazy Horse**, stabbed in the back by an American soldier in 1877 whilst fighting for his people's land and rights. Hewn from a mountain, partly by blasting, it will eventually become the world's largest sculpture, and it was intriguing to capture the progress of its development against an alabaster scale model of the proposed work in the foreground. This showed the chief seated astride a mount, his left arm extended and forefinger pointing. The dimensions of the head and arm will be 87½ft (nine storeys) high and 263ft long respectively, and the whole will ultimately stand 563ft tall, overwhelming its surroundings when completed many years hence. Begun in 1947, the task has been taken over by his family since the death of the sculptor, Korczak Ziolkowski, in 1982.

An on-site museum displayed a hide with beautiful illustrations portraying Indians, a rabbit, raccoon, beaver, bison, deer and dog.

painted hide

Also in the compound, wonderfully executed in metal and silhouetted against the light, were the **Black Hills Nature Gates**. These depicted a deer, ram and mountain lion, ducks, a stork, other birds perched or in flight, including a raptor with prey in its talons, a squirrel, bear and fox, eagles, a leaping stag, swallows or swifts, an upright prairie dog, a mountain goat, an elk, and plants. We were shown a black bear, fortunately in a large enclosure, and a log trading post called, unimaginatively, The Fort.

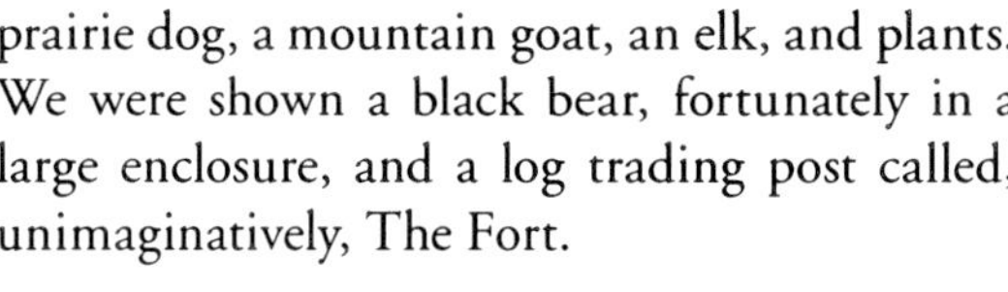

Nature Gates

Back on board, we drove past the white railing fence of a farm and down narrow roads lined with yellow aspen and green firs, the grey mountains looming above. Passing **Sylvan Lake** with its interesting granite formations, we came to what was known as **Needles Highway**. This self-explanatory carriageway was bordered by big boulders and breathtaking stone spires, one featuring the eye of a needle 30 to 40 feet high but only 3 to 4 feet wide. Again, these looked striking when viewed against the sun, and in two places the road cut a passage through the middle; barely the width of the bus, it was necessary to negotiate with care.

Needles Highway

We traversed more avenues of gold, looking incredible against the gigantic tors and blue of the sky, and drove through **Custer State Park**. Named after General George A. Custer, we stopped here to survey bison, bighorn sheep, donkeys wandering the road looking for a handout, and a pretty bubbling brook surrounded by tall trees. We passed through yet another square rock-hewn tunnel, where the presidential statues were magically revealed as we emerged from the darkened interior into the light. We drove back to Rapid City past more green and gold scenery with splashes of red groundcover – hardly the Black Hills of Dakota referred to in the song! Incidentally, the name was attributed to the hills because the thick ponderosa pine forest made them appear black from the plains.

Deadwood

The following day, I was given a private car tour of that famous name from historical annuls, **Deadwood**, so called because of the dead timber on surrounding hills. Originally named Deadwood Gulch, in 1876 gambling halls and brothels sprang up as fast as bars, but when the gold played out all that remained were the drinking and gambling dens and houses of ill repute – plus a reputation as one of the wildest towns in the American West. Now it has been restored, and attractions included a carriage display. Although still with a Wild West flavour, buildings were decidedly different, being mainly higher more-substantial brick constructions without much colour. They included such romantic venues as the **Bullock Hotel**, built in 1895 by Sheriff Seth Bullock who was killed in the 1800s and whose ghost is reputed to remain, and **No. 10 Saloon** (relocated after being burnt down) with its sawdust-covered floor, where **Wild Bill Hickok** was shot in the back in 1876 by Jack McCall. James Hickok's colourful career included service as an army scout, stagecoach guard, hunting guide, and marshal, but his passion was gambling. Legend has it that he was killed whilst holding eights and aces, a full house that became known as 'The dead man's hand'. His actual **Death Chair**, a gun belt slung across the back, was exhibited in a niche above the doorway, along with moose and deer heads on rafters, and long-barrelled rifles and old photographs, including those of Indians, on walls – in total contrast to the multitude of coruscating lights on poker machines! There was also an Indian tomahawk, a sabre, powder horn, rifle and other artefacts arrayed on and around a hide decorated with tepees, men on horseback, and scenes of fighting between Native Americans and white men.

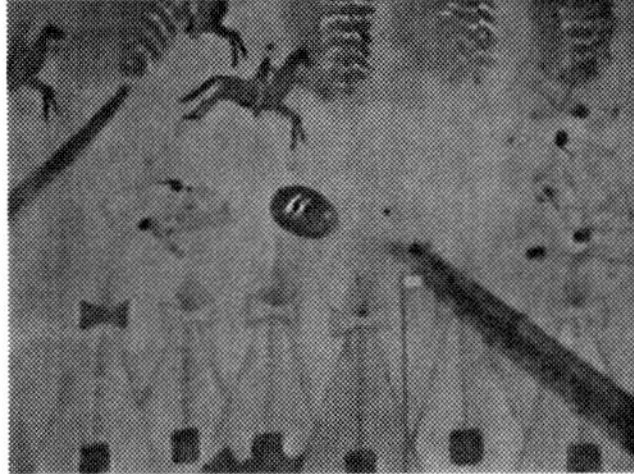
illustrated hide

Another well-known Deadwood identity was Martha Jane Canary (**Calamity Jane**), a Wild West show performer and prostitute who looked, dressed, drank, cursed and shot like a man and in 1876 drove a bullock train from Cheyenne. She was buried in **Mt Moriah Cemetery** on **Boot Hill** alongside Wild Bill and other legendary figures of the Gulch. Lesser known characters included Dora Du Fran, a kind-hearted brothel madam who was buried with her parrot Fred (gargoyles were stationed at each corner of the plot), Potato Creek Johnny, Henry 'Preacher' Smith, Deadwood's first ordained minister, killed by Indians, Seth Bullock, the town's first sheriff and friend of Theodore Roosevelt, and 'Vinegar Bill' shot dead in a brothel and buried naked in a coffin several inches too short! Nowadays the town survives on tourism and gaming, of which latter there were a great many establishments. Colourful names included Legends, Gold Strike, Pink Palace, Eagle Bar, Gold Nugget, Cody's, Gold Dust, Wild Bill Bar, Silver Dollar, Stockade, and French Quarter, with a cancan girl on the sign.

Once playing host to dignitaries including Calvin Coolidge, an imposing hotel with sturdy white pillars was built in 1903 at a cost of $100,000, and other structures featured a tower, turret, and coloured canopies. Picturesque old wooden houses lined upper terraces, and on the outskirts I saw a little white wooden church with a spire. A group of false-fronted wooden buildings included a bright blue shop with a navy and white striped awning and the Lady Luck Saloon with red, white and blue cloth rosettes around the parapet – a real touch of the Old West. Other appropriate names included Stagecoach, Lucky Miner, Starlight, Jackpot Charleys, Wilderness Edge, and Miss Kitty's (The Belle of Deadwood) with mirrored ceilings, crystal chandeliers, and a blaze of flashing lights. One saloon was illustrated with a large bison, a 'cowboy' (live) stood twirling six-guns outside Cousin Jacks, and 'Wild Bill' sat for perpetuity in a chair near the Deadwood Livery.

paper tableau

At the time of my visit, they had just completed the restoration of cobbled roads and installed copies of original streetlamps.

Spearfish Canyon

Not far from Rapid City lay a beautiful replica of the 840-year-old tiered stave church in Borgund, Norway, with steep shingled roofs and an intricately carved dragon's head at the apex of each gable. The interior was also an excellent example of craftsmanship. Surrounded by stone walls and set amongst grass, garden and trees, the site also held a sod-roofed wooden house and a log dwelling with red-flowering plants in window boxes.

A life-sized image of an Indian spearfisherman was located at **Spearfish Creek**, its quiet waters reflecting golden trees. Named by the Indians, it was one of only two in the world to freeze from the bottom up. Again on a private tour, we traversed the length of **Spearfish Canyon**, in the upper reaches of which footage of *Dances with Wolves* was filmed. Mile after mile of absolutely spectacular scenery unfolded before us as we continued along a winding road through this superb wilderness of sheer white rock faces and a multitude of trees with golden autumn foliage amongst the pines. Forested slopes below bare precipices formed the backdrop to abundant streams flowing over stony beds and through dense stands of mostly green and yellow timber interspersed with some apricot tones. A waterfall plummeted down a sheer wall, there was the occasional red plant, and a mammoth white boulder had fallen into one section of the river almost creating a dam. The road was surprisingly free of traffic as we drove enthralled at the glorious vistas, which included whole hillsides of glaring yellow (almost orange) aspens – and always the encompassing mountains.

South Dakota had much to offer and I did not get to see all the attractions, but one exceptional exhibition included a beautiful Indian tableau created entirely from white paper. It depicted a man, a feather in his hair and adorned with fringed leggings, mounted on a horse and carrying a rifle, a woman, her long hair also ornamented with feathers and wearing a bone necklace, riding a horse pulling chattels lashed to a *travois*, and a figure walking behind two children riding bareback. His right hand upraised towards an eagle with outspread wings on a dead tree, one rider sported a bear claw necklace and a feather in his braided hair. Another, in full headdress and carrying a pole decorated with feathers, rode in the lead, and all were beneath a rocky overhang on which lay a dead tree and the skeleton of a beast. Sitting astride a horse and holding aloft the skull of a steer, a solitary figure wore a fringed shirt and a breastplate created from bones. Facial features were extraordinary. Even the rocks and exposed roots of a pine had been crafted from the same material, and the effect produced a ghostly scenario.

WYOMING

Devils Tower

From Rapid City, courtesy of Powder River Transportation, I also visited the 1,267ft **Devils Tower** in Wyoming, the first National Monument in the United States and the world, dedicated by congress in 1906. This grey granite monolith, with strange markings resembling the gouges of giant claws, featured in the film *Close Encounters of the Third Kind.* A Native American legend states that the brother of seven sisters was suddenly transformed into a bear, to escape which the girls, running for their lives, climbed a tree stump that rose into the air. The bear clawed at the bark trying to reach them, and the sisters were borne into the sky to become the stars of the Big Dipper. However, up close the 'score marks' appeared more like elongated crystal-type formations or clustered pillars of rock. In reality it was actually the core of a volcano formed when fiery magma

Devils Tower

erupted through sandstone, cooled underground, contracted, fractured into columns, and was exposed after millions of years of erosion by weather and the **Belle Fourche** (Beautiful Fork) **River**, on one bank of which it sat.

It was clear when I arrived, but it began to rain and a light mist endowed it with an eerie aura. The surrounding terrain featured patches of brilliant red rock, dry grasses, red and yellow trees, and the inevitable green pines. From a distance, it was uncanny the way the monster emerged like an enormous thimble above gentle gradients covered in red and yellow grasses and a few firs. I had been fortunate because it commenced raining heavily and the mountain faded into the background, only to do its reappearing trick when zooming in with the camera. I had been provided with another private car tour because there was no public conveyance, and as we drove back a couple of deer ran across in front of our vehicle and leapt the roadside barrier.

This was a region that attracted such characters as Butch Cassidy and the Sundance Kid.

COLORADO

Denver

It was necessary to go through **Cheyenne**, capital of Wyoming, to reach Denver, but the city had absolutely nothing to recommend it, I did not even take one photograph.

I celebrated my birthday on the train to **Denver**, **Colorado**; a fellow lady passenger purchased a cupcake and added a candle, whilst the crew packaged an Amtrak blanket in newspaper and sang Happy Birthday!

Originally founded as a gold mining camp, the city was made up of three separate towns, an argument over the naming rights being settled by the city fathers, the purchase price being a barrel of whiskey! My introduction to the capital, known as **The Mile High City**, was a collection of boxlike skyscrapers reflected in glass façades and an old church with a tall steeple, looking incongruous in their midst. Other premises included the wedge-shaped **Brown Palace Hotel** (1892), which had a nine-storey atrium covered by a Tiffany stained-glass skylight, and the Capitol Building with a statue in a yellow garden bed in the forecourt. An interesting two-storey red stone building had a yellow door, emerald green window frames and roof ornamentation, and a red tiled roof. I saw a free-standing stone colonnade and, set in lawns and gardens, a huge semicircular edifice with a clock tower on top and plain pediment above the massive Ionic-columned portico.

The lovely **Denver Botanic Gardens** provided a tranquil and relaxing hour with their extensive moat-like waterways and unusual plants. Water cascaded over twin stone pillars in the centre of a pool, and fountains complemented by lilies and different-coloured rushes graced another. Clumps of dry grasses made an interesting and attractive feature, and I came across a rotunda, yellow reeds growing in a stepped pool with white urns at the edge, and even a vegetable garden with an enormous bright orange pumpkin. A pergola faced a contemporary statue in another lily-covered pond, which reflected city buildings. The highlight was the **Japanese Garden of Pine Wind** (*Shofu-en*), with stone lanterns, lawns, willows, stunted green trees interspersed with red and yellow, full-sized conifers, a winding path, and a pond with rocks and lilies. On one bank, beneath the drooping yellow foliage of a tree with a white trunk and branches, stunning vibrant crimson shrubs stood amongst green, the entire scene mirrored in the water. The authentic teahouse, constructed in Japan, was shipped across the Pacific and reassembled by skilled artisans.

stone building and church spires

Coming to an area of substantial homes, the spires and spiky twin steeples of a church rose up behind an imposing rough-textured stone building, the appeal of its warm tan tones augmented by a turret, sculpted stone gables, an eyebrow window in the shingled roof, and iron-railed balconies.

The church contained a carved marble altar, a rose window, and beautiful stained-glass scenes and representations of saints in rich colours of purple, red, green, blue and yellow.

stained glass

Here also was the Victorian home of the 'Unsinkable' **Molly Brown**, heroine of the *Titanic* disaster. This affluent-looking edifice of rough-textured grey stone featured a carved pediment and deep-pink woodwork that included ornamented gables and eaves. With the addition of pink stone balustrades and pink coping on walls, it was flamboyant like the lady herself, and I noticed an embossed white plaque, white stone lions, and a white urn enhanced with relief. Other buildings near the centre were more traditional, almost European in appearance, and I found a wall around a construction site painted with colourful frogs, exotic parrots, and flowers in vibrant hues.

Writer Square held a modern clock tower and a raised garden bed with a bust, probably that of a famous author, amongst the flowers. Located in one of the buildings was possibly the most unusual and fascinating exhibit that I have ever seen: a display of Michael Garman's unique works. Referred to as the storyteller sculptor, his miniature images were set in the streets and alleys of a magical town from a bygone era, with 'live' action by holograms: images created using stage illusion techniques with mirrors, lights and sound. A bar scene in the Darby Hotel depicted patrons sitting at tables cluttered with cans and other items, or seated on barstools placed on a black and white checked linoleum floor. A moose head, advertisements, including one for Camel cigarettes, a calendar, and the faces of Bud Abbot and Lou Costello adorned peeling walls, a man played a Wurlitzer jukebox, another leant against it whilst perusing a paper, an old-fashioned telephone was mounted on the wall beside a door, and minute bottles of J&B whiskey stood on mirror-backed shelves behind the bar, which even had a foot rail. An old-fashioned till sat on the counter. Attention to detail was remarkable, even to each tiny brick appearing individually made and laid.

scene in the Darby Hotel

Below a sign stating Leroy & Bertha's bar and grill, a man slouched against the doorframe reading a newspaper; a broom, overflowing battered bin and litter lay around the step. Gas and electricity meters, the room tariff and graffiti blighted the red brick wall, a sash window was propped open with a can, and green plants appeared behind a wooden gate. Later this scenario was transformed to night, and in lighted windows I could see a coloured girl in a bedroom and a guest talking on a wall phone.

A pool hall scene portrayed men around the table with a dog curled up underneath, a Budweiser mirror, a moose head, a scantily clad woman playing the jukebox, and a customer emerging from a door marked MEN. Complete with miniature globes, working old-style street lighting illuminated walls, and gas lamps stood on the footpaths. The interior of Harry's Barber Shop featured a man sitting reading the paper whilst people conversed in the street outside and a figure leant over a balcony. A Pepsi sign was painted on the wall and dormer windows opened from the shingled roof. Men stood in an alley, one sat on steps with his chin resting in his hands, some congregated at the corner of Court Street, another leant against a lamppost, and two sat on a bench seat with a Pepsi advertisement on the back – Pepsi must have been a sponsor!

a town street by Michael Garman

A lineman was up a pole outside an apartment block where washing hung on rope strung between buildings, and a man in underclothes was yawning and stretching on an iron-railed balcony whilst a woman shook a duster from the fire escape. A pot plant stood on a windowsill. A man was talking on a public telephone outside a pizzeria with dogs on the steps and a coloured man seated on a bench nearby. A man on the paved pathway carried a child on his shoulders, and the scene was completed by cats and two red-and-yellow fire hydrants.

An illusionary couple interacted in a cobbled street, and a girl stood on a balcony singing *When the Wind Blows*. This scene faded and was replaced periodically by a wall with a fanlight window. But I think the most outstanding achievement was the Crown Theatre with its flashing neon sign above the announcement for the current showing of *Casablanca* starring Humphrey Bogart and Ingrid Bergman. Through the open doors, across the heads of moviegoers, it was even possible to view the actual film being screened! Other patrons and a box office stood in the tiny foyer with a miniature advertisement for the coming attraction: *Ox-Bow Incident* starring Henry Fonda. Outside, more coloured people, one eating a hamburger, sat on another bench advertising Pepsi.

There was a garage with an antiquated petrol bowser, and a moving image behind the counter of Ruthie's Café: a red brick building dated 1920 with stone quoins and a sculpted parapet. The surround of its shopfront window was carved, as were the porch posts. A dog was curled up at the feet of a man at the entrance, another man leant on a lamppost, and a salesman or traveller was seated on a bench in the street, his case at his feet. The adjacent duplex had iron-railed steps leading to the doors, tiny oval windows with floral metalwork, and symmetrical bay windows, from one of which leant a lady, curlers in her hair and clad only in a petticoat. Bins stood in the street, and a man in a leather jacket, tie and hat stood near the foot of the steps, but most of the characters wore jeans and casual attire. The red brick walls had solid stone foundations, and letterboxes, pipes for plumbing, and electricity wiring all added to the reality. Rubbish including cardboard boxes littered a lane, and a brush rested on top of a can of paint next to a screwdriver on a sill. A figure leant from an upstairs sash window above Gails Dance Studio, figures were visible in the lighted interior, and a pot with pink flowers sat on the windowsill.

Back in the real town, I took pictures of a tall traditional clock tower and the modern **Tabor Centre** shopping mall on three levels in a 168m greenhouse. The city skyline formed a backdrop to the huge expanse of **Civic Centre Park** with its lawns and colourful flowerbeds. A cheeky squirrel hopped happily and nibbled food held in its front paws. A red brick and white slab 'causeway' separated the **Capitol Building** from the immense semicircular edifice mentioned earlier. Modelled on that in Washington, the former had a carved pediment above a pillared portico and a dome containing the world's entire supply of Colorado onyx, covered in 24-carat gold. An obelisk stood in a circle between the two structures. Side paths, one flanked by equestrian statues, led to small colonnades, one of which had a lion sitting beside the steps. Rough-textured stone seemed to be a feature of Denver, and another such building in warm ochre tones had a partially shingled domed turret, wood-turned verandah posts, a bay window, and gables.

Colorado Springs

On a tour to **Colorado Springs** (6,035ft), I went from a traditional stone church with stained glass to the ultramodern chapel of the **Air Force Academy**. This enormous futuristic structure raised a row of 17 identical steel-and-glass spires to heaven, and the stark interior contained only a plain altar, wooden pews, and a simple tall crucifix comprised of two thin metal crosspieces. Composed of tiny panes, vertical lines of multi-coloured glass framed triangular windows; also inserted in the towering ceiling, they shone like stars.

Surrounded by russet blades of autumn grasses and low shrubs, jagged red sandstone walls and occasional white tors announced the **Garden of the Gods**, an awesome spectacle silhouetted against the light. Needle-sharp spires projected above pines that grew amongst this forest of fantastic formations sculpted by time and weather up to 300 million years ago. We drove through

balancing rock

a rock-filled valley to the site of a mammoth balancing boulder and other undermined monoliths beside the road. Wonderful views of cloud wafting in vales were visible between these erosion-sculpted monuments to nature's grandeur, and a few yellow trees provided a fabulous colour contrast.

The road passed more interesting shapes to arrive at the charming town of **Manitou Springs** (6,336ft) at the foot of 14,110ft **Pikes Peak**. Although a small community, it featured a couple of grand Victorian buildings, including one with two turrets and several gables and the colossal four-storey **Miramont Castle** built by a wealthy French priest in 1895. An architectural curiosity, it had 2ft-thick walls and 46 rooms incorporating nine major building styles. Set in lawns spread with a carpet of yellow from fallen leaves, a lovely old wooden home had a turret, shingled roof and carved woodwork, which included the trim around eaves and the balustrade and posts of a wide verandah.

house in Manitou Springs

Colour was introduced to the streets by flowers in tubs, and a mountain stream from a spring ran through the centre and under a stone bridge. There was a strong Indian influence with names such as Navajo Store and Eagle Dancer. This was also apparent in adobe buildings with log corbels, one being the hotel with its rustic wooden balcony and ladders to access the parapet. A drinking fountain in the form of a kneeling Indian maiden had water pouring from a container in her hands.

Continuing on, we paused at a viewpoint above **William's Canyon** where Rocky Mountain junipers grew and at another with a town far below. We were heading for the **Manitou Cliff Dwellings**, village remains of the ancient **Anasazi** Indian culture, with log reinforced adobe-brick buildings built from AD 1100 to 1300 under the overhang of a red precipice, the only openings being those for doors and ventilation. The substantial remains blended perfectly with the overpowering daunting cliff face into which they were built. Again, external ladders provided access to upper levels, from where exceptional vistas to misty mountains were obtained. There was a mysterious round tower and a ceremonial *kiva*, a meeting house for men. Pervading the village, muted haunting sounds of pan pipes, like the spirits of long dead ancestors, sent shivers down the

Manitou cliff dwellings

spine. A couple of dwellings featured rudimentary decoration, and one had a hollow scooped out of the floor for a fire.

A model in **The Pueblo**, a three-storey building demonstrating the architecture of the Taos **Pueblo** Indians of today, reconstructed a room with chillies and woven woollen shawls hanging on walls, clay jars around a fireplace, and wooden utensils. An exhibition of pottery showed examples applied with different geometric designs (some fairly sophisticated), one depicting birds, and a few with colour. Wooden and stone tools were used in the production of corn, a robust variety with hard kernels that took a long time to cook but withstood drought and was resistant to disease and mould when stored.

We travelled a beautiful mountain highway and stopped at a place with the apt title of **Point Sublime** to photograph a panorama with a series of mountains fading into the distance. Below, framed by rock and waving grasses, was a valley with a lake and pines. My witty guide declared 'This isn't actually real; I had it painted just so that you could see it'. We drove through a roughly hewn stone tunnel where yellow trees emerged from the glare at the other end like developing film. Other stops were made for pictures of a waterfall flowing down a smooth sloping rock face to the valley floor in gentler pine-clad mountains and a second fall cutting its way through more-rugged rock with yellow and apricot-tinted trees in the foreground. As we continued, the walls on either side became higher and introduced a little red foliage. We spent a short while in the small town of **Pine Creek**, with three interesting adjoined buildings: red brick with blue and white woodwork, white clapboard with green and white striped awnings, and a half-timbered structure. Tables and chairs sat on the sidewalk and art adorned a nearby façade.

Denver

The streets of suburban Denver were lined with lovely wooden homes displaying some colour and the usual features of bay windows, attic rooms, porches and turrets. Surrounded by pale green trees with black trunks, they were set on green lawns with yellow carpets of fallen autumn leaves. I utilised the **Cultural Connection Trolley** and visited historic **Byers-Evans House** (1883), the sitting room featuring a beautiful ceiling with a floral edge and designs in the corners, a chandelier suspended from a central rose, period pieces, and a fireplace with a tiled surround; silver candlesticks, vases and a gilt clock stood on the mantel. The study/drawing room was furnished with a grand piano, a lace cloth on a small table set for tea, brass implements by a lovely firescreen, a cabinet, pictures, a tapestry-upholstered armchair, a bookcase, and carpets on polished wooden floorboards. A bedroom contained an elaborately carved canopy bed, period chairs, fussy wallpaper, lace curtains, and a dresser with knick-knacks on a lace runner. The dining room featured plates on mantels, ornate Art Deco papering, leadlight windows, a table with seating for six, a buffet and two side tables, and a crystal chandelier hanging from the gleaming, highly polished wooden ceiling. The house itself was a large brick construction with a small-paned bay window in the centre of the symmetrical façade and an iron-railed balcony.

Another tour showed me more red rock, a red tunnel, red boulders, and the red wall defining the **Red Rocks Amphitheatre**, a natural looming (400ft) formation of what else but red-hued rock; colour relief on its sloping strata was provided by yellow lichens and green trees at the base. Man-made seating climbed the lower incline within this perimeter, and wonderful views extended to small green trees on fairly barren beige-coloured hills. Eagles flew overhead, one bare tree was lodged in a cleft, and it was an area of amazing balancing rocks. There was also the very red, **Red Rocks Trading Post**, which looked striking with the black branches of a lacy green tree against one wall. Back on the coach, we followed a small river and passed dun-coloured hills with sparse pine trees, brilliant yellow foliage, white rock, and a range of snow-capped mountains on the far horizon.

I took film of the city high-rise lit at night and, joining the train again next morning, headed for **Glenwood Springs**.

Glenwood Springs

The track progressed from gradual gradients to a route along pine-clad gorges with the blue **Colorado River** at the bottom. As the walls became higher, huge pines literally grew from crevices in the rugged rock, and the clear river changed to rapids rushing over white stones. There were many canyons and photographic opportunities marked on the Amtrak California Zephyr route map. Leaving the passes behind, and many tunnels varying in length from 78ft to the Moffat at 6.2mi, we traversed a russet plain bounded by yellow and fir-forested slopes with low cloud above and encountered our first snow. The **Moffat Tunnel**, under **Rollins Pass**, opened in 1928 and cut a five-hour journey over the pass – a route called Giant's Ladder reaching a dizzying height of 11,600ft, which required 'helper' engines for the long steep haul – to little more than ten minutes. Now we came across bare trees, small amounts of yellow with the perennial pines, and gradually increasing precipitation. At one stage, we watched the flakes falling, and conifers were cloaked in a glistening white mantle with snow-topped peaks as a backdrop, like typical Christmas card scenes. It was a picturesque wonderland appreciated even more from the warmth of the heated carriage.

We came to an area of purple-hued brush wending its way between the pines like a mauve river, a white plain created by a layer of snow on red grasses, and the small community of **Fraser** (elevation 8,574ft) with single-storey wooden buildings, one steeple, and little colour. It proudly called itself the 'Icebox of America' because winter temperatures dropped to minus 50°F. Nearby, was the rock formation of the **Devil's Thumb**. We alighted briefly before continuing on beside the **Fraser River**, bordered now by rust-coloured grasses and yellow bush with a background of pines; a dusting of snow lay on the grey earth, and the slopes of valleys were clothed in tones of purple. This was a particularly enjoyable ride, presenting a beauty different from the eternal dense green and yellow of previously – a pleasant change.

After many miles the terrain altered yet again to a river bed full of massive boulders dislodged and fallen from rock walls. I took film of the train as it curved around bends and passed isolated cabins, yellow and orange banks, and the last leaves of autumn clinging to black branches. Subtle deviations included empty grassy plains, dense yellow vegetation, lines of bare trees like skeletons, distant snow-capped mountains, a wider more-peaceful river, and a few cattle. Entering another ravine, the river narrowed, became busier, and fell in small chutes between rust-coloured grassy verges, vibrant yellow trees and less greenery; all superimposed on the dull brown canvas of the mountains. We gradually ascended to survey an emerald waterway winding between alternating banks of glaring yellow or sheer rock to the waterline. I found a place at the open rear of the carriage, where the only sounds were the monotonous and hypnotic clickety-clack of the wheels and the screech of iron on iron as the brakes were applied around bends.

The walls became craggier, with lofty peaks reaching heights of 1,500ft above the river in **Gore Canyon**, followed (after 22 miles) by **Red Canyon**, the reddish rock under the grey surface inspiring the Spanish to name the river and countryside Colorado – colour red. Forty-six minutes west of Red Canyon, at the Colorado and **Eagle** Rivers junction, was a town with the peculiar name of **Dotsero**, so called because it was marked on survey maps with '.O' – dot-zero! After more vistas comprised of reds, yellows, greens and grey, I captured film of the train as it curved around the base of a towering perpendicular red rock wall. The stone became redder, the trees more orange, and the river a deeper green, changing from still sections to rapids, with lonely farms in areas where the land opened out. Flat-topped red ranges with a distinct band of white at the summit were striking, and altered again as we entered breathtaking 27km **Glenwood Canyon** and the **White River National Forest**. Narrower and higher, vertical grey rough-surfaced and rugged rocks were adorned with spruce, aspen and majestic pines dwarfed by the tremendous size of their host. The colour of the river changed to milky green and due (I assumed) to the restriction in width, the freeway running alongside was a massive elevated bi-level concrete structure with over 40 bridges and viaducts. Stunted green, yellow and sienna-coloured brush covered lower slopes, and low cloud touched some peaks. The track followed the narrow gorge, sometimes looking down at the river, sometimes alongside, and I filmed the engine as it entered a rock tunnel.

There was nothing outstanding about **Glenwood Springs**, where the **Fork River** met the Colorado, but it was a tidy town and I noted a shopfront with designs created by brickwork and Doc Holliday Tavern, its sign in the shape of an ammunition belt and six-gun with red neon simulating flames issuing from the barrel. The grave of this legendary hero (or infamous gunslinger) lay above the town. The 'teddy bear' was born when President Theodore (Teddy) Roosevelt stayed at the Hotel Colorado. A craft store displayed clever tableaux created from driftwood and dried grasses. They included miniature models of timber houses with gables and attics: one with a bent chimney pipe and another, behind a railing fence, even equipped with a tyre swing suspended from the branch of a tree. Cloud hung even lower and it was raining as I investigated further. A quaint wooden store, appearing to be a converted home, had flowerboxes displaying mixed colours, and I had obtained lodging in a most intriguing guesthouse called Adducci's Inn. My room in this blue and white shingle-walled establishment held two beds with frilled apricot-and-white floral spreads, pillows and matching curtains. Pictures included a delightful composition depicting two posteriors seated side by side on a plank above a bathing pool: that of a naked white child with a bare bottom and a black dog of the same height, its tail hanging down behind.

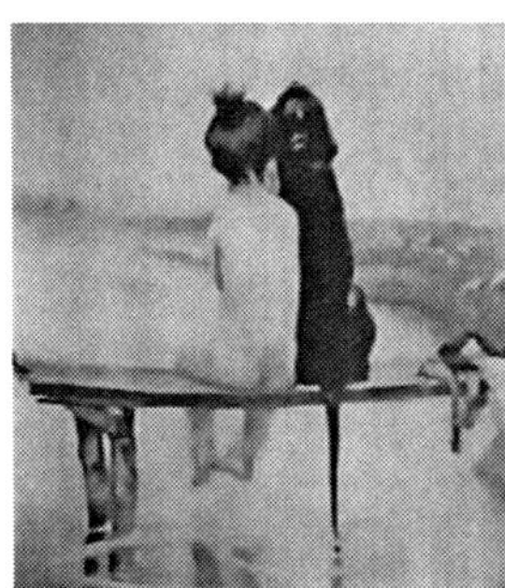
cute picture

However, the amazing thing was the bathroom, with a black mirrored ceiling, plain black and black and white patterned shower curtains, a gilt edged oval mirror and frilly white lampshades above a black sink in a white cabinet, a black and white bath, a black mat on white tiles, and black and white wallpaper covered with large interwoven images of naked Egyptian, American Indian and Grecian ladies. This theme was repeated on the cupboard doors and a curtain, but the pièce de résistance was a large replica of Michelangelo's *David* on the sink, a fig leaf in the appropriate place and holding a red hand towel – the only colour introduced in the room!

my bathroom

The sitting room was furnished with a lovely painted screen, lace antimacassars on a chair and the striped Regency lounge, ornaments on the mantel of the marble fireplace, ruched lace curtains, a small table, and a standard lamp.

The actual springs had a daily flow of 3,500,000 gallons and the water temperature was approximately 51°C (124°F).

Aspen

Snow lay on crests as I made my way by bus on a day trip to **Aspen**, but the ski slopes in this resort city were now covered in grass and the ski lift was not functioning. Aspen was first founded by miners seeking their fortune in silver in the 1880s, when it was nothing more than a shanty settlement. Now ritzy and high priced, it was nevertheless attractive, with Victorian buildings, autumn trees laying carpets of a new type of gold on cobbled streets, and distant snow apparent on the lofty mountain backdrop. Typical alpine architecture had steeply pitched roofs, and older wooden buildings included adjacent structures in pink and blue respectively, the first with the date 1923 on its freestanding gable. Two dogs, one black and one white, sat patiently outside the entrance to one of the tallest structures, the red brick **Elks Building**, with a flag flying from the silver dome on one corner. At the opposite end of the scale was tiny photogenic **Little Annie's Eating House**, a frontier type timber construction with carriage lanterns, window boxes and red trim, wedged between two larger brick buildings. Painted on the brickwork of another structure was an elaborate illustrated sign reading Patriotic Order Sons of America Smuggler Mining Co.

I found a canopy incorporating stained-glass panels, a square with fountains erupting directly from the pavement, a shop with incredible glassware, an establishment entitled Silver Nugget, white wooden **St Mary's Church** with a belltower, **Pitkin County Courthouse** with a brick tower, and statues depicting a black bear, brown horse, and two donkeys, radiating a coppery sheen, both laden with miners implements such as a pickaxe, flagons, and sluicing pan. The well-known and expensive **Hotel Jerome** was a showpiece; the looming exterior visible through the glass ceiling of a lounge area, which contained deer heads on pink walls with a decorative cornice, period furniture including tapestry-upholstered carved chairs, palms and other potted plants, chandeliers, and pictures. The dining room featured maroon chairs and matching tied-back drapes with heavy pelmets. A corridor with contemporary ceiling decoration and swagged curtains led to a bar featuring a light fitting created from antlers hanging from an identical ceiling, a grand piano with colourful inlay work, the head of a bison, and an ornate carved table on an elaborately patterned carpet.

Walking on the outskirts brought me to small wooden buildings with a splendid mountain background, a pleasant river, and ducks and geese at a lake surrounded by brown and orange grasses.

rural scene

Amongst yellow trees and pines, I came across a live eagle perched on a branch, but it must have been restrained because it did not fly off when I approached close enough for photographs. Another eagle, this time in metal, 'flew' above a chimney. This was an area of expensive brick-and-shingle housing with turrets, gables, porches, and balconies; a gazebo stood alone in a meadow. One timber and shingle house featured leadlight glass, carved verandah posts and balustrade, and a fancy iron fence; a blue and white all shingle home had a matching picket fence. An interesting red-roofed half-timbered white building had muntined windows, carriage lamps, a red door, vibrant green trim including a belvedere with a needle spire in the centre, and a colourful garden with nasturtiums. Other points of interest included colourful planters, a log house with a wagon wheel leaning against the façade, a three-storey mansion with all the usual features and the inclusion of attic windows, and numerous homes featuring fretwork.

Aspen house

An unusual aspect was the many shingled gables in contrasting colours: one in vivid pink on a grey building with a belvedere and red brick chimney on the brown shingled roof. Another grey house had a mauve and lilac gable, the colours repeated in a wide horizontal facia across the front, and both in a different style of shingle to the rest of the house. Silent leaves were gently falling like flakes of gold, and a little shingled house in brown and lemon was tucked behind a white paling fence beneath lofty brown-and-yellow trees. Literally pretty as a picture, and set on a cloak of leaves behind a picket fence, a little pink wooden house had pink shutters, a grey roof, and a tiny portico with fretwork, turned posts and flower boxes. Of two adjacent homes, one had a mauve gable, the other bands of peach, pink and green with a fretwork insert at the point of the eaves; both had carved posts.

pretty cottage

Glenwood Springs

Returning to Glenwood Springs, I had a look at the famous World's Largest Hot Springs Pool producing 15,000,000 litres of 51°C water daily (the main pool at 90°C), and my last sights were of a well-worn outsized boot hanging from a sign reading Complete Shoe and Boot Repair above the blue and white striped awning of a window containing a pair of bright red boots, The Candlestick Maker in a timber building with an old-style street lantern on the sidewalk, a colourful rock garden outside a blue and white house, stained glass in a residence with a sign saying Wipe Your Paws near the doorstep, and the view from my window of mountains beyond a little wooden cottage with smoke wafting from the chimney.

Grand Junction

Next morning, I continued on Amtrak to **Grand Junction** (elevation 4,591ft), where the Gunnison and Colorado Rivers meet and where I disembarked to join one of my Great Train Journeys of the World: the riveting Silverton to Durango authentic steam-powered narrow gauge railroad established in 1881. Originally hauling cargos of prospectors, gamblers, merchants and ladies to make or break their fortunes at the 'end of the line', it underwent the familiar cycle of boom and bust experienced by many due to the economy, fluctuating ore prices, wars and depressions. Surviving until the first decade of the 20th century, in the late 1950s it was rejuvenated, and the little train now transports thousands of tourists.

Leaving Glenwood Springs there was a dramatic change in scenery: drier more open country with scant low scrub, bare mountains exhibiting a variety of colours, and a still river with yellow trees lining the banks. Twenty-nine miles after departure we went through **New Castle** where, in 1896, an explosion in the nearby Vulcan mine killed 59 miners and threw timbers 400ft into the river. A second explosion in 1931 levelled the works, killing all 39 men – and the mine was still on fire! As ever, I was enthralled with the constantly changing terrain as the shallow river widened and the now closer ridges appeared golden when struck by the rays of the sun. These became a flat-topped red barricade perched on grey slopes above green and yellow banks and appeared uncannily like the Great Wall of China. On one stretch it was perfectly reflected in the river, together with clumps of green on the hillside and even the brilliant blue of the sky. As before, isolated pinnacles pointed to the heavens, and ploughed ridges of farm fields echoed the creviced faces of flat-topped mountains behind. We passed orchards and green crops before reaching our destination, where I stayed at the Hotel Melrose Hostel.

Silverton

It was still dark when the bus departed for Silverton the following morning, and we drove through the quiet town before entering more stunning mountains, the river taking on the semblance of a creek far below and green pines appearing black amongst massed yellow trees, which were bright even in the predawn conditions. In fact, they assumed an even more intense radiance as the only colour in a completely black and grey world. The road had been hewn into the rock of steep mountain sides with no guardrail at the sheer drop. There were colours in the rock, but the pines looked dark and foreboding without sunlight, and the ominous brooding peaks crept closer, almost encroaching on the highway.

Silverton, a well-preserved silver mining town at 2,840m (9,318ft), was actually bigger than it looked at first sight prior to sunup, at which time it was transformed into one of the most photogenic and certainly most colourful places that I had ever visited. However, in the glow from the first faint blush of dawn, my impressions were of a town consisting almost exclusively of single-storey wooden buildings, one with a square turret reading American Legion Post 14, another, the distinctive shingled gable in turquoise and white. Horses grazed in a snow-covered corral with a little cabin and snow-topped peaks behind. Apart from birds flying across a bell tower, they were the only creatures awake; it was totally silent, not even the barking of a dog or crowing of a rooster disturbed the serenity.

As the rising sun lit yellow crests, causing their icy surface to glisten, the blue sky and some colour began to emerge, and smoke began to issue from tall metal chimneys as people stirred in the sleepy town. Standing on stone foundations, a pale pink house had a grey roof and trim, gables, and a little porch; another had stained-glass inserts in the door and window of its tiny red-roofed portico. A rustic shingled shack with turned posts on its tiny verandah was called The Sun House, and the two-storey Bent Elbow Restaurant, in gaudy pink and bright yellow, was a typical construction with a balcony forming a covered verandah over the boardwalk. A rough wooden sign on the patched and rusted corrugated iron and timber false-fronted façade of the Olde Time Photography shop announced Notorious Blair St. This trader stood on one corner of the **Old Town Square**, its boardwalk lined with log buildings, one with a wagon wheel leaning against the façade and a life-sized wooden Indian in full headdress. A mustard-coloured false-fronted building called Old Arcade had a sunburst on top and stood next to a wooden structure abutting a brick building, which in turn stood beside the Hitchin Post adjacent to the Candle Shop – with a false front in deep pink!

Silverton

A stone store titled The Hummingbird Shop was next to the red brick Swanees, which featured blue awnings and a juxtaposed tiny blue and white wooden annexe called Swanees Sweets, with iron trim on the roofline. This mixture of wood, stone and brick included the yellow Zhivagos Restaurant with a wooden balcony, and the **Town Hall** (1908) with its clock tower. One block was a veritable rainbow, with adjacent yellow, garish pink, pale green, pumpkin-yellow, grey (with an upper bay window), and bright blue buildings.

Two ethnic establishments went by the names of Indian Trading Post and Storyteller Indian Store, with a full-sized bear (stuffed) standing upright at the entrance to the latter. The first contained pelts (with tails intact), artefacts, a bearskin, and an assortment of clothing; the other, decorated containers, dolls, and dream catchers with feathers, one with a genuine fox head in the centre. There was a shop called simply Train Store, and two of the colourful buildings had embellishment on their false fronts. On the opposite side of the street stood facades of vivid pink and white, green and tan, and red and yellow, the latter a hotel with striped canopies. A sign illustrated with an ebullient curling moustache announced Handlebars Food and Saloon, and there was the Silverton Mint, Rocky Mountain Cakes, Silverton Pioneer Star

Newspaper, and the purple-accented Rusty Cowboy Steakhouse Saloon. A sculpture portraying a man on a horse stood on top of a stone structure.

I had reached the opposite end of town, where a pretty chuckling brook had the grandiose name **Rio de las Animas**, and dry reddish-brown and yellow hills were defined by a line of green firs at the summit, with snow lying on crests beyond. A few houses clustered amongst bare and yellow trees beside the stream made an attractive picture, one with a vintage truck and red and green wagon out front. Others included a blue dwelling with a bright red roof, a white clapboard house with hanging baskets and a railing fence, and one with carved woodwork and bright orange pumpkins on the doorstep.

early automobile

The tiny brown and yellow wooden station informed that we were at 9,302ft; the elevation varied considerably depending on the source. Back in the centre, I discovered what must have been one of the first ever motorcars, with a bar for steering, the brake at the side, and metal wheels without tyres; Whistle Stop Trading Post was printed on the door.

A few more novel names were The Pickle Barrel Restaurant, High Noon Hamburgers and The Fudge Mine. The Iron Horse Indian Shop had a painting on the façade, an adobe structure was named Restaurante y Cantina Romeros, one building sported lace curtains, and another was constructed with wooden slats laid diagonally to create a pattern. A church with a small tower was framed by the steeple on a white wooden church in the foreground. The weathered photography shop, horseshoes adorning the façade, advertised antique portraits; a penny-farthing cycle stood on the boardwalk in front and an old-style lamp with a beaded fringe sat in the window.

penny-farthing

And in every direction snowy peaks dominated. At the Old Town Square, I spoke with an artist who explained the location for one of his works hanging in the gallery, a painting illustrating the wonderful scenery that I have been describing. An interesting bar housed a vast conglomeration of articles such as horseshoes, harness, pictures, an old clock, a standard lamp and paraffin lanterns, moose antlers, clothing, utensils and tools. Animals and heads demonstrated the skill of the taxidermist. The entire town was declared a

National Historic Landmark in 1966, the name ostensibly credited to a miner who bragged 'We have no gold, but silver by the ton'.

The train had arrived and stood belching steam outside the Old Arcade, right in the centre of town; colourful buildings in the vicinity included one with a candy-pink roof. Originally used to haul ore, the black coal-fired engine with its tail of yellow wooden carriages looked magnificent against the backdrop of a pine-clad snowy crest. A second locomotive puffed and chugged into town beside the first, and it was not necessary to be a train buff to appreciate the spectacle.

steam train

My final picture was of an overgrown gravestone bearing the inscription:

Here Lies
Lester Moore
Told a Lie no Les no More

And so the journey began. Leaving the township behind, the train entered a wide valley with a shallow blue river, reddish slopes, and snow on summits in the background. The waterway became narrower, taking on a milky green hue, and steeper sides were composed of white rock bearing the inescapable pines. This changed again as we approached a sheer chasm with rapids and boulders at the bottom. I obtained graphic film of the train snaking around curves below the encompassing red, grey and (in places) bright orange rock – we were engulfed by mountains.

headstone

We passed a waterfall, tall conifers, and yellow brush that, together with the rock walls, took on a copper glow. The track traversed the **Rio de los Animas Canyon**, and from my position at the open end of a car, with only the clatter of the wheels for company, I managed to acquire extraordinary film of the entire trip.

en route

As the environs changed yet again, the river flowed between iron-coloured vertical walls, and a section of delicate plant life looked like purple mist. At one stage, the train halted and it was possible to compose perfect pictures incorporating all the features of blue sky, grey mountains, snow, yellow, amber and green vegetation, and teal-blue and white water tumbling over orange boulders – it was an explosion of colour.

unrivalled splendour

Confined by rugged rock faces and peaks, the course of the river fluctuated between broad and narrow stretches of calm and rough water, one wider section with a stony bed heralding the appearance of an even greater density of yellow trees mingling in an area of thickly forested pine. We passed one lonely cabin and a wooden suspension bridge. The black and yellow train blended well with the surroundings, and the whistle sounded from time to time, although the only other traffic would have been wildlife. In places, enormous firs achieved a foothold in white rock, and sunlight glinted and sparkled off the shimmering surface of the water. Nearing the completion of the rocky ride, a few puffs of white cloud settled above mountains with a light covering of snow, and a solitary startling white peak like Switzerland's Zermatt rose up behind us. The route climbed, and we peered straight down the perpendicular walls of the narrow canyon to a river that was now a rich blue. Riveting film showed the train negotiating bends on a shelf with wild water surging through a cleft of red-and-grey rock below and a sheer precipice to the right.

hugging the cliff

Durango

Durango, at 6,512ft and gateway to the **San Juan Mountains**, was a more progressive town than Silverton, with many statues in the streets. These included an eagle perched beside a modern fountain, a shining silver bison, and a boy of bronze reading a book from the pile at his feet. One of the big disappointments of my trip was the fact that I arrived here on a Sunday and, my contact being absent, was unable to avail myself of a prearranged personal tour of the ancient Anasazi remains at **Mesa Verde**. However, I did manage a full day excursion to the Colorado National Monument and Black Canyon of the Gunnison, both extraordinary attractions. No two canyons are alike, certainly the case here because both were distinctly different destinations.

Colorado National Monument

With a small group of five, I spent a few hours hiking through the **Colorado National Monument** with towering red rock looming 1,000ft overhead. Stopping first at an overlook, we could trace a meandering line of lime-green vegetation, indicating the presence of water, at the base of red escarpments atop grey slopes with sparse darker green growth.

the escarpment

There were several huge pillars and it was easy to see where an enormous section had fallen away, like a red iceberg calved from a glacier, and lay in a heap of rubble. Although it was warm as we began our trek, wind whistled through the canyon, which extended towards a hazy horizon. The twisted black or white trunks of dead trees made dramatic foregrounds to the rugged red surroundings.

an ancient landscape

Formations like gigantic wide-stemmed mushrooms with flat white caps, fingers of rock, high shallow caverns, beehive formations, and weathered towers made up the remainder of the superb terrain in this valley enclosed by vertical walls with a vivid blue sky above. In places, it was incredibly smooth (like Uluru in Australia's Northern Territory) with overhanging lips of rock. Foliage differed inasmuch as I only saw *one* yellow tree. We came to an area of red earth and a colossal natural amphitheatre, where eagles flew overhead. The beginning of a natural arch, such as I was to see many years later, was pointed out. We crossed a small stream with larger trees and passed a group of symmetrical but conjoined formations. Two opposing free-standing red walls and an immense 600 ton balancing block completed the highlights of the park, where the only other inhabitants were three climbers tied together with rope and scaling a sheer face, the only sound that of the engine of a small plane flying overhead. The formations were achieved by different types of rock being eroded to different degrees by the actions of wind, water and frost, the

future towers

vibrant colours of red, orange and brown obtained by iron and other mineral deposits.

Black Canyon of the Gunnison

We moved on to the 53mi-long **Black Canyon of the Gunnison**, narrowest (396m) and sheerest in North America, more jagged than the Colorado and, as the name implies, black in colour. Whereas the previous one rose 2,000ft above the Colorado River, this abyss *dropped* 2,500ft (762m) from a flat broad plain, like a mighty schism in the earth's crust, the **Gunnison River** appearing like a stream, just visible on the floor of dark awe-inspiring depths shrouded in mystery. Except for a few bushes, the austere rocks were almost devoid of vegetation. An area of natural square pillars looked like a tessellated pavement from above, growth of yellow lichens provided a little colour, and the surrounding countryside was greener. A few pillars were toppled and other formations of rock spurs, spikes and spires rose up from the canyon floor.

tessellated pavement

In order to peer into the bottom it was necessary to venture near the brink and this completely unspoilt site was without any man-made intrusions such as safety fences – scary stuff! Light only reached the deepest parts of this ravine, appearing cut with a giant saw, at noon when the sun was directly overhead. Cautiously approaching the rim, it was then possible to detect the blue of the water, some pale greenery, and a group of pines thriving, almost unbelievably, on a ledge in the dimness of the rift. I saw white birds flying below, and one sheer face was reflected so that it appeared twice its height. Bare, blackened and twisted trunks and branches contributed to the drama-filled atmosphere. As we left this sombre intimidating place behind, shadows of clouds created patterns on the surrounding brown-and-white hills.

steps and stairs

dramatic scenery

UTAH

Canyonlands National Park

I was moving through a succession of spectacular national parks and crossed into **Utah** for **Canyonlands National Park**, encompassing the confluence of the **Green** and Colorado Rivers and composed of stone pinnacles banded in orange, red and white. Scenery en route included a solitary stark white wall of stone and it was back to swathes of brilliant yellow and orange bushes livening dried hillsides of grey and brown, with snow lingering on far mountains. We stopped at a lake with densely forested surrounds, a little snow on the ground, and a community of log cabins with shuttered windows and stone or brick chimneys on iron or shingled roofs.

From here, we followed the course of a brown river, its green banks bounded by sheer red walls with a heavy overcast sky above. Visible above stony slopes, we saw our first fingers of rock in the distance, and the red earth was covered with clumps of spinifex-like vegetation, sparse green brush, and flat-topped mesas scored with both horizontal and vertical cracks, making them appear striated. Approaching closer, we discovered incredible (almost impossible) balancing rocks and huge red boulders making remarkable silhouettes against the light; again I obtained wonderful photographs utilising twisted dead trees as a foreground. There were occasional white stones that served to highlight the rich red colour, and I filmed tors framed by tors in an open area where buttes stood like islands in a red sea. Shrouded in haze, the eerie sun made an interesting picture beside the silhouette of a black tower beneath the ominous brooding cloud canopy.

Arches scenery

Arches National Park

We proceeded, via **Moab**, to **Arches National Park**, which as the name suggests, enveloped an area of monumental orange sandstone arches and windows, together with the features described earlier.

Within its boundaries was the world's largest concentration of natural arches (2,400 named), which because of their near perfect form explorers first thought were the work of a lost civilisation; the people in our small party were dwarfed by the immense formations. Again, I composed superb pictures incorporating the artistry of dead trees, and filmed arches through arches; even the dark cloud appeared sculpted. Of exceptional width (100m/328ft), **Landscape Arch** looked fantastic beside the outline of a bare black tree and with vistas of other monoliths through the opening.

Landscape Arch and others

Unfortunately, I ran out of film before reaching the most impressive, **Delicate Arch**, 15m (49ft) high and with a 10m (33ft) span, erupting from the precipitous edge of a sheer abyss.

We paused for a brief look at grey mudflats, which almost looked like a mirror image of the bruised overcast sky. An extraordinary building featuring onion domes and Arabic style windows appeared behind a paddle wheeler moored at a landing.

Delicate Arch

Salt Lake City

Reaching **Salt Lake City**, established in 1847 and nestled at the foot of the **Wasatch Range**, I encountered a complete change of pace. Grand brick and timber homes featuring attics, turrets and verandahs were set in green lawns shaded by autumn trees, a stone church with a sculpted façade had a rose window and a blue spangled ceiling inside, and the State Capitol lay at the end of a long broad avenue; founder Brigham Young decreed that the streets had to be wide enough for a team and wagon to turn without having to back up. The **Capitol Building**, constructed from Utah granite in 1912, featured a copper dome above a circular colonnade of 24 Corinthian columns. Inside walls held large canvases and murals dramatising the state's history. The domed ceiling was painted with seagulls in flight, the official state bird, honouring those that saved the Mormon crops from grasshoppers in the 19th century.

Again, the city was a mixture of traditional and modern, with a plain arch called the **Eagle Gate** enhanced by a 6,000lb bird with a 20ft wingspan and a large Venetian-looking edifice, its patterned brickwork adorned with a sculpted frieze of naked cherubs under the eaves. Bearing lamps upon their shoulders groups of three stood on a ledge, others amongst colourful sculpting above arched windows. Classical terracotta countenances completed the embellishment. The multi-spired **Mormon Temple**, a gold statue of the angel Moroni blowing a horn on top and the **Brigham Young Monument** in front, rose in the background behind an enormous concrete bowl planted with yellow flowers. Begun in 1853 and hand-hewn by pioneers, the church took 40 years to complete. Situated in ten acre **Temple Square**, also housing the **Tabernacle** of the famed choir, this was the headquarters of the Church of Jesus Christ of Latter Day Saints, and I took a guided tour that demonstrated the marvellous acoustics: a dropped pin could be heard 750ft away. The temple was also effectively lit in the evening. The domed tabernacle contained an organ with 11,623 pipes and seated 6,500 people. The original pipes were fashioned by an Australian organ builder from tall straight-grained pine hauled 300 miles by ox-pulled wagons. The choir had its beginnings with the trek across the prairie when hymns were sung around the campfire at night. Members come from many diverse backgrounds and have performed all over the world. I also visited the **Beehive House** (1854), residence of Brigham Young who led the group of Mormon pioneers and named for the beehive, Mormon symbol of industry, perched on the cupola.

Brigham Young was born in 1801 in a log cabin in Vermont. Apart from being taught to read by his mother, he had little formal schooling – 11 days of instruction under a travelling schoolmaster – yet went on to lead thousands of people in covered wagons across the Great Plains to Utah and establish Salt Lake City. Never before had such a large mass of people braved the hostile terrain and attempted the long arduous journey across the prairies; George Bernard Shaw later referred to him as an American Moses leading his people through the wilderness into an un-promised land. He took over as leader of the church when the Prophet Joseph Smith was martyred in Illinois in 1844, established peaceful coexistence with the Indians, and became the first governor of Utah in 1851. He dug canals, imported plants and animals, built railways and telegraphs, established industries and banks, constructed theatres, and erected temples and tabernacles; he founded two universities, and fathered 56 children by more than one wife. He was both spiritual leader and the ultimate statesman, and died in 1877.

Twenty-two miles south of the city was located the **Bingham Canyon Copper Mine** from which I have a specimen of ore. Where once stood a mountain, now lay the largest man-made excavation in the world: one half mile deep, two and a half miles across, and covering 1,900 acres. The Sears Tower, at that time the world's tallest building (1,454ft), would have reached only half way up the side of the open pit mine, the world's first. At the time of my visit it could seat nine million people, and approximately 300,000 tons of material was removed daily. The mine began operations in 1906, and most of mankind's copper came from Bingham Canyon mine. Also producing gold, silver and molybdenum, it had been dubbed The Richest Hole on Earth.

The **Great Salt Lake** has a saline content almost seven times that of any ocean.

NEVADA

Las Vegas

From the religious fervour of Salt Lake City, I went by train to its complete antithesis: the gambling fantasyland that is **Las Vegas** in **Nevada**. The casinos never close in this city that is so bright at night it can be seen from space; there is no other place like it in the world. It began life as Indian territory until, in 1833, white settlers formed a town on the west bank of the river. When the railroad arrived, rowdy New Town developed on the east bank, attracting unsavoury characters like Billy the Kid, which the west bank vigilantes cleaned out.

I secured a room in the **Vacation Village** (that no longer exists) at the extreme end of **The Strip** (**Las Vegas Boulevard**) for $22 per night, and caught a bus from the railway station, also no longer functioning, which was located in the **Union Plaza Hotel**. The conveyance travelled the long straight stretch of this town dumped slap-bang in the middle of the desert, past a rotunda, the Flamingo with its gigantic red flowers, which started it all when built by **Bugsy Segal** in the 1930s, a neon flashing 'BIG' (as was everything in this larger-than-life place!), Treasure Island, Casino Royale, the Sands, Mirage, **Frontier**, **MacDonald's** (of course!), **La Concha**, and **Stardust**. Gaily coloured metal umbrellas were arrayed on the pavement just before Circus Circus, which was followed by El Rancho, the **Candlelight Wedding Chapel**, **Algiers Hotel**, and **Thunderbird**, all punctuated by palms. The town throbs 24 hours a day, 365 days a year.

After depositing my luggage, I caught a bus back to the top end and returned by foot – some eight to ten kilometres. At that time, the now enclosed **Fremont Street** was open to the blue ceiling of the sky, and sights included the famed cowgirl above the words Glitter Gulch and the neon cowboy on the **Pioneer Club**, featured in most travel brochures on America. This was the older original part of town where a goose wearing a hat and sitting on golden eggs revolved beneath the cowgirl, and casinos included **Binion's Horseshoe**, **Golden Nugget**, **Smart Sally's**, **Four Queens**, **Lady Luck** and **Fremont**. The Strip was dotted with wedding chapels bearing names such as **Hitching Post** and **Silver Bell**, with flashing neon bells. A building with a British theme displayed a sign incorporating a bulldog, the Union Jack, and a shield featuring three lions. Altogether it was tacky, artificial, brash and brassy, but I had more fun here than anywhere else and finished up spending eight days, with a break in the middle because rates rose considerably for the weekend. However, food was amazingly cheap, with buffets to encourage high rollers and even a Denny's (also since gone) in the centre of the main street.

Continuing my exploration, I came to more tiny white wooden chapels with small steeples. Enclosed by a low white picket fence, **Graceland** had a bell tower and a white wooden bridge, which led to a green arbour and a fancy arch in a white wall with a garden visible beyond. The larger **Cupid's Wedding Chapel** was announced by gaudy red hearts, and a square white adobe building with turquoise doors was called **Mission of the Bells**. One called simply **Little White Chapel** had white fountains with classical statues of a boy on a pedestal and doves respectively; cherubs and hearts appeared on stained-glass windows behind. It also featured a garden with white trellis, a wrought-iron pergola, and a sign in a heart reading 24 HR DRIVE-UP WEDDING WINDOW! Slightly different was the pink and white **Victorian Chapel** with San Francisco Sally's Olde Tyme Parlour Wedding emblazoned across the front and wedding dresses in the windows. Finally, I found the **Little Chapel of Flowers** and **L'Amour Chapel**, with its own flower shop, white arches covered with plants, and a large white gazebo. All the chapels were situated on the very busy main road with noisy traffic continually whizzing by, a location hardly conducive to quiet weddings. Something else different was a small blue **Palmistry Studio**.

Vegas World casino had a space theme indicated by a planet on the mirrored wall of the entrance and an astronaut engaged in a space walk on the façade rearing behind. This was where I indulged in the only gambling experience for the duration of my stay. There was a promotion that cost $2 to enter and participants were issued with a $5 voucher at the beginning of each hour for four hours. At the suggestion of the management, I won the $2 back on a slot machine and thereafter tried my luck at blackjack. Unfortunately, there was never a space at the $1 table and I rapidly lost my stake at the higher priced betting arenas. I guess the idea was to then invest your own money, but I left to investigate nearby attractions and returned just before each hour! Finally despairing of success, I asked a professional player to place my bets, which he duly did, and I finished up walking away with US$11 (at that time worth AUD22) for no outlay!

The town was a fun-lovers paradise with heaps of giveaways available everywhere: vouchers, key rings, dice, caps, fridge magnets, torches, popcorn, margaritas, and mugs. In fact, one pink motel was even called **Fun City** and stood next to the **Chapel of the Bells**. A black and white cow stood with a crescent moon above the **Holy Cow Casino**, also featuring white pillars with black patches and a sign advertising 'Cowlectables' and the Freshest Beer in Town. The **Sahara** announced Neil Sedaka in concert, with coming attractions being Cybill Shepherd, Steve Allen, Merle Haggard and Zsa Zsa Gabor. The **El Rancho** complex embraced a Western theme with stuccoed and false-fronted wooden buildings. These included a boarding house in pink and pale lemon with mock stained glass, a red general store, a bank, a sheriff's office, a white livery with more simulated coloured glass, a bingo parlour, a red gambling hall, a card room, and two tiers of small, iron-railed viewing platforms above a façade labelled Sports and Race Book. A mammoth clown sporting multihued patterned shoes, each as large as a car, and holding a lollypop stood outside **Circus Circus**, which had flags flying above its pink and white striped circus tent featuring free acts. The venue was so large that it had its own monorail, which travelled around the perimeter and past a red mirrored dome. Beneath the big top, on the mezzanine midway overlooking the flashing lights and bedlam of the gambling below, I watched world-class performers executing double somersaults and twists in mid air from a trapeze. One artist released a flyer and caught another almost simultaneously on the same swing, the first bouncing from the safety net back to the bar. There was a sideshow alley with a merry-go-round and funfair games, which included ball throwing skills and a water race with prizes of stuffed cartoon characters. I watched a juggler who executed a somersault whilst tossing batons, skipped with a rope whilst bouncing a ball on his head, and balanced balls on his hands whilst doing a backward somersault. He also performed acts with Frisbees and hats. It was all exceedingly noisy.

I arrived at the huge metal umbrellas (in colours of yellow, red, blue and green with lacy iron 'fringes') on red paving tiles outside **Westward Ho**, which was advertising a half pound hot dog and beer for 99 cents! Opposite, next to a restaurant with a small onion dome, was the sign for Silver City. The umbrellas, together with the stars on the bowed façade of **Riviera**, were reflected in a mirrored surface, and sunlight glinted off the original stars to create its own rayed formations. The huge Circus Circus screen was constantly changing with pictures and script; World's Fare Buffet, Jazz on the Strip, and a show starring Joe Pecsi and Sharon Stone were advertised in lights beneath a Splash sign on Riviera, and the Westward Ho sign promoted an all you can eat buffet, with beverage included, from 7am to 12pm. Inside **Silver City**, 'miners' laboured overhead: climbing a ladder with a crate on one shoulder, pushing a laden ore cart, or working at a sluice box; casks hung in a net. **Desert Inn** advertised the Four Tops with special guest star Kevin Pollak, but the grandest show of all (and free!) was at **Treasure Island**, with its smiling skull sign, full-sized galleons on an artificial lake in the street, and a man-made mountain with real palm trees. The show had just finished when I arrived, and rising from the depths, one of the ships presented a carved stern depicting a visage between naked images on dolphins.

British galleon

Behind was a Mediterranean-type town called Buccaneer Bay Village with colourful pink, blue, white and green adobe buildings, and a blue and white rowing boat high and dry on rocks.

the village

Slightly more elegant two- and three-storey structures featured pillars, plants grew on roof tops, and there was a stone tower. Palm trees and other greenery were lodged in rocks at the waterline, from where wooden steps leading to boardwalks completed the romantic scenario. The 'sunken' ship, HMS *Buccaneer* – blue with horizontal pink stripes, some sails furled, and the colourful figurehead of a skirted figure on a seahorse – sailed into view.

figurehead

I looked away and when I turned back the ship was now under full sail and had passed a tarnished copper bell on a weathered wooden post reinforced with metal rings. There was an ochre-coloured building and blackened walls, the result of cannon fire, behind a moored galleon with tattered sails, extensive rigging, crow's nests, and boarding nets over the side. It was all accompanied by music including, appropriately, the *Sailor's Hornpipe* and *Rum and Coca-Cola*.

I crossed a bridge to enter the 'town', ensconced behind façades with lanterns, multi-paned windows and balconies, one created to resemble the prow of a ship with a female figurehead, another composed of skulls and bones. Its elaborate brick doorway was flanked on one side by a sculpted Neptune holding a trident and mounted on a sea serpent, on the other by seahorses with a winged figure like a mermaid. Greenery cascaded overhead.

Neptune

The bow of the moored vessel featured two fearsome dragons, their twisted bodies clothed in colourful scales, and one with its mouth open to reveal cruel fangs and a long curled tongue. A basket of fish sat alongside a barrel and hemp-wrapped parcel on the dock, and implements hung around a fire burning in a grate with a cauldron suspended over the flames. Inside, beneath a black ceiling, full-sized figures stood next to imitation lighted windows with shutters. Rugs hung over the wood or iron balcony railings and statues stood in niches.

I moved outside for the commencement of the next show, heralded by dramatic music and two men paddling a rowing boat.

let the battle begin

Dialogue between the two protagonists began with one of the pirates announcing (as they lowered gold bullion to the deck) that a fully rigged 14-gun British man-of-war was bearing down on their starboard beam. A pompous voice from the advancing vessel commanded 'Heave to and take the sail off her' as a man slid down a rope from a mast head. A cockney accent replied 'Aye aye sir', and ensuing conversations included a call to battle by the pirate captain (armed with a telescope), which was greeted with resounding cheers, whilst the English, in immaculate white uniforms, shortened their sails and climbed rigging. On the pirate ship sailors were ordered to 'Lower that net back into the hold' and 'Avast, up the main topsail yard with ye'. The British commander, in a black jacket with gold braid, bellowed through a bullhorn proclaiming 'In the name of His Majesty, stand by to receive a marine boarding party'. In answer, the pirates declared that the only thing they would receive would be their swords, valuables and 'whatever rum you might have on board'. The Pirate captain bawled to his crew 'Are you ready for the English sword? Then raise the gunports me lads'. Referring to the British officer as 'the son of a woodsman's goat', he mounted the rigging and fired a pistol. The conflict commenced with a cannonball creating a huge splash in the choppy blue 'sea' as flame and smoke issued from gunports in the side of the British galleon. Other orders issued by the British included 'In the name of the crown stand to and surrender', 'Rifles to the ready' and 'Fire number four and five, get set for a broadside'. On the pirate ship smoke billowed overhead and the top of a mast toppled as fire broke out on deck. Then a call from the British to 'Elevate your cannon and fire a broadside into their powder warehouse' resulted in a pyrotechnic conflagration of great magnitude, with clouds of black smoke and flames silhouetting masts, rigging, and sails. 'That will teach the cheeky scoundrels'. 'Yes, perhaps next time they will be more obedient to orders given from the poop deck of a British ship of the line'. This was answered by a wicked laugh and a blast of cannon to 'His Royal Highness' that scuttled the English vessel, whereby the crew jumped overboard in response to the cry 'All hands abandon ship'. Amid flames and sparks (extinguished by the boiling water), the captain went down with his sinking vessel whilst his crew swam to safety.

the battle

From the victorious pirate captain the invitation went out 'Ahoy ye landlubbers, it's time to enter our fair village and share in our victory celebrations, so onward to Treasure Island'. And this was back to where I first came in – with a few residual flames, blackened buildings, and the British boat (the captain standing on the deck!) rising from the waves. The buccaneer boat, a large skull and figures on its stern, was called *Hispaniola*, and a skeleton reposed on a plundered wooden chest in the rocks onshore.

the pirate ship

The **Mirage**, with the blue glass façade of the **Sands** opposite, also had a spectacular display, but not on the same scale: extensive stepped waterfalls cascaded below palm trees to a lake with boulders and full-sized 'leaping' dolphins, and a central volcano erupted every 30 minutes at night.

cascade by day and night

A cluster of colourful European-type buildings made up **Casino Royale**, and **Harrah's** was in the form of a colossal paddle steamer. **Caesars Palace** featured four golden chargers above the entrance, flanked by winged sphinxes, to the **Forum** Shops, and water poured from beneath the stallions. Inside, a revolving tableau had automated figures portraying, amongst others, a courtier playing a lyre and Bacchus, god of wine, drinking from a gold goblet whilst seated on a throne mounted on a dais (that looked extraordinarily like a decorated layer cake!) in the centre of a very blue pool with bubbling fountains. Strobe lighting illuminated the images and created pictures that included a galloping horse on the red ceiling.

Bacchus

Elsewhere, the painted sky and cloud overhead changed regularly from day to night, there was a flowing fountain formed from flickering lights, numerous statues, and both black and white marble columns with gold capitals, their high sheen glowing in the blaze of light and colour. Outside, a travelator moved past fountains in a large pool and pillars surmounted by angels blowing horns. People parachuted into the courtyard, but I was prevented from taking more film indoors. Added to the traffic noise, the blare of amplified announcements was a constant accompaniment in the streets.

Fishers was a half-timbered edifice next to the **Imperial Palace**, and the main entrance to Caesars depicted forum ruins with the statue of a naked male in the centre. The **Flamingo Hilton** boasted iridescent multihued flamingos, made even more vibrant by the sun. It stood next to the striking red **Barbary Coast**, which in turn was next to **Ballys** – advertising the upcoming appearance of Frankie Valli and the Four Seasons – and opposite **Aladdin**, with fountains and a winged statue adding interest to a pool in front. As I continued making my way back (still walking), I passed Aladdin and the massive **MGM Grand**, accessed through the open jaws of a mammoth golden green-eyed lion. This complex alone was like a mini Disneyland, with theatres, rides and themed areas. Next was the medieval compound consisting of towers with red, blue and gold spires that constituted King Arthur's **Excalibur**, one occupied by Merlin in the form of a hologram. Made up of a series of quaint, particularly colourful houses reminiscent of the Caribbean, **Tropicana** was located behind two gigantic stone heads, replicas of those on Easter Island. Lush vegetation and stone masks were secreted amongst waterfalls tumbling over glistening rocks, with rushes in the foreground and flashing lights climbing a towering building behind. Filmed with the waterfall in the forefront, and lit up at the approach of evening, Excalibur looked tremendous; neon jousters announced a round table buffet where I had a fantastic and cheap meal – just $5!

By the time I left it was night, and strobe lighting played on fountains exhibiting different patterns of spray at the **Luxor**. Comparatively new at the time, it featured a figure between the paws of a colossal sphinx, statues of Ramses, palm trees, and the 'Nile River'. It was also home to an avenue of ram-headed sphinxes like the original in Egypt and an obelisk with images around the base and engraved with the usual hieroglyphs, including cartouches, birds, snakes, *ankhs* and hares. I was now near my hotel and another chapel called **Little Church of the West**, the oldest on The Strip. Las Vegas demonstrated the epitome of extravaganza, even more apparent at night when it was transformed into a glitzy but magical fairyland. I met up with a couple who drove me the length of The Strip in their car and my comment, recorded on film, was 'It's like daylight, it's so bright'. Coloured lights cascaded in waves like glowing waterfalls, and names that I had not noticed earlier in the day stood out: **Las Vegas Club**, **Golden Gate**, **Coin Castle**, **California**, **Olympic Garden**, and a **Travelodge**. Westward Ho and Stardust had exuberant displays, the effulgent stars on Riviera looked fantastic, and even MacDonald's was elaborate. As did the paddlewheel of Harrah's, the lollypop of the Circus Circus clown had rapidly alternating illuminations making it appear to revolve.

We called into a dimly lit restaurant with fire burning in a huge bowl of water but I was not permitted to take photographs; it seems that it was a venue for clandestine assignations! We drove past the forceful Mirage cascade, the fountains outside Aladdin (now spouting water turned blue by coloured globes), flashing red flowers on the Flamingo, the changing hues of the pillars of light outside Ballys, and the piercing green eyes, lit from behind, of the Easter Island statues, also a feature of the sphinx. Finally, we drove to the top of a nearby hill for a stunning overview. However, next day I wandered backstreets behind the glitter and found it to be a dull, depressing and almost sordid town. I was led to believe that the local populace did not enjoy living there because essentials and commodities such as white goods were expensive and sometimes scarce, everything being geared to gambling and the tourist dollar.

CALIFORNIA

Death Valley

Las Vegas was a good base for many attractions in the region, and I was provided with a day tour to **Death Valley**, the lowest point in the United States, approached via miles of flat desert terrain with cacti, clumps of dried grass-like scrub, and interesting coloured hills in the background. The actual valley, a national monument, lay 86m (282ft) below sea level at **Badwater**. It was the driest place in North America and reputedly one of the hottest on earth, the highest recorded temperature reaching a staggering 134° Fahrenheit (57°C). Much of the landscape had been likened to Viking photographs of Mars, the reddish crags of the canyon serving to make its totally flat floor, which appeared like a vast white lake, even more remarkable. Although I believe that the roadrunner and coyote exist here, the only wildlife I observed in this desolate but starkly beautiful area was a couple of eagles, and except for the hardiest species, it was even devoid of plant life. An example of the rare beauty was the **Artist's Palette**, a series of contoured hills coloured red, white, yellow, brown and green by mineral deposits. Surrounded by chocolate-coloured terrain, another unique section, almost exclusively of light-coloured sandstone, was weathered into rounded slopes and serried ridges.

Driving onwards, we came to a shallow, absolutely still blue salt lake with incredible reflections, the straight black ribbon of road disappearing into the distance between multihued hills turning golden and rust coloured. Still further, there was even less vegetation, and pure white hills were topped in startling contrast by red earth. Into this isolated wilderness there emerged an Indian-operated casino. We passed a large mesa, more cacti, and plains of bluish sagebrush before arriving back in Las Vegas.

Death Valley was a borax desert but founded, like many other regions, on gold. Most prospectors used burros or mules, and supplies in 1849 included potatoes (up to $2 a pound) and flour – at $50 a barrel, as much as he could afford – which had mostly soured and provided extra protein from the worms it contained! If they could be acquired, eggs at $1 each were nestled in the flour to 'keep' and prevent breakage. The list continued with onions at $1 each and whiskey, also a dollar. Coffee, cornmeal, beef, maple syrup and canned peaches were a luxury. In addition to foodstuffs, the jackass carried a water canteen, pick, shovel, rock wedge, hammer, gold pan, coffee pot, blanket and frying pan.

NEVADA

Las Vegas

I went for yet another evening ramble (strangely, one of the few places that I felt entirely safe), and was enthralled by the vision of the Mirage's thundering volcano erupting high into the air from the centre of the fall, and even turning the water red with its glow. A blimp flew overhead, and fire ran down the steps of a side cascade and across the boulder-filled lake, it was a spectacular display.

fire above and below

Inside, more wonders unfolded. The famous white tigers were enclosed in a fanciful glass-fronted environment, with waterfalls flowing into a bubbling blue pool, synthetic palm trees, stone elephants, and hanging vines overhead. In spite of its grand appearance, it was still a concrete cage, with one tiger lying listlessly on a platform at the top of steps leading to a large brilliantly coloured flower mosaic. A second bored-looking tiger gave a tremendous yawn and lethargically groomed itself as it sat between pillars bearing images of sacred Egyptian cats by the elaborately shaped pool. Except for the pond, mural, vines, and intermittent blue and pink lights on the ceiling, everything in the enclosure was white – even the palm trees! Both animals were totally disinterested in the noisy crowd gathered around their artificial world, and the latter rose slowly to lap at water in a bowl placed beside the pool.

Ensconced in palms, bromeliads and other exotic plants, a more natural rock waterfall was located near a huge aquarium that held small sharks (including a spotted species), fish with black-and-yellow stripes, red fish, and blue varieties. Outside again, the red, blue and white Casino Royale sign was striking against the dark background of the night sky as I waited for the volcano to 'perform' again, its flames, preceded by weird music, primitive chanting and smoke, belching from the depths. Fire exploded in sequence from each terrace of the side cascade and spread to form a sea of fire below. As it receded on top, it left behind a fountain of water that spurted high into the black firmament; the green searchlight of Luxor also reaching skyward behind. Inside once more, I was drawn back to the tigers; the one on the ledge having merely turned its head, whereas its mate now paced restlessly to and fro. Flaming torches also featured around the horses on top of Caesars, and the **Planet Hollywood** sign rotated above the angels atop their columns.

The Imperial Palace **Auto Collection** exhibited beautifully restored black vehicles with gleaming brass (including side lamps), a white car with a dickie seat, a vibrant red sports car with a white hood and tall mascot, a long white convertible, and automobiles of celebrities including Hitler's Mercedes and Liberace's cream-coloured car – sporting a candelabrum on the bonnet! Next morning, hot air balloons flying over Vegas included one in the shape of a bottle.

vintage car

Planet Hollywood

Pueblo Grande de Nevada

I joined another tour to see Nevada's **Lost City**, **Pueblo Grande de Nevada**, an Anasazi (Ancient Ones, ancestors of the Pueblo Indians) civilisation extending back to AD 800 when, at its height, they raised maize and cotton, created weavings from dog hair, mined salt and turquoise, and gambled with stone dice. Once again, the way was lined with low scrub and red, grey, white, brown and yellow hills with a hint of green, and later we began to encounter remarkable red roadside formations. We stopped at a site with ducks and a shoal of milling catfish before continuing past red earth and more rock manifesting amazing shapes.

The museum was in **Overton**, 60 miles northeast of Las Vegas, but the original inhabitants once populated the length of the valley from Warm Springs to the Virgin River. We came across remains of a settlement: stone houses nestled at the foot of, and blending into, the looming red rock. Nearby, primitive petroglyphs depicted concentric circles, animals, and what appeared to be snakes etched into the black surface to reveal the red stone. This was a unique area with a small canyon composed of rock that was alternately smooth or rough and jagged; the latter with sloping strata, the former pitted with strange holes. Some of these were large enough to be classified as caves, and a few had formations like the stalactites in limestone caverns. We paused at the crest of a hill, where we surveyed a valley floor littered with mounds of red rock and a panorama extending to the **Virgin Mountain Range** and 8,075ft **Virgin Peak** near the border of Arizona.

The museum site traced a history of development from BC nomadic desert culture to a sophisticated society based on agriculture 1,000 years later. Several crumbling wattle and daub houses with weathered timber struts had been reconstructed on original foundations, and plants such as mesquite and screwbean, traditionally gathered by the Indians, formed part of the surroundings. The low dwellings had ladders to access flat roofs.

ancient adobe

The earliest residents, the Basketmakers (100 BC to AD 500), wove baskets from willow and yucca, which served many purposes: carrying water, sifting seeds and flour, and storage of grain, personal effects or ceremonial items; meals were prepared by dropping hot stones onto food in pitch lined baskets. They collected wild amaranth, piñon nuts and Indian rice grass, and used an *atlati* (spear thrower) to hunt deer, bighorn sheep, rabbits, lizards and birds. Between AD 500 and 700 they turned to agriculture, primarily corn, squash and beans, and began to make pottery; the *metate* and *mono* (stones for grinding) were developed, and gourds were often used as utensils. The turkey was domesticated, but mainly for feathers when the bow and arrow replaced the spear and *atlati*. Pits for subterranean storage were evident, and interior decoration etched into adobe walls included hands, figures, circles and animals.

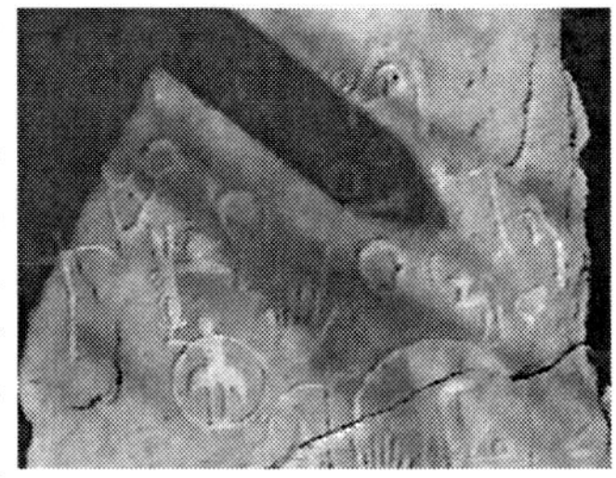

primitive engravings

A mock-up of a living area showed pottery vessels and corncobs on open fireplaces fashioned from clay. From AD 700 on, the pueblos developed, but the people disappeared around AD 1150. The reason is a matter of conjecture with several theories put forward: climate change, nomadic tribes, drought, famine, disease, or soil erosion due to overuse of resources. They were followed by the **Paiutes**.

We passed Wayne Newton's property on the way back to Vegas.

Las Vegas

Inside the Luxor with its 30-storey atrium, I found excellent reproductions of ancient Egyptian paintings on carved temple façades mingled with a modern 'Cairo'. Below the immense ceiling of the pyramid, next to rocks and genuine palms, animated camels were pure Hollywood – they even spoke! It was possible to take a boat ride down the indoor 'Nile River' but this I did not do. My hotel, Vacation Village, was also a casino but not as flashy as most. In front, an impressive statue of a cougar stood on huge boulders surrounded by Joshua tree cacti. Planes flew overhead because it was opposite the airport, but it is a sound that, along with traffic noise, never disturbs me. I attended three shows whilst in Las Vegas: *Viva Las Vegas*, a matinee starring Debbie Reynolds and, back to back, the dynamic *Hit City* and adults only *High Voltage*, voted Show of the year two years running. I caught a bus at night but did not feel at risk.

ARIZONA

Flagstaff

I left this amazing city of make believe (Vegas) at the weekend and made my way to **Flagstaff, Arizona**, which I used as a base for the Grand Canyon, journeying each morning by bus. Although boasting a nice stone church and an attractive railway station, the town was nothing special, but it was a convenient option with a beautiful drive to the canyon and certainly considerably cheaper than staying near the park; I found a room at the Monte Vista Hotel. A few dainty deer with pretty markings, enormous ears, soft brown eyes with long lashes, and white backsides with black-tipped tails frequented the railway yard, but sadly they had become accustomed to people and had turned into scavengers with moth eaten coats.

a dear little deer

Flagstaff received its name when settlers stripped a pine tree to make a flagpole. It was interesting for the fact that the planet Pluto was discovered by astronomers at **Lowell Observatory** here in 1930.

Grand Canyon

My first impression of the **Grand Canyon** was one of disappointment – it looked exactly like every picture that I had ever seen; in fact, the entire panorama appeared just like a painted canvas. That was the Grand Canyon, so what; it had nothing new to show. The many ancient strata of red and white flat-topped and sculpted rock, cut by the courses of long dried up rivers, were covered in places with trees that appeared minute from the height. Against one vertical red wall, the bare branches of a nearby blackened tree looked fantastic, and far below, a meandering line of green growth marked the passage of a current water source.

Grand Canyon

In the far distance, the crest on the opposite side stood out as a white band, its surface tinged with green. Lodged beneath a protective overhang, interesting but faint primitive art depicted long-horned deer. White monoliths also stood out against the red, and an artist wearing a typical French beret was working at his easel on the rim.

The different strata exhibited various tones of red, the topmost layer being white and other permutations achieved by changing light. Tame squirrels frequented the area, and paths crisscrossed the canyon floor between its sheer walls, circled flat-topped 'tables' with green cloths, and passed formations crowned with white. I did not attempt the hot and strenuous climb down, instead taking a ranger tour of the rim. Even here, snow-capped mountains were evident on the extreme horizon, and again a dead tree, this time bleached, provided a stunning foreground for one of the red precipices.

trees provided an excellent foreground

A formation named **Red Butte** was actually a volcanic core; aeons ago there were more than 5,000 active volcanoes in the region. There were few places where the river was visible at the bottom of the ravine that it had carved, and it did appear as red as its name indicated, but when lit by the sun it assumed the guise of a silver ribbon. Strangely, where the river cut its path, the walls that enclosed it were black. One of the attractions

canyon resident

of the park was the lack of man-made intrusions, it was just a vast plateau with the massive nine mile wide cleft, which was itself divided into myriad passageways, rugged walls within walls, and slopes studded with clumps of low growth beneath a clear blue sky. A glorious flaming sunset burst across the deep blue of the heavens as I left that first evening.

Man never made his presence felt here to any great extent; however, there was evidence of habitation as early as 2000BC, and the Anasazi came later.

Montezuma Castle

My next diversion was the more than 600-year-old **Montezuma Castle National Monument**, the site of another remarkable culture, **Sinagua**, located in a high recess of a black and white rock wall in the **Verde Valley**, with remnants of other ancient stone structures along the base. Built around AD 1100 for defence against invaders, it was a five-storey, 20-room dwelling place. An interesting cutaway model illustrated the interior levels of this cliffside habitation, which housed many families and had a lookout on top. The Sinagua were farmers, hunters and gatherers, the valley supplying abundant water for crops (the staple being corn), and game such as deer, antelope, rabbit, bear, muskrat, turtle and duck. They made pottery, stone tools and bone needles, dried skins and wove cotton. Ornaments for personal decoration were fashioned from shells, turquoise, and a local red stone. Food was kept in storehouses on the lowest level, upper floors were accessed by ladder, and they used friction for creating fire. The misnomer Montezuma Castle was applied by pioneers who mistook the ruins for those of an early Mexican civilisation.

Montezuma Castle

Jerome

We continued on to the historic copper town of **Jerome**, which featured tall brick chimneys on typical wooden houses tucked amongst greenery and weathered stone or timber buildings with names such as Rickeldoris Candy and Popcorn Company, Jerome Basket, Bird's Nest (in the Central Hotel), English Kitchen, Designs On You, Turquoise Spider, an ice-cream outlet called ZIP (a cone forming the letter I), and Copper Shop. The Daisy Hotel stood open to the sky, its roof having been removed during WWII for the copper it contained. A red brick establishment carried a sign with a leg clothed in a black and white striped stocking and the words House of Joy. Old-time benches lined the sidewalk. The town being built on the steep slopes of Cleopatra Hill, an elevated street looked out over the flat roofs of the main thoroughfare (where a man walked a pair of poodles: one black, one white) to empty wilderness beyond. It was fascinating to note that Winston Churchill's mother, Ginny Jerome, once lived here, and the town was named for her brother, Eugene, who backed the mining operations.

Sedona

From Jerome we headed for **Sedona**, just south of **Oak Creek Canyon**, a spectacular region of bright rust-red buttes, bluffs and tors, most with the peculiar cap of white limestone on the red sandstone, which created an impact even in an area full of such scenery. Pausing at a rise on the outskirts of town, it appeared as if cocooned in a gigantic basin with a cracked rim. Sedona was a tidy, well-laid-out town featuring stuccoed and timber buildings with tiled or shingled roofs, many flying the flag. Names included Golden Nugget, Corral, Western Trading Post, Delightful Muddle, Desert Dancer, Stage Stop, and Book Loft. The whitewashed English Kitchen had red geraniums on the window sills. I saw wooden verandah posts, an impressive statue of a figure on horseback, topiary trees, garden beds, and a few fountains, one making a great foreground to the red monoliths. We enjoyed lunch at tables with red and white checked cloths on a covered wooden verandah overlooking this splendid terrain.

Sedona

The awesome scenery that followed combined tall timber of predominantly ponderosa pine with the red background, and introduced brilliant yellow foliage with black trunks, which looked startling against red rock that actually began to diminish in favour of sheer white walls dotted with green. We paused for pictures at a quietly gurgling, clear stony brook with attractive long-leaved plants, yellow trees, and banks of red earth.

rivulet

Changing again as we climbed to a height, an overview presented vistas of pine-draped craggy and creviced cliffs with splashes of red and yellow amongst the verdant greenery. Gone was the red rock, replaced completely by white peaks. Far below we could see a creek bed and, to the right, the winding road snaking its way uphill.

Painted Desert

Interspersed between visits to the Grand Canyon was a tour through the **Painted Desert** to Monument Valley. The former was an extraordinary vision of gently rounded hills composed of multihued earth in perfect layers, with snowcaps in the far distance. Uncanny tones in the sandy slopes included everything from palest pink bordered by narrow bands of black and grey, to beige, red, yellow and white. We passed two isolated golden towers standing like a massive gateway with a dramatic purple sky overhead.

pillars

Further on, red tors erupted abruptly from a landscape transformed to flat parched earth in which dry red and yellow grasses struggled to survive. As we neared our destination, incredibly red mesas, buttes, and spires started to emerge, horses stood at the roadside, and we passed one solitary dwelling.

Monument Valley

Monument Valley needs no introduction because it is well recognised from countless cowboy movies. Rising 305m (1,000ft) from the Colorado Plateau, two famous formations like hands with opposing thumbs pointing skyward were indeed named as such – **The Mittens**.

The Mittens

The region was inundated with scattered monoliths, towering red walls like crenellated castle battlements, and wondrous needle-fine spurs of vibrant red rock emerging directly from the scarlet earth like sandstone stalagmites, the highest being the **Totem Pole**, 91m/298ft high and only 2m/6ft wide.

The authentic Wild West atmosphere was augmented by a derelict wagon and wheels propped against railing fences.

This was **Navajo** country and we were handed over to an Indian guide for our four-wheel-drive tour through the park. Being the first real Red Indian that I had met, he obligingly posed for pictures sitting on a gnarled and twisted branch of a blackened tree with the colourful formations in the background.

the Totem Pole

Replicas of *hogans* (dome-shaped indigenous houses) were created from overlapping logs sealed with red mud, the pipe of a central stove jutting from the roof. Sitting in the open interior of one such abode, an Indian woman was carding and spinning wool in the time-honoured method: twisting, stretching, and winding it onto a spindle by hand. The purple sky persisted and the glaring red-and-orange surroundings were charged with an electrifying sensation of suspense. The only vegetation was dried spinifex-like grasses, the stone needles produced stunning silhouettes, and the composition of the rock seemed to vary between massive smooth boulders and shale-like stone. This was the 'real' West, which Lewis and Clark pioneered and whetted appetites to 'Go West' when they set out on their 8,000 mile, two and a half year epic journey to the Pacific in 1804. Between 1842 and 1860, the biggest peacetime migration in history saw followers in their footsteps forge the Oregon and Santa Fe Trails. Travelling barely 15 to 25 miles per day, with wagons containing all their possessions, they faced gruelling treks across rugged mountains and ravines, ploughed through deep canyons, and forded perilous rivers in an untamed wilderness, guided by such as Jedediah Smith, Kit Carson, and many others.

shades of the old West

The Navajo language, one of the most difficult to master, was used by the US Marine Corps as a code to transmit messages during WWII; it was never broken by the Japanese.

We travelled back through the Painted Desert, and I also have film of a river bordered by a conflagration of claret, crimson, gold and amber growth.

Grand Canyon

The following morning was heralded by a delicate pink and pale blue sunrise as I headed back to the Grand Canyon to embark on an 80-minute complimentary plane ride with Air Grand Canyon. This exhibited a different aspect and provided a new appreciation of this awesome spectacle that was totally exhilarating; it jolted me out of my ho-hum lethargy with regard to this grandest of nature's displays. The first impression that assailed me was the mile after mile of flat open plain split by this monumental rift in the earth's crust.

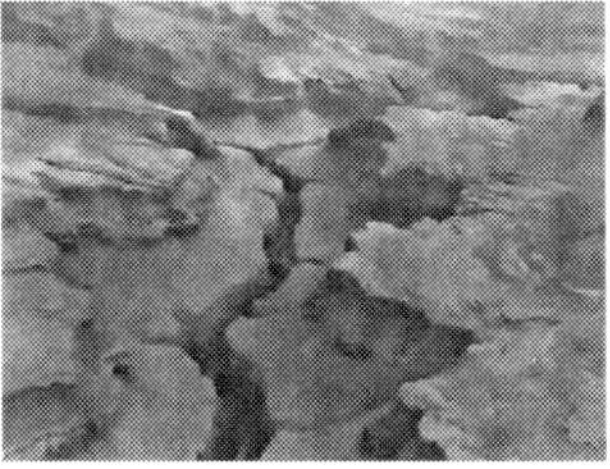
canyon from the air

The next thing to strike me was the colour as the cracked green mantle descended in giant red steps or fell in green slopes below sheer precipices to narrow fissures with water at the bottom. The mighty **Colorado River** was still only visible when flying directly above, and overpowered as it was by the tremendous size of its surroundings appeared little more than a stream. At times it was a deep blue, at others dark emerald green, probably reflecting trees along its banks, as we followed the bends and turns at its widest parts.

following the river

I saw one waterfall, and we flew on to a forested area with snow on the ground before turning for a return circuit. Occasionally the colours were inverted: green below, red on top and white strata between, the different hues seeming to swirl as the river negotiated massive U-bends.

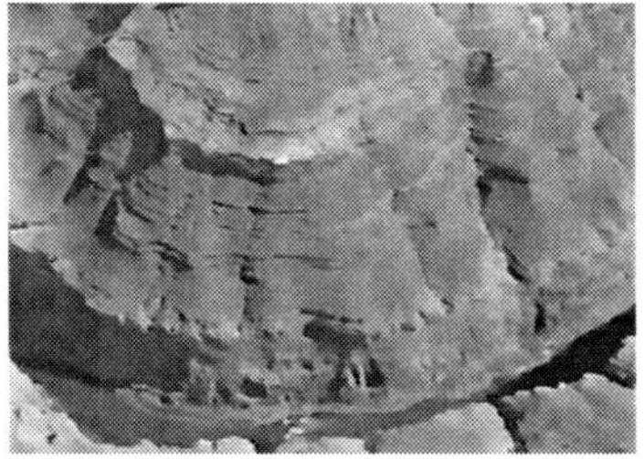
U-bend in the river

There were secondary plateaus, pyramids, walls and spires within the canyon rim, and the ground was cleaved with an infinite number of deep jagged cracks, some with tributaries feeding the main water course. As before, the vegetation varied from a smooth topcoat of unblemished green to clusters of bush on limestone outcrops. Just prior to landing, a beautiful rainbow formed a bridge from the heavy descending cloud to earth.

I returned to the park again the following morning, but even though I took a different rim tour it was an anticlimax after the flight. Nevertheless, I saw some memorable sights: a large yellow and white column photographed against a red precipice, stepped pyramids within the canyon, horizontal bands of colour like a gigantic layer cake, striking pictures with dead trees, and a closer encounter with the river, which emphasised its earthy red tones. A stone structure was decorated with Indian art depicting figures, patterns, tepees, birds, deer, and a hunter with a bow and arrow. This building incorporated a most unusual attraction: a mirror that had the capacity to turn the reflected image upside down.

a white tor made a statement against the red background

At 360km (223mi) long, 16km (9mi) wide and 1,700m (1 mile) deep, it was difficult to see how even the awesome Colorado River, appearing so small and quiet from the height, could have sculpted the yawning chasm with its looming walls of limestone, sandstone and shale. Its strata of yellow, red, green, magenta and gold documented the earth's formation dating back two billion years, and sunlight on its surfaces created an ever-changing character. Even with all the time available in and around Flagstaff, I did not make it to Hoover Dam or Lakes Mead and Powell; the latter closed for the season. All are described in a later book.

NEW MEXICO

Albuquerque

Next day, I left by train for **Albuquerque**, founded in 1706 and situated astride the **Rio Grande** in **New Mexico**. The track traversed dry plains past tepees set up at the foot of immense ochre cliffs and a few houses beneath towering escarpments and red monoliths. Because we were crossing a reservation, we had on board an Indian host who gave the commentary and provided interesting stories of herbal medicines, marriage and myths; he also played a reed flute and sang tribal songs for his captive audience. He pointed out the snow-capped **Brother and Sister Mountain** on the far horizon, but I forget the reason for the appellation. Leaving Flagstaff on the route of the old **Santa Fe Trail**, the train crossed **Canyon Diablo** on a 544ft-high bridge and passed the **Red Cliffs of New Mexico**, noted for their changing colours in the bright desert sun. Legend has it that the once grey rocks acquired their red hue from the blood of a wounded great stag as it fled through the hills. We also passed Indian pueblos many hundreds of years old, the low stone houses with beehive-shaped *hornos* (ovens) in front, and just before our destination, crossed the Rio Grande.

The **Old Town** of Albuquerque was an authentic desert community with cactus, old wagons, and adobe buildings with wooden verandah posts. Names on shopfronts included Silver Sun, Treasure House, Roadrunner, High Noon, and Thunderbird. Wooden tubs held flowering plants, benches of iron and wood sat on sidewalks, and chillies hung everywhere; light shining through the clusters produced a red glow, making them appear translucent and creating wonderful subjects for pictures. There were many craft outlets. The huge ochre-coloured adobe church, with shadows of the cross on its walls and small birds flitting to and fro, featured symmetrical white-topped towers. A wooden sign amongst yucca and prickly pear cactus in its rock garden read **Iglesia de San Felipe de Neri 1706**. The hub of the Old Town, it was built by early Spanish settlers. A line of attractive shops included one called Covered Wagon, which had an old wooden Indian (like that in the song) and wooden wagon wheels out front. It was a bright sunny day, but welcoming tree-shaded patios and covered verandahs made it very pleasant.

There was a smattering of two-storey buildings with wooden balconies, two courtyards with fountains in garden beds, old-fashioned lanterns, and one glorious yellow tree lit by the sun. Replica clay ovens stood in front of a rustic ladder leaning against a red wall hung with chillies, and brilliant plum-coloured creeper festooned the similarly toned posts and beams of a verandah sheltering another wagon wheel and a cast-iron bench. Selling very colourful garments, a shop titled Desert Sunset was located at the end of an alley carpeted in fallen leaves and lined with green plants and flowers, which included bright orange nasturtiums and blooms of vivid pink. In front of the Old Town Cat House, a yellow garden bed contained a white fretwork cat on top of a notice reading Cat Crossing, and an alert dog eyed a black feline obeying the sign! Other snippets on my film include vine-covered paved pathways and patios, art on a wall, the Old Town Music Box (a store), and a shop called Dream Catcher with rose-pink walls (also hung with chillies), its door and window painted turquoise – the latter compartmented to hold artefacts. Softly tinkling wind chimes were suspended from a vine-draped pergola at the entrance to a street where lacy iron tables and chairs were shaded by yellow creeper – chillies hanging behind were bordered by flashing lights!

My film shows an establishment called The Harvest with a sheaf tied to a post and a wagon wheel on the roof, small birds darting around a rust-coloured adobe premises with a wooden chair and rustic ladder in front, the

Indian Trading Post, and a long white building with white verandah posts facing large yellow trees with black trunks. A neon sign depicting a cowboy and cactus announced the Rio Bravo restaurant, ceramic plaques adorned a two-storey white stuccoed structure, and I noticed signs for Garcia's, Route 66, made famous by the television series of the same name. Two shady courtyards were enclosed by walls with delicate floral sprays painted around iron-gated entrances and trailing across walls: Catalina's Court in blues, white and lemon, the other with green leaves and tiny flowers in soft pastel shades. Finally, I encountered a wide multicoloured mosaic path.

chillies galore

I came across a musical quartet (two guitars, fiddle and castanets) playing and singing the nursery rhyme *Cat and the Fiddle* whilst grouped around a vintage automobile parked in front of a fountain beside the metal sculpture of a cowboy riding a bucking bronco. Other members included a character with a long beard wearing a Stetson. I also found a wooden rotunda and tree-shaded lawns with cast-iron benches; it was a very appealing town.

Colonisation by Spaniards in the late 1500s ceased when they were driven out by the Indians. Returning twelve years later, together with a Mexican contingent, the three races lived in peace until Mexico became independent from Spain in 1821, when a brief period saw the land ruled by Mexico. It was annexed by the United States in 1846 and gained statehood in 1912.

During the Civil War, two cannon now in the museum were buried behind the church by retreating Confederate soldiers.

Chimayó

I took a tour to Taos, passing interesting brown formations and stopping en route at the **Sanctuario de Chimayó** (1813), an adobe church renowned for its sacred sand, of which I have a small phial. Tradition has it that a religious object (from memory a cross) was found in the desert and transferred to a chapel whence it mysteriously kept relocating back to its original site; soil from the area was accredited with remarkable healing powers, attested to by numerous letters of gratitude. Secluded behind rustic wooden doors in adobe walls, the unassuming exterior of the small church, with tiny twin towers and a wooden cross in the yard, belied its elaborate interior featuring carved woodwork, unsophisticated paintings of saints, and heavy exposed beams. The ornate altarpiece, with intricate patterns and slender spiral pillars, encompassed a carved crucifix, and uprights in the wooden altar railing exhibited different designs. The sculpted panels of side altars were adorned with artwork and incorporated statues, simple carving decorated the pews, and the small Stations of the Cross were painted. A separate sanctuary lined with religious pictures, statues and votive candles had a small circular hole filled with the blessed earth in the centre of the floor. Even here, chillies were suspended beside paintings in the vestibule!

Taos

Continuing towards Taos, we came to a large white adobe church with a wooden balcony between the twin towers and a cross above the gateway to the churchyard. Inside were the same exposed beams, larger painted Stations in ornately carved frames, and almost gaudy coloured art behind the altar. This depicted Christ, saints and angels (the latter with green wings and dressed in red tunics over bright green shorts!), each segment framed by flowers. Also bordered by flowers, one wall held a portrayal of the Holy Trinity standing on a globe. Symbols including plants and animals appeared to have been burnt onto the wooden ceiling by poker.

Sights worth noting in the town of **Taos** (founded 1617) included a white adobe called Horse Feathers: Where the West Lives On, with turquoise frames and chillies hanging on spiral wooden verandah posts, El Rincón Trading Post (1909) with a bell mounted above an Indian eagle motif on the façade, and the interior of a house with a grill, coal-heated iron and stone jar on ledges of the adobe fireplace in the kitchen. This room also contained a wooden table holding pastry, a rolling pin and vegetables. Corn hung on a wall below dried herbs or grain, stoneware jars and jugs sat on shelves, ladles were suspended, together with a copper basin (and a single black stocking!), on pegs underneath, and wooden bowls placed below them again. An old wooden well stood in the crazy-paved courtyard. This was the home for 25 years of legendary frontiersman Kit Carson who led the way to the Pacific Coast. Built in 1825 with 30in. adobe walls and traditional beams, it was purchased in 1843 as a wedding gift for his 14-year-old second bride; he married three times altogether.

Leaving home at 17 to join a wagon train heading for Santa Fe, Kit Carson worked as a cook, interpreter – he had a working knowledge of several Indian languages – fur trapper and mountain man from 1829 to 1842, when he was asked by John Fremont to guide the first of three major exploratory expeditions that mapped the West. During this period, Fremont and Carson participated in the Bear Flag Revolt (1846), which wrested control of California from Mexico. At the conclusion of his scouting career, from 1847 to 1853 Carson tried ranching, driving 6,500 sheep from New Mexico to California through hostile Indian country and turning a handsome profit of $35,000. In 1859, he became a federal Indian agent and earned a reputation for honesty and fair dealing. With the advent of Civil War, he entered his final career as a military officer, rising to the rank of brigadier-general. His campaigns against the **Apache**, Navajo, and tribes of the southern plains brought peace to the frontier. His last appointments were as commander of Fort Garland and superintendent of Indian affairs for Colorado. He died in 1868 from an aneurysm and is buried in **Kit Carson Park**, Taos.

A wide boulevard had a gazebo, gardens in adobe surrounds, a memorial with a cross on top, yellow trees like spun gold on black trunks, and wooden lamp standards. Coloured illustrations of workers decorated cast-iron seats, and similar to Albuquerque, buildings were predominantly adobe in shades of red, brown and yellow. Large bunches of chillies hung from protruding wooden corbels, and ladders leant against walls. A weathered wooden image stood beside a doorway with a sign above featuring a buckjumper and the words Old Taos. The same street led to an attractive restaurant called El Patio, with a lacy iron gate, flowers in wooden tubs, and a cart loaded with pumpkins. Incongruously, a colourful wooden Indian in full headdress, his arms folded, stood majestically alongside a Coca-Cola vending machine!

the old and the new

Indicating the season, a few trembling leaves reflecting the colour of the adobe walls clung tenuously to a branch, and snow was visible in the distance beneath a brilliant blue sky. Using a play on words, a bookshop was called Moby Dickens. Scenes of chillies on a burnt-orange wall with a blue door and awning, a violinist performing beneath leaves falling silently like golden snowflakes, a three-tiered fountain, a coloured glass cupola, and massed birds on a stepped gable topped by a cross completed my sightseeing. Even the Holiday Inn was a classic pueblo adobe structure.

We continued to **Taos Pueblo**, an Indian community unchanged since 1540, and where parts of the present structures were built between AD 1000 and

1450. A designated National Historic Monument, it had New Mexico's highest mountain, 13,151ft **Wheeler**, as a backdrop. Archaeologists believe that Taos Indians lived in the valley before Columbus discovered America and hundreds of years before Europe emerged from the Dark Ages. Constructed entirely of adobe – earth mixed with water and straw and shaped into sun-dried bricks – the pueblo walls were frequently several feet thick. Here, the roof of the stepped five-storey structure was supported with *vigas* (log beams) across which *latillas* (smaller timbers) had been placed and packed with dirt. Outside surfaces were continuously maintained by replastering with thin layers of mud, the insides coated with thin washes of white earth. The complex was comprised of many individual homes with common walls but no connecting doorways. In earlier days, there also being no doors or windows to the outside, entry was gained only from the top. Still living traditionally, the villagers elected not to install electricity or indoor plumbing; they baked bread in dome-shaped outdoor *hornos*, and drew water from the **Rio Pueblo de Taos**.

pueblo

It was an expensive exercise to visit this pueblo of arrogant aggressive people; as well as the entry fee it cost $10 for a video permit, and even then much was prohibited. There was even a fee of $15 to sketch or $35 for painting! I managed to obtain photographs of the Morning Talk Indian Shop with a steer skull on a post, the many mounds of clay ovens, and numerous rustic ladders. Fresh Oven Bread Cooked Pies was crudely printed on a sign, as were the words Do Not Climb up Here at the head of steps, and it was forbidden to film the populace. A large covered log structure was presumably a marketplace, and the only colour was introduced by a few door and window frames; according to folklore, painting these turquoise kept the devil away from the household. A shop called Songs of the Indian Flute had paintings of an Indian and a jar on the doors, metal chimneys (some smoking) jutted from roofs, wood for fires was stacked on the ground, and

Indian houses

a long ladder protruded from the top of an underground ceremonial cave or *kiva*.

The village was situated beside a pretty river lined with yellow grasses and bare trees, its stony bed spanned by a narrow plank bridge. With its brown and white finish and plain crosses, **San Geronimo (St Jerome) Church** (1850) looked almost new. Chillies hung together with a dream catcher outside one dwelling, and a traditionally patterned rug on the wall of another, which also had large decorated bowls near the oven.

interior Indian church

Probably in anticipation of sales, one man reluctantly agreed to photographs whilst he played a large flute followed by a tin whistle. Their economy was based on tourism and craft; they were traditionally hunters but the only animals appeared to be a couple of dogs.

Santa Fe

Ten miles west of Taos, the **U.S. 64 Bridge**, at 650ft the second highest span in the nation, crossed the ravine of the **Rio Grande Gorge**. Because of its narrow width and almost perpendicular sides, this abyss looked like a rift caused by earthquake rather than a chasm created by erosion, and extensive views along its length, from both sides of the bridge, stretched across level plain to distant mountains still harbouring pockets of snow. Our route followed the smaller upper reaches of the Rio Grande, and was once again lined with vibrant orange and yellow trees.

I was deposited in **Santa Fe**, the oldest and highest capital in the United States (founded in 1610 as La Villa Real de la Santa Fe de San Francisco de Assisi!), but still with the same ambience encountered throughout New Mexico, and the same preponderance of low adobe buildings. In fact, city ordinance demanded that all construction must be in the 17th-century adobe-style and one of 23 approved shades of brown. **The Palace of Governors** (1610) was the oldest public building in the United States, and Indians spread blankets to display their wares under its long timber-columned porch. The oldest church still in use in the United States, **San Miguel Mission** (1610), was also here, and the unusual **State Capitol** was built in the shape of a Zia sun symbol. **Zia** Indians regard the sun as sacred and their symbol takes the form of a red circle with rays pointing in four directions; it features on the flag of New Mexico.

I obtained a makeshift private room at the white adobe Santa Fe Hostel, a fun place with kitchen facilities and a great crowd of young people. One night, I inadvertently locked myself out of the room and it was quite a game to find anyone to let me back in, but we all had a good laugh at my expense and I was made so welcome that I enjoyed my stay tremendously. The dining area had a bizarre wall featuring a big bright yellow ceramic sun with a smiling face, its painted rays superimposed on a blue sky. It reigned over a scene with yellow figures in a flimsy russet-coloured boat, its white sail billowing, on a rough blue ocean at the base of towering red cliffs. Cloud was cleaved by lightning overhead and other figures stood on the opposite shore. Arched recesses in a nearby exterior stone wall were illustrated with scenes that could have been heaven and hell or the apocalypse. One portrayed a green vale with beautiful mountains, snow and blue sky, the other, a mushroom cloud erupting from rugged dark stone mountains with fires and the black empty eye sockets of a white steer skull at the foot. Above was a vista of cloud or ice containing images of primitive man and an arm reaching out (maybe the hand of God?) in a black firmament.

Bandelier National Monument

Next day, I was provided a tour with an Indian guide to **Bandelier National Monument**, stopping to film six donkeys hauling an antiquated wooden caravan with chillies hanging in the window, a skull with long horns above, a goat on a trailer at the back, and a hen and rabbit sitting on the running board! We passed brilliant yellow trees, pitted pink-hued basalt walls with vertical cracks and natural caves, more adobe dwellings and a church, and an adobe-walled underground *kiva* as described earlier, with steps to access the long ladder.

The monument was in a secluded forested site (with more golden trees) surrounded by enormous taupe, pink and white cliffs and once inhabited by prehistoric peoples. Remains of stone dwellings littered **Frijoles Canyon**, which was cut by a blue stream named **Rito di las Frijoles** (Bean Creek). One foundation, in the shape of a large circle, had strange rock lined cavities in the floor, others were divided into many rooms and built in open spaces or along the base of the mountain by which, being constructed of the same material, they seemed absorbed.

ruins at the base of the precipice

Yet more, reminiscent of the cave dwellings of Cappadocia in Turkey, had been hewn from the tuff (compressed volcanic ash) and basaltic lava by tools of harder stone. From inside one of the latter, accessed by ladder, I looked out over tan tors and another large circular ruin attributed to the **Tyuonyi**, circa 1500s.

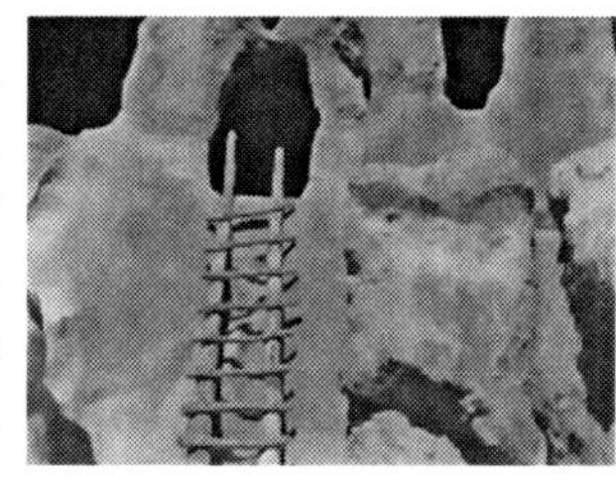
cave dwelling

Faded blue colour was apparent on one ceiling, and walls had carved faces illustrating a story, narrated by our guide, of identical twins. Other engraving included a fish, concentric circles and birds, a panel featured a stepped design in ochre and white, and there was a primitive interpretation of a macaw with a disproportionately large head. Many small holes puncturing the walls would have originally supported log struts, and boulders were used to seal doorways. The people grew corn, beans and squash, and used cotton cloth, as evidenced by remains found in caves, which indicated that they had the loom; although, the growing season being short suggested that they may have obtained the cotton by trade. Yucca provided fibres for sandals, baskets and rope; soap was made from the roots, and the flowers were eaten. They made pottery with decorations in colour or black and white and, at a later period, glazed. It is surmised that drought, soil depletion and erosion, famine and disease, singly or in combination, forced the canyon dwellers to seek new lands.

the only inhabitants today

Our lady guide demonstrated the use of stones for grinding. Strange cacti flourished, and a busy charcoal-grey squirrel with a beautiful bushy white tail was the only inhabitant in the ghostly stillness of a long deserted city, the demise of which even the trees accentuated with their falling leaves. As the day lengthened, I captured some striking pictures: a tower in the background of an autumn leaf caught in the web of a spider almost its equal in size and a red mushroom-shaped rock formation, the latter eventually filmed as a black silhouette against an eerie, almost black sky with black clouds edged in silver by an unseen light source.

rock formation

ARIZONA

Phoenix

My next destination was **Phoenix, Arizona**, a surprisingly clean and green city established on ruins of the ancient AD 300 **Hohokam** (Vanished Ones) Indian culture in the desert **Valley of the Sun**, fulfilling the prophecy of early settlers that it would rise like the legendary bird for which it was named. Next to a modern edifice with a sunburst above the entrance, a large stone building displayed small figures in niches and broadly smiling countenances in circles within ornately carved squares.

Phoenix façade

Sails created a shaded area in **Patriot Square Park** with its skyscraper backdrop, and a three-storey red brick house opposite a reserve was resplendent with attic windows in decorative gables, a turret with a shingled spire, ironwork roof capping, tall chimneys and a picket fence. Although still a collection of stuccoed buildings, by contrast the **Mercado** (meaning market in Spanish, the language mainly spoken in states near the Mexican border) was extremely modern with extensive use of colour. Its white towers, façades, pillars and arches were accented in mauve, honeycomb, peach, emerald to lime green, a variety of blues, lemon, and powder pink through to salmon. Red awnings completed the display. Palms were in abundance, and courtyards featured a three-tiered fountain with reptiles spurting water, statues in coloured niches, and a tile picture panel depicting rocks, water and verdant vegetation in vivid hues. Crossed by curving pathways, the adjacent garden featured beds of succulents and patches of lawn with shady canopies of green foliage. A large pool reflected palm trees, and a forecourt to one side had fan-shaped traveller's palms, a many-jetted fountain, and huge metal frogs: one on a lily pad, others leaping flowers. Filtered sunlight cast a pale green glow and a round tower reared in the background.

Tucson

I did not spend much time in Phoenix but moved on to **Tucson**, the oldest continually inhabited settlement in the United States, founded in 1776 as a supply depot for the nearby Mission San Xavier del Bac and where I stayed at the Congress Hotel (1919), which numbered amongst its past guests the infamous John Dillinger gang. There was more of a desert ambience here.

Behind a stand of palms I found an adobe church with symmetrical towers, and sunset produced delicate swirls of pink cloud swept across a pale blue sky with mountains visible in the distance. There were many open spaces, including an area with flowering tubs lining a broad staircase leading to pink stuccoed buildings, seating, a rotunda, and an impressive gleaming copper-toned high-rise behind. The **Pima County Courthouse** was a little different from the usual inasmuch as it sported a large flower in relief above the doorway and a highly decorative, mostly green dome tiled in a geometric design. To one side, a pale pink and white arched colonnade bounded a courtyard containing a large saguaro cactus. Another ornate pink façade featured iron-railed balconies and a small statue in a circular niche surrounded by intricate carving. The kitchen of a historic home had gourds and candlesticks on the adobe-brick mantel, a wicker basket, a camp stool, a clay jar and bowl, and a skin covering the floor.

Continuing my wandering, in a parklike setting facing a busy street I stumbled across life-sized stark white religious figures that included a tableau of the Last Supper and a crucifix. The city centre also contained an impressive feature with water cascading over rocks, quiet channels, bubbling fountains, and a large blue reflecting pool that mirrored lights at dusk. Modelled on the Cathedral of Queretaro, Mexico, the **St Augustine Cathedral** (1896) featured elaborate sandstone embellishment on its white façade. Above the entry, a bronze statue of the saint was portrayed with the saguaro, yucca and horned toad of the Arizona desert. Framed by palm trees, it looked lovely against the vivid blue sky of evening.

Saguaro National Monument & Arizona-Sonora Desert Museum

A day trip with Coyote Tours to the **Arizona-Sonora Desert Museum** was a worthwhile experience. Approached through the **Saguaro National Monument**, named after the cactus that can live up to 200 years, weigh over ten tons, grow up to 50ft (15m) tall, and the roots of which can store up to 2,000 gallons of water, the museum was also a reserve for other interesting varieties of cactus; some flowering. There was a fascinating metal frieze demonstrating the evolution of prehistoric beasts and birds from fish.

evolution frieze

Amongst the comprehensive avian collection in cages and a walk-through aviary, I saw a russet variety, a red hummingbird seeking nectar from red blossoms, a grey and white bird with a long fine beak, black head and purple flash, and a green hummingbird, its wings flapping so rapidly that they were a blur; the name derives from the sound caused by this action. A bright yellow bird with black and white wings and a black tail was pecking fruits, and I observed an inquisitive indigo bird with a maroon breast, a grey species like a parrot with a red bill and crest, and a brilliant crimson variety. Many were puffed up because of the cold wind, and a jet-black bird with beady white eyes and rich cobalt blue wings and tail looked stunning perched on a white branch of a dead tree. A pair with long black tails, white chests and blue backs had topknots of two black feathers that were blowing in the blustery conditions. A larger black and white bird of prey had beautiful markings on its white collar, bright green parrots had red faces, and a motionless sleepy brown and white owl was caged next to one with tufts of feathers like ears, which was more alert and stared at the camera without blinking. A curious busy brown woodpecker with a red crown and black and white striped wings and tail hopped up and down a trunk. Most were so colourful and active that I was tempted to take photographs even through the wire.

Animals from the region included spotted jaguarundis in a stony enclosure with dead timber and cactus, and an ocelot on a rocky ledge, grooming just like a tame tabby, the one spot of colour in its compound provided by a Halloween pumpkin! Others creatures were an ugly looking peccary, white-tailed deer, Mexican wolves with attractive markings, a glossy black bear asleep in a rocky nook, a bobcat licking its jaws and peeking warily from behind boulders, and foraging coatis with long banded tails, long snouts, and long claws with which they groomed each other.

coatis

Finally, there was an interesting display of ever fascinating rocks, minerals and crystals with names such as Chrysocolla, Bioptase, Lamarite, Hemimurphite, Azurite and Calcite, in colours of emerald, purple, cobalt blue, pink, coral, red and yellow. There were round crystals, long crystals looking like the tall cactus, and square orange crystals like glowing coals from a fire. One particularly striking core featured turquoise, violet and blue tones, and all were shown to great effect on a black background.

Old Tucson Studios

One of the best tours was to **Old Tucson Studios** where more than 300 movies, television shows and commercials had been filmed since it was built by Columbia Pictures, as an exact replica of Tombstone in the 1880s, for the 1939 movie *Arizona* starring William Holden. It was authentic even down to 1,400 head of cattle, 750 horses, 80 oxen, 125 mules and burros, 40 hogs, 50 stray dogs from the Tucson pound, 200 chickens and 20 buzzards! More recent projects included the movie *Tombstone*, John Wayne's *Rio Lobo* and *El Dorado*, *Posse* with Kirk Douglas, two Clint Eastwood films, and episodes of *High Chaparral*, *Little House on the Prairie* and *Highway to Heaven*.

mission building

Much like Disneyland, a programme was distributed on entry for various shows throughout the day. Comparatively free of crowds, it emanated a genuine Wild West feel with its adobe or false-fronted timber buildings, dirt streets, boardwalks, railed verandahs, hitching posts, wagon wheels, and the OK Corral Freight Depot built in 1957 for the film *Gunfight at the OK Corral.* There was also a decrepit adobe mission (from many a movie) with a cannon, two-tiered stone fountain, two covered wagons and a cart in the foreground.

The Rio Lobo River and the adobe Cantina with its wooden verandah posts were constructed for the film of the same name (*Rio Lobo*); it was fascinating to learn how, by the magic of film, a small body of water could be endowed with the illusion of a large river. Crossing a rustic wooden bridge, I entered the bar with its lanterns and wooden tables and chairs. The General Store had barrels, mops, brooms and implements on the verandah, and pumpkins were placed under a sheaf of grain tied to a signpost in the street. Lowering storm clouds added to the atmosphere.

General Store

There was a substantial adobe with billowing cloth rosettes draping railing on the upper level, and the two-storey Red Dog Hotel – used as a saloon in the TV series *High Chaparral* and John Wayne movies *McLintock* and *El Dorado* – with a covered balcony, bottles on the bar and shelves, and wooden tables and chairs. The Chinese Laundry, built of unrendered adobe brick with a false wooden gable on top, had a stable half door and sign announcing 'I do good job you come back again you pay in Yankee money and not in yen'. The name Lum Sing and 'very good washing ironing' was also painted on the lids of barrels mounted beside the door. Inside was an assorted jumble of paraphernalia including an old-time wooden washboard, a paraffin lantern, and amusing crudely written notices on boards that read: Lum Sing wash both man and lady laundry, Lum use fresh soap it never been in water, Lum not fix shirts just wash and then white like snow. It also was built for the film *Arizona*, as was the mission and adobe schoolhouse, a replica of the first in Tucson. Next to the laundry was a store with wooden barrels on the verandah and items hanging from beams. A wooden bench advertised Austin's Dog Bread, banners and flags flapped in a stiff breeze, and amongst the false-fronted buildings was the yellow Valley National Bank and the Marshall's or Sheriff's office, also built for John Wayne's *Rio Lobo*, which had at times held captive Clint Eastwood, Kirk Douglas and Glenn Ford. An authentic atmosphere was created with wagon wheels and cactus, a large two-storey timber structure had a columned portico and a plain pediment, and at the end of the street I could see the bell tower of the small white wooden church from *Little House on the Prairie*.

An amateurish gunfight was enacted around barrels and a carriage in the street outside the swing doors of a saloon next to the Wells Fargo & Co Express and Bank, used as a general store in *McLintock*, as a bank during the movie *Monte Walsh* starring Lee Marvin, and in a chase scenario with John Wayne and Maureen O'Hara. Three combatants acted out a scene with punching, kicking, and blazing six-guns; one character in a Stetson and chaps, who had killed his victim, twirling his revolver and stating 'I just made your day' – sound familiar? I made my way to the church and schoolhouse originally built for the 1968 film of *Young Billy Young* with Angie Dickinson and Robert Mitchum, but more recognisable as that from Little House. Inside, I found wooden desks, a blackboard (with Black Hills Dakota written in chalk), a photograph of George Washington, and an easel. Blue sky had started to emerge, and looking up, the white cross on the shingled spire appeared merged with fluffy white cloud. Gas lamps lined the streets, and some buildings only had small window panes, glass probably being a luxury item in the period portrayed. I passed a barbershop and an undertaker, the latter with a hearse inside, red curtains, and gaps in the wooden façade. I found broken wagons, the Dolan Murphy Freight Company, wooden balconies, a Dry Goods store, and a red brick Emporium with floral curtains backing displays in its bay windows, above which was painted Quality

studio street

Suits and Imported Hats respectively. Wooden water troughs stood on the road in front.

The Reno, oldest operating steam locomotive in the United States (1872), was purchased in 1970 from MGM Studios and was situated near a small wooden railroad station, the Old Tucson Stage Depot, a log building with a palomino pony in an enclosure, and a wagon – a modern jet plane flew overhead! Clint Eastwood drove the engine through the Valley National Bank in the movie *Joe Kidd*, filmed at Old Tucson in 1971.

the Reno

There was a second freight depot, and the location of *High Chaparral* (1966–71) featured remains of a wagon, adobe ruins and flowering cacti. The site was surrounded by mountains, cactus and scrub, horses were penned in a corral, and a blacksmith shop (built for *Arizona*) contained a bellows, fireplace and harness. It was used as a hideout by Dean Martin in *Rio Bravo*, which starred John Wayne and also featured Ricky Nelson. Amongst the final sights, Akters Trading Post had skulls on the ends of joists, cans suspended from a beam, and a wheelbarrow, barrels and boxes on the verandah; inside, I observed a treadle sewing machine, fabrics, cottons, and an old illustration. The Southern Pacific Depot, also built for *Rio Bravo*, bore a sign with the commemoration: Ronald Reagan 40th president of the United States acted here in the 1950 film *The Last Outpost*. Located just within the entrance, it was moved from Amado, Arizona, in 1959 and featured in the film *Yuma* (1970) and the remake of *Red River* (1988).

Other buildings in town were the Doctor's Office (displaying frontier medicines and period equipment), an Assay Office, Courthouse, the Golden Nugget Saloon, another cantina, and the Gold Dust Theatre from *Joe Kidd*. Amongst the list of movies (in chronological order) were *The Bells of St. Mary's*, *Gunfight at the OK Corral*, *The Lone Ranger*, *Have Gun Will Travel* (the inspiration for the alternate name for my books), *Bonanza*, *Gunsmoke*, *Mark of Zorro*, *Posse*, *A Star is Born*, *How the West was Won*, *Hart to Hart*, *Calamity Jane*, *The Three Amigos*, *Desperado*, *Billy the Kid*, and more recently (in 1990) *Tales from the Crypt* and *Unsolved Mysteries*. The venue also included an amusement park called Silverlake. We drove back to Tucson through stony brown mountains and hillsides covered in brush, flowering cactus, prickly pear, and tall saguaro like a veritable forest.

I completed the day with a walk to the colourful **Barrio Historico District** not far from my hotel, passing on the way a contemporary interpretation of Arches, Bryce and Mesa Verde parks painted in red, vibrant pink, mauve and blue. More-subdued art depicted Indian mythical figures, Bandelier National Monument, and an eagle standing on a cactus, a snake in its beak and talons. This was one side of a central globe with a wing on the left and rays on the right, and on the other were Spanish conquistadors, one armed with a halberd. A chained man sat astride a horse, and a hunter armed with a spear chased his quarry (a deer full of arrows) on horseback. A plant superimposed with the faces of a family grew above skeletons buried in rocks beneath the surface of the earth. This decorated the wall next to a bright yellow building, and the intriguing area featured a beige building with turquoise frames, adjacent rose-pink and blue houses, crooked walls, and a striking pink residence with blue pillars, shutters and porch railing. A teal-blue house had white shutters, and a pink and apple-green dwelling abutted one in a lurid green. A vivid blue house, its yellow door and green steps flanked by prickly pear cactus, had a huge imitation gecko clinging to a corner below its flat roof, and a red brick house with a shingled roof had a blue door and a bright red and yellow gable. A salmon-pink façade featured a blue door and purple step. Another red brick home had green frames, a pale blue and white iron fence, and a garden full of gay petunias. Finally, I found two more blue houses, one with a yellow door.

Tombstone

Next day, I followed up my studio tour with a visit to the real **Tombstone**; known as The Town too Tough to Die, one street was even called Toughnut! With all original 1880s buildings, it looked just like a movie set, and Big Nose Kate's Saloon stood in the main street, this time sealed and lined with parked cars. Conversing on the sidewalk, one of two local identities wore a black Stetson, black suit and white shirt with a black ribbon bow tie, and carried an ivory-handled gun in a holster. Flags fluttered from false-fronted buildings, and I came to the original **OK Corral** described on a sign as:

FEED & LIVERY STABLES
HORSES, MULES, BOUGHT, SOLD, & TRADED
HAY & GRAIN HORSE SHOEING BLACKSMITH

In and around the yard was a collection of wagons (including a glass hearse!), the Jail – next to the Total Wreck Saloon – and wax models of well-known protagonists positioned for the legendary shootout on October 26, 1831, which was narrated by a taped commentary. On one side were **Ike** and **Billy Clanton**, supposed rustlers and highwaymen, with **Tom** and **Frank McLaury**, hardworking ranchers. On the other were Tombstone Chief of Police **Virgil Earp**, his brothers **Morgan** and **Wyatt**, reputed deputy and US marshal, and their friend **Doc Holliday**. When the smoke cleared after only 30 seconds of gunplay, Frank and Tom McLaury, together with Billy Clanton, were dead and Virgil and Morgan Earp seriously wounded. Other infamous names associated with the town were those of **Bat Masterson**, **Billy Claiborne** and **Johnny Ringo**. I was given free entry to **Historama**. Located next to the OK Corral, this was the story of Tombstone narrated by Vincent Price, which employed animated figures on a revolving stage and film showing licking flames engulfing the town in the fire of 1882, surging swollen waters flooding the mines, and gun battles; it also reproduced the piercing sounds of Apache war cries.

Back in the street, I passed a picturesque house with white railing, vines, a pretty garden – and chillies hanging in the porch. Balconies gracing some false-fronted wooden façades created cover for plank boardwalks, and a museum was housed in the first **Telephone and Telegraph Office** (1902). Drawn by two black horses, a red stage coach with yellow wheels made its way down the street, and a two-storey brick establishment with stone quoins had a white portico, pediment, and rooftop belvedere.

the West lives on

The interior of a bar was decorated with wagon wheels, a collection of clocks, figures standing on a mezzanine balcony, and Western paraphernalia including hats, the confederate flag, long steer horns, and a reward notice on a post. Just as picturesque were some of the names such as the Tombstone Tumbleweed (the local newspaper) and a hair parlour called Curl Up 'N Dye!

The name of the town originated from derision afforded a miner who ventured into the hills and was told that all he would find would be his tombstone; his eventual wealth realised around $1,000,000! The townsite was laid out on March 5, 1879, and by June 20, 1880 there were 3,000 people in the camp; in the 1890s it reached 15,000, and today numbers approximately 1,200 residents. Traders included the OK Café, Stetson Saloon, Wells Fargo Express Office (1880) – with the picture of a bearded miner panning for gold

– Sourdoughs, Tombstone Trailblazers and Outfitters, Campbell and Match Billiards, Medicine Bow, and Kate's:

A Legend in Her Own Time Restaurant & Coffee Corral
The Most Original Cowboy Saloon in Tombstone

This was written on a sign beneath a beam of the verandah. Printing on the window of a brick building with a wooden balcony read Virgil W Earp City Marshall & Deputy, and another saloon, featuring a singing cowboy, had a bar mirror with a deeply carved surround – and a roulette wheel on the ceiling! The name of Nellie Cashman (Angel of the Camp) appeared frequently in annuls and around town, including a restaurant and beauty shop, and a bowlegged character bearing side arms and wearing spurs, a waistcoat and ten-gallon hat strode purposefully along the timber decking. A sign on the white wooden balcony of the two-storey Silver Nugget depicted a jubilant miner, and the stone **Bird Cage Theatre** (1880), once an infamous Bawdy House, was the town's most authentic building. This featured old photographs, portraits and billboards, an illustration of an exotic Eastern dancer accompanied by a man playing a lute, several clocks, steer horns, a wooden ceiling, figures sitting in curtained boxes between which sets of antlers were mounted, and a couple of pianos in the dark cluttered interior. One of the boxes was furnished with a carved chair, a gambling table still holding scattered playing cards, and the strange combination of a steer skull and a painting of genteel society in an ornate carved frame on the walls. Above the box was a sign stating 'This box was occupied by 'Russian Bill' every night for 2 yrs, at $25 per night. Bill was not an outlaw but just wanted to appear tough, so he stole a horse, for which he was hanged. He was really a Russian nobleman and was pitied by most of the citizens.' Glass cabinets held a wealth of other memorabilia. More businesses included Old Miners BBQ Café with a picture of crossed tools, and the Tombstone Epitaph newspaper building.

I watched the Helldorado gun slinging entertainment, which included a re-enactment of an altercation between Virgil Earp and the McLaury's, where the former was shot in the back from the balcony of the Grand Hotel to which the latter had retired. It was another amateurish production in a dirt street with a boardwalk, hitching posts, an open-fronted mock-up Oriental Saloon (where beer was 5c and whiskey 25c), a Barber, the blue and white Grand Hotel, a Boot/Shoes Shop, a Gun Shop, Lees Laundry, a Cantina, and combined Doctor and Dentist. There were a lot of drunken bodies reeling around, fisticuffs and gun duelling; it was an enjoyable diversion with quite a bit of humour.

I was on a private car tour and we progressed to fascinating **Boot Hill Cemetery**, with a few plants in the dry ground and plain wooden crosses atop stone cairns. A wooden epitaph read:

Here lies George Jackson
Hanged by mistake in 1882
He was right
We was wrong
We've strung him up
And now he's gone

Words on crosses stated: Red River Tom shot by Ormse, Killeen 1880 shot by Leslie, Marshal White shot by Curly Bill, and some, such as James M Martin 1881, with name and date only. Another wooden tombstone had similar wording to the one found in Silverton, which led me to believe that one (or both) was not authentic. This one claimed:

Here lies Lester Moore
Four slugs from a .44
No les no more

One weathered board that did appear genuine read John Heath taken from County Jail and lynched by Bishee Mob in Tombstone Feb 22 1884. Others included: Cowboy Bill King shot by Burt Alvors, and Billy Kinsman 1888.

San Xavier del Bac

A tour to the wonderful **Mission San Xavier del Bac** (1783–87), nicknamed White Dove of the Desert for its shining white exterior, revealed paintings on walls and in spandrels and domes. These included a large illustration of the Last Supper and a haloed Mary, surrounded by angels, standing on a pedestal with the Christ Child in her arms. Fancy capitals crowned pilasters, and ornate coloured stuccowork adorned cornices. Statues appeared in niches or on brackets (many below sculpted curtains), and there were three altars with elaborate and colourful carved stonework. A fluted canopy lay above the intricate gilded main altar, its entrance flanked by bronze lions and colourful ceramic angels. The second altar featured a crimson-robed figure standing above a silver image lying in a glass case, and the third carried a statue of Mary garbed in blue. The entire interior was filled with decoration in gold and various shades of red, blue and green.

Alone in a desert wilderness, surrounded by palms, aloe, prickly pear, saguaro and spindly trees, and with a flat topped mountain beyond, this striking white church featured a stunning entrance sculpted from brown stone.

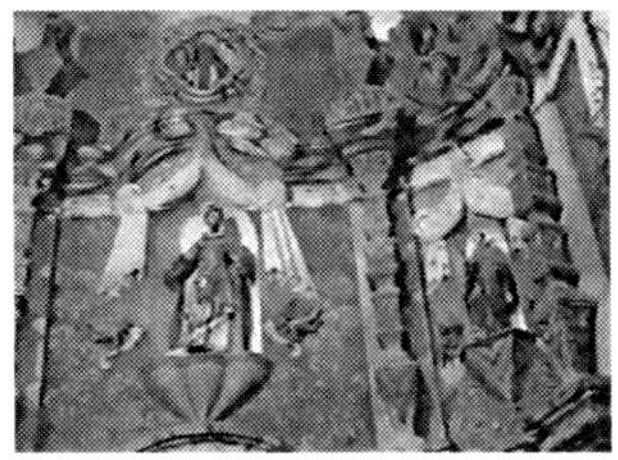

interior San Xavier del Bac

This also contained statues in 'curtained' niches, and a separate white tower housing three bells appeared above the high exterior stone wall. The white was almost blinding against a deep blue sky, and I obtained good pictures through a multi-arched gateway at the rear, with a simple cross on top and a small statue in an opening. A four tiered-fountain sat in the courtyard.

church façade

The view from a height showed a helicopter coming in to land and the city of Tucson unfurled on a timeless flat desert plain surrounded by mountains, resembling a giant caldera with grey skyscrapers like fingers of smoke in the centre. We approached **Sabino Canyon** through more stony brown hills studded with 200-year-old saguaro and past quiet reflecting pools ringed by white boulders. Joining an open-air shuttle, I made a couple of laps of the park. That evening, I came across a jazz band consisting of a pianist, saxophonist, and Negro drummer in a white suit and hat playing the classic *Don't get around much any more.*

MEXICO

Nogales

I embarked on a tour to the border town of **Nogales** in **Mexico**, which was dirty and untidy but extremely colourful and, with its lively atmosphere, refreshing. It was a return to colourful flat-topped adobe structures: a red building next to the blue and yellow Fiesta del Sol, attached houses of deep pink, pastel green and blue, and others in lemon, pink and pale green. I was confronted by steep stepped streets, cobbled roads and a horde of cats, which surprised me. Donkeys in gay striped blankets (one with a purple cap!) pulled gay yellow carts displaying brightly painted scenes that included palm trees, houses, a church, and a snowy mountain behind a huge orange flower on a stony outcrop. The blue Bar Los Amigos stood next to a café with a red and yellow rainbow, and an incongruous edifice glorying in a pediment and life-sized statues on the upper façade stood next to a powder-pink drug store with white trim and pillars.

A woman was sorting produce on the pavement, there were many big, noisy and colourful old American cars, and I found a café called Kahlua, like the drink. Bright rugs were displayed under an awning, and a row of shops in blue, baby pink, yellow and salmon pink was almost garish. The words Super Tortas were painted in yellow alongside El Oasis, which had a vivid blue awning on a glaring lilac wall. A large painting of a galloping horse and a red canopy distinguished the next street, and abutting another yellow façade, La Finca de Adobe was the name on a brilliant blue building with hot-pink guttering. Other streets revealed adjacent apple-green and bright pink walls, a large structure with mosaic motifs, and a fountain and blue umbrellas in front of turquoise and pink buildings. A two-tiered blue fountain provided the foreground to an illustration of a Mexican in a sombrero sitting beneath a cactus, a hawker cart stood outside a stone church, and a large red, yellow, blue and green sunshade identified the entrance to a street market selling, amongst other things, very colourful Mexican dolls, ponchos, and artificial fruits and flowers.

AMERICA

ARIZONA

Tubac

On the return to Tucson we stopped at historic **Tubac**, first settled by Hohokam Indians from the year 300, then the Spaniards with Father Kino in 1691, followed by the Mexicans in 1821, and finally, since 1853, becoming part of the United States. Tubac was the site of Arizona's first European settlement, its first schoolhouse (1885), newspaper, and state park: the

Presidio (fort), established in 1959. The Spanish constructed the fort in 1752 to protect settlers and missions from attack by **Seri** and Apache Indians and to extend their presence along the frontier in the face of potential colonisation by Russia, France and England. The commander of the Presidio (**El Presidio de San Ignacio de Tubac**), Bautista de Anza, and explorer Fray Francisco Garces, led a party of 240 colonists and over 1,000 head of horses, cattle and mules westward, eventually founding the city of San Francisco in June of 1776. In that same year the military authorities moved the garrison to Tucson and unprotected settlers left their land. In 1787 a company of Indian soldiers under Spanish officers was posted at Tubac, Apache reservations were established, and peace maintained by providing supplies, but when Mexico gained independence in 1821, the new government lacked funds to continue supplying the Apaches, and many resumed a life of raiding. That, together with the lure of gold in California, led to the town being abandoned once again. In the tides of change, it prospered to become the largest town in Arizona, but the Civil War drained the region of troops, leaving it vulnerable, and it was once more deserted. Although resettled following the war, silver strikes around Tombstone and the routing of the railroad through Tucson again saw its demise, and it never regained its former importance. In succeeding years Tubac had become a boom town, ghost town, mining town, and now an artist colony.

Small **St Ann's church** (1920) stood opposite the **Presidio State Historic Park**, its buildings including a kitchen with an adobe-brick fireplace, shelves holding utensils and a wicker basket, garlic and chillies hanging on the wall, and a long wooden table with bowls containing food items and a large platter full of fruits and vegetables. A rough adobe dwelling, its verandah roof supported by crude logs and a huge saguaro cactus in front, also stood in the park, but more interesting were the homes of local artisans with their shady verandahs. One occupant sat in a rocking-chair on a covered porch with a metal wagon wheel leaning against one of the rough-hewn timber posts. Located near a small shrine, prickly pear cactus grew beside salmon-pink adobe benches decorated with white flowers. In the main street of the small town, al fresco dining could be enjoyed near an adobe building with blue trim and large decorative iron gates. Another enormous saguaro towered above the light blue Mi Casa Su Casa, an ochre structure had a round turret, and prickly pear flourished in the dry soil. Quaint figures occupied places above and beneath a shop sign reading Cloud Dancer. A white adobe with projecting log corbels stood starkly against a very blue sky, a bell hung in a small arch above a brick entrance, and we visited the mission (San Xavier del Bac), visible in the near distance, to which I had been the previous day.

NEVADA

Las Vegas

I headed back to Las Vegas on the train, passing a wind farm with hundreds of three-armed steel windmills in perfect rows, like some alien army on the flat red desert floor. Defying the odds, I found Las Vegas just as exciting the second time around, and walking down The Strip from Vacation Village, I took film of a rainbow in the spray of the fountain in front of the colossal sphinx outside Luxor. Drawn in perpetuity by two life-sized model horses, a coach with a golden lion emblazoned on the side stood in front of Excalibur, and passing under the portcullis beneath the towers with their colourful spires was like entering the magical kingdom of King Arthur. Inside, the décor was lit to represent a castle at night, with turrets beneath clouds in a painted sky and crenellated walls bearing banners and coats of arms. There was a huge living tree, and a two-storey structure stood in the centre of a fountain ringed by coloured lights in the water.

Exiting here, I came to the waterfall outside Tropicana with its colourful buildings and entered MGM Grand, at that time the world's largest hotel, casino and theme park. Here, I saw the setting of *The Wizard of Oz* with Dorothy, the Tin Man, Scarecrow and Cowardly Lion walking arm in arm down the yellow brick road as it weaved its way through a field of red flowers; a shining green castle in the background appeared to be composed of vertical elongated crystals. A hot air balloon with a figure speaking from the basket floated overhead in the blue dome of a sky rent by thunder and lightning. Surrounded by plants and lit with coruscating lights, the little wooden house of Dorothy's aunt revolved on a turntable; pink and blue flowers and enormous red toadstools with white spots were scattered around, and flashing lights cascaded in sequence, like falling raindrops, through a canopy of leaves. Dorothy, a basket on her arm, was holding a conversation with an animated tree, the Tin Man, carrying his axe, was talking to the lion in a forest, the Witch made an appearance, and the Scarecrow, his arms extended, was nodding in a corn crop. Directly in front of this fairy story re-enactment, patrons were playing slot machines!

Beneath the glittering dome in the reception area of the hotel, people sat on a circular bench with statues in the middle. Partitioned off with simulated swagged curtains, the long front desk was ablaze with the glare from an enormous multi-panel screen behind, the pictures rapidly changing along its entire length. Dressed in a black suit and bow tie, the realistic animated figure of actor and comedian Foster Brooks was relating stories and jokes beside a huge wall mural, and another bench surrounded an artificial tree with a broad girth and a canopy of bronze leaves. Vines adorned a wall with arched openings containing a small fountain and planter boxes. An illuminated mural was shown to effect behind dark arches, and on a wide brightly lit concourse, draped white statues flanked the entrance to Leonardo's.

In the massive theme park portraying glimpses of different cultures, I first encountered Casablanca Plaza: an Arabian concept with onion domes flanking a white arch decorated with blue tiles. An arcaded building called Casablanca lay to one side, and a red and yellow Arabic tent stood in the court along with palm trees. This led to a street that could have represented any era or locality, followed by a visit to contemporary New York Street with its Central Park Wedding Chapel, Pawn Shop, and Outer Space Voyage. Gas lamps lined this thoroughfare, and I came across the end of a musical production like a scene from *South Pacific* being enacted on the sidewalk. Billboards advertised Empire Cold Cure and a soap product. Olde England Street featured half-timbered structures, a replica of 12th-century Glastonbury Abbey ruins, a brick arch, lighted lanterns, lead-latticed windows, and a brick and stone building that, according to its title, took one behind the scenes. This was followed by New Orleans Street with a full-sized gleaming coal-black railway engine at a station and a food stand with a red and white canopy.

Seeing the funnels of a paddle wheeler at the end of the avenue, I made my way to the 'Mississippi River' where again I just caught the end of a performance, this time jazz. I had been issued with a timetable on arrival but did not have a chance to consult it. Here, I found the *Cotton Blossom* steamer, an impressive metal statue, and a stone bridge leading to the Salem Waterfront, which could have been anywhere in Europe with its towers, half-timbered buildings, and white lighthouse. I wandered past the riverboat, a green windmill with a waterwheel alongside a wooden wharf, and a small humpbacked bridge. My investigations took me inside a large theatre, and past more half-timbered structures with shutters and window boxes, a stone turret with a shingled roof, and clapboard shops with gables. In this conglomeration of cultures and periods in time, distant artificial snow-clad mountain peaks suggested a place on the Continent.

Entering the Asian Village, I encountered pagodas, plants on pedestals, buildings with curled corners on the roof, and a green and gold edifice with the tall thin spire typical of Thai architecture. Two characters from Popeye, the villain and Olive Oyl, were posing with eager fans, and I backtracked to

French Street displaying a most attractive medieval stone building with a tower, shingled roof, arched windows and doorways, dormers with shutters, and flower boxes.

Olive Oyl and friend

The Old West Supply Co. and a timber construction with attic windows denoted other locales. I passed in front of the shingled windmill, small bridge and green pool, at the edge of which, old-style street lighting and narrow brick buildings with shutters and decorative free-standing gables indicated Amsterdam and its canals.

Crossing a small wooden bridge brought me to Tumbleweed Gulch where a troupe of players known as 'Grandmosphere' was performing a skit in front of a tepee and the Tumbleweed Hotel. It consisted of a Western comedy and dance routine with cowboys, Indians, cartoon characters (one in a gigantic Stetson and one with a huge headdress), and the obligatory fair young maiden, who was actually a make believe animal wearing frilly pantaloons and a petticoat under a pink and white spotted dress with puffed sleeves and a full skirt; a flat straw hat decorated with a green ribbon and yellow flowers sat on her head. Calling for his bow and arrow, the cartoon cowboy was presented with an outsized bow tie and an Arrow shirt by a 'real' cowboy in a gaudy red ten gallon hat, red bandana, black shirt, and black and white leopard-print chaps and waistcoat. Another cast member aimed a miniature bow and arrow. I walked by the Rio Grande Cantina and retraced my steps to the entrance.

Amsterdam

Back on The Strip, diagonally opposite Harrah's I came to the huge pool with its statue and series of fountains outside Aladdin and a billboard advertising David Copperfield at Caesar's, which this time I managed to capture on film. Wall panels bore deep relief of Roman soldiers in helmets and tunics, waging hand to hand combat with spears, swords and shields, or on horseback with near-naked bodies being trampled underfoot and naked women abducted.

There was a perfect reproduction of Michelangelo's *David*, and lighted figures in recesses behind a large galleon, a figurehead forming its pointed bow, floating at full sail under a darkened firmament illuminated by 'stars'. A blue and pink sunset 'sky', which changed as I watched to the purple and black canopy of night, lay above a simulated marble forum. This was composed of buildings circling a tumultuous fountain with ornate columns and imposing figures. These consisted of Neptune with his trident astride a fish, four images of Pegasus, a naked female and one in flowing robes, a Roman soldier wearing nothing but a helmet (and strategically draped cloth) wielding a shield and spear, and a central figure, maybe one of the gods, with a bare torso, long beard, and bearing a Roman-like ceremonial standard. Other life-sized images lined the parapet above lighted arches around the perimeter of the room.

wall panels

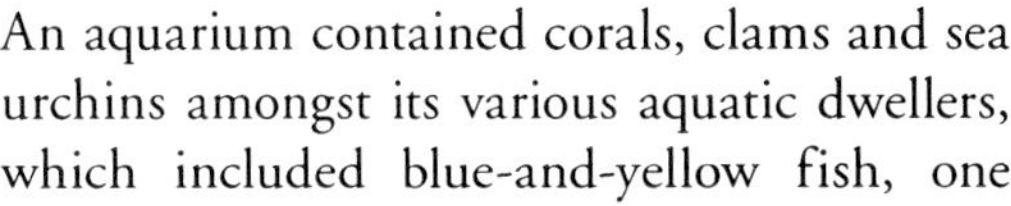

An aquarium contained corals, clams and sea urchins amongst its various aquatic dwellers, which included blue-and-yellow fish, one species with a long 'snout', a bright pink variety with a yellow tail, brilliant yellow fish, striped and spotted fish, a single striking red fish, and one banded in red, white and blue like a patriotic flag. The central animated character in the tableau described previously announced 'I am Bacchus, god of merriment and wine' as he sat on his throne drinking from a gold goblet, tapping a finger, and shaking with raucous laughter. Sprays of coloured water played, as did the image with his lyre. I returned to the fountain, which was then under 'daylight'.

Caesar's fountain

Leaving here, I strolled past Harrah's enormous 'riverboat' and Casino Royale to re-enter the Mirage, where a brown Bengal tiger had joined the white one still languidly lounging on the ledge beneath the lovely floral mosaic. I discovered another indoor waterfall tumbling over boulders and enhanced by exotic vegetation, which included palm trees, banana plants, orchids, ginger, and bromeliads sprouting from the trunk of a dead tree fallen across the cascade. Continuing on past Treasure Island, the day darkened and a fairy-tale world of moving coloured lights emerged against the night sky. The brilliantly hued steel umbrellas were outlined in flashing globes and the Westward Ho sign was crowned with sparkling rainbow towers, their radiance flowing upwards and flaring at the top like fountains of light. Silver City and the onion dome atop the adjacent restaurant (offering a variety of international cuisine) stood out more than in daylight. Stardust literally lived up to its name with myriad heavenly illuminations. The kaleidoscope that was Riviera was also festooned with winking blinking stars and coruscating colour, and the entrance to Circus Circus was just one vast canopy of red and white twinkling points of light rolling in different directions. The lollypop of the red-haired multihued clown was twirling as I went inside to enjoy more of the entertainment. This time an artiste was performing amazing bodily contortions whilst held by a man hanging upside down from the bar of a trapeze. At one stage, the girl was held only by their entwined legs, and in another part of the act her body was suspended horizontally from a strap around her partner's neck and vigorously spun. With a brief squeal, she released the end around her neck (amid gasps of dismay from the audience who thought that she was going to fall), to remain hanging by just one foot and spinning vertically. Acrobatic tricks included performers being catapulted from a board onto the shoulders of one riding a unicycle, a girl executing a double back flip on stilts, and gymnasts doing complete back flips on the spot.

UTAH

Zion National Park

I left for a tour of **Zion** (established 1919) in **Utah**. Whenever I began to think that I had seen it all, something else would come along to impress, and I was overawed by this majestic park. Traversing a black chasm with a return to the beautiful yellow trees, the terrain gradually assumed reddish hues, finally becoming a true red crowned with white as we entered spectacular canyon country featuring towering formations, which together with the foliage and sky produced an artist's palette of colours. The beginnings of a rock arch were pointed out on a far slope. According to our guide, 14 types of lizard and around 200 bird species, including eagles, falcons and spotted owls, inhabited the area. Reaching speeds of more than 200 miles per hour, the peregrine falcon is the world's fastest bird.

Our first stop was the **Visitor Centre**, which was ringed by impressive peaks including **West Temple** and **Tower of the Virgin**, the second at a shallow sandy creek bed with the strange vertical faces capped by white Navajo sandstone looming above and a few white flowers amongst the yellow trees with their black trunks. Climbing to a position above the treetops and beneath an overhang, we stood behind a gently falling veil of water like a beaded curtain; rays of sun shining through produced colours in the prismatic drops, and it was almost possible to count each one. It was an inspirational sight. A white monolith shone in the glare of the sun, but the subdued lighting in a narrow cleft produced many shades of red (iron oxide) through to apricot and almost pink, and various greens from jade to a lovely lime. Other colours were introduced by lichens and mosses. Lacy black branches of a dead tree looked stunning against the red, and all was surmounted by an exceedingly blue sky.

Zion

Deeper into the park, awesome 3,000ft walls were almost intimidating as they overpowered the surroundings and constricted the field of vision; mammoth firs on high ridges were dwarfed into insignificance. We had our first sighting of the partially obscured **Great White Throne** (750m/2,460ft) looming above its neighbours and came to a faster flowing, but still shallow, stony **Virgin River** confined by massive 2,400ft perpendicular cliffs. Incredibly, the mighty **Zion Canyon** was carved by this small river, which could turn violent in a flash flood.

Virgin River

Adding to the rich warm tones, glorious red trees lined a narrow ravine, and the soft murmur of the stream was the only sound as yellow leaves fell in a silent shower. Sun's rays peeping over a crest shone through the yellow and red foliage, accentuating black trunks and casting an ethereal glow in God's red cathedral with its blue dome overhead. The red leaves shimmered like bright flames of fire or molten lava, it was indescribably beautiful.

The multitude of sculpted formations included iron-capped tors (called hoodoos), arched recesses, and the **Great Arch of Zion**, a blind arch high up on a vertical surface. Numbered amongst the trees were cottonwoods, willows and velvet ash. As if by sleight of hand, the Great White Throne appeared once again in the camera lens when zooming in to the red and black cliff faces that framed it. We came to a small cataract in the perceptively bluer river, now wider but still enclosed by sheer precipices with shining yellow and amber trees at the water's edge. As well as a few hoodoos and surfaces that looked as if sliced by a gigantic knife, the Throne was visible here also, behind white peaks and red mountains that were thrown into relief as the monument became apparent by zooming towards it. This was an enthralling environment, with the burbling brook, trees like liquid gold in the shadowy interior of the red canyon, white summits, and blue overhead.

In a nearby small settlement, a red brick building with a white steeple provided the foreground for natural spires behind. Red pinnacles also appeared in the background of picturesque houses, one with smoke issuing from the chimney, a white picket fence, and clumps of pampas, their fronds glowing in the sunlight.

glowing pampas

We returned to Las Vegas through changing colours and configurations, finishing with the black canyon and a flaming sunset.

Las Vegas

Also outside the Vacation Village were a tall saguaro and a group of life-sized metallic horses with flying tails, running forever on gravel beside boulders. My final excursion downtown revealed a ridiculous life-sized pink elephant which looked like a papier-mâché creation, Tropicana advertising Folies Bergère and, in MGM, a second artificial tree, an animated queen waving a wand and speaking beside flowers her equal in height, and the vibrantly coloured Oz rainbow forming the ceiling of an arcade lined with slot machines. Another walk through the 'enchanted forest' produced a more severe thunder and lightning storm, with clouds swirling on the domed ceiling above the toadstools, flowers and castle. A smaller more-intimate castle had a turret and gate posts adorned with pink hearts, and the Scarecrow was still nodding in the cornfield. Lights twinkling like stars overhead were outshone by the blaze from slot machines, and back on The Strip the continuous stream of traffic roared past a Treasure Island now lit with intense colour. The spectacle of the Mirage waterfall, its flames (reflected off passing cars, turning them pink!) and central spouts of water higher than the surrounding palm trees, never palled, and flaring torches illuminated Caesars.

CALIFORNIA

Yosemite

I departed Las Vegas to return to California and onward to **Yosemite National Park** in the **Sierra Nevada** mountain range, leaving behind the flat desert landscape and outlying casinos of Nevada Landing with its tower and imitation paddle wheelers, and the frontier inspired Gold Strike – the last civilisation for a while. We traversed miles of terrain with coloured sands and one stark white section, which underwent a complete transformation on my film to be replaced by *snow*!

It was winter in Yosemite, and the splendour was unsurpassed. My first views were of 914m (2,998ft) **El Capitán**, one of the largest granite monoliths in the world; **Half Dome**, a 670m (2,198ft) granite massif sheared in half by glaciation, and 740m (2,427ft) Yosemite Falls, narrow but the highest in North America and sixth highest in the world.

Yosemite falls

Deer inhabited white fields, the firs and grey mountains were dusted with snow like icing sugar, and a tiny red church provided a rare touch of colour. There were a few yellow trees, snow covered logs, and a tranquil clear unfrozen stream reflecting the mountains and green of conifers along its banks. With only small patches of blue, the colour of the sky matched that of the grey rock, and the world appeared inverted in the flawless mirror of the water. At our next stop, where snow lay more thickly, **Bridal Veil Falls** dropped 227m (744ft) and provided another awesome spectacle. To paint a composite picture: snow-coated logs formed the foreground to a solitary yellow tree on the far bank of a quiet watercourse that reflected huge green pines dwarfed in a gap of the lightly sprinkled mountains, the falls down an almost smooth face to one side and white El Capitán on the other.

Bridal Veil Falls

Another stunning picture shows pines at the base of these same crests filmed beyond the last orange leaves clinging to a bare branch. We crossed a stony stream and followed the road beneath Christmas card trees, their branches weighed down by a white mantle.

Our next stop, **Glacier Point** (2,199m/7,214ft), revealed a farther valley view, this time from above: copious scenes with deep pockets of snow and white trees, as yet lush green slopes, the massive bare El Capitán again to the left, and Bridal Veil waterfall to the right. There were many vantage points for magnificent photography in this incredibly beautiful park. Framed by branches of a fir, this one also presented pictures with a cloth of delicate cloud on snow-crowned summits. We drove closer to the cascade, which fell from a U-shaped depression that it had probably helped forge directly down the sheer face to the **Merced River** on the valley floor. The monolith was still on the left, but it was easier to appreciate the many peaks to the right of the falls from this location.

Christmas card scenery

We progressed through changing vistas to the bigger **Yosemite Falls**, where two tiers plunging down a cliff with evergreens at the base were visible across a wide white meadow dotted with yellow and orange trees. As it plummeted silently in the distance, the towering second drop gave an indication of the immense height of the much larger one above. The river, with small snowy islands in the middle, coloured trees on its banks, and the still surface reflecting firs and a mountain covered by mist-like cloud, wound through one side of the white field. Yet another view of the energetic falls revealed a third, even higher drop, spilling into a hanging lake between it and the next level. We walked to the base, where only the lowest fall was visible as it thundered over boulders at the bottom and along the rocky bed of the river. Living up to its name, **Sentinel Rock** stood watch in the background.

Merced River

A quiet section of the waterway was bounded on one side by a striking white cliff face, and turbulent stretches were surrounded by massive broken slabs of rock, snow-covered fallen logs, moss-cloaked trunks, and copper-coloured leaves. Many summits appeared through low mist wafting in the background, and rows of pines like serried ranks of soldiers crowned one precipice. These were the mighty giant redwood, also called sequoia after the Cherokee leader Sequoya. Nature's largest living thing is the General Sherman Tree, the equivalent of a 27-storey building! With the introduction of colour, it differed from the regular black and white world of winter and was therefore extremely beautiful. But the most superlative site of all, viewed from different vantage points, was that of snowy rocks and russet, yellow and green trees in front of a U-shaped depression between the sheer faces of two white monoliths, rolling cloud over the top, snow-covered slopes in the gap, and the whole superbly duplicated in a still body of water. It was an outstanding sight that literally took my breath away and I stood transfixed. The park lodge was enhanced with beautiful floral arrangements, and late in the day the scene was made even more bewitching by falling snow, through which the lights of the building shone.

the ultimate picture

Next day, I ventured back to the park by bus, past pine-dressed mountains that extended right to the road and a tiny church with a white steeple, through small communities, beside the rock-strewn river, and beneath **Arch Rock**, an entrance created by one of the monstrous boulders that now lined the route, riverbed and banks. I spent the time amid more entrancing scenery with its magic meadows, marvellous mirror images, snow-draped trees, and a different aspect of Bridal Veil Falls, which dislodged an amount of snow like a mini avalanche, but on this occasion under bright blue skies. I crossed a snow-covered wooden bridge across the river for additional views of Yosemite Falls.

NEVADA

Reno

The blue of the sky was reproduced in the river on the return trip, which this time concluded in **Reno**, its autumn-decked streets lined with attractive housing. Reno by night was, if possible, even more brilliant than Las Vegas: a dazzling, gleaming and twinkling blaze of oscillating, revolving and changing colour, flowing upwards, outwards, and in every conceivable direction on the **Sands**, **Flamingo**, **Fitzgerald's** with its shamrock and wall with vertical green bands of moving light, the **Virginian**, **Riverboat** with funnels, sparkling rainbow arches, and flashing card suits, the **Calneva** (California and Nevada) and **Comstock** casinos. Even a huge Free Parking sign and that announcing loans on jewellery were brightly illuminated! An arch across the main thoroughfare, **Virginia Street**, had the name Reno in big, bold, bright pink neon letters, and Biggest Little City in the World in blue below. Other casinos were **Bandstand**, **Horseshoe**, **Harrah's** and **Harold's**, the last featuring a gigantic painting of a dramatic landscape containing a 'flowing' waterfall created with white lights and a team of plodding pink neon bullocks pulling a yellow covered wagon with pink wheels. On the second floor, I found an impressive array of more than 2,000 weapons: antique guns, spears and shields, duelling pistols, Winchesters, Colts and Derringers. **El Dorado** had a tower block and lights like a literal kaleidoscope of changing patterns, and **Circus Circus** featured a multihued clown vibrating with colour; like Vegas, a monorail ran past the huge striped big top. Prices advertised breakfast for $2.79, lunch at $3.49, and dinner $4.79; a one pound prime rib was $7.95 and steak and lobster $9.95. Inside, I found the bizarre mock-up of a saloon, with a guitar and a picture of a sheriff, his moustache moving and star of office twirling, on a wall, a bar mirror, imitation flowers, a neon flashing 'Hotel', a character like Daffy Duck, a miner's pan on a post, and animated figures and objects. These included a mechanical piano player, bottles that toppled and righted themselves, the lid of a jack-in-the-box opening and closing, a critter popping up from a barrel, a rocking basket, dripping water, a rearing grizzly, a dog nodding its shaggy head to keep time, and a pair of disembodied boots tapping to the music! The midway incorporated a sideshow alley with prizes of fluffy dolls and Looney Tunes characters including Tweety, the Roadrunner and Coyote.

By day it was a nondescript town situated on the picturesque **Truckee River**, which was crossed by a nice arched bridge. There was a green park beside a dam, its placid water spilling over a small cataract to rocks. I took a casino tour where I spent the day accompanied by a charming Negro related (nephew, I think) to Rodney King, who made international news when severely beaten at the hands of police. He was very solicitous of my welfare (lending me a coat and gloves) but refused to be photographed because he was apprehensive of reprisals if recognised. It was a free gambling tour offering gaming credits, food and drink, but neither of us were interested in participating and just went for the sights, which included a dark church with white cupolas on its twin towers, a huge sundial, a bottle-green and purple hall, **Silver City Casino**, and two interesting turrets, one hexagonal in shape and decorated in pink and blue.

That night, there was an exciting interlude when an announcement was piped throughout the hotel requesting guests to vacate their rooms due to a fire alarm. Because I sleep naked, I scrambled into slacks and a T-shirt (without underclothing) and proceeded to the foyer where elderly men and women were congregated in all forms of undress: women with curlers in their hair and men in striped pyjamas. Everyone was milling aimlessly around unsure of what to do and mingling with the elaborately dressed casino crowd – it was hilarious!

Because nobody seemed to take charge, I organised cups of tea for distressed people, and when the big, beefy, brawny firemen in their orange suits and yellow helmets arrived I requested to go back to my room for the camera. Permission was initially refused but eventually granted if I was escorted by one of the fire fighters, which I duly accepted. It all turned out to be a false alarm but was very entertaining.

Lake Tahoe

I had stayed in Reno's twin town of **Sparks**, and next morning the city, ringed by snowy mountains, was spread out below my window, with birds flying across apricot-tinted clouds in the first rays of sun and lingering street lights. With Gray Line I set out on a tour to **Lake Tahoe** – the largest alpine lake on the North American continent, third deepest in the world, and spanning the border of two states – and Carson and Virginia Cities. The weather had deteriorated again, with falling snow blowing across a stream to form heavy banks, and cloud closing in so that the sky appeared to touch the earth.

Several communities comprised Tahoe, the first being **Squaw Valley**, site of the 1960 Winter Olympics, a typical attractive alpine village with steeply roofed buildings, a ski lift, and a snow-covered bridge across a rivulet meandering through deep expanses of white. We continued following the icy river through **Tahoe City** and on past false-fronted timber structures to **Emerald Bay**. With mist hanging on the surface, the windswept dark-coloured lake was anything but green, and it lashed at a stony shore protected by sturdy pines. We stopped for lunch at **Caesar's Casino** in **South Lake Tahoe** (1,897m/6,223ft above sea level), with a view over snow-covered roofs and a solitary boat on the dull lake. Derived from a Native American word, Tahoe means Water in High Place (or Big Water depending on the reference), and was inhabited by **Washoe** Indians for centuries before being 'discovered' by Captain John Fremont and Kit Carson in 1844.

Carson and Virginia Cities

Underway again, in foggy conditions and with snow banked on road verges, we pressed on to **Carson City**, named after legendary frontiersman Kit Carson. Here, the day underwent a complete transformation; we were greeted by brighter light, green lawns, autumn trees and conifers, and a few impressive edifices, as befitted a state capital, but I found it singularly uninteresting.

At a higher elevation, **Virginia City** was a different story: full of character and with old-time constructions along wooden sidewalks. Originally chasing the lure of gold, prospectors found that the sticky mud that clung to picks and shovels proved to be silver, assayed at $2,000 a ton in 1859! The resulting boom turned Virginia City into the most important settlement between Denver and San Francisco, and grubby miners into millionaires who built mansions, imported furniture and fashions from Europe and the Orient, and financed the Civil War. At its peak the city was a boisterous 24-hour town, both above and below ground, with visiting celebrities, Shakespearean plays, opium dens, newspapers, competing fire companies, over 100 saloons, at least five police precincts, and a thriving red light district. The International Hotel was six storeys high and boasted the West's first elevator – called a 'rising room'! Wiped out by a devastating fire in 1875, which destroyed more than 2,000 structures, the town was rebuilt in just a year and many of today's buildings date from that period. For over half a century it held the attention of the world, pouring more than $400,000,000 in gold and silver into the economy of an expanding nation.

Buildings included the imposing white-walled **Fourth Ward School** with its central tower, **St Mary of the Mountains** with a white steeple, several spires and a rose window, the **Mackay Mansion**, and a few other three-storey structures with wooden balconies creating covered verandahs. Snow lay in the streets of this town with its authentic Western ambience, which also featured the **Delta Café and Saloon** (1876) containing the original **Sawdust Corner Restaurant** and **Suicide Table**. The cluttered interior with its wooden ceiling was decorated with old Tiffany-style bead-fringed lamps, guns and swords, pictures including a sailing ship and portrait, bottles, and a framed knife collection. The second section, established in 1863, contained pictures and portraits, a glass-fronted cabinet with an assortment of knick-knacks, a player piano, antique cash registers, deer heads, beaded light shades, a mantel clock, paraffin lanterns – and modern slot machines!

Virginia City

Other interesting buildings included the red brick and white clapboard **Bucket of Blood Saloon** with an old-fashioned bar, a second church with a steeple, the **Julia C. Bulette Saloon and Café** incorporating the **Red Light Museum**, the red brick **Molinelli's Hotel** with a sign reading Silver Queen outlined in lights, intriguing **Piper's Opera House**, which looked more like a converted fire station, The Wild West Museum, red and yellow buildings, the Trading Post, and Buckskin. There were the usual false-fronted timber façades, and rough-hewn posts supported balconies. The streets were on different levels, the highest devoted mainly to white wooden houses with white picket fences, their mountain backdrop almost obscured by mist. Called The West It Was, an old timber-built museum with a shingled roof had tools and a mill wheel out front, and I came across of a couple of bay windows, the Shooting Gallery with elaborate fretwork, the Gold Room and Brass Rail Saloons, Wild Horse Souvenirs, and a shop titled Solid Muldoon. In keeping with the ambience, a yellow vintage car was parked outside the Bucket of Blood.

A light flurry of snow was falling as I came to a boardwalk alley, a room off which contained an enamel bathtub, a toilet pedestal, bottles on a shelf, umbrellas, a lace cloth on a makeshift table, and patterned linoleum on the floor. Feather boas, men's hats and ladies fancy chapeaux, a frilly garment, the confederate flag and framed pictures all hung on a wall papered with stripes. The reconstruction of a barroom displayed a feather boa on a rack and bottles on shelves, as well as a revolver in the holster of a gun belt hanging on a post, a board reading 'just hitched', posters, and the stars and stripes. A painted sign on a brick wall read: This is the Territorial Enterprise Building, home of Nevada's first newspaper, still published from this building weekly. The newspaper began printing in 1861, and one of its early reporters was Samuel Clemens – alias Mark Twain! There was a Glass Blowers Workshop, a bell tower, the Virginia City Mercantile, the **Red Garter Saloon & Gambling Hall**, and Comstock Cowboy Western Wear. Snow had blown onto sidewalks, covered wooden stairs, and also coated steps with stone balustrades leading to an impressive three-storey wooden residence with a bay window, turret and carved porch on solid stone foundations.

From an upper level, I looked across the tops of buildings, one with a belfry on its steeply pitched shingled roof, another with a crooked chimney wired for support! Except for bare trees and a few parked cars the streets were practically deserted, which made for good photography. I came to the rear of the ramshackle Red Garter (with pipes, patched tin walls and a paling fence), yards blanketed in snow, and a row of houses in blue, red, and green, the latter with a yellow door and trim. It began to snow again as I came to the 1859 **Territory Prison and Marshal's Office**, now the **Museum of Wax**, with a boarding house of the same year overhead. Next, I saw a line of gabled buildings with attic windows and the interior of the **Washoe Club** (1875),

Virginia City's oldest Saloon, its walls adorned with old-time photographs, antlers, and a large frame holding pictures clipped from old newspapers; an incongruous crystal chandelier and beaded lampshades hung from the wooden ceiling with its carved cornice. Signs outside the club announced **Historic Winding Stairs** and **Museum of the Macabre**. A wooden Indian with braided hair and a full feather headdress stood in another doorway, street posts were decorated for Christmas, and a bath tub, possibly used as a planter in summer but now filled with snow, resided on the boardwalk alongside wooden benches. There were 750 miles of tunnels underneath the streets of the city, once the Richest Place on Earth! Calamity Jane's Bar was the subject of the last photograph that I took before boarding the bus back to Reno, stopping briefly at a casino featuring an interior of make-believe façades.

Lake Tahoe

a black and white world

The following day, I rejoined the train past snow-coated river scenery in an even more black and white winter world, with grey skies again reaching to the ground, isolated houses covered in the white precipitation, bare trees with black trunks (the yellow foliage now gone), dull dried brush, pines, and an occasional bluish tinge to the black ribbon of water. Even the train appeared grey as it rounded bends and blended into its surroundings, and my film looks like old black and white footage.

Through water spattered windows, I photographed a small community with a couple of colourful stores and iced-over parked cars. A white house with fretwork trim like giant snowflakes matched the frosted features of the landscape. Progressing further, trees became lost beneath their white mantle, and I glimpsed a shrouded lake. This was **Donner Lake**, about one and a half hours out of Reno, where a party of 89 Illinois pioneers were stranded when caught in a snow storm en route to California. All but 47 died of starvation, and those that survived had resorted to cannibalism.

At one stage, I became aware of an eerie bronze glow from a hidden sun trying to penetrate the dense cloud cover. Like sand, snow blew in a fine powder off rocks embedded in deep banks, and from the rear of the train I filmed the single track cutting the white surface.

tracks in the snow

The bare branches of delicate lacy trees were trimmed with snow, a blue sky began to emerge along with yellow and green trees on hillsides reflected in still water, and by the time we pulled into **Colfax** the snow had all but gone. Eight minutes before Colfax the train crossed **Long Ravine Trestle** from where **Cape Horn** was visible; the steepest slope on this line, rail crews had lowered Chinese labourers down in baskets to hack away a narrow ledge for the track.

It had been necessary to make a huge detour to Sacramento in order to return to South Lake Tahoe by Amtrak thruway bus service. Very early in my trip, whilst waiting at San Louis Obispo station for the train to Monterey, I had met a gentleman who insisted that I come to stay when I reached Tahoe. He was farewelling his sister and she reiterated the invitation saying 'He really means it'. Hence, when I contacted him, he put me up in **Caesar's** because being a 'high roller' he had accumulated many points for accommodation. He joined me for breakfast and both he and his wife were most hospitable, although it was not possible to venture further than their home in the almost blizzard conditions. Even worse than my prior visit, the view from the restaurant was practically obliterated, and everything was white: buildings, roads with a small amount of slow moving traffic, and even the unseen lake, with snow still falling and forming dense drifts. However, the room was cosy and one of my better lodgings, even to a large circular bath beside the bed!

I briefly braved the conditions to take pictures of the hotel façade and the snow-coated statue of a pony express rider (Tahoe was on the fabled route), but was quickly forced back indoors because of the intense cold, which rapidly numbed my fingers and prevented me filming. Nothing much beyond the immediate vicinity was visible.

pony express

Inside, the décor presented a similar theme to Las Vegas: a figure standing in the centre of a forum and a brightly coloured Egyptian figure holding a notice, with deep relief of naked and near-naked images in various poses on the wall behind. All that could be seen from my window was a solid bank of unblemished snow. On departure, my generous hostess presented me with a leather bag to hold my ever increasing load of brochures.

I stayed two nights, and the day that I left it was magnificent: white clouds in a deep blue sky and brilliant sunshine glinting off deep white banks on the verge, which caused even the bus driver, who sees it regularly, to exclaim that it was like a picture postcard. We followed a camper van with a foot of precipitation blowing off the roof, and for the first time, the lake was blue. Cabins banked high with snow were almost concealed beneath tall white trees, and a red snow plough stood out, as did a blue and yellow building. We passed a small church with a white steeple, a tattered flag flapping from a pole, a man shovelling snow (who gave a cheery wave), buried fences, an icy stream, and an illuminated sign stating Poor Visibility Chains Required, which our driver alighted to comply with. At a second sign, reading Chains Required Over Summit 25mph, traffic was pulled over at an obligatory stop for inspection. We climbed the pass with glistening banks of smooth snow reaching overhead on one side, and a valley with fields of white ringed by snowy mountains to the other. As we descended, homes were snuggled beneath branches of trees bowed down with the weight of the load they carried, which caused our coach captain to comment 'all the little houses … just like you see in the Christmas cards'. We began to follow a small river filled with snow-covered rocks, and more of the beautiful trees, their glistening ice crystals making them appear made of lace, created a breathtaking sight.

lacy trees

By the time we stopped to remove the chains there was not a cloud in the sky, and the fine tracery of the trees looked stunning against the rich blue. Apparently, the area had been destroyed by fire and the houses were all new in the last few years, but there was no evidence of the disaster in this gorgeous white fairy-tale land.

a white world

Finally leaving the snow behind, we came to a street appropriately called 'Spring', and drove down a thoroughfare with fancy but narrow false-fronted wooden buildings in pastel tones of pink, green, beige and blue, which included a tobacco shop, ice-cream parlour, Sam's National Bank, and a barber. I acquired a room with rows of pigeons roosting on the sill and a horizontal pole outside my window, and a view that included a nearby pink and white wooden mansion resplendent with fretwork on gables, a tall chimney, balconies, a bay window, turret, and wooden balustrades.

village shops

I travelled by car through dry, gently rolling hills shadowed by cloud, with sparse growth, a few yellow trees, and *no* pines! My memory fails me as to with whom I was driving, or indeed the town that we visited, although one of the prettiest residential areas that I saw, featuring colourful wooden and shingled houses with paling fences, decorative gables, carved verandah posts, attic windows and small porches. One had a creeper-covered arch leading to the doorway, above which was a weird figure seated astride the tiny but colourful shingled portico. A second had a miniature windmill, its sails spinning, and a two-tiered white fountain, a large pink and white house had a cascade of pink and red flowers over a stone wall, and a lolly-pink dwelling with a picture window stood next to a cream and brown residence with hedgerows, topiary trees, and a hexagonal belvedere on the roof of the verandah. Other colours amongst the small and large homes were red with white trim behind a bright yellow tree and blooming pink magnolia, and blue and white. One of the biggest, on a corner block with a large garden, was grey and white with a red dome on one corner, wooden trim around the shingled upper storey, and transoms with leaded glass. A pale pink cottage with white shutters and a grey roof had dainty fretwork pillars, and a yellow and white house had an octagonal belvedere and an attic window in the gable above the porch.

attractive houses

An elaborate white shingled mansion with tall red brick chimneys featured a carved pediment over the porch and a gable with a 'moon' opening leading to a tiny balcony; it was set off by a brilliant liquid amber tree in the grounds. Others exhibited a round turret and an attic window, a multi-paned bay window, an ornamental arrangement including shells, driftwood and dried flowers behind plate glass, and a large window with a half-curtain in lace and a straw hat trimmed with artificial red flowers and red ribbon hanging on the door. Tall blue flowers reared in front of a house with a fanlight in a small gable, and a white urn behind a yellow hedge fronted a house endowed with amazing leadlight windows. Elsewhere, white flowerboxes were filled with colourful impatiens.

CALIFORNIA

San Diego

I made my way south to **San Diego** and from a tour bus took film of a gay commercial centre. Amongst its colourful façades I noticed a yellow building with green trim and red-and-yellow awnings next to a red building with a bright pink edifice in the background. We drove past upmarket housing, a pastel pink and blue complex, and the attractive pink-toned Mediterranean-style La Valencia Hotel with maroon awnings, set in a lush garden that included tree ferns. We continued down a long boulevard lined with tall palm trees, through an area of small shops, past boats in the bay with the city skyline beyond, and along **North Harbor Drive** where the three-masted sailing ship **Star of India** was berthed. The oldest square-rigged merchantman afloat, in 1863 she made 21 trips around the world and was now part of the **Maritime Museum**. Next was kitschy **Seaport Village** with its wooden buildings (one sporting huge antlers), a lighthouse, clock tower, and exclusive condominiums. Entering the city proper, impressive buildings amongst the high-rise included the elliptical and concave edifices comprising the Marriott Hotel, another with cascading glass tiers, and the tentlike construction that was the **Convention Centre**.

We came to the **Historic Heart of San Diego** where the **Old Spaghetti Factory** was located, traversed the downtown area, and crossed the **Cabrillo (Suicide) Bridge** with the **California Tower** and **Balboa Park**, housing the **Aerospace Centre**, **Museums** and **Art Gallery**, at the end. Passing a semicircular colonnade and bandstand in a garden setting, we continued on to **Heritage Park** and adjacent **Old Town State Park**, site of the first European settlement in California. This featured a collection of old-time brick, timber and stuccoed buildings, including one called simply Groceries & Provisions, and a Tobacco, Cigar and Pipe shop, its rustic posts supporting a shingled canopy over the plank sidewalk on which stood a wooden Indian. Sequestered amongst palms was a white Spanish-style mission with a blue-domed tower, and the park was invitingly laid out with white railing fences and a green tree-shaded common in the centre, the sound of a train hooter adding atmosphere. There was a building called El Fandango with umbrellas in the courtyard, a three-tiered fountain in the compound of the Bazaar del Mundo, a long low white building with a small bell tower above the entrance, and flags hanging limply from flagpoles behind a vibrant orange and yellow garden in front of the **Mormon Battalion Memorial** building.

The beautiful, very elaborate two- and three-storey Victorian homes included one with a spired white turret next to a pumpkin-yellow timber edifice with carved woodwork and a porch. Beside this again was a tan, rust and white mansion with a square tower, a tiny carved pediment, and woodwork embellishment; all were in immaculate surroundings with old-fashioned lighting and paved roads.

grand house

On **Old Town Avenue** I found a bell on a parapet, the **Old Town Saloon**, historic **Whaley House**, paintings outside a small gallery behind a white picket fence, and finally, an old shingle house with a sign reading Dentist and Physician. A harbour trip showed the modern city skyline with a cruise ship, ferries and boats at the **Santa Fe Pier**, small yachts in the bay, a flock of birds flying low across the water, a bridge, and an old fishing trawler.

MEXICO

Tijuana

I took a tour with Gray Line to **Tijuana**, impossible to mistake for any other destination because Mexicans love colour. The main drag, **Avenida Revolución**, was a riotous mix of crowded discos, restaurants, seedy bars, bellowing hawkers, and tacky souvenir shops. We parked near the only substantial structure, its pinkish façade featuring a delicately sculpted parapet and a tripartite entrance, with a *jai alai* player balanced on a globe of the world in a pool outside. Also called *pelota*, the game is one of the fastest on earth and played with a *cesta*: a curved wicker basket strapped to the wrist and used to hurl a leather or rubber ball. A girl wearing a purple top and riding on a banana decorated an entrance beneath a red cupola, with a red and yellow building one side, and red, blue, lilac and yellow walls the other. Vivid lime and orange were used together, and pink appeared under the eaves of a building enhanced with alternating large blue and green diamonds.

Wearing striped blankets and pulling illustrated carts, the donkeys of street photographers were very much in evidence, along with vendors holding enormous bunches of large multihued paper flowers. Everywhere, I was assailed by colour. A green Bar, Grill & Dance hall was hung with fluttering flags and different-coloured balloons – it also had a full-sized yellow school bus on the canopy above the sidewalk! Many Third World countries used old United States school buses for their transport systems. Another flower seller sat on the pavement with yellow paper sunflowers, a sign beneath the dance hall read Dentista, and there was a bright pink gable, an apple-green building, a pink tower, and more huge multicoloured flowers, even the litter bins were bright red! Cars were mostly antiquated and rattly.

I saw a building called simply 'Terror' and an old pedestal clock on the footpath. A clock face also appeared in one of twin towers, their bells ringing merrily, of a church with two-toned pink-hued stonework and statues in niches on the façade. De Dulces was illustrated with samples of its wares (confectionary), and I came to a large blue and mauve building and two open-fronted food shops. The first, with a flaming fire and a cheery merchant wearing a red apron, made tacos; the second, the name Tropical spelt out in fruits and vegetables, sold *ensaladas*, *frutas*, *tortas* and *hamburguesas*, the vendor also in a red apron. A girl walked by carrying a cage containing a live green and yellow parrot, and a man outside a stall with a red awning was sweeping the pavement between white plastic tables with garish striped cloths placed beneath a tree, its trunk painted red, green and white. Next door, another man was painting a storefront vivid blue and yellow.

It was all very lively, and I reached a square with a three-tiered fountain, tree-shaded pergolas, and colourful shops, the sounds of amplified music blaring from a fiesta in progress nearby. Making my way towards it, past a small plot growing bananas, I found another square, this one with multicoloured streamers overhead, decorative bells and artificial flowers, fairy floss sellers (even some of this was multihued!), a band playing, and other performers walking around with instruments: a double bass, piano accordions, and guitars, one being strummed in competition with the act on stage. Another vendor was cooking meat on a hotplate, there was a red Licores (liquor) store, men wore Stetsons (it seemed the sombrero was no longer favoured), and a gaudy blue statue sat on a maroon pedestal. It was very noisy and I did not linger long.

A magenta building decorated with a row of wagon wheels and green trim stood next to the yellow **Hard Rock Café**, the words The Border Of Rock above the entrance and the rear end of a big old American car sticking out of the wall overhead. There were more *mariachis* here, and the streets resounded with music.

typical Hard Rock Café

The next photographs I took were of a vibrant green and yellow building and others embellished with checks or stripes. Chess sets were for sale amongst figurines with work-worn faces wearing scarves and carrying baskets of chillies or bright jars.

Mexican figurines

A bell above the corner of the ochre-coloured adobe Margaritas Village (1982) rang out, a sign on the front advertising Coyote Joe Exotic Skin Boots. It was strange to see two onion domes on a glaring pink building; reminiscent of those in Russia, one had red checks, the other curved bands of black and white. Boarding the bus again, we drove past the statue of an Aztec-type warrior silhouetted against the orange cloud of sunset, a pale pink stone wall daubed with graffiti, and the depressing shanties of a *favela* (slum), showing just a sprinkling of pastel colours, wending their way up hillsides. I imagine their life to be such that the inhabitants would have little regard for the usual beautification of homes.

AMERICA

CALIFORNIA

San Diego

From my window in San Diego, I observed a whale wall, bay vistas, and the city skyline. My next excursion was to the **Zoo** (world's largest) where I was given a complimentary guided double-decker bus tour. At the entrance I was greeted by a large long-legged bird with a long fine beak, ducks, spoonbills, a crested white bird, and a flock of glorious crimson flamingos, one continually swaying its long neck to and fro. Exotic plants such as orchids grew in trees, and amongst the exhibits were restless hyenas with striking black and white stripes, various deer including a species with long backward curving horns like a sable antelope, lions (one rolling on its back and lying spreadeagled like a domestic cat!), and a polar bear pacing with its pigeon-toed gait in a concrete enclosure whilst its mate did a back flip in the pool. According to our guide they spend 70% of their life in water and this female stood 6ft tall, weighed over 700lb, and had 6in. claws in both front and back paws. A Kodiak, the world's largest bear, was penned in a similar compound, as were smaller glossy-coated black bears. A white rhinoceros still retained two respectable horns, and a cage held magnificent scarlet birds. I am always enthralled by the antics of comical meerkats with their alert, cute and cheeky faces, upright stance and quick movements. A ram with massive curled horns was housed next to a shaggy white mountain goat with small black horns, and very active lynx' had long pointed ears with the signature tufts of fur on the ends. A pair of beautiful white foxes with bushy tails had delicate shadings, and lovely golden-brown ferret-like animals were fascinating to watch as they continually bounded over rocks and leapt up and down a tree. Two cheetahs on leashes were being walked around the grounds by keepers – accompanied by a red setter dog!

Next, I came to yellow-billed and orange-crested toucans, and a lush walk-in rain forest aviary with bird's nest ferns and moss-covered rocks. Pecking at the fruit of a monstera, a white bird with a tall crest and shrill cheep was answered by the raucous call of a peacock perched on the railing of a bridge. It was feeding time for the seals, and gorillas inhabited a beautiful area with a waterfall splashing over rocks, plenty of greenery, and trees. After having experienced them in their natural habitat it was never the same to see animals in captivity, especially these largest relatives of man that are very human-like in behaviour. There was one huge silverback, a mother with a babe on her back, and a juvenile watching an adult strip and eat bamboo. In a second aviary, with a nice cascade, I found waterbirds with stilt-like legs and a beautiful turquoise variety with a russet back; its wings, when spread, were blue and black. A tiger (behind glass) lazed by a pool and had a stout branch to climb on; most enclosures contained dead trees, which I always find attractive for their artistic value. An appealing swamp area was also enhanced with the skeletal trunks, as well as long-leaved plants. Back at the entrance, a rainbow-coloured macaw (that said 'Hello') was perched in front of yet another dainty waterfall surrounded by palms, the flock of flamingos further along.

the artistry of dead trees

The Amtrak conductor that I had met on the train took me to lunch at a restaurant with magnificent views of the harbour and city. Afterwards we drove through a pleasant suburb with a couple of large half-timbered houses: one very English with a bird bath on the lawn, the other with multi-paned windows and an iron-railed platform between gables on the roof. There were stone houses, white paling fences, and a large pink residence with white columns and trim. When I commented on the number of timber houses in America, my host astounded me by stating his impression that Australia did not have many forests and had to import all its wood! Americans are really very ignorant about the rest of the world.

Our destination was the renowned red and white **Hotel del Coronado** with its long verandahs, towers, and domed ceilings, one with chandeliers in the form of crowns. I was informed that the royal yacht was brought in every several years and stayed for a few days. In fact, it was rumoured that King Edward VIII met his future wife Wallis Simpson at a dinner here in 1920. The hotel had hosted 12 presidents and featured in the 1959 film classic *Some Like It Hot*. Returning to the city, I captured one of the most glorious sunsets that it has been my privilege to see: flaming across the sky in purple, pink and yellow streaks that coloured the entire bay, deepened to crimson, and finally turned orange.

Capistrano

I took a bus to historic **Capistrano**, where the swallows return from their annual migration, and its mission church (1776). Although with minimal decoration on the outside, the colourful interior featured a statue in a niche with painted red, green and yellow surrounds, flowers and faces in spandrels, tiny carved Stations, and crystal chandeliers. Artwork around a framed picture simulated curtains in soft green and red, and painted flowers in urns were further enhanced by a frieze below and a pattern beneath the cornice above. Its **Serra Chapel** was the oldest building in the state. The white exterior, with a red dome on the three tiered tower, looked stunning against a deep blue sky. The mission grounds were not open, but looking over the wall I glimpsed nice gardens, a colonnaded cloister and a fountain. Other interesting attractions in town were the Trading Post, a stone tower with a white dome behind vibrant red maple trees, and an old red railway carriage used as a depot.

Disneyland

I caught the train to **Anaheim**. How does one begin to describe **Disneyland**? It is billed as 'The happiest place on earth' and in truth it was impossible to spend the day without a smile on your face and was one venue enhanced by noisy crowds. The entrance was marked by yellow flowerbeds on green lawns in front of a red brick building with a clock tower and white stone quoins. Just inside, a cannon stood in front of a green square surrounded by traditional buildings and towers; red bows and holly decorated lampposts (an indication of the approaching festive season), and a band marched by, its members dressed in white trousers, red jackets, and plumed hats.

I boarded a horse-drawn carriage for the ride down Main Street, U.S.A., representing any turn of the century thoroughfare and lined with picturesque narrow adjoined façades. These included the mauve and blue American Pastime with a gable containing a circular white window and fretwork around eaves, the red brick façade of the Main Street Cinema with tiny red window awnings and a fancy yellow entrance canopy announcing Steamboat Willie, a pink wooden façade the width of one room with leaded windows, fancy eaves and a black and white striped awning, the Candy Palace, the pink brick Disneyana with an awning and small window canopies in blue, and a blue and white timber Canned Goods & Spices store with a fancy gable. This in turn was beside a dark brick Preserves and Coffee shop with white awnings, which abutted the powder-green and white square turret of Market House on the corner, both with ironwork parapets on their flat-topped red shingled roofs. On the opposite corner, Disney Clothiers featured a hexagonal turret, someone walked by holding a balloon with Mickey Mouse ears, there were stalls in the streets, Christmas garlands on façades, and fancy gables. Sandwiched between brick and lemon timber frontages, a narrow pale green wooden building had a decorated pediment and a yellow awning above a green planter full of bright yellow flowers. The clip-clop of the horses' hooves and clanging of the bell accompanied our leisurely progress. Men in boaters and striped blazers of different colours stood amongst the crowd, and we passed a futuristic complex and beautifully maintained lawns and gardens with the Matterhorn bobsled ride in the background.

Disneyland street

I alighted at the entrance to **Fantasyland** and **Disney Castle**, the grey stone walls, fine pink central tower and spired turrets of which need no introduction. White swans floated on the moat, and stately blue firs stood either side of the drawbridge. Two white trees, suggesting snow, were adorned with a silver star and coloured baubles, and a tiny rotunda, together with trimmed bushes and a wooden bridge, was reflected in the water. To the right, Snow White and

Bambi stood above a waterfall with alabaster dwarfs at the bottom. Further on, I came to a shop called Tinker Bell with a window in the half-timbered gable, dormers in the shingled roof, a turret, and a square tower with stone quoins. Similar buildings nearby were a fantasy of spires, and the Wicked Queen from *Snow White* (and one of the dwarfs, dressed in green and looking like Robin Hood!) stood behind a window. Located near a merry-go-round, a half-timbered clock tower boasted a tall steeple, and a shingle-roofed half-timbered turret and bay window completed a stone archway. A nearby shingled roof featured an onion dome and a contemporary rendition of George and the Dragon acting as a wind vane. Merlin, a long white beard to his knees and dressed in a purple robe and matching peaked hat, was performing next to Excalibur – buried deep in the stone.

There were patterned chimneys on rooftops, muntined windows, coloured spires, and the thatched half-timbered Mad Hatter's cottage with crenated hedges. Pastel paper lanterns were suspended above a ride of brightly hued cups and saucers decorated with hearts and flowers, the white bobsled mountain again appearing behind. Continuing on, I arrived at one of my favourite attractions: the towers, domes, spires, spinning wheels and numbers of the complicated compilation that makes up **It's a Small World**, like something constructed from a giant meccano set in every conceivable delicate shade. A round smiling face swayed in time to a loud tick-tock, and whilst the catchy signature tune played, doors below opened to parade a galaxy of tiny international figures. At the conclusion, shutters above opened to reveal the time, and automated drummers performed to one side. It was accessed via boat on a canal that flowed between large topiary animals and designs created with plants.

a small world

From here, I sought out **Toon Town**, a bizarre but appealing assortment of fanciful buildings in brilliant colour, with crooked walls, windows and chimneys, the name displayed on an artificial garish green mountain behind. There was a bright red fire station with a tilted tower on top, a huge animated toad leaning from a hole in the wall above a doorway, a building with rockets protruding and smoke issuing from the roof, and the gaudy blue and red Jolly Trolley stop. Daisy's Diner had a hotdog on the roof, City Hall was topped by Mickey Mouse (his arms revolving), and through it all strutted Donald Duck in an aviator's outfit.

Totally lopsided, in fact canted in all directions, an indigo timber structure had a red shingled roof, white trim, a duck on the chimney, and even a twisted topiary tree in front!

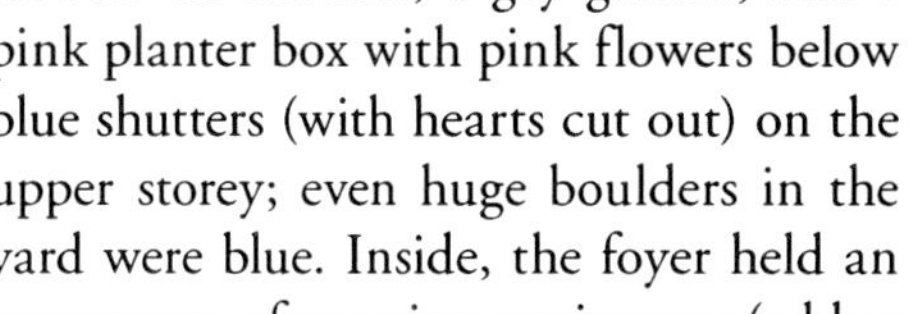

Mickey Mouse made another appearance on top of a waterfall located near the route of the rattly Toon Town Trolley, which lurched by with its clockwork key turning on the roof. Minnie's delightful white house with its crooked lilac shingled roof, had solid pink posts and balustrade, lilac-and-mauve window frames with potted flowers on the sills, a gay garden, and a pink planter box with pink flowers below blue shutters (with hearts cut out) on the upper storey; even huge boulders in the yard were blue. Inside, the foyer held an assortment of sporting equipment (a blue racquet, yellow football and green fishing rod) bulging from behind the partially closed rounded door of a cupboard, the lounge had pictures angled on the wall, articles in a cabinet, and a piano, and the kitchen was furnished with a half-curtain, checked walls and floor, a stove, brooms, and jars on a shelf, all made to simulate items from a cartoon. Mickey Mouse was greeting children with hugs and signing autographs; he obliged one big kid with a dance, a wave for the camera, a pinch on the cheek, a kiss and a gracious bow – me!

Toon Town

Mickey and me

A cornfield behind a paling fence had a 'Goofey' scarecrow – hardly a deterrent because a bird was perched on its head! Donald's white boat, *Miss Daisy*, had a blue and yellow cabin and a red and white horizontally striped funnel, and a house with red and green shingles had a plant (Jack's beanstalk?) growing out of a minute window in a tiny turret with a weathervane on top. This was followed by a red, green, yellow and white house (even to a bright green street lamp in front), a narrow blue insurance building, and a rounded green edifice; the whole town was constructed with bowed rather than straight surfaces.

By now, I was back at the bobsled mountain, water cascading down its side, and entered **Tomorrowland**, where animated robots with flashing lights, like R2D2 from the space movie *Star Wars*, were talking. I took a voyage on a yellow submarine (to the North Pole and back!), which sailed past a blue lobster, colourful waving weed, small and large fish, moray eels revealing fang-filled jaws, shells clinging to unusual rock formations, a blue starfish, a swimming turtle, an octopus, corals, moving crabs, and clams opening and shutting their fluted shells. Of course, it was all artificial, but in reality giant clams are the largest bivalve mollusc in the world, they can weigh up to a quarter of a ton, and their average lifespan is more than 100 years.

Next, I secured a great corner position for the **Lion King Parade**, preceded by two plodding rhinoceroses lowering their heads and batting long eyelashes at bystanders. These were followed by cavorting and leaping Africans in bird masks, colourful grass skirts and ankle decoration, two others carrying floral banners with a lion in the centre, another with a yellow feather headdress and banging a drum, and two, coloured feathers in their hair, wearing green and yellow jumpsuits resembling jesters. A float carrying an old white-maned lion, a toucan, and two talking giraffes came next, followed by another drummer and two more figures in purple and yellow jumpsuits respectively. Deer with long striped horns, in the form of dancers in costume, came behind, trailed by a float with rearing antelope surrounding a typical flat-topped African acacia tree hung with wind chimes and pushed by Africans in long-fringed garb with buffalo horns on their heads. Swaying from side to side, a waddling elephant with long tusks and waving trunk preceded more figures in bird masks, black-and-white feathers in their hair and wearing skirts and collars of black-and-white pelts. Standing above a waterfall surrounded by colourful flowers, an enormous elephant with huge ears occupied a float preceded by a slithering crocodile. Dancers in leopard costume led a jungle float with monkeys swinging from vines and an ugly warthog on the back. Garish figures on stilts came next, followed by African drummers on a float constructed to resemble rocky terrain with trees bearing coloured gourds. Finally, taking up the rear, a majestic Simba stood triumphantly on his rock ledge, also inhabited by birds, a deer, lizards and a snake. A white lion waved from below the Lion King's perch, and his image revolved above a tor behind. The float was heralded by dancing zebras and leopards and flanked by Africans in feathered headdresses carrying totems on tall bamboo poles. All the while the stirring music of the film was amplified above the crowd.

Walking past an Indian in full headdress, I moved on to **Frontierland**, its wooden façades so typical of the many towns that I had visited: there was the Pioneer Mercantile, Bonanza Outfitters, Dry Goods Store, and Golden Horseshoe Saloon. It was getting late and I had not even taken a toilet break – there was just not enough time! Turning towards adjoining **Adventureland**, I saw a full-sized paddle steamer with smoke issuing from twin funnels as it moved on the 'river', the banks of which were lined with rushes, drooping trees, timber buildings, and a working mill wheel. There were also riverside tables and chairs. A three-masted galleon called *Columbia*, with a crow's nest and female figurehead, pulled into the wharf where wooden barrels stood next to a bollard, and a man walked by in a black tricorn hat decorated with a white feather.

I took a boat ride through a dark pirate's grotto, which reproduced a plundered town in flames, a raging gun battle, lusty singing, and a peg leg character. Opposite, were timber mansions like something from *Gone with the Wind*, and a nine-man band, its members in black hats, played jazz music on trombones, saxophones, drums, guitars and trumpets. They performed a popular number recorded with Marvin Gaye a few years back. I had entered **New Orleans Square**, with old-fashioned streetlamps, typical scrolled-iron balconies, lacy iron posts, and a large pink and blue building with blue shutters. Lights had begun to come on when I found an artist working at the foot of a curved staircase lined with flowering plants. This was accessed through an arch with an overhead balcony (also enhanced with flowers) below a fanlight window. A mansion had colonnades of iron tracery and a portico with white columns reaching two storeys high. Having since visited New Orleans, I could appreciate in retrospect how authentic this representation of 'Bourbon Street' was.

Critter Country featured a ride called **Splash Mountain** with a moss-covered shingle-roofed entrance and a steep water chute issuing from the jumble of tangled roots beneath an old tree. One could not escape the screams of participants, and I was not brave enough to attempt any of these scary, more adventurous 'enjoyments'. The most daring that I accomplished was a rotating machine with chairs on chains, which flung one out horizontally at tremendous speed – it was exhilarating. I watched the ship set sail amid its picturesque environs of lush tree ferns, long-leaved plants – and a mass of ducks paddling on the water in its wake. Similar greenery and mossy rocks bordered a rivulet. I attended the **Country Bear Playhouse** with its comical 'bear-itone' singers. The show was introduced by talking moose, bison and elk heads mounted on a wall, the remainder of the entertainment performed by 'bears'. One sang *It's Beginning to Look a Lot Like Christmas* accompanied by another playing a piano decked out for the festive season, with a festooned tree alongside. A painted backdrop with the words Christmas Greetings portrayed a scene with bears on a toboggan, a deer, a snowman, and a snow-covered house and firs. A bear band attired like hillbillies (one with a Santa hat) played country songs on a banjo and rustic instruments, and one dressed as Father Christmas played rock on a green electric guitar shaped like a pine tree. A mournful polar bear in red earmuffs and a long red scarf bemoaned a soul-searching lament to a penguin encased in a block of ice! Others in a variety of colourful Christmas costumes sang *Walking in a Winter Wonderland*. Buildings were illuminated when I left the theatre, and I retraced my steps past the group of men in boaters and striped jackets with matching trousers seen earlier, who were performing *Whistle While You Work* on tinkling instruments.

Taking up a position near sellers holding huge bunches of coloured balloons, I joined the crowd to watch the **Christmas Pageant**. The start was heralded by a fanfare of trumpets blown by men dressed entirely in red, their instruments hung with red banners, and followed by drums, cymbals, trombones and a tuba. They played *O Come All Ye Faithful* as men holding standards and garbed in medieval trappings rode by on caparisoned horses, their tossing heads crowned with ostrich plumes. These were followed by a float accompanied by dancing couples: the women in flowing dresses and swirling capes in a rainbow of colours, the men attired in matching suits, and one woman wearing the tall cone-shaped medieval hat with the long veil. This gleaming golden float, with twinkling transparent spires of coloured glass, disgorged a company of jesters and was then boarded by the dance troupe. All the time, the magical scene was further lit by winking flashes from a multitude of cameras.

The next float belonged to the Wicked Queen from *Snow White*, dressed in rich purple and casting spells with her wand as she rode. She was trailed by another fairy-tale character on a float with a tree house surrounded by flowers. Coming next was the incongruous sight of a red and gold boat with a pirate swinging from the rigging, pirates parading in front, and pirates wielding glinting cutlasses. This was followed by dancing cups and saucers, a teapot, clock, spoons, knives and forks, which were probably from the Mad Hatter's Tea Party because a table coming behind was laden with twirling cakes and bottles. The rear of this float carried Beauty and the Beast, separated by double doors in an arbour of flowers. Sitting on the rim of a flower-decked wishing well, a singing Snow White was accompanied by the seven dwarfs, three playing piano, accordion and lute respectively.

three dwarfs

A collection of gyrating animals came next: ostriches with pretty faces and pink bows in their 'hair', pink hippopotami with long eyelashes in shiny short skirts with matching bows on their heads, and green crocodiles, their jaws full of fearsome teeth, wearing swirling black capes lined with red. Reclining on a bed, one hippopotamus, smiling to reveal huge molars, used a powder puff whilst gazing at herself in a hand mirror.

The appropriate music announced dancing figures from Mary Poppins, including colourful chimney sweeps and the lady herself, with case and umbrella, who stood on the roof of a house with a smoking chimney. This preceded a troop of 'wooden' soldiers with red cheeks and pointed noses dressed in tall red hats with white plumes, red jackets, white trousers, long black boots, and playing trumpets. Roger Rabbit pranced on top of a stack of children's alphabet blocks decorated with painted animals, 'teddy bears' danced with other toys, and Pinocchio, together with Jeppo in his toyshop, sat beating time to the band, surrounded by (amongst other things) a stuffed dog, more teddy bears, an engine, building blocks, and Christmas decorations. Coming behind bears accompanied by a large pink tiger, a mermaid with a sparkling green tail sat with a red toy car atop another pile of blocks, closely followed by spinning gingerbread men. Goofy and Donald were cooking outside a twinkling candy house created from biscuits, dripping icing, piped decoration, candy sticks and coloured lollypops. Hopping snowmen carried peppermint sticks and preceded colourful snowflakes on roller skates whirling to the tune of *Walking in a Winter Wonderland*. Next was a delightful float: winking lights on a white Christmas tree and Mickey and Minnie Mouse, attired in gorgeous glittering blue outfits with white trim, gliding over ice enclosed by a rustic fence. Couples dressed in shiny gold satin (the men also wearing gold top hats) danced by, followed by red reindeer and, finally, Father Christmas in a brilliantly lit sleigh hovering above the decorated gilt rooftop of a house and wishing all a Merry Christmas, Happy New Year and Happy Holiday. It had been a wonderful show.

I walked back past the pink and grey castle, now lit with sparkling lights and the firs illuminated, and took the boat ride through Small Small World, which presented a blaze of pastel colour against the black of the night sky. Inside was a collection of fascinating small tableaux from all lands. The first thing to greet me was an overhead montage of rainbows, butterflies, the sun and flowers, followed by a boat crammed with people on a sea full of fish. A bear paddled a kayak in front of a blue 'ice' castle with a tower from which an Eskimo was fishing. In succession, I came to a wooden soldier, dancing figures, a trio of musicians with flute, accordion and fiddle surrounded by flowers, and a regimental band in busbies playing amongst green trees with blinking lights. Figures stood on a crescent moon amid stars in the sky, a beefeater stood in the archway of tower with the turrets of a castle behind, and a yellow cow, turning its head, wiggling its ears, and moving its tail, stood on top of a building.

Holland was represented by a windmill and tulips, Italy by the leaning tower of Pisa, Rialto Bridge and St Peter's dome, and veiled Arabian belles beat tambourines. Thai dolls were featured with a *gamelan* orchestra and typical umbrellas, Japanese dolls wore *kimonos* fastened with *obis*, and a Mexican tableau had a sun with flashing rays and figures parading beneath a large sombrero. These were followed by a rocking kangaroo with a joey in its pouch, Hawaiian girls swaying in grass hula skirts, masked drummers in a South Sea Island setting, girls in white veils, a shepherdess with a crook and sheep, and another band. Alice was portrayed with the white rabbit, and Russians strummed balalaikas. Most scenes were enhanced with bright flowers and leaves, and final tableaux were of French cancan girls, an American cowgirl with an Indian in a full feather headdress banging a drum, another bevy of beauties in white veils playing tambourines, Spanish troubadours, and choristers with black faces.

In a complete change of pace, the time frame reverted to show long-horned rams and dinosaurs beneath sombre red-and-black skies in stony and primeval swampy settings respectively, the latter chomping on weed dredged from the water. Prehistoric flying pterodactyls were resting near a small waterfall, triceratops browsed, brontosaurus drank from a jungle pool, and a T-rex challenged an opponent. As distinct from the beginning of the tour, when 'It's a small world after all' played continuously, dramatic music accompanied the changing vistas, rising to a crescendo when one of the mammoth monsters stood poised at the brink of a flaring red fissure in the earth's crust. Back at the entrance, the silhouette of a train engine made an interesting picture moving in front of the multihued façade.

I came to a performance of **Beauty and the Beast** in which figures from the parade – a cup and saucer, plates, the clock, candle and cutlery – executed a maypole dance with ribbons hanging from a crystal chandelier. There was a segment with smoke and coloured lights, and it concluded with dancing to the beautiful tunes of the show in a lovely ballroom setting.

The spectacular climax of my day, which words must surely fail to describe, was undoubtedly the **Fantasmic** production, presaged by coloured fountains transforming into a sheet of fine white spray onto which were projected images of a boat or whale being swamped with water and cartoons of Mickey Mouse as the sorcerer's apprentice. Exploding colour in a tremendous burst of water accompanied by fireworks was greeted with Ooh's and Aah's, and kaleidoscope patterns were displayed on the misty screen along with opening blooms like camellias and daisies in gorgeous crimson and blue. Black and white strobe images included an elephant, which changed to become a row of orange elephants blowing trumpets for two indiscriminate animals to dance together. These were followed by a colourful Pinocchio worked by 'strings' of light and flanked by two girls dancing to the tune of the *French Can Can*. Dainty goldfish with beatific faces chased each other around a bowl filled with flickering stars and bubbles, Jiminy Cricket appeared trapped in one of these watery capsules, which eventually burst to release him, and fish were terrified by the massive eye of an unseen sea monster. A violent storm erupted, in which the open jaws and tail of a gigantic predator emerged, the tempest finishing with a whirlpool and tsunami.

Flying the skull and crossbones, the galleon sailed into view, with sailors in the crow's nest and sliding down ropes. This was followed by three barges decorated with large flowers, each bloom outlined by a blaze of coloured lights. One carried Beauty and the Beast, the theme from the film playing whilst green and blue fountains towered in the background. A second held the mermaid from the pageant and a partner, the other ferried Snow White and the Prince. A mirror reflecting the face of the Wicked Queen was projected onto the curtain of water, and other cartoon images interpreted flights of fantasy and frightening figments of imagination. The surface of the lake erupted into fiery red flames, and Mickey used a laser to fight a dragon in a dream sequence that concluded with flashes of lightning; it could have been quite scary for little ones. The riverboat drifted by in a glow of fluctuating pastel pink colour, all the characters from the parade waving scarves on deck. A vibrant red cloud of smoke exploded across the sky and Mickey, wearing a red costume in his guise as Merlin, appeared in a fan of white light. Mingling with the smoke, the glare of incandescent and sparkling fireworks jetted high into the heavens accompanied by a tumultuous climactic fanfare of cymbals and brass. I made my weary way back to the entrance (still not having availed myself of a rest room!) through Adventureland, denoted by crossed tusks above the gateway, past the Wicked Queen in her castle, and down Main Street U.S.A., which now rivalled Las Vegas with its galaxy of glittering lights; a large Christmas tree stood at the end.

Hollywood

Next day, again with Gray Line, I took a tour to **Hollywood** through downtown **Los Angeles**, a sprawling uninteresting city where the only things to remark upon were a white clock tower, a plethora of palm trees, glass buildings, and a wide stairway with water flowing over rocks down a central channel, an archway at the top and a skyscraper looming beyond. Because it was Sunday there was little traffic. We passed the famous 50ft Hollywood sign on **Mt Cahuenga**, originally erected in 1923 as an advertising sign for a real estate company, and drove down shabby streets with low buildings and tinny stars suspended across the roadway to the **Walk of Fame** outside the red and green **Mann's Chinese Theatre**. Amongst the more than 2,500 names in the bronze-edged pink stars set in black terrazzo pavement, with a camera or record in the centre to signify the genre of entertainment, were those of Glenn Ford, the Carpenters, Glenn Miller, Charles Bronson, Elvis Presley, Marilyn Monroe, Joan Collins (a book in the middle), and Olivia Newton-John. The signed imprints of hands and feet, in concrete, spanned many decades and included legendary names of people probably unknown to today's youth, who pioneered the film industry. Some also had dedications written by the stars, and I was fascinated by the litany, copied verbatim, that follows:

Meryl Streep Sept. 25 1994, Eddie Murphy Be Free 5/14/87, GIANT 56 Elizabeth Taylor, IN SINCERE APPRECIATION Jean Harlowe Sept-29-33, Susan Hayward Aug-10-51, THANKS SID Betty Grable, 8/21/84 You Made My Day Clint Eastwood (who else!), 5-16-84 Steven Spielberg, and Ava Gardner Oct 21-52. It was interesting to note that most of the women wore spiked heels. Continuing I found: For Mr Grauman All Happiness Judy Garland, Thank you Sid Fred Astaire, Good Luck Sid. Douglas Fairbanks, Eddie Cantor, Julie Andrews 3:26:66, and Frank Sinatra. The name of Sid Grauman (new to me) featured prominently; there was even a memorial to his mother that read 'In eternal memory of my dear mother Rosa Grauman Mar. 24-40 Sid Grauman', and apparently the theatre once bore his name.

Other inscriptions were Cecil B deMille Aug 7 1941, Paul Newman and Joanne Woodward His and Hers Thanks May 25 1963, and Jimmy Durante Oct-31-45. As the great comedian he was, he had also imprinted his nose and written 'dis is my schnozzle wish I had a million of em'. One signed Roy Rogers and Trigger, with the message 'To Sid Many Happy Trails April 22 1944', also bore imprints of shod hooves. Richard Widmark wrote: To

Walk of Fame

Sid With Sincere Thanks April. 24-1947, Jack Lemmon just put the date 5/29/63, and Deborah Kerr 'The King and I 3-22-56'.

A plaque showing the spaceship Enterprise and the name of the producer, Gene Roddenberry, was signed by the cast members of the original Star Trek including D Forest Kelley. Sid a great guy was Clark Gable's contribution, and Gregory Peck wrote TO MY FRIEND SID MR. HOLLYWOOD DEC. 15th. 1949. Marilyn Monroe put Gentlemen Prefer Blondes, Charlton Heston said simply Thanks 1/18/62, and other names included Sophia Loren 7/26/62, Van Heflin, Kirk Douglas, Anthony Quinn, Steve McQueen, Doris Day Jan 61, Joan Crawford 9-14-29, Cary Grant, Rock Hudson, and Harrison Ford. Jeanne Crain used the words: My Greatest Thrill OCTOBER 7th 1949, Hayley Mills just wrote FAB, and finally, Rita Hayworth said To Sid Grauman Thanks.

Hollywood, with legendary **Vine Street** and **Sunset Strip**, was a tacky town, but **Beverly Hills** was full of classy shops, one with a galaxy of stars names emblazoned across the front. We did the usual touristy circuit down **Melrose Avenue** and **Santa Monica Boulevard**, past the homes of the Rich and Famous behind high stone walls, and along landscaped streets with trees and a fountain. **Rodeo Drive**, with elegant stores like Louis Vuitton and one with bright yellow awnings and clipped trees in tubs, culminated at the venerable **Beverly Wilshire Hotel**. Progressing down a boulevard lined with tall stately palms and past neat more-modest housing we reached the **Hard Rock Café**. This was full of guitars, gold records, Elvis posters, a silver lamé costume and a blown-up cover of Life magazine showing a pouting Marilyn Monroe (the two latter framed behind glass), a gleaming motorbike, a large picture of some celebrity's car – and noise! A poignant copy of the Mirror newspaper had headlines saying 'In peace at last…' above a photograph of Elvis in his coffin, '…the troubled King' written below. Along with its trendy boutiques, Melrose Avenue boasted Subway and Big Mac!

Venice Beach

En route to quirky **Venice Beach**, we passed mastodons with enormous curling tusks in simulated swampland, Twentieth Century Fox Film Corporation, and **Malibu**, with palms lining the esplanade. Reminiscent of hippie days, Venice was an eye-opener. A Negro in a shiny blue suit was executing jerky movements to taped rap music, watched by a lady in a long coat who bent to speak to a none-too-friendly Doberman dog. Art covered a wall behind lairy souped-up motorbikes with stretched front chassis, and framed pictures were displayed on the sidewalk beside a grassed area of the foreshore (with the inevitable palms) that extended to the sand. There were many birds and a 'one man band' playing a saxophone, beating a drum with a stick attached to his elbow, and clicking castanets with a foot. One man rolled up on skates to watch. Wearing a long black cape, a fortune teller squatted behind her array of charms and/or tarot cards, and an artist was creating bright contemporary pictures with spray cans and a palette knife.

The main promenade was bordered by cafés and colourful shops with canopies. A 'mechanical' man with a robotic voice performed for donations, and a Dalmatian dog, sitting on its haunches, was wearing a red bow tie and sunglasses! It appeared quite happy with all the attention it was receiving. Mythical castles, planets, trees and fish formed the subjects for more futuristic paintings, the spheres achieved by spraying around the lid of a bin, and other effects created by rubbing with fingers. I watched as the artist created a fascinating blue, black and white scene depicting an eclipse, with white rays fanning out from one side of the obscured globe and orcas frolicking in an ocean underneath. A man tickling the ivories of a piano on the pavement forced another on roller skates to deviate from the pathway. A wooden boardwalk between the lawn and sand was also a venue for skating and pushbikes.

Flying flags added to the festive feel, and a man was sitting at a sidewalk table with two great Danes tethered beside his chair, the latter watching with disdain as a person strolled by with a Chihuahua on a leash. Another dog, standing on hind legs at a window of the Venice Bistro, was being fed tidbits by an employee. It was a popular venue for walking dogs, and two more interacted in the roadway, which had been converted to a pedestrian mall. A long blue wall was illustrated with a fiddler performing in front of a red and white building, a second façade in beautiful blues and pinks incorporated whales, and other wall art included a classic face. Rastafarians displayed articles on the pavement, a man played a didgeridoo (that appeared to be made out of metal piping!), T-shirts were printed with the 'Big Five' – leopard, elephant, lion, rhino, and tiger (instead of buffalo) – and far-out figures were painted on the front of a shop with equally way-out garments for sale. Another alert Doberman was restrained on a lead opposite more people offering to predict one's future, and figures with stark white masks, dressed all in black, mimed scenarios; I have no idea of the message that they were attempting too convey. A street artist was creating portraits, people paraded with large and small dogs, a man played a guitar, and other buildings included a Saloon and the colonnaded Penny Lane, housing a tattoo shop. San Diego was a convenient base and proved a much nicer place to stay than Los Angeles; we drove back past luxury housing along a canal.

Universal Studios

Next day saw another highlight, **Universal Studios** in 'Tinsel Town', and the first thing to accost me in front of Christmas-decked brick buildings was Harry the gorilla. I walked past wooden façades of 'Deadwood', which included a hardware store displaying an assortment of goods on the verandah. Above a canopy at the end of the thoroughfare, and wearing a red Christmas cap, was a huge model of the head, lolling tongue and forepaws of a sad-eyed St Bernard. I also found the *River Princess* paddle steamer in the upper level **Entertainment Centre**, before riding the StarWay escalator to **Studio Centre** on the lower level. Here, I joined the **Backlot Tram Tour**, which wound through old city streets with names like Brownstone and New York St., between buildings with stone balustrades on staircases, and past a corner store. Green lawn in front of a white-pillared red brick building with a clock on the pediment denoted Courthouse Square, and we continued through a setting with a spotlight directed on a wall – and the 30ft-tall 30,000lb of a ferocious roaring King Kong (with gleaming red eyes and close enough to touch!) ripping down electricity wires, thereby causing a helicopter to crash and creating fierce fires.

Escaping from this inferno, we drove down more city streets, passing a stone church and buildings such as Jose's Auto Shop, Hennessy's, and a Post Office with a steeple in the background. Consisting solely of stone and brick façades with fire escapes snaking up walls, they were supported at the back by scaffolding! With awnings over sash and bay windows in front, they gave the illusion of substantial constructions. We crossed a wooden bridge that 'collapsed' (to a chorus of screams) under the weight of the tram, and righted itself as we moved off. Gaily decorated and vintage cars from films included a huge pink Chevrolet. We travelled through Bedrock, home of the Flintstones, passing Barney and Betty Rubble's red stone house utilising a clam shell for its porch roof, a technicolour bus with Bedrock R.T.D. written on the side, and the log car that Fred peddled with his feet on the ground.

flash flood

One of the most realistic effects occurred when we parked beside an adobe bridge and it began to 'rain'. A flash flood raged down the rough rocky roadway lined with pampas and dirty whitewashed adobe houses (one with blue trim, another with a grass-covered shingled roof), knocking down a dead tree as it made its way to a culvert. On the command 'Sit up boy!' the tree resumed its upright position when the water subsided, the guide saying 'You guessed it, it's a dogwood'!

We came to a section called Old Mexico, with sculpted pillars flanking a statue in a carved recess, arched colonnades, red tiled roofs, a well, a crumbling adobe wall, cactus, and a bell tower. We entered 'Texas', with music from Dallas playing and reproductions of old timber and brick buildings, the latter including the two-storey Star of the West with wooden balconies and verandah posts. There was a Dry Goods store, a shop selling Gents Valises & Travelling Bags Wholesale & Retail, and the red Cheyenne National Bank with white stone quoins, a wooden balcony and turned posts, again just a brick façade braced by struts. We were informed that windows were created from sugar so that when the actors crashed through shattered like glass but without causing damage or injury.

Other structures included one with a wooden bell tower, and we passed through an area with a rusted car body and old boats, which gave the impression of being the studio dump but I believe was somehow connected to *Gilligan's Island.* Coming to the 'Parting of the Red Sea', it was interesting to learn that the effect was achieved by splicing the film with scenes of water pouring from tanks and running the footage backwards. After crossing the 'sea' we arrived at an ancient stone city with broad staircases, columns and balustrades, and entered an old French quarter featuring iron-railed balconies, striped awnings, archways, colourful doors and shutters, and names such as Madame Odette. We then came to an area of medieval stone buildings with a paved courtyard containing an elaborate fountain. Movies filmed here included *The Hunchback of Notre Dame* and *Frankenstein's Monster.*

Next, we drove through a subway station and experienced an 8.3 earthquake, which caused an oil tanker to crash, the upheaval of the concrete platform, electricity poles to tumble, bells to ring, lights to flash, flames to erupt, and flood to inundate the area. Safely departing this catastrophic zone, we passed the backs of false façades and an old locomotive numbered 67 to reach Cabot Cove (*Murder She Wrote*), with piped *Jaws* music and a monstrous artificial-looking grey shark that attacked a figure in a rowboat – resulting in a spout of blood! It also created havoc by being the means of exploding drums of gasoline stored on a jetty, with the resultant fiery conflagration. Crossing the bay via a bumpy ride over a wooden pier (also a target for the massive monster), we came to sets from country films, suburban locations,

TV series (including *1313 Mockingbird Place*), and homes in well-maintained grounds that had housed James Garner and Doris Day, in *The Thrill of it All*, and James Stewart. More large buildings included a town hall followed by the moulding grey timber *Psycho* house (Bates Motel) – equally as eerie in daylight! Finally, we experienced an 'avalanche' as we traversed an 'ice' tunnel that revolved around us to deliver an uncanny sensation of falling or spinning.

Back at the Entertainment Centre, people were taking photographs with their heads in the jaws of a shark, and a beautiful blue parakeet, real in this world of fantasy, was perched amid lush ferns and philodendrons beside a pond with a small cascade. I walked to the working windmill of Moulin Rouge in an area of white stone buildings with brown quoins, red roofs, multi-paned windows, dormers, small iron-railed balconies, and red flowers in window boxes. A lady wandered by carrying two immense garishly coloured stuffed toys, and a shop called Silver Screen Collectibles sold tributes to 'The King', James Dean and Marilyn Monroe, in the form of posters, videos and apparel.

I made my way to the first of many entertainments on offer throughout the day, the rough and tumble of **The Wild Wild Wild West Stunt Show**. The setting was a town consisting of the usual accumulation of brick and timber buildings, such as Dillon's Livery Stable and the Gilded Lily Saloon, with a banner strung across the street in front announcing: Square Dancing and Hanging Saturday Night. It began with a cowboy galloping along the street to the accompaniment of the William Tell Overture and another swinging down from a loft atop a bale of hay, and degenerated into a slapstick comedy routine with a balcony collapsing under a girl who fell onto a pile of straw, acrobatic mock fighting, and tosses and spills to show how it was done. A cowgirl cracked a whip, and a man escaped from the upper storey of an exploding building by sliding along the wire holding the banner, which ripped when he grabbed it and carried him to the ground. At one stage, dynamite was tossed from hand to hand and eventually thrown into a well where it detonated with a mighty splash, whereupon one of the cowboys raised his hands and stated 'Oh *well*'! Cowboys were dashing in and out of windows and doors like a vaudeville farce, the villain in black and white checked trousers and the hero encouraged by interjections from the audience. There were demonstrations of trick riding, plenty of shootouts, and people tripping and falling all over the place. An explosion on a rooftop resulted in clothing being flung over the parapet, followed by a man falling off an adjoining rooftop and the entire façade of the first building collapsing outward, the open doorway 'fortuitously' falling across a man seated underneath. In the finale, a man vaulted onto the back of a horse, which knelt to applause and was then ridden 'off stage'.

Next venue was the **Flintstone Show**, with stone buildings, a vendor selling rocky road ice cream from a stone cart, Dino, a TOY.S.AURUS shop, and Fred yelling his expressive 'Yabba dabba doo', sliding down the neck of the dinosaur excavator in the quarry, and running to join Barney in the car. The Water Buffalo Lodge featured in the story, and from a stone television set with antlers sitting on top to act as an antenna a newsreader announced that: The substance formally known as 'argh!' will now be known as fire. The storyline described a trip to 'Univershell' Pictures in 'Hollyrock' involving a flight on Pterodactyl Airlines, which creature leisurely flapped its wings and flew above the heads of the audience. The last segment involved dancers in tiger costumes, smoke belching from a fiery volcano, fluttering fabric flames, and a woolly mammoth waddling across the stage.

Dino in the Flintstone house

The next show I attended was **Beetle Juice's Graveyard Revue**, as crazy as its name implies, with grotesque characters (including one like Lurch from *The Adams Family*), loud music, and a host of pyrotechnics including flashing lights, smoke and fireworks. The 'monstrous' show featured performances of rock and heavy metal, with drums, an electric guitar and energetic dancing. The compare wore a black and white suit with wide vertical stripes (looking like a prison outfit), and sported yellow hair, a whitened face, and blackened eyes. Because of the title, I wondered if he was supposed to represent the walking dead. He later executed a comedy act manipulating two dummies to the *Banana Boat Song*. Another, with long black hair, wore a long black and red cape, and a figure in a glittering purple jacket stood at a piano and belted out Jerry Lee Lewis' *Great Balls of Fire.*

At the completion, I moved on to the **Miami Vice Spectacular**, enacted under a black night sky in a setting with a large bungalow and wooden outbuildings beside a lagoon. It began with a man tying a rowboat to the jetty and running towards a barn-like structure, followed by a man running from weapon fire on a trawler and a figure with an automatic rifle driving a racing speedboat – explosions erupting in the water behind it. People were running every which way, tumbling, sliding and firing guns; it was difficult to know where to look to follow the confusing action, which incorporated fist fights, a flying fox, and falling bodies. Apparently, the scenario portrayed the

Caribbean and sleazy smugglers. A jetty collapsed and there were burning buildings, more explosions, gunfire, and skidoos or wave skis escaping in the lagoon followed by towering spurts of water from explosives. A couple fled the smoke and flames of a burning building in a speeding mine wagon on rails (shades of Indiana Jones), which also exploded in flames, the occupants catapulted into the water. A zodiac (rubber inflatable raft) burst out of nowhere to blazing guns and spouts of foam, and a tower toppled amid a scene lit by walls of flame. Eventually, the goodies achieved supremacy, and the act was climaxed by sombre music as a helicopter, its spotlight shining like a beacon, rose from behind the house. It was continually bombarded by gunfire as it hovered, and ultimately crashed in a gigantic ball of fire, but not before destroying a tower that released thousands of gallons of water, creating a raging torrent.

conflagration

But the show I remember most vividly was **Backdraft**, from the movie with Kurt Russell, where one actually experienced a fierce fire and felt the intense heat. Standing on an iron balcony overlooking a warehouse full of metal drums, we were first aware of smoke, and then different points bursting into flame, which rolled as it raced along walls and overhead. Flaring sparks rained down, steam erupted from exploding pipes, and parts of the building (including the deck on which we were standing!) collapsed. It was a scary and realistic conflagration.

The next venue was the complete antithesis and began with a mouse skittering along a tightrope and into a hole. This was followed by a dog pulling on a rope to raise a basket containing a miaowing cat, which scampered along rooftops and released a sign reading Welcome to the **Animal Actors Stage**. There was another big droopy-eyed St Bernard in a Christmas cap gazing down, and the tail of a live one disappeared behind a green curtain in a doorway with a yellow star reading Beethoven overhead. A chimpanzee swung from a rope to join its trainer sitting on a bench. Aping the man's posture with hands between knees, the compare commentated 'Like father, like son'. After a short routine, completed with clapping and waving, the chimp retired and a brightly coloured bird was released to hover in the strong breeze from a powerful fan, I guess to demonstrate its strength and ability.

The next event was a dog act with the alert canine turning circles, begging, standing on hind legs, bowing, backing up, sitting, lying, raising and lowering its head, crawling, rolling on sides and finally hiding its face in its paws when told that it should be ashamed of itself, all in response to spoken commands. It obviously enjoyed performing because its tail wagged continuously. Other animals included the real St Bernard, a collie like Lassie, and a huge hog! An orange orangutan in a purple T-shirt and turquoise pants gave the most amazing performance, it was difficult to realise that it was not human. Emerging with a most sorrowful expression on its face, it was instructed to wave and smile, complying with a massive grin revealing big teeth. Told to show its tongue it duly did, and then pursed huge rubbery lips on command. It responded to the trainer with a hug and kiss before acting out a series of directives initiated by conversation; at no time did it receive food rewards as in the dog act. The interaction went something like this:

Trainer: Don't be embarrassed, you look nice. Reaction: Hiding eyes
Good looking folks this evening, huh? Vigorous nods
Pretty exciting bunch of people. Bored yawn with hand over mouth
That's not nice, you like these people. More vigorous nods
You like me. Emphatic shaking of head from side to side
Tell them what you think about me, go ahead. Takes microphone and blows raspberries
That's not funny, is it? Laughs

The trainer pushed the orangutan, which slapped him back and then imitated hands on hips. Smacking the trainer's backside, the animal then lay down to avoid threatened retaliation. When the audience was asked for a big hand for Jethro, the creature also clapped. It was extremely funny and very clever.

The Universal Studios sign was illuminated as I strolled down **City Walk**, where I discovered a bizarre window display with an enormous pink rooster, its head turning, perched on the back of a black, yellow and white cow. A multicoloured pterodactyl and a blue dinosaur or crocodile were both opening and closing their jaws. Inside, it was a blaze of whirling flashing lights, colourful shapes, and striped tents. The rear of a golden lion was cut away to reveal the revolving cogs in its mechanism, a red horse was outlined with coruscating neon lighting, a weird instrument played automatically, a multihued bird and giraffe also turned their heads, and a barking dog stood behind a pig that opened its mouth and jumped up at a gaudy parrot in a tree. In the midst of all this zany craziness was a touching tribute to Lucille Ball, incorporating excerpts from home movies and classic shows.

Back in the street, which was as bright as day with flickering coloured lights, a neon baseball bat was striking a neon ball, a roaring 'fire' blazed above a pizza parlour, and Santa's reindeer galloped across the night sky. I did two very different rides: **Back to the Future** was a thrilling heart stopping adventure using special effects to create a sensation of soaring over (and into!) brick walls, and **E.T.** was a gentle ride on an automatically steered pushbike, which took one above rooftops and scenes from the movie, at the end of which each rider was farewelled by this appealing alien using their name – 'Goodbye Faye'!

old engine

Knott's Berry Farm

Knott's Berry Farm in **Buena Park**, America's first theme park, was introduced by the figures of a pair of square dancers revolving on top of the water tank below a windmill, and a man (live) with a long white beard and dressed in a black suit and hat, using his burro, its teeth bared, as a ventriloquist dummy saying 'Welcome to Knott's Berry Farm'. Wearing hats and shoes to match their dresses, models of a couple of girls from the 1950s were seated on a bench in the Ghost Town section, which was filled with authentic-looking adobe and wooden buildings including a blacksmith.

Knott's Berry Farm

In **Wild Water Wilderness**, I found a huge Indian visage sculpted from stone, with an impressive water feature called **Thunder Falls** plunging over a rock wall in the background. This was the venue for a show entitled **Mystery Lodge** where, enhanced by strobe lighting and special effects, an elderly Indian related fascinating folklore, tales and myths.

Next things of interest were a life-sized wooden toy soldier guarding a red wooden store, bright red poinsettias amongst green ferns and foliage inundating a wagon in front of Grandma Botts Hand-Done Bonnets and Dresses, and a glassblower in a rural marketplace full of craft shops, flowers in barrels, and shady trees, which included Australian eucalypts. **The Birdcage Theatre**, dated 1881, was playing Charles Dickens *A Christmas Carol.* A lovely yellow-green tree, made even brighter by the sun, grew in front of its peeling brick wall, a false-fronted wooden building stood next door, and a wild water ride beyond. On stage, the interaction between Scrooge and the ghost (in chains) provided a chance to cheer the hero and hiss the villain. A second windmill was also enhanced with poinsettias, the wooden structures all had shingled roofs, windows had simulated snow on panes, and there were many Christmas garlands. Clothing and hats were for sale, a building with a crooked chimney pipe on the roof and the word ROOMS on the wooden façade had paintings arrayed in front, and an old locomotive 'pulled' wagons full of red flowers and greenery.

Walking past wagon wheels, more coloured foliage in tubs, and a livery stable, I arrived at a courtyard surrounded by adobe buildings with chillies hanging from corbels and a ladder to access the flat roofs. Here, an Indian girl performed tribal dances to the beat of a drum and chanting. Her extravagant costume consisted of sparkling sequined moccasins featuring birds, a white skirt, a beaded waistcoat, and an enveloping white shawl decorated with embroidery, a glittering design, and a long coloured fringe. This area, called **Indian Trails**, was next to **Old West Ghost Town** where I saw a lariat-whirling cowboy in chaps and a white Stetson, the Calico Saloon, a cowboy in black twirling a six-gun, and the Chow House.

I saw fake mountains, an old covered wagon, a fountain, flags flying, and a seal performing in a pool with a yacht on a painted ocean backdrop, the creature leaping to touch a ball suspended high above with its rostrum (snout/beak). A sign indicated 'Hitchin' License here', and I attended a vaudeville show in the Calico Saloon, its stage flanked by bars with old pictures and an assortment of bottles on shelves. Introduced by a top-hatted man with mutton chop whiskers wearing a red shirt and singing a comical ditty, the first act featured a lady in an elaborate costume with flounces, boas and bows. Accompanied by skimpily dressed showgirls, the next to perform was a tenor singing a selection of Christmas songs including *Let it Snow, Let it Snow, Let it Snow* and *Silver Bells* – one of which was tinkled by a comedian standing behind. The troupe returned to sing several numbers including *Winter Wonderland*, and two girls, feathers in their hair, wearing pink-and-black full circle skirts with lots of ruffles and sparkles, danced a bawdy cancan to reveal garters and frilly knickers. All the costuming was in hot-pink and black and very effective.

From a station in front of a cluster of wooden buildings, one stating Wagons Built & Repaired, and yet another windmill, I rode behind an old locomotive with a bell on the front, which I had heard clanging periodically throughout the day. At the conclusion, I came to a large lake where, beyond tall palm trees on the opposite bank, I observed the loop-the-loop ride in **Fiesta Village** and a riverboat, its paddlewheel turning as it disappeared around a bend. At the side of this lake, called **Reflection**, a white heron stood beside a white weatherboard church with a small steeple, and from here I watched one of the most spectacular water, light and music productions that I had ever seen. Beginning with fanned jets, it progressed through a series of changing patterns with arcing and revolving sprays like a gigantic sprinkler system, combining these different effects to mingle with fountains spurting as high as the surrounding palms. Swaying veils of water were further enhanced by a rainbow, and the white heron stood motionless, as if entranced by the music to which the display seemed to keep time. Also beside the lake, surrounded by an iron fence, a brick church with a belfry on its tiled roof was set in a lush garden containing a fountain.

Located at one end of the lake, **Camp Snoopy** had flags at the entrance and a clock, its works and pendulum exposed, above the door, together with a figure of the dog for which the camp was named. White rocks, ferns and long-leaved plants bordered a pond containing koi and ducks. The camp had its own animal show, with a white mouse (appearing as two with its shadow) running along a wire – followed by a cat! There was also a dog act. There were quaint wooden buildings, a wagon advertising Beary Good Wares, and Snoopy, wearing a Christmas hat, posed for photographs with children, one apprehensive tot in arms saying an emphatic 'No!'

Leaving the camp, I came across a wooden Town Hall and a brass band performing near more massed poinsettias, its members dressed in top hats and long grey jackets. Standing beneath the loop ride I could appreciate the immense height as the carriages laboriously inched their way up and plummeted down to execute two loops, but I opted for something tamer in a time machine that travelled back through a period of fierce winds, molten rock and monsters, with a roaring tyrannosaurus rex illuminated directly in front by a flash of lightning! I witnessed a street 'gunfight' before dusk descended, and calling 'Merry Christmas', a parade of characters including Snoopy and the Peanuts gang marched down dimly lit avenues and past the blacksmith to the Birdcage Theatre, its lights flashing, where they stopped with the brass band to sing *Gloria In Excelsis Deo* and carols, and where the donkey was wending its weary way home.

Sea World

Next day, I attended **Sea World**, where I was just in time for the first performance of whales and dolphins together in a show called **One World**. This commenced with a 36-year-old 25-ton black whale leaping from cobalt blue water as gulls flew above, followed by silver-grey dolphins leaping in tandem and then making a supreme effort to jump twice their body length to reach a flag flying overhead. I walked past colourful gardens to the **Shamu Show**, where a sleek black and white orca (killer whale) balanced, its flukes (tail) in the air, on a platform at the edge of the pool. It then slid off backwards to engage in leaps, spy hopping, and propelling a diver to the opposite side. Again spy hopping, it revolved slowly as if waltzing to the music, with a trainer clinging to its head. The two then surfed together, the swimmer balanced on the whale's rostrum, before the orca mounted the platform for a second time and, flukes in the air, spun on its side. To the accompaniment of squeals, it deliberately splashed the audience and then lifted its entire body upright from the water with the trainer standing on its rostrum. Together with a companion, the two leapt completely out of the water (breached) and then, with a calf, lay on the platform with their flukes raised. The action was all projected onto a massive screen behind.

In a section referred to as **Forbidden Reef**, I found a tank with huge twisting and turning moray eels, slithering, writhing and weaving in and out of rocks, accompanied by throbbing music. The only other occupants of the tank were a starfish and few bright red fish. Together with silvery shoals and waving weed, another tank contained bat rays, lying on the bottom, gracefully gliding or gently flapping 'wings'. Outside, beautifully landscaped Japanese-style gardens had traditional buildings, rocks, trimmed trees and a stone bridge, all nicely reflected in a pond. Another exhibit showed shoals of glinting golden fish circling in unison as if waltzing to the background music. Amongst coloured corals, which included varieties like dainty bronze-toned lace, yellow with a frilled edge, and bright pink resembling feathers, the next tank held plain and striped fish in colours of blue, purple, yellow, and red. Spotted species included a black fish with pouting yellow lips, a black and white banded tail, and large perfect white spots on its belly. One particularly stunning fish had alternating curved bands of yellow and purple, and many featured distinctive horizontal or vertical stripes. In contrast, one exhibited gorgeous colours of soft pink, turquoise, apricot and lemon that melded together. Ranging from delicate pastels to bold hues, all the inhabitants of this marine world appeared to dance to the mood music. A display of larger specimens included one like a spotted grouper.

Inhabiting a lovely pond with rocks, mossy banks, drooping foliage and philodendrons, many brightly hued flamingos were standing on one leg, an expedient said to conserve body heat, reduce fatigue or enable them to take flight more easily. Back indoors, tanks held an array of fragile corals in pinks, mauve through to purple, and blues, like an exotic undersea garden but the colours all too vivid to be real. Clown fish and black-and-yellow butterfly fish were weaving amongst the tentacles of different-coloured anemones, and the striking species clothed in the combination of subtle colours stood out against brown rocks and clumps of branched yellow coral. Some darted rapidly hither and thither, others swam leisurely, and yet others were furiously flapping fins. Fascinating striped lion fish had dorsal and side fins like spread fans, and brilliant iridescent blue fish swam in and out of pure white coral. A black, white and pale lemon fish with indistinct markings sported an excellent form of deception: a large white-rimmed black 'eye' near the tail. Varying from tiny to large, anemones included varieties with long fine tentacles or a flaring frilled top on gracefully bowing stalks. One part was a profusion of pinks, even to bright pink starfish also inhabiting the pool. The whole display was like a symphony of movement. One of the most enrapturing exhibits was a tank full of translucent jellyfish gently drifting and pulsating in very blue water, their frilled tentacles swaying as if in a graceful water ballet; there was even soothing music in the background. When caught by the light they were transformed to the palest pink.

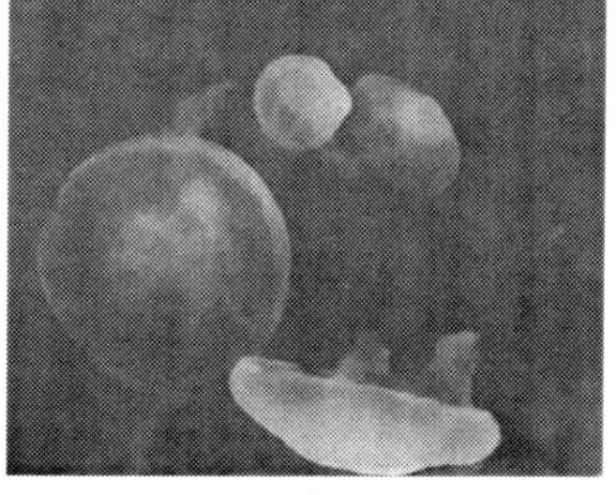

jellyfish

A lush tropical setting of water, rocks and greenery held rich red ibis and large white birds. An incongruous sight was that of a team of eight Clydesdale horses hauling a Budweiser wagon; a Dalmatian standing in an attitude of expectancy on top of the load. A large enclosure behind glass was home to dozens of magellanic penguins wearing their black and white suits, flapping and calling with their peculiar caw in a simulated icy terrain. Always fun to watch, some were just lying, others porpoising, many alternately hopping and waddling with their awkward gait, or wagging stumpy tails. They were stretching, clapping flippers backwards, shaking, diving to and hopping from the water, or simply swimming. Less active were groups of emperors, largest of the penguin family, grooming and shaking heads. It was quite well done, the environment appearing almost authentic.

Held on a green sward surrounding a pool, **Wings of the World** included a demonstration of birds of prey. Eagles swooped in seconds from a blimp high overhead, and one species illustrated how they smashed booty on rocks to break shells or tenderise meat. With the inducement of food, bird calls were initiated, a parrot imitating a wolf whistle on cue! A pair of crowned cranes made an entrance, followed by a colourful macaw and a white cockatoo with yellow underwings. We had a close encounter with a huge fierce-looking brown owl, flapping its four foot wingspan as it roosted on the keeper's gloved hand. In a more peaceful environment, a magnificent indigo parrot, perched on a branch of a dead tree beside a pool surrounded by a mass of greenery, 'conversed' in harsh tones with a white companion.

indigo parrot

A walk through a glass tunnel showed sharks gliding overhead, their tails barely moving, and starfish, corals and anemones displaying almost iridescent colours that glowed in the dark interior. Again, there was the thrumming of sound like a heartbeat that, with the staring unblinking eyes and open jaws revealing double rows of cruel sharp-pointed teeth, conveyed an ominous aura. My final film was of gleaming fish appearing fashioned from pure gold, superb electric-blue fish swimming amongst tall grass-like weed, dark-coloured fish with shinning silver spots like sequins, and playful sea otters rolling over and over.

Los Angeles

I returned to my starting point, Los Angeles, where the historic **El Pueblo District**, birthplace of the city in 1781 and originally named El Pueblo de Nuestra Senora la Reina de Los Angeles (The Town of Our Lady the Queen of the Angels), was conveniently located near the Amtrak **Union Station**. Itself the scene of many movies and last of the great old stations to be built (1939), it displayed Spanish and Art Deco styles. Preserving a number of buildings from the Spanish and Mexican eras, **Olvera Street**, one of Los Angeles' first roads, featured a large cross beside a white church with symmetrical towers and a carved stone entrance. I filmed a tower through the lacy ironwork of a rotunda and old metal plaques inserted in a wall below an arched recess. The buildings, constructed with small bricks, were enhanced with trees and flowering vines, and accordion music provided a festive atmosphere in the street market.

I visited **Avila Adobe** (1818), the oldest house in the city, with a feminine bedroom containing a carved ebony four-poster bed with a white canopy, a table with a lace cloth set for tea, and a candlestick and painted fan on the sill. A more masculine domain held a saddle, a carved chair in front of a desk, a trunk, a jacket and hat hanging on a wall, and boots. The kitchen had an adobe-brick oven with a cauldron to one side and pans on the mantel above; garlic and utensils hung on walls, produce sat on a wooden table, a shelf held crockery, and a pitcher stood on the floor. There was also an outdoor clay oven and a large dining room with a crucifix on the wall.

Casa de Sousa, a grey brick building with metal railing, was brightened by red flowers; old-fashioned lampposts lined the brick-paved paths, colourful costumes were displayed for sale, and al fresco diners were entertained by a gaucho band consisting of vocalists accompanied by an accordion, guitar and bass, all wearing Stetsons. I observed a fountain, a holy statue on a wall-mounted bracket beneath a canopy, a planter created with ceramic tiles, a popcorn wagon, the model of a donkey (wearing a hat) attached to a wooden cart, and a second band of troubadours in brown jackets.

After taking a photograph of downtown skyscrapers, I came across a sight that gave meaning to the word pathos. In a deserted seedy area of dirty bare concrete blocks, I found a dead tree, its spindly naked branches hung with a plastic bottle, bits of rag, old shoes tied by the laces, a candle, a small silver bell, a blue ball, and two tattered stuffed toys, one a blue elephant. I guess it was meant to be a Christmas tree but it looked sad and lonely and made an impression that I have never forgotten.

poignant tree

I was apprehensive in this poor part of town and left hurriedly, coming to a wall with a colourful painting depicting a confusion of multicultural images, a unique 'pond' with water swirling in a whirlpool towards a totem in the middle, and a modern metal sculpture, seemingly a reflection of the mullioned wall behind.

Returning to the old quarter, steps led below street level to a candle shop decorated with colourful paper flowers and a bearing a sign that read Gonzalez Candles Hand Made Since 1956. **Casa California** was covered with creepers, and there were trees, pigeons, palms, and a planter filled with red flowers in the centre of an avenue. Music played, and I saw more costumes, stuffed toys and bright paper flowers for sale; there was even a lost and found kiosk. My last two pictures were of a stark white church with a square clock tower surrounded by palm trees and superimposed on a blue sky, and a large religious artwork portraying snow white doves, a monk, and a group of people including a minstrel, babe in arms, and three leading a goat, horse, and dogs respectively.

At one stage, en route to Los Angeles, I passed through **San Bernadino** where the McDonald's hamburger was born 50 years ago – and sold for 5 cents! A couple of the many fascinating snippets gleaned whilst travelling aboard Amtrak: a hotel in Wabasha provides complimentary shoe shines, hot bricks to warm feet, and house cats for company, and the town of Deeming is home to the world's only duck race.

HAWAII

Oahu

On my return trip to Australia, I stopped over in **Hawaii** where I stayed at **Waikiki Beach** on the island of **Oahu**. This was an idyllic location with **Diamond Head**, where Captain Cook first made landfall, on one side of a bay revelling in yellow sand, palm trees, and a catamaran on blue sea beneath white cloud in a very blue sky. On a street near the hotel, trams trundling past, I found a man with red-and-yellow and blue-and-yellow macaws. The hub of this area was the attractive and enticing two-storey **International Market**. Dolphins 'leapt' on top of a waterfall tumbling over rocks planted with lush tropical greenery and bright red foliage. It plunged to a blue pond containing metallic fish being hunted by a metallic fisherman wielding a trident. A large Christmas tree stood near a stage decorated with flowers and green plants where, previewing the *Legends in Concert* show, two Negro performers, dressed respectively in a silver coat with red trousers, and a gold jacket with black trousers, sang Little Richard's *Johnny Be Good* and *Tutti Frutti*. A second fall flowed over rocks between trees, ferns, and exotic red and variegated leaves. Shops sold paper flowers and vibrant coloured candles, which I watched them creating by paring and twisting the layers of wax to reveal different hues. Inside, another pond had a fountain in the centre and red flowers on its bamboo bridge.

A band played soft lilting Hawaiian music at beachside tables in one of the luxury hotels, where I caught a magnificent sunset that lit the clouds from below and silhouetted umbrellas and palm trees against an orange sky. In the interior of a store selling Western gear, I noted wagon wheels, a rider on a full-sized automated horse (it turned its head), and a figure leaning over a balcony. It was raining as I rode a bus back to the hotel through boulevards bordered by trees coiled with red, green and white lights and past a large winking Christmas tree. Reflecting the illuminations, raindrops on the windscreen were turned into myriad sources of colour.

Hawaii

The capital, **Honolulu**, did not have much to recommend it so I flew to **Hilo** on the big island, **Hawaii**, because the 4,000ft **Kilauea** volcano was erupting. Being the only natural phenomenon that I had not witnessed, I was anxious to experience it. However, I lost my nerve when it came to flying overhead for a close encounter because I understood that there had been a number of helicopter crashes in the preceding weeks due to the corrosion of rotors by the volcanic ash. Instead, I took a tour that began at a high viewpoint overlooking a white church and steeple; water lapping the shore in the foreground. A beachside collection of historic native structures included many totem poles: around a building with a steeply pitched roof, in the courtyard of the **Hale-o-Keaweheiau**, on posts between the pointed stakes of its surrounding palisade, and a pair at the water's edge. Most depicted images of ancient gods, many with grotesque faces, and one had a wooden bird on its head; they glared down to warn people against intrusion.

totem poles

Situated on the white beach sand of a rocky blue bay surrounded by palm trees and backed by green hills, the structures included a wood-framed shelter thatched with leaves or grass, which protected produce hanging to dry. An outrigger canoe rested in front. Ancient craft were made of *koa* wood lashed with coconut fibres, and the cove had a *ki'i* (image) in the water warning that it was the canoe landing for royalty only. The **Great Wall**, its stones of lava fitted together like a jigsaw, was built without mortar some time in the mid 1500s. Logs and levers were probably used to position the stones and it separated royalty from the commoners.

With the unpronounceable name of **Pu'uhonua o Honaunau** (Place of Refuge), the complex was a relic of life before outsiders came in the late 1700s. For people who had broken *kapu* (sacred laws) such as getting too close to the *alii* (chief), touching his possessions, letting their shadow fall on the palace grounds, or even fishing at the wrong time, the penalty was death, unless they could reach this sanctuary where a ceremony of absolution was performed by the *kahuna pule* (priest). It was believed that to break the *kapu* brought violent reaction from the gods in the form of lava flows, famine, tidal waves or earthquake. To prevent these catastrophes, the *kapu* breaker was pursued and put to death, but if he reached the sanctuary and was given absolution the offender could return home safely, usually within a few hours. Others who sought refuge were women and children, those too old, young or infirm to fight, and the defeated in times of war because this place was considered inviolable.

Everyday activities were also regulated by the *kapu*: women were forbidden to eat offerings to the gods (although presumably men had no such restriction!) and at certain times could not prepare meals for men or eat with them. They were not permitted to eat pork, coconuts, bananas, or a variety of other foods. The religion of the people included the belief that royal chiefs had a special power (*mana*), both in their person and possessions, which remained in their bones after death. Superb voyagers, Polynesians from the Marquesas migrated to Hawaii over 1,600 years ago, navigating by sun and stars, and reading winds, currents and the flights of seabirds. They sailed across 2,400 miles of open ocean in great double-hulled canoes carrying items essential for survival: pigs, dogs, chickens, taro roots and sweet potato, seeds, and saplings of coconut, banana, sugarcane and other edible and medicinal plants. Like bamboo, the coconut had many uses: it provided food and oil, fibres of the husk were used to make rope, mats and brushes, the trunk produced spears, posts and drums, and from the leaf was made thatch, baskets and fans.

Driving past lush vegetation, our next stop was a complete contrast: an awesome desolate volcanic area with fields of jagged bare black lava and nearby **Punalu'u Beach**, where blue water and white-capped waves pounded the black volcanic sand. Although surrounded by greenery, the stark landscape of the lava fields had few plants struggling through the sharp stones. We drove to an interpretive centre for an overview of a steaming caldera within the rim of a massive crater. Closer inspection revealed a range of colours: red from iron, yellow sulphur, and the greenish tinge of copper, with wafting smoke and waving russet grasses. Completing the picture, smouldering cairns, clouds of steam, and deep belching fissures with vivid red-and-orange sides were interspersed with patches of green. Ferns seemed to be the best equipped to survive. One lonely red flower like

fumaroles

waratah made a bright splash in its sombre surroundings, and a strong wind ruffled the grasses as we came to a rift caused by an upheaval in the earth's crust.

Another view from a distance showed the caldera as a black hole and cloud on the blackened horizon like plumes of smoke. It was an eerie landscape of grey, white, black and brown, and we drove past an area of smooth lava with glazed surfaces of obsidian (glass), which were shining even in the dull conditions. Parking near the edge of the crater, the floor far below appeared as a mass of crazed cracks, steam issuing forth like wraiths escaping into the air from the very bowels of hell. We stopped at an exhibition of ginger bracts, glossy red and white anthuriums, and gorgeous orchids. Colours included pink, orange, purple, mauve with spotted petals, sprays of small yellow blooms, and one white flower with a maroon and yellow centre and frilled edge. Over 90% of Hawaii's native flora and fauna are endemic, found nowhere else on earth.

Even from a distance of six to seven miles we were able to see the impressive display of the volcano spewing a great volume of ash into the atmosphere as we moved on to a far more friendly environment, that of **Rainbow Falls**. Ensconced in lush jungle, they fell with a roar and clouds of spray, and there were several smaller drops in the vicinity. Underway again, we crossed rivers and passed more falls amidst thick ferns and greenery, one plummeting directly to the ocean. The volcano of **Mauna Loa** was the most massive mountain on earth, occupying an area of 10,000 cubic metres and rising 30,000ft from the ocean floor, more than 1,000ft higher than Everest.

Rainbow Falls

Oahu

Arriving back on Oahu at night, it had stopped raining, and we drove through beautiful fairyland streets with trunks and limbs outlined with strings of lights so that they appeared to be exquisite trees of refulgent whiteness or colour.

The Christmas tree had a star on top and was a mass of blinking light, with huge illuminated characters nearby – snowmen in Hawaii!

illuminated trees

My choice for accommodation was the Outrigger Waikiki Tower, less than half a block from the beach, and one of 25 Outrigger Hotels in Hawaii.

Pearl Harbor

Early Polynesians discovered the Hawaiian Islands around AD 500, and Cook arrived in 1778. On yet another trip, I made a moving visit to the **Arizona**, settled in its watery grave on the floor of **Pearl Harbor**. Bombed during the attack on the morning of December 7, 1941, which brought America into WWII, she lay as a memorial to the 1,177 seamen on board who lost their lives and remain entombed for eternity. The United States flag flew from a pole attached to the severed mainmast. Although causing much damage and loss of life, the attack was not a total success, and in the words of Japanese Admiral Yamamoto 'Awakened a sleeping giant and filled him with a terrible resolve'. As commander-in-chief of the combined fleet, he was also instrumental in planning the Battle of Midway, where he sustained his most prominent defeat, and the development of an airfield in Guadalcanal in an attempt to cut the American lifeline to Australia and short circuit the threat posed by General Douglas MacArthur and his forces in New Guinea. He was killed when flying from Rabaul to the Solomon Islands in 1943.

I attended a **Paradise Cove** luau, which as well as the good food (and plenty of potent blue mai tai's!), included the ceremonial pulling of fish nets accompanied by the blowing of the conch shell and island chants.

The mai-tai is a cocktail based on rum, Curaçao liqueur and lime juice. On this occasion, I had gone with my boyfriend at the time, Mark Rhodes (related to Cecil), and we had been commissioned to sell gemstones brought from their mines in Zimbabwe by his brother Richard. The traditional luau was cooked in an *imu* (underground oven) lined with stones. The stomach cavity of a pig was stuffed with fire-heated stones, the animal wrapped in *ti* and banana leaves and placed in the centre of the *imu*. Bundles of food such as fish and chicken were also wrapped in *ti* leaves and placed around the pig. The whole was covered with more leaves and hot stones, sealed with dirt, and left to cook for several hours.

Addendum

I would like to add a few extra words about cities and places mentioned above.

Albuquerque lies in the shadow of the **Sandia** (Watermelon) **Mountains**, so called because of their red hue at sunset.

The **Black Hills of Dakota** are actually 7,000ft mountains covered in ponderosa pine, spruce and aspens. It was here that Custer and his troops were massacred by the Sioux at the **Battle of Little Big Horn**.

In a similar scenario to other US towns, **Denver** evolved from a tent city which sprang up overnight with the discovery of gold.

Las Vegas has been described as dazzling, dynamic, lavish, luxurious, decadent, indulgent, raunchy and chic, but where else can you experience the Grand Canal of Venice, the pyramids and enigmatic Sphinx of Giza, the Eiffel Tower, souks of Morocco and Roman antiquities in one day.

The **Mission San Xavier del Bac** is also known as the Sistine Chapel of North America.

Mt Rushmore: Washington's nose on this Shrine of Democracy is 20ft long.

The first colony in **San Francisco** founded the **Presidio** and **Mission Dolores** in 1776. 1848 saw a gold rush and much of today's financial district is built on acres of ships abandoned during the stampede.

San Jose: More facts about the **Winchester House**. There were 13 steps to the 13th bathroom which had 13 wall panels with 13 windows; other windows had 13 panes. There were 13 globes in the chandeliers, 13 coat hooks in the séance room, 13 steps on most flights of stairs, 13 glass cupolas on the greenhouse roof, 13 palms lining the driveway, and Sarah's will, containing 13 clauses, was signed by her 13 times. She wore a veil and only her Chinese butler was allowed to see her face; two servants who accidentally did were dismissed with a year's wages. To confuse the spirits, every night she slept in a different bed in one of 40 bedrooms. Carved posts were inserted upside down.

San Simeon: More facts about **Hearst Castle**. It contained 26 bedrooms, 32 bathrooms, 14 sitting rooms, 2 libraries, a 2,000ft dining room, a billiard room, 30 fireplaces and a beauty salon. The 3rd century sarcophagus depicted Apollo accompanied by 9 muses. As well as this property, Hearst owned an even larger estate on the McCloud River, a triplex in Manhattan, a million acre ranch in Mexico, a 14th century castle in Wales, a 100-room beach house in Santa Monica, and several houses in Beverly Hills. In addition to newspapers, his empire included magazines, radio stations and an immense art collection. Guests included aviators Charles Lindbergh and Amelia Earhart, the Duke and Duchess of Windsor, film moguls Louis B. Mayer and the Warner Brothers, statesmen Calvin Coolidge and Winston Churchill, authors George Bernard Shaw, H. G. Wells and Aldous Huxley, and film stars Greta Garbo, Jean Harlow, William Powell, Gloria Swanson, Buster Keaton, Leslie Howard, Cary Grant, Clark Gable, Carole Lombard, Loretta Young, James Stewart, Joel McCrea, Joan Crawford, Gary Cooper, Douglas Fairbanks Jr. and David Niven.

Santa Fe: The Zia sun symbol is a circle representing life and love without beginning or end. Four rays, one at each compass point, represent the four seasons, divisions of the day (sunrise, noon, evening and night), and four stages of life: childhood, youth, adulthood and old age.

Seattle: The settlement was named after a local Indian chief, Sealth. In 1897 it was a gateway to the Klondike; supplying prospectors was the foundation that made it a prosperous city. The original 'skid road' was Seattle's Yesler Way, down which logs were skidded to the sawmill. The 184m (603ft) Space Needle offers sweeping 360° views of today's city and the underground tour from a restored 1890s saloon provides glimpses of the centre before the great fire of 1889.

Zane Grey brought world attention to **Sedona** in the 1920s with his book *Call of the Canyon*. It was also the venue for more than 65 motion pictures including: *Angel and the Badman* and *Tall in the Saddle* starring John Wayne, *The Rounders* with Glenn Ford and Henry Fonda, and films with Elvis and Burt Lancaster.

The **Silverton** to **Durango** railroad and **La Plata County** have featured in a score of films starring some of the biggest names in Hollywood. Beginning in 1949 with Virginia Mayo and Dorothy Malone in Warner Brothers *Colorado Territory*, the list reads like the who's who of the movie world. Marilyn Monroe, Rory Calhoun, Walter Brennan, Anne Baxter and Dan Daily starred in 20th Century Fox *Ticket to Tomahawk* (1950), Dean Jagger and Sterling Hayden in *Denver and Rio Grande* (1952) in which two engines were deliberately wrecked in a head-on collision and, also in 1952, Marlon Brando appeared with Anthony Quinn in *Viva Zapata!*, for which the latter won an Oscar. The roll call continues with Mitzi Gaynor, James Cagney, Ernest Borgnine and Barbara Stanwyck. *Around the World in Eighty Days* (1956) with David Nivan, Shirley MacLaine and Marlene Dietrich won an Oscar for best picture, and James Stewart featured with Audie Murphy and Dan Duryea in *Night Passage* (1957). Jimmy Stewart also appeared amongst the huge cast – including John Wayne, Debbie Reynolds, Gregory Peck, Henry Fonda and George Peppard – in the Metro Goldwin Mayer classic *How the West Was Won* (1963). 1969 saw Paul Newman and Robert Redford in *Butch Cassidy and the Sundance Kid* and, finally, James Garner and Suzanne Pleshette starred in *Support Your Local Gunfighter* (1970).

Tombstone's Bird Cage Theatre was the scene of 16 gunfights and 26 killings, but on a gentler note, was the origin of the song *Bird in a Gilded Cage.*

Tucson was under Spanish rule until Mexico gained independence in 1821. Known as a rowdy frontier town, it became part of the United States with the Gasden purchase of 1853, except for a brief period when Confederate soldiers seized the city during the Civil War.

CHINA 1995

'Exotic and mystical China, the world's second largest and most populace country, alone containing over one quarter of the earth's people, has the oldest continuous civilisation with a recorded history of nearly 5,000 years. The famous Peking Man, whose relics were found in caves near Beijing, lived about 500,000 years ago. Culturally, scenically and architecturally unique, it is also an adventure in cuisine! A journey through China is one of the most fascinating and rewarding travel experiences on earth'. This quotation is from the brochure that I wrote for a group tour to China, which I organised after having tasted its wonders for myself.

Beijing

We began in **Beijing**, settled as early as the Xia and Shang dynasties 3,000 years ago, and my first photographs on this occasion were of the chaotic traffic, bicycles (often with carts attached), and a busload of laughing and waving children. We followed the latter past a duty pointsman on a covered dais, beneath an archway with a bamboo-tiled roof, along a street lined with attractive trees, their black branches bare of leaves, and past a building with an arched entrance, decorative brick façade, and typical curled corners on the roof. Outside one grand edifice, a street market featured clothing hung on lines strung between trees and goods on carts or the pavement. At other roadside stalls, vendors were stretching dough to make noodles, and corncobs were cooking in steaming boilers alongside a table and benches set up under spreading branches that provided little shade.

roadside cuisine

Great Wall

On our very first tour we were besieged, even before leaving the bus, by hawkers selling such items as pottery teapots and mirrors with embossed silver backing. At **Badaling**, we approached the **Great Wall** through a marble gateway topped with green tiles, which framed the famous monument behind. One of the wonders of the world and the only man-made structure visible from space, it was originally a series of feudal defences built in the fifth century BC. Linked during the reign of Emperor Qin (221–207 BC) to form a 5,000km barricade, it was the greatest such undertaking constructed by mankind on earth and the scene of incredible bloodshed. At this point, the wall was 7.8m high and 6.5m wide at the base. It was a stupendous feat of engineering, unrivalled to this day, sweeping and snaking up and down mountains as far as the eye could see, with bastions at regular intervals and in places the steep slopes necessitating steps. Belying its haphazard construction, the surveying technique followed by its engineers was to send ponies dragging saddles behind them over the hills and peg out the path that they chose. It was interesting to contemplate these points when standing on this magnificent monolith – which ultimately faced the wrong direction!

Great Wall

Looking over the wall, we had our first glimpse of cherry blossom, and this visit differed from my previous one inasmuch as we encountered large crowds, which had been absent when I had been there in winter. We stopped at a retail outlet (an indulgence in which I never partake when travelling alone) displaying extremely beautiful vases decorated with brightly coloured flowers and, adjourning to a restaurant, enjoyed a meal seated at round tables, the lazy Susan in the centre crammed with an array of meat and vegetable dishes of which I recognised only bananas! Food was always inclusive of beer or soft drink and tea. Outside, images of tiny creatures sat along the roof capping, and a typical Chinese tree with gnarled, curled and twisted branches, also bare of leaves, made a striking silhouette against an overcast sky with a misty veiled sun behind.

artistic tree

After lunch, we visited a factory where artisans were using fine long-handled brushes to paint scenes, in black and white or colour, on the *inside* of bottles.

Summer Palace

Travelling behind a caravan of covered trishaws we visited the **Summer Palace**, where gardens incorporated the special natural sculpted rock taken from Taihu Lake and used in Chinese landscaping the world over. More of the contorted trees stood outside a pavilion with red pillars, decorated panels, and a bamboo-tiled roof.

temple and unique trees

Courtyards featured metal urns and auspicious lions and dragons. Walking towards us, two ladies dressed in red-and-gold with elaborate headdresses were, according to our guide, concubines. We entered a pavilion with exquisite floral screens, lanterns, and a painted scene depicting black-and-white long-necked long-legged birds above a delicately carved wall panel inserted with mirrors. In the grounds, a gorgeous deep pink cherry tree caused one member of my touring party to exclaim 'It almost looks unreal', and because I was wearing pink slacks I was requested to pose in front of it.

Reclining on the shore of **Lake Kunming**, this palace, built in the Manchu reign*, was destroyed by an Anglo-French force in 1880 and damaged again in the Boxer Rebellion. Each time restored by the Empress Dowager (Dragon Lady), it was now a public recreation spot with pavilions, temples, wooden and stone bridges, and a long 7,228m covered corridor: a gallery of vivid blue, red, green and white artwork depicting miniature scenes and mythical themes. Ensconced amongst the greenery, its splendid gardens featured wisteria and a magnificent tree covered with white magnolia blossoms. Plying the lake, enclosed brightly painted dragon boats had fearsome heads at the prow, and the pagoda-like **Tower of Buddhist Incense** was visible from a shore lined with willow trees.

dragon boat

Tower of Buddhist Incense

Near a bridge guarded by stone lions, an incredible white marble steamboat 'floated' on the water; built as a summerhouse for the Empress Dowager Ci Xi, it was complete with 'paddle wheels' on the sides and intricate stained-glass panels. Immersed amongst vibrant pink

* In 1644 a Manchu prince was crowned as the first Qing Emperor of China.

cherry blossom, a Chinese mother wearing a charcoal-grey suit, and holding an infant dressed in a pale blue outfit and yellow mandarin hat, made for good film, as did a stone 'moon' bridge with a marble balustrade. Normally, such structures were reflected to form a perfect circle (hence the name), but the dull day prevented this eventuating.

Our next stop, at a canal lined with shophouses, was an outlet displaying the exquisite embroidery for which the country is famed, much of it reversible. Stitched onto transparent material, a fluffy white kitten wearing a red bow and sitting on green grass appeared absolutely lifelike, even to the bright eyes.

moon bridge at Summer Palace

Leaving here, we visited a temple with many bells flanking the pathway and larger bells arrayed within the entrance. More gnarled and twisted trees made a great picture in front of a decorated squat round tower to one side. Travelling along streets with low buildings, we passed one of the many-tiered city gates and children riding as pillion passengers on bicycles negotiating the heavy traffic. Reflecting a white stupa on the hillside opposite, another large lake featured a stone-and-marble bridge, willows, pavilions, and a balustrade with lotus-topped columns around its perimeter.

embroidered kitten

A tiered archway provided access to a garden setting with cherry trees, a gazebo, and a girl in traditional dress. Here, we had a meal before attending a fascinating cultural show featuring artists with heavily made-up faces, elaborate costumes and headdresses, and the sounds of strident voices and oriental music with clashing cymbals. A dance executed with blue banners, shaken at one stage to represent waves, told a story, and figures holding staffs paraded before a character with a long white beard and crown, who sat motionless whilst a clever baton twirler wearing a grotesque mask performed in front of him. This was followed by a display of acrobatics for which the Chinese are justifiably renowned: skilled performers executed cartwheels and backward flips across the stage, in some instances without using hands! The finale included a simulated battle between 'forces' wielding swords and long-handled weapons respectively, others somersaulting over a large flag whilst armed with two long swords, and an acrobat returning, with alternating feet, poles tossed by two people.

Forbidden City

A wall with a colourful modern mural was in complete contrast to the next venue: Tiananmen Square and the **Forbidden City**, imperial palace of both the Ming and Qing dynasties for 500 years. This massive complex, covering 180 acres and comprising 800 individual wooden buildings with with, supposedly, a total of 9,999 rooms, was begun in AD 1406 and completed in 1420. The world's largest palace, as well as ceremonial halls and private quarters, it contained a vast treasure house of priceless jewels and objets d'art added to by emperors over centuries and unmatched by any ruling family in the world. The whole was surrounded by 10m-high walls and a 52m-wide moat. Beyond the **Meridian Gate** (**Wumen**), originally for the exclusive use of emperors, five marble bridges led to the **Supreme Harmony Gate**, which opened to a gigantic courtyard that could hold 100,000 people and led in turn to the three great halls of **Supreme Harmony**, **Complete Harmony** and **Preserving Harmony**. Lying between steps was an immense slab of stone sculpted in the Ming dynasty and refurbished in the reign of a Qing emperor. With a length of 16.57m, width of 3.07m, and 1.07m thick, it weighed over 200 tons, and the border of interlacing lotuses surrounded curling waves at the bottom and nine dragons amongst clouds in the middle. An elderly couple dressed in black (the man with a white beard) posed for photographs. We first encountered a series of gilded and carved thrones, one of which, flanked by gold pillars and large metallic birds, had pedestals bearing *samovars* (tea urns) in front. The huge halls featured heavily embossed ceilings.

North of the halls were the living quarters: 40 mansions surrounding the **Palace of Heavenly Purity** (**Qianjing Hall**). The courtyard garden at the back of the palace contained a red feature wall, ancient trees (two with bonded trunks to create one), a few flowering bushes, golden lions, and a tall incense urn.

China is the home of dragons

Much of the treasure was stripped from the Forbidden City by Chiang Kai-shek and taken to Taiwan, where most was on display in the National Palace Museum. What remained included a suit of jade, Qing dynasty sedan chairs in the **Hall of Middle Harmony**, terracotta warriors, a water clock in the **Hall of Union**, traditional painting in the **Palace of Peaceful Old Age**, and costumes, jewelled ceremonial swords, gold Buddhas encrusted with precious gems, a five-ton block of carved jade, bronzes, flowers fashioned from semiprecious stones, and arts and crafts in the **Palace of Mental Cultivation**. Outside the walls of the Forbidden City, tiered roofs and the moat made wonderful subjects viewed through lacy pale green trees with black trunks. At one time, the price of admission to the city was instant death, but this has dropped to a mere ten yuan!

We adjourned to another delightful venue for lunch: a red building with red lanterns hanging beneath the curled corners of its eaves. The garden forecourt contained decorative Taihu Lake stone, blossoming cherry trees, willows, shrubs with red, white and crimson blooms, and a marble balustrade fencing a pool with a covered stone bridge and fountains.

Tiananmen Square

The vast expanse of **Tiananmen Square** covered and area of 98 acres and could hold up to one million people, making it the largest public square in the world. It was bordered on three sides by austere buildings and on the fourth by the **Gate of Heavenly Peace**, the entrance to the Forbidden City surmounted by a tiered pavilion. This was dominated by a huge portrait of an inscrutable Chairman Mao, in front of which great multitudes would rally to applaud his speeches with thunderous slogan-chanting acclaim. Ornate pillars, a stone lion, high-spurting fountains, marble balustrades, and the massive **Memorial to the People's Heroes**, commemorating the 1949 communist revolution, were almost lost in the enormous open space, where a popular pastime was the flying of silk or paper kites in shapes of butterflies, birds and other objects.

People's Monument

Peoples Monument

Temple of Heaven

Moving on to the 15th-century **Temple of Heaven**, the main monument was actually the round multi-tiered highly decorated red **Temple of Prayer for Good Harvests**. This mammoth religious icon, 38m high and 30m in diameter, was built entirely without nails or cement; in fact, the only metal used in its construction was gold! Deep relief covered the ceiling, and it was accessed via several stairways between white marble balustrades that circled the base at different levels. It was preceded by a series of structures individually revealed and photographed through successive arched entrances. An artist, who obligingly held up his work for inspection, sat creating a lovely watercolour of the imposing final edifice.

copper steamboat

For lunch we were treated to Peking duck, which I had not previously sampled because it was very expensive. Carved into thin slices at our table, pieces were selected with chopsticks, dipped into sauce, and wrapped with a vegetable accompaniment in a type of pancake, the traditional method of serving. In the evening (unfortunately after we had eaten!) we strolled past a long row of ever-fascinating food stalls with tantalising aromas, steaming boilers, grilled meats, fried fish, and huge copper steamboats (like *samovars*) containing hot soup, which was added to bowls of rice mixed with other ingredients.

Meals were composed of selections from an assortment of dishes, which included a variety of sausage, spring rolls, different dumplings like *dim sum*, noodles, kebabs (including whole quail!), shaved meat, and various vegetables tossed over charcoal burners. I saw dumplings threaded on long skewers, arrays of small jars containing condiments that were added to fried foods, bowls of beans, stir-fried bean sprouts, a type of red jelly, bananas fried in hot fat, and other sweet concoctions. Much of it (although not all!) looked delicious and was probably incredibly cheap; money changed hands and was stuffed into an old biscuit tin. The bustle of activity made for an absorbing diversion, and with the smoke, smells, and vendors in long white coats and caps calling out, chopping with cleavers, stirring, pouring, and serving into bowls with china spoons, it was one of the best food markets that I had experienced.

a row of chefs

The Chinese are very superstitious and endow certain foods with many curative powers; for example, a certain variety of peach is credited with healing piles, premature grey hair, leprosy, hepatitis, rheumatism, indigestion and paralysis! In Beijing we stayed at the Jin Tai Hotel.

Datong

I had organised private compartments on the overnight train to **Datong**, where we arrived at 6.46am and transferred to the Yungang Hotel. I was fortunate to have utilised the Yunnan Overseas Tourist Corporation, a relatively small but enthusiastic organisation that gave me excellent and unstinting service, and highly recommended in a country where all tourism was controlled by the government. My purpose in visiting Datong was the awesome spectacle of the **Yungang Grottos**, one of three greatest examples of Buddhist cave art in China, starting from AD 398 and constructed over a period of 60 years. Cut into a mountain, the caves stretched for one kilometre and contained 53 niches and 51,000 statues, the tallest 17m, the smallest only a few centimetres.

entrance to grottos

The multistorey wooden structure built into the cliff face at the entrance was also an attraction, with the heads of mythical beasts adorning its many pillars.

The grottos, some with columns roughly hewn from the stone and many with surprisingly intense colours of blue, red, green, yellow and white enhancing the images, were shallow and therefore most were easily observed with natural light. Other relief included embossed designs and lotus petals. Seated and standing figures, some with hands raised as if in benediction, had elongated earlobes and inscrutable, serene or benign countenances that had been smiling for hundreds of years. They graced every surface and were even ensconced amongst deeply sculpted flowers on particularly entrancing ceilings. A couple had three heads and several arms, and where the colour endured, most were clothed in garments of turquoise. One exceptionally large image, a small figure standing on its knee to support an upraised arm, had tiny birds nesting above, and the entire complex was overshadowed by a 13.4m (44ft) seated **Sakyamuni** (historical) **Buddha**. The myriad beautifully executed statues were surely one of the wonders of the world, and I am privileged to have seen several such sites. It was distressing and a great tragedy to hear of others being destroyed.

Yungang Grottos

We paused for photographs of an ancient grey-stone monastery with a beautifully shaped roof, latticework fashioned with bricks, stone images, and a striking **Three**

Dragon Wall in blue and gold. Dragon walls came in odd numbers (3, 7 or 9), which must also be auspicious.

The busy streets of Datong were packed with people and bicycles, one man even free-wheeling a second whilst riding. Stalls selling fruits, clothing and much unrecognisable produce were set up on the footpath, vendors cooked kebabs over charcoal braziers mounted on bicycles (both smoking!), and people walked along reading the newspaper.

bicycle vendors

dragon wall at old monastery

Xuankong Temple

We set out by car, past a multi-tiered city gate, to visit the **Xuankong (Hanging) Temple**. Traversing desolate empty terrain, we stopped to photograph flat-roofed adobe houses, many literally built into the barren hillsides of stark desert surroundings with just a few bare trees.

The village, with steps leading up from a stonewalled dry riverbed, appeared almost swallowed by the earth from which it had been constructed. Wood was stacked for winter, straw feed for donkeys (I saw three idle beasts) lay drying on roofs, long poles, a rustic ladder, a broom and shovel leant against walls, a dog barked, a chicken strutted up a street (others gathered around dwellings), and a cart sat in a yard of this seemingly deserted community.

primitive village

adobe houses

There was a small attempt at decoration on one house from which an old lady emerged. I noticed sapling and log enclosures, outdoor ovens, and a fireplace with utensils and food or fuel in a large pan to one side. In the middle of the riverbed stood a stone-lined well from which a man with buckets suspended at the ends of a pole across his shoulders stooped to collect water. Clay chimneys, one with smoke issuing forth, sprouted from mud-packed rooftops. In a reversal of reactions, an elderly gentleman in the blue cap and jacket smiled broadly as he posed with a young boy, but doubt and suspicion registered on the face of the latter and was reflected in the worried visages of other inquisitive children who appeared, as usual, from nowhere. Script lay around their doorway, which led to a kitchen with pictures pasted on a wall, a brick oven, and an assortment of containers such as pottery jars, bottles, barrels, and a huge hemp sack that could have contained rice.

bemused faces

Disused and abandoned cave dwellings, with decorative woodwork framing entrances, remains of stone walls in front, a grindstone, and a chicken emerging from a roost also cut into the rock, provided a basis for interesting film.

cave dwellings and hen house

On the move again, we passed several donkey carts and one man leading two of the beasts tethered by rope, small motorised vehicles carting lengths of wood (one with the driver sitting on top), a man with a rolled carpet on his back, a farmer tilling with donkeys and age-old wooden apparatus, grain drying by the roadside, and produce on the verge.

Ours was one of few vehicles to negotiate around bicycles weaving down the muddy road of a fascinating country town. Children in woollen caps with 'ears' or pompoms rode as pillion passengers on bicycles, which were even the mode of transport for army personnel. One rider carried two children and his purchases; at times it was a revelation to see how much could be accommodated on one machine! Rubble lay in heaps, ancient small shops, their bamboo-tiled roofs covered with moss and/or grass, proved very photogenic, and goods were arrayed on handcarts. A common sight was that of horses pulling wagons, the trays equipped with a structure like

loaded cart

a low elliptical barrel made from staves and carrying, amongst other things, stone or coal.

As usual in China, children were gaily dressed whilst the adult populace were drab, although in the equally dreary surroundings and bleak wintry conditions, racks of coloured pants (that I never saw anyone wearing), and a display of brightly hued skeins of wool were exceptions providing splashes of colour.

rural street

the bicycle is king

The paved centre contained larger buildings and a big market. We took our lunch break here, and I was able to observe men in suits playing billiards at several tables lined up in the main thoroughfare, men with metal drums on poles hoisted across their shoulders in narrow side streets, sacks of vegetables, a cart displaying meat, and one with either cooked ducks or chickens.

side streets

Another billiard table was located behind a clothing stand, and I saw hens in baskets outside a ramshackle corrugated iron construction where food preparation was in progress. Along the roadway in front, a man trundled indeterminate items on a crude handcart with a wobbly wooden wheel.

I noticed Chinese characters around the entrance to a cluttered private yard, and yet another billiard table, this one placed near baskets and a mound of produce opposite a hardware store offering a jumbled assortment of goods such as brooms, metal utensils, and large bulging sacks piled on the sidewalk.

village life

A tot in a yellow jacket and mandarin hat leant against a wall, and amongst the roadside vendors were two men sitting on the pavement surrounded by wares that included shiny brass kettles and basins. Holding a billycan, another man sat on the street verge conversing with a companion. Strident music rent the air, and I was still an object of much interest in this rural locality.

More billiards anyone?

everything but the kitchen sink

We progressed to the hanging temple perched high up and clinging to the side of a sheer cliff face, an amazing sight consisting of up to four levels, the orange roofs prominent beneath massive rock overhangs. Although an extensive complex, it was dwarfed by its surroundings, appearing like an eagle's nest on a rocky ledge and supported in part by flimsy timber pilings.

Xuankong Temple

Crossing a wide dry riverbed via a makeshift rickety bridge with wooden slats and leaning concrete pylons (maybe the victim of flood), we climbed the steep ascent to the magnificent monastery built (partially) on solid foundations cut from stone. I had not been here before and it came as a total surprise; the complex, nondescript from afar, was covered with exquisite brightly hued carving and painted designs. The curved eaves, created from bamboo and painted a beautiful shade of turquoise, their corners carrying images of dragons, were hung with brass temple bells that continually chimed in a rhythm of discordant tones.

Carved screens covered many openings, and ornate decoration included illustrations framed in electric blue, smaller scenes below floral patterns, red framework inset with green panels and lattice, and joists graced with intricate designs in vivid blue, maroon, white and green. Interlocking pieces (in blue) formed wooden brackets.

intricate woodwork

A yellow curtain was drawn aside to reveal a recess holding seated wooden images in red-and-gold garb, the ceiling featuring beautiful flowers and birds in bright pink panels, a theme repeated on beams.

artwork on beams

An alcove held golden and alabaster deities with a spot in the middle of the forehead (maybe indicating a third eye), one wearing a red cloak, another in a multihued costume, and a blue figure with fearsome features; a forest of wooden prayer 'flags' in many colours hung overhead.

deities

As I ascended and descended up and down steps and along corridors that followed the line of the precipice, I came across an image with a long beard in a gold robe, two large seated figures in front of painted surrounds, others with a background of colourful intricately carved three-dimensional fretwork, panels enhanced with beautiful scenes, and floral patterns below lattice on doors. Two particularly beautiful carved panels featured green-and-gold birds of paradise with flowing pink tails nestled amongst pink flowers and green leaves.

Another group of figures (two with fierce faces) was backed by a gilded fretwork screen containing colourful flowers, and the ceiling was again decorated with pink panels. From an elevated passageway, I looked down on orange-toned roofs with finely executed shapes and carved yellow flowers on ridgelines. Although ancient and dusty, the temple exuded an aura of faded splendour.

beautiful panel

even the roofs were a picture

A flock of sheep crossed the road in front of us as we drove through more isolated communities to arrive at a metalwork factory. Here, copper and brass were being beaten into utensils and ornaments, embossed, and buffed to a radiant sheen. Following this, we visited a silk factory, where we traced the journey of the delicate material from the cocoon and winding of the thread to weaving and printing by both screen and hand. A length measuring some 50 to 100m was pegged onto trestles, and splotches of paint from enamel mugs applied to the billowing fabric with a brush. It was excessively noisy and workers toiled without the benefit of protection for the ears. We also stopped at a green tea plantation.

Another venue new to me was an open-air complex of Buddhist art, with stunning stone sculptures that I found fantastic in spite of rain. The first, a mammoth carved rock with greenery cascading over the top, had stylised faces above a fall of water tumbling in front of a figure of Buddha. Other images of the teacher and philosopher appeared each side. A walkway between sculpted surfaces and past beautiful autumn foliage led to a wall with a Buddha image in high relief surrounded by a host of smaller characters interacting in scenes of everyday life. This entire work was situated beneath a rock overhang, the canopy completed by a spread of glorious bright green leaves cloaking dark branches opposite.

Buddha

An immense reclining Buddha, eyes closed, earrings in the elongated lobes, and a row of figures above, was also shaded by an overhang complemented by these beautiful trees, light shining through the leaves enhancing their colour and endowing them with a subtle glow. The next carvings depicted a man with a huge black buffalo, seated Buddha images, and a frieze of graceful robed figures in shadow. Five tall stately images with more-sombre visages were surrounded by tiny sculpted figures and embossed designs. One, his right hand raised, wore a crown, a second, with bare shaved head, had hands clasped in prayer, and two others, with ugly countenances, had the appearance of temple guardians. Giving an impression of their height, one held a pagoda in his right hand and trampled a life-sized figure underfoot.

Perspective was also indicated by a woman with a bright purple-and-pink umbrella who only came to the top of the pedestal on which one of the larger statues stood. An even taller seated image, with hands on knees, towered above the stone from which it was hewn, and a man standing on a rock to one side of another seated Buddha (this

religious images

one surrounded by carving) only reached from the elbow halfway to the shoulder. A little different was the six-tiered stone pagoda located in their midst. A lovely grotto contained images of Buddha in niches cut into a rock face with bushes and greenery growing from crevices. Of these, a laughing Buddha displaying the fat tummy with which Westerners are more familiar, sat above a low waterfall and fast-flowing stream with the soulful sound of a flute in the background, all of which offered plenty to provide pleasure and engender his obvious merriment. This enjoyable visit concluded with scenes of a tall temple, dragons in silhouette on its roofline, cradled in a lovely thicket that included a unique self-explanatory snowball tree.

Hangzhou

We took the overnight train back to Beijing, arriving next morning and transferring to the airport for a flight to **Hangzhou**. In the 13th century this was the largest and richest city on earth, the opulence of which astounded even Marco Polo who said 'Hangzhou is the most elegant and graceful city in the world'. It lasted until the Mongol armies of Kublai Khan put it to the sword and destroyed it. The quote varies but it was certainly the biggest and wealthiest. The Ming emperors restored the city but it was sacked again by the Taiping rebels in the 1880s. The most renowned age of refinement was born in Hangzhou and an old saying stated that: *Above there is heaven, below there is Suzhou and Hangzhou.*

Today it is a big modern city and yet the China of dreams. A peaceful oasis in this tumultuous country, placid **West Lake** was created by a local governor in the eighth century and featured picturesque islands, pleasure craft (rowed or motorised), towering pagodas, teahouses and humpbacked bridges set against a backdrop of gently rolling hills. It was captured in wonderful photographs, framed by branches, showing misty mountains beyond a pavilion with curled eaves in the centre of a wooden bridge, both reflected in the water. Surrounded by stately trees, a stone moon bridge also provided an idyllic scene with white blossoms in the foreground.

Around the lake and on its islands, a wide variety of trees in differing shades of green included willows, flowering cherry, and a tall conifer-like species. The lawns, walkways, gardens, tree-shaded green banks, and gazebos were favoured by ducks as well as people, and a group of soldiers, one playing a flute, walked along the

West Lake

foreshore. Nets were placed in the lake to prevent fish from damaging the lotus. Accessed via a bridge, a pavilion built over the water was enveloped by trees that included a striking willow with black branches and trunk, its foliage almost yellow with the sun behind. Across a lovely tree-lined street, an edifice with many coloured flags fluttering overhead, a stone lion and gardens in front, and beautiful lacy trees against the white wall composed a most attractive picture, its moon gate revealing tantalising glimpses of a classical garden with stone steps, deep pink flowers, green plants, and a tile-roofed pavilion.

The itinerary that I had planned included a cruise in an ornate boat with a gilt dragon at the bow, a roof displaying the curled corners, beautifully carved chairs, and an exquisite large wooden relief, like the famous willow pattern of old crockery, depicting the lake, boats, bridges, people, trees and temples.

dragon boat

We sailed to an islet with a rotunda and pavilions encompassed by lovely trees at the end of a zigzag walkway crossing the water, which reflected the scene in its entirety. A giant piece of the famed Taihu rock stood in the lake near a gazebo, also in the water, with an artificial stork perched on the apex of its roof. White walls featured a moon gate and decorative openings, which provided perfect frames and proved a popular place for photographs. I took a self portrait, which happened to include a busy sweeper, in a large mirror at the entrance. Hangzhou also saw the beginning of the Grand Canal, built to eventually link it with Beijing. We stayed at a hotel with the popular Chinese name of Lily, and the lake was also endowed with lyrical names such as Orioles Singing in the Willows, Autumn Moon Over Calm Lake, Lotus Flower in Crooked Courtyards, and Melting Snow at Broken Bridge!

Suzhou

Next on my programme was **Suzhou**, to where we travelled by train and checked into the Suzhou Hotel. I found the many gardens of this ancient city the best in China and a sheer delight, as were the many narrow canals, crossed by 168 bridges, of China's 'Venice'. Situated in the heart of the rich Yangtze Delta, it was known as the Land of Fish and Rice, and one third of the country's silk, which was first transported on the fabled Silk Road, came from Suzhou.

If one could turn a blind eye to the refuse and raw sewage emptied into the water, it was a totally fascinating experience. From a steep stone bridge, we surveyed a canal and barges, shophouses, a pagoda, a humpbacked bridge enhanced with greenery, and ancient beautifully landscaped fortifications. From a second vantage point I filmed a classic building through the rounded arch of another bridge. Opposite, encased in the concrete of the canal path, green trees and one a mass of glorious white blossom were making a valiant effort to survive. Similar views, with the inevitable washing, were obtained from another embroidery outlet. Here, a carved screen was inserted with silk panels portraying elegant women dressed in colours of pink and blue, yellow, and pink and red respectively. Pictured amongst different floral sprays, they showed a lady using an embroidery hoop, one with flowers in her hair, and another with an elaborate coiffure and a floral garland around her neck. Again stitched onto transparent cloth, a cuddly looking white kitten was on display here also; it was a favourite theme. A wooden screen was illustrated with humpbacked bridges and zigzag walkways, pavilions, figures, flowers and trees, a pagoda, a long wall, and boats.

The ancient narrow streets, where I came across a display of art, were lined with the same struggling trees mentioned earlier, and shophouses backed onto canals where boats plied up and down. Rain developed, and colour magically appeared on bicycles in the dull dreary streets, vendors doing a roaring trade in hooded plastic capes, which evolved like rainbows in hues of vivid pink, red, yellow, purple, green and various shades of blue. The green trees were magnificent even under these adverse conditions, which did not ease when we visited our first garden. Simulating a landscape of trees and mountains, plants mingled with tall rocks made a dramatic picture against a white wall draped with greenery, as did curtains of purple wisteria over a covered pathway crossing a pond, the latter viewed through lattice in a wall. Even the heavy drip of constant rain sounding a plink plonk on the water could not spoil the ambience of gazebos, bamboo sighted through an octagonal wall opening, the decorative rock sculpted by nature, mossy trunks, covered corridors, bamboo-tiled roofs, green and red shrubs, and bonsai seen through a moon gate. Enclosed by ivy-covered walls, this extensive collection featured many varieties of trees in different sizes and one vibrant pink azalea in a ceramic pot. The art of bonsai utilises wire to encourage branches to develop artistic and appealing shapes. In a stunning representation of the Stone Forest in Kunming, stunted shrubs were planted amongst fluted grey rock pinnacles standing in water and surrounded by floating lilies.

A pavilion held screens embroidered with gorgeous fantail goldfish; once again worked on transparent fabric, they literally appeared to be swimming. Black-and-white water birds were depicted with trees, flowers and rushes, and yet another irresistible fluffy white kitten, walking with tail erect, even had blush-pink inner ears, a pale grey nose, and the illusion of gloss embroidered into its coat – it was so inviting to touch!

artistry with stone

Our next venue also featured a pond, in the centre of which loomed a piece of the ornamental Lake Taihu rock surrounded by yellow flowers and green plants; an autumn tree, rotunda, and large green trees graced the perimeter. The interior of the rotunda contained lovely reliefs of birds and figures, doors with embossed scenes below latticework panels, a filigree partition with a round doorway, and a large colourful ceramic vase. Outside, a procession of theatre players in costume greeted us with a cheery '*Ni hao*' – 'Hello, how are you?'. In another area, multihued crowned temple guardians stood watch: two benign (one carrying a furled parasol) and two with dark scowling countenances guaranteed to strike terror into the hearts of wrongdoers. In spite of rain dripping from trees, flames and smoke issued from incense burners in the courtyard of a second temple, this one containing many golden images of Buddha. Red poles with gilt characters supported a decorated ceiling from which hung red lanterns; a red banner was appliquéd with a gold dragon, and a ferocious guardian, holding a pagoda in his left hand, had a face at his middle! A multi-armed goddess was amongst tiny alabaster figures located above a colourful tableau and two rows of larger gilded images. Life-sized golden statues, including another with many arms, stood around the walls. People bowed foreheads to the floor in obeisance to an army of gold deities.

Suzhou rose to prominence after the completion of the Grand Canal 1,300 years ago, when its network of waterways became an important trading link, especially for its most valuable product, silk. The city had weathered many upheavals: in the 1800s most of it was decimated, 70% of its population killed, and the silk industry devastated by horrific fighting in the Taiping Rebellion, but it survived the carnage and, since then, the Japanese military occupation, civil war, the 1949 Cultural Revolution, and latter day industrialisation. At one time, it gloried in almost one hundred landscaped works of art, built mostly in the Ming dynasty and designed for harmony, meditation and tranquillity for nobles, but only six have been preserved for posterity.

The most beautiful, **West Garden** (**Xiyuan**, first built 1271–94), had a zigzag pathway leading to a white rotunda standing in water, its bi-level curved roof, delicate green trees around the edge of the pool, and the last vestiges of wisteria clinging to lacy bare branches on a covered walkway mirrored to absolute perfection. In these almost monochrome surroundings of white walls and pale trees, where even the sky had lost its hue, colour was provided by a group of gay umbrellas and two huge artificial red water lilies floating on the surface of the water.

even the rain could not detract from the beauty of the gardens

In keeping with Chinese tradition, halls and pavilions in the garden had appealing descriptive names, of which I shall only give the English translations: Stones Listening to the Lute, Stone-Worshipping, Green-Locking, Lotus Fragrance, and Chinese Parasol Upon Which the Phoenix Rests! Incorporated into the garden, the **Jiezhuanglu Temple** had a large hall containing gold statues around the base of a tall rock with colourful figures inserted in natural nooks. Five hundred more images of gilded clay *arhats* resided in glass cases, one trio with colourful finely crafted wooden dragons in front.

dragons et al

Interesting and unusual statues included a Buddha with two faces back to back, an intriguing guardian deity displaying changing moods from laughter to sadness when observed from different angles, and three many-armed back to back images with 1,000 eyes in total. However, as always, my favourites were the multihued wooden guardians, one holding a musical instrument, all wearing crowns, and two conveying expressions of extreme anger.

a real charmer

The temple, built around 1271 in the Yuan dynasty, was destroyed in the Taiping Rebellion and restored in the latter part of the Qing dynasty.

We spent considerable time standing on a bridge to watch the activity on a canal lined with shabby houses built right on the waterway, their pipes draining directly into the canal and some with unguarded steps leading to the surface. Walls were crumbling, one window was covered with a sheet of plastic, and a couple had overhead balconies protected with makeshift awnings of corrugated iron. Weeds sprouted from stone foundations, one had a few plants in tin cans on a concrete ledge, a tree appeared to sprout from a roof, and a lady squatted on a set of steps leading between houses to scour her wooden nightsoil pail.

scouring her night soil pail

Heavy barge traffic occasionally caused congestion as captains sounded hooters, waved directions, and fended their vessels off other boats and walls with the long poles sometimes used to propel the craft.

Steam engines at the stern of barges intermittently belched black fumes into the atmosphere. Many of these decrepit-looking vessels were operated by families and had crude living quarters, one had a dog on board, and all appeared to carry little in the way of cargo. Some had canvas tarpaulins covering the hold, and except for the absence of sails and the fact that they were motorised or poled, I could have attributed them with the origin of the term Chinese '*junk*'! Here, the canal was barely wide enough for two barges to pass, and there seemed to be scant regard to the laws of passage because they went by on either side, the right-of-way degenerating into Rafferty's rules! One side of our viewpoint looked towards a humpbacked bridge, the others to towers in the distance and, below, a broom and pots on a tiny concrete patio outside a dwelling. At least 20 or more vessels passed underneath in the time we spent watching, and from further along we looked down on the street in front of the canal where plane trees, a pink bicycle, an attic window, a lacy iron balcony and people constituted the view.

traffic jam

Back in our car, I observed a butcher chopping meat with a cleaver next to a teahouse with red lanterns. Driving beneath an old triple-arched gateway we eventually arrived at another embroidery factory, called Academy of Silk, with a red maple bonsai at the moon gate entrance. These outlets never failed to enthral as rows of girls, faces almost on their fine work, toiled to produce exquisite pieces of art. At least they laboured under better conditions than those in the factory, where clattering machines produced the fabric in a process commencing with the winding of silk from cocoons; here music played and there was laughter and chatter. Silk was prized as long ago as 2500 BC and China was still the world's largest producer, although to avoid having to travel the hazardous route, it was established in Italy when Emperor Justinian sent two monks to discover the secret and they managed to smuggle the silkworm eggs back in their canes. I watched and filmed as they laboriously created a spray of cherry blossom, a black-and-white bird on a twig with cleverly shaded red maple leaves, and a scene executed in black and white showing mountains rising from incredibly realistic mist. Other subjects included autumn leaves in pink and red, which appeared almost as if one could reach out and pick them up, glossy-looking grapes worked in purple, lilac and mauve, small fish swimming amongst weed, butterflies, and more white Persian kittens: one with shell-pink inner ears and shiny tinsel around its neck, another on a branch with autumn-toned leaves. A pair of tabby kittens with black-tipped ears appeared so life-like that people viewing my photographs assumed them to be real. There were red flowers, large fish, and various other cats, which were a popular and appealing topic. Many subjects were copied from pictures set up beside their work. Finished items included pink salmon exhibiting a silver effect created with grey and white cottons, an elegant traditionally attired lady with a bouffant hairstyle teasing a kitten, spotted deer nuzzling each other, trailing sprays of red-brown leaves, a stork in flight, cute puppies, goldfish, a peacock with roses, long-tailed white birds on a twig with red leaves, and yellow birds on pink blossoms. Worked in silk, a framed portrait of Prince Charles turned to reveal Princess Diana on the other side! My camera had been malfunctioning and the film rolled considerably, which spoilt much of my photography.

realistic kittens and puppies

I acquired some private time to further investigate Suzhou's fascinating streets, where I passed a food stall, an appealing scene of a young boy feeding grain to tiny chickens on a step beside the pavement, more houses backing onto a canal, trishaws, a few bicycles with carts attached, one with cane panniers, and literally thousands ridden by well-dressed people and even men in uniform.

food stall, trishaw and the occasional car

I saw a man delving into a drum with tongs, and small open-fronted shops selling all manner of goods, such as cane baskets, rope, plastic bottles, a bamboo bed frame, and brooms, with oddments strung overhead. A lady carried a sloshing bucket of liquid past a bicycle barrow with whole pineapples, pieces of which were sold by weight from handheld scales.

Reaching a market I discovered ladies gutting eels (also sold by weight), tomatoes, Chinese greens, cucumbers and melons, a man weighing offal, and a strange root vegetable being shaved with a cleaver. A store displayed all sorts of paraphernalia, including raincoats, rope, cane chairs and assorted containers.

selling pineapple

small market and local shop

I watched a couple in a room below street level working with kapok, which they processed in a primitive wooden box-like mechanical apparatus and formed into mattresses compacted and smoothed by hand with the aid of a heavy round metal plate with a handle; it was most interesting. Some canals were so narrow that one could almost reach from windows across the intervening space to shake hands, and the perfectly calm water, although was choked with rubbish, still afforded perfect reflections. I came to an area where live chickens were sold, their legs trussed with string in order to weigh and carry them, and another pedlar was carving some product with a cleaver.

Back by the waterways, I found an attractive bridge with very shallow steps and a moored boat with a rusted corrugated iron roof, plywood partitions, and firewood stacked on the back; another arched bridge crossed in front of the bow.

barge and bridge

Mossy-roofed houses were shaded by trees growing in the street behind, and one sprouted from foundations just above the water.

reflections

I was on a narrow paved pathway and three small boys were so engrossed by something in bushes that they were oblivious to me taking pictures of them. A house on the opposite side of the canal had steps leading to the water from a tiny back porch with a few items of clothing and an umbrella hanging to dry. From another doorway, directly above the canal, a person was drawing water in a can attached to a length of rope.

Anchored opposite, a boat had its side flaps raised to reveal a bicycle and a man sitting to read the paper, whilst covered bowls sat on top of a stove from which smoke issued – instead of from the bent chimney pipe supported by wire!

drawing water straight from the canal

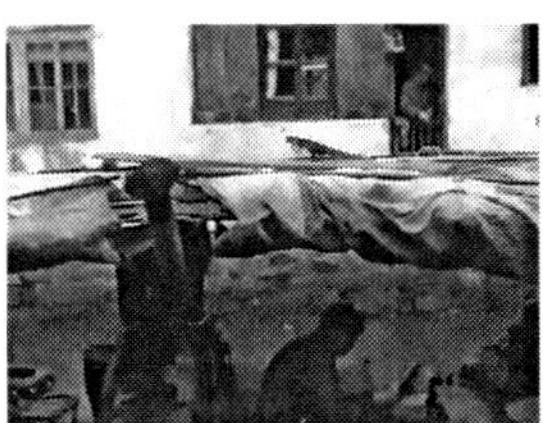

reading the morning news whilst breakfast is cooking

A smiling couple on yet another boat were sitting on the open deck; the man had his shirt off and was washing whilst enjoying the brief sunshine. I could see into the kitchen of one dark dwelling where utensils sat on a bench and an enamel basin, obviously for washing and the preparation of food, sat in a stand.

Back in the main streets, a broom and baskets lay outside a home with articles of apparel pegged on a line, framed paintings were displayed in front of a shop also selling textiles, and

another canal scene

fish were arranged in trays, behind which a man was divesting himself of gumboots in order to don sneakers.

cluttered doorway

I saw teahouses, items on shelves in a store with a small counter opening to the street, a colourful florist displaying many lilies and, in a window of the shop next door, two large ceramic vases illustrated in green and white. There were many steep stepped bridges and altogether, in spite of the garbage, it was a photogenic town with quaint buildings and picturesque waterways. A man sat on a tiny chair at a tiny table on a tiny balcony drinking soup directly from a bowl, and across a humpbacked bridge from where I took the photographs, pink lanterns hung from eaves above caged birds in the open windows of a shop on the canal. Other people sat on cane chairs in the street, also a popular pastime in the evening after a hot day.

step bridge

That evening, we went to the **Garden of the Master of the Nets** (**Wangshi**) for a cultural show. The first act featured a performer wearing a long black beard, a flowing red outfit, and a tall headdress incorporating two extremely long feathers, and a girl in a red *cheongsam*, also with elaborate headgear. They were singing Chinese opera, and for once I was almost grateful for the spasmodic performance of my camera because the piercing sounds were intermittent on the playback!

performers

A magician disguised by a golden mask was the next item on the programme, followed by a singer in a glittering dress accompanied by a trio playing traditional instruments resembling a fiddle, xylophone, and many-stringed guitar. Seated in front of traditional pictures adorning the wall, these three also gave solo performances. Each act was set in a different lighted pavilion reflected in the pool, and even these bore imaginative names: Pine Viewing and Painting Appreciating.

A girl with beautiful features, trinkets in her hair, and a long powder-blue dress with sequins on the skirt and yoke, performed a graceful dance with fans composed of white feathers, the only other colour provided by a flowering pink azalea in a pot. Two more, with sparkling diamante headdresses, danced with small quivering fans, and a flautist played in one of the open corridors on the opposite side of the pond, the sound floating across the limpid water in the stillness of the quiet garden. He was followed by a soloist with a type of clarinet. In the next room, a lady wearing a white dress with a gold neckline played a type of zither, her nimble fingers tripping and flying rapidly across the strings. I regretted the lack of sound for these last three acts. The final performance featured two more traditional instruments like a banjo and guitar, the latter with an exceedingly long slender neck and appearing to have only a couple of strings. Again sounding like a yowling cat, the vocalist obviously rendered a sad song because she exhibited a mournful expression. A lovely screen provided the backdrop.

Next day, as we again made our way by car, washing hung outside houses opening immediately onto the footpath, and a mop was propped near a doorway where a man was seated on a bench to read the newspaper. Morning on the canals had produced film of a man washing his face, ears and hair in a basin set on top of a clay oven at the head of steps leading from the water. Opposite, a person threw liquid from a doorway into the canal, and people were cycling and walking across a bridge nearby. It must have been washing day because clothes hung in streets, on balconies, and from poles extending from windows. Standing on steps below another stone bridge, this one with an ornate marble balustrade, a woman was washing and wringing out her mop.

morning ablutions and washing the mop

Zhuozheng, the **Humble Administrator's Garden**, one of the four most famous in a land of glorious gardens, was established in 1522 around a pond and narrow waterways with small bridges. The banks were lined with trees in a soft shade of green and paved paths that were regularly swept. Autumn foliage introduced colour, and one red tree glimpsed behind the decorative grille in a white wall was particularly outstanding. Colour was also provided by a solitary umbrella beside the main pool, which was crossed by a bridge leading to a moon gate in a white wall beyond. Around the edge, willows lowered weeping fronds into the water. Walking along a covered passageway we encountered a large group of Korean women in their unmistakable national dress with a voluminous skirt falling from the bust line, the many hues of their identical costume providing a kaleidoscope of colour: apple green, bright and pale pink, yellow, apricot, various blues and chartreuse. Posing amongst vibrant pink, red and white azaleas, one lady in shimmering pink was the focus of many photographs.

More pavilions, rotundas, bridges and zigzag walkways were the subjects of magnificent mirror images, the **Mandarin Duck Hall**, once a theatre, had unusual leaded windows with small panes of both indigo and clear glass, and the garden contained an ancient teahouse. Bamboo made a statement amongst delicate trees and Lake Taihu rock, and another bonsai collection included a wisteria with one delightful spray of the drooping mauve blossom. Some of these miniature exhibits were obviously very old, their gnarled and twisted trunks emphasised by beds of bright green moss. I never tired of the various vistas of trelliswork, water, willows, bridges and curled eaves, often framed by moon gates to form composite pictures, and I took film of three of us reflected in a large mirror, which caused a few laughs. The remainder of the garden consisted of gazebos interconnected by pathways, rock arrangements with plants in crevices and trees on top, and two tiny courtyards: one with a miniature red maple, budding green shoots on black branches, and two slender upright stones, the second containing the sculpted rock. A fact not acquired before was that the stone was deliberately submerged in the lake by one generation, and retrieved by the next for the purpose of creating such monuments.

pavilion and Lake Taihu rock

Photographed through an ornate window, the ten-tiered **North Temple Pagoda** made an excellent picture, as did a stunning red maple, bamboo, palm trees and greenery in the surrounds. Tiny figures on a curled roofline (believed to ward off evil spirits) and lanterns under eaves also made an interesting frame for the towering pagoda. A wind had sprung up and white cherry blossom was blowing like flakes of snow and settling in drifts. I climbed to the top of the wooden structure for a tremendous panorama over landscaped gardens that featured different species of conifer, low box hedges, flowering trees, and a combination of artistic bare branches and thick foliage. I was also able to appreciate decorative roof capping, not visible from below, and the perimeter of the garden, beyond which spread streets of white housing with grey bamboo-tiled roofs.

Returning in daylight hours to the beautifully maintained Wangshi Garden, we were enthralled by a glorious display of azaleas viewed through a moon gate, a grassed courtyard with tall Lake Taihu rock and small trees, many additional pieces of the sculpted stone scattered around, an undulating white wall with greenery in front, covered corridors with rectangular openings manifesting different patterns of grille, autumn foliage, artistically shaped naked branches amongst the various shades of green, and rock walls around a pool.

undulating wall

There were ponds reflecting zigzag walkways, pavilions, and a simulated rocky mountain with a rotunda on the summit.

Snaking its way along a second white wall, dark dragon coping arched above a moon gate through which a palm tree, shrubs and lawn were visible.

rotunda

gate in wall with dragon coping

The dragon was draped with ivy, tendrils of which extended down the wall behind ornamental stone, attractive trees and palms. Another white moon gate had a red tree to one side, its curved trunk conforming to the shape of the opening, a little stone bridge was enhanced with creeper clinging beneath its arch, and a perfectly round doorway framed more bright pink azaleas, trees and green plants. Displaying yellow leaves and in full bloom, the thick branches of an old wisteria threaded their way over a high brownstone wall, through a hole in which the curled eaves of a rotunda could be seen. Overlooked by a pavilion with a string of red lanterns suspended from one corner, more pretty autumn foliage grew beside a pond containing water lilies, and a gazebo surrounded by greenery was viewed through an octagonal opening. A small nook contained rocks and a brilliant red tree, whilst an area with widely spaced pavers was a picture in red, pink and green. Bamboo, latticework under eaves, and a tall pillar of rock completed my filming in this venue of abundant charm. The various apertures were designed to frame alluring scenes, and words fail to impart the exquisite beauty of this garden.

Grand Canal

Before joining our boat along the **Grand Canal** to Wuxi, another stroll in the streets revealed a corner fruit shop and a pedlar with a charcoal burner on a bicycle barrow. Begun in the 12th and 11th centuries BC and widened during the 7th (Sui Dynasty) and 14th (Yuan Dynasty), the 1,794km canal reaching Beijing ranked with the Great Wall as a symbol of ancient Chinese civilisation. We travelled past the aforementioned fortifications and stone bridge, flowering cherry trees, tumbledown shacks and lines of laundry, and looked down on a barge with the roof seemingly held in place by blocks of wood. A lady was doing her washing in the canal, and busy water traffic included a barge loaded with logs. Moored beside banks, others were hung with laundry, and a figure tossed waste from a basin into the already murky chocolate brown water. Sometimes covered by tarpaulins, which were often secured by old tyres, many appeared to carry soil, gravel-like white stone, or timber, and were so weighed down that water almost lapped over the gunwales. Anchored beside a green bank, a red-and-blue vessel stood out amongst nondescript craft. The canal was wide at this point and both large and small boats, often towing or tied together in a long convoy, their loud hailers blaring, klaxons sounding, and men standing in the prows, moved in a continual stream, with women doing their washing or cooking on board. Many had lengths of wood on the roof (maybe extra fuel), steam billowed from engines, and a barge laden with full sacks was moored to one side. We passed some type of factory or kiln where men were running down a wooden plank to load obviously heavy sacks strung on a pole carried between two. Interesting barges were laden to overflowing with bundles of rags, scrap paper and/or cardboard.

loaded with cardboard

long line of barges

We had a masseur on board, and one of my group members had her neck vigorously massaged. One man was shovelling something overboard, a dog ran along the embankment, we passed beneath modern steel bridges, and ladies were washing clothes – one using a straw broom to clean a bucket – at the foot of steps leading from a stone-walled promenade harbouring cherry blossoms, open-fronted shops, and of course the ubiquitous bicycle, of which China has over 700 million. A figure scrubbed utensils beside ramshackle

pots onshore

corrugated iron sheds, and another scoured a pail on more steps by the canal. There was a scarcity of trees, a few patches of green that were probably weeds, a lot of rubble, and large clay jars and pots arrayed on the roadside.

We came to more bridges, which spanned side canals as well as the main waterway, and began to encounter heavier barge traffic. But there were surprisingly few people in the tree-lined street fronting housing in the village of **Xushuguan**, although some were washing utensils or clothes in the canal, from which they also collected water! The occasional beautiful show of blossoms helped to brighten decrepit buildings.

A barge carried bamboo almost its own length lashed to the sides, and many men were employed unloading sheafs of grain or straw. Using pitchforks, they tossed it onto wagons where others stood atop the load to stack it. Some just sat on their vessels chatting, and in a puttering barge laden with tons of cardboard, its engines emitting clouds of smoke, the helmsman, perched up high in order to see over his cargo, sat at an enormous wheel. Laundry provided colour in a row of berthed boats, and terracotta pottery was lined up on the shore. With only a basin, a lady was washing clothes that were then hung on a line strung from the cabin in the stern to the bow.

washing day

A long row of adjoined craft had people preparing and eating food and lines of washing flapping in the breeze created by their movement. At times, we passed close enough to almost scrape sides and I could look down into one hold where a man was shovelling. On other extremely long convoys I noticed a solitary unhealthy-looking plant in a tub, a man cleaning with a mop, women executing the eternal chore of washing, which was also spread on tarpaulin covers, one red boat and several blue (most were bereft of colour), and one with vegetables stored on deck.

washing en route

We passed another intriguing paper and rag boat and followed a promenade with garbage along the waterline and at the foot of steps. Rubbish, rubble and washing added to the generally untidy appearance of the street fronting houses. Although some showed evidence of having once been whitewashed, all the buildings here were monotonous grey concrete with grey smokestacks belching behind; on the whole, China and its people were very drab.

A second member of my group volunteered for a shoulder massage, which she endured with an expression of agony on her face! Nearing Wuxi, we came to a neat stone-walled embankment, moored boats in side canals crossed by small concrete and wooden bridges, lengths of timber stacked on shore and being loaded onto a barge, a tender bobbing alongside a bigger boat, vessels carrying full sacks, and others bearing soil taken from large mounds by a bridge. Several places had lines of men running up and down planks with loads suspended from poles across their shoulders. We passed fish traps consisting of nets suspended from crossed poles that were lowered manually into the water, which I had seen many times in Asia, ducks on rocks in shallows, a barge with washing on a length of bamboo and two dogs, barges with logs, and a line of barges conveying a cargo of some white substance in holds; most had a clutter of ropes, poles, anchors and other equipment on their prows. It had been a relaxing (but noisy!) experience.

Wuxi

Passing a traffic circus containing a modern statue depicting a girl, her hair streaming, leaping in the centre, we were transferred to the delightful Lakeside Hotel. Driving to yet another beautiful park, **Turtle Head Peninsula**, so called because of its resemblance to the head of that reptile, we passed people sitting in small fishing boats and fish traps in a wide expanse of calm water over which stood shacks on stilts. There was nothing to differentiate this garden, but it was still enjoyable: rocks, delicate trees, water, a stone lantern, the **Everlasting Spring** humpbacked bridge, pavilions, and the bare tree with writhing branches in striking silhouette. Amongst the infinite poetic names were the Broad Happiness Temple and Chanting Fragrance Hall. Water plants floated on the surface of a pond with Lake Taihu rock in the middle, walkways led to rotundas, and there were copious reflections. In an illustration of the old and the new, a speedboat roared past a large dragon boat leisurely sailing on **Lake Taihu**, its huge head at the prow, tail on the stern. Taking advantage of a holiday were hordes of well-dressed people, including one young lady in a large picture hat and three small, very shy girls in, respectively, a glittering frock with gold and silver flounces, a dress with an ornate patterned yoke and tiered skirt, and elaborate hair adornment.

Our next destination was a gaudy complex like a miniature Disneyland, and was indeed a Chinese amusement park, also called **Taihu**. Gay umbrellas lined the route to the entrance, and a pagoda on a distant hill was apparent between pink and lemon spires crowning towers that rose above lime-green battlements on its white perimeter wall. Inside was a replica (supposedly) of the Arc de Triomphe. A second archway was located beyond a group of statues on a pedestal in the middle of fountains projecting different water displays. Formal gardens led to a Scandinavian stave church and a castle. We left via another gateway beyond which many turrets were visible; a stone bridge to one side crossed a moat.

En route to an exhibition of figurines, we passed a European-style symmetrical colonnaded edifice with statues around the roofline and a traffic circle containing a modern clock tower and a huge fanciful dragon, its head created from concrete and its serpentine body from green plants. Amongst the collection, a sequence of effigies portrayed an old long-bearded Chinese fisherman under a broad-brimmed hat, his trousers rolled up above bare feet, and a container by his side. He was depicted in different actions of landing and jubilantly displaying the catch at the end of his line. In keeping with the Chinese penchant for exotic names, one figurine was title Monkey Wreaks Havoc in Heaven!

delightful figurines

We visited a different type of garden with the emphasis on flowers. At the entrance, red trees behind beds of pink and white azaleas bordered by orange blooms and greenery made a great impression. Once inside, other beds with tall conifers had verdant mountains in the background. Steps led to a yellow wall with three arches and bamboo-tiled coping on its staggered top. In front, maples rose up behind massed purple, pink and white flowers again edged by the orange and green combination. Potted palms were arrayed around a similar display at the rear of the wall. A stone bridge was flanked by red maple trees and pink and white azaleas, whilst a pagoda on a hill formed the backdrop to pavilions reflected in a pool.

pagoda in the background

A covered walkway with octagonal openings led to a rotunda, the curled corners of its roof enhanced with filigree. A second stone bridge, also flanked by flowers, crossed a pond covered with water lilies and led to a two-tiered white pavilion set in green lawns under the awning of a gorgeous green shade tree. A dragon wall reared above another covered walkway, a pavilion with trelliswork under the eaves had multi-paned glass windows, and a glorious display of wisteria cascaded down a white wall with the sculpted stone in the foreground. In front of this again, a stone retaining wall with greenery in crevices bounded a pond, its reflections undisturbed by almost motionless carp. Making an eye-catching picture, tall pinnacles of pale grey, almost white rock soared above bright pink flowers, red foliage and green shrubs.

We passed the inevitable food stalls and headed back to our hotel, also set in magnificent grounds, which featured beautiful foliage, bridges crossing a large pond, Lake Taihu rock, rotundas, and a small pagoda. In the lobby, red, pink and purple azaleas lined a small pool containing bubbling fountains lit by coloured lights to create shimmering orbs of red, blue and green; a monstera deliciosa flourished in rocks behind. From my window I obtained wonderful vistas of the lake, trees, houses and distant hills.

In the town, known locally as Radiant Pearl in the Lake, many men carried heavy loads in baskets suspended from poles across their shoulders, a lady washed dishes in a basin on the pavement, and carts were loaded with timber. Taking up a position opposite a row of open-fronted food shops, one with a white-coated cook busily stirring the contents of a steaming cauldron, I remained stationary whilst the moving panorama passed me by: a man staggering under the weight of his baskets, a woman carrying shopping in one hand and leading a child by the other, a man on a bicycle with plants in his carrier, trishaws, bicycles with carts carrying bamboo or greenery, one with panniers filled with tomatoes, and a lady with greens in a basket over her arm.

steaming cauldron

A man with bananas for sale sat on the verge whittling wood, and another, wearing the traditional cap, sat on a cane chair mending an umbrella; a bird fluttered in a cage above, and bicycles were parked to one side. A young lady carried a covered bowl and chopsticks, and I saw *one* car. Many were suspicious of the camera and reluctant to be photographed, although one family group, with clothing hanging overhead and seated around a stove outside their home, posed proudly: the elderly gentleman with a bowl of food and a broad smile, but a young girl seemingly apprehensive. Around them on the pavement were basins, a stack of wood, a cane basket, bicycles – and a Marlborough advertisement. Neater two-storey homes appeared along the canal, and en route to the railway station we passed logs on a hand-pulled cart in the busy street.

Shanghai

On board the train to China's largest city, Shanghai, it was interesting to watch the attendant pouring a long stream of boiling water from a kettle held high above glasses.

pouring water for tea

Free hot water was always provided on Chinese trains, mostly in thermos flasks, and passengers carried their own tea in a jar, a habit I acquired on my first visit. Passing haystacks and small fishing boats, one with occupants thus engaged, we travelled alongside the waterway and on arrival checked into the Huaxia Hotel before negotiating tree-lined avenues to visit a handcraft factory. Here, we witnessed something else that I had not previously seen – paper cutting. Using no pattern, it was fascinating to watch as butterflies and strutting roosters evolved from precise, cleverly executed incisions made with sharp scissors. Other creations included flowers and figures.

artistry with paper

Worked in fine stitches, unbelievably beautiful embroidery featured subjects such as elegantly garbed ethnic ladies with elaborate coiffures. There were demonstrations (and naturally items to purchase!) of the internal decoration of glass bottles and painting on large canvases. Delicate watercolours showed ladies in traditional attire, and arresting art in subtle colours depicted mountains, a waterfall, red and green trees, clouds, and reflections in shining water; canal scenes were rendered in black and white.

We drove past an extremely long and bustling street market where meat, fruits, vegetables and other commodities, displayed in hessian sacks, baskets, buckets, boxes, bags, bowls, crates and tubs, and on trays or simply cloth on the ground, were purchased by customers on bicycles. A glass case contained what appeared to be cooked ducks, and I could distinguish celery, potatoes, cucumbers, a long variety of purple aubergine, dry looking roots, fungi, peppers, peas, bamboo shoots, red and green apples, bananas, mandarins and oranges, watermelons, and the reddest of tomatoes weighed on handheld scales, but only one person was preparing food. At another intersection, cooking was being carried out below washing hanging on a line, which would surely have been infused with savoury odours!

Our first tour was to a temple complex containing gleaming golden images, one holding a gold lotus flower; ceramic vases and a lidded container were arrayed at their feet. Lighted candles stood before a many-armed figure, there were smoking incense urns in courtyards, and a multi-tiered pagoda reared above elaborate rooflines in the grounds.

Seated in front of an altar holding many objects, monks dressed in black-and-maroon, a golden canopy decorated with dragons overhead, were chanting and beating gongs placed on an intricately carved red and gold stand. Reciting from a book, an older monk in yellow was seated in front of a black image lodged before a second altar on which stood burning candles. Both altars held blue-and-white ceramic joss stick bowls. Inserted in a yellow wall, a round stone carving with an embossed edge portrayed mountains, trees, and a flautist seated cross-legged above heavy relief of a reclining bull.

many hands make light work

In another pavilion, the ever-colourful crowned guardians stood beneath decorative lanterns. Dressed in elaborate garb, carrying a parasol and small shrine, one had blue faces at his stomach and knees, another held a musical instrument. The ferocious guardians had black and red visages respectively, the black figure with a beard.

stone carving

temple guardian

Yet other pavilions had more gold images. I came across a young girl with an incredible painted face: chalk-white foundation had been overlaid with bright crimson above cheeks and around kohl-accented eyes, the boldly drawn black brows flaring upwards. Dark red lips and two black spots on the bridge of her nose completed the makeup, and she was dressed in a glaring yellow costume, her black braids fastened with red frippery. A boy with similar countenance had a tick or check mark on his nose. More busy scenes in narrow streets revealed open-fronted shops, food cooking, people and goods on the pavement, one lady knitting whilst waiting for custom, washing strung on bamboo poles overhead, tables and chairs on the roadway, fruits, a bunch of bright balloons, and decrepit buildings.

waiting for customers

The **Yu Yuan** (**Mandarin**) **Garden** (1559–77) was the finest example of a Ming Court garden and consisted of a series of scenes and pavilions connected by covered corridors, stairs and bridges to create the illusion of great size in a quite small area. Its central feature was the **Temple of Town Gods**, which failed to protect it in the Opium War of 1842, the Taiping Rebellion, and the Boxer Rebellion in 1900, and it also housed the pleasant **Wuxinting Teahouse**. Entered via a zigzag pathway across a pond containing a white statue, the garden was a veritable oasis in the centre of this frenetic teeming metropolis. Landscaped with the usual water, rocks, and brilliant red trees amongst the green, it also presented magnificent opportunities for reflections. A stunning fall of mauve wisteria cascaded over white stone that harboured azaleas and greenery in crevices and enclosed a pool containing water lilies and carp. Framed by a moon gate, I captured the idyllic scene of a gazebo, its curved roof shaded by a lacy tree, situated above the white stone retaining wall of a pond crossed by a small bridge, opposite which drooping willows dipped long tendrils into the water. In colours of red and mauve, large double blooms of China's national flower, the peony, made a superb foreground to a pavilion surrounded by delicate foliage and mirrored in the water.

peony flowers

A red pavilion with glass windows was reflected in a pond with plants in its rocky boundary, and hundreds of carp formed a solid orange mass as they milled around a rotunda in anticipation of being fed. Dragons decorated roof capping, and the monstrous mythical beasts also peered down from their position atop an undulating wall threading its way around the grounds, levelling out (sans dragons) at the end of a waterway, and continuing behind a forest of white stone with a striking red tree and vibrant pink blooms amongst the vegetation. With the aid of another large mirror, I inserted myself into a magnificent setting of autumn foliage and greenery. A room contained tables and chairs crafted from the roots of trees, and high relief on a wall portrayed figures in a pavilion overlooking a scene with mountains, trees, a swan, and two people on a bridge spanning a body of water. Probably the illustration of a tale in Chinese folklore, other figures standing on cloud above included one with a horrific expression and a dagger in the hand of an upraised arm.

folkloric relief

Two jar-shaped doorways in walls either side of a small paved patio opened onto lovely scenes, and another aperture in a white wall was inset with black ironwork depicting, as if in silhouette, a twisted tree and a long-legged long-necked bird perched on rock; a gazebo and green garden were evident behind.

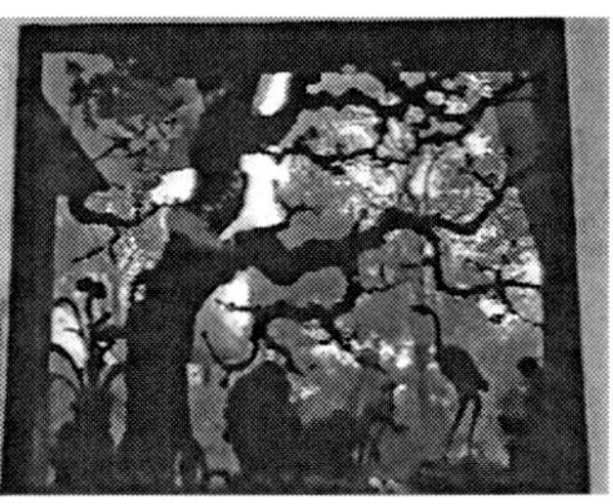

beautiful inset

A metal lion was the subject of my last picture, and once again outside, we came across a bevy of colourful children. Because of China's one child policy, I often found them to be spoilt by lavish attention and consequently cheeky, as distinct from Japanese children who were always impeccably behaved.

We were serenaded at lunch by a xylophone and traditional stringed instrument held between the knees and played with a bow. After the meal, and views (between the first multistorey buildings we had encountered) of the **Television Tower**, China's largest and at that stage third highest in the world, but almost obliterated by shrouding mist, we proceeded to **The Bund**. Paralleling a wide boulevard, this bustling waterfront promenade was landscaped with paving, trees, low hedges and lawns, and amongst the crowds I found two girls holding a cute white puppy with black button eyes and nose. It was not raining, but the whole area was enveloped in fog and it was extremely cold. Colonial buildings in this merchandise 'Mecca' featured a dome and clock tower.

China's most Westernised city, it was once one of the richest, most frenzied, exciting and wicked on earth, where opium-based businesses rubbed shoulders with branches of respectable Western institutions. The Yangtze River provided a natural conduit for cotton textiles from the interior, an industry based on cheap labour, and Shanghai revelled in wealth, flamboyant materialism, snobbery and vice. In the late 1930s, the dream collapsed into a nightmare of Japanese military repression, starvation, atrocity, and finally the struggle for supremacy between Mao Zedong and Chiang Kai-shek, from which it was never to fully recover. There was little in this city of 11 million to show for its past notoriety; however, it still had more stores and consumer goods and was more fashionable than even the capital. On the opposite side of the **Huang Pu River**, perched on splayed legs, the TV Tower was now visible.

Passing views of an attractive bridge reminiscent of the Golden Gate in San Francisco, we drove to a carpet factory – surely every country on the globe must have at least one of these establishments! These were particularly impressive, with intricate and very colourful designs, one with traditional figures again probably illustrating a Chinese fable. A beautiful screen showed groups of ethnic ladies involved in leisure pursuits like reading, and another had individual ladies indulging in such activities as grooming or embroidery in settings of various blossoms or bamboo.

elegant ladies

Superb black-and-white illustrations pictured rocky tors emerging from mist or reflected in water behind the silhouette of a bare tree. A colourful scene of jollification included a man with a stringed instrument, a white-bearded figure on a donkey, a group of women, and large red water lilies.

Moving on to an after school care centre, we passed a handcart loaded with bamboo that must have been close to 25ft in length. The institution was an eye-opener because talented children were engaged in making origami birds with flowing curly tails, practising calligraphy, studying music and creating art. One tiny tot, so small that she had to sit on a book placed on top of the stool, played a sophisticated tune on a piano, which caused one of my ladies to shake her head in wonder. Others played violins, three performed a recital with lute-like instruments, and two performed Strauss waltzes on piano accordions. A girl with beaded decoration at the ends of her plaits had a look of extreme concentration on her face whilst painting, some practiced typing on antiquated machines, and yet others danced rudimentary ballet – if not excelling in technique, at least enthusiastically!

We ate dinner that evening at a restaurant where ingredients were selected individually, passed to the open-view kitchen, stir-fried on large hotplates by men in chef's hats wielding long chopsticks, and then tossed into bowls that were whirled with a flourish overhead.

China had an infinite number of handcrafts, and we embarked on a visit to a jade outlet where the precious stone was shaped with the aid of a tiny electrically operated spinning disk whilst held under running water; being continually immersed must have proved extremely detrimental to hands. Items both large and small, translucent and opaque, in colours of pink, purple, white, a variety of greens, brown, and grey to almost black were produced. Amongst the finished products, one huge tableau in deep relief depicted trees, mountains, a rotunda, a bridge, graceful water birds and a cascade. Individual pieces included a laughing Buddha with an extremely high sheen (and a fat belly), flowers, trees, birds, horses, and one dragon boat, its tall masts complete with fragile sails and rigging.

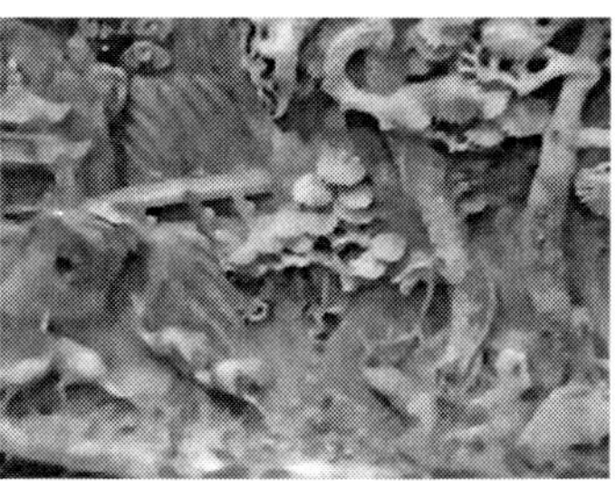

jade sculpture

We were again entertained, this time in a theatre (Lan Xin), by a comedy act involving dancing 'lions' picking up a tinkling ball, scratching behind an ear with a hind leg, walking on rear legs, performing tricks, and being ridden by other performers. There were several clever acrobatic routines, including a girl twirling plates at the end of a stick in her right hand whilst balancing with her left on the head of an accomplice standing on a board mounted on a rolling cylinder, itself on a small dais. In the next act, astride the same cylinder, another balanced stacked trays, separated by glasses, on the end of a stick held between her teeth. On this same apparatus, two performers head to head (one upside down) twirled rings on arms and legs. A vocalist was followed by trick riding that became progressively more complicated. After getting the bicycle moving, the first balanced with just one foot on the central bar. Others rode with their body crosswise over the seat and peddled with one hand, executed handstands holding the seat and handlebars, or stood with one foot on the seat, the other steering. A duo propelled the machine with one lying across the handlebars, feet in the air, and peddling with hands, the second with one foot on the seat, the other in the air, and steering with hands. A girl peddled with hands whilst sitting in the V of the framework, her partner standing on the seat and handlebars to steer. The finale was a group of seven fanning out from the central figure on one machine and then up to 12 in a triangular formation. This was followed by a child with a trick bicycle that split in two and left him riding a unicycle, propelling the other half, and then carrying it over his shoulder! An impressive balancing act featured a man supporting on his head (by one leg!) five interlocking small sawhorses that protruded in front as well as above. He sat and turned full circle by performing complicated manoeuvres and then increased the number of benches to seven, which he balanced whilst twirling rings from his arms. Finally, he achieved an almost impossible task by holding on his head an unwieldy arrangement of 11 sawhorses whilst climbing steps to mount a huge ball that he proceeded to roll with his feet! The next act involved dancers in sequined tops, spinning ropes (made taut by weights) like batons, even whilst executing cartwheels, back flips, somersaults and several other feats. Other remarkable balancing acts included a contortionist twisting and turning whilst supporting girls on his hands and feet. High flyers were catapulted from a springboard to an elevated chair or spun backwards from the board to create a stack of four people standing on shoulders, a couple even performing the backward flip on stilts! Jugglers tossed ninepins, plates, knives and rings. Amazing stunts performed on a flexible bamboo pole supported on the shoulders of a man and woman included bouncing from a sitting to standing position, and flipping backwards and forwards from a standing position. The show concluded with a turning human pyramid, which was also shown in silhouette by clever lighting effects. There was a flag act similar to that at the previous show, and the theatre was the repository for another exquisite silk screen. Most of the artistes were very young.

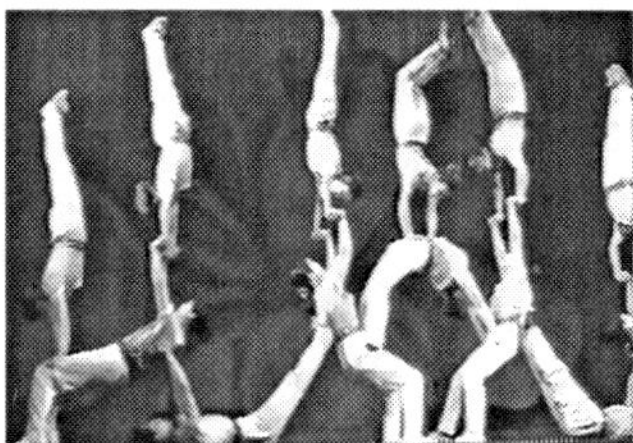

behind the curtain and finale

Kunming

The following morning saw us on a flight to **Kunming**, and the afternoon at an interesting market where a vendor,

flower seller and sweeper

flowers in a carrier on the back of his bicycle, stood negotiating with a customer, and a worker with a straw broom was sweeping around hot-food carts, from one of which a seller emptied a bucket onto the street. The street sweeper, a cigarette dangling from his mouth, approached the woman buying flowers for money, a rare sight in China.

I saw the same lady making purchases at a vegetable market displaying strawberries, tomatoes, cucumbers, leeks, celery, zucchinis, beans, the elongated eggplant, peas (some shelled), peppers (capsicum), roots and fungi, and also selling dumplings, uncooked noodles, fish and poultry.

Hens were confined in wire cages, and I heard a rooster crowing. Fish from the size of sardines to salmon were flapping about in tubs of water aerated with hoses, and from a large tank, a man with a long-handled scoop was selecting and extricating others, which he left floundering on the ground.

Small turtles also swam in the plastic containers. Women sat filleting fish and gutting eels, and a lady had a type of leafy green vegetable in her carrier basket. A handcart was trundled through the middle of the noise and confusion. In other sections, I found nuts, olives and cheeses next to plucked ducks, their heads and yellow feet intact. Alongside was a clothing stall, in front of which a lady was paring a strange root vegetable.

fresh fish

butchers in the background

oodles of noodles

feet, giblets and heads

Vendors were cooking over fires in metal drums, which were set up behind an elderly man squatting on the sidewalk with a small pile of potatoes and spring onions. A food cart was erected in front of a barber, also on the footpath, using a cutthroat razor to shave a customer seated in a cane chair.

at least I could recognise beans

A group of ethnic minority people in traditional garb congregated outside a building; of the 55 minority tribes in China, 22 were native to this province of **Yunnan**.

a shave and then breakfast

Dragon Gate

Situated at 6,280ft, the city had a yearlong mild climate, which made it pleasant for the walking entailed to experience its many sights. The first was **Dragon Gate**, a bit of a misnomer because it was actually comprised of a series of gateways and altars built up the sheer face of a mountain and accessed via a narrow pathway (and many steps!) cut into and through the rock. Constructed some two centuries ago in the reign of Qing emperor Qianlong, the grottos took 72 years to hack out of the stone and a further eight for a sculptor to fashion the images, which included the god of literature adorning the main cave. The first altar contained three guardians, one with pleasant features and two intimidating. The central figure, a fierce face lodged at his middle, was flanked by two holding packages, and the surrounds were decorated with painted panels and carved woodwork.

another intimidating face

The views from different levels were superb, although obscured in the distance due to pollution or smog, but from the top an uninterrupted panorama of houses, lakes and mountains unfolded. Lower vantage points were impeded by trees, elaborate roofs with artwork on gables under heavy bamboo eaves, and stone gateways, one with lions atop pillars also supporting a lintel bearing Chinese characters. A second altar in its rock-hewn alcove had joss sticks burning before a golden deity seated amongst smaller figures and flowers, all in deep relief on the stone wall. Large Chinese characters were embossed on a rock face, and looking up, the entrance to the highest altar could be viewed through branches of trees clinging to the perpendicular surface. Revered by many pilgrims, this last place of devotion contained a golden image depicted in motion, standing on the back of what appeared (by its wings and tail) to be a dragon, and flanked by two larger seated figures in nondescript grey with faint vestiges of colour and sombre gilded countenances, one holding his long beard in the right hand.

gilded faces

These were surrounded by smaller images, also sculpted from the stone, as was decoration on the ceiling, and there were offerings of flowers and lighted candles, which even though it was open, made the cave smoky. Making my way down again, I came to a gateway with a stepped top and, semi-hidden by dry growth and tangled roots, heavy relief of a huge bird, its wings spread, above a recess with an unusual image standing to one side. Black and white scenes were painted on panels inserted under the eaves of a bamboo-tiled roof near a similarly stepped gateway through which trees and the lake far below were visible. A green and coppery-coloured image, only the right half of his body armoured, had one foot on the head of a beast whilst holding what resembled a giant kebab!

Cars vied with many cyclists, their backs erect, riding along a beautiful lakeshore drive. Rimmed by tall trees and with boats on the water, this was **Lake Dian**, second largest freshwater lake in China.

Kunming

Amongst the inner city congestion, I observed stallholders that included purveyors of flowers under large red umbrellas and women with goods in baskets on a pole suspended across their shoulders, a mode of carrying that I had always associated with China but was surprisingly more synonymous with Vietnam and the rest of Asia.

We had a meal at a theatre restaurant where we were entertained by four dancers dressed in identical ethnic costumes but in different colours. The first, executed with waving handkerchiefs in complementary shades of green, pink, blue and lemon, was followed by a fan dance. Strangely, a table was produced on stage, and with a commentary in Chinese, one girl in a gorgeous gown gave a demonstration of carving a duck! Next to be introduced was a man playing a bamboo flute, then pretty girls in different minorities dress. A youth in gold trousers, a white shirt under a gold-trimmed red waistcoat, a red and gold pillbox hat and long black boots, partnered an exotic dancer wearing shimmering shorts beneath a diaphanous red skirt, a black and gold sequined top with flowing red sleeves, and a pillbox hat with dangling ornamentation and a long veil trailing down her back; it was like something from the Arabian Nights. A fascinating act featured a man blowing tunes on a leaf! He wandered amongst the diners in this busy and noisy venue, played *Auld Lang Syne* for our group, and presented a member of my party with one of his 'instruments'. The next act was a beautiful rendition of a dance that could have done justice to *Swan Lake* ballet. A girl wearing trousers beneath a full circle glittering mirrored skirt, a feather and flowers in her hair, performed graceful movements with feet, arms, head, hands and body to resemble the actions of a bird. It was a convincing interpretation, even lit to throw shadows on a screen. More tribal dancers followed, the girls looking like Robin Hood in pink trouser suits with beaded hats. The final act was a vocalist singing 'Should Auld Acquaintance be Forgot' – also in Chinese!

We were served bowls of hot soup then shown how to add ingredients from the selection of meats, vegetables and vermicelli on the table, the resultant concoction mixed with chopsticks. The only disagreeable aspect was the smoking of other patrons. The décor included two magnificent jade pieces depicting figures and trees on a mountain and animals in head to head combat in a similar setting. From an upstairs window, I looked down on a lamp-lit scene with a crazy-paved path winding between a pool and a waterfall surrounded by greenery. Steps led up the side of a simulated mountain created from rocks, which overlooked two teardrop-shaped pools in the background.

Sani Village and the Stone Forest

Following the course of a river, we drove beneath a high overpass and through a tall narrow chasm that eventually opened out to a patchwork of brown and green fields, crops, and old stone bridges, over one of which a man jogged toting containers suspended from a length of the ubiquitous bamboo. The sound of ducks came to my ears as workers laboured in plots that included lettuce, healthy-looking cabbages, and rice seedlings to be transposed to larger paddies. Carts pulled by trotting horses with jangling harness and tinkling bells went by, and further on, white ducks revelled in the brown water of the river. Traversing rickety footbridges, farmers with hoes over their shoulders crossed to an adobe village with a couple of whitewashed houses behind very green vegetable patches. The rich earth extended right to the water's edge where I also saw a couple of buffalo. One field worker wore a coolie hat, also an article more prevalent in Vietnam. The delightful rural picture was completed by a few autumn trees, green hills, and white butterflies flitting over the banks and bushes separating neat plots.

rural China

We paused to take photographs of ducks (dead) hanging by the neck beside a roadside clay oven that a man stoked to a roaring fire, after which the ducks were lowered in their entirety (beaks and all!) into the top and a heavy metal lid reinstated.

duck barbeque

Stopping at another farming community, it was easy to see the irrigation channels between rows of vegetables, and a large herd of long-horned white goats (and half a dozen brown) were moving down the path towards us – some looking for greener pastures in lush crops to the side!

goats and green fields

We were heading for the **Stone Forest** (**Shilin**), as the name implies, a unique forest of upright stony outcrops believed to have been formed by the earth's crust pushing up and being sculpted into fantastic shapes by aeons of weathering. Projecting above intervening treetops, they formed a natural maze of bizarre grey mushrooms and limestone columns up to 100ft high, interspersed with pockets of water. It never ceased to amaze me how no two of the

Stone Forest

planets features were the same: no two mountain ranges, no two deserts, rivers, waterfalls, forests or oceans.

We first visited the primitive **Five Tree Village** of the **Sani Zhu** clan of the **Yi** minority tribe, its houses settled around a small lake, also containing standing stones, at the entrance to the forest.

entrance to Stone Forrest

Here we were besieged by beautiful girls in costume carrying gay umbrellas, colourful embroidered 'hill tribe' bags, and items that they all clamoured to sell – even *I* succumbed!

colourful costume

Narrow winding streets between the mud-brick houses were littered with rubble, ladders stood against walls, and I saw haystacks, unthreshed barley and the odd bucket.

A man leading a buffalo cart stopped to shovel dirt, and huge pigs had backsides protruding from a precarious brick shelter with straw on top. This was within a crude log and rock-built enclosure with a large round vessel carved from stone at one end.

houses and a typical yard

A lady was washing clothes behind a fence of roughly piled rocks and another carried a baby in a sling on her back. Washing hung on lines, strings of corn in trees, and a man was stacking watermelons into a cart. Another lady was doing her laundry in a yard

leading and loading the cart

pig sty

containing a large basket, a red rug slung across a bamboo pole, sheaves of straw leaning against a wall, and an old bathtub, which surely served some purpose other than that originally intended!

One yard contained a none-too-friendly dog, children (one waving Mickey Mouse!) ran around, and a woman almost disappeared beneath an enormous load of grass on her back.

washday

not a happy dog

Smoke issued from chimneys on the bamboo-tiled roofs, a mother goat with two white kids wandered freely, a white hen roosted on a pile of timber, and there were even a few flowers amid the squalor.

One street featured tors of the forest rock; I guess it was easier to build around rather than remove it. We had to run the gamut of souvenir stalls (where we saw the amusing but practical sight of a child with bottomless pants!) before adjourning for lunch served by local girls in colourful traditional attire. After our meal and a brief introduction to the stone immersed in the lake, we were surrounded by a cacophony of sound as we again had to do battle with the souvenir sellers. One girl wore a different tribal dress consisting of a skirt with wide horizontal bands of blue, pink and red topped by a red waistcoat over a white shirt; a red headscarf to which long strands of beads were attached completed the outfit. Another was outstanding in vibrant pink with yellow-and-purple cuffs, and many wearing beaded and embroidered hats carried the embroidered bags and colourful sunshades. We observed a huge formation with a hole in the centre, in front of which local tourists, dressed in hired costumes, were posing for photographs.

walking grass

goats and rocks

Finally entering the park proper, we walked between the towering rock walls of a narrow chasm only teased by the sun, but still extremely hot because for the most part we had to compete with huge noisy crowds. However, even this could not detract from the spectacle of pinnacles, formations with craggy serrated ridges and fluted sides, caves, balancing rocks, and tors crowned with caps of stone.

balancing rocks

A tiny pavilion, which turned out to be a viewing platform, was visible on a distant summit. Weed covered one pool, prohibiting reflections in the still water, and at others it was difficult to find a position along the narrow passageways to focus on the entire scene and its mirror images.

Some trees actually thrived in crevices whilst others, searching for a foothold, probed with twisted roots. From the viewing point, I looked down on a trail of people like a file of ants. Some rocks produced a ringing tone when struck, indicating that they were hollow, and minimal red colour appeared in one group, but most were grey, nicely offset by a blue sky.

reflections

within the forest

Retracing our steps back to Kunming, past stands of bamboo beside a stream and houses with vegetable plots, we stopped at a venue where a screen inlaid with mother-of-pearl portrayed a man riding a buffalo, a simple shelter, palms and other trees, a man tilling with buffalo in a field, and one carrying a load across a rudimentary wooden bridge.

Arriving at our hotel (the Golden Dragon, how original!) we found the staff dressed in different ethnic costumes and lined up to greet some dignitary. In the street outside, I watched for sometime as a large group, using all parts of the body, executed the slow motions of *tai chi*. Isolated from the main gathering, one lady was working with fans. Lines of cyclists about 15 abreast were waiting for the change of traffic

mother-of-pearl inlay

lights at the intersection, one carrying bloody butchered carcasses across his rear carrier and others peddling (or pulling by hand) carts loaded with goods. Large helium balloons floated in the air, and when I returned to the hotel the welcome gathering was still waiting.

We experienced the other side of the coin on a visit to the **Golden Temple**: dirt streets, a horse-drawn cart, and a corrugated iron roof on a ramshackle building where food was cooking in woks over fires in metal drums. At the temple, some of my group members chose to ride in gay flower-decorated carts – pulled by goats! It was the usual conglomeration of pavilions, burning joss sticks in front of a shrine in the courtyard, golden images, ancient carved woodwork in deep relief, temple bells, flowers viewed through a moon gate, and a stone lion.

stone lion and temple

There was also a display of wax figures in traditional dress, and an artist was creating interesting and attractive pictures by the unusual method of blowing paint across paper, causing it to spread and form images resembling trees, their branches and twigs.

Guilin

We flew to **Guilin** (founded 214 BC), an area of unique karst scenery that has inspired poets and painters for centuries. An upheaval of the earth's crust millions of years ago exposed limestone deposits in the seabed, which over the years had weathered into the breathtakingly beautiful roller coaster hills of today, with romantic names such as Duxiu Feng (Solitary Beauty) and Decai Shan (Piled Silk Hill).

Guilin

Before joining our boat for a trip on the **Li River**, I observed

full load

anytime is meal time

a man squatting on the sidewalk eating rice and another hauling a cart piled high with furniture.

Although highly commercialised, one felt isolated from the commotion once on the river. As part of a flotilla, we sailed 83km (51mi) past lush banks and incredibly green hills with a few faces of exposed white rock to the village of Yangshou. Yellow pebbles on the shore contrasted with towering cones and rounded fingers of stone, softened by a thick mantle of vegetation, which fell steeply to form valleys that framed other formations. We passed ancient villages of adobe houses (some whitewashed), crude wooden shacks with grass roofs, wooden walkways and ramps to the water, and a set of steps at the foot of which a person was washing. I observed buffalo in the river, people engaged in various activities, fishing boats, and clumps of striking soft-green feathery bamboo. The different colours lent depth and diversity, and row upon row of peaks were shrouded in veils of mist.

mist-shrouded peaks

A rooster crowed, cattle grazed in unbelievably green meadows, and a waterfall cascaded into green water. A local ferry, fishermen, the occasional stone retaining wall, a shore temple, beautiful green spreading trees, solitary towering needles of stone, and the vessel of a cormorant fisher with washing hanging outside the cabin and baskets sitting on bamboo rafts lashed to its side provided supplementary visual attractions.

We were served lunch on board, for which I was reluctant to leave the awesome passing panoramas and take the time to enjoy. It is difficult to convey the idyllic aura of this special place; the overall impression that remains with me is one of outstanding beauty: scenes composed of jade-green water, stony banks, vivid green meadows with browsing cattle, and whitewashed houses surrounded by dainty bamboo and trees of different shades as a foreground to majestic creations covered with darker verdant vegetation. Other views showed the formations thrown into remarkable silhouette against the sunlight, and strangely there was not the familiar bird life usually associated with rivers (I only remember seeing two), the stillness only disturbed by the

questing fingers

occasional blast of the boat's horn rather than the cries of our feathered friends.

Just prior to pulling into **Yangshou**, we began to encounter the cormorant fishermen standing to paddle their bamboo rafts with long oars. The time-honoured method employed by these men uses tame birds to dive for fish, their long necks collared to prevent them swallowing the catch. The banks widened and houseboats of the fishermen were moored alongside the edge.

I could not get enough of this scenery

Arriving at the village, one of these men, wearing a broad-brimmed coolie hat, was posing for pictures with his birds on the ends of a pole. An imposing set of marble stairs led up to an unimpressive town, one of the worst tourist traps that I had ever encountered, until then or since. It was filled with naught but souvenir stalls, vendors even under umbrellas lining the steps, where one could expect to be constantly badgered and hassled. The only photograph I took was of a beautiful caged pheasant. We journeyed back to Guilin by bus, past the wonderful peaks rising behind miles of rice paddies and fields full of water, which could have been fish or eel ponds.

houseboats of the cormorant fishers

Whilst in Guilin, we also visited the **Reed Flute Caves**, exhibiting the usual formations lit to great effect by coloured lighting and where legend has it that the Dragon King housed his maidens. We were entertained at the Hoover Theatre Restaurant, and in keeping with the poetic Chinese titles, we stayed at the Ronghu Wintersweet Hotel. Not quite so appealing in the name stakes was the Gorge of Ox's Liver and Horse's Lung on the Yangtze!

Guangzhou

We departed by air for **Guangzhou**, formerly **Canton**, also called City of Rice Eaters and City of Rams, where we stayed at the Landmark Hotel. China's most modern and progressive city, it lay on the **Pearl River Delta** and only 111km (69mi) from capitalist Hong Kong. It was here that China first opened her doors for Western trade and where began the infamous Opium Wars of the 19th century, which precipitated the downturn of imperial power. As with the rest of the country, there were colourful markets displaying everything from rare aromatic spices and traditional medicines (deer antler, starfish and mosses) to dazzling songbirds and tropical fish, and which included every species of animal, bird and fish offered for the dinner table – it resembled a takeaway zoo! Here, I filmed caged birds before we embarked on a city tour that took in one of the best temples in the whole of Asia: **Guangxiao** (**Bright Filial Piety**) dating back to the third century BC. There were stone lions in the forecourt and the plain exterior was hung with red lanterns, but the outstanding attraction was the intricate decoration on the roofline, ridges and under the eaves. Portraying aspects of daily life, superb colourful ceramic tableaux showed many beautifully executed figures occupying elaborate buildings and inserted amongst an ornate assemblage of dragons, trees, rocks, hideous faces, flowers, animals and birds, which included peacocks or the mythical phoenix. One scenario portrayed a family gathered around a table, and another appeared to depict a court setting with dignitaries in astonishing headgear and learned-looking scribes.

temple detail

roof detail

It was an extraordinary artistic work. Inside, a modern interpretation of a warrior-like guardian was painted on a black door, and delicate carved wooden panels also incorporated scenes. Created from white jade, a standard lamp featured filigree arms and a complicated arrangement of clouds swirling around flowers, trees, pavilions, and figures: one holding a whisk, another a miniature lantern, and a third a cane.

picture created with dried grasses

A final handcraft outlet exhibited a tableau (behind glass) created from cork, a red and white plate with a most intricate pattern, a large painting showing a peacock with white lilies, and another, in subtle tones, of a pheasant and colourful flowers. A horse, birds flying above trees, and a fisherman mending his nets were all created with dried grasses, and of all things, I found pale-coloured jade prawns!

From here, we went to the **Liurong** (**Six Banyan Tree**) **Temple** with its octagonal 57m nine-storey (from the outside, 15 inside) **Flowery Pagoda**. A temple was founded here in the year 537 but rebuilt twice, and today's pagoda dated from 1097 in the Northern Song Dynasty. By this time, I was slightly jaded and found the most interesting sight to be a laden miniature orange tree!

The neighbourhood of **Liuhua Park** was the location for a landmark of Canton: the huge fanciful **Sculpture of the Five Rams**, said to have appeared 2,000 years ago carrying rice in their mouths and ridden by five gods who vanished and the rams turned to stone. Boats sailed past an impressive white edifice standing in the water, and from my window I had a great view of various craft and one of the bridges on the **Zhujiang** (**Pearl River**). The hotel had a lavish patio garden with bridges, pathways through greenery, and a small rotunda on top of a fabricated mountain from which flowed a wide waterfall. A drab concrete monstrosity in the centre of a traffic roundabout was a gigantic monument to a Chinese revolutionary figure, and my final pictures were of people, some with bicycles, lined up to read the daily newspaper attached to a wall (a common occurrence in China), and a park where a man and woman were performing *tai chi* with swords.

the daily news

Conclusion

Because the government did not welcome individual travellers (there was still much of which they were ashamed), bureaucracy and officials had made my first journey in China difficult, creating obstacles to discourage tourists entering embarrassing sensitive areas. At that stage, I felt that they would have to make a decision to either allow free access or ban lone travellers altogether; it seemed that the latter applied on my second visit.

I had organised an itinerary allocating free time for shopping or individual pursuits, but the Chinese government was very reluctant to have foreigners moving around unsupervised, so my agent had slotted tours into every available space. One involved a visit to a hospital, which sounded strange and uninteresting but turned out to be totally fascinating. Seated like students in a lecture theatre, we were given a demonstration of *chi kung* or *qigong*, whereby the doctor concerned performed a series of intricate arm and hand movements causing his body to become electrically charged, which he verified by illuminating a globe held in the hand. Volunteers were given small jolts on pressure points to relieve stress, and we all joined hands in a circle to experience the uncanny transference of current from one to another; it was an absorbing couple of hours. I acquired a brochure on a tea infused with *qigong* that claims to cure every ailment known to man, from piles, obesity and insomnia, to coronary heart disease, rheumatic arthritis and cancer, also deafness, migraine and both diarrhoea *and* constipation!

The most striking aspect of my second visit to China was the emergence of a huge middle class of well dressed people, no longer in the drab blue but wearing jeans and colourful Western gear as a result of the evolution of free markets. Many also possessed sophisticated electronic equipment. Apparently (I was informed), traders were refusing to pay tax, but the government still encouraged their enterprise because input of the foreign dollar, whilst increasing the wealth of the individual, also contributed greatly to the national economy. In between my two visits, I had witnessed an alarming decline in American society, which became cause for reflection on a change of power in the world, and disquieting contemplation of how we would fare under Chinese rule as a consequence.

INDEX

A

B

C

E

Lightning Source UK Ltd.
Milton Keynes UK
UKOW08f1120240417
299768UK00002B/840/P

9 781514 444627